HAESTAD METHODS

WASTEWATER COLLECTION SYSTEM MODELING AND DESIGN

First Edition

OTHER BOOKS FROM HAESTAD PRESS

Advanced Water Distribution Modeling and Management, first edition
   Haestad, Walski, Chase, Savic, Grayman, Beckwith, and Koelle

Computer Applications in Hydraulic Engineering, sixth edition
   Haestad, Walski, Barnard, Durrans, and Meadows

Floodplain Modeling Using HEC-RAS, first edition
   Haestad, Dyhouse, Hatchett, and Benn

Proceedings of the First Annual Water Security Summit, first edition
   Haestad

Stormwater Conveyance Modeling and Design, first edition
   Haestad and Durrans

Water Distribution Modeling, first edition
   Haestad, Walski, Chase, and Savic

To order or to receive additional information on these or any other Haestad Press titles, please call 800-727-6555 (US and Canada) or +1-203-755-1666 (worldwide) or visit www.haestadpress.com.

HAESTAD METHODS

WASTEWATER COLLECTION SYSTEM MODELING AND DESIGN

First Edition

Authors
Haestad Methods
Thomas M. Walski
Thomas E. Barnard
Eric Harold
LaVere B. Merritt
Noah Walker
Brian E. Whitman

Managing Editor
Thomas E. Barnard

Project Editors
Kristen Dietrich, Adam Strafaci, Colleen Totz

Contributing Authors
Christine Hill, Gordon McKay, Stan Plante, Barbara A. Schmitz

Peer Review Board
Jonathan Gray (Burns and McDonnell), Ken Kerri (Ret.),
Neil Moody (Moods Consulting Pty, Ltd.), Gary Moore (St. Louis Sewer District),
John Reinhardt (Massachusetts Department of Environmental Protection),
Reggie Rowe (CH2M Hill), Burt Van Duin (Westhoff Engineering Resources)

HAESTAD PRESS
Waterbury, CT USA

Wastewater Collection Sytem Modeling and Design
First Edition

© 2004 by Haestad Methods, Inc. All rights reserved. Haestad Methods, Inc. is a wholly owned subsidiary of Bentley Systems, Inc.

Printed in the United States of America. No part of this publication may be reproduced, stored in a retrieval system, or transmitted, in any form or by any means, electronic, mechanical, photocopying, recording, or otherwise, without the prior written permission of the publisher.

Graphic image reprinted courtesy of ESRI and is used herein with permission. Copyright © ESRI. All rights reserved.

Indexer: Beaver Wood Associates and Ann Drinan
Proofreaders: Beaver Wood Associates

Special thanks to *The New Yorker* magazine for the cartoons throughout the book.
© The New Yorker Collection from cartoonbank.com. All Rights Reserved.

Page 3 - (1989) Bernard Schoenbaum	Page 255 - (2002) Frank Cotham
Page 27 - (2000) Mike Twohy	Page 283 - (1971) Chon Day
Page 53 - (1991) Robert Mankoff	Page 295 - (2002) Mick Stevens
Page 82 - (1994) Leo Cullum	Page 339 - (1999) George Booth
Page 94 - (1988) James Stevenson	Page 351 - (1987) Donald Reilly
Page 101 - (1970) James Stevenson	Page 393 - (1993) Donald Reilly
Page 108 - (1997) Danny Shanahan	Page 400 - (1999) Mort Gerberg
Page 115 - (1994) Bruce Eric Kaplan	Page 444 - (1997) Leo Cullum
Page 129 - (1994) Edward Koren	Page 458 - (1988) Mischa Richter
Page 142 - (1999) Donald Reilly	Page 481 - (2002) Barbara Smaller
Page 159 - (1991) George Booth	Page 534 - (1994) Mischa Richter
Page 185 - (1992) Mick Stevens	Page 541 - (2001) Donald Reilly
Page 193 - (1995) Al Ross	Page 548 - (1997) Leo Cullum
Page 235 - (1989) Mick Stevens	

ClientCare, Flowmaster, HAMMER, SewerCAD, StormCAD, WaterCAD, and WaterGEMS are trademarks, service marks, certification marks, or registered trademarks of Haestad Methods. All other brands, trademarks, and company and product names belong to their respective holders.

Library of Congress Control Number: 2004112826
ISBN: 0-9657580-9-5

Haestad Methods, Inc.
37 Brookside Rd.
Waterbury, CT 06708-1499
USA

Phone: +1-203-755-1666
Fax: +1-203-597-1488
e-mail: info@haestad.com
Internet: www.haestad.com

"Similar to Haestad's earlier publications, *Wastewater Collection System Modeling and Design* will become a classic over time. Well written, this book clearly links engineering theory to practical modeling applications and offers many technical nuggets for experienced professionals."

-Bert van Duin
Westhoff Engineering Resources, Inc
Canada

"Traditional sewer design methodology suffers from old age. This book is a tremendous step forward in modernizing the sewer design process. Both novice and experienced designers should find this book an invaluable resource."

-LaVere B. Merritt, PhD, PE, DEE
Brigham Young University
Provo, Utah

"*Wastewater Collection System Modeling and Design* provides a unique blend of the principals and practices of engineering for academia and professional engineers. This text provides its readers with modeling guidance that is both technically sound and relevant for improving the performance of existing systems."

-Gary Moore, PE
Metropolitan St. Louis Sewer District
USA

"*Wastewater Collection System Modeling and Design* is a great addition to what has become my Haestad Methods library. This book is a must for all practicing engineers that work in sewer system design and is a great reference for use by college students. Finally, a single book that links fundamental sewer hydraulics to practical sewer design and modeling practiced by professional engineers."

-Brian E. Whitman, PhD
Wilkes University
USA

Acknowledgements

Wastewater Collection System Modeling and Design is the culmination of the efforts of many individuals, the most significant of which are the thousands of engineering professionals around the world who dedicate their careers to managing wastewater and providing basic sanitation services to ensure the health of the public. Haestad Methods has been serving wastewater engineers around the world for over 20 years, and our discussions with the community have provided the inspiration to write this book.

Many authors contributed to the success of *Wastewater Collection System Modeling and Design*. Primary credit goes to Tom Walski, Eric Harold, LaVere Merritt, Noah Walker, and Brian Whitman. Significant contributions were also made by Christine Hill, Gordon McKay, Stan Plante, Barbara A. Schmitz, and the staff of Haestad Methods. Information on the individual authors and the chapters to which they contributed is provided in the next section, "Authors and Contributing Authors." It is the synthesis of everyone's ideas that really makes this book such a practical resource. Extra special thanks to the project editors, Kristen Dietrich, Adam Strafaci, and Colleen Totz for their countless hours of hard work and dedication to weave the information from many authors and reviewers into a cohesive and accessible textbook.

We greatly appreciate the efforts of our peer reviewers Jonathan Grey, Ken Kerri, Neil Moody, Gary Moore, John Reinhardt, Reggie Rowe, and Bert van Duin. They provided exceptional insight and shared practical experiences that added enormously to the utility of this book.

Many engineers at Haestad Methods contributed to editing, reviewing, content development, exercise review, and fact checking for this book, making its final delivery a company wide effort. Their input played an enormous role in shaping the text into its final form. Special thanks to Brian Bauer, Jack Cook, Ryan Cournoyer, Norelis Florentino, Michael Glazner, Sharavan Govindan, Andres Gutierrez, Juan Carlos Gutierrez, Jennifer Hatchett, Gregg Herrin, Keith Hodsden, Ming Jin, Tasneem Khomusi, Elizabeth Lipovsky, Douglas Maitland, Christopher Moks, Guillaume Pelud, Richard Sappe, Mal Sharkey, Angela Suarez, Karthik Sundaresan, and Somchit Thor. Brian Whitman and Tom Walski contributed to the discussion topics and exercises at the end of each chapter.

The illustrations and graphs throughout the book were created and assembled under the direction of Mike Campbell with the assistance of Caleb Brownell. We also wish to thank the following individuals and organizations for providing us with additional illustrations and photographs: Tom Walski, Getty Images, Cole Publishing, University of Iowa, Maria do Céu Almeida, John Barton, Daniel Sztruhar, Duncan Mara, Peerless Pump Company, Aquacraft, LNEC, MGD Technologies, Thel-Mar Company, Campbell Scientific, Marsh-McBirney, Unidata, Renaissance Instruments, Water Environment Research Foundation, Pearson Education, R.D. Zande & Associates, ITT Flygt Corporation, and Environment One Corporation. Special thanks to Meredith Miller at cartoonbank.com for the *New Yorker* cartoons throughout the book.

Others involved in the production process for the book include Lissa Jennings (publishing logistics), Rick Brainard and Jim O'Brien (cover design), Matt Cole (web page design), Jeanne and David Moody (indexing and proofreading), David Klotz (formatting and page layout), and Ann Drinan (indexing).

Finally, special thanks to Haestad Methods executive vice president, Niclas Ingemarsson, who provided the human resources and management guidance to get the job done, and to the company president, John Haestad, who provided the vision and motivation to make this collection of ideas a reality.

Tom Barnard
Author and Managing Editor
Haestad Methods, Inc.

Authors and Contributing Authors

Wastewater Collection System Modeling and Design represents a collaborative effort that combines the experiences of over fifteen contributors and peer reviewers and the engineers and software developers at Haestad Methods. The authors and contributing authors and the chapters they developed are:

Authors

Thomas M. Walski
Haestad Methods, Inc. (Chapters 1, 3, 12, 13)

Thomas E. Barnard
Haestad Methods, Inc. (Chapter 15)

Eric Harold
Buchanan Street Consulting (Chapters 7, 11)

LaVere B. Merritt
Brigham Young University (Chapters 2, 4, 6, 10)

Noah Walker
Dudek and Associates (Chapters 8, 9)

Brian E. Whitman
Wilkes University (Chapter 5)

Contributing Authors

Christine Hill
XCG Consultants, Ltd. (Chapter 15)

Gordon McKay
Hong Kong University of Science and Technology (Chapter 15)

Stan Plante
CDM (Chapter 14)

Barbara A. Schmitz
CH2M Hill (Chapter 14)

Haestad Methods

The Haestad Methods Engineering Staff is an extremely diverse group of professionals from six continents with experience ranging from software development and engineering consulting, to public works and academia. This broad cross section of expertise contributes to the development of the most comprehensive software and educational materials in the civil engineering industry. In addition to the specific authors credited in this section, many at Haestad Methods contributed to the success of this book.

Thomas M. Walski, PhD, PE, DEE, F. ASCE

Thomas M. Walski, PhD, PE, Vice President of Engineering for Haestad Methods, has been named a Diplomat by the American Academy of Environmental Engineers. Over the past three decades, Dr. Walski has served as an expert witness; Research Civil Engineer for the U.S. Army Corps of Engineers; Engineer and Manager of Distribution Operation for the City of Austin, Texas; Executive Director of the Wyoming Valley Sanitary Authority; Associate Professor of Environmental Engineering at Wilkes University; and Engineering Manager for the Pennsylvania American Water Company. Over the past decade, he has also taught more than 2,000 professionals in Haestad Methods' IACET-accredited hydraulic modeling courses. His experience in wastewater collection systems ranges from operating a large regional system made up of a mixture of sanitary and combined collection systems to evaluating small pressure sewer systems.

A widely published expert on hydraulic modeling, Dr. Walski has written several books, including *Analysis of Water Distribution Systems*, *Water Distribution Simulation and Sizing* (with Johannes Gessler and John Sjostrom), and *Water Distribution Systems – A Troubleshooting Manual* (with Jim Male).

He has served on numerous professional committees and chaired several, including the ASCE Water Resources Systems Committee, ASCE Environmental Engineering Publications Committee, ASCE Environmental Engineering Awards Committee, and ASCE Water Supply Rehabilitation Task Committee. He also served on the committees that produced the Water Environment Federation's *Pump Station Design* (FD-4) and *Energy Conservation* (MFD-2) manuals.

Dr. Walski has written over 50 peer-reviewed papers and made roughly 100 conference presentations. He is a three-time winner of the best paper award in Distribution and Plant Operation for the *Journal of the American Water Works Association* and is a past editor of the *Journal of Environmental Engineering*. He received his MS and PhD in Environmental and Water Resources Engineering from Vanderbilt University. He is a registered Professional Engineer in two states and a certified water and wastewater plant operator.

Thomas E. Barnard, PhD, PE

Thomas E. Barnard, PhD, PE, is a senior engineer with Haestad Methods. He has more than 20 years of experience in environmental engineering working as a consultant, researcher, educator, and author. He holds a BS in civil engineering from the University of Vermont, an MS in environmental engineering from Utah State University, and a PhD in environmental engineering from Cornell University. His expertise include water and wastewater treatment, hazardous waste management, surface water hydrology, and water quality monitoring systems. His major consulting projects include RCRA permitting for hazardous and radioactive wastes at the Rocky Flats Plant in Colorado; water quality modeling of receiving wastes and analysis of wastewater treatment/disposal alternatives in Alexandria, Egypt; and investigations of regional water quality monitoring programs in the Chesapeake Bay watershed of the United States.

Dr. Barnard is a contributing author to *Computer Applications in Hydraulic Engineering* and *Stormwater Conveyance Modeling and Design*. He has contributed chapters to *Principles of Environmental Chemistry* and *Chemometrics in Environmental Chemistry*. He has also served as a book reviewer for Water Environment and Technology and as a peer reviewer for the *Journal of the American Water Resources Association*. He is a registered professional engineer in Pennsylvania.

Eric Harold, PE

Eric M. Harold, PE, currently serves as Director of Buchanan Street Consulting. Mr. Harold is an environmental engineer with over 13 years experience in combined sewer overflow (CSO) and sanitary sewer overflow (SSO) analysis, hydrologic and hydraulic modeling, sanitary sewer and stormwater flow monitoring, water quality monitoring and modeling, and database management. He has made numerous presentations in hydraulic and hydrologic modeling. Mr. Harold holds a BS degree in Civil and Environmental Engineering from the University of Cincinnati. He is a registered professional engineer in Maryland, Virginia, and the District of Columbia.

LaVere B. Merritt, PhD, PE, DEE

Dr. Merritt, Professor of Civil and Environmental Engineering at Brigham Young University, has broad research and design experience in sewer systems. Of particular note is his experience in design optimization, cost sensitivity to design parameters, design flow rates, infiltration and inflow analysis, and tractive force approaches to self-cleansing. His publications include over 10 peer-reviewed technical papers and over 50 research and consulting reports. He has made numerous technical presentations, mainly on water quality and computer-aided sanitary engineering design.

Noah Walker, PE

S. M. Noah Walker, P.E. is the Principal Utility Planner for Dudek and Associates, Inc. and Chief Technical Officer of 3-Waters Technical Services. Over the past 25 years, Mr. Walker has served as Process Engineer for Continental Grain Co.; Assistant Director of Systems Planning and Systems Services (IT) for the Water and Wastewater Utility in Austin, Texas; Chief of Collection Systems, City of Las Vegas; and Regional Engineering Manager and Product Line Manager for software at ADS Environmental Services. Over the past decade, he has taught hundreds of engineering professionals to use leading collection system modeling software including through Haestad Methods' IACET-accredited sewer modeling course. His career focus has been on applying rapidly changing hardware and software technologies to improve the management of water, wastewater, and storm water utilities.

During his career, Mr. Walker has been involved in the implementation of large scale data networks and temporary and permanent wastewater flow measurement installations. He has also developed graphical user interfaces for hydraulic models, developed software for the analysis and integration of wet weather flows, and contributed significantly to most of the major collection system modeling software applications in use today. Mr. Walker has been responsible for the preparation of over fifty utility master plans and over one hundred inflow and infiltration analysis reports.

He has served on numerous professional committees, including the Standard Construction Specifications Committees for the City of Austin, Texas and Clark County, Nevada; the GIS Management Committee for Clark County, NV; and the Growth Management Utility Committee for the City of Austin. He was also a contributor to the Water Environment Federation *Manual of Practice 7, Wastewater Collection Systems Management*.

Mr. Walker has written numerous professional articles and conducted presentations including *Data Infrastructure Planning for Large Water Utilities, Implementing Highly Integrated Capital Improvements Programs with GIS, Costs of SSO Management – The Australian Experience, Inspection of Military Industrial Waste Systems, USEPA CMOM Compliance*, and *Hybrid Collection System Modeling*. Additionally, he was the primary author of training materials for Haestad Methods' SewerCAD program and has prepared training materials for other collection system models. He has served as a technical reviewer for the *ASCE Journal of Hydraulics*.

Mr. Walker received his B.S. in Agricultural Engineering from Auburn University. He is a registered professional engineer in Texas.

Brian E. Whitman, PhD

Brian Whitman, PhD, is an Associate Professor of Environmental Engineering at Wilkes University in Wilkes-Barre, PA. He holds a MS in Civil Engineering and PhD in Environmental Engineering from Michigan Technological University. He has extensive experience teaching hydraulic modeling software for use in water distribution system design, wastewater collection system design, and water resources engineering.

Christine Hill, M.Eng., P.Eng

Christine Hill is an Associate and Manager of the Municipal Infrastructure Group at XCG Consultants Ltd. Ms. Hill obtained a Masters of Engineering Degree from the University of Toronto in 1994. She is an expert modeler with extensive experience in the use of hydraulic models for the purposes of facility planning and evaluation and has been involved in many combined sewer overflow, sanitary sewer overflow, and infrastructure needs studies. Over the past 15 years, she has worked on many large multi-disciplined projects in a number of jurisdictions in both Canada and the United States, including major projects in Toronto, Ottawa, Thunder Bay, Halton, Windsor, Welland and Hamilton, Ontario; Edmonton, Alberta; and Cincinnati and Cleveland, Ohio.

Gordon McKay

Professor Gordon McKay, currently with the Department of Chemical Engineering, Hong Kong University of Science and Technology, has over 30 years experience in academia and industry.

He established his own company, Consultancy Process Engineering and Management Systems, in 1987, and from 1991 to 1995 he was a subcontractor for Project Management Ltd. – Foster Wheeler Ireland. He was appointed as their Senior Process Specialist to head up the Process Safety and Environmental Management teams and acted as Project Manager for certain key projects. His work in the safety area included performing Safety Audits and serving as Hazop Chairman and Process Safety Training Manager. In the environmental area, his work included responsibility for environmental impact statements, environmental audits, acquisition audits, IPC license applications, and implementation of environmental management systems.

Prior to establishing his own consultancy, Professor McKay was in the Chemical Engineering Department at Queens University, Belfast for 17 years. He has published over 300 research papers and authored/contributed to five books in the fields of environmental management systems and the design of environmental treatment systems. He is currently Chairman of the Chemical Discipline for the Hong Kong Institution of Engineers.

Stan Plante, PE

Stan Plante, PE, is a principal engineer with CDM and directs various information technology projects in Ohio and surrounding states. Throughout his career, Mr. Plante has focused on development and application of hydraulic models to support water distribution and wastewater collection master plans. He has managed many water and sewer master plan projects for both slow- and rapid-growth situations, and has also provided technical direction and troubleshooting on modeling efforts around the United States, particularly for water distribution projects. In the last few years, Mr. Plante has worked on GIS implementation projects for a variety of environments (large city, small city, airports, etc.), several of which have included modeling integration components.

Barbara A. Schmitz

Barbara A. Schmitz is a senior GIS consultant and project manager with more than 18 years of experience in developing and applying geospatial technologies. She is the firm-wide technology leader at CH2M Hill for GIS applications related to water, wastewater, and water resources management projects. Ms. Schmitz has expertise in the integration of GIS technologies with water and wastewater utility maintenance management systems for facilitating utility system inventories and digital mapping, condition assessments, combined sewer overflow and sewer infiltration/inflow management, and general utility maintenance and management planning. She integrates GIS databases with modeling applications, such as hydraulic models, to support system design, analysis, and optimization. Ms. Schmitz also provides training in GIS and related technologies for CH2M Hill clients and in-house staff.

Ms. Schmitz has authored several peer-reviewed papers and conference presentations on a variety of GIS topics. She has also contributed chapters on GIS applications to several books about sewer and water system modeling and to a manual of practice for implementing geographic information systems in utilities.

Foreword

Libraries are wondrous institutions. Rows and rows of books create a feeling of awe as they rise high above the floors of the great libraries of the world, such as the Bibliothèque Nationale in Paris, The John P. Robarts Research Library at the University of Toronto, and the Library of Congress in Washington, D.C. But, the true magnificence of libraries lies in their ability to set in motion imagination and excitement in learning. The books and other materials they house provide the opportunity to understand and benefit from what others have experienced, and expand our ability to make informed decisions. Indeed, the mission statement of the Library of Congress states the Library's aim to "sustain and preserve a universal collection of knowledge and creativity for future generations."

Study of the decisions, actions, and results of others' past activities under conditions analogous to one's own situation helps in predicting the results of current decisions. Social science scholars study human behavior and develop hypotheses or explanations of what to expect from humans in certain group interactions. Military scientists explore the principles that control the conduct of war, and then apply those principles to battle conditions. Scientists study the research and experiments of other scientists to better understand the causes and effects of material, force, and environment variation. Each of these examples represents the premise of simulation and model software development, which is that the past helps predict the future when combined with scientific or mathematical principles.

Like libraries, models can activate the imagination and generate excitement because they provide information and knowledge that, in turn, enables more informed decisions or solutions. Decision makers use modeling tools to simulate actual conditions and generate performance and functional assessments significantly more quickly than with real-time observations. Generally, the only technical restriction on what can be simulated is the complexity and power of the model.

The value and benefit of using models is increasingly being recognized. In the wastewater industry, utilities use hydraulic models in all phases of the collection and treatment system's life cycle: planning, design, construction, and operation. Hydraulic models allow costly and complicated collection systems to be comprehensively evaluated prior to expending a community's limited resources to solve service or regulatory issues. Proposed infrastructure components can be assessed against the risk of not achieving a utility's mission and goals, or of incurring harmful health and environment consequences due to poor or unexpected performance.

Once wastewater collection and treatment systems have been built and put into service, their performance can be measured. Utility decision makers can then use the measurement information to gauge earlier decisions and expectations. Knowledge gained from past experience will aid the utility in achieving future goals, and can assist others in similar situations if documented and exchanged in technical publications, manuals, or reference books.

This book has done an excellent job of capturing and communicating the knowledge of several experienced hydraulic modelers. It presents a good, balanced perspective of the alternatives and informational needs of a modeler starting a modeling project, including how to build and assemble the hydraulic components and apply the software tool efficiently.

Undoubtedly, this book too will appear in libraries and be on the shelves of hydraulic modelers who want to gain from the knowledge and experiences of their peers and predecessors.

Reggie Rowe, PE
CH2M Hill

Table of Contents

	Preface	xi
	Continuing Education Units	xv
	About the Software	xvii

Chapter 1 Introduction to Wastewater Collection System Modeling 1

- **1.1 Wastewater Collection System Overview** — 1
  - Terminology — 2
  - Sources of Wastewater — 2
  - Types of Conveyance — 3
- **1.2 Modeling** — 5
  - Applications of Collection System Models — 5
  - Types of Collection System Modeling — 7
- **1.3 Historical Perspective on Collection System Analysis** — 7
  - Collection Systems — 7
  - Hydraulics History — 11
  - Historical Summary — 16
- **1.4 The Modeling Process** — 16

Chapter 2 Steady Gravity Flow Hydraulics 23

- **2.1 Fluid Properties** — 24
  - Density and Specific Weight — 24
  - Viscosity — 24
  - Fluid Compressibility — 27
  - Vapor Pressure — 27
- **2.2 Fluid Statics and Dynamics** — 28
  - Static Pressure — 28
  - Absolute Pressure and Gauge Pressure — 29
  - Velocity and Flow — 30
  - Reynolds Number — 31
  - Velocity Profiles — 31

	2.3	**Fundamental Laws**	32
		Conservation of Mass	32
		Conservation of Energy	33
		Conservation of Momentum	36
	2.4	**Hydraulic Design Variables**	38
		Flow Rate or Discharge	38
		Channel/Pipe Slope	38
		Depth of Flow	38
		Velocity	39
	2.5	**Energy and Head Losses**	40
		Energy Equation	41
	2.6	**Hydraulic Elements**	44
		Open-Top Cross Sections	44
		Closed-Top Cross Sections	46
		Noncircular Cross Sections	49
	2.7	**Manning's n Variation**	49
		Calculating n with the Darcy-Weisbach Equation	50
		Variation of n with Depth	52
		Recommended Values of Manning's n	53
	2.8	**Minor Losses in Junction Structures**	54
		Energy-Loss Method	55
		Composite Energy-Loss Method	60
	2.9	**Tractive Force Self-Cleansing**	63
		Tractive Tension	63
		Sediment Carrying Capacity – Experimental Analysis	65
		Camp Formula	69
		Yao's Method	69
		Abwassertechnische Vereinigung (ATV) Method	71
		Additional Considerations	71
	2.10	**Specific Energy and Critical Flow**	72
		Specific Energy	72
		Froude Number	74
		Subcritical and Supercritical Flow	74
		Hydraulic Jumps	75
		Flow Profiles	76
		Backwater Curves	77
	2.11	**Hydraulics of Flow-Control Structures**	78
		Orifices	79
		Weirs	79
		Gates	84

Chapter 3 Unsteady Gravity Flow Hydraulics 91

	3.1	**Basics of Unsteady Flow Analysis**	93
	3.2	**Types of Routing**	94

	3.3	**Hydrodynamic Equations**	**95**
		Saint-Venant Equations	95
		Approximation to Hydrodynamic Equations	96
		Diffusion Analogy	97
		Kinematic Wave	97
		Muskingum Routing	98
		Muskingum-Cunge Routing	98
		Convex Routing	100
		Weighted Translational Routing	100
		Level Pool Routing	100
		Summary of Methods	101
	3.4	**Complications to Routing Methods**	**101**
		Manholes and Junction Tables	103
		Surcharging	103
		Overflows and Diversions	104
		Parallel Pipes and Loops	105
		Flow Reversal	106
		Dry Pipes	107
		Drop Structures	107

Chapter 4 Force Main and Pumping Hydraulics 113

4.1 Friction Losses 113
Darcy-Weisbach Equation ... 116
Colebrook-White Equation and the Moody Diagram ... 117
Hazen-Williams Equation ... 118
Swamee-Jain Equation ... 120
Manning Equation ... 120
Pipe Roughness Changes ... 121
Comparison of Friction Loss Methods ... 121

4.2 Minor Losses 122
Minor Loss Valve Coefficients ... 123

4.3 Energy Addition – Pumps 125
Pump Head-Discharge Relationship ... 125
System Head Curves ... 126
Other Pump Characteristic Curves ... 128
Fixed-Speed and Variable-Speed Pumps ... 129
Affinity Laws for Variable-Speed Pumps ... 129
Power and Efficiency ... 130

Chapter 5 Model Construction 137

5.1 Developing the Modeling Plan 137

5.2 The Modeling Process 138
Purpose and Objectives of a Model ... 138
Develop Alternatives ... 141
Scales of Models ... 141
Software Selection and Training ... 143

		Define Data Requirements	143
		Identify Data Sources	144
		Collect Data	146
		Validate the Data	147
		Build the Model	148
		Identify Data Gaps	148
		Sensitivity Analysis	148
		Calibrate the Model	148
		Validate the Model	148
		Run Simulations	149
		Develop Solutions	150
		Bookkeeping	151
	5.3	**Constructing the Sewer Model**	**152**
		Level of Detail	153
		Subbasin Delineation	154
		Pipes	154
		Manholes	160
		Pumps	164
		Wet Wells	168

Chapter 6 Dry Weather Wastewater Flows — 173

6.1	**Definition of Flow Rates**	**175**
	New Systems	175
	Existing Systems	176
6.2	**Unit Load Factors**	**176**
	Residential	176
	Commercial Sources	177
	Industrial Wastewater Flows	179
	Fixture Unit Method	181
	Land-Use Methods	183
	Measured-Flow Methods	185
	Assigning Loads to a Model	187
6.3	**Peaking Factors**	**187**
	Peaking Factor Charts and Equations	188
	Minimum Flows	190
	Selection of Flow Generation Rate and Peaking Factor	191
6.4	**Time-Varying Flows**	**193**
	Diurnal Curves	193
	Developing Systemwide Diurnal Curves	195
	Defining Usage Patterns Within a Model	196

Chapter 7 Wet Weather Wastewater Flows — 203

7.1	**Wet Weather Flow Definitions**	**204**
	What Is Wet Weather Flow?	204
	Components of Flow in Wastewater Collection Systems	204
	Modeling Wet Weather Flows	206

	7.2	**Wastewater Collection System Hydrology**	**208**
		Combined Sewer System Hydrology	208
		Modeling Combined Sewer Systems	210
		Separate Sanitary Sewer System Hydrology	212
		Modeling Separate Sanitary Sewer Systems	213
		Continuous versus Event Hydrology	216
	7.3	**Rainfall**	**217**
		Rainfall Data	217
		Selecting Model Simulation Events	218
		Calibration Events	219
		Design Storms	219
		Continuous Records	228
	7.4	**Modeling Runoff**	**229**
		Rainfall Abstractions	230
		Horton Equation	233
		Green-Ampt Equation	233
		Rational Method	234
		NRCS (SCS) Method	236
	7.5	**Determining Hydrographs from Runoff Volumes**	**239**
		Determining Peak Flow and Time to Peak	240
		Snider Triangular Hydrograph	240
		Unit Hydrograph Approach	242
		NRCS (SCS) Dimensionless Unit Hydrograph	243
		Nonlinear Reservoir	246
	7.6	**Empirical Methods for Generating Hydrographs**	**248**
		Percentage of Rainfall Volume (R-Factor)	249
		Unit Hydrographs from Flow Measurements	249
		Simplifications to Unit Hydrograph	250
		Inflow Coefficient Method	250
		Rainfall/Flow Regression	252
		RTK Hydrograph Method	254
		Unit Loads for Design Studies	261
	7.7	**Snowmelt**	**262**
		Runoff Potential	262
		Snowmelt Models	263
Chapter 8		**Data Collection and Flow Measurement**	**271**
	8.1	**Flow Measurement Considerations**	**271**
		Components of Flow	272
		Review of Existing Information	273
		Selection of Metering Locations	273
		Safety Considerations	274
	8.2	**Flow Measurement**	**275**
		Hydraulic Control Sections in Open Channels	275
		In-Pipe Methods	280
		Manual Methods	281

8.3	**Instrumentation**		**283**
	Depth		284
	Velocity Meters		287
8.4	**Precipitation Measurement**		**292**
	Precipitation Data Acquisition		293
	Measurement of Rainfall		293
	Gauge Operation Considerations		294
	Radar Imagery		295

Chapter 9 Model Calibration 301

9.1	**Basic Calibration Concepts**	**302**
	Overview of Calibration	302
	Calibration Parameters	303
	Building-Block Approach	305
	Steady-State and Extended-Period Simulations	305
9.2	**Dry Weather Flows**	**305**
9.3	**Wet Weather Flows**	**309**
	Constant Unit Rate Method	310
	Percentage of Rainfall Volume (R-Value)	312
	Percentage of Stream Flow	313
	RTK Hydrograph	315
	Predictive Equation Based on Rainfall-Flow Regression	316
9.4	**Special Considerations in Calibration**	**320**
	Volume Differences	321
	Shape Considerations	322
	Timing Shifts	323
9.5	**Understanding Overflows**	**324**
	Estimating Combined Sewer Overflow	325
	Estimating SSOs	326
	Detecting Overflows with Scattergraphs	326

Chapter 10 Design of New Gravity Wastewater Collection Systems 333

10.1	**Materials**	**334**
	Pipes	334
	Manholes	335
	Other Appurtenances	336
10.2	**Initial Planning**	**337**
	Decision to Provide Sewer Service to an Area	337
	Types of Conveyance	338
	Separate versus Combined Systems	338
10.3	**Preliminary Design Considerations**	**339**
	Data Requirements	340
	Alternatives	341

	10.4	**Initial System Layout**	**341**
		Gravity Sewer Layout	342
		Manhole Location and Spacing	342
		Location of Pumping Facilities	343
		Sewer Easements	343
		Example of a Sewer Network Layout	344
	10.5	**Flows in Sanitary Sewers**	**346**
		Low Flows in Early Years	346
		Allowances for Infiltration and Inflow	346
		Phased/Staged Construction	348
	10.6	**Horizontal and Vertical Alignment**	**348**
		Pipe Slopes	348
		Curved Sewer Alignment	349
		Minimum Depth of Cover	349
		Maximum Depth	352
	10.7	**Hydraulic Design**	**352**
		Pipe Sizing	354
		Manholes	355
		Computer Modeling for System Design	356
		Steady Flow versus Extended-Period Simulation (EPS) Analysis	356
		Design Maximum Flow Rates with Pumping	358
	10.8	**Special Installations**	**358**
		Sewers in Steep Terrain	358
		Sewers Along Streams	359
		Elevated Crossings	359
		Inverted Siphons (Depressed Sewers)	360
	10.9	**Wastewater Collection System Optimization**	**361**

Chapter 11 Wastewater Collection System Evaluation and Rehabilitation   371

	11.1	**Planning for System Characterization**	**372**
		Performance Requirements	373
		Current Performance	374
		Approach to System Characterization	375
	11.2	**System Characterization**	**376**
		Review Existing Records	376
		Update System Inventory	378
		Collection System Condition Investigation	379
		Inspection of the Condition of Controls and Ancillary Structures	382
	11.3	**Hydraulic Investigations**	**384**
		Field Data Collection	385
		Data Analysis	386
		Application of Hydraulic Modeling	390
		Assess Hydraulic Performance	394

	11.4	**Evaluating Rehabilitation Strategies**	**395**
		Preventive Maintenance Program 399	
		Source Controls 399	
		Sewer Separation.. 400	
		Pipe Rehabilitation/Replacement 401	
		Inflow/Infiltration Control.. 402	
		Interbasin Transfers 405	
		Real-Time Controls 405	
		Storage Facilities 406	
		Wet Weather Treatment Facilities... 407	

Chapter 12 Force Mains and Pump Stations — 419

12.1 Need for Pump Stations — 420

12.2 Pump Station Overview and Design Considerations — 423
Components.. 423
Design Decisions 425
Pump Capacity 425
Pump Station Configuration 426
Pump Types and Selection.. 427
Wet Well Sizing 432
Net Positive Suction Head 433
Appurtenances 435

12.3 Force Main Sizing with a Single Pump Station — 435
Determining Pipe Sizes 436
Developing System Head Curves 437
Selecting Economical Pipe Size 438

12.4 Modeling Pumped Systems — 441
Modeling Pumps.. 442
Downstream Flow Attenuation 442
Identifying Potential Problems 443
Modeling a Pipeline with Multiple High Points 444

12.5 Efficiency Considerations — 448
Constant-Speed Pumping... 448
Variable-Speed Pumping 451
Automated Energy Calculations 455

12.6 Force Mains with Multiple Pump Stations — 455

12.7 Hydraulic Transients — 457

Chapter 13 Low-Pressure Sewers — 467

13.1 Description of Pressure Sewers — 468
Storage Tanks.. 470
Service Lines 470
Pressure Mains 471
Air-Release/Vacuum-Breaker Valves 471
Discharge Points... 471

13.2	**Estimating Flows**	**472**
	Empirical Approaches	473
	Poisson Distribution to Estimate Loads	475
13.3	**Pressure Sewer Design Considerations**	**478**
13.4	**Modeling Pressure Sewers**	**479**
	Modeling to Size Pressure Mains	480
	Representing All Service Connections as Nodes	481
	Detailed Models	482

Chapter 14 Utilizing GIS 489

14.1	**GIS Fundamentals**	**490**
	Data Management	491
	Geographic Data Representations	494
14.2	**Developing an Enterprise GIS**	**495**
	Keys to Successful Implementation	495
	Needs Assessment	496
	Design	497
	Pilot Study	504
	Production	504
	Rollout	505
14.3	**Model Construction**	**505**
	Model Sustainability and Maintenance	506
	Communication Between the GIS and Modeling Staff	507
	Network Components	508
	Wastewater Loads	510
	Building the Model	515
	Pitfalls in Constructing Models from GIS	517
	Loading Model Results to GIS	520
14.4	**GIS Analysis and Visualization**	**520**
	Basic GIS Uses and Examples	520
	Advanced GIS Uses and Examples	522

Chapter 15 Regulatory Issues 529

15.1	**United States Laws and Regulations**	**529**
	Clean Water Act	530
	U.S. Federal Regulations	531
	Water Quality Standards and Total Maximum Daily Loads (TMDLs)	537
	Section 404 Dredge and Fill Permits	538
15.2	**Canadian Laws and Regulations**	**538**
	Sanitary Sewer Systems	539
	Combined Sewer Systems	539
15.3	**European Union Laws and Regulations**	**546**
	Urban Wastewater Treatment Directive (UWWTD)	546

Water Policy Framework Directive (WPFD) 549
Integrated Pollution Prevention Control Directive (IPPC) 549
Product Directives 549
Control of CSOs in EU Member States 549
Design Criteria for CSOs 550

15.4 Use of Models for Regulatory Compliance — **551**

Appendix A Symbols — 557

Appendix B Conversion Factors — 563

Appendix C Physical Properties — 567

Bibliography — 573

Index — 589

Preface

Wastewater conveyance facilities are usually an overlooked part of urban infrastructure—that is, until they do not perform well. Then they receive the wrong kind of attention. Good designers and operators of such systems keep their systems quietly and efficiently working out of the public's eye. This book is intended to help those individuals who design and operate wastewater collection systems do so effectively. It considers the range of wastewater collection system types, from strictly sanitary sewer systems to combined systems.

There are many aspects of wastewater collection systems including regulatory, inventory, personnel, and property ownership. This book focuses on the hydraulic aspects of collection systems. The hydraulic calculations needed for good design and analysis of systems are very cumbersome and nearly impossible to perform manually. As a result, use of computer models has become the standard for collection system work.

While this book concentrates on hydraulic models of wastewater collection systems, it is not solely a book on modeling, but one that takes the reader from basic hydraulics and model building to load estimation, data collection, calibration, design, and rehabilitation of systems. Even though the emphasis is on gravity systems, the book also covers force mains and pressure sewers, use of Geographic Information Systems (GIS), and regulatory issues.

The process of modeling a collection system varies from one situation to another. Tools and assumptions that work when designing a new system for a land development project are different from those used to analyze overflows from an aging urban system. This book seeks to capture that breadth.

Writing this book was especially challenging in that we had so many authors and reviewers, and there are so many ways to approach collections system modeling. It was not uncommon for an author to write about topic x, and another author to comment, "Why are we discussing topic x? No one does it that way." So we'd delete it and a reviewer would say, "Why don't you discuss topic x? That's how I solve these problems." There is really no single "right" way to do things, so we tried to cover as much ground as possible.

Chapter Overview

Chapter 1 provides general background information on wastewater collection systems and lays the historical groundwork for the remainder of the book.

Chapter 2 presents steady gravity flow hydraulic theory from the most basic principles to somewhat more advanced topics such as tractive forces and gradually varied flow.

Chapter 3 presents the basics of unsteady flow, from the most theoretically correct approach using the full Saint-Venant equations to various simplifications of those equations. It includes issues posed by appurtenances such as manholes and problems caused by surcharging in pipes that normally flow partly full.

Not all wastewater collection system pipes can flow by gravity. The principles of pumping and pressurized flow are presented in Chapter 4.

Chapter 5 continues with an overview of the process of creating hydraulic models for a variety of situations. It then discusses the practical aspects of obtaining and using the data needed for sound hydraulic analyses.

Design and analysis of collection systems are driven by the loads placed on the system. Dry weather loads, presented in Chapter 6, are especially important in new sanitary systems, and a variety of methods for estimating them are discussed. Wet weather flows (Chapter 7) tend to be most important in combined sewer systems and older systems with a good deal of infiltration and inflow. These contributions to loading can be as simple as unit loads or as complicated as hydrologic runoff models.

Models need data for calibration and verification, and the methods to collect this type of flow and precipitation data are presented in Chapter 8. When working with existing systems, Chapter 9 describes how these measurements are used to calibrate and validate the model so that model behavior closely mimics the behavior of the real collection system over a range of conditions.

Chapter 10 presents how new collection systems are designed, with an emphasis on the application of hydraulic models.

With most existing systems, the concern is not so much with installing new sewers but in assessing the capacity and performance of the systems and in using modeling to answer questions about the available capacity and the need for rehabilitation. Chapter 11 describes the requirements for this type of study, which are considerably different from those encountered when installing new sewers.

There are two ways in which pumping and pressure pipes are used in collection systems. The first consists of force mains and pumping stations as described in Chapter 12, while the second is a pressure sewer system with individual pumps at each customer as described in Chapter 13.

Utilities are increasingly relying on GIS data for model building. Chapter 14 discusses use of GIS data in wastewater modeling.

Collection systems must be designed and operated in compliance with increasingly strict regulations. An overview of regulatory practices is presented in Chapter 15.

Convention

While this book is entitled *Wastewater Collection System Modeling and Design* and the word "wastewater" is used frequently in the book, some prefer the term "sewage." These words are used interchangeably throughout the text, as are the terms "wastewater collection systems" and "sewage systems." The word "sewer" is used to describe the piping in the systems.

For units, English units are used first, with equivalent metric values given alongside. There is an extensive set of unit conversion tables in Appendix B.

Continuing Education and Problem Sets

Also included in this text are approximately 100 hydraulics and modeling problems to give students and professionals the opportunity to apply the material covered in each chapter. Some of these problems have short answers, and others require more thought and may have more than one solution. The accompanying CD-ROM in the back of the book contains an academic version of Haestad Methods' SewerCAD software (see "About the Software" on page xvii), which can be used to solve many of the problems, as well as data files with much of the given information in the problems pre-entered. However, we have endeavored to make this book a valuable resource to all modelers, including those who may be using other software packages, so these data files are merely a convenience, not a necessity.

If you would like to work the problems and receive continuing education credit in the form of Continuing Education Units (CEUs), you may do so by filling out the examination booklet available on the CD-ROM and submitting your work to Haestad Methods for grading.

For more information, see "Continuing Education Units" on page xv, "About the Software" on page xvii, and "CD-ROM Contents" in the back of the book.

Haestad Methods also publishes a solutions guide that is available for a nominal fee to instructors and professionals who are not submitting work for continuing education credit.

Feedback

The authors and staff of Haestad Methods have strived to make the content of *Wastewater Collection System Management and Design* as useful, complete, and accurate as possible. However, we recognize that there is always room for improvement, and we invite you to help us make subsequent editions even better.

If you have comments or suggestions regarding improvements to this textbook, or are interested in being one of our peer reviewers for future publications, we want to hear from you. We have established a forum for providing feedback at the following URL:

www.haestad.com/peer-review/

We hope that you find this culmination of our efforts and experience to be a core resource in your engineering library, and wish you the best with your modeling endeavors.

Thomas M. Walski, PhD, PE, DEE
Vice President of Engineering
Haestad Methods, Inc.

Continuing Education Units

With the rapid technological advances taking place in the engineering profession today, continuing education is more important than ever for civil engineers. In fact, it is now mandatory for many, as an increasing number of engineering licensing boards are requiring Continuing Education Units (CEUs) or Professional Development Hours (PDHs) for annual license renewal.

The chapters in this book contain exercises designed to reinforce the hydraulic and hydrologic principles covered in the text. Many of these problems provide an excellent opportunity to become further acquainted with software used in sanitary sewer modeling. Further, these exercises can be completed and submitted to Haestad Methods for grading and award of CEUs.

For the purpose of awarding CEUs, the chapters in this book have been grouped into several units. Complete the following steps to be eligible to receive credits as shown in the table. Note that you do not need to complete the units in order; you may skip units or complete only a single unit.

Unit	Topics Covered	Chapters Covered	CEUs[1]	Grading Fee (US $)[2]
1	Introduction, Open Channel Hydraulics	1 & 2	1.5	$75
2	Unsteady Flow, Pressure Flow	3 & 4	1.0	$50
3	Model Construction, Sanitary Loading	5 & 6	1.0	$50
4	Wet Weather Flows, Monitoring Calibration	7, 8 & 9	1.0	$50
5	Design of New Sewers, Rehabilitation of Existing	10 & 11	1.5	$75
6	Force Mains, Low-Pressure Sewers	12 & 13	1.5	$75
7	Utilizing GIS and Regulatory Issues	14 & 15	0.5	$25
All Units	All	All	8.0	$400

[1] 1 CEU = 10 PDHs
[2] Prices subject to change without notice.

1. Print the exam booklet from the file *exam_booklet.pdf* on the CD-ROM in the back of this book or contact Haestad Methods by phone, fax, mail, or email to have an exam booklet sent to you.

   Haestad Methods
   37 Brookside Road
   Waterbury, CT 06708
   USA
   Attn: Continuing Education

   Phone: +1 203 755 1666
   Fax: +1 203 597 1488
   email: ceu@haestad.com

2. Read and study the material contained in the chapters covered in the unit(s) you select.
3. Answer the exercises at the end of the relevant chapters and complete the exam booklet.
4. Return your exam booklet and payment to Haestad Methods for grading.
5. A Haestad Methods engineer will review your work and return your graded exam booklet to you. If you pass (70 percent or higher), you will receive a certificate documenting the CEUs (PDHs) earned for the successfully completed units.
6. If you do not pass, you will be allowed to correct your work and resubmit it for credit within 30 days at no additional charge.

Notes on Completing the Exercises

- Show your work, where applicable, to be eligible for partial credit. You may include separate pages to show your calculations.
- Many of the problems can be done manually with a calculator, while others are of a more realistic size and are much easier to solve if analyzed with sewer modeling software.
- To aid in completing the problems, a CD-ROM is included inside the back cover of this book. It contains an academic version of Haestad Methods Sewer-CAD software, software documentation, and computer files with much of the given information from the problem statements already entered. For detailed information on the CD-ROM contents and the software license agreement, see the information page in the back of the book.
- You are not required to use SewerCAD to work the problems.

About the Software

The CD-ROM in the back of this book contains an academic version of Haestad Methods SewerCAD Stand-Alone software. The following provides a brief summary of the software. For detailed information on the software and how to apply it to solve wastewater collection system problems, see the help system and tutorial files included on the CD-ROM. The software included with this textbook is fully functional but is not intended for professional use (see license agreement in the back of this book).

SewerCAD Stand-Alone

SewerCAD Stand-Alone is a powerful, easy-to-use program for the design and analysis of wastewater collection systems. SewerCAD Stand-Alone has a CAD-like interface but does not require the use of third-party software in order to run. SewerCAD provides intuitive access to the tools needed to model complex hydraulic situations. Some of the key features allow you to:

- Design and analyze multiple sanitary sewer networks in a single project
- Examine your system using gradually varied flow algorithms or a standard capacity analysis
- Automatically design the entire system, a selected portion, or just a single element using user-defined constraints for velocity, cover, and slope
- Load your model with unit sanitary loads based on contributing population, service area, total sanitary flow, or your own customized loading type
- Peak your loads using the Babbitt, Harmon, Ten State, or Federov equation, or use your own formulas or tables
- Calculate infiltration based on pipe length, diameter, surface area, length/diameter, or user-defined data
- Generate plan and profile plots of a network and customize their format to match your presentation standards
- Perform extended-period simulations that include time-variable loads and hydrologic routing
- Analyze pressure or partial (free surface) flow conditions automatically, including transitions
- Perform gravity structure head loss calculations using Standard, Absolute, FHWA HEC-22, or AASHTO methodologies
- Assess the costs associated with the sanitary sewer collection and pumping system automatically

- Recommend future improvements based on both hydraulic impact and construction cost
- Draw on existing pipe data, network topology, and digital terrain models within Autodesk Land Development Desktop / Civil Design (LDD/CD) projects
- Connect your SewerCAD model to GIS systems, SCADA systems, or other data management tools including databases and spreadsheets
- Analyze the trade-offs of different capital improvement plans to find the most cost-effective solution
- Efficiently manage large data sets and different "what if" situations with database query and edit tools
- Generate fully customizable graphs, charts, and reports
- Animate plans and profiles showing sanitary sewer system performance over time

CHAPTER

1

Introduction to Wastewater Collection System Modeling

Growth in world population and urbanization presents a host of challenges to the engineers and planners who design, maintain, and operate wastewater management systems. In developing regions, unprecedented growth and the accompanying increase in wastewater production mean that the environment is progressively less able to absorb pollution loads. Developed countries face additional challenges related to maintaining or improving the level of service in the face of aging wastewater infrastructure, new customers in need of sewer service, and increasingly strict environmental regulations.

Those tasked with meeting today's wastewater management challenges are aided by computer models and other technologies developed in recent decades. Hydraulic analysis programs can perform the detailed hydraulic calculations necessary to accurately model wastewater collection systems, freeing the modeler to consider a wider array of system conditions and alternative solutions. Designers and operators can now get a far more detailed picture of system behavior and more accurately predict how the system will react under various circumstances.

The focus of this book is the application of hydraulic models to the design, rehabilitation, and operation of sanitary and combined sewer systems. It presents the fundamental equations for flow in pipes, discusses the construction of wastewater collection system models, and describes the application of these models in practical situations. This chapter serves as an introduction to the text by describing basic terms and concepts and providing an overview of the history of collection systems, hydraulics, and computer modeling.

1.1 Wastewater Collection System Overview

Wastewater collection systems convey domestic, commercial, and industrial wastewater (and in many cases stormwater and groundwater) from its sources to a location where it may be treated and ultimately reclaimed for reuse or recycling, discharged to a receiving water body, or applied to the land. Wastewater is defined as "the spent or used water of a community or industry which contains dissolved and suspended matter." (American Society of Civil Engineers. 1982). The words *wastewater* and *sewage* are used interchangeably throughout this book. The pipes conveying the wastewater are referred to as *sewers*.

Terminology

A wastewater collection system consists of a network of pipes, connecting manholes or access chambers, pump stations, and pressure mains. The terminology used for these components varies from one location to another. Following are definitions of the most common elements.

- The largest sewers are usually referred to as *trunk sewers* or *interceptors*, although in some places the word interceptor is reserved for those sewers that intercept flow that formerly was discharged directly into streams but is now transported to treatment facilities.
- A *main* (sometimes called a *collector*) is the term used to describe most sewers.
- In some locations, *laterals* are the smallest sewers; in others the term refers to the piping from the customer to the main in the street.
- A *relief sewer* describes a sewer installed to provide extra capacity to a part of the system that was overloaded.
- Pressurized pipes fed by centralized pump stations are referred to as *force mains* or *rising mains*.
- Pressurized pipes fed by pumps from individual customers are called *pressure sewer* systems.
- *Vacuum sewers* use vacuum pumps to convey wastewater.
- Pumps are contained in structures known as *pump stations* or *lift stations*.
- *Wet wells* are underground chambers that store wastewater waiting to be pumped.
- *Manholes* or *access structures* provide access to the sewer for cleaning and other maintenance activities.
- *Diversion chambers* and *junction chambers* are structures in which flow can be mixed or split. In combined sewers systems, flow can be split between that going to treatment and that going to an overflow.
- *Storage facilities* may consist of oversized pipes, surface ponds, or underground tunnels.

Wastewater collection systems are usually laid out in treelike (dendritic) patterns with smaller sewers flowing into progressively larger sewers. Thus there is generally only one flow path from any point of entry to the terminus of the sewer system.

Sources of Wastewater

Wastewater collection systems are designed to collect and transport wastewater from domestic, commercial, and industrial sources. However, inadvertent or illegal connections frequently result in entry of additional flows into the system. *Infiltration* is water that enters the system from the ground through defective pipes, pipe joints, connections, or manhole walls. *Inflow* is water discharged into the sewer from sources such as building and foundation drains, drains from wet or swampy areas, manhole covers, cross connections, catch basins, or surface runoff. Collectively, these flows are referred to as *infiltration/inflow* or *I/I*. These nonwastewater flows may be separated into dry- and wet-weather components. *Rainfall-derived inflow and infiltration* or *RDII* is the component of the sewer flow that is above the normal dry-weather flow pattern. It represents the sewer flow response to rainfall or snowmelt in the system.

Types of Conveyance

Although most sewer systems are designed and operated for partially full gravity flow, there are actually five types of flow conditions that can exist in a collection system, as illustrated in Figure 1.1.

- *Partially full gravity flow* – there is a free water surface in the pipe.
- *Surcharged gravity flow* – the depth of flow in the gravity pipe is above the pipe crown because of a downstream control.
- *Pressure flow in force mains* – sewage is pumped along stretches where gravity flow is not feasible, such as from one gravity drainage basin to another.
- *Pressure sewers* – each customer has a pump that discharges to a pressure sewer.
- *Vacuum sewers* – flow is pulled through the system by vacuum pumps.

Even though most collection system pipes fall into the first category, systems can have a combination of all five types of flow.

Pipe materials used in sewage systems include reinforced concrete, prestressed concrete, cast iron, ductile iron, vitrified clay, polyvinyl chloride, and polyethylene. Due to the corrosive nature of sewage, metal pipes and, in some cases, concrete pipes may be lined to reduce the effects of corrosion.

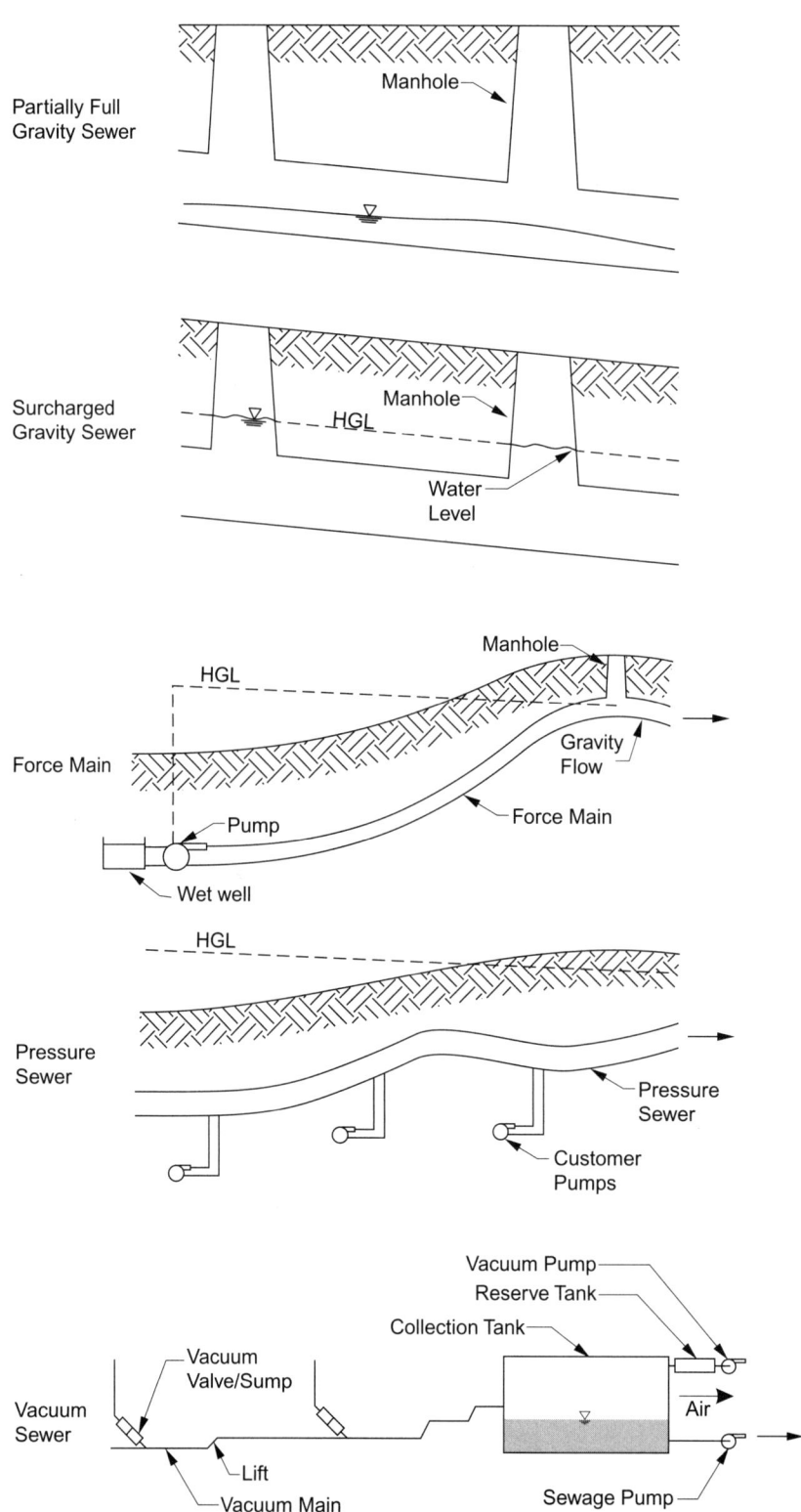

Figure 1.1 Flow conditions found in various types of sanitary sewers.

1.2 Modeling

The words *model* and *modeling* are used in so many ways that it is helpful to distinguish among the many types of models. The *American College Dictionary* (Random House, 1970) defines a model as "a physical or mathematical representation to show the construction or operation of something." With regards to wastewater collection systems, there are actually several kinds of models.

- A *mathematical model* is a set of equations that describes some physical process. The Manning equation is an example of a mathematical model describing the relation between velocity, size, roughness, and hydraulic grade line slope in a pipe or channel. Mathematical models can be solved either analytically or numerically.

- A *computer model* is a computer program representing a physical system that approximates or reflects specific behaviors of that system. The numerical representation allows for computational numerical analysis. A computer model usually contains one or more mathematical models. A program such as SewerCAD can model flow in a sewage collection system.

- A *system model* consists of the computer model plus all of the data necessary for a particular system model. For example, SewerCAD, plus the data files describing the collection system in City A, comprise the sewer system model for City A.

In addition to these three types of models, the words *model* and *modeling* are also often used in software design to describe how data are structured. An *object model* is a graphical representation of the structure of objects (components) that make up a software package including their attributes, functions, and associations between other objects. A *data model* or *data schema* refers to the way that data are organized in database files and database tables. With a defined formal data schema, users and programs know exactly where to place or find the data. Once data are located, the schema further describes its type, size, and constraints.

In this book the word *modeling* is most often used to describe the process of creating and using a wastewater collection system model for a specific system.

Applications of Collection System Models

Sanitary sewer models are used for design, long-range master planning, water quality investigations, operational analysis, capacity assessments, and regulatory compliance. The development, calibration, and maintenance of a model comprise a continuous process for the system operator. Some applications are described below.

Long-Range Master Planning. Planners and engineers investigate a wastewater collection system and its projected flows to determine which capital improvement projects are necessary to ensure quality of service for the future. This process, called *master planning* (also referred to as *capital improvement planning* or a *comprehensive planning study*), usually includes an activity to project system growth and wastewater flows for design horizons of 5, 10, 20 years, or more. System growth may occur because of population growth, industrial expansion, annexation, acquisition, or wholesale agreements between wastewater collection utilities. The ability of the collection network to serve its customers adequately must be evaluated whenever system growth is anticipated. Not only can a model be used to identify potential capacity problems (such as overflows), but also to size and locate collectors, pumping stations, and force mains, so that those problems will never occur.

Design. In the design of new sewer systems or the expansion of existing systems, hydraulic models simulate the performance of the individual components and the collection system as a whole. During the design process, numerous configurations, alternatives, and loadings may be evaluated to determine pipe sizes, elevations, and alignments. Checking the size of a pipe or the performance of a proposed pump under anticipated conditions are examples of how a model is used in design.

Rehabilitation Studies. As with all engineered systems, the wear and tear on a sewage collection system usually leads to the eventual need for rehabilitation of portions of the system. Pipe joints crack and develop leaks, allowing infiltration. Uneven settlement causes misalignment of pipe sections, and sediments may clog pipe sections. To counter these effects of aging, a utility may choose to clean or reline a pipe in an attempt to restore it to its original hydraulic condition. Alternatively, the pipe may be replaced with a new (possibly larger) pipe or another pipe may be installed in parallel. Manholes may be replaced or rehabilitated. Hydraulic simulations can be used to aid the design of rehabilitation efforts, to assess the effects of such rehabilitation, and to determine the most economical improvements.

Water Quality Investigations. The quantity and quality of flow that a sewer collection system delivers to a treatment plant affects the treatment efficiency and, ultimately, the water quality of the receiving body. Some wastewater collection models can track various constituents within the flow. High levels of I/I in a sewer system can reduce treatment plant efficiency and lead to discharge of high levels of pollutants into receiving bodies. Overflowing sewers release untreated wastewater into the environment. Today, many environmental regulatory agencies have severe restrictions, with possible enforcement actions for such overflows. Overflows must be eliminated in sanitary systems, while in combined systems they must be minimized to reduce water quality impacts. Models can help us to understand where, when, and why sewers overflow and to assess mitigation measures, which can improve water quality.

Operations. System operators are generally responsible for ensuring that the system provides a continuous flow of sewage to the treatment plant. Unexpected peaks or unusual patterns in the flow may indicate an illegal discharge to the sewer. An unusual decrease in flow may indicate an overflow, a break or washout of a sewer main, or a malfunctioning pump station. A model can simulate different daily operation schemes to determine the effect of various actions, such as modifying pump station operation, providing the operator with better information with which to make decisions. If the model contains information related to the changes in flow throughout the day, it can be used to schedule the best time to visit a site. Considering the velocity and depth changes throughout the system can help to predict areas of increased hydrogen sulfide generation.

Regulatory Compliance. Hydraulic sewer models are an extremely useful tool for assessing and demonstrating compliance with environmental regulations. As discussed in Chapter 15, operators of sanitary sewer systems must comply with many constantly changing regulations. Models can demonstrate whether the system has adequate capacity and its effect on water quality. For example, the US EPA's Combined Sewer Overflow (CSO) policy (US Environmental Protection Agency, 1999) states the following:

> Modeling of a sewer system is recognized as a valuable tool for predicting sewer response to various wet weather events and assessing water quality impacts when evaluating different control strategies and alternatives. EPA supports the proper and effective use of models, where appropriate, in the evaluation of the nine minimum controls and the development of a long-term CSO control plan. (Section II.C.1.d)

Types of Collection System Modeling

Two kinds of modeling are used in collection systems, steady-state and unsteady flow. *Steady-state* models assume constant flow rates at each point in the system and can be thought of as a snapshot in time of the changing conditions of the system. Although flow in a wastewater system is not actually steady, the primary interest of the designer is to determine whether or not there is sufficient capacity to convey the peak flows. Steady-state models are ideal for predicting these peak flows. In addition, steady-state models can be used to determine if the velocities at lower flow rates are sufficient for self-cleansing.

For most design work, this steady-state approach is adequate. For larger systems or systems with widely varying flows, such that pump cycling or storage in the pipes is significant, simulation of *unsteady-flow* conditions becomes important. This is accomplished by routing flows through the system using either a hydrologic routing technique or by solving the more complex hydrodynamic equations. Chapter 3 discusses unsteady-flow routing in detail.

1.3 Historical Perspective on Collection System Analysis

The history of collection system analysis follows two paths:
- The development of collection systems
- The development of hydraulic analysis techniques and software.

Collection Systems

The earliest drainage systems date back to as early as the third century B.C. with the Indus civilization followed by the Mesopotamians (Mays, 2001). The systems from this period were developed primarily for stormwater drainage, but frequently conveyed sanitary waste as well. During the second century B.C., the Minoan civilization developed extensive drainage systems on the island of Crete. These included the first documented separate sewer system in Knossos (Mays, 2001). Between 1100 and 700 B.C., the Greeks began constructing the first sewers under streets. The Romans did the same adding crude stone manhole lids with bronze rings for lifting (Mays, 2001).

There was little progress in sewage collection systems in western Europe during the Dark Ages. Collection systems were primarily intended for stormwater, while night soil from chamber pots was disposed of as solid waste, if possible. Often, night soil was simply discarded through an open window with a shout of *"garde l'eau,"* which translates as "watch out for the water" (Ecenbarger, 1993). Metcalf & Eddy (1972) reported that human waste was banned from the London sewer system until 1815 and from the Boston system until 1833. Hamburg, Germany, made it mandatory to connect houses to the sewer system in 1843 (Foil, Cerwick, and White, 1999).

A major technology was introduced in the period 1800–1865: a continuous supply of running water (Tarr, 1996). Wastewater flows changed considerably with the advent of the flush toilet in the mid-1800s. Although there were numerous designs, the first that was widely accepted is credited to Thomas Crapper in 1884 (Ecenbarger, 1993; Reyburn, 1971). By 1880, roughly one third of the urban households in the United States had flush toilets (Tarr, 1996). The development of the water closet meant that dry weather sewage flows increased significantly, while the quality of water entering receiving streams deteriorated significantly. Cities began constructing systems to remove wastes with no consideration for treatment. Three of the more noteworthy projects of the nineteenth century are noted here.

The original Paris storm sewer was constructed in the Middle Ages as the streets were paved (Delluer, 2003). Under Napoleon I, a vaulted sewer network was built, as shown in Figure 1.2. It was approximately 30 km long. In 1850, Georges Haussmann and Eugene Belgrand designed the present sewer and water-supply network. It was built to discharge flow downstream of Paris. The system worked by gravity, with pumping stations in low neighborhoods. The sewers were large enough to allow room for potable-water mains, cables, and pneumatic tubes. Most of the main collectors had a rounded lower section called a "cunette" and inspection sidewalks on each side. Many portions had egg-shaped cross sections. The Paris sewers were the prototype for most other sewer systems around the world and became a tourist attraction in the late 1800s. The tour included *Wagan-vannes*, the boats used to clean the sewers by increasing flow velocity around their hulls. The sewers of Paris are the subject of a book by Reid (1991).

In London during the early 1800s, most residences had cesspits beneath the floors (Gayman, 1996). The pits were designed to overflow into street drains when filled to capacity. Problems with odors, explosions, and asphyxiation from sewer gases, as well as disease, caused the Commission of Sewers to develop a comprehensive plan. Joseph Bazalgette designed the systems. The Main Drainage of London began in 1859 and was completed in 1865. The combined drainage system had 3-in. laterals, 9-in. intermediate pipes, and egg-shaped mains, as illustrated in Figure 1.3.

In the United States, a significant sewer-construction project was the Sanitary and Ship Canal in Chicago, (first phase, 1892–1900) (Zurad, Sobonski, and Rakoczy, 2002). The project was conceived in response to the polluting of Lake Michigan, the source of Chicago's drinking water, by untreated sewage. As the city grew in the second half of the nineteenth century, the intakes were moved farther from the shore. In 1885 a major storm flushed runoff and wastewater far beyond the intakes and epidemics killed thousands during the mid 1880s. As a result, the Sanitary District of Chicago was created to safeguard Lake Michigan. The problem was solved by reversing the flow of the polluting rivers and redirecting them to the Mississippi River basin. A system of three canals totaling 70.5 mi (113 km) was constructed. Figure 1.4 shows some workers in one of the tunnels.

Hager (1994) described the history of wastewater hydraulics with an emphasis on German systems. He wrote that the first German system was designed by Walter Lindley for the City of Hamburg in the mid-1800s. Systems in Danzig, Berlin, and Zurich followed. Bechman (1905) and Frühling (1910) wrote about French and German collection systems at the beginning of the twentieth century. Imhoff's (1907) pop-

Figure 1.2 Cutaway view of a Paris sewer, 1830.

ular pocket guide on sewer design contained primarily graphical solutions to sewer design problems.

Initially, sewers discharged directly into receiving waters. The earliest wastewater treatment facilities were developed in England in the 1860s (Metcalf & Eddy, Inc., 1972). Early research into treatment in the United States was conducted at the Lawrence Experiment Station in Massachusetts in the late 1800s.

Most sewer systems in the early twentieth century were constructed as combined sewer systems, sized primarily to convey stormwater flow and carrying sanitary sewage as an afterthought. Because treatment facilities could not handle large wet-weather flows, these systems had diversions, or overflows, installed to discharge combined sewage directly to the receiving water during high-flow events.

One of the earliest US design books on collection system practice was Metcalf and Eddy's (1914) *American Sewage Practice*. Other important references were Babbitt and Bauman's *Sewerage and Sewage Treatment* (1922), Steel's *Water Supply and Sewerage* (1938), and papers by Camp (1946) and Shields (1936). For many years, the standard reference for collection system design was the joint American Society of Civil Engineers (Manual 37) and Water Pollution Control Federation's (Manual of Practice 9) *Design and Construction of Sanitary and Storm Sewers* (1930), which was later divided into two publications.

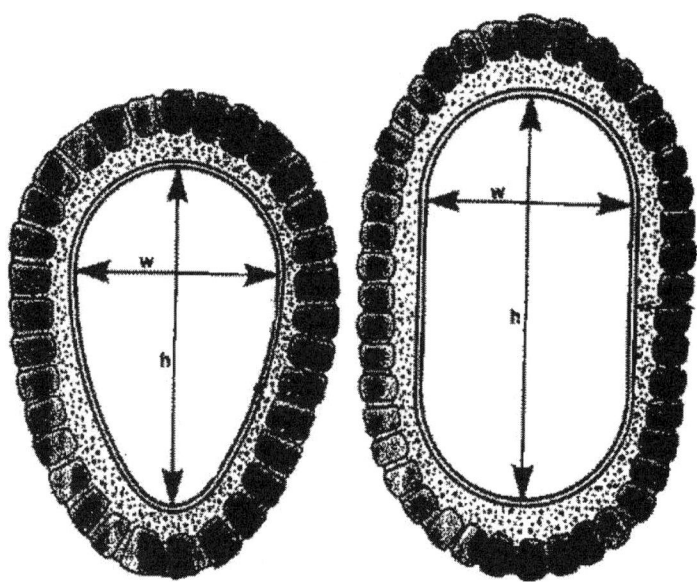

Graphic reprinted with permission from Cleaner Magazine (A Glimpse into London's Early Sewers), March 1996
©1996 COLE Publishing Inc. www.cleaner.com

Figure 1.3 Oval sewer designs used in London.

Courtesy of The Metropolitan Water Reclamation District of Greater Chicago

Figure 1.4 Chicago Ship and Sanitary Canal.

In post–World War II United States, separate sewer systems were installed in most communities constructing new systems. Steel (1947) described circumstances where separate sewers would be preferable to combined sewers,

> ...where there is an immediate necessity for collection of sanitary sewage but not for the larger conduits required for the storm flow; where conditions are favorable for carrying storm sewage long distances over the ground surface; where disposal of the

combined flow would necessitate pumping but where the separated storm sewage would not; where mixture of storm and sanitary sewage would need to be pumped; where the mixture of storm and sanitary sewage would necessitate the treatment of both while separation would allow disposal of storm flow without treatment; where an existing system of storm or combined sewers is inadequate in capacity and can be used for sanitary sewage alone....

By the 1960s, no new combined sewer systems were being installed in the United States. Public Law 92-500 (1972) made it virtually impossible to obtain a discharge permit for any combined system. The very high costs of separating existing combined sewers means that many combined systems will continue to operate as such for the foreseeable future in the United States.

The first modeling of collection systems consisted of tabular forms with manual calculations of flows, water levels, and hydraulic grade lines (American Society of Civil Engineers, 1982). As computer programming became feasible, these manual calculations were computerized to simplify the work of iterative calculations. With the advent of microcomputers and spreadsheet programs, these calculations were often moved to the microcomputer.

The first dynamic computer model was the US EPA Storm Water Management Model (SWMM) (Heaney, Huber, and Nix, 1976). Since that time, many other models have been developed to simulate the performance of wastewater collection systems. Recent years have seen the implementation of powerful graphical user interfaces in these models. Users no longer need to scroll through long text listings of model inputs and results.

Even though separate systems are currently the norm in developed countries, excess infiltration and inflow still cause problems with wet weather flows. In addition to installation of new sewers, existing sewers continue to require considerable rehabilitation due to hydrogen sulfide corrosion, root intrusion, uneven settlement, and poor-quality joints. Also, areas become redeveloped with new land uses and densities increasing the loads on existing sewers. Currently, regulatory agencies are emphasizing minimization of wet weather collection system overflows as a key item in improvement of water quality (US EPA, 2000).

Recent advances in wastewater collection systems include portable flow metering, improvements in efficiency of variable-speed pumps, and greater reliance on small-diameter pressure and vacuum sewers (US EPA, 1991). Some systems have adopted strategies that include storage of wet weather flows so that they can be treated later. New methods for in situ rehabilitation of sewers have extended the useful lives of sewers. SCADA (Supervisory Control And Data Acquisition) technology has greatly improved the monitoring and control of wastewater collection systems.

In recent years, research in combined sewers has moved away from hydraulics to the development of treatment methods to minimize the effects of overflow on receiving waters. Such technologies include sediment traps, vortex regulators and concentrators, high-rate treatment processes, maximizing wastewater treatment plant performance, and disinfection (Field, Sullivan, and Tafuri, 2004).

Hydraulics History

The existence of functioning sewer systems more than 2000 years ago indicates that some ancient civilizations understood rudimentary hydraulic principles. The follow-

Combined vs. Separate Sewers

In the 1800s, cities in western Europe and North America abandoned cesspools and pit privies and constructed sewer systems for the removal and disposal of wastes. The original urban sewers in Great Britain and Europe were for stormwater only. With the installation of running water and water closets, houses were connected to the existing storm sewers, which evolved into a combined system. This approach was adopted in many large cites in the United States.

George E. Waring Jr. was a sanitarian and a proponent of the theory that "sewer gas," produced by putrefying fecal wastes, was the cause of infectious diseases such as typhoid, cholera, and yellow fever, which were common in urban areas. He developed the concept of the separate sewer system with flush tanks placed at the upstream terminal of each lateral. The tanks had a mechanism to insure that 112 gallons were flushed every 24 hours. Household connections were 4 in. in diameter and no more than 300 homes were to be connected to each 6-in. main. The systems contained no manholes. In 1875–76, Waring built the first separate sewer system in the United States in Lenox, Massachusetts. The best known example of the Waring system was built in Memphis, Tennessee in 1880.

In 1881 the National Board of Health sent sanitary engineer Rudolph Hering to Europe to report on sewage practices. Hering submitted an exhaustive report that suggested a model for choosing between separate and combined sewers. Both systems improved sanitary conditions, with the choice depending on local conditions and financial considerations. Combined sewers were best suited for densely built-up cites, while separate systems were best suited for smaller cites where underground removal of stormwater was not required. Hering had attempted to develop a rational engineering basis within a cost-benefit framework for decisions about sewer design. Hering's model was used to select the type of sewer system and both types were built in the late 1800s.

Waring remained a strong advocate of the separate sewer system. He obtained patents on his design and formed his own company to sell it to cities across the United States. By 1892, 22 municipalities had constructed separate Waring systems. The perceived danger of sewer gas was a primary justification for removing sewage as quickly as possible. In 1887, Hering performed an evaluation of the Memphis system. He found that the small pipes did not flow smoothly and resulted in frequent stoppages. Since there were no manholes, streets had to be torn up to clear blockages. The flush tanks were inefficient and unnecessary because of the steep slopes of the sewers.

The debate between combined and separate sewer advocates continued into the twentieth century. The concept of design choice rested on the assumption that large cities could safely dispose of their sewage in waterways, since the ability of receiving waters to dilute and purify wastes was not well understood. Many engineers thought that water filtration plants could safely protect the public from the diseases associated with sewage and that wastewater treatment plants were not required.

Eventually, the construction of combined sewers ceased. Through the twentieth century there was an effort to separate sewer systems and treat and/or temporarily store the discharge from combined sewers. The overflow of untreated wastes from combined sewers (CSOs) remains a significant environmental problem today. In the United States, there are 859 CSO permits in 32 states. The regulation of CSOs and the management strategies implemented to mitigate their effects are described in Chapter 15.

Sources:

Schladweiler, J. C. 2002. "Tracking Down the Roots of Our Sanitary Sewers. www.sewerhistory.org/chronos/roots.htm.

Tarr, J. A. 1996. *The Search for the Ultimate Sink: Urban Pollution in Historical Perspective*. Akron, OH: University of Akron Press.

US Environmental Protection Agency (EPA). 2001. *Report to Congress: Implementation and Enforcement of the Combined Sewer Overflow Control Policy*. US Environmental Protection Agency 823-R-01-003. Washington, DC: US Environmental Protection Agency.

ing section, which documents some of the key events in hydraulic history was adopted primarily from Rouse and Ince (1957).

Archimedes (c. 250 B.C.) is the best-known hydraulics researcher of ancient times. He is credited with the invention of the screw pump (Archimedes screw) and the discovery of the principles of buoyancy. However, the science of hydraulics wasn't established until the time of Leonardo da Vinci (c. 1500). He experimented with weirs, orifices, and flow resistance in open channels. Dialogues Galileo (c. 1620) extended some of Da Vinci's work and studied vacuums and hydrostatics. Later (c. 1640), Benedetto Castelli developed the principle that flow, velocity, and area are related as $Q = AV$. Evangelista Torricelli (c. 1644) extended Castelli's and Galileo's work and showed that the velocity of flow from an orifice is proportional to the square root of the head. Torricelli is also credited with the invention of the barometer and some of the earliest experiments with vacuums.

Edme Mariotte (c. 1680) applied the results of his experiments to decrease flow resistance by avoiding abrupt bends and increasing pipe diameters to allow for deposits. Domenico Guglielmini (c. 1700) introduced the principle of equilibrium between the velocity of a fluid in a channel and the resistance of the channel.

In addition to developing the first mechanical "arithmetic computer," Blaise Pascal (c. 1660) developed Pascal's principle, which states that in a fluid at rest, pressure acts equally in all directions. Figure 1.5 illustrates some of Pascal's experimental appararatus.

With the publication of *Principia Mathematica Philosophiae Naturalis* in 1687, Sir Isaac Newton brought mathematics to the description of physical phenomena in a way that had not been seen before, thus laying the groundwork for modern hydraulics. His three laws of motion are essential to all later mechanics, but his law of viscosity is particularly important to hydraulics.

Daniel Bernoulli's publication of *Hydrodynamicae* in 1739 (see the title page in Figure 1.6) was a compendium of the hydraulic principles known at that time. He is best known for the Bernoulli principle, which describes the drop in pressure of a fluid in motion. While Bernoulli explained the ideas behind what is known as Bernoulli's equation, his colleague Leonhard Euler (c. 1760) actually wrote out the Bernoulli equation in the form used today.

While the science of hydraulics progressed, practical application was based to a large extent on the experimental work of Claude Couplet (c. 1710) at Versailles and the publication of *Architecture Hydraulique* by Bernard de Belidor in four volumes between 1737 and 1753. Another French hydraulic engineer, Henri Pitot (c. 1750), developed the principles of measuring velocity in a fluid by observing the velocity head in a Pitot tube.

Several investigators studied the resistance of channels to flow, but it was Antoine Chézy (c. 1780) who determined that velocity is proportional to the square root of the channel slope. A similar equation was also developed by Johannes Eytelwein at roughly the same time. Pierre du Duat (c. 1800) was one of the first to explicitly use the factor $2g$ in hydraulic equations and to theorize on the interactions between fluids and boundaries.

The science of flow measurement advanced with the development of the current meter by Reinhard Woltman (c. 1780) and the Venturi meter for closed-pipe flow by Giovanni Venturi (c. 1795).

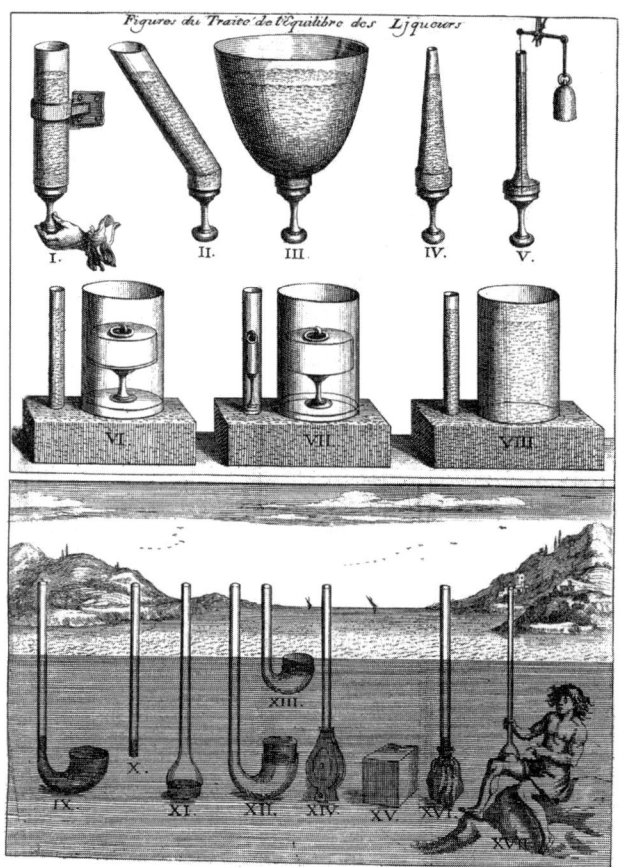

Figure 1.5 Sketch of Pascal's experimental equipment for demonstrating the principles of hydrostatic pressure.

Although the hydraulic jump had been known for some time, Giorgio Bidone (c. 1820) is credited with being the first to systematically study it. A contemporary of Bidone, Giuseppe Venturoli, is credited with developing the first backwater curve for nonuniform flow. Work on backwater curves was extended by Jean Belanger in 1828.

Several investigators in the early 1800s, including Louis Navier, Augustin de Cauchy, Jean Barre de St. Venant, and George Stokes, sought to develop general equations for the motion of fluids. The resulting equations are generally referred to as the *Navier-Stokes equations*, and the one-dimensional form is referred to as the *St. Venant equation*.

In 1839, Gotthilf Hagen described two flow regimes, later known as *laminar* and *turbulent*, and developed equations for head loss in both types of flow. His work was substantiated in 1841 by Jean Louis Poiseuille, who was primarily interested in the flow of blood. The theory behind the Hagen-Poiseuille law was later developed by Franz Neumann and Eduard Hagenach (c. 1860).

Julius Weisbach (c. 1845) developed the general formula for head loss that still bears his name and was a proponent of nondimensional coefficients. Henry Darcy also conducted experiments on head loss in a wide variety of pipes. This work, published in 1857, led to his name also being associated with Weisbach's equation.

Figure 1.6 Title page of Daniel Bernoulli's *Hydronamica*.

In Ireland, T. J. Mulvaney (1851) investigated the relation between rainfall and streamflow, which became the rational method. These techniques were introduced to the United States by E. Kuichling (1889), as described in (Chow, 1964).

Henri Bazin (c. 1870) published extensive experimental studies on flow in open channels and over weirs. An improvement to Chézy's equation for head loss in open channels was published by Emile Ganguillet and Wilhelm Kutter in 1869 and was verified against Bazin's work. A different equation was published by Phillippe Gauckler in 1868, and a subsequent equation was developed by Irish engineer Robert Manning (c. 1889). The equation referred to today as the *Manning equation* more closely resembles that of Gauckler.

The principles of similarity were advanced in the late 1800s with Osborne Reynolds and the father-and-son team of William and Robert Froude receiving credit for the advances in this area. Neither of the Froudes actually developed or used the dimensionless number associated with their name. Although Reynolds is most often associated with the description of laminar and turbulent flow, he also conducted considerable work in cavitation and the equations for turbulent flow. William Thomas (Lord Kelvin) is credited with coining the term *turbulence* in 1887.

Sir Horace Lamb wrote the most comprehensive work in hydrodynamics with his *Treatise on the Mathematical Theory of Fluid Motion*, first published in 1879. The title was changed to *Hydrodynamics* in subsequent editions.

The early 1900s saw the development of empirical equations for head loss in the United States by A. Hazen and G. S. Williams (c. 1900) and Charles Scobey (c. 1915). Ralph Leroy Parshall (c. 1915) developed a measuring flume based on Venturi's principles that today bears Parshall's name.

The primary advances in the early 1900s were made in the understanding of boundary layer theory, which deals with the interactions between fluids and solids. Much of this work, centered at the Kaiser Wilhelm Institute für Strömungsforschung, was led by Ludwig Prandtl. Some of Prandtl's more notable students included Paul Blasius, Theodor von Karman, Johann Nikuradse, and Herman Schlichting. This group provided the theoretical basis for the head loss equations developed empirically by Weisbach during the previous century.

Meanwhile in England, Thomas Stanton (c. 1920) developed what were known as *Stanton Diagrams*, relating the friction factor, roughness, and Reynolds number, although such diagrams were first developed by Blasius. Today, these are referred to as *Moody Diagrams*, after the work of US researcher Lewis Moody (1944).

While not as exciting as hydraulic research, others did considerable work on the estimation of sewage flow rates. For large systems, H. E. Babbitt proposed methods for determining average and peak flows and Hunter (1940) developed the fixture-unit method for estimating sewage flow rates for plumbing systems. The Johns Hopkins Residential Water Use Program developed additional data for estimating flows (Geyer and Lentz, 1964). R. D. Pomeroy (1974) developed methods to predict and control hydrogen sulfide generation in sewers.

Current research has focused more on the computerization of hydraulic design calculations and the development of sophisticated software packages, rather than the development of new equations.

Historical Summary

Wastewater collection system modeling represents the marriage of wastewater technology, hydraulic analysis, and computerization to develop tools that can be used to efficiently solve practical sewer system design and analysis problems. New innovations in GIS, SCADA, optimization, and graphical user interfaces should continue to help engineers and operators more effectively operate and manage their systems.

1.4 The Modeling Process

Modeling can be used to quickly perform a large array of "what-if" analyses to investigate optimal facility sizing, I/I control, and operational changes before such changes are made in the actual system. Modeling is not a single linear process, but a series of steps, some of which can be performed in parallel (see Figure 1.7). The importance of some steps depends on the nature of the project. Moreover, each of the steps can be repeated. For example, even after a model has been used to design a project, the modeler may go back to the loading step and determine the effects of other loads.

The complexity of a system model depends on the application, software, availability and extent of data, budget, and skill level of the modeler. The modeling process illustrated schematically in Figure 1.7 begins with a clear definition of purpose and scope for the project. It is important to have all wastewater collection utility personnel

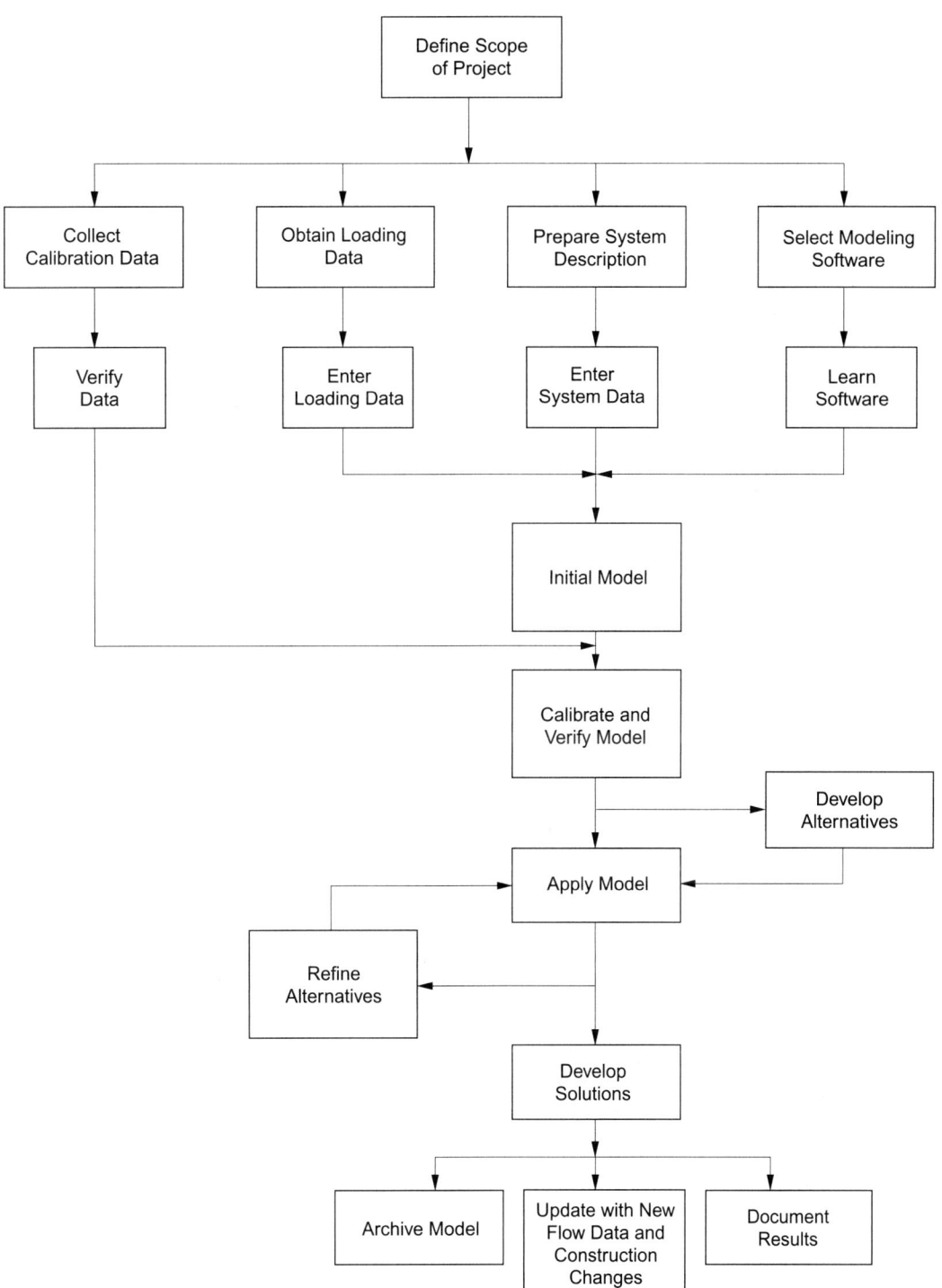

Figure 1.7 Flow chart of the steps in modeling a wastewater collection system.

including upper management, engineering, operations, and maintenance commit to the modeling effort in terms of human resources, time, and funding. Modeling cannot be viewed as an isolated endeavor by a single modeler, but rather as a utility-wide effort with the modeler as the integrator. Once the vision of modeling is accepted by the utility, key decisions on issues such as flow rate generation, data accuracy, and calibration precision may be addressed.

As shown in Figure 1.7, the initial development of the model is accomplished in four parallel tracks. These steps may be conducted by different personnel, but they must be coordinated. The actual calibration of the model is the responsibility of the lead modeler. Often the calibration step reveals deficiencies in the system or in the loading (flow rate) data and requires that additional data be obtained.

When the model has been calibrated and verified, simulations may be performed for other configurations, loadings, and pipe sizes. Results from these simulations may lead to the development of additional options. The end product of modeling is a recommended master plan, design, operating plan, or rehabilitation plan. When the task has been completed, it is important that the model and results be documented and the model stored so that it can be readily updated when the sewer configuration or the loadings change.

The modeling process is described in great detail in the remaining chapters of this book. A network model is just another tool (albeit a very powerful, multipurpose tool) for an experienced engineer or operator. It is still the responsibility of the user to understand the real system, understand the model, and make decisions based on sound engineering judgment.

References

American Society of Civil Engineers (ASCE). 1930. *Design and Construction of Sanitary and Storm Sewers*. ASCE Manual 37 and WPCF MOP 9. New York: American Society of Civil Engineers.

American Society of Civil Engineers (ASCE). 1982. *Gravity Sanitary Sewer Design and Construction*. ASCE MOP 50 (WEF MOP FD-5). Reston, VA: American Society of Civil Engineers.

American Society of Civil Engineers (ASCE). 1992. *Design and Construction of Urban Stormwater Management Systems*. ASCE MOP No. 77 (WEF MOP-FD-20). Reston, VA: American Society of Civil Engineers.

Babbitt, H. E., and E. R. Baumann. 1922. *Sewerage and Sewage Treatment*. New York: John Wiley & Sons.

Bechman, G. 1905. *Hydrologique agricole et urbaine (Agricultural and Urban Hydraulics)*. Paris: Belanger.

Camp, T. R. 1946. Design of sewers to facilitate flow. *Sewerage Works Journal* 18, no. 3.

Chow, V. T. 1964. *Handbook of Applied Hydrology*. New York: McGraw-Hill.

Delluer, J. W. 2003. The evolution of urban hydrology: Past, present and future. *Journal of Hydraulic Engineering* 129, no. 8: 563–573.

Ecenbarger, W. 1993. Flushed with success. *Chicago Tribune*, 4 April.

Federal Water Pollution Control Act [commonly referred to as Clean Water Act], Public Law 92-500, October 18, 1972, 86 Stat. 816; 33 *US Code* 1251 et seq. Amended by PL 100-4, February 4, 1987.

Field, R., D. Sullivan, and A. N. Tafuri. 2004. *Management of Combined Sewer Overflows*, Boca Raton, Florida: Lewis Publishers.

Foil, J., J. Cerwick, and J. White. 1999 Where we've been—wastewater collection. *Missouri Water Environment Association Newsletter* (Fall).

Frühling, A. 1910. Die entwasserung der stadte (Drainage of Cities). In *Handbuch der Ingenieurwissenschauften (Handbook of Engineering Studies)*. Leipzig: Englemann.

Gayman, M. 1996. A glimpse into London's early sewers. *Cleaner*, March.

Geyer, J. C., and J. L. Lentz. 1964. *An Evaluation of the Problems of Sanitary Sewer System Design*. Baltimore, MD: The Johns Hopkins University Press.

Haestad Methods and R. Durrans. 2002. *Stormwater Conveyance Modeling and Design*. Waterbury, CT: Haestad Press.

Hager, W. H. 1994 (English edition 1999). *Wastewater Hydraulics*. Berlin: Springer.

Heaney, J. P., W. C. Huber, and S. J. Nix. 1976. *Stormwater Management Model, Level I, Preliminary Screening Procedures*. EPA 600/2-76-275. Cincinnati, OH: US Environmental Protection Agency.

Hunter, R. B. 1940. *Methods of Evaluating Loads on Plumbing Systems*. Report BM865. Washington, DC: National Bureau of Standards.

Imhoff, K. 1907. *Tashenbuch der Stadtentwasserung (Pocket Guide for City Drainage)*. Berlin: Oldenburg.

Kuichling, E. 1889. The relation between rainfall and the discharge in sewers in populous districts. *Transactions of the American Society of Civil Engineering* 20, no. 1.

Mays, L. W. 2001. *Stormwater Collection Systems Design Handbook*. New York: McGraw-Hill.

Metcalf, L., and H. Eddy. 1914. *American Sewerage Practice*.

Metcalf & Eddy, Inc. 1972. *Wastewater Engineering*. New York: McGraw-Hill.

Moody, L. F. 1944. Friction factors for pipe flow." *Transactions of the American Society of Mechanical Engineers* 66.

Mulvaney, T. J. 1851. On the use of self-registering rain and flood gauges in making observations of the relation of rainfall and of flood discharges in a given catchment. *Transactions of the Institute for Civil Engineers, Ireland* 4, Part 2: 18.

Pomeroy, R. D. 1974. *Process Design Manual for Sulfide Control in Sanitary Sewerage Systems*. EPA 625/1-7-005, US Environmental Protection Agency.

Random House. 1970. American College Dictionary, edited by C. P. Barnhart. New York: Random House.

Reid, D. 1991. *Paris Sewers and Sewermen: Realities and Representations*. Cambridge, MA: Harvard University Press

Reyburn, W. 1971. *Flushed with Pride: The Story of Thomas Crapper*. Englewood Cliffs, NJ: Prentice-Hall.

Rouse, H., and S. Ince. 1957. *History of Hydraulics*. Iowa Institute of Hydraulic Research.

Shields, A. 1936. Anwndung der aehnlichkeitsmechanik und der turbulenz forschung auf die geschiebebeweung (Application of Similarity Mechanics and Turbulence

Research upon Bedload Movement). *Mitteilungen der Preussischen Versunchsanstalt fur Wasserbau und Schiffbau* (Prussian Research Institute for Hydraulic Engineering and Shipbuilding) 26.

Sirapyan, N. 2001. A history of personal computing. *PC Magazine* 20, No. 15.

Steel, E. W. 1938 & 1947. *Water Supply and Sewerage.* New York: McGraw-Hill.

Tarr, J. A. 1996. *The Search for the Ultimate Sink: Urban Pollution in Historical Perspective.* Akron, OH: University of Akron Press.

US Environmental Protection Agency (US EPA). 1991. *Alternative Wastewater Collection Systems.* EPA 625/1-91/024. US Environmental Protection Agency.

US Environmental Protection Agency (US EPA). 1999. *Combined Sewer Overflows, Guidance for Monitoring and Modeling.* EPA 832-B-99-002. US Environmental Protection Agency.

US Environmental Protection Agency (US EPA). 2000. *Compliance and Enforcement Strategy Addressing Combined Sewer Overflows and Sanitary Sewer Overflows.* US Environmental Protection Agency.

Zurad, J. T., J. P. Sobonski, and J. R. Rakoczy. 2002. The metropolitan water reclamation district of greater Chicago: Our century of meeting challenges and achieving success. In J. R. Rogers and A. J. Fredich, eds. *Environmental and Water Resources History.* Reston, VA: American Society of Civil Engineers.

Problems

1.1 Match the name with the works in the following table. Place the letter in the blank.

1	___	Wrote *History of Hydraulics*	a	Manning
2	___	Early calculating machine	b	Navier-Stokes
3	___	Boundary Layer Theory	c	Newton
4	___	Flow measuring flume	d	Pitot
5	___	Open channel head loss equation	e	Reynolds
6	___	Laminar vs. Turbulent Flow	f	Venturoli
7	___	Head loss in laminar flow	g	Archimedes
8	___	1-D open channel flow equations	h	Parshall
9	___	Velocity measurement	i	Pomeroy
10	___	Punch cards	j	Rouse and Ince
11	___	Patent for flush toilet	k	Huber, Heaney, Nix
12	___	Hydrogen sulfide corrosion in sewers	l	Hunter
13	___	Fixture unit method	m	Venturi
14	___	Equations for fluid motion	n	Prandtl
15	___	Law of Viscosity	o	Pascal
16	___	Backwater curves	p	Hollerith
17	___	Buoyancy principle	q	Woltman
18	___	SWMM model	r	Crapper
19	___	Closed pipe flow meter	s	Hagen-Poiseuille
20	___	Current meter	t	St. Venant

1.2 What law passed in 1972 requires discharge permits for any discharges in the United States?

1.3 What is I/I and what are its adverse environmental impacts?

1.4 Name five types of flow conditions in sewer systems.

1.5 How can SewerCAD and the Manning equation both be considered "models"?

1.6 Why are graphical user interfaces important?

1.7 Where are relief sewers used?

1.8 Moody diagrams are based on what diagrams developed by an earlier researcher?

1.9 How did the invention of the flush toilet change the nature of sewage?

CHAPTER

2

Steady Gravity Flow Hydraulics

The flow of liquid in a conduit may be classified as *full pipe* (or *closed conduit*) or *open channel,* depending on whether the free liquid surface is subject to atmospheric pressure. In open-channel flow, gravity alone provides the force to move the fluid. It is the most common flow condition in sewers, and engineers attempt to effectively use the work done by gravity to move sewage through the network.

Open-channel flow may be further categorized as steady or unsteady, and uniform or nonuniform. With *steady flow,* there is no significant variation in flow rate with time. Under *uniform flow* conditions, flow properties remain constant along the channel length. *Uniform flow* occurs in long inclined channels of constant cross section (i.e., prismatic channels) when the energy loss due to fluid friction is exactly supplied by the reduction in potential energy due to the downward slope of the channel. The depth of uniform flow is called the *normal depth*.

Because uniform flow can only occur if the flow is also steady, the term "uniform flow" is often used as shorthand to denote what is actually steady, uniform flow. This condition is often assumed in the hydraulic design of sewer systems. The analysis of steady, uniform flow requires the application of continuity and energy conservation principles.

Steady, nonuniform flow is constant over time, but a variation does occur along the channel length. This type of flow can occur in a channel with a transition in cross-sectional shape or slope. *Gradually varied flow* is the term for gradual changes in flow properties along a channel.

2.1 Fluid Properties

Fluids can be categorized as either gases or liquids. The most notable differences between the two states are that liquids are far denser than gases and that gases are highly compressible compared to liquids. The most important properties of liquids are specific weight and fluid viscosity.

Domestic sewage is considered to be water in terms of its hydraulic characteristics. However, some characteristics of sewage require special consideration, including the following:

- Pipe corrosion and/or coating and grease buildup need to be addressed in establishing pipe roughness factors.
- Transport and settlement of solids may affect hydraulics in some situations.
- Centrifugal pumps used in sewage pumping must be wastewater rated, which indicates that they include more corrosion protection and clogging-prevention features than normal, clean-water pumps.

Appendix C contains tabulations of the physical properties of water, including specific weight and viscosity.

Density and Specific Weight

The *density* of a fluid is its mass per unit volume. The density of water is 1.936 slugs/ft^3 (998.2 kg/m^3) at standard pressure of 1 atm (1.013) bar and temperature of 68.0° F (20.0° C). Changes in temperature or pressure affect the density, but are generally insignificant for design purposes. Tables in Appendix C give physical properties of water at other temperatures.

The property that describes the weight of a fluid per unit volume is called *specific weight*, which is related to density by gravitational acceleration as

$$\gamma = \rho g \qquad (2.1)$$

where
- γ = fluid specific weight (lb/ft^3, N/m^3)
- ρ = fluid density (slugs/ft^3, kg/m^3)
- g = gravitational acceleration constant (32.2 ft/s^2, 9.81 m/s^2)

The specific weight of water, γ, at one atmosphere and 68° F (20.0° C) is 62.32 lb/ft^3 (9789 N/m^3). Since temperatures in water and wastewater systems are typically colder than 68° F (20.0° C), a slightly higher specific weight (62.4 lb/ft^3, 9800 N/m^3) is commonly used for engineering analysis and design.

Viscosity

Fluid *viscosity* is the property that accounts for a fluid's resistance to deformation due to shear stress. Figure 2.1 shows the relation between the velocity gradient and shear stress for various types of fluids. Fluids that exhibit a linear relationship between shear and the velocity gradient are called Newtonian fluids. The slope of the plot velocity gradient vs. shear stress is viscosity, μ, described by Newton's law of viscosity:

$$\tau = \mu \frac{dV}{dy} \qquad (2.2)$$

where
- τ = shear stress (lb/ft², N/m²)
- μ = absolute (dynamic) viscosity (lb-s/ft², N-s/m²)
- $\frac{dV}{dy}$ = velocity gradient (ft/ft-s, m/m-s)

The physical meaning of this equation can be illustrated by considering the two parallel plates shown in Figure 2.2. The space between the plates is filled with a fluid, and the area of the plates is large enough that edge effects can be neglected. The plates are separated by a distance y, and the top plate is moving at a constant velocity V relative to the bottom plate. Liquids exhibit an attribute known as the no-slip condition, meaning that they adhere to surfaces they contact. Therefore, if the magnitude of V and y are not too large, then the velocity distribution between the two plates is linear.

From Newton's second law of motion, for an object to move at a constant velocity the net external force acting on the object must be zero. Thus, the fluid must be exerting a force equal and opposite to the force F on the top plate. This force within the fluid is a result of the shear stress between the fluid and the plate. The velocity at which these forces balance is a function of the velocity gradient normal to the plate and the fluid viscosity, as described by Equation 2.2.

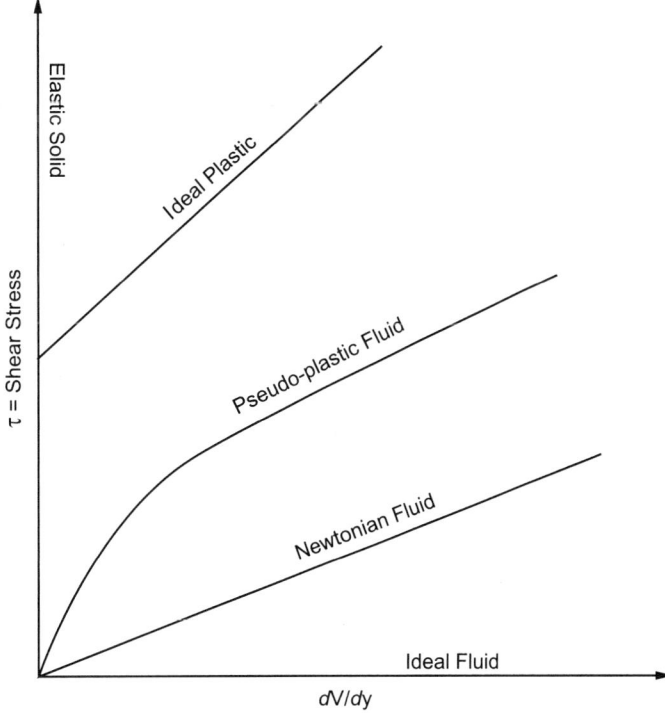

Figure 2.1 Shear stress versus velocity gradient for Newtonian and plastic fluids.

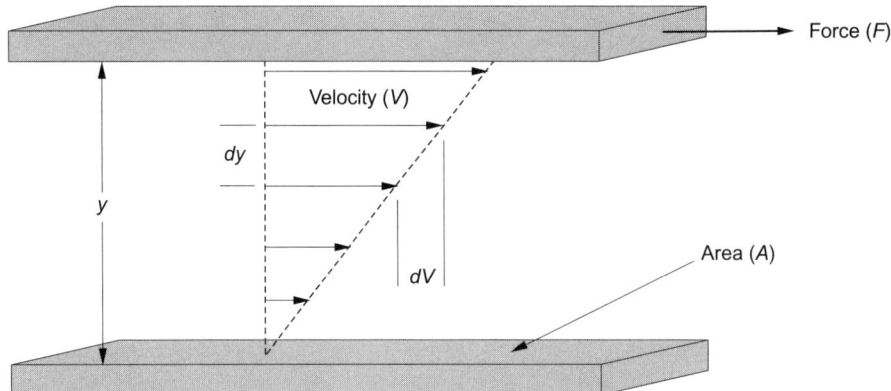

Figure 2.2 Physical interpretation of Newton's Law of viscosity.

Thick fluids, such as syrup and molasses, have high viscosities. Thin fluids, such as water and gasoline, have low viscosities. For most fluids, the viscosity remains constant regardless of the magnitude of the shear stress that is applied to it.

As the velocity of the top plate in Figure 2.2 increases, the shear stresses in the fluid increase proportionately. Fluids that exhibit this property conform to Newton's law of viscosity (Equation 2.2) and are called *Newtonian fluids*. An ideal plastic has a definite yield stress and a constant linear relation between τ and dV/dy. Water and air are examples of Newtonian fluids. Some types of fluids, such as inks and sludge, undergo changes in viscosity when the shear stress changes and are classified as non-Newtonian. A thixotrophic substance, such as printer's ink, has a viscosity that is a function of its prior deformation. Sludges may exhibit plastic or pseudoplastic behavior depending on the concentration of solids.

Relationships between the shear stress and the velocity gradient for typical Newtonian and non-Newtonian fluids are shown in Figure 2.1. Because most distribution system models are intended to simulate water, many of the equations used consider Newtonian fluids only. Water, typical wastewater, and many other fluids exhibit shear stress that is adequately described by a linear relationship between shear stress and velocity gradient.

Viscosity is a function of temperature, but this relationship is different for liquids and gases. In general, viscosity decreases as temperature increases for liquids, but increases as temperature increases for gases. The temperature variation within wastewater collection systems, however, is usually quite small, so changes in water viscosity are negligible for this application. Generally, hydraulic analysis software treats viscosity as a constant for a temperature of 68° F (20° C).

The viscosity derived in Equation 2.2 is referred to as the *absolute viscosity* (or *dynamic viscosity*). For hydraulic formulas related to fluid motion, the relationship between fluid viscosity and fluid density is often expressed as a single variable. This parameter, called the *kinematic viscosity*, is expressed as

$$\nu = \frac{\mu}{\rho} \qquad (2.3)$$

where ν = kinematic viscosity (ft²/s, m²/s)

Fluid Compressibility

Fluid compressibility is described by the *bulk modulus of elasticity*, given by

$$E_v = -V_f \frac{dp}{dV} \qquad (2.4)$$

where
E = bulk modulus of elasticity (lb/in², kPa)
V_f = volume of fluid (ft³, m³)
p = pressure (lb/in², kPa)

All fluids are compressible to some extent, but density differences are negligible for the range of pressures normally experienced in water resource and sewage facilities. Water has a bulk modulus of elasticity of 410,000 psi (2.83×10^6 kPa) at 68° F (20° C); therefore, for example, an extreme pressure change of 2000 psi (1.379×10^4 kPa) causes only a 0.5 percent change in volume.

Compressibility of water is important in the analysis of *hydraulic transients*, a phenomenon caused by extremely rapid changes in velocity (when, for instance, a check valve suddenly closes or a pump stops operating). The momentum of the moving fluid can generate pressures large enough that fluid compression and pipe-wall expansion can occur and generate potentially destructive transient pressure fluctuations in water systems (Haestad Methods et al., 2003). In steady gravity flow in sewers, wastewater can be considered incompressible.

Vapor Pressure

Vapor pressure is the pressure at which a liquid will boil. The vapor pressure of a liquid increases with increasing temperature, and boiling occurs when the vapor pressure exceeds the confining pressure. These properties are illustrated by the fact that water boils at a lower temperature at higher elevations due to the lower atmospheric (i.e., confining) pressure. For example, the vapor pressure of water at 212° F (100° C) is 1 atm, but at 68° F (20° C), it is just 0.023 atm.

THE WATER DESK

If water in a confined area experiences pressures below its vapor pressure, even just locally, the water boils and forms a vapor pocket. *Cavitation* occurs in pumps when the fluid being pumped boils because of a drop in pressure, forming a vapor pocket that then collapses when a higher pressure is encountered. When cavitation occurs, it sounds as if gravel is being pumped. Severe damage due to fatigue failure of pipe walls and pump components can result if this situation persists or occurs frequently.

2.2 Fluid Statics and Dynamics

Hydraulic properties of interest in gravity sewer analysis include pressure, velocity, flow, Reynolds number, and velocity profile.

Static Pressure

Pressure is the normal (perpendicular) force applied to the surface of a body per unit area. In the US customary system of units, pressure is expressed in pounds per square foot (lb/ft^2), but the water and wastewater industry generally uses lb/in^2, abbreviated as psi. In the SI system, pressure has units of N/m^2, also called a *pascal*. In water and wastewater systems, units of kilopascals (kPa = 1000 Pa) or bars (100 kPa) are commonly used.

For incompressible fluids at rest, pressure variation with depth is linear and is referred to as a *hydrostatic* pressure distribution, as illustrated in Figure 2.3 and described by

$$p = \gamma h \qquad (2.5)$$

where p = pressure (lb/in^2, kPa)
h = depth of fluid measured from the free surface (ft, m)
γ = fluid specific weight (lb/ft^3, N/m^3)

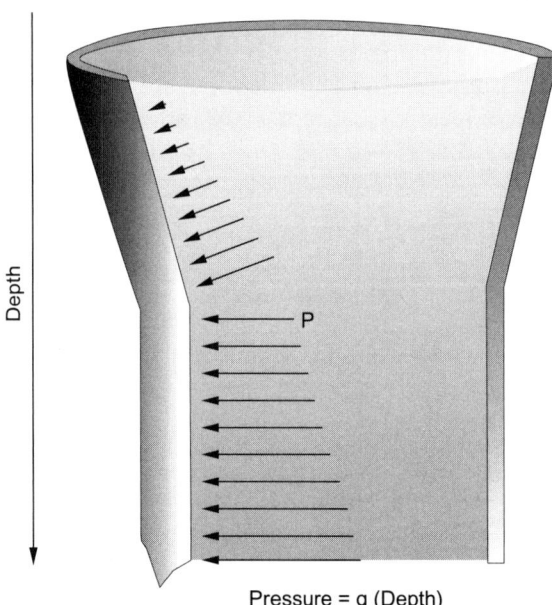

Figure 2.3 Static pressure in a standing water column.

Thus, the pressure in an unconfined fluid at a given point is due to the weight of the fluid above that point. The weight of the earth's atmosphere is the cause of *atmospheric pressure*. Although the actual atmospheric pressure depends on the elevation and weather, standard atmospheric pressure at sea level is 14.7 lb/in² or 101 kPa, defined as 1 atm.

Equation 2.5 can be rewritten as

$$h = \frac{p}{\gamma} \tag{2.6}$$

The quantity p/γ is called the *pressure head*, which is the potential energy resulting from water pressure. Recognizing that the specific weight of water in US customary units is 62.4 lb/ft³, a convenient conversion factor for water is 1 psi = 2.31 ft (1 kPa = 0.102 m) of pressure head.

Example 2.1 Pressure calculation

Consider the wet well for the sewage pump station illustrated in the following figure, in which the water surface elevation is 5 ft above a pressure gauge. The pressure at the base of the tank is due to the weight of the column of water directly above it and is given by

$$p = \gamma h = \frac{62.4 \frac{\text{lb}}{\text{ft}^3} 5\,\text{ft}}{144 \frac{\text{in}^2}{\text{ft}^2}}$$

$$p = 2.1\ \text{lb/in}^2$$

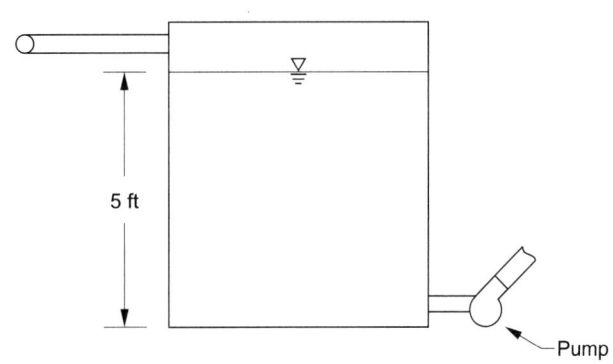

Absolute Pressure and Gauge Pressure

There are two pressure reference points that are commonly used in hydraulics. *Absolute pressure* is the pressure measured with absolute zero (a perfect vacuum) as its datum, while *gauge pressure* is the pressure measured with ambient atmospheric pressure as its datum. The two are related to one another by

$$p_{abs} = p_{gauge} + p_{atm} \qquad (2.7)$$

where p_{abs} = absolute pressure (lb/in², kPa)
p_{gauge} = gauge pressure (lb/in², kPa)
p_{atm} = atmospheric pressure (lb/in², kPa)

Note that when a pressure gauge is open to the atmosphere, it registers zero on its dial. Gauge pressure is used in most hydraulic applications; the atmospheric pressure component usually does not need to be considered. Figure 2.4 illustrates absolute and gauge pressures.

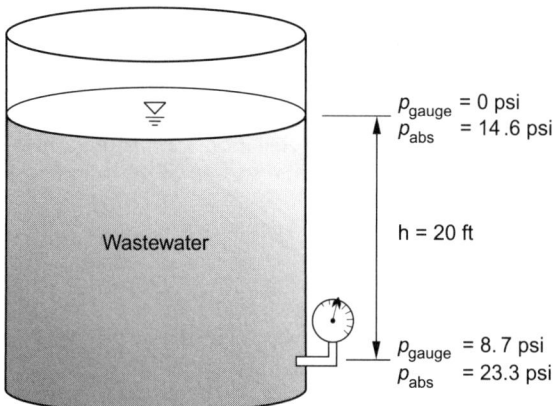

Figure 2.4 Gauge pressure and absolute pressure compared.

Velocity and Flow

In typical flow, velocity varies across the area of a cross section; thus, a velocity profile exists. In practical applications, however, average velocity can be used, which is defined by

$$V = \frac{Q}{A} \qquad (2.8)$$

where V = average fluid velocity (ft/s, m/s)
Q = pipeline flow rate (ft³/s, m³/s)
A = cross-sectional area of flow (ft², m²)

The cross-sectional area of a full circular pipe is $\pi D^2/4$, so the velocity equation can be rewritten as

$$V = \frac{4Q}{\pi D^2} \qquad (2.9)$$

where D = pipe diameter (ft, m)

Reynolds Number

The *Reynolds number* is the dimensionless ratio between inertial and viscous forces in a fluid. It can be used to classify the flow as laminar, transitional, or turbulent. For full circular pipes, the Reynolds number is given by

$$\text{Re} = \frac{VD\rho}{\mu} = \frac{VD}{\nu} \qquad (2.10)$$

where   Re = Reynolds number
D = pipeline diameter (ft, m)
ρ = fluid density (slugs/ft^3, kg/m^3)
μ = absolute viscosity (lb-s/ft^2, N-s/m^2)
ν = kinematic viscosity (ft^2/s, m^2/s)
V = velocity

The Reynolds number ranges that define the three flow regimes are listed in Table 2.1. The flow of water in sewer systems is nearly always in the transitional or turbulent range.

Table 2.1 Reynolds number for various flow regimes.

Flow Regime	Reynolds Number
Laminar	<2000
Transitional	2000–4000
Turbulent	>4000

Example 2.2 Reynolds Number

A full pipe with a diameter of 1 m has a flow rate of 1.5 m^3/s. The water temperature is 20° C. What is the flow regime?

Solution

The velocity is

$$V = \frac{Q}{A} = \frac{1.50 \text{ m}^3/\text{s}}{\pi \left(\frac{1}{2} \text{ m}\right)^2} = 1.91 \text{ m/s}$$

Thus, the Reynolds number is

$$\text{Re} = \frac{VD}{\nu} = \frac{(1.91 \text{ m/s})(1 \text{ m})}{1.02 \times 10^{-6} \text{ m}^2/\text{s}} = 1.87 \times 10^6$$

Therefore, the flow regime is turbulent.

Velocity Profiles

Figure 2.5 illustrates the variation of fluid velocity within a pipe. Such plots are referred to as *velocity profiles*. In laminar flow, the head loss through a pipe segment is primarily a function of the fluid viscosity, not the internal pipe roughness. Turbulent flow is characterized by mixing and eddies that produce random variations in the velocity profiles, thus making the profile flatter than that of laminar flow.

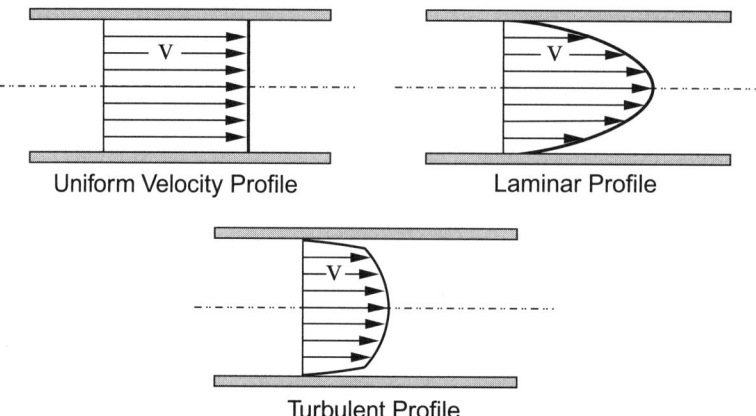

Figure 2.5 Velocity profiles in different flow regimes.

2.3 Fundamental Laws

This section discusses the basic physical laws underlying fluid flow: conservation of mass, conservation of energy, and conservation of momentum.

Conservation of Mass

The principle of conservation of mass states that matter is neither created nor destroyed. The mass entering a system is equal to the mass leaving that system, plus or minus the accumulation of mass (i.e., storage) within the system.

In typical engineering analyses, the properties of flow change both in space and time. For example, the amount of wastewater present in a given segment of a trunk sewer may change over time; therefore, accounting for the accumulation (or loss) of wastewater during any time interval is essential.

Consider an *incompressible fluid* (that is, a fluid having a constant density, so that volume and mass are proportional) that flows through a fixed region (a *control volume*) and denote the volume of fluid, or *storage*, in that region at time t by the quantity $S(t)$. The fixed region might correspond to a lake or reservoir, wet well, or manhole. If $I(t)$ represents a volumetric flow rate into the region, then a volume $I(t)\Delta t$ of additional fluid flows into the fixed region during the time interval Δt. If the volumetric flow rate out of the system is $Q(t)$, then a volume of fluid equal to $Q(t)\Delta t$ flows out of the region during the time interval.

According to the conservation of mass, at the end of the time interval (that is, at time $t + \Delta t$), the storage $S(t + \Delta t)$ of fluid in the fixed region is equal to the initial contents, plus the additional fluid that entered during that time, less the amount of fluid that left during that time. This is expressed mathematically as

$$S(t + \Delta t) = S(t) + I(t)\Delta t - Q(t)\Delta t \qquad (2.11)$$

where t = time (s)
$S(t + \Delta t)$ = storage at the end of the time interval (ft^3, m^3)
$S(t)$ = storage at the beginning of the time interval (ft^3, m^3)
$I(t)$ = volumetric inflow rate at time t (ft^3, m^3)
$Q(t)$ = volumetric outflow rate at time t (ft^3, m^3)

A volumetric flow rate, typically denoted by Q, is referred to as a *discharge* in hydrologic and hydraulic engineering.

Rearranging Equation 2.11 yields

$$\frac{S(t+\Delta t) - S(t)}{\Delta t} = I(t) - Q(t) \qquad (2.12)$$

As Δt approaches zero, this equation becomes

$$\frac{dS}{dt} = I(t) - Q(t) \qquad (2.13)$$

Equation 2.13 is the differential form of the mathematical expression for conservation of mass. An integral form may be obtained by multiplying both sides of the expression by dt and integrating to get

$$\int_{S_1}^{S_2} dS = S_2 - S_1 = \int_{t_1}^{t_2} I(t)dt - \int_{t_1}^{t_2} Q(t)dt \qquad (2.14)$$

If a flow is *steady*—that is, if the flow characteristics do not change with time—then the time derivative in Equation 2.13 is zero and conservation of mass may be expressed by simply stating that the inflow and outflow discharges to and from a control volume are equal. In other words, $I(t) = Q(t)$.

Conservation of Energy

In the most formal sense, a discussion of conservation of energy for a fluid begins with the First Law of Thermodynamics. That law states that the rate of change of stored energy in a system is equal to the rate at which heat energy is added to the system, minus the rate at which the system does work on its surroundings. In typical sewer flow, the stored energy consists of *kinetic energy* from the motion of the fluid, *potential energy* due to its position relative to an arbitrary datum plane, and *internal energy*.

In the vast majority of civil and environmental engineering applications, flow is considered steady and incompressible, and it is generally sufficient to apply the principle of conservation of energy in a much simpler way using what is commonly known as the *energy equation*. The expression most commonly applied expresses energy on a unit-weight basis (that is, as energy per unit weight of fluid), so the change in energy between two points 1 and 2 is given byc

$$\frac{p_1}{\gamma} + Z_1 + \frac{\alpha_1 V_1^2}{2g} = \frac{p_2}{\gamma} + Z_2 + \frac{\alpha_2 V_2^2}{2g} + h_L - h_P + h_T \qquad (2.15)$$

where
- p = fluid pressure (lb/in^2, kPa)
- γ = specific weight of the fluid (lb/ft^3, N/m^3)
- Z = elevation above an arbitrary datum plane (ft, m)
- α = velocity distribution coefficient
- V = fluid velocity, averaged over a cross section (ft/s, m/s)
- g = gravitational acceleration constant (ft/s^2, m/s^2)
- h_L = energy loss between cross sections 1 and 2 (ft, m)
- h_P = fluid energy supplied by a pump between cross sections 1 and 2 (ft, m)
- h_T = energy lost to a turbine between cross sections 1 and 2 (ft, m)

The first three terms on each side of this equation represent, respectively, the internal energy due to fluid pressure, potential energy due to elevation of the fluid, and kinetic energy. Because the dimension of each term is in units of length (resulting from division of energy units by fluid weight units), the three terms are generally called the *pressure head*, the *elevation head*, and the *velocity head*. The terms on the left side of the equation with the subscript 1 refer to an upstream cross section of the fluid, and those on the right side with the subscript 2 refer to a downstream cross section.

Because the velocities along individual streamlines generally differ due to the effects of pipe walls or channel sides, the velocity head terms in Equation 2.15 are corrected with the velocity distribution coefficient (α) if an average cross-sectional velocity is used.

Because each term in Equation 2.15 has units of length, qualitative aspects of the energy equation can be shown graphically. Figure 2.6 shows energy and hydraulic grade lines in a Venturi meter.

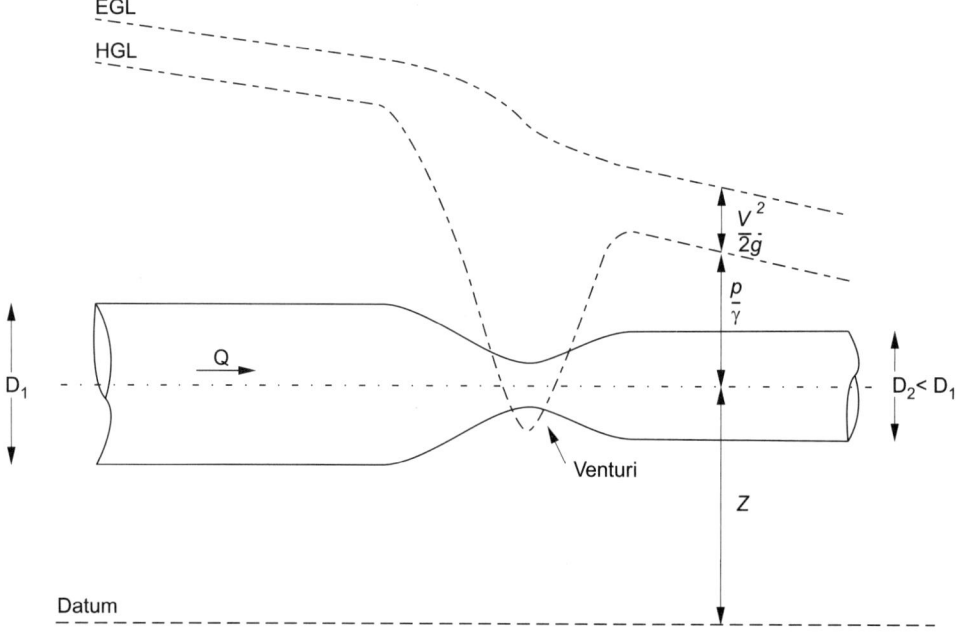

Figure 2.6 Profile of EGL and HGL through a Venturi section.

In Figure 2.6, the elevation head (Z) represents the vertical distance from the datum to the pipe centerline. The *hydraulic grade line* (HGL) represents the height to which a column of water would rise in a standpipe placed anywhere along the length of the pipe and is the sum of the pressure head and elevation. The height of the HGL is sometimes called the *piezometric head*. The vertical distance from the pipe centerline to the HGL is the pressure head, p/γ, and the distance from the HGL to the *energy grade line* (EGL) is the velocity head, $V^2/2g$. The vertical distance from the datum to the EGL is representative of the sum of the first three terms on each side of Equation 2.15 and is called the *total head*. Flow always moves in the direction of decreasing total head (not necessarily decreasing pressure), and hence is from left to right in the figure.

According to conservation of mass, the velocity must be greater in the throat of the Venturi than in the upstream pipe; thus, the distance between the HGL and EGL is greater for the downstream pipe. At the throat of the Venturi itself, where the flow velocity is the highest, the distance between the EGL and HGL is the greatest. In the regions upstream and downstream of the Venturi, where the HGL is above the pipe centerline, the fluid pressure (gauge pressure) in the pipe is positive. In this example, the HGL falls below the pipe centerline at the Venturi and the fluid gauge pressure is negative. Note that while the fluid pressure just downstream of the Venturi is greater than that in the throat of the Venturi, flow is still from left to right since that is the direction of the energy gradient.

The EGL in the figure has a nonzero slope because energy is lost to friction and turbulent eddies as fluid moves through the pipe. In other words, the total head decreases in a downstream direction along the pipe. In Figure 2.6, because neither a pump nor turbine is present, the difference in the elevation of the EGL between any two locations (cross sections) along the pipe is representative of the head loss h_L between those two cross sections. The loss rate of total energy in a fluid flow increases with the velocity of the flow. Thus, in the figure, the magnitude of the slope of the EGL is larger for the smaller pipe than for the larger pipe.

In open-channel flow problems, the energy equation is somewhat different from that presented in Equation 2.15. The difference arises in the pressure head term, which, instead of p/γ, is $d\cos\theta$, where d is the depth of flow normal to the channel bottom and θ is the angle of inclination of the channel. Thus, the energy equation for flow in an open channel is

$$Z_1 + d_1 \cos\theta + \frac{\alpha_1 V_1^2}{2g} = Z_2 + d_2 \cos\theta + \frac{\alpha_2 V_2^2}{2g} + h_L \qquad (2.16)$$

where Z = channel bottom elevation (ft, m)
  d = depth of flow normal to the channel bottom (ft, m)
  θ = channel slope angle
  α = velocity distribution coefficient (dimensionless)
  V = flow velocity (ft/s, m/s)
  g = gravitational acceleration constant (32.2 ft/s^2, 9.81 m/s^2)
  h_L = energy loss between section 1 and section 2 (ft, m)

Figure 2.7 illustrates the terms in Equation 2.16.

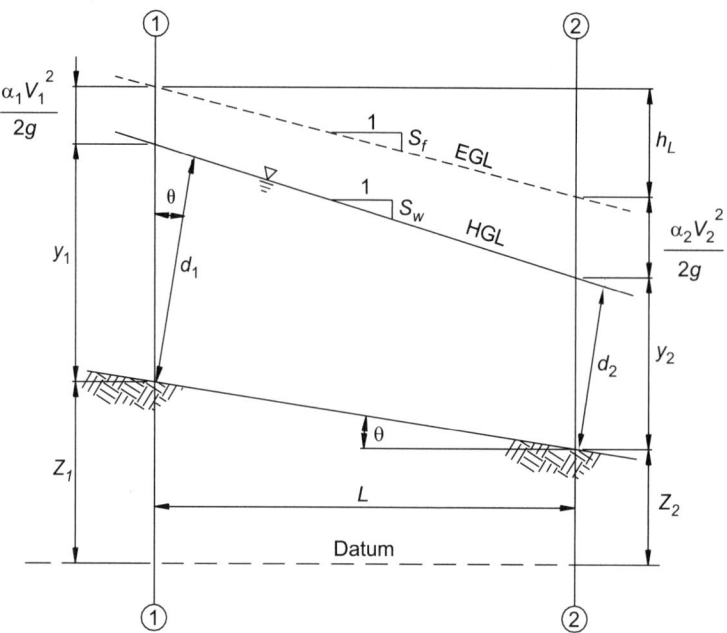

Figure 2.7 Definitions for the energy equation in open channel flow.

Because $d = y\cos\theta$ (see Figure 2.7), an alternate form of the energy equation for open channel flow is

$$Z_1 + y_1\cos^2\theta + \frac{\alpha_1 V_1^2}{2g} = Z_2 + y_2\cos^2\theta + \frac{\alpha_2 V_2^2}{2g} + h_L \qquad (2.17)$$

When the angle of inclination, θ, is small, this equation becomes

$$Z_1 + y_1 + \frac{\alpha_1 V_1^2}{2g} = Z_2 + y_2 + \frac{\alpha_2 V_2^2}{2g} + h_L \qquad (2.18)$$

Conservation of Momentum

The principle of conservation of momentum states that the summation of the external forces acting on a system is equal to the time rate of change of momentum for the system. The physical principle of conservation of momentum is generally more difficult to apply in practice than either conservation of mass or conservation of energy. The added complexity is that momentum is a vector quantity (that is, it has both magnitude and direction), whereas mass and energy are scalars (represented by magnitude only). Momentum equations must therefore be written separately for each coordinate.

In its most general form, conservation of momentum in the x-direction is expressed as

$$\sum F_x = \frac{\partial}{\partial t}\int_{cv} \rho V_x dS + \sum (M_{out})_x - \sum (M_{in})_x \qquad (2.19)$$

where $\quad F_x =$ force acting on the water in a control volume in the x-direction (lb, N)

t = time (s)

cv = control volume (ft³, m³)

ρ = fluid density (slugs/ft³, kg/m³)

V_x = x-component of the velocity of the fluid in the control volume (ft/s, m/s)

S = fluid volume (ft³, m³)

M_{out} = momentum outflow rate from the control volume (lb, N)

M_{in} = momentum inflow rate into the control volume (lb, N)

This expression, which is written for the *x*-coordinate, can be written for other coordinates as needed. It states that the sum of the external forces acting on the water in a control volume is equal to the time rate of change of momentum within the control volume (the volume between points 1 and 2 in Figure 2.7), plus the net momentum outflow rate (in the *x*-direction) from the control volume. In this expression, the sums of M_{out} and M_{in} account for the possibility of more than one inflow and/or outflow pathway to/from the control volume. A *momentum flow rate*, in the *x*-direction, can be written as

$$M_x = \beta \rho Q V_x \tag{2.20}$$

where M_x = momentum flow rate in the *x*-direction (lb, N)

β = velocity distribution coefficient (dimensionless)

Q = discharge (ft³/s, m³/s)

The numerical value of β is close to 1 for turbulent flow.

If a fluid flow is steady (its characteristics do not change with time), Equation 2.19 reduces to

$$\sum F_x = \sum (M_{out})_x - \sum (M_{in})_x \tag{2.21}$$

Further, if there is only a single inflow stream (that is, a single inflow pipe) and a single outflow stream from the control volume, Equation 2.21 can be rewritten as

$$\sum F_x = \rho Q \, \Delta(\beta V)_x \tag{2.22}$$

Equation 2.22 states that the vector sum of the *x*-components of the external forces acting on the fluid within a fixed control volume is equal to the fluid density times the discharge times the difference between the *x*-components of the outgoing and incoming velocity vectors from and to the control volume. As in Equation 2.20, the velocity terms should be modified using a velocity distribution coefficient if one chooses to use the average velocity at a cross section.

The forces due to change in momentum plus the pressure forces on bends require that bends, especially in force mains, be restrained to prevent movement using either thrust blocks or restrained pipe joints. A force main with a restrained joint is shown in Figure 2.8.

Figure 2.8 Installing a restrained bend on a large force main.

2.4 Hydraulic Design Variables

In the hydraulic design of sewers, the basic design variables are flow rate, maximum velocity, minimum velocity for self-cleansing, pipe slope, depth of flow, and head losses. Various equations have been developed to relate these variables. Commonly used equations are described later in this chapter.

Flow Rate or Discharge

While flow rates are typically reported in units of cubic feet per second (ft^3/s) in US customary units and cubic meters per second (m^3/s) in the SI system, the units actually used depend on local and industry conventions. Treatment facilities often use million gallons per day (mgd) or megaliters per day (ML/d). Pump curves and pressure flows are generally given in gallons per minute (gpm), liters per second (L/s), or cubic meters per hour (m^3/hr), and customer loads are discussed in gallons per day (gpd) and liters per day (L/d).

Channel/Pipe Slope

Channel slope is defined as the invert (lowest point in the cross section) drop per unit length of channel. It is typically expressed as a unitless value (i.e., length/length), but units may be provided (e.g., ft/ft or m/m). Often, slope is expressed as a percent or in units such as ft/1000 ft of m/km.

Depth of Flow

Depth of flow is measured from the lowest point in the channel bottom to the water surface. For a pipe, the ratio of the depth of flow *(y)* to the inside height is often called the *partial depth* or depth/diameter ratio *(d/D)*. This ratio is sometimes multiplied by 100 and referred to as the *percent full depth*. Equations for calculating the depth in terms of size, slope, and flow are given later in this chapter. Figure 2.9 shows a sewer with a fairly low depth of flow.

For some problems, the *hydraulic depth* y_h is defined as the cross-sectional area A, divided by the top width T.

$$y_h = \frac{A}{T} \tag{2.23}$$

Courtesy of Maria do Céu Almeida/LNEC

Figure 2.9 Partly full flow in a sewer.

Velocity

For incompressible flow, volumetric flow rate (also called discharge) is usually used in conservation of mass expressions, so flow rate and velocity are related by the conservation of mass equations. The average velocity is given by Equation 2.8 on page 30.

Maximum Velocities. Impact, pipe erosion, and manhole nuisance and safety issues have resulted in maximum sewage velocities commonly being limited to about 15 ft/s (4.6 m/s) unless special requirements are met, such as the use of ductile-iron pipes and/or special energy-dissipation features at the downstream manhole. At simple, straight-through manholes, higher velocities are acceptable, perhaps as high as 20 ft/s (6.1 m/s). Conversely, at multiple-inlet and/or direction-change manholes, lower maximum velocities on the order of 8 ft/s (2.4 m/s) or lower may be appropriate.

Minimum Velocities. Sanitary flows carry a wide variety of inert and putrefactive particles. To avoid long-term deposition and accumulation of these materials, the wastewater must carry these particles to the treatment facility. The traditional approach to self-cleansing is to require a full-pipe velocity of at least 2 ft/s (0.61 m/s).

This approach has proven adequate to avoid serious sediment buildup in most sewer lines, but it does not address self-cleansing as accurately as does the tractive force method described later in this chapter. Minimum slopes to achieve a velocity of 2 ft/s (0.61 m/s) are tabulated in Table 2.2 for Manning's n = 0.013. Due to the difficulty in precise invert placement and the very small invert elevation gain from flatter slopes, a minimum slope of 0.050 is recommended for large pipes. The velocities resulting from this minimum slope are shown in Table 2.2 for pipe sizes 36 in. (915 mm) and larger.

Table 2.2 Minimum slopes for various pipe sizes.

Pipe Diameter		Slope, ft/100 ft (m/100 m)	
in.	mm	Calculated[1]	GLUMRB[2]
6	152	0.49	—
8	203	0.34	0.40
10	254	0.25	0.28
12	305	0.20	0.22
15	381	0.15	0.15
18	457	0.12	0.12
21	533	0.093	0.10
24	610	0.077	0.08
27	686	0.066	0.067
30	762	0.057	0.058
33	838	0.050	0.052
36	915	0.050 (2.1)[3]	0.046
39	991	0.050 (2.2)[3]	0.041
42	1067	0.050 (2.3)[3]	0.037

[1] Calculated with the Manning Equation, n = 0.013, velocity = 0.61 m/s (2 ft/s)

[2] Great Lakes Upper Mississippi River Board (1997)

[3] Recommended that 0.050 be the minimum slope for larger-diameter pipe; number in parentheses indicates velocity in ft/s.

Minimum slopes recommended by the Great Lakes Upper Mississippi River Board Standards (GLUMRB, 1997) are presented in the last column of Table 2.2. For pipes 12 in. (305 mm) and smaller, the GLUMRB recommendations are greater than the calculated values. For pipes 36 in. (915 mm) and larger, the recommended slopes are less then the calculated values. An analysis that considers the tractive force and associated self-cleansing power of the flow is presented in Section 2.9.

2.5 Energy and Head Losses

The most common approach to the analysis of flow in sewers is to construct an energy balance for open channel flow as in Equation 2.18. In most sewer networks, the major cause of head losses is the friction exerted on the sewage by the walls of the pipe or channel. Minor losses, as the name implies, are often small in comparison to frictional losses. This section discusses head loss caused by channel friction. Minor losses are described in Section 2.8.

Energy Equation

The energy equation, introduced in Section 2.3, may be reduced for turbulent gravity water flow (since α is usually very close to one) to the form

$$Z_1 + y_1 + \frac{V_1^2}{2g} = Z_2 + y_2 + \frac{V_2^2}{2g} + h_L \qquad (2.24)$$

where
- Z = elevation of the channel bottom at point 1 or 2 (ft, m)
- y = depth of flow at point 1 or 2 (ft, m)
- V = average velocity at point 1 or 2 (ft/s, m/s)
- g = gravitational acceleration (ft/s², m/s²)
- h_L = energy losses between points 1 and 2 (ft, m)

In uniform flow, the channel invert profile, the water surface profile, and the energy grade line (friction slope) profile are parallel. This may be formally stated as (see Figure 2.7):

$$S_o = S_w = S_f \qquad (2.25)$$

where
- S_o = slope of the channel bottom (ft/ft, m/m)
- S_w = slope of the hydraulic grade line (ft/ft, m/m)
- S_f = slope of the energy grade line (ft/ft, m/m)

Over a given length of pipe, the head loss in the last term of Equation 2.24 is equal to the product of the length and the channel slope, or

$$h_L = S_f L \qquad (2.26)$$

The Manning equation, the Darcy-Weisbach equation, and the Kutter-Chézy equation are the most commonly used methods for computing head losses in sewers.

Manning Equation. The Manning equation may be stated as

$$Q = \frac{k}{n} A R_h^{2/3} S^{1/2} \qquad (2.27)$$

where
- k = 1.49 for US customary units
-     = 1.0 for SI units
- A = cross-sectional area of the flow (ft², m²)
- R_h = hydraulic radius (ft, m) = p/A
- p = wetted perimeter (ft, m)
- S = slope of the energy line = S_o for uniform flow (ft/ft, m/m)
- n = Manning's roughness coefficient

The Manning equation is used almost exclusively for open-channel design in the United States, while the Darcy-Weisbach and Kutter-Chézy equations are sometimes used in other parts of the world. The Manning and Kutter-Chézy equations are slightly handicapped by the common assumption that the roughness coefficient is merely a function of the physical roughness of the channel walls (a property of the pipe material). This assumption is not strictly accurate, since n varies slightly with hydraulic radius and therefore diameter, and Reynolds number (Re) varies with velocity, diameter, and temperature (viscosity). In most open-channel design, the assumption that n is determined only by the physical roughness is adequate, given the range of uncertainty in the other equation variables along a channel. However, in sewer design, where the variables are more tightly bounded, n should be considered a function of these other variables, as well as the pipe material. Section 2.7 covers variations in Manning's n.

Table 2.3 shows traditional Manning's n values. Note that a fairly large range is listed for each channel and material type. Generally the smallest n value in the range is appropriate for a high-quality channel or pipe, such as in a well-constructed sewer. The factors that affect the value of n are discussed in Section 2.7.

Table 2.3 Manning roughness (n) values for various conduit materials.

Conduit Material	Manning's n[1]
Closed conduits	
Asbestos-cement pipe	0.011–0.015
Brick	0.013–0.017
Cast iron pipe	
Cement-lined and seal coated	0.011–0.015
Concrete (monolithic)	
Smooth forms	0.012–0.014
Rough forms	0.015–0.017
Concrete pipe	0.011–0.015
Corrugated metal pipe ½ in (13 mm) × 2⅔ in (68 mm) corrugations	
Plain	0.022–0.026
Paved invert	0.018–0.022
Spun asphalt	0.011–0.015
Plastic pipe (smooth)	0.011–0.015
Polyethylene	0.009[2]
Polyvinyl chloride	0.010[2]
Vitrified clay pipe	0.011–0.015
Vitrified clay liner plates	0.013–0.017
Open channels – lined	
Asphalt	0.013–0.017
Brick	0.012–0.018
Concrete	0.011–0.020

[1] modified from American Society of Civil Engineers (1982) unless
[2] French (2001)

Although the form of the Manning equation given as Equation 2.27 is useful for most open channels, it may be difficult to apply to more complex cross sections. For pipes, the equation is typically applied to a full pipe and the properties then adjusted for partial flow using hydraulic elements relationships, as discussed in Section 2.6. Some materials like brick as shown in Figure 2.10 can show a wide range of n values depending on their age and the way they were installed. For a full pipe, it is possible to replace hydraulic radius terms with diameter/4. The full-flow form of the Manning equation is

$$Qn = C_f D^{8/3} S^{1/2} \qquad (2.28)$$

where C_f = unit conversion factor
  = 0.3117 for Q in m³/s, D in m
  = 0.4632 for Q in ft³/s, D in ft
  = 0.275 for Q in gpm and D in in.
 D = pipe diameter (ft, m)
 S = slope of the energy line

Photo courtesy of R. D. Zande and Associates

Figure 2.10 Wastewater flow through a brick sewer.

Darcy-Weisbach Equation. The Darcy-Weisbach equation was developed using dimensional analysis and by balancing wall drag and gravity/pressure forces. It is valid for Newtonian fluids, which include most common gases and liquids. The equation for full-pipe flow is

$$h_L = \frac{fLV^2}{D2g} \qquad (2.29)$$

where h_L = head loss (ft, m)
 f = Darcy-Weisbach friction factor (dimensionless)
 L = pipe length (ft, m)
 V = average pipe velocity (ft/s, m/s)
 g = gravitational constant (32.2 ft/s², 9.81 m/s²)

The *friction factor, f,* is a function of several variables, expressed as

$$f = \text{func}(\text{Re}, \varepsilon/D) \qquad (2.30)$$

where ε = equivalent sand grain roughness (ft, m)
 Re = Reynolds number, defined in Equation 2.10

Details about using the Moody diagram and the Colebrook-White equation to obtain f are presented in Chapter 4.

Kutter-Chézy Equation. The Chézy equation, in conjunction with Kutter's equation, was developed around 1769 by the French engineer Antoine Chézy and is probably the oldest constitutive relationship for open channel flow. The roughness component, C, is a function of the hydraulic radius, friction slope, and lining material of the channel. The Chézy equation is

$$V = C\sqrt{R_h S} \qquad (2.31)$$

where
- V = mean velocity (ft/s, m/s)
- C = roughness coefficient (see following calculation)
- R_h = hydraulic radius (ft, m)
- S = friction slope (ft/ft, m/m)

The roughness coefficient, C, is related to Kutter's n through Kutter's equation, as follows. (Note that the n in Kutter's equation is the same as Manning's n.)

$$C = \begin{cases} \dfrac{41.65 + \dfrac{0.00281}{S} + \dfrac{1.811}{n}}{1 + \dfrac{\left(41.65 + \dfrac{0.00281}{S}\right)n}{\sqrt{R_h}}} & \text{for U.S. customary units} \\[2em] \dfrac{23 + \dfrac{0.00155}{S} + \dfrac{1}{n}}{1 + \dfrac{\left(23 + \dfrac{0.00155}{S}\right)n}{\sqrt{R_h}}} & \text{for SI units} \end{cases} \qquad (2.32)$$

where n = Manning's roughness coefficient (dimensionless)

Some authors suggest omitting the term 0.00281/S (0.00155/S in SI units) from the equation, because it was originally included to account for calibration data now known to be inaccurate.

2.6 Hydraulic Elements

In open-channel flow, relationships between the physical and hydraulic variables vary with depth of flow in the channel. Table 2.4 lists the hydraulic properties for commonly used cross sections.

Open-Top Cross Sections

For the open-top sections (rectangular, trapezoidal, and triangular) shown in Figure 2.11, the depth of flow, y, is measured from the water surface to the deepest part of the channel. If the depth of flow is known, cross-section properties may be calculated using the relationships in Table 2.4. If the area is known, the depth of flow is determined by solving for y with the appropriate relationship in the second column.

Table 2.4 Cross-section properties of prismatic open channels with depth of flow, y.

Channel Description	Area, A	Wetted Perimeter, P	Hydraulic Radius, R_h	Top Width, T	Hydraulic Depth, h_D
Rectangular with base, B	By	$B+2y$	$\dfrac{By}{B+2y}$	B	y
Trapezoidal with base B and equal side slopes, z	$By+zy^2$	$B+2y\sqrt{1+z^2}$	$\dfrac{By+zy^2}{B+2y\sqrt{1+z^2}}$	$B+2yz$	$\dfrac{By+zy^2}{B+2zy}$
Trapezoidal with base B and unequal side slopes, z_1 and z_2	$By+0.5y^2(z_1+z_2)$	$B+2y(\sqrt{1+z_1^2}+\sqrt{1+z_2^2})$	$\dfrac{By+0.5y^2(z_1+z_2)}{B+y(\sqrt{1+z_1^2}+\sqrt{1+z_2^2})}$	$B+y(z_1+z_2)$	$\dfrac{By+0.5y^2(z_1+z_2)}{B+y(z_1+z_2)}$
Triangular with equal side slopes, z	zy^2	$2y\sqrt{1+z^2}$	$\dfrac{zy}{2\sqrt{1+z^2}}$	$2yz$	$\dfrac{y}{2}$
Triangular with unequal side slopes, z_1 and z_2	$0.5y^2(z_1+z_2)$	$2y(\sqrt{1+z_1^2}+\sqrt{1+z_2^2})$	$\dfrac{0.5y^2(z_1+z_2)}{2y(\sqrt{1+z_1^2}+\sqrt{1+z_2^2})}$	$y(z_1+z_2)$	$\dfrac{y}{2}$
Circular with diameter D flowing full	$\pi\dfrac{D^2}{4}$	πD	$\dfrac{D}{4}$	0	$\dfrac{D^1}{4}$
Circular with diameter D flowing partially full[2]	$\dfrac{D^2(2\theta-\sin 2\theta)}{8}$	$D\theta$	$\dfrac{D}{4}\left(1-\dfrac{\sin 2\theta}{2\theta}\right)$	$D\sin\theta$	$\dfrac{D}{8}\left(\dfrac{2\theta-\sin 2\theta}{\sin\theta}\right)$

[1] Hydraulic mean depth $= A/R_h$
[2] $\theta = \cos^{-1}\left(1-\dfrac{2y}{D}\right)$

Rectangular or square sections are sometimes encountered in sanitary sewers; however, the relative economy and better strength characteristics of circular pipe make noncircular sections less desirable for sewers, in most cases. For irregular or compound cross sections, procedures described by Haestad Methods and Durrans (2003) may be used to determine cross-section properties.

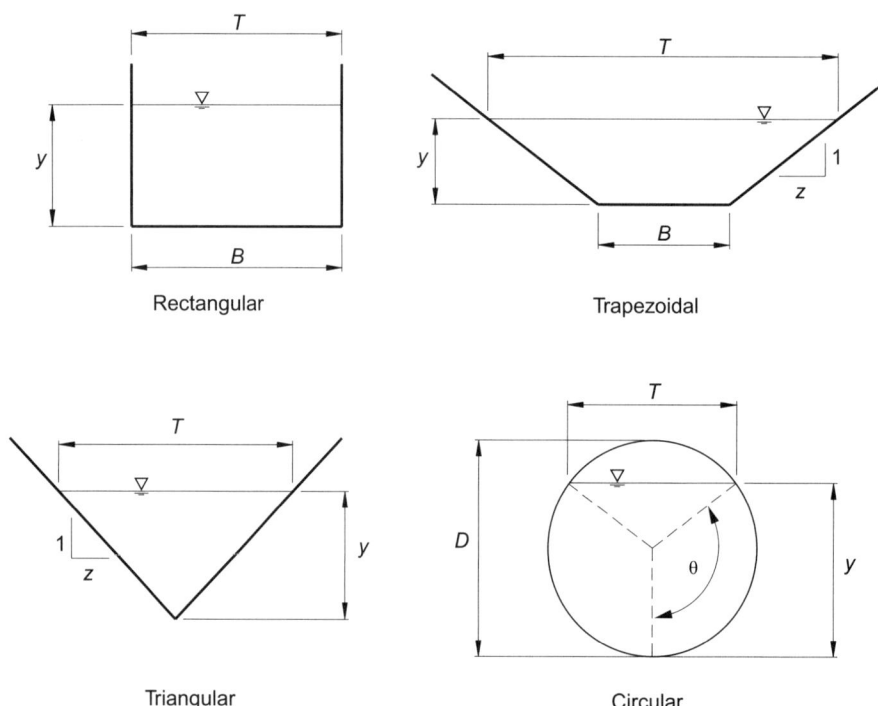

Figure 2.11 Definitions of terms used in Table 2.4.

Closed-Top Cross Sections

A special category of cross sections has gradually closing tops. The most commonly used section in sanitary sewers, which rarely flow full, is circular pipe. Thus, the analysis of partially full circular pipes is frequently required. The equations in the last row of Table 2.4 describe the hydraulic properties in terms of the angle θ (defined in Figure 2.11). If the depth of flow, y, is known, θ is given by

$$\theta = \cos^{-1}\left(1 - \frac{2y}{D}\right) \quad (2.33)$$

where θ = angle (radians)
 y = depth of flow (ft, m)
 D = diameter of circular section (ft, m)

The use of these equations is demonstrated in Example 2.3.

Because these calculations are tedious, the hydraulic element chart (Figure 2.12) is frequently used. This figure presents the partially-full/full-pipe ratio for each hydraulic property as a function of the depth-to-diameter ratio (y/D). The variation of n with depth is discussed in Section 2.7. Use of the hydraulic element chart is demonstrated in Example 2.3.

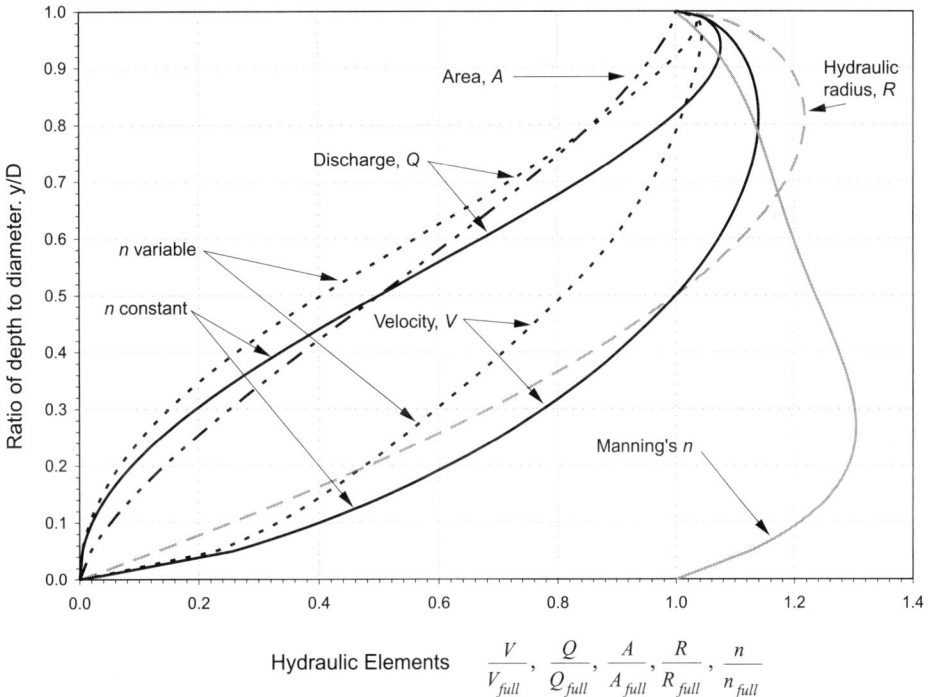

Figure 2.12 Geometric and hydraulic ratios for a circular cross section.

Example 2.3 Flow in a partially full circular pipe.

Assume that a 10 in. pipe with a slope of 0.006 and Manning's $n = 0.011$ is to carry a design minimum flow rate of 0.10 ft³/s. What are the depth of flow, hydraulic radius, and velocity?

Solution

An analytical solution may be developed by substituting the partially full expressions for A and R_h into Equation 2.27 to get

$$Q = \frac{k}{n}AR_h^{2/3}S^{1/2} = \frac{1.49}{0.011} \times \frac{\left(\frac{10}{12}\right)^2(2\theta - \sin 2\theta)}{8} \times \left[\frac{D}{4}\left(1 - \frac{\sin 2\theta}{2\theta}\right)\right]^{2/3} \times 0.006^{1/2} = 0.10 \text{ ft}^3/\text{s}$$

A trial-and-error solution gives $\theta = 0.801$. The depth of flow is found by solving Equation 2.33 for y and substituting values for D and θ to get

$$y = \frac{D}{2}(1 - \cos\theta) = \frac{10/12}{2}(1 - \cos 0.801) = 0.127 \text{ ft} = 1.52 \text{ in.}$$

The hydraulic radius is found with the formula from Table 2.4 to be

$$R_h = \frac{D}{4}\left(1 - \frac{\sin 2\theta}{2\theta}\right) = \frac{10/12}{4(2)}\left(1 - \frac{\sin 2(0.801)}{2(0.801)}\right) = 0.078 \text{ ft}$$

The flow velocity is found by combining Equations 2.8 and 2.27 and substituting values for n, R, and S to get

$$V = \frac{1.49}{n}R^{2/3}S^{1/2} = \frac{1.49}{0.011} \times 0.078^{2/3} \times 0.006^{1/2} = 1.92 \text{ ft/s}$$

The graphical solution using the chart in Figure 2.12 is as follows. The full-pipe values for R_{hf}, V_f, and Q_f needed for a graphical solution, are

$$R_{hf} = \frac{10/12}{4} = 0.208 \text{ ft}$$

$$V_f = \frac{1.49}{0.011} \times \frac{(10/12)^{2/3}}{4} \times 0.006^{1/2} = 3.68 \text{ ft/s}$$

and

$$Q_f = \frac{1.49}{0.011} \times \frac{\pi(10/12)^2}{4} \times \frac{(10/12)^{2/3}}{4} \times 0.006^{1/2} = 2.01 \text{ ft}^3/\text{s}$$

The ratio $Q/Q_f = 0.10/2.01 = 0.0498$. From Figure 2.12, this ratio corresponds to $y/D \cong 0.15$, or $y = 10 \times 0.15 = 1.5$ in. This value of y/D gives $R_h/R_{hf} = 0.38$, or $R_h = 0.208 \times 0.38 = 0.079$. The corresponding ratio $V/V_f = 0.52$ gives $V = 3.68 \times 0.52 = 1.9$ ft/s.

Graphs may be developed to show the relations among y, D, and Q. For example, a graph for depth of flow versus flow for various slopes for a 12-in. (300-mm) sewer is shown in Figure 2.13.

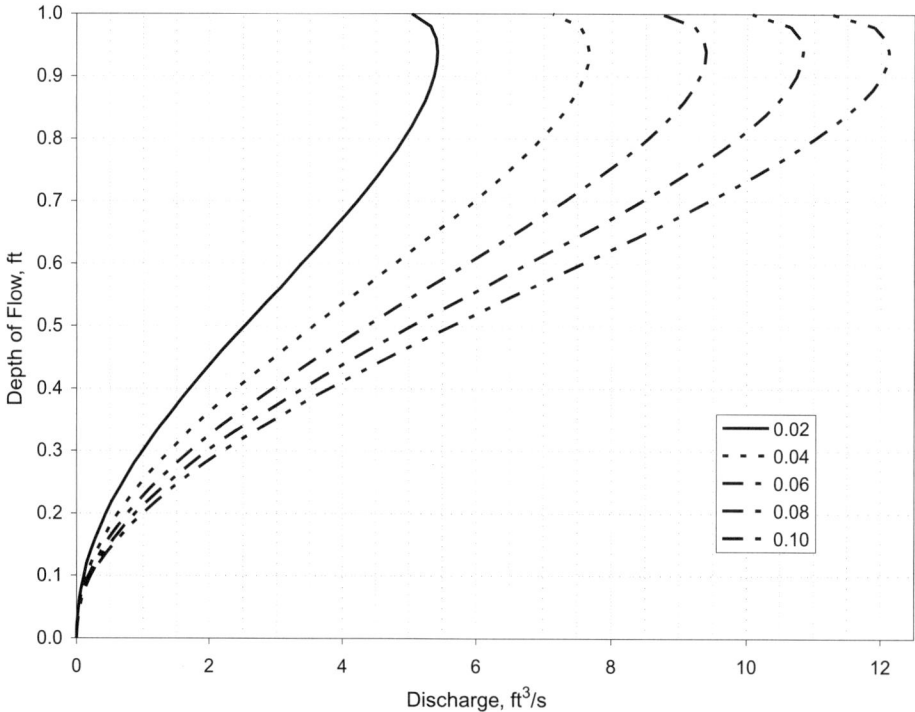

Figure 2.13 Flow depth versus flow rate for various pipe slopes, with $n = 0.013$ and $D = 1$ ft.

Noncircular Cross Sections

Although not commonly used in sewer mains, noncircular cross sections are occasionally used in trunk sewer construction, especially older brick sewers.

Inverted egg and elliptical pipes are quite common in parts of Europe. Inverted egg pipes are also found in some cities in the United States. With narrowing walls near the bottom of the pipe, a greater depth of flow can be maintained for smaller flow rates, resulting in a larger hydraulic radius and higher velocity, and thus better self-cleansing than a comparable circular pipe section. The hydraulic properties of partially filled egg-shape sewers are described by Gill (1987) and Hager (1999). Formulas for calculating flow and velocity in elliptical sections are presented in Haestad Methods (2001).

For a more detailed discussion of the exact dimensions of noncircular conduits and methods for determining flows in those pipes, see Hager (1999).

2.7 Manning's *n* Variation

At a minimum, designers need to be aware of the following factors that affect the value of Manning's *n*:

- *Wall roughness* – For most commercial sewer pipes, actual wall roughness is so small that flows are at or near the hydraulically smooth boundary. This means that commercial pipe material roughness differences have negligible effect on Manning's *n*. Thus, for the same diameter and flow velocity, a finished concrete pipe with $\varepsilon = 0.0001$ ft has essentially the same *n* as a PVC pipe with $\varepsilon = 0.000,005$ ft, since they are both hydraulically smooth. However, *n* for a rough concrete pipe with $\varepsilon = 0.005$ ft would be 20 to 25 percent higher.

- *Viscosity* – Water temperature, and thus viscosity, affects *n*. However, the effect is negligible for the range of water temperatures normally found in sewers.

- *Diameter* – Calculated values of *n* vary significantly with diameter. At a typical 3 ft/s, $n = 0.0090$ for an 8-in. pipe and $n = 0.010$ for a 36 in. pipe, which is 11 percent higher. Experimental and field data indicate that *n* does increase with increasing diameter (Tullis, 1986; Schmidt, 1959).

- *Velocity* – For hydraulically smooth flow at all diameters, the calculated Manning's *n* decreases as the velocity increases. (At least theoretically, *n* should be independent of velocity in rough pipes; that is, the flat zone of the Moody diagram.) Experimental data indicate that *n* decreases with increasing velocity (Tullis, 1986).

- *Manning's n variation with depth of flow* – With $D = 4R_h$, calculations of *n* for partial depths of flow using the Darcy-Weisbach relationship show negligible variation with decreasing depth of flow until about 10 percent partial depth, where *n* begins to increase significantly as the hydraulic radius rapidly decreases.

- *Age and alignment* – The *n*-value for sewer pipes gradually increases over time depending on design, construction, installation practices, system O&M, and environmental conditions. Environmental concerns include fluctuating groundwater elevations, nearby construction practices, and the shifting of soils due to sediment, slippage, and earthquakes. All of these factors contribute to sags, humps, and other shifts in sewer alignment. The apparent *n*-value can increase significantly due to the higher turbulence that accompanies bad alignment, cracks, protrusions, etc.

- *Deposition* – deposits of sediment, debris, grease, and other materials can increase the value of *n*.

The subsections that follow present methods for computing Manning's *n* and provide recommended values.

Calculating *n* with the Darcy-Weisbach Equation

It is generally accepted that the Darcy-Weisbach equation (see Chapter 4) is theoretically the most accurate equation describing head loss for a wide range of conditions. It is informative to observe the variation in Manning's *n* as determined by the Darcy-Weisbach equation. Setting $S = h_L/L$ in the Manning equation and $D = 4R_h$ (for circular pipes) in the Darcy-Weisbach equation, combining the two equations, and solving for Manning's *n* gives

$$n = k R_h^{1/6} f^{1/2} \tag{2.34}$$

where k = 0.0926 for US customary units or 0.1129 for SI units
  R_h = hydraulic radius (ft, m)
  f = Darcy-Weisbach friction factor (dimensionless)

Values for *f* may be obtained from the Moody diagram (see Chapter 4). In addition, several explicit expressions have been developed for *f*; the *Swamee-Jain equation* is frequently used:

$$f = \frac{1.325}{\left[\log\left(\dfrac{\varepsilon}{3.7D} + \dfrac{5.74}{\mathrm{Re}^{0.9}}\right)\right]^2} \tag{2.35}$$

where ε = equivalent sand grain roughness (ft, mm)
  Re = Reynolds number
  D = pipe diameter (ft, mm)

With Equation 2.35, *f* may be determined as a function of water velocity, pipe diameter, pipe roughness, and water viscosity. The result for *f* is then substituted into Equation 2.34 to find *n*.

Example 2.4 Calculation of Manning's *n*

Determine Manning's *n* for a 6-in. concrete pipe with ε estimated as 0.0001 ft and velocity = 2.2 ft/s.

Solution

Equation 2.10 is used to find the Reynolds number for 60° F water:

$$\mathrm{Re} = 2.2 \text{ ft/s} \times 0.5 \text{ ft}/(1.22 \times 10^{-5} \text{ ft}^2/\text{s}) = 90{,}164$$

Equation 2.35 is then applied to find the friction factor as

$$f = \frac{1.325}{\left[\ln\left(\frac{0.0001}{3.7 \times 0.5} + \frac{5.74}{90164^{0.9}}\right)\right]^2} = 0.0193$$

This result is substituted in Equation 2.34 to get

$$n = kR_h^{1/6}f^{1/2} = 0.0926 \times (0.5/4)^{1/6} \times 0.0193^{1/2} = 0.0091$$

It is interesting to note that the Manning's n computed in Example 2.4 is considerably lower than $n = 0.013$, which is the value traditionally used for concrete sewer-pipe design. Figures 2.14 and 2.15 show the n variation in a 12-in. pipe over various roughness and velocity values. Figure 2.14 shows that in rough pipes, n is essentially constant for velocities ranging from 1 to 13 ft/s (0.3 to 4.0 m/s). However, for smooth pipes, n decreases from 0.010 to 0.080 over the same velocity range.

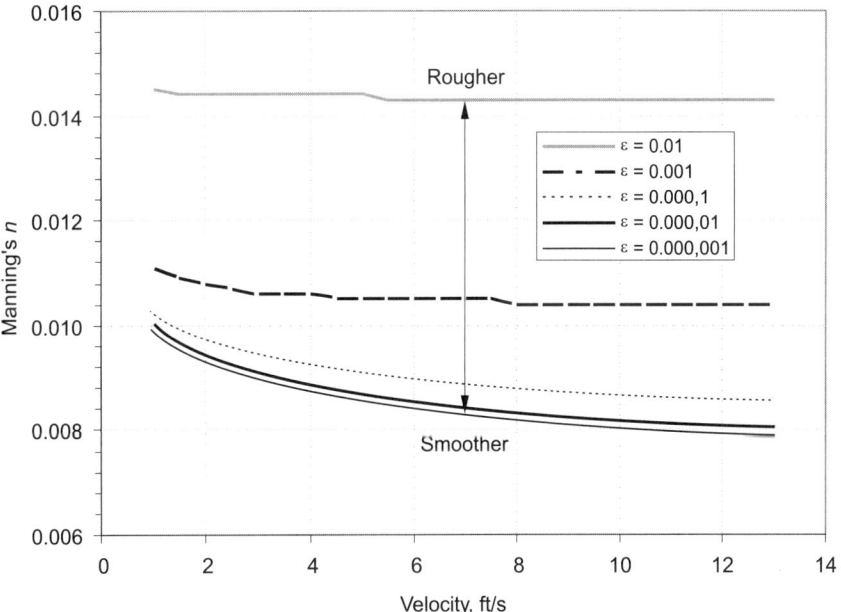

Figure 2.14 Variation of n with velocity for various roughness values (ft) in a 12 in.-pipe.

Figure 2.15 shows that there is a strong relation between roughness and n for rough pipes ($\varepsilon = 0.01$ to 0.001 ft). For smoother pipes, the relation is affected by viscous forces in the pipe, and n is actually more a function of the Reynolds number than the roughness height. These graphs suggest that n is more appropriate for rough pipes than for smooth pipes.

It should be noted that for values of ε ranging from approximately 0.0001 ft (0.03 mm), which corresponds to smooth-finished concrete, to about 0.000005 ft (0.0015 mm), which corresponds to plastics, the flow regime for typical sewer diameters and velocities is at or near the hydraulically smooth boundary identified by the Colebrook-White equation. Thus, for a given pipe diameter and flow velocity, there is a large range of pipe roughness for very little difference in n. For the hydraulically smooth

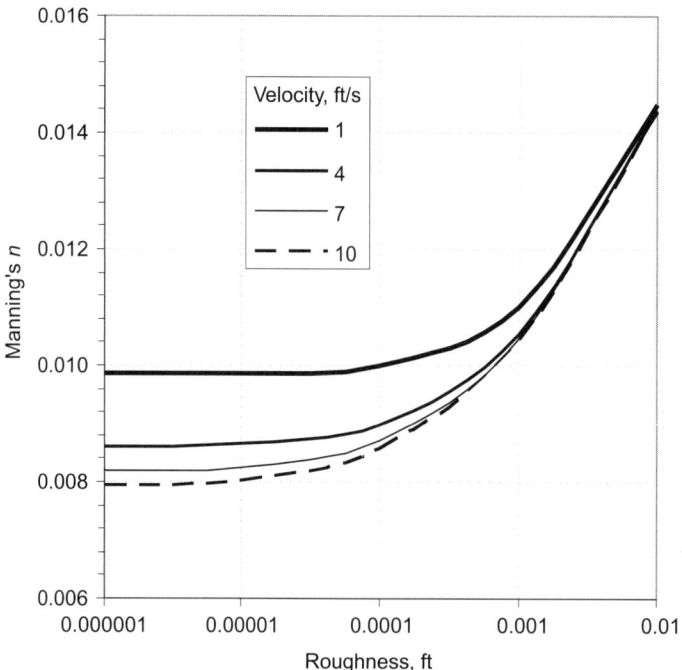

Figure 2.15 Variation of n with pipe roughness for various velocities (ft/s) in a 12-in. pipe.

condition, the laminar sublayer along the pipe wall is thicker than the range of physical roughness. Some concrete pipe-forming methods leave rough surfaces with values of ε higher than 0.005 ft (1.5 mm). Such high values of ε move the hydraulic regime in the pipe significantly away from the hydraulically smooth boundary and cause a significant increase in n—as much as 20 to 25 percent higher than for smooth-finish concrete.

In general, n increases with increasing diameter and decreases with increasing velocity. Therefore, n is lowest for small diameters and high velocities and highest for large diameters and low velocities. For example, with ε = 0.0001 ft and water temperature of 60° F (15.6° C), n ranges from about 0.008 for a 6 in. (152 mm) pipe at 10 ft/s (3 m/s) to n = 0.011 for a 72 in. (1830 mm) pipe at 2 ft/s (0.61 m/s). In practice, these values might be increased by about 15% to allow for the less-than-ideal hydraulic flow conditions in sewer pipes. Some regulations require use of n = 0.013 for design.

Variation of *n* with Depth

Experiments conducted to determine the effect of variation of depth of flow on Manning's n have shown that n is greater in partially filled round sewer pipe (ASCE, 1982 and WPCF, 1969) than in a full pipe. This variation is indicated in Figure 2.12. An empirical relationship for n as a function of depth of flow is (Schmidt, 1959)

$$\frac{n}{n_f} = 1.0 + 2.75\frac{y}{D} - 8.55\left(\frac{y}{D}\right)^2 + 10.0\left(\frac{y}{D}\right)^3 - 4.22\left(\frac{y}{D}\right)^4 \qquad (2.36)$$

"Counselor, please advise your client that, issues of personal safety aside, gravity is the law."

where:
- n = Manning's n for a partially full pipe
- n_f = Manning's n for a full pipe
- y = depth of flow (ft, m)
- D = pipe diameter (ft, m)

Calculated n values for partial-flow depths, based on the more-accurate Darcy-Weisbach equation and experimental results (Schmidt, 1959, Camp, 1940 and Tullis, 1986), show essentially no variation in n with depth of flow until the flow is very shallow (less than 10 percent full), at which point n increases significantly. Thus it is questionable whether the variation in n as shown on many traditional charts is properly represented as simply a function of flow depth. The practice of varying n with depth of flow is not recommended, but it makes little difference in actual design. However, Manning's n does vary with water temperature, pipe diameter, and velocity of flow, as described in the following section.

Recommended Values of Manning's *n*

Most design codes recommend $n = 0.013$ for all pipe sizes. Many experiments on full-scale sewer-line installations, including operating sewers, report $n \approx 0.009$–0.011 (Tullis, 1986; May, 1986; Straub, Bowers, and Puch, 1960; Wing and Kerri, 1978). Most of these tests were on 8 to 18 in. sewers, so reported values are about the same as the values calculated with Equations 2.34 and 2.35. In operating sewers, however, such factors as serious misalignment, pipe interior deterioration, joint separation, cracks, protruding connections, buildup of sediment, and buildup of coating materials may result in much higher n values.

If local regulatory agencies require use of the traditional $n = 0.013$, the designer should recognize that with good installation and cleaning maintenance when needed, velocities and pipe capacities are considerably higher than indicated by the design calculations. If the regulatory agency allows discretion in selecting n values, the values in Table 2.5 should be considered.

Table 2.5 Suggested values of Manning's n for sewer design calculations.

Condition	Diameter, in. (mm)					
	6 (152)	8 (203)	10 (254)	12 (305)	15 (381)	18 (457)
Extra care	0.0092	0.0093	0.0095	0.0096	0.0097	0.0098
Typical	0.0106	0.0107	0.0109	0.0110	0.0112	0.0113
Substandard	0.0120	0.0121	0.0125	0.0125	0.0126	0.0127
Condition	**24 (610)**	**30 (762)**	**36 (914)**	**48 (1219)**	**60 (1524)**	**72 (1829)**
Extra care	0.0100	0.0102	0.0103	0.0105	0.0107	0.0109
Typical	0.0115	0.0117	0.0118	0.0121	0.0123	0.0125
Substandard	0.0130	0.0133	0.0134	0.0137	0.0139	0.0142

The "extra care" values in Table 2.5 are the calculated theoretical n values; "typical" values are 15 percent higher; and "substandard" values are 30 percent higher. The extra-care values correspond to clean water flowing in a clean, well-aligned pipe. It seems reasonable to increase them by about 15 percent to allow for good—but less than ideal—conditions in the pipe. The type of pipe, the care taken during construction and in making connections, and cleaning maintenance determine whether extra-care, typical, or substandard conditions actually exist in a sewer pipe over its lifetime.

2.8 Minor Losses in Junction Structures

This section discusses an additional head loss, called minor loss, that occurs when there are local flow restrictions and/or disturbances at manholes, lateral inlets, flow-measurement sections, and similar pipe appurtenances. The total head loss along a pipe is the sum of the frictional and minor losses.

Bends and valves are rare in gravity sewer systems; thus, most of the minor losses are attributed to manholes. Traditionally, the head loss is expressed as the product of a minor loss coefficient and the absolute difference between the velocity heads upstream and downstream of the appurtenance. This approach is reasonable for many types of minor loss calculations. For most situations, the minor loss coefficient for manholes ranges from 0.1 to 1.0, and head loss ranges from 0 to roughly 0.2 ft (0.06 m). From a hydraulic point of view, the most important detail of a manhole is the bottom channel, which can provide for a smoother flow transition.

Because flow geometries are often complex at manholes and junction structures are often complex, specialized methods have been developed for minor loss prediction, as presented by Brown, Stein, and Warner (2001). These approaches, known as the energy-loss and composite energy-loss methods, are described in the subsections that follow. Other methods for determining head loss at manholes are described in Hager (1999).

Energy losses in manholes add to losses in pipes. Depending on the flow condition, these losses are added to the EGL when moving upstream or subtracted from the EGL when moving downstream.

Energy-Loss Method

The inlet pipe(s) to a manhole or junction structure in a sewer have one of a few possible configurations with respect to their invert elevations, as follows:

a) All inlet-pipe invert elevations may lie below the elevation of the predicted depth of water in the structure.

b) All inlet-pipe invert elevations may lie above the elevation of the predicted depth of water in the structure.

c) One or more of the inlet-pipe invert elevations may lie above the elevation of the predicted depth of water in the structure, while one or more are below this elevation.

For structures in which all inlet-pipe invert elevations lie above the predicted free water surface elevation within the structure (so that there is *plunging flow* from all of the inlet pipes), the outlet pipe behaves hydraulically as a culvert. In that case, the water-surface elevation within the structure can be predicted using the methods presented in Norman, Houghtalen, and Johnston (2001), and the water-surface elevations in each of the upstream pipes can be determined independently as free outfalls.

The *energy-loss method* (Brown, Stein, and Warner, 2001) for estimation of head losses at inlets, manholes, and junctions applies only to configuration (a) and to the pipes in configuration (c) whose invert elevations lie below the predicted free water-surface elevation within the structure. When one or more inlet pipes meet these criteria, the method may be applied to each to determine the corresponding head loss. This method is applicable to manholes constructed with or without benches to provide smooth transitions in flow.

For inlet pipes to which the energy-loss method is applicable, the head loss through the structure can be computed with

$$h_L = K \frac{V_o^2}{2g} \qquad (2.37)$$

where V_o = velocity in the outlet pipe
K = adjusted minor loss coefficient

Laboratory research has shown that K can be expressed as

$$K = K_o C_{D1} C_{D2} C_Q C_p C_B \qquad (2.38)$$

where K_o = initial head loss coefficient based on the relative size of the structure
C_{D1} = correction factor for the pipe diameter
C_{D2} = correction factor for the flow depth
C_Q = correction factor for relative flow
C_P = correction factor for plunging flow
C_B = correction factor for benching

Equations 2.37 and 2.38 can be applied to each of several inlet pipes at a structure, provided their invert elevations lie below the predicted water-surface elevation within the structure.

The initial head loss coefficient, K_o, depends on the size of the structure relative to the outlet-pipe diameter and on the angle θ between the inlet and outlet pipes (see Figure 2.16) and is given by

$$K_o = 0.1\left(\frac{B}{D_o}\right)(1 - \sin\theta) + 1.4\left(\frac{B}{D_o}\right)^{0.15}\sin\theta \qquad (2.39)$$

where
B = structure diameter (ft, m)
D_o = outlet pipe diameter (ft, m)

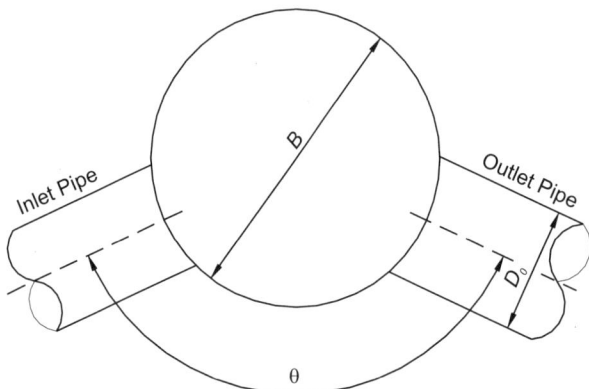

Figure 2.16 Plan view of inlet structure.

If the structure is not circular, an *equivalent structure diameter*, which is the diameter of a circular structure having the same area as the actual noncircular one, should be used. For example, if the inside dimensions (plan view) of a junction chamber are 3 ft (0.91 m) by 6 ft (1.8 m), with an area of 18 ft² (1.66 m²), the equivalent diameter used in Equation 2.39 is $B = (4A/\pi)1/2 = [4(1.66)/3.14]1/2 = 4.79$ ft (1.46 m).

The correction factor for pipe diameter, C_{D1}, is important only when the predicted water depth in the structure is at least 3.2 times as great as the outlet pipe diameter. In such cases, C_{D1} is given by

$$C_{D1} = \left(\frac{D_o}{D_i}\right)^3 \qquad (2.40)$$

where D_i = inlet pipe diameter (ft, m)

When the predicted depth in the structure is not at least 3.2 times the outlet pipe diameter, $C_{D1} = 1$. When applying correction factors, the depth of water, d, in the structure should be determined as the difference between the hydraulic grade line at the upstream end of the outlet pipe and the invert elevation of the outlet pipe.

The correction factor for flow depth, C_{D2}, is important only when the predicted depth in the structure is less than 3.2 times the outlet pipe diameter; otherwise, $C_{D2} = 1$. The correction factor is given by

$$C_{D2} = 0.5\left(\frac{d}{D_o}\right)^{0.6} \qquad (2.41)$$

The correction factor for relative flow, C_Q, is required when there are two or more inlet pipes at a structure. Note that this calculation is performed for each inlet pipe, yielding a C_Q for each inlet. When there is only one inlet pipe, $C_Q = 1$. The correction factor depends on the angle θ between the outlet pipe and the selected inlet pipe and on the ratio of the flow in the inlet pipe to the outlet pipe:

$$C_Q = 1 + (1 - 2\sin\theta)\left(1 - \frac{Q_i}{Q_o}\right)^{0.75} \tag{2.42}$$

where Q_i = discharge from the inflow pipe

Q_o = flow in the outflow pipe

When an inflow pipe to a structure has an invert elevation higher than the elevation of the free water surface in the structure, it is said to have a *free outfall*, and the water plunges into the structure. The resulting turbulence and energy dissipation within the structure affect the head loss of other inlet pipes whose invert elevations lie below the free water surface. The coefficient C_P is computed and applied in the head-loss calculations only for the pipe(s) whose flow is not plunging. The coefficient is given by

$$C_P = 1 + 0.2\left(\frac{h}{D_o}\right)\left(\frac{h-d}{D_o}\right) \tag{2.43}$$

where D_o = outlet-pipe diameter (ft, m)

d = depth of water in the structure (ft, m)

h = difference in elevation between the highest inlet pipe invert and the centerline of the outlet pipe (ft, m)

In cases with no plunging inlet pipes or where $h \leq d$, $C_P = 1$.

Benching of the invert of a structure, as illustrated in Figure 2.17, can reduce head losses by effectively directing the path of the flow through the structure. The correction factor for benching, C_B, depends on the depth of water in the structure relative to the outlet pipe diameter and is listed in Table 2.6 for various conditions. Submerged flow is defined as $d/D_o \geq 3.2$, while unsubmerged flow is defined as $d/D_o \leq 1.0$. For values of d/D_o between 1.0 and 3.2, C_B is linearly interpolated between the tabulated values.

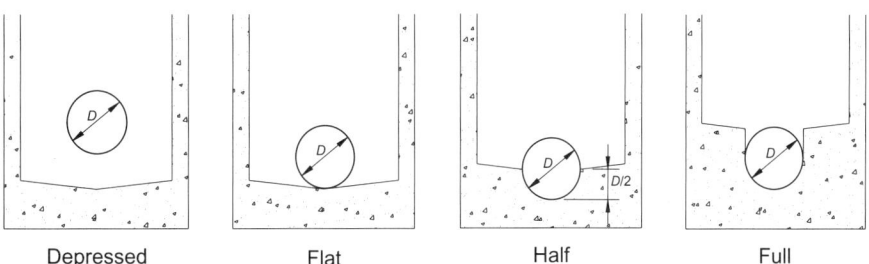

Figure 2.17 Benching the invert of a structure.

Table 2.6 Correction factors for benching.

Bench Type	Submerged	Unsubmerged
Flat or depressed floor	1.00	1.00
Half bench	0.95	0.15
Full bench	0.75	0.07

Example 2.5 Computing hydraulic grade elevations within a manhole using the energy loss method

Consider a manhole with two inlet pipes, as shown in the following figure. The inlet-pipe invert elevations have been set so that their crown elevations match the crown of the outlet pipe. If the HGL elevation at the upstream end of the outlet pipe is 104.43 ft and the velocity is 7.37 ft/s, determine the HGL elevations for pipes 1 and 2 at the point of entry to the manhole. Calculate the HGLs for a flat-benched and full-benched manhole.

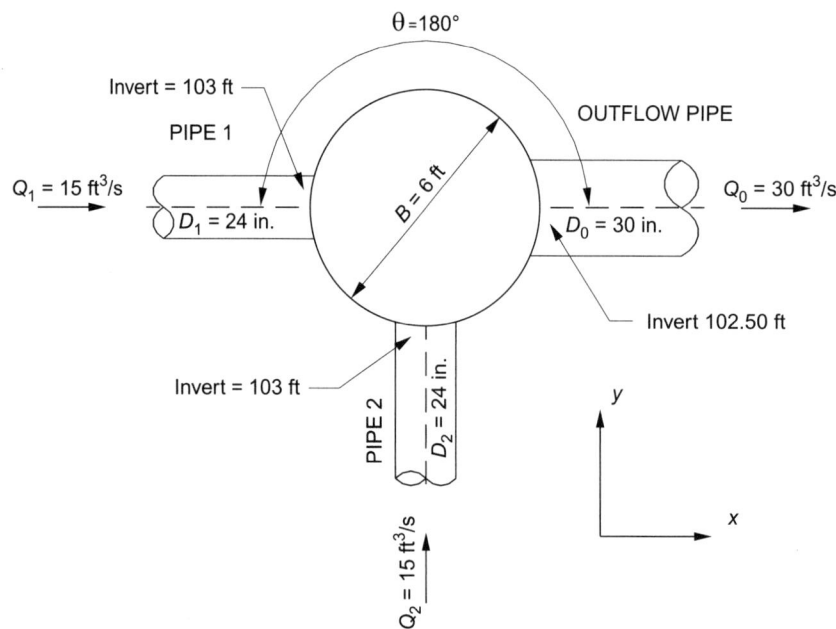

Solution

For Pipe 1, $\theta = 180°$, so the initial head loss coefficient is found using Equation 2.39 as

$$K_o(1) = 0.1\frac{6}{2.5} = 0.24$$

Similarly, for Pipe 2, where $\theta = 90°$, the head loss coefficient is

$$K_o(2) = 1.4\left(\frac{6}{2.5}\right)^{0.15} = 1.60$$

The depth of flow, d, in the manhole structure is the difference in elevation between the outlet HGL and its invert, or 1.93 ft, so $d/D_o = 1.93/2.5 = 0.77$. Since $d/D_o < 3.2$, the correction factor for pipe diameter is 1 for both inlet pipes:

$$C_{D1}(1) = C_{D1}(2) = 1$$

The correction factor for flow depth is determined using Equation 2.41 for each of the inlet pipes:

$$C_{D2}(1) = C_{D2}(2) = 0.5\left(\frac{1.93}{2.5}\right)^{0.6} = 0.86$$

The correction factor for relative flow, C_Q, is given by Equation 2.42. The angle for the first pipe is $\theta_1 = 180°$, so $\sin\theta_1 = 0$. For the second pipe, $\theta_2 = 90°$, so $\sin\theta_2 = 1$. Thus, the correction factors are

$$C_Q(1) = 1 + (1-2(0))\left(1-\frac{15}{30}\right)^{0.75} = 1.59$$

$$C_Q(2) = 1 + (1-2(1))\left(1-\frac{15}{30}\right)^{0.75} = 0.41$$

Because there is no plunging flow is in this example, the correction factors are

$$C_P(1) = C_P(2) = 1$$

For a full bench the correction factor is $C_B = 0.07$ and for a flat bench it is $C_B = 1.0$.

The adjusted loss coefficient for Pipe 1 is, for a full bench,

$$K(1) = K_o(1)C_{D1}(1)C_{D2}(1)C_Q(1)C_P(1)C_B(1) = 0.24(1)(0.86)(1.59)(1)(0.07) = 0.02$$

and for a flat bench,

$$K(1) = K_o(1)C_{D1}(1)C_{D2}(1)C_Q(1)C_P(1)C_B(1) = 0.24(1)(0.86)(1.59)(1)(1.00) = 0.33$$

For Pipe 2, the loss coefficient for a full bench is

$$K(2) = K_o(2)C_{D1}(2)C_{D2}(2)C_Q(2)C_P(2)C_B(2) = 1.64(1)(0.86)(0.41)(1)(0.07) = 0.10$$

and for a flat bench is

$$K(2) = K_o(2)C_{D1}(2)C_{D2}(2)C_Q(2)C_P(2)C_B(2) = 1.64(1)(0.86)(0.41)(1)(1.00) = 0.58$$

The head loss for Pipe 1 with a full bench is

$$h_L(1) = 0.02\frac{(7.37)^2}{2 \times 32.2} = 0.02 \text{ ft}$$

so the HGL is

$$HGL = 104.43 + 0.02 = 104.45 \text{ ft}$$

With a flat bench the head loss for Pipe 1 is

$$h_L(1) = 0.33\frac{(7.37)^2}{2 \times 32.2} = 0.28 \text{ ft}$$

so the HGL is

$$HGL = 104.43 + 0.29 = 104.71 \text{ ft}$$

For Pipe 2, the HGL for a full bench is

$$HGL = 104.43 + 0.10\frac{(7.37)^2}{2 \times 32.2} = 104.51 \text{ ft}$$

and for a flat bench is

$$HGL = 104.43 + 0.58\frac{(7.37)^2}{2 \times 32.2} = 104.92 \text{ ft}$$

Composite Energy-Loss Method

The composite energy-loss method can be used in situations similar to those to which the energy-loss method applies (Brown, Stein, and Warner, 2001). However, the composite method is better suited to analyzing losses in structures with many inflow pipes. It is applicable only to subcritical flows in pipes.

The method is used to compute a unique head loss through the junction structure for each of the incoming pipes. This head loss is then added to the energy grade at the upstream end of the outlet pipe (EGL_o) to obtain the EGL at the downstream end of the incoming pipe (EGL_i). The velocity head for the incoming pipe can then be subracted from EGL_i to obtain the hydraulic grade, HGL_i. The head loss through the structure for a particular inflow pipe is given by

$$h_L = K \frac{V_o^2}{2g} \tag{2.44}$$

where K = the adjusted minor loss coefficient for the composite energy-loss method

The adjusted minor loss coefficient K is defined as

$$K = (C_1 C_2 C_3 + C_4) C_B \tag{2.45}$$

where C_1 = coefficient for the relative access-hole diameter
C_2 = coefficient for the water depth in the manhole
C_3 = coefficient for lateral flow, the lateral angle, and plunging flow
C_4 = coefficient for the relative pipe diameters
C_B = coefficient for benching (as before, given by Table 2.6)

Empirical equations describing these coefficients were developed from laboratory studies and analyses. These equations are presented in the following subsections.

Computing C_1 (Relative Access-Hole Diameter Coefficient). The energy-loss coefficient related to the relative access-hole diameter, expressed as the ratio of access-hole diameter, B, to outlet-pipe diameter, D_o, is given by

$$C_1 = \begin{cases} \dfrac{0.9 \dfrac{B}{D_o}}{6 + \dfrac{B}{D_o}}, & \dfrac{B}{D_o} < 4 \\ 0.36, & \dfrac{B}{D_o} \geq 4 \end{cases} \tag{2.46}$$

Thus, the value of this coefficient increases with increasing relative access-hole diameter, up to a value of $B/D_o = 4$, after which it remains constant at 0.36. Note that the value of C_1 is the same for all incoming pipes.

Computing C_2 (Water Depth in Manhole Coefficient) and C_3 (Lateral Flow, Lateral Angle, and Plunging Flow Coefficient). The coefficients C_2 and C_3 represent the composite effect of all the inflow pipes, the outflow pipe, and the manhole. Their calculation is affected by and also affects the calculation of the access-hole water depth, d. Because of this interdependence, an iterative method is used to calculate these coefficients. The first step is to compute an initial estimate of d with the equation

$$d = HGL_o + C_1 C_B \frac{V_o^2}{2g} - Z_o \qquad (2.47)$$

where HGL_o = hydraulic grade elevation at the upstream end of the outlet pipe (ft, m)
Z_o = elevation of the outlet pipe invert (ft, m)

This value is used to calculate an estimate of C_2 with

$$C_2 = \begin{cases} 0.24\left(\frac{d}{D_o}\right)^2 - 0.05\left(\frac{d}{D_o}\right)^3, & \frac{d}{D_o} \leq 3 \\ 0.82, & \frac{d}{D_o} > 3 \end{cases} \qquad (2.48)$$

The analysis of the factors affecting energy losses for lateral flows resulted in an equation for C_3 that is the most complex of any of the coefficients. For a simple, two-pipe system with no plunging flow, $C_3 = 1.0$. (A pipe has plunging flow if the critical flow depth elevation in the pipe, $y_c + Z_i$, is higher than the access-hole depth elevation, $d + Z_o$.) Otherwise, C_3 is expressed in the form

$$C_3 = 1 + C_{3A} + C_{3B} + C_{3C} + C_{3D} \qquad (2.49)$$

The calculations for C_3 consider the angle θ_i between the inlet and outlet pipes. As this angle deviates from 180° (straight-line flow), the energy loss increases because the flow cannot smoothly transition to the outlet pipe. All inflow pipe angles are measured clockwise from the outlet pipe. The calculation of C_3 accounts for inlet-flow plunging by considering the inlet as a fourth, synthetic inflow pipe with the corresponding angle set to 0°.

C_3 can have a value ranging from 1 for no lateral flow to potentially very high values for greater plunge heights. Because empirical studies do not support this result, a value of 10 is set as a realistic upper limit on C_3.

Term C_{3A} represents the energy loss from plunging flows and is valid for up to three inlet pipes plus the plunging flow from the inlet:

$$C_{3A} = \sum_{i=1}^{4} \left(\frac{Q_i}{Q_o}\right)^{0.75} \left[1 + 2\left(\frac{Z_i}{D_o} - \frac{d}{D_o}\right)^{0.3} \left(\frac{Z_i}{D_o}\right)^{0.3}\right] \qquad (2.50)$$

where Q_1, Q_2, Q_3 = discharge from inflow pipes 1, 2, and 3 (ft³/s, m³/s)
Q_4 = discharge into the manhole from the inlet (ft³/s, m³/s)
Z_1, Z_2, Z_3 = invert elevations of the inflow pipes relative to the outlet pipe invert (ft, m)

Term C_{3B} represents the energy loss due to change in direction between the inlet and outlet pipes. If the horizontal momentum check HMC_i, given by

$$HMC_i = 0.85 - \left(\frac{Z_i}{D_o}\right)\left(\frac{Q_i}{D_o}\right)^{0.75} \qquad (2.51)$$

is less than 0, then the flow is assumed to be falling from such a height that horizontal momentum can be neglected and $C_{3B} = 0$. If $HMC_i \geq 0$, then C_{3B} is given by

$$C_{3B} = 4 \sum_{i=1}^{3} \frac{\cos\theta_i \times HMC_i}{\left(\frac{d}{D_o}\right)^{0.3}} \tag{2.52}$$

where $\theta_1, \theta_2, \theta_3$ = angle between the outlet main and inflow pipes 1, 2, and 3 (degrees)
 HMC_i = horizontal momentum check for pipe i

If there is more than one inflow pipe, C_{3C} is calculated for all combinations of inflow pipes that have $HMC_i > 0$. The pair that produces the highest value is then used for the calculations of C_{3C} and C_{3D}.

$$C_{3C} = 0.8\left(\frac{Z_A}{D_o} - \frac{Z_B}{D_o}\right) \tag{2.53}$$

where Z_A, Z_B = invert elevation, relative to the outlet pipe invert, for the inflow pipes that produce the largest value of C_{3D}, given by

$$C_{3D} = \left|\left(\frac{Q_A}{Q_o}\right)^{0.75}\sin\theta_A + \left(\frac{Q_B}{Q_o}\right)^{0.75}\sin\theta_B\right| \tag{2.54}$$

where Q_A, Q_B = discharges for the pair of inflow pipes that produce the largest value of C_{3D} (ft³/s, m³/s)
 $\theta_{A, B}$ = angle between the outlet main and inflow pipes for the pair of inflow pipes producing the largest value of C_{3D} (degrees)

With the initial estimates of C_2 and C_3, the access-hole depth is recalculated with

$$d = HGL_o + \frac{V_o^2}{2g} + C_1 C_2 C_3 C_B \frac{V_o^2}{2g} - Z_o \tag{2.55}$$

where HGL_o = hydraulic gradeline at the upstream end of the inlet pipe (ft, m)
 Z_o = invert elevation of the outlet pipe at the upstream end (ft, m)

This new value of d is compared to the previous estimate and the entire procedure for calculating C_2, C_3, and d continues until the method converges on the value of d.

Computing C_4 (Relative Pipe Diameter Coefficient). The last coefficient to be determined in Equation 2.49, the coefficient related to relative pipe diameters, C_4, is computed for each inflow pipe with

$$C_{4i} = 1 + \left(\frac{Q_i}{Q_o} + 2\frac{A_i}{A_o}\cos\theta_i\right)\frac{V_i^2}{V_o^2} \tag{2.56}$$

where A_i, A_o = cross-sectional areas of the inlet and outflow pipes (ft², m²)
 θ_i = angle between the outlet pipe and inflow pipe i (degrees)

Because this term represents an exit loss from each inflow pipe, C_{4i} is set to 0 for each pipe with plunging flow. In addition, if θ_i is less than 90° or greater than 270° for any inlet pipe, the corresponding term $\cos \theta_i$ is set to 0 in Equation 2.56. The upper limit for the value of C_4 is 9.0.

Because of the complex, iterative nature of the composite energy-loss method, its application is not well suited to manual calculations and thus it is not illustrated here through an example problem. However, it is readily adaptable to computer solutions.

2.9 Tractive Force Self-Cleansing

Wastewater contains suspended particles. Tchobanoglous, Burton, and Stensel (2003) state that medium-strength domestic wastewater contains 210 mg/L of suspended matter with 160 mg/L of fixed (inorganic) and 50 mg/L of volatile (organic) particles. Sewers that collect surface-water inflow may experience periods of significantly higher sediment load. Suspended matter may be cohesive or exist as discrete particles with a range of sizes. Butler, May, and Ackers (2003) state that typical average particle size (d_{50}) values in combined sewers in the United Kingdom are 10, 40, and 50 μm for wastewater with low, medium, and high sediment loads. The specific gravity ranges from 1.01 to 1.6.

Sanitary sewers must be designed so that sediment does not accumulate during periods of low flow without providing some period with enough flow to clean out the pipes. To assure that sewers will carry suspended sediment, two approaches have been used: the minimum (or self-cleansing) velocity described in Section 2.4 and the minimum boundary shear stress method, also called the "tractive force" method.

Tractive Tension

The forces acting on a fluid element are shown in Figure 2.18. In steady flow, the gravitational force of the fluid must equal the friction force along the pipe wall. The component of the gravitational force parallel to the axis of the pipe per unit boundary area is known as the *tractive tension*, tractive force, or boundary shear stress. This tension is given by

$$\tau = \frac{W \sin \theta}{pL} \tag{2.57}$$

where τ = tractive tension (lb/ft², Pa)
W = weight of fluid (lb, N)
p = wetted perimeter (ft, m)
L = length of pipe (ft, m)

The weight of fluid is given by

$$W = \rho g a L \tag{2.58}$$

where ρ = fluid density (slug/ft³, kg/m³)
g = gravitational acceleration (32.2 ft/s², 9.81 m/s²)
a = area of fluid section (ft², m²)

Since $a/p = R_h$, the tractive tension is given by

$$\tau = \rho g R_h \sin \theta \tag{2.59}$$

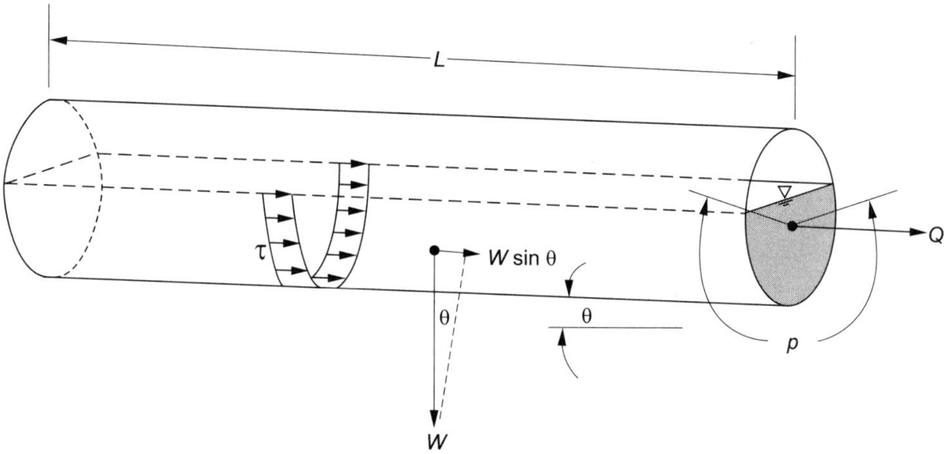

Figure 2.18 Definition of parameters for tractive tension in a circular sewer.

When θ is small, it is approximately equal to the slope, S, and the tractive tension is given by

$$\tau = \rho g R_h S \qquad (2.60)$$

The equations for tractive tension can be rearranged to give the minimum slope for any tractive tension and flow rate. Mara, Sleigh, and Taylor (2000) developed the following relationship for minimum slope, based on the assumption that $y/D = 0.2$ and $n = 0.013$:

$$S_{min} = 2.33 \times 10^{-4} \tau^{1.23} Q^{-0.461} \qquad (2.61)$$

where S_{min} = minimum slope to move particles
τ = tractive tension (Pa)
Q = flow (m³/s)

When flow is stated in L/s, the coefficient 2.33×10^{-4} is replaced with 0.0055. When flow is stated in ft³/s and τ is in lb/ft², the coefficient is 0.141.

In some locations (for example, see Brazilian Standard 946/1986), an assumption of $\tau = 1$ Pa (0.0209 lb/ft²) tractive force reduces Equation 2.61 to

$$S_{min} = 2.33 \times 10^{-4} Q^{-0.461} \qquad (2.62)$$

When the flow is stated in ft³/s, the coefficient 2.33×10^{-4} is replaced with 1.21×10^{-3}. In Brazil, the recommended minimum design flow is 1.5 L/s (24 gpm), even if the actual flow is less.

Example 2.6 Tractive tension design

Given a minimum flow of 10 L/s, use the Brazilian Standard to determine the minimum slope for a gravity sewer pipe and the size of pipe for which the assumptions are applicable.

Solution:

The minimum slope is given by Equation 2.62 as

$$S = 0.055 \times 10^{-461} = 0.002 \text{ m/m}$$

The standard assumes that $n = 0.013$ and $y/D = 0.2$. Applying the Manning equation to find a depth of flow at this minimum flow rate yields the results in the following table.

Pipe Diameter, in. (mm)	y/D
15 (380)	0.24
18 (460)	0.18

Thus a 15 in. (380 mm) or 18 in. (460 mm) pipe set at a slope of 0.002 will meet the standard. The size selected depends on the peak flow.

Sediment Carrying Capacity – Experimental Analysis

In a series of experiments, Raths and McCauley (1962) assessed the ability of an 8-in. (205-mm) sewer pipe to convey sand particles with sizes ranging from 0.15 to 7.9 mm and a specific gravity of approximately 2.7. The pipe slope ranged from 0.0015 to 0.0050 and y/D varied from 0.10 to 0.57. For each set of operating conditions, the tractive tension was calculated using Equation 2.60. The results are displayed in Figure 2.19.

These results were linearized to yield

$$\tau = 0.867 \, d^{0.277} \tag{2.63}$$

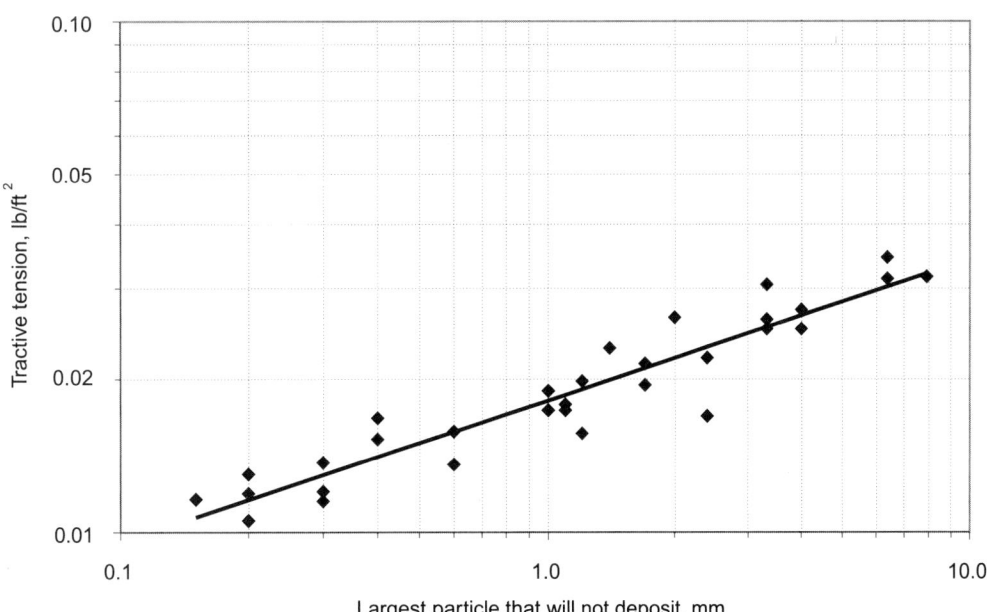

Figure 2.19 Comparison of sediment-carrying capacity with tractive tension.

where τ = minimum tractive tension (Pa)
d = particle size (mm)

For τ in units of lb/ft², the coefficient becomes 0.0181. Note that the assumption of 1 Pa (0.02006 lb/ft²) in the Brazilian Standard results in movement of a 1.45-mm particle.

For a given particle size and tractive tension calculated with Equation 2.63, the minimum slope is a function of flow and, hence, the depth of flow. Figure 2.20 shows the minimum slope (given by Equation 2.60) of a pipe that has the tractive tension to move a 0.5 mm particle. The minimum slopes for a full pipe and a pipe with a y/D of 0.2 are shown.

In Figure 2.21, the minimum slopes for full-flowing pipes with diameters ranging from 6 in. (150 mm) to 36 in. (915 mm) are shown for 0.5 and 10 mm particles. The slopes were calculated using Equations 2.63 and 2.60. The slope required for a velocity

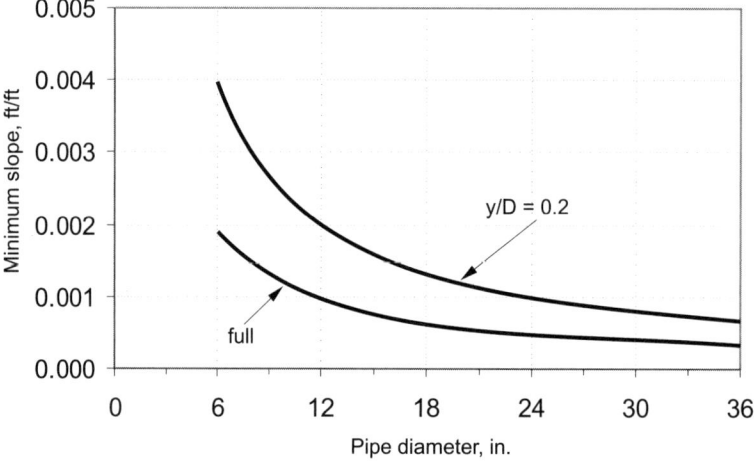

Figure 2.20 Minimum pipe slope to move a 0.5 mm particle.

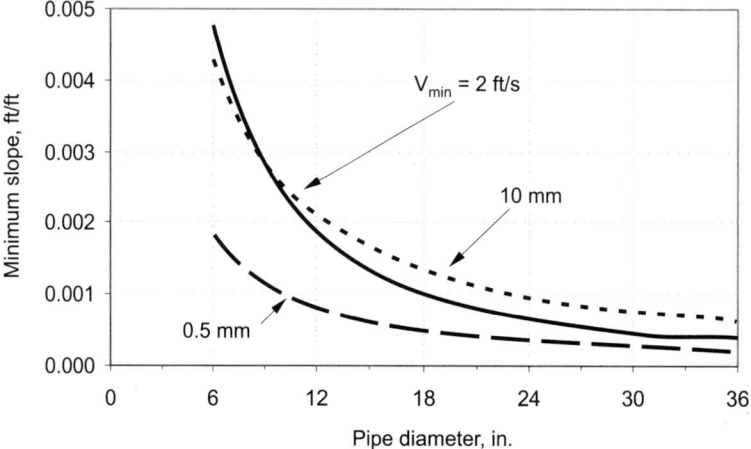

Figure 2.21 Minimum slopes as a function of pipe diameter. Calculations assume the pipe is flowing full.

Section 2.9 Tractive Force Self-Cleansing 67

of 2 ft/s (0.6 m/s) (from Table 2.2) is also shown on Figure 2.21. In this figure, the 2 ft/s (0.6 m/s) line for pipes flowing full is close to the 10 mm curve for a 6-in. (150 mm) pipe and approaches the 0.5 mm curve as the pipe diameter increases to 30 in. (760 mm). This analysis suggests that the 2 ft/s (0.6 m/s) minimum-velocity standard removes progressively smaller particles as the pipe diameter increases.

An important observation from tractive tension considerations is that the full-pipe velocity must increase with increasing pipe size to give the same tractive force, and hence cleansing power, as smaller diameter pipes. Many researchers have noted that larger-diameter sewers need higher velocities to reduce sediment buildup (Schmidt, 1959; Yao, 1974; May, 1994). When designing pipes in areas with minimal slope, engineers may increase the pipe size to convey larger maximum flows, but this has the side effect of making it more difficult to move sediment at low flow.

This phenomenon may be demonstrated by the following example. For a 12-in. (305 mm) pipe flowing full at a slope of 0.002, the tractive force (from Equation 2.60) is 0.322 lb/ft^2. A 24-in. (610 mm) pipe has the same tractive force when placed at a slope of 0.001. The velocity in a pipe is given by the Manning equation:

$$V = \frac{k}{n} R_h^{2/3} S^{1/2} \quad (2.64)$$

For the 12-in. (305 mm) pipe, the velocity is

$$V = \frac{1.49}{0.013} \left(\frac{12}{12 \times 4}\right)^{2/3} 0.002^{1/2} = 2.03 \text{ ft/s } (0.62 \text{ m/s}) \quad (2.65)$$

and for the 24-in. (610 mm) pipe, the velocity is

$$V = \frac{1.49}{0.013} \left(\frac{24}{12 \times 4}\right)^{2/3} 0.001^{1/2} = 2.28 \text{ ft/s } (0.69 \text{ m/s}) \quad (2.66)$$

Example 2.7 Minimum slope calculation

Find the minimum slope needed for self-cleansing a 1 mm particle with a specific gravity of 2.7 for a design minimum flow rate of 0.20 ft^3/s in a 10-in. concrete pipe.

Solution

The required tractive tension is given by Equation 2.63 as

$$\tau = 0.0181 \times 1^{0.277} = 0.0181 \text{ lb/ft}^2$$

Table 2.5 gives Manning's $n = 0.0109$ for "typical" conditions.

Equations 2.27 and 2.60 and the equations for a partially full circular conduit in Table 2.4 are solved simultaneously to yield the slope corresponding to the required tractive tension. In this solution, the value of y is assumed, R_h is found with the equation in Table 2.4, S is calculated with Equation 2.60, and Q with Equation 2.27. The results of a trial-and-error solution are listed in the following table.

y, ft	θ, radians	R_h, ft	S, ft	A, ft	Q, ft^3/s
Assume	$\cos^{-1}\left(1 - \frac{2y}{D}\right)$	$\frac{D}{4}\left(1 - \frac{\sin 2\theta}{2\theta}\right)$	$\frac{\tau}{\rho g R_h}$	$\frac{D^2(2\theta - \sin 2\theta)}{8}$	$\frac{k}{n} A R_h^{2/3} S^{2/3}$
0.2	1.024	0.118	0.0023	0.101	0.138

y, ft	θ, radians	R_h, ft	S, ft	A, ft	Q, ft³/s
0.24	1.133	0.138	0.0021	0.130	0.182
0.25	1.159	0.142	0.0020	0.138	0.194
0.255	1.172	0.145	0.0020	0.141	0.200
0.256	1.175	0.145	0.0020	0.142	0.201

For $Q = 0.20$ ft³/s, the minimum slope is $S = 0.0020$ with $y = 0.255$ ft.

Based on the traditional criteria of 2 ft/s and $n = 0.013$, the minimum slope for a 10 in. pipe is 0.0025; however, based on tractive force the minimum slope is 0.002 for the 0.20 ft³/s minimum design flow rate in a 10-in. pipe.

The analysis presented in Example 2.7 may be extended to cover the range of pipe diameters encountered in gravity sewers. Figure 2.22 is a plot of the minimum pipe slope (S_{min}) as a function of the minimum flow (Q_{min}). The minimum slopes are shown for flows greater than 0.053 ft³/s (1.5 L/s) and extend until the slope reaches 0.0005. The lower limit of flow was suggested by Mara, Sleigh, and Taylor (2000) as the lower limit for tractive force analysis. The minimum slopes are calculated for $n = 0.013$ or $\varepsilon = 0.00001$ ft (0.000003 m) and a 1-mm particle with a specific gravity of 2.7.

Figure 2.22 indicates that for any pipe diameter, S_{min} is varies from 0.037 at $Q_{min} = 0.072$ ft³/s (2.04 L/s) to 0.00105 at $Q_{min} = 0.773$ ft³/s (21.8 L/s). Also note that the GLUMRB S_{min} of 0.0022 for the 12 in. (305 mm) pipe corresponds to $Q_{min} = 0.18$ ft³/s (5.1 L/s).

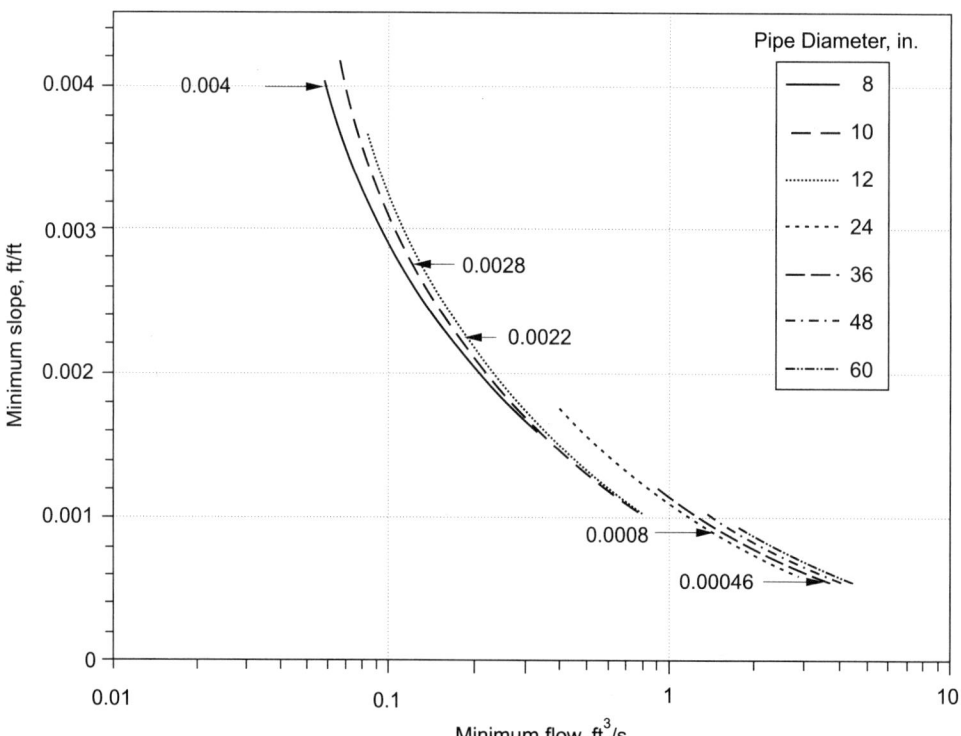

Figure 2.22 Minimum slopes as a function of flow rate for various pipe diameters. Minimum slopes from the GLUMRB standards for each diameter are indicated by the arrows.

For the 8-in. (205-mm) diameter pipe, the graph indicates that slopes less than the GLUMRB S_{min} (0.004) are adequate when Q_{min} is greater than 0.06 ft³/s (1.7 L/s). However, based on tractive force analysis, Figure 2.22 shows that the minimum slopes in the GLUMRB standards may not provide adequate self-cleansing in large-diameter gravity sewers. For the 36-in. (915-mm) pipe, the 0.00046 minimum GLUMRB slope requires a minimum flow of 3.8 ft³/s (110 L/s) to provide adequate scour.

Camp Formula

The American Society Civil Engineers (1982) recommends the Camp formula for calculating the minimum velocity required to move sediment in a sewer pipe. The equation was first proposed by Camp (1946). Applying the Manning equation to Equation 2.60 with results of studies by Shields (1936) on sediment transport yields

$$V_{min} = \frac{C_f}{n} R_h^{1/6} [B(s-1)d]^{1/2} \tag{2.67}$$

where C_f = conversion factor of 1.486 for US units or 1.0 for SI units
V_{min} = minimum velocity (ft/s, m/s)
R_h = hydraulic radius (ft, m)
s = specific gravity
d = particle diameter (ft, m)

B is a dimensionless constant with a value of about 0.04 to start motion of a clean granular particle and 0.8 for adequate self-cleansing of a cohesive material. Equation 2.67 is valid for a pipe flowing full. Graphs for analyzing self-cleansing in partially full pipes were prepared by Geyer et al. (1957).

Example 2.8 Minimum velocity calculation

Calculate the minimum velocity and minimum slope required to transport a 1-mm (0.00328-ft) diameter particle with a specific gravity of 2.7 in a 12-in. (305-mm) sewer pipe. Use $B = 0.04$ for a granular particle.

Solution

$$V_{min} = \frac{1.486}{0.013}\left(\frac{1}{4}\right)^{1/6} [0.04(2.7-1)0.00328]^{1/2} = 1.36 \text{ ft/s}$$

The minimum slope is calculated by solving Equation 2.64 for S to get

$$S = \left[\frac{1.36 \times 0.013}{1.486 \times \left(\frac{1}{4}\right)^{2/3}}\right]^2 = 0.00090$$

Yao's Method

Yao (1974) developed methods for determining minimum velocity based on shear stress much like Camp. For full pipe flow, the velocity required is given by

$$V = 0.79 \frac{D^{1/6}}{n} \left(\frac{\tau_o}{\rho}\right)^{1/2} \qquad (2.68)$$

where V = minimum velocity (m/s)
D = pipe diameter (m)
n = Manning's n
τ_o = minimum shear stress (Pa)
ρ = fluid density (kg/m^3)

Yao extended this to sewers that were partly full. For sewers less than one-half full, the minimum velocity becomes

$$V = 0.935 \frac{D^{1/6}}{n} \left(\frac{\tau_o}{\rho}\right)^{1/2} y^{1/6} (1 - 0.08y) \qquad (2.69)$$

where y = depth of flow (m)

Yao recommends using critical shear stress of 0.1 to 0.2 Pa for sanitary sewers and 0.3 to 0.4 Pa for combined sewers that may have larger solids. Figure 2.23 shows the velocity needed to transport the solids in a sewer with very low flow based on Equation 2.69. This velocity can be used to check designs to ensure that scouring will occur.

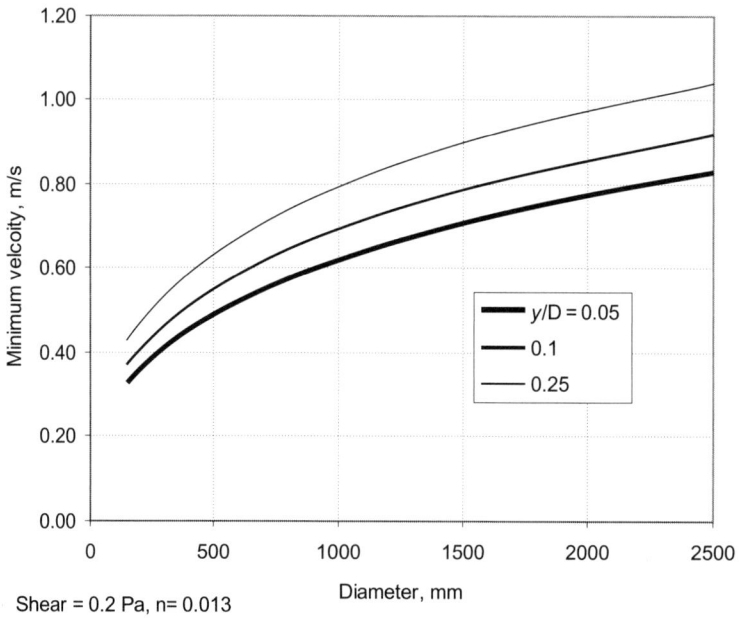

Figure 2.23 Minimum velocity to ensure solids transport at low flow.

Example 2.9 Minimum velocity for partly full sewers

Given a 0.5-m diameter sewer with Manning's n = 0.013 carrying water with a density of 1000 kg/m^3, determine the minimum velocity versus depth for depths of 0.0–0.25 m and minimum shear stress of 0.1–0.4 Pa.

The solution is shown in the following graph.

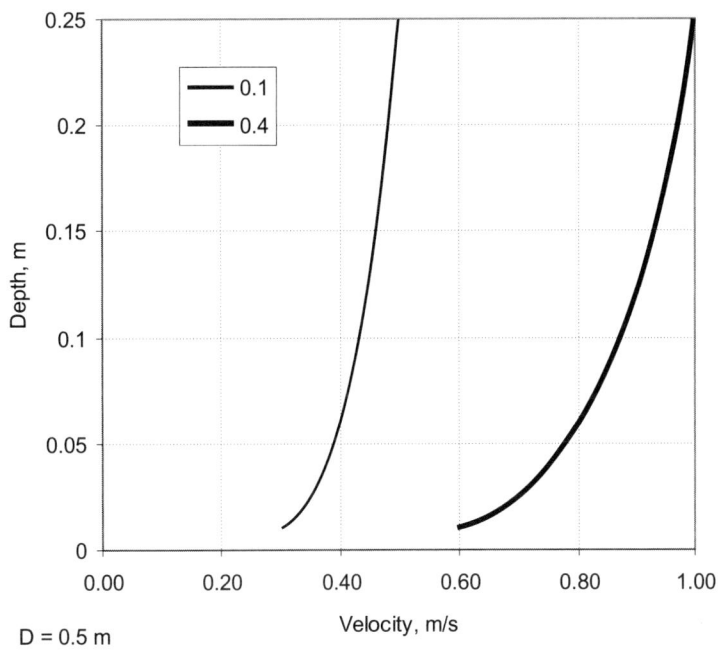

D = 0.5 m

Abwassertechnische Vereinigung (ATV) Method

What is referred to as the ATV (1988) method is based on work by Macke (1983) and Sander (1994). It states that the minimum velocity at half full can be given by

$$V = 0.5 + 0.55D \qquad (2.70)$$

where
V = minimum velocity at half full (m/s)
D = diameter (m)

The minimum bottom slope can be given by

$$S = \frac{0.0012}{D} \text{ for } D < 1 \qquad (2.71)$$

where S = minimum bottom slope

For diameters greater than or equal to 1, the minimum bottom slope is 0.0012.

Additional Considerations

If a pipe is designed to self cleanse at Q_{min} using tractive force principles, in concept the deposition of particles will not occur for a long enough period of time to allow the deposited material to become highly scour resistant. If the material were to become scour resistant, very large tractive forces might be required for cleansing. Sometimes grease buildup, gravel deposition, etc. make self cleansing a practical impossibility, and sewer cleaning equipment must be used.

The methods presented in this section may be used to assure that a gravity sewer pipe will move a discrete (noncohesive) particle of a defined size and density. This analysis does not consider the scouring of deposited material. In order for erosion of deposited material to occur, the hydrodynamic lift and drag forces acting on the solid material must overcome the restoring forces of submerged weight, particle interlocking, and cohesion. More detailed analyses of sediment transport in sewers are provided by Delleur (2001) and Butler, May, and Ackers (1996).

Considerable research has been conducted in recent years in the movement of sediment in sewers. In 2003, the *Journal of Hydraulic Engineering* published a special issue on the Hydraulics of Sediment Movement in Urban Drainage Systems. As a detailed presentation of this work is beyond the scope of this book, the reader is referred to papers by Ashley, Crabtree, Fraser and Hvitved-Jacobsen (2003); Butler, May, and Ackers (2003); Coleman, Fedele, and Garcia (2003); DeSutter, Rushford, Tait, Huygens, Verhovern, and Saul (2003); Knigth and Sterling (2000); Ota and Nalluri (2003); Pisano, O'Riordan, Ayotte, Barsanti, and Carr (2003); Rushforth, Tait, and Saul (2003); Saul, Skipworth, Tait and Rushforth (2003); and Tait, Chebbo, Skipworth, Ahyerre, and Saul (2003).

2.10 Specific Energy and Critical Flow

In open-channel flow, topics such as specific energy, subcritical and supercritical flow, flow profiles, hydraulic jumps, and backwater curves are important. In sanitary sewers, particularly for small diameters, the flow regime is of consequence in only a few situations in sanitary sewer design.

Specific Energy

In open channels, *specific energy* is the energy with respect to the channel bottom:

$$E = y + \frac{V^2}{2g} \tag{2.72}$$

where
- y = depth of flow (ft, m)
- V = average velocity (ft/s, m/s)
- g = gravitational acceleration (32.2 ft/s^2, 9.81 m/s^2)

A plot of depth of flow versus specific energy is shown in Figure 2.24.

In general, two different depths of flow, called *conjugate depths*, may exist for a given specific energy.

For a given flow rate, the depth at which minimum specific energy occurs is called the *critical depth*, y_c. Of special note is the fact that near critical depth, relatively small changes in energy cause significant depth changes in the depth of flow. However, when the specific energy is not near this minimum value, it takes relatively larger changes in the specific energy to cause significant changes in the depth.

Equation 2.72 (specific energy) can be differentiated with respect to y, and then set equal to zero to define the minimum E point on the curve that is the critical depth. The resulting relationship for any channel cross section with an open top may be written as

Section 2.10　Specific Energy and Critical Flow

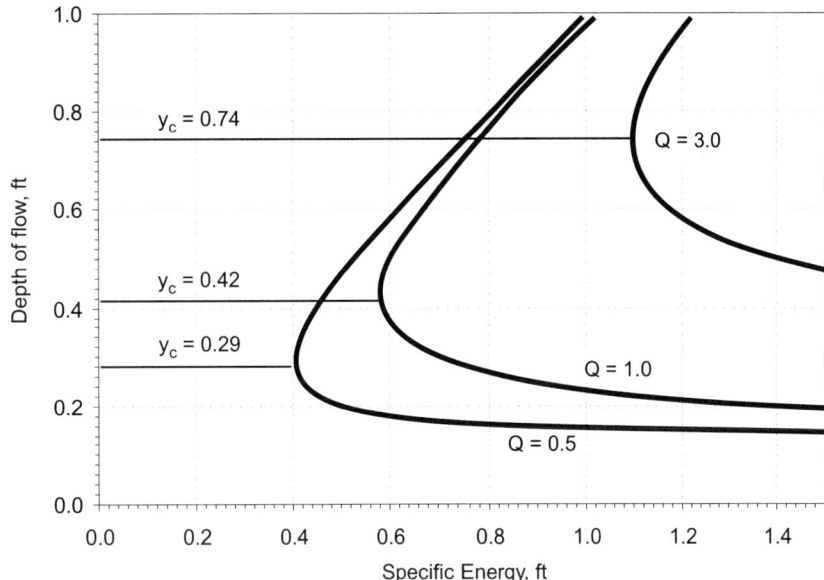

Figure 2.24 Depth of flow vs. specific energy for a 12-in. pipe at various flow rates.

$$\frac{Q^2}{g} = \frac{A_c^2}{T} \quad \text{at } y = y_c \quad (2.73)$$

where Q = flow rate (ft³/s, m³/s)
A_c = cross-sectional area of the flow at critical depth (ft², m²)
T = top width (ft, m)

The complexity of the geometry of circular sections discourages an explicit mathematical solution for determining critical depth in pipes. A semiempirical equation (French, 2001) is

$$y_c = \frac{1.01}{D^{0.26}} \left(\frac{Q^2}{g}\right)^{0.25} \quad (2.74)$$

where y_c = critical depth (ft, m)
D = pipe diameter (ft, m)

Example 2.10 Determine critical depth

Given an 8 in. pipe carrying 0.5 ft³/s, determine the critical depth.

Solution

Equation 2.74 gives the critical depth as

$$y_c = \frac{1.01}{\left(\frac{8}{12}\right)^{0.26}} \left(\frac{0.5^2}{32.2}\right)^{0.25} = 0.33 \text{ ft}$$

An alternate approach is to determine y_c by plotting y as a function of E and graphically determine y_c. Specific energy is given by

$$E = y + \frac{V^2}{2g} = y + \frac{\left(\frac{Q}{A}\right)^2}{2g}$$

where

$$A = \frac{D^2(2\theta - \sin 2\theta)}{8}$$

$$\theta = \cos^{-1}\left(1 - \frac{2y}{D}\right)$$

Select values of y from 0 to 0.667. The plot in the following figure shows that E has a minimum at $y_c = 0.33$ ft.

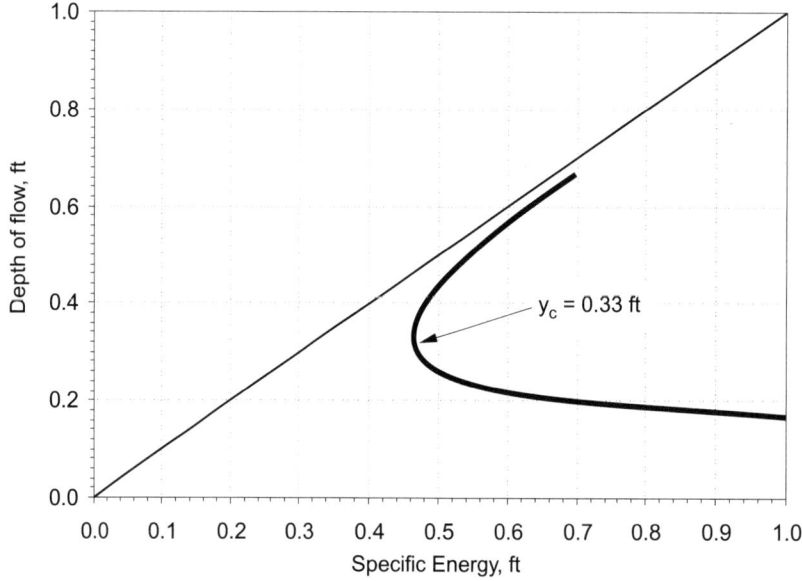

Froude Number

The *Froude number* is a ratio of the inertial forces to the gravity forces in the flow, given by

$$\text{Fr} = \frac{V}{\sqrt{gD_h}} \qquad (2.75)$$

By substituting the critical depth conditions from Equation 2.73 into Equation 2.75, we show that Fr = 1 at the critical flow depth, y_c.

Subcritical and Supercritical Flow

Under conditions of normal flow, when the depth of flow is deeper than y_c, the Froude number is less than 1, the flow is called *subcritical* (or *tranquil*), and the channel slope, S_0, is *mild*. If depth of flow is shallower than y_c, then the Froude number is greater than 1, the associated flow is called *supercritical* (or *rapid*), and the channel slope is called *steep*.

The existence of subcritical or supercritical flow depends primarily on the slope of the pipe. For most pipe slopes, the flow is always either supercritical or subcritical. However, for a narrow range of slopes, the type of flow depends on whether an increase in flow increases the velocity or depth more. Subcritical flow may exist at low flow rates, supercritical flow may exist when the pipe flows half full, and subcritical flow may return as the pipe nears full. Thus, a particular pipe may be classified as steep for some flow rates and mild for others.

Hydraulic Jumps

When the flow regime changes from supercritical upstream to subcritical downstream, a fairly abrupt change in water depth called a *hydraulic jump* occurs. Unless the upstream velocities are high, hydraulic jumps are very small; typically, they are only as high as a few inches. In sewers, a jump occurs when a steep pipe flows into a mild pipe at a manhole. Whether the jump occurs in the upstream pipe or the downstream pipe depends on the flow rate and pipe slopes. For a particular geometry, the jump location can shift with a change in flow rate; however, the jump is usually either always upstream or downstream for the normal range of flow rates in the sewer.

The impulse-momentum principle describes hydraulic jumps. The relationship may be expressed as

$$Q\rho V_1 + \sum F = Q\rho V_2 \tag{2.76}$$

where Q = the volumetric flow rate (ft³/s, m³/s)
ρ = mass density (slug/ft³, kg/,m³)
V – vector velocity (ft/s, m/s)
ΣF = vector sum of the forces acting on the fluid element, including its weight (lb, N)

In general, for a given flow rate, two depths exist that satisfy Equation 2.76. These depths occur before and after a hydraulic jump and are called *sequent* or *conjugate* depths.

The energy lost in the turbulence of a hydraulic jump, which is in addition to the very small uniform flow loss, can be determined by applying the specific energy equation (Equation 2.72) across the jump:

$$y_1 + \frac{V_1^2}{2g} = y_2 + \frac{V_2^2}{2g} + h_L \tag{2.77}$$

or

$$h_L = y_2 - y_1 + \frac{(V_2^2 - V_1^2)}{2g} \tag{2.78}$$

In closed conduits, sometimes the downstream conjugate depth "needs" to be deeper than the pipe height. So after the jump, the downstream pipe flows full with a slight pressure. When this condition occurs in sewer pipes, except when there are extremely high velocities and/or excessive flows in the upstream section, this pressure is quite small and would normally not exceed a few inches of head. This situation also represents a condition in which the flow rate exceeds the pipe's open channel flow capacity. In that case, the jump occurs in the upstream manhole or upstream pipe and results in ponding in the manhole. In sewers, such jumps are most likely to occur where there is a transition to a milder slope.

Another consideration is that hydraulic jumps induce turbulence, which can release dissolved gases such as hydrogen sulfide and cause odor problems. For a more extensive discussion on hydraulic jumps in sewers, see Hager (1999).

Flow Profiles

With open channel flow through a series of pipes, the water surface often makes a transition from one depth to another as flow asymptotically approaches uniform conditions. Most of these depth changes occur in the vicinity of manholes where flows combine and slopes change. The profile defined by the water surface through these sections of changing depth is referred to as the *water surface profile* or *flow profile*; the profile most commonly encountered is called *gradually varied flow*. The slope of the water surface is described by dy/dx, with energy and head loss relationships integrated to obtain the depth y as a function of the distance x along the pipes. Since direct integration of these expressions is difficult, they are generally solved by finite-step numerical integration. A common approach in developing the finite-step equations is to apply the energy equation to the ends of the section being considered, as follows.

The energy equation for points 1 and 2 along a channel was given as Equation 2.24, repeated here:

$$z_1 + y_1 + \frac{V_1^2}{2g} = z_2 + y_2 + \frac{V_2^2}{2g} + h_L \qquad (2.79)$$

where z = elevation of the channel bottom (ft, m)
 y = depth of flow (ft, m)
 V = average velocity (ft/s, m/s)
 h_L = energy loss across the element (ft, m)

Note the following relations for the terms in Equation 2.79:

$$E_1 = y_1 + \frac{V_1^2}{2g} \qquad (2.80)$$

$$E_2 = y_2 + \frac{V_2^2}{2g} \qquad (2.81)$$

$$S_o = \frac{z_2 - z_1}{\Delta x} \qquad (2.82)$$

$$h_L \cong S\Delta x \qquad (2.83)$$

where E = specific energy (ft, m)
 S_o = channel slope (ft/ft, m/m)
 S = average energy line slope (ft/ft, m/m)
 Δx = distance along the channel (ft, m)

Equations 2.79 to 2.83 can be combined and rearranged to the form

$$\Delta x = \frac{E_1 - E_2}{S - S_o} \qquad (2.84)$$

Equation 2.84 is a common way of describing relationship between y and x for gradually varied flow. One of the flow equations, such as the Manning equation, is used to determine S, which is an estimate of the average energy line slope for the section. A rearranged Manning equation is often used, where V_m and R_{hm} are the averages of the velocities and hydraulic radii at the ends of the section, in the form

$$S = \left(\frac{nV_m}{kR_{hm}^{2/3}}\right)^2 \qquad (2.85)$$

where n = Manning roughness coefficient
V_m = average of the velocities at sections 1 and 2 (ft/s, m/s)
R_{hm} = average of the hydraulic radii at sections 1 and 2 (ft, m)
k = 1.49 for US customary units
1.0 for SI units

When one considers surface profile curves, it is helpful to note that for water depths greater than y_c the flow is subcritical. Calculations begin at a known water depth downstream called a *control point* and the curve goes back upstream. Conversely, for water depths less than y_c, calculations begin at a control point upstream and the curve proceeds downstream. Examples of profile calculations are presented by Haestad Methods and Durrans (2003) and other open channel references.

Backwater Curves

When flow conditions deviate from normal depth owing to a change in channel geometry, flow will eventually approach a new normal depth. The water surface profiles describing this transition back to normal depth are referred to as *backwater curves*. If the flow transition is gradually varied, then Equation 2.84 can be used to determine the depths through the transition. If the flow transition is rapid, then that section experiences *rapidly varied flow* and Equation 2.84 does not work well, since a good relation between head loss and depth is not available. An example of rapidly varied flow is the hydraulic jump. Rapidly varied flow occurs when flow passes through critical depth.

Most sewer system design models will calculate backwater curves, although in most cases, flow approaches normal conditions fairly quickly after pipe geometry changes. Backwater curves might be of interest at the downstream end of a large-diameter sewer when the water depth downstream is deeper than normal depth of flow in the sewer: for example, a pipe discharging into a wet well. In this situation, a backwater curve can be calculated in the upstream direction to determine extent of backwater effects.

Figure 2.25 is a profile of a sewer discharging into a wet well. Note that the tailwater in the wet well, at elevation 102.3 ft, causes the flow in the pipe to back up so that the backwater effect extends into the upstream pipe. The calculation of the surface elevation begins at the downstream elevation (102.3 ft) and continues to the upstream end of the pipe. In this case, the normal depth is 1.82 ft and the depth of flow at the upstream end is 1.86 ft. Therefore, the backwater effect extends the full length of the pipe.

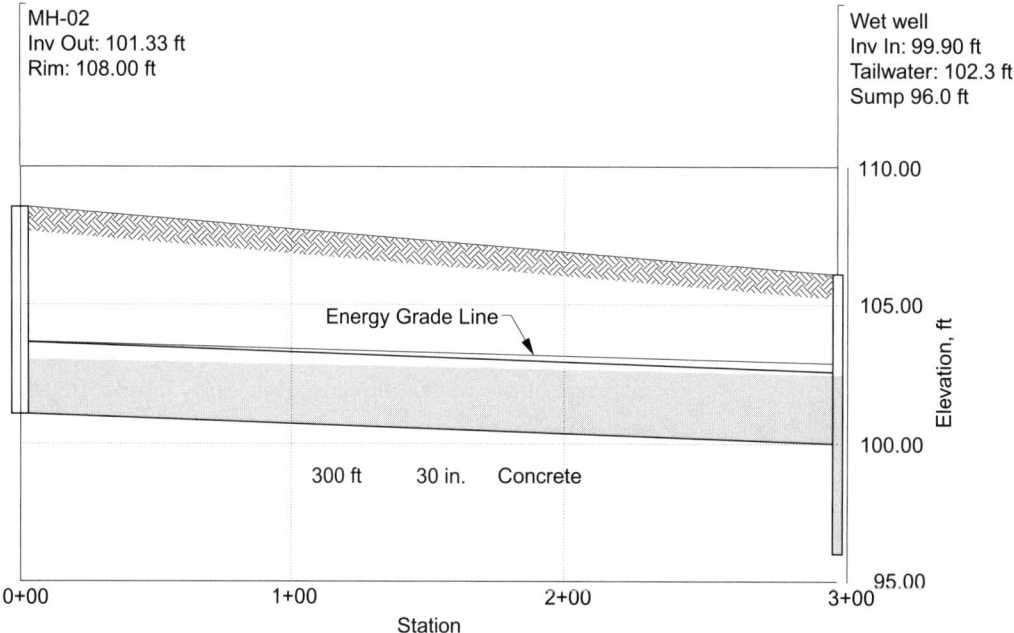

Figure 2.25 Example backwater profile in a sewer with a submerged outlet.

2.11 Hydraulics of Flow-Control Structures

In sanitary and combined sewers, a variety of structures can be used to restrict flow or to split the flow into two portions. Flow may be diverted from the sewer for temporary storage and treatment or it may overflow to the receiving water. Commonly used control structures include orifices, weirs, siphons, and gates. The design of these structures is discussed in manuals of practice prepared by American Society of Civil Engineers (1992) and Water Environment Federation (1999). This section reviews the fundamental equations used to quantify flow through these structures.

Some systems may contain parallel relief sewers that were installed because upstream loading increased in excess of the capacity of the sewer. There is no "flow control structure" for these flow splits. These can be modeled as parallel sewers, or in some cases, replaced by a single equivalent sewer with the same head loss versus flow relationship as the parallel sewers.

Open-channel flow control structures, particularly those used in flow measurement, are described by Bos (1976) and French (1985). Unfortunately, structures in actual sewers tend to not exactly correspond to ideal laboratory weirs and orifices. Some of these structures are described in Water Environment Federation (1999), and flow equations for these structures are discussed in Hager (1999).

Orifices

Orifices may be used to measure or control flow. In sewers, they are oriented either horizontally or vertically, as illustrated in Figure 2.26. Because they usually discharge small flows, orifices are often used in combination with other control structures. The discharge through a single orifice depends on the area of the opening, the effective head on the orifice, and the edges of the opening. The relationship among these variables is expressed as

$$Q = C_d A_o \sqrt{2gh_o} \qquad (2.86)$$

where
Q = discharge (ft^3/s, m^3/s)
C_d = discharge coefficient (depends on the orifice edges)
A_o = area of the opening (ft^2, m^2)
g = acceleration due to gravity (32.2 ft/s^2, 9.81 m/s^2)
h_o = effective head (ft, m)

Brown, Stein, and Warner (2001) indicate that $C_d = 0.60$ if the edges of the orifice opening are uniform and square. For ragged edges, such as those resulting from using an acetylene torch to cut an opening, $C_d = 0.40$ should be used instead.

The effective head on an orifice depends on whether it has a free or submerged discharge. If the discharge is a free outfall, the effective head is the difference between the upstream water surface elevation and the elevation at the centroid of the orifice opening. If tailwater submerges the outlet of an orifice, the effective head is equal to the difference between the water surface elevations immediately upstream and downstream of the orifice.

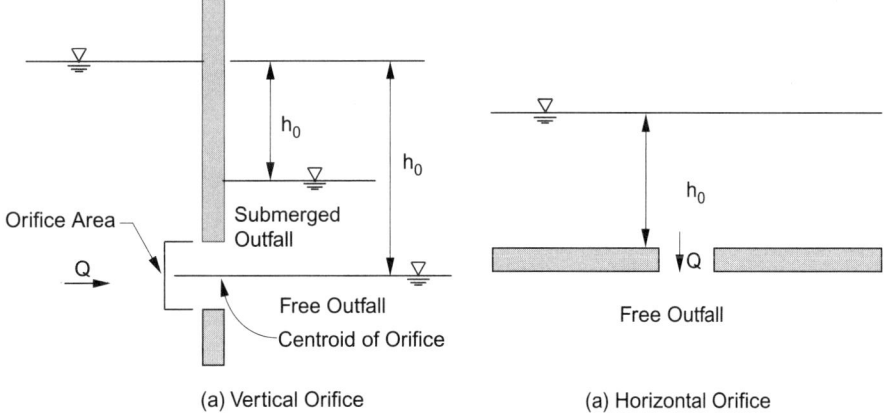

Figure 2.26 Orifice in vertical and horizontal orientations.

Weirs

Weirs may be found in sewers in the variety of configurations shown in Figures 2.27, 2.28, and 2.29. Weirs are usually classified as being either *sharp-crested* or *broad-crested*. A relatively thin plate forms the crest of a sharp-crested weir. For a broad-crested weir, the weir crest thickness is relatively large and flow over the weir crest is critical.

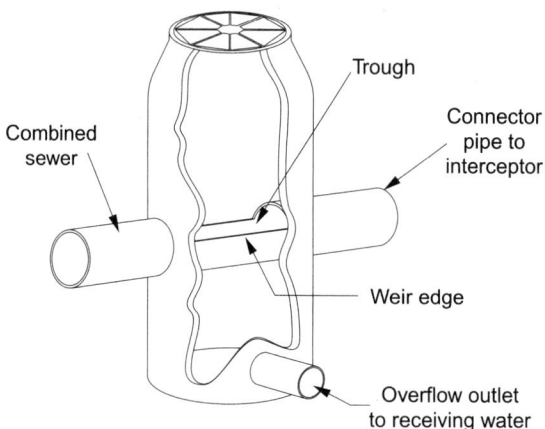

Figure 2.27 Example of a side weir.

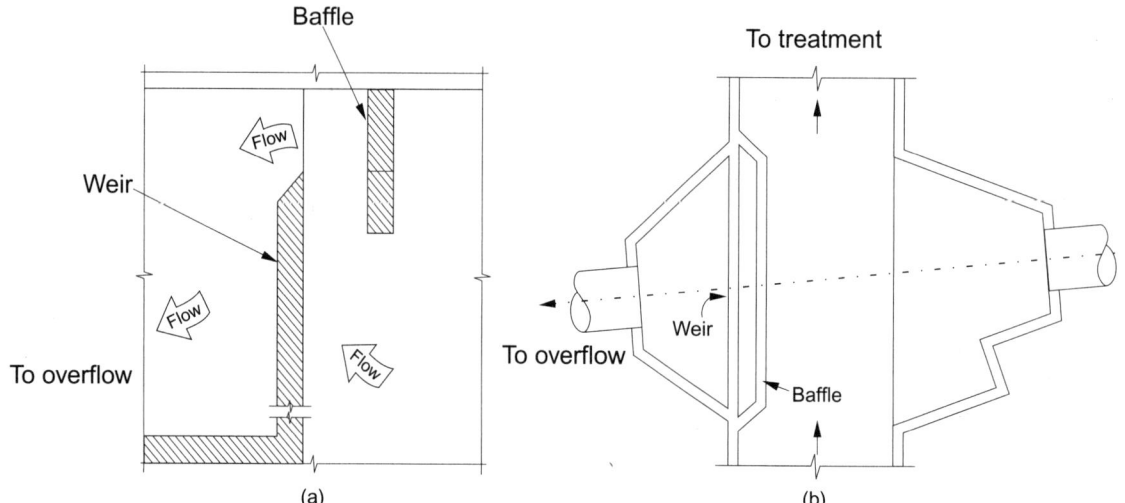

Figure 2.28 Example of a baffled side weir showing (a) elevation and (b) plan views.

Additional types of weirs involve the attributes of the crest cross section (rectangular, triangular, trapezoidal) and whether there are flow contractions at the ends of the weir. A *contracted* weir causes the flow to contract. Flow over a *suppressed* or *uncontracted* weir has no end contractions.

Sharp-Crested Rectangular Weirs. The discharge over a sharp-crested weir may be determined via the energy equation. The procedure amounts to equating the total energy head upstream of the weir to the total energy head on the weir crest. The resulting equation for discharge in terms of the upstream energy level depends on the cross-sectional shape of the weir and inevitably also involves some simplifying assumptions. An empirical weir-discharge coefficient, C_d, is introduced to account for the simplifying assumptions and to correct the theoretical discharge.

Section 2.11　　　Hydraulics of Flow-Control Structures　　81

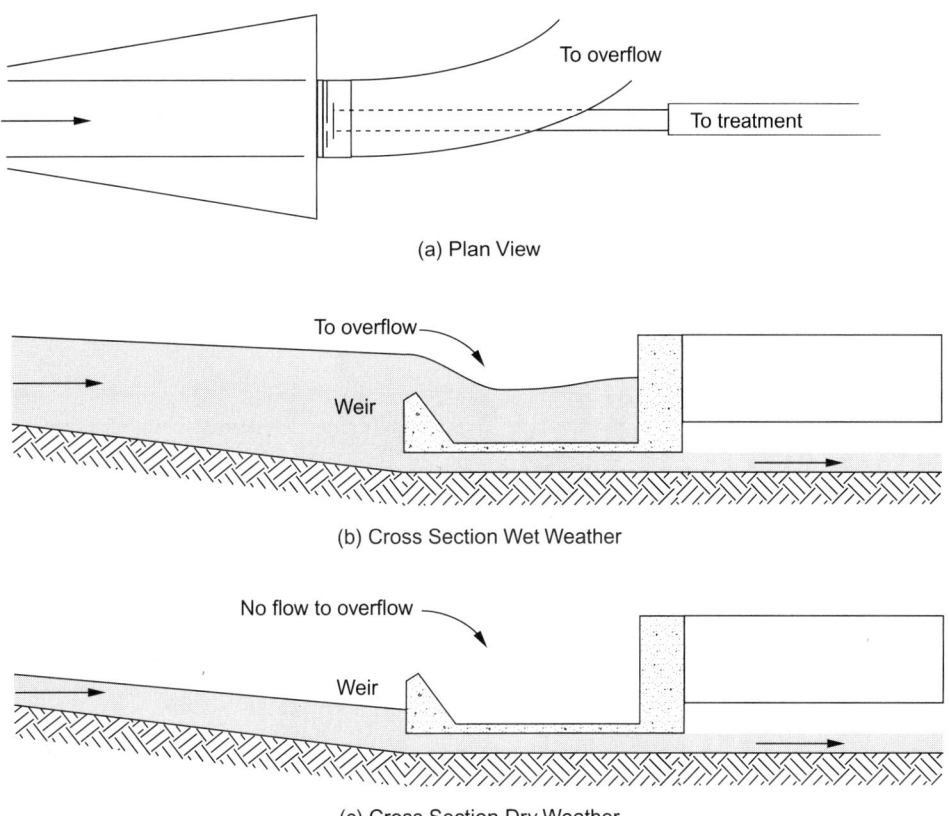

Figure 2.29 Transverse weir showing (a) plan, (b) wet weather cross-section, and (c) dry weather cross-section views.

The discharge, Q, over a fully contracted (no bottom or side effects) rectangular sharp-crested weir may be expressed in terms of the head H on the weir as

$$Q = \frac{2}{3} C_d \sqrt{2g} L H^{3/2} \tag{2.87}$$

where　　C_d = discharge coefficient
　　　　　L = length of the weir crest (ft, m)
　　　　　H = height of water above weir crest (ft, m)

It is assumed in this expression that the velocity head of the flow upstream of the weir is negligible and, hence, that the head, H, on the weir is the difference in elevation between the upstream water surface and the weir crest.

Fundamentally, the discharge coefficient in Equation 2.87 depends on the Reynolds and Weber numbers of the flow (i.e., viscous and surface tension effects are negligible) and on the dimensionless head H/H_w, where H_w is the height of the weir crest above the bottom of the channel, as shown in Figure 2.30. However, experiments have shown that the discharge coefficient can be represented by (Rouse, 1946; Blevins, 1984)

$$C_d = 0.611 + 0.075\frac{H}{H_w} \qquad (2.88)$$

This expression is accurate for values of H/H_w less than 5 and is approximate up to $H/H_w = 10$. For $H/H_w > 15$, the discharge can be computed from the critical flow equation by assuming that $y_c = H$ (Chaudhry, 1993).

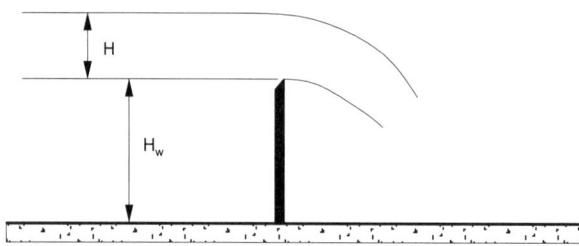

Figure 2.30 Elevations of sharp-crested weirs.

When flow occurs over a contracted rectangular weir, the end contractions cause the effective crest length of the weir to be reduced from the actual crest length. In this instance, the head-discharge relationship for the weir is

$$Q = \frac{2}{3}C_d\sqrt{2g}(L - 0.1NH)H^{3/2} \qquad (2.89)$$

where
C_d = discharge coefficient determined from Equation 2.88
N = number of weir end contractions (usually, $N = 2$)

This equation assumes that L is greater than $3H$. Note that the effective length of the weir is $L - 0.1NH$, which is $0.1NH$ shorter than the actual length of the weir crest.

Broad-Crested Weirs. The flow profile over a broad-crested weir can be evaluated using the concepts of specific energy and critical depth. Figure 2.31 illustrates a broad-crested weir of height H_w with an approaching flow of discharge Q and depth y_1. The thickness of the weir crest in the direction of flow is Δx, and the cross section is rectan-

Section 2.11 Hydraulics of Flow-Control Structures 83

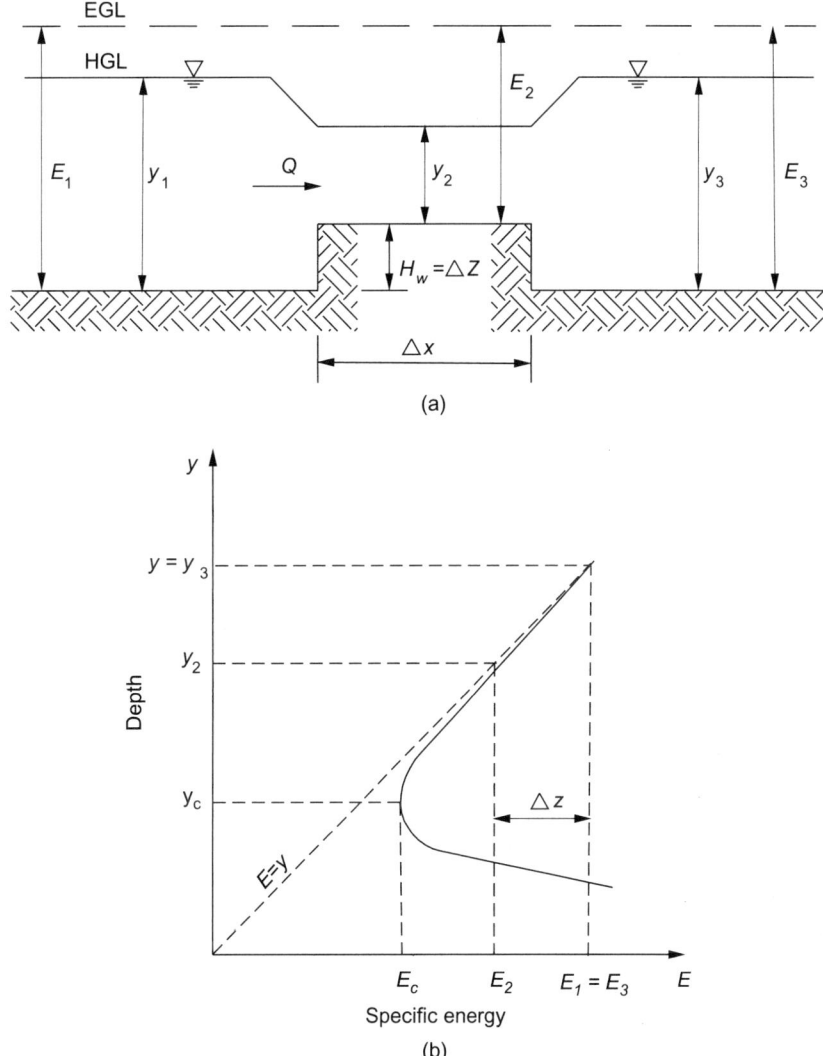

Figure 2.31 Broad-crested weir (a) definition figure and (b) specific energy curve.

gular with a weir crest length of L normal to the plane of the page. For example, a roadway embankment containing a culvert behaves as a broad-crested weir if the water is high enough to flow over the roadway surface.

The specific energy upstream of the weir is E_1. If there is no energy loss, the specific energy on the crest of the weir is E_2, from which the depth y_2 may be determined using the depth-specific energy relationship (Figure 2.31). Thus, if the weir crest height H_w is not excessively large and zero energy loss is assumed, then the flow profile over the weir may be evaluated using a specific energy curve. If desired, a minor loss could be introduced to account for the actual energy loss.

If, for the assumptions that E_1 and y_1 are fixed values and that $H_w = \Delta Z$, E_2 is found to be less than E_c, then the assumptions described in the preceding paragraph are not valid. This is because E_c represents the lowest energy on the specific energy curve (see Figure 2.31b). What actually occurs is that the flow is *choked*, meaning that a backwater effect is created by the weir. In such a case, one must set $y_2 = y_c$ and $E_2 = E_c$. The specific energy upstream of the weir is then found as $E_1 = E_c + H_w$, and the depth y_1 is determined from the specific energy.

When a flow is choked (that is, when a structure behaves as a broad-crested weir), the discharge may be computed as a function of the head, $H = E_1 - H_w$, as

$$Q = C_d \sqrt{g} L \left(\frac{2H}{3}\right)^{3/2} \tag{2.90}$$

Values of the discharge coefficient can be estimated with

$$C_d = \frac{0.65}{\left(1 + \dfrac{H}{H_w}\right)^{1/2}} \tag{2.91}$$

These expressions are valid if $0.08 < (y_1 - H_w)/\Delta x < 0.50$. Head losses across the crest of the weir cannot be neglected if $(y_1 - H_w)/\Delta x < 0.08$. If $(y_1 - H_w)/\Delta x > 0.50$, then streamlines over the weir crest are not horizontal.

Side Weirs. A weir parallel to the wastewater flow in the side of the sewer pipe is known as a side weir (see Figure 2.27). Discharge over side weirs is a function of the geometry and the slope of the flow in the sewer. Analysis requires determining the flow profile in the pipe. Details are given in Mays (2001) and Hager (1999).

Gates

Gates have hydraulic properties similar to orifices. Discharge through gates, either free or submerged, is given by (Mays, 2001)

$$Q = CA\sqrt{2gH} \tag{2.92}$$

where C = discharge coefficient
A = area of opening (ft^2, m^2)
H = effective head (ft, m)

The discharge coefficient is a function the size of the opening, the depth of water above the orifice, and the characteristics of the discharge (free fall vs. along prolonged bottom). Values for C range from 0.487 to 0.712 (Metcalf & Eddy, Inc., 1981).

References

Abwassertechnische Vereinigung (ATV [Wastewater Technical Association]). 1988. *Richlinien für die Hydraulische Dimensionierung und den Leistungnachweis von Abwasserkanalen und Leitungen* (Guidelines for Hydraulic Design of Sewers). Arbeitsblatt A110 (Worksheet A110). St. Augustin, Germany: Abwassertechnische Vereinigung.

American Society of Civil Engineers (ASCE). 1982. *Gravity Sewer Design and Construction.* ASCE Manuals and Reports of Engineering Practice No. 60. Reston, VA: American Society of Civil Engineers.

American Society of Civil Engineers (ASCE). 1992. *Design and Construction of Urban Stormwater Management Systems*. ASCE Manuals and Reports of Engineering Practice No. 77, WEF Manual of Practice FD-20. Reston, VA: American Society of Civil Engineers.

Ashley, R., B. Crabtree, A. Fraser, and T. Hvitved-Jacobsen. 2003. European Research into sewer sediments and associated pollutants and processes. *Journal of Hydraulic Engineering* 129, no. 4: 267.

Associação Brasileira de Normas Técnicas (ABNT). 1986. Projeto de redes coletoras de esgoto sanitario. *Brazilian Design Standard 9649/1986*. Rio de Janeiro, Brazil: Associação Brasileira de Normas Técnicas.

Barnes, D., P. J. Bliss, B. W. Gould, and H. R. Valentine. 1981. *Water and Wastewater Engineering Systems*. London: Pitman.

Bos, M. G., ed. 1976. *Discharge Measurement Structures*. Wagemingen, Netherlands: International Institute for Land Reclamation and Improvement.

Brown, S. A., S. M. Stein, and J. C. Warner. 2001. *Urban Drainage Manual*. Hydraulic Engineering Circular 22, 2nd ed. Washington, DC: Federal Highway Administration.

Butler D., R. W. P. May, and J. C. Ackers. 1996. Sediment transport in sewers Part 2: Design. *Proceedings of the Institution of Civil Engineers: Water, Maritime & Energy* 118: 113–120.

Butler D., R. W. P. May, and J. C. Ackers. 2003. Self-cleansing sewer design based on sediment transport principles. *Journal of Hydraulic Engineering* 129, no. 4: 276–282.

Camp, T. R. 1940. Discussion – Determination of Kutter's n for sewers partially filled. *Transactions of the American Society of Civil Engineers*. 109: 240–247.

Camp, T. R. 1946. Design of sewers to facilitate flow. *Sewage Works Journal* 18, 3.

Chaudhry, M. N. 1993. *Open-Channel Flow*. New York: Prentice-Hall.

Coleman, S. E., J. J. Fedele, and M. H. Garcia. 2003. Closed conduit bed-form initiation and development. *Journal of Hydraulic Engineering* 129, 856.

Delleur, J. W. 2001. Sediment movement in drainage systems. In *Stormwater Collection Systems Handbook*, edited by L. W. Mays. New York: McGraw-Hill.

DeSutter, R., P. Rushford, S. J. Tait, M. Huygens, R. Verhovern, and A. J. Saul. 2003. Validation of existing bed load transport formulas using in-sewer sediment. *Journal of Hydraulic Engineering* 129, 325.

French, R. H. 1985. *Open Channel Hydraulics*. New York: McGraw-Hill.

French, R. H. 2001. Hydraulics of open-channel flow. In *Stormwater Collection Systems Handbook*, edited by L. W. Mays. New York: McGraw-Hill.

Gill, M. A. 1987. Hydraulics of partially filled egg shaped sewers. *Journal of Environmental Engineering* 113, no. 2: 407–425.

Great Lakes-Upper Mississippi River Board of State Public Health and Environmental Managers (GLUMRB). 1997. *Recommended Standards for Wastewater Facilities*. Albany, NY: Great Lakes-Upper Mississippi River Board.

Haestad Methods and S. R. Durrans. 2003. *Stormwater Conveyance Modeling and Design*. Waterbury, CT: Haestad Press.

Haestad Methods, T. M. Walski, D. V. Chase, D. A. Savic, W. Grayman, S. Beckwith, and E. Koelle. 2003. *Advanced Water Distribution Modeling and Management.* Waterbury, CT: Haestad Press.

Haestad Methods. 2001. *StormCAD User's Guide.* Waterbury, CT: Haestad Methods.

Hager, W. H. 1998. Minimalgeschwindigkeit und sedimenttransport in kanalisationen (Minimum velocity and sediment transport in sewers). *Korrespondenz Abwasser (Wastewater Correspondence)* 36, no.1: 29.

Hager, W. H. 1994 (English edition 1999). *Wastewater Hydraulics.* Berlin: Springer.

Knight, D. W. and M. Sterling. 2000. Boundary shear in circular pipes running partly full. *Journal of Hydraulic Engineering* 126, no. 4: 263.

Macke, E. 1983. Bemenssung ablagerungsfier stromungszustande in kanalisaationsleitungen (Design flows with no deposits in sewers). *Korrespondenz Abwasser (Wastewater Correspondence)* 30, no. 7: 462.

Mara, D., A. Sleigh, and K. Talyor. 2000. *PC-Based Simplified Sewer Design.* http://www.efm.leeds.ac.uk/CIVE/Sewerage/sewerage_index.html (accessed May 13, 2004).

May, D. K. 1986. A Study of Manning's coefficient for commercial concrete and plastic pipes. Edmonton, Alberta, Canada: T. Bench Hydraulics Laboratory, University of Alberta.

May, R. W. P. 1994. Transport of sediment in sewers: Application to design of self-cleansing sewers. *European Water Pollution Control* 4, no. 5: 57–64.

Mays, L. W. 2001. Storm and combined sewer overflow: Flow regulators and control. In *Stormwater Collection Systems Handbook,* edited by L. W. Mays. New York: McGraw-Hill.

Metcalf & Eddy, Inc. 1981. *Wastewater Engineering: Collection and Pumping of Wastewater.* New York: McGraw-Hill.

Norman, J. M., R. J. Houghtalen, and W. J. Johnston. 2001. *Hydraulic Design of Highway Culverts.* McLean, VA: Federal Highway Administration.

Ota, J. J., and C. Nalluri. 2003. Urban storm sewer design: Approach in consideration of sediments. *Journal of Hydraulic Engineering* 129, 291.

Pisano, W. C., O. C. O'Riordan, F. J. Ayotte, J. R. Barsanti, and D. L. Carr. 2003. Automated sewer and drainage flushing in Cambridge, Massachusetts. *Journal of Hydraulic Engineering* 129, no. 4: 260

Raths, C. H., and R. R. McCauley. 1962. Deposition in a sanitary sewer. *Water & Sewage Works* (May): 192–197.

Rushforth, P. J., S. J. Tait, and A. J. Saul. 2003. Modeling the erosion of mixtures of organic and granular in-sewer sediments. *Journal of Hydraulic Engineering* 129, 308.

Sander, T. 1994. Zur dimensionierung von ablagerungsfreien abwasserkanalen unter besonderer berücksichtigung von neuen erkenntnissen zum sedimentations – varhalten (The design of sewers with no deposits with particular attention to new results relative to sedimentation). *Korrespondenz Abwasser (Wastewater Correspondence)* 37, no. 6: 689.

Saul, A. J., P. J. Skipworth, S. J. Tait, and P. J. Rushforth. 2003. Modeling total suspended solids in combined sewers. *Journal of Hydraulic Engineering* 129, 298.

Schmidt, O. J. 1959. Measurements of Manning's coefficient. *Sewage and Industrial Wastes* 31, no. 9: 995.

Shields, A. 1936. Application of similitude mechanics and turbulence research to bed load movement. *Mitteilungen der Preussischen Versuchsantalt fur Wasserbau und Schiffbau*, no. 26.

Straub, L. G., C. E. Bowers, and M. Puch. 1960. Resistance to flow in two types of concrete pipe. Technical Paper No. 22, Series B. Minneapolis: St. Anthony Falls Hydraulic Laboratory, University of Minnesota.

Tait, S. J., G. Chebbo, P. J. Skipworth, M. Ahyerre, and A. J. Saul. 2003. Modeling in-sewer deposit erosion to predict sewer flow quality. *Journal of Hydraulic Engineering* 129, 316.

Tchobanoglous, G., F. L. Burton, H. D. Stensel. 2003. *Wastewater Engineering: Treatment and Reuse.* New York: McGraw-Hill.

Tullis, J. P. 1986. Friction factor tests on concrete pipe. Hydraulic Report No. 157. Logan, Utah: Utah Water Research Laboratory, Utah State University.

Water Environment Federation (WEF). 1999. *Prevention and Control of Sewer System Overflows.* 2d ed. Alexandria, VA: Water Environment Federation.

Yao, K. M. 1974. Sewer line design based on critical shear stress. *Journal of Environmental Engineering* 100, no. EE2: 507–520.

Problems

2.1 You are to design a concrete rectangular channel with a design discharge of 100 ft³/s on a 1/310 grade. If the depth of water in the channel is not to exceed 4 ft, determine the minimum width of the channel bottom.

2.2 Determine the Froude Number and flow classification (e.g., supercritical, critical, subcritical) for Problem 2.1.

2.3 A 610 mm corrugated metal pipe (CMP) on a 1/100 slope has a depth of 330 mm. What are the wetted perimeter, cross-sectional area of flow, hydraulic radius, velocity, discharge and specific energy?

2.4 Determine the Froude Number and flow classification (e.g., supercritical, critical, subcritical) for the conditions of the pipe described in Problem 2.3.

2.5 Determine the depth and specific energy in a 42-in. concrete sewer pipe on a 1/500 grade with a discharge of 36 ft³/s.

2.6 An 8-in. vitrified clay pipe (n = 0.013) on a 1 to 300 grade had a measured discharge of 0.30 ft³/s with a measured water depth of 3.5 in. Manually calculate the velocity using the Manning equation. Compare the computed velocity from the measured Q and A to the predicted velocity from the Manning equation and explain why the velocity values would be different.

2.7 Estimate the Manning's roughness value, n, for a 6 in. plastic corrugated pipe on a 1/500 grade with a measured discharge of 0.136 ft³/s when half full.

2.8 Determine the critical depth for a 610 mm concrete pipe carrying 0.185 m³/s.

2.9 Determine the critical slope and flow conditions for the pipe described in Problem 2.6.

2.10 For a rectangular concrete channel (n = 0.015) with a channel bottom width of 1 ft, a discharge of 1.18 ft³/s, and depth of 6 in., the specific energy is 7.0 in. (Fr = 0.59). As you know from the specific energy profile, there can be two possible depths for a given specific energy as long as the flow is not critical. For this channel geometry and flow rate (1.18 ft³/s), determine the channel slope for both the subcritical and supercritical condition if the specific energy is 7.0 in.

2.11 Consider the manhole pictured in the following figure. If the depth of water in the manhole is 2.5 ft, determine the head loss for each inlet pipe using the energy-loss method. The manhole floor is constructed with a half-bench design to reduce the head loss, and the crown elevations of the inlet pipes match the crown of the outlet pipe.

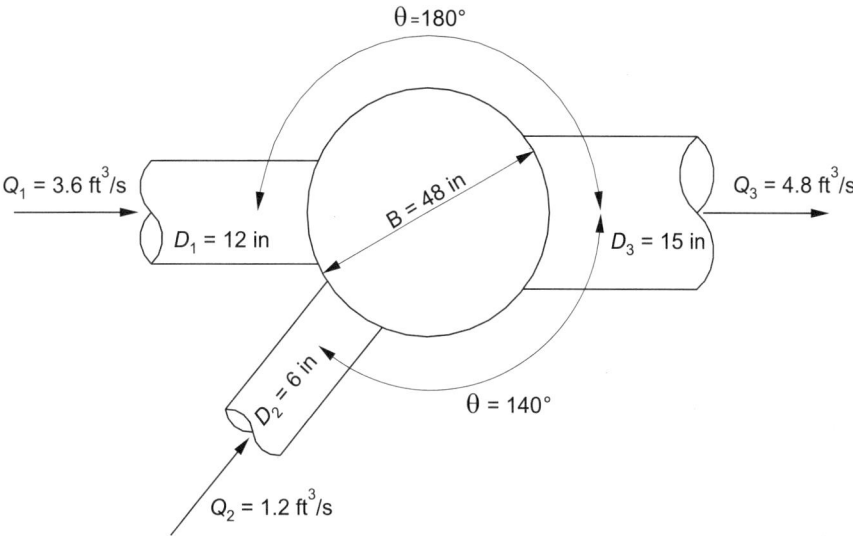

2.12 For the manhole pictured in the figure, determine the head loss for the manhole using the power-loss method and the same conditions described in Problem 2.11.

2.13 Determine the minimum slope to clean a 305 mm concrete sewer pipe for a granular particle with an equivalent diameter of 2.5 mm using the Camp formula. The particle density is 2.78 g/cm^3

2.14 For a design flow rate of 0.01 m^3/s and the granular particle described in Problem 2.13, use the Raths and McClauley experimental relationship to estimate the minimum cleaning velocity and slope for a 305 mm concrete pipe. Assume that the y/D ratio is 0.2. Compare this slope to the estimated minimum slope using the Mara, Sleigh, and Taylor relationship.

2.15 Determine the discharge through a 3-in. uniform, square-edged orifice for 10 ft of head.

2.16 Determine the discharge over a 1.2 m wide sharp-crested, rectangular weir with a weir crest 0.60 m above the channel bottom and a measured water level behind the weir of 0.65m.

2.17 Determine the discharge over a 1.2 m wide sharp-crested, contracted rectangular weir with a weir crest 0.60 m above the channel bottom and measured water level behind the weir of 0.65 m.

2.18 Determine the discharge from a 1.2m wide broad-crested weir with a weir crest 0.60 m above the channel bottom and measured water level behind the weir of 0.65 m.

CHAPTER

3

Unsteady Gravity Flow Hydraulics

While most collection system design is based on steady-state hydraulics, flow in sewers is inherently unsteady. The flow does not remain steady because of the following conditions:

- Normal variation in loading due to domestic and industrial diurnal water use patterns

- Variations in inflow and infiltration during wet weather

- Cycling on and off of pumps

- Behavior of flow-regulating devices

- Changes in tailwater level in wet wells

These time-varying dynamic conditions are illustrated in Figure 3.1. They are especially important when analyzing capacity limitations and overflows in existing sewer systems. Unlike the problems in designing sewers for new land developments, unsteady flow and overflows become critical issues in older systems. The analysis of pump stations also requires quantification of the time variation of flows.

Changes in flow move gradually through the collection system. As the flow in a pipe increases at the upstream end, the water level and velocity increase, which in turn move downstream. In addition, the flow regime may change. In response to a storm, flow in a combined sewer begins partly full but may change to full flow, then becoming pressurized as the tailwater rises at the downstream end or a restriction downstream limits the flow.

92 Unsteady Gravity Flow Hydraulics

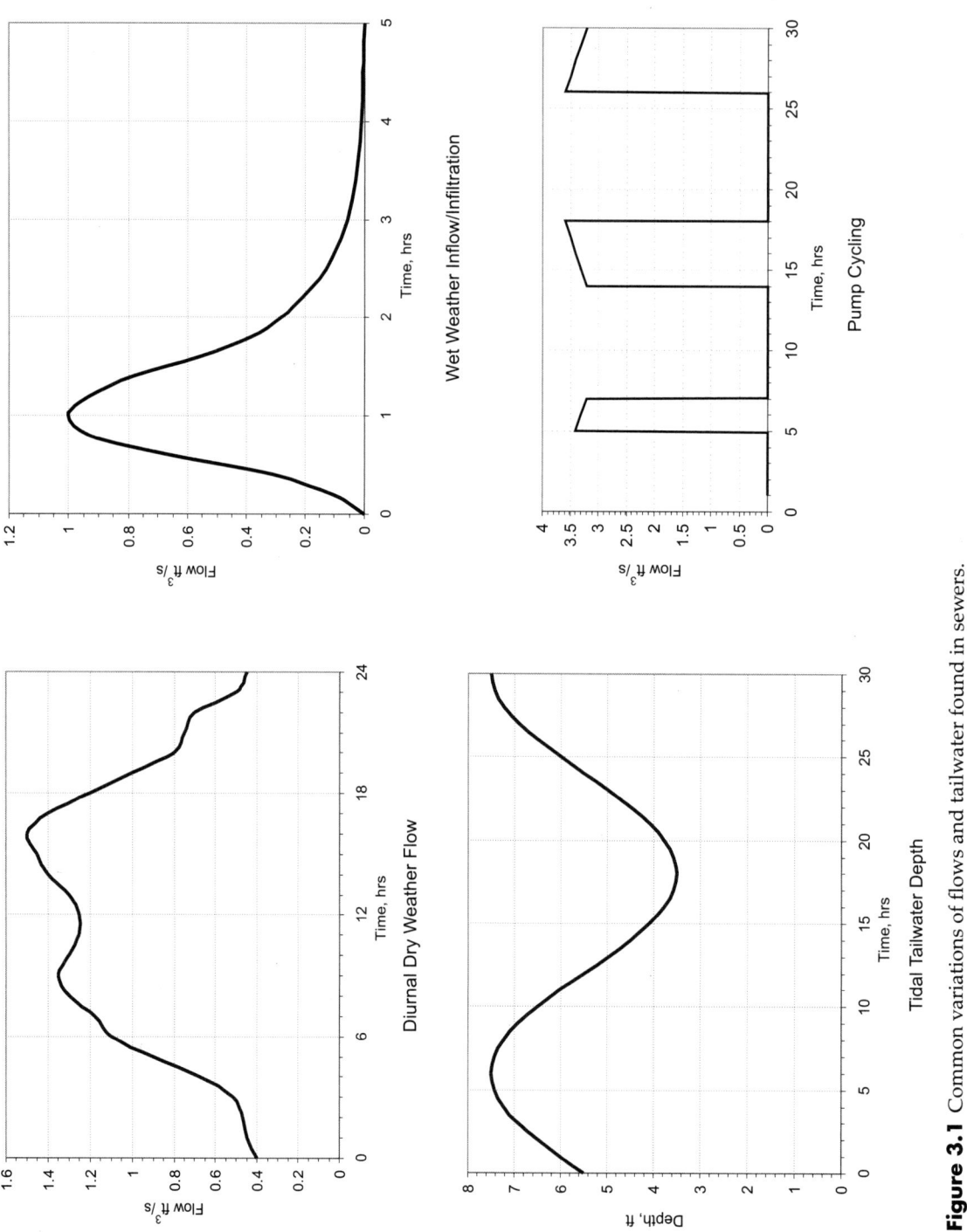

Figure 3.1 Common variations of flows and tailwater found in sewers.

3.1 Basics of Unsteady Flow Analysis

The process of modeling an unsteady flow through a sewer system is referred to as *routing* the flow. The *National Engineering Handbook* (US Soil Conservation Service, 1972) defines routing as, "Computing the flood at a downstream point from the flood at an upstream point, taking storage into account." As a disturbance from the steady flow moves downstream, the peak of the disturbance tends to flatten out as some of the water goes to increasing depth in a process known as *attenuation*.

In steady flow there is a unique relationship between depth and flow rate (i.e., normal depth, with water surface parallel to the channel bottom). This relationship is referred to as a *rating curve*. For unsteady flow however, the depth deviates from the normal depth. The slope of the water surface during increasing (rising) flow is greater than the channel bottom slope and is flatter than the channel bottom slope during decreasing (falling) flow. This results in a looped rating curve, as illustrated in Figure 3.2.

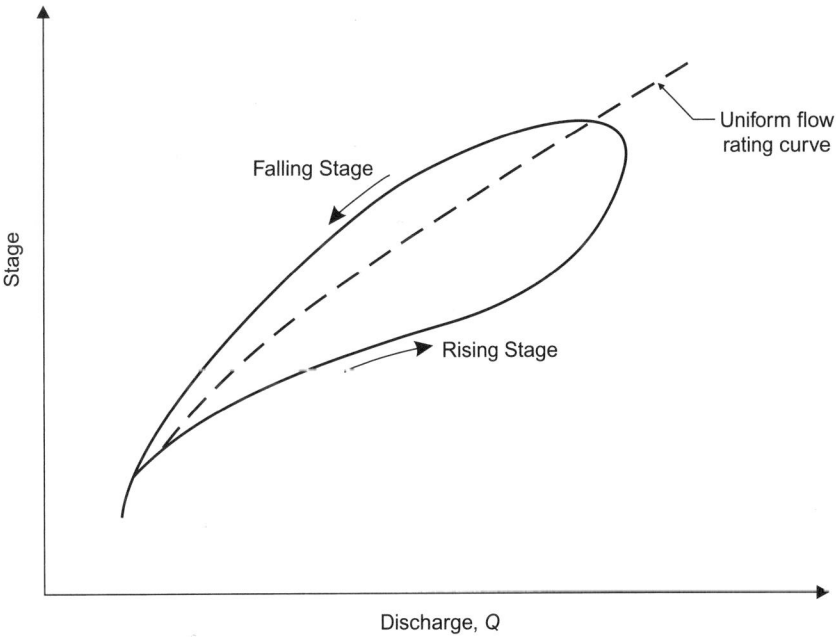

Figure 3.2 Example of a looped stage-discharge curve.

There are a variety of ways to solve for unsteady flow in collection systems, ranging from the theoretically complete St. Venant equations (Section 3.3) to simple hydrologic routing methods (described in later sections). The methods used to determine sewer flows have evolved from those developed for solving flooding problems in streams. However, they are considerably more complicated because of the potential for sewers to transit between full-pipe pressurized flow and going dry.

The remainder of this chapter describes the equations used to solve unsteady flow problems and the application of those equations to real collection systems.

3.2 Types of Routing

Hydraulic models track both the flow and hydraulic grade through the system, while *hydrologic* models track flow and use a simplified approximation to account for momentum effects. Hydrologic routing methods are also referred to as *lumped* models because they calculate flow at one location (the downstream end) of a reach. Hydraulic routing models are referred to as *distributed* models because they calculate flow at several cross sections simultaneously (Fread, 1993).

Attenuation of flows in pipes is due to temporary storage in each pipe reach. Hydraulic methods explicitly consider the depth of water in determining the volume stored. In many cases, the geometry of a pipe is so complex that the work needed to determine storage is excessive, so storage is approximated by simplified storage equations. Hydrologic methods assume that knowing the inflows during the present and previous time step and the outflow during the previous time step are sufficient for determining outflow from a reach. Once the inflow and outflow are known, water depth can be determined, if needed, using gradually varied flow methods, or even normal depth.

Hydrologic routing methods rely on the storage equation, which is

$$I - Q = \frac{dS}{dt} \qquad (3.1)$$

where I = inflow (ft³/s, m³/s)
Q = outflow (ft³/s, m³/s)
S = storage (ft³, m³)

Various methods have been developed for calculating the outflow from a stream or pipe reach given the inflow. Such methods are generally accurate if downstream conditions do not back up the flow; that is, if tailwater depth and flow restrictions do not significantly reduce the downstream flow rate. When there is a downstream limitation, hydrologic routing methods tend to predict peaks that are higher than hydraulic models and arrive earlier because they do not adequately account for all factors leading to attenuation.

3.3 Hydrodynamic Equations

The most commonly used equations for modeling unsteady flow in sewers are based on the assumption that the flow is one-dimensional, the pressure distribution is hydrostatic, the length of the channel is much greater than the depth, and the water density is constant. Disturbances in a fluid under such conditions are referred to as *shallow-water* or *translatory* waves (Linsley, Kohler, and Paulhus, 1982).

Saint-Venant Equations

One-dimensional flow in sewers is best described by the equations attributed to Jean-Claude Barre de St. Venant. (They are a simplification of the three-dimensional Navier-Stokes equations.) They are based on the assumption that the average velocity in a cross section is adequate to describe the flow and the water surface only slopes in the direction of flow. The Saint-Venant equations consist of two partial differential equations—one for continuity and a second for momentum—and have many different forms. French (1985) gives the continuity equation as

$$\frac{\partial y}{\partial t} + y\frac{\partial u}{\partial x} + u\frac{\partial y}{\partial x} = 0 \qquad (3.2)$$

and the momentum equation as

$$\frac{\partial u}{\partial t} + u\frac{\partial u}{\partial x} + g\frac{\partial y}{\partial x} - g(S_o - S_f) = 0 \qquad (3.3)$$

where
- u = velocity in the longitudinal direction (ft/s, m/s)
- x = distance in the longitudinal direction (ft, m)
- y = water depth (m, ft)
- g = gravitational acceleration (32.2 ft/s^2, 9.81 m/s^2)
- S_o = slope of the channel bed in the longitudinal direction (ft/ft, m/m)
- S_f = friction slope (ft/ft, m/m)

Initial and boundary conditions are required to solve these equations. The boundary conditions are usually the inflow hydrographs and tailwater conditions at the outlet and the initial condition is the gradually varied flow profile (or normal depth) based on some predetermined flow at the start of the analysis.

The Saint-Venant equations cannot be solved analytically, so a variety of numerical solutions have been developed. The methods can be classified as either finite-difference methods or the method of characteristics. While the method of characteristics works well for sudden abrupt waves, finite-difference methods are preferred for the type of flow variations encountered in sewer systems.

Finite-difference solutions divide space and time into a grid, as illustrated in Figure 3.3, and approximate derivatives as finite differences, such as

$$\frac{\partial u}{\partial x} \doteq \frac{\Delta u}{\Delta x} \qquad (3.4)$$

There are many articles describing methods for solving these equations, including Abbott, 1979; Chow, 1973; Cunge, Holley and Verwey, 1980; Fread, 1993; French, 1985; NOAA, 2000; Ponce, Li, and Simons, 1978; Price, 1973; Roesner, Aldrich, and Dickin-

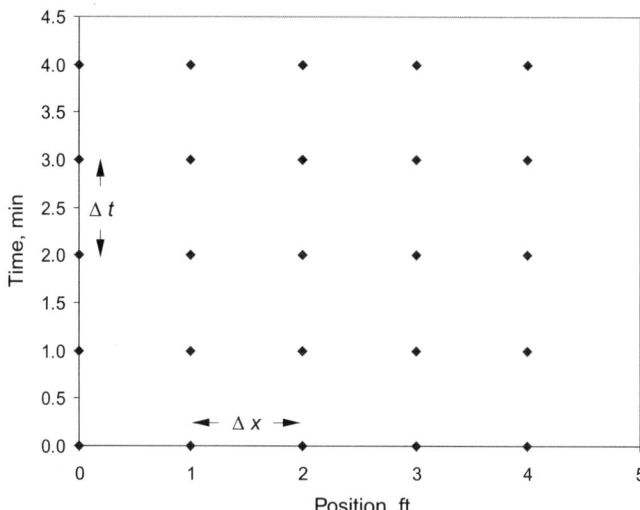

Figure 3.3 Finite difference grid.

son, 1989; Yen, 1996; and Yen, 2001. All involve discussions of whether implicit or explicit methods should be used. Explicit solutions are easier to program, but implicit solutions tend to be more stable. The number of points used in the numerical solution also affects convergence and accuracy.

In particular, explicit methods need small time steps (on the order of 10 seconds for wet-weather conditions) (Roesner, Aldrich and Dickinson, 1989). Numerical stability problems can manifest themselves as oscillations in flow and surface elevation, excessive velocities, or continuity errors. The time-step size should be based on the time it takes for a surface wave to travel the length of a pipe, which is approximated by

$$\Delta t = \frac{L}{\sqrt{gD}} \tag{3.5}$$

where Δt = time for the wave to travel the length of the pipe (s)
    L = length of the pipe (ft, m)
    g = gravitational acceleration (32.2 ft/s^2, 9.81 m/s^2)
    D = diameter of the pipe (ft, m)

Successful solution of the finite-difference equations depends on the selection of time and distance step sizes. Large step sizes result in faster solutions, but have more potential for instability and imprecision. Numerous computer programs are available, so manual calculation of unsteady flow in sewers is generally not practiced.

Approximation to Hydrodynamic Equations

Because of the difficulty of solving the Saint-Venant equations, numerous approximations have been developed. Most involve eliminating terms from the momentum equation to improve stability. It is possible to rearrange and simplify the St. Venant momentum equation to find the discharge as a function of the discharge under normal flow and the terms in the momentum equation (Weinmann and Laurenson, 1979; French, 1985).

$$Q = Q_N\left(1 - \frac{1}{S_f}\frac{\partial y}{\partial x} - \frac{u}{S_o g}\frac{\partial u}{\partial x} - \frac{1}{S_o g}\frac{\partial u}{\partial t}\right)^{1/2} \qquad (3.6)$$

where Q = actual unsteady flow (ft^3/s, m^3/s)
         Q_N = flow under normal conditions (ft^3/s, m^3/s)

When all the terms in the parentheses are considered, then Equation 3.6 corresponds to the Saint-Venant equations. When the final term in the parentheses is neglected, the models are referred to as a *diffusion analogy* and flows do not change abruptly, as in a pump cycling upstream. When only the first term is considered, the model only determines normal depth and is called *kinematic wave routing*. With each successive level of approximation, the equations become easier to solve, but lose some of their ability to represent real phenomena.

In some instances (NOAA, 2000), modelers have developed methods to turn off troublesome terms in the equations under specific conditions, while leaving them in the solution most of the time.

Diffusion Analogy

In the diffusion analogy or diffusion wave (Ponce, 1986), the continuity and momentum equations are combined into the single equation

$$\frac{\partial Q}{\partial t} + c\frac{\partial Q}{\partial x} = D\frac{\partial^2 Q}{\partial x^2} \qquad (3.7)$$

where c = wave celerity (ft/s, m/s)
         D = coefficient for wave attenuation (ft^2/s, m^2/s)

The coefficients c and D can best be estimated from observed hydrographs and can be calculated for regular channels as

$$c = \frac{1}{T}\frac{dQ}{dx} \qquad (3.8)$$

and

$$D = \frac{Q}{2TS_o} \qquad (3.9)$$

where T = top width (m, ft)

The diffusion analogy works well when the slope is relatively large and the depth small. The coefficient c is often referred to as the *kinematic wave speed*.

Kinematic Wave

If the conditions during the unsteady flow event do not deviate significantly from normal flow, then most terms in the right-hand side of Equation 3.6 can be eliminated to give

$$\frac{\partial Q}{\partial t} + c\frac{\partial Q}{\partial x} = 0 \qquad (3.10)$$

This equation is referred to as a *kinematic wave* solution.

Kinematic wave routing works well when flow changes are slow and the stage discharge relationship is not significantly looped.

Muskingum Routing

A commonly used form of hydrologic routing is the Muskingum method, which assumes that the storage in a reach is given by

$$S = K[XI + (1-X)Q] \tag{3.11}$$

where
- S = storage (ft³, m³)
- K = storage constant (s)
- X = relative importance of inflow and outflow in determining storage
- I = inflow (ft³/s, m³/s)

For most streams, X is approximately 0.2, while K is an approximation to the travel time in the reach. A graphical method to determine X and K based on field data is given in Linsley, Kohler, and Paulhus (1982). While, in general, the theory behind the kinematic wave method makes it more appropriate for an open channel with no top rather than a sewer, Samani and Jebelifard (2003) have shown how, with some modification, it can be applied to circular pipes.

The discharge from a reach is given by

$$Q_2 = c_0 I_2 + c_1 I_1 + c_2 Q_1 \tag{3.12}$$

where the subscripts refer to time steps 1 and 2. The duration of a time step is t. The coefficients are given by

$$c_0 = \frac{0.5t - KX}{K - KX + 0.5t} \tag{3.13}$$

$$c_1 = \frac{KX + 0.5t}{K - KX + 0.5t} \tag{3.14}$$

$$c_2 = \frac{K - KX - 0.5t}{K - KX + 0.5t} \tag{3.15}$$

As a check, note that

$$c_0 + c_1 + c_2 = 1 \tag{3.16}$$

Typical hydrographs from Muskingum Routing are shown in Figure 3.4.

Muskingum-Cunge Routing

The Muskingum-Cunge method, a variation of the Muskingum method proposed by Cunge (1969), allows the routing coefficients to change based on changes in the top width and flow. It combines the desirable features of the kinematic wave method with benefits of the Muskingum method, in that it allows a limited amount of attenuation. This routing method is discussed in Ponce, Li, and Simons (1978), HEC (1990), and Yen (2001). It is especially desirable in pipe-flow problems where the top width of

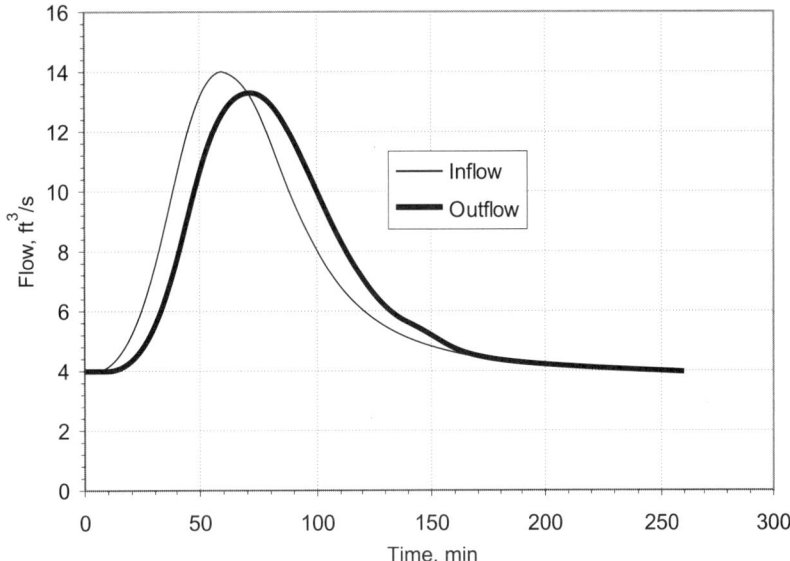

Figure 3.4 Example of flow routing.

flows changes dramatically with flow in some ranges. The simplified form of the hydrodynamic equations for the Muskingum-Cunge method is given by

$$\frac{\partial A}{\partial t} + c\frac{\partial Q}{\partial x} = \mu\frac{\partial^2 Q}{\partial x^2} + cq_L \qquad (3.17)$$

where
- c = wave celerity (ft/s, m/s)
- μ = hydraulic diffusivity (m²/s, ft²/s)
- q_L = lateral inflow (m³/s, ft³/s)

The Muskingum coefficients can be given by

$$K = \frac{\Delta x}{c} \qquad (3.18)$$

and

$$X = \frac{1}{2}\left(c\Delta t + \frac{Q}{TS_o c}\right) \qquad (3.19)$$

where
- Δx = distance step (ft, m) (approximately $c\Delta t$)
- T = top width (ft, m)

This can be solved (for $K = \Delta t$ and $\alpha = 1 - 2K$ to give the following relationship for flow

$$Q_2 = \frac{2-\alpha}{2+\alpha}I_1 + \frac{\alpha}{2+\alpha}(I_2 + Q_1) \qquad (3.20)$$

The coefficient α is given by

$$\alpha = \frac{KQ}{S_o(\Delta x)^2 T} \tag{3.21}$$

where Δx = length of reach (ft, m)

Convex Routing

Another variation in hydrologic routing is convex routing, which only uses flows from the previous time step to determine the outflow from a reach (US Soil Conservation Service, 1972). The flow equation is

$$Q_2 = cI_1 + (1-c)Q_1 \tag{3.22}$$

where c = convex routing coefficient

The convex routing coefficient is not the same as the wave speed c (Equation 3.8). It is the ratio of the time step to the travel time in the reach. The time step should be less than the travel time (i.e., $c < 1$). The travel time, however, is not a constant but is a function of velocity. It is usually determined for a velocity corresponding to 50 to 75% of the maximum flow. The coefficient is given by

$$c = \frac{V\Delta t}{L} \tag{3.23}$$

where V = representative velocity (ft/s, m/s)
Δt = time step size (s)
L = length of pipe (reach) (ft, m)

Weighted Translational Routing

Although the travel time should generally be greater than the time step, sometimes there are a few very short pipes that would force the time step to be unrealistically small. For such cases, when it is necessary to have a method that works when $c > 1$, the discharge can be calculated with

$$Q_2 = \frac{1}{c}I_1 + \left(1 - \frac{1}{c}\right)I_2 \tag{3.24}$$

In small systems with steep slopes, disturbances essentially slide down the pipe with little or no attenuation. To determine the flow at a given time, it is only necessary to look upstream to the flow one time step earlier at position $V\Delta t$. This value will most likely not be at a location between points where the flow is known. Therefore, interpolation is needed to determine the flow passing downstream.

Level Pool Routing

Level pool routing (sometimes called *Modified Puls*) is not a pipe-routing method but a method to route flows through storage ponds or reservoirs. In sewer flow, this can be applied to basins that store wet weather flows. This method is appropriate for modeling elements when the head-loss is not nearly as important as the volume of storage.

Summary of Methods

The methods used to approximate the full dynamic equations are summarized in Table 3.1, which is based on a similar table in Haestad Methods, et al. (2003). This table presents the assumptions that are built into the simplifications and when they are appropriate.

In general, most of the simplifications to the Saint-Venant equations can be used for wastewater collection systems as long as the collection system does not have backups and flow reversals. In such cases, the full Saint-Venant equations are needed. In design situations, however the engineer is not building the sewers so that they back up and reverse flow, so the simplified routing methods work fine. In small systems, even simple routing methods are not needed, since steady, peak-flow analysis is usually adequate.

3.4 Complications to Routing Methods

While the methods discussed in the previous section can account for unsteady flow in channels and pipes not flowing full, real wastewater collection systems may include complications that are not accounted for in these methods.

Each of these complications, which are discussed in this section, requires an adjustment to the flow routing. The adjustments depend on the routing method being used.

"So that's where it goes! Well, I'd like to thank you fellows for bringing this to my attention."

Table 3.1 Summary of hydrologic routing methods.

Method	Theory/Equation	Assumptions	Information Needs/Parameters	Appropriate Applications
Kinematic Wave	$\frac{\partial Q}{\partial t} + c\frac{\partial Q}{\partial x} = 0$	• No allowance for backwater effects. • No allowance for varying conveyance between the main channel and overbank areas.	• Shape of cross section. • Length of reach. • Slope of the energy line. • Manning's n.	• Pipe slope exceeds 0.002.
Level Pool (Storage or Modified Puls)	$\frac{\partial Q}{\partial x} + \frac{\partial A}{\partial t} = 0$	• Lateral flow is insignificant. • Water surface in the storage area is horizontal.	• A functional relation between storage and outflow is required to solve the finite-difference approximation.	• Storage basins. • Significant time-invariant backwater influence on the discharge hydrograph.
Diffusion Wave	$\frac{\partial Q}{\partial t} + c\frac{\partial Q}{\partial x} = D\frac{\partial^2 Q}{\partial x^2}$	• No abrupt changes in flow with time.	• Shape of cross section. • Length of pipe reach. • Slope of energy grade line. • Manning's n.	• Should not be used for rapidly varying backwater.
Muskingum	$I - O = \frac{dS}{dt}$	• Storage in the reach is modeled as the sum of prism storage and wedge storage. • Prism storage is defined by a steady-flow water surface profile. • No allowance for backwater.	• K (travel time through the reach). • Weighting factor X ($0.0 \leq X \leq 0.5$).	• Situations with little or very crude channel geometric data, but some calibration data (observed hydrographs at two or more points).
Muskingum-Cunge	$\frac{\partial A}{\partial t} + c\frac{\partial Q}{\partial x} = \mu\frac{\partial^2 A}{\partial x^2}$	• No allowance for backwater. • As it omits the acceleration term of the momentum equation, it should not be used for rapidly varying hydrographs.	• Shape of cross section. • Length of reach. • Channel slope. • Manning's n.	• Slow hydrograph through reaches with flat slopes.
Weighted Translational Routing	Outflow is based on inflow from current and previous time steps.	• Empirical method. • Flows are not attenuated.	• Representative velocity.	• Pipes that don't surcharge.
Convex Routing	Outflow is weighted sum of previous step's inflow and outflow.	• Empirical method.	• Representative velocity.	• Urban drainage pipes. • Steep slopes.

Manholes and Junction Tables

Most unsteady-flow routing methods were developed for streams, which obviously do not have manholes. In some models, the effects of manholes can be ignored and the upstream and downstream pipes can be treated as if they were contiguous. This works well when the flow passes through the manhole at normal depth and there is minimal head loss.

Accounting for head loss in manholes is better handled through some form of the energy equation, rather than the momentum equation. The inlet to the manhole is the downstream boundary condition for the upstream pipe and the outlet of the manhole is the upstream boundary condition for the downstream pipe. The continuity equation is replaced by a storage equation that tracks the volumes into and out of the manhole. This is especially critical when the manhole is surcharged or overflowing, because the pipe continuity equation cannot account for storage or diversion in these situations.

Manholes are also convenient places to account for changes in flow regime from super- to subcritical. Saint-Venant equation solvers have a difficult time accurately locating hydraulic jumps. Placing the transition from super- to subcritical flow at a manhole makes solutions proceed more smoothly.

Surcharging

Even though wastewater collection systems are designed and usually operated to flow partly full, modelers are most interested in high-flow conditions for which some pipes may flow full. In this case, the pipe is pressurized and is said to be *surcharged*. The equations for full-pipe flow, as presented in Chapter 2, are applicable in this situation. The difficulties with the full-pipe hydraulic equations arise when a pipe is pressurized during one time step and not during another, or when it is pressurized for a portion of its length. These transition cases between full and partly full flow can be difficult for models to handle.

The most common approach is to use the equations for partly full flow and place an imaginary vertical slot above the pipe to keep track of the hydraulic grade line, as shown in Figure 3.5. This slot, which is attributed to Preissmann (1960), must be narrow enough to not contain an appreciable amount of water, yet not be so small that it causes instability. The Preissmann slot is sized so that the wave celerity in the slot is comparable to the speed with which an elastic pressure wave moves through a full pipe.

A typical value used for slot width is

$$b = \frac{\pi g D^2}{4c^2} \quad (3.25)$$

where b = width of the Preissmann slot (ft, m)
 g = acceleration due to gravity (32.2 ft/s^2, 9.81 m/s^2)
 D = diameter of the pipe (ft, m)
 c = speed of the pressure wave (ft/s, m/s)

Values of c in pressure pipes depend on the pipe material, type of joint, nature of pipe anchoring, and amount of entrained gases. Wave speed can vary from 4700 ft/s (1440

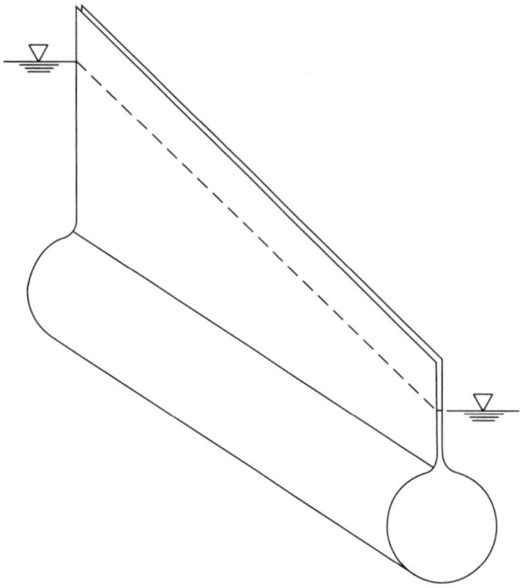

Figure 3.5 Preissmann hypothetical open slot.

m/s) down to speeds on the order of 600 ft/s (200 m/s). Fluids in rigid pipes tend to have higher wave speeds, while fluids with entrained gases have speeds at the lower end of the range. More information on wave speed can be found in Chaudhry (1987), Haestad Methods et al. (2003), and Wylie and Streeter (1993).

Overall, the wave speed tends to decrease when surcharging is present. Because hydrologic routing methods do not explicitly consider whether or not the pipe is full and they use the same routing coefficients even when there is no storage available in the pipe (there can be storage in the manholes), hydrologic routing may show the peak arriving faster when surcharging is present.

A special case of a surcharged sewer is an inverted siphon, which is intended to flow full at all times. The Preissmann slot works well for these situations. Because there are changes in slope along an inverted siphon, several model nodes (either nonmanhole nodes or "sealed" or "bolted" manholes) may be required. Difficulties in routing can occur when there are multiple barrels in the siphon. Methods for handling this are described in the discussion of parallel pipes on page 105.

Overflows and Diversions

Wastewater can leave a collection system through a diversion facility specially constructed to regulate the overflow, or simply by flowing out through an open manhole cover. When the water level in the sewer reaches an opening, whether it is a weir, valve, manhole lid, or catch basin, water will leave the sewer. The rate of the water loss is usually approximated by an outflow whose volume is based on a weir or orifice equation. At best, this is a crude approximation, since these openings are seldom represented accurately by equations. Each situation must be analyzed individually to determine what water levels and flows correspond to the start of a diversion and how the flows are split thereafter.

Hydrologic routing models are less capable of representing overflows, since they do not link flow rate directly with water level. They must therefore base the volume of overflow on a relation between inflow to the model node and volume diverted. This is usually presented in the form of a rating table. The modeler is responsible for developing the rating table based on flow measurements or a theoretical calculation.

One of the difficulties in handling any overflows is deciding on the fate of the water that leaves the collection system. It can be

- Lost to a receiving water body
- Ponded and then flowed back into the sewer when water levels in the sewer drop below the pond surface
- Moved overland to the next catch basin or other inflow point
- Some combination of the above

In diversion chambers constructed to handle overflows, the overflows usually are directed to a receiving stream. However, when a manhole overflows, the fate of the water depends on the topography at the overflow. Since many overflows occur at depressions, the water may be ponded and then return after the flow peak passes. With combined or storm sewers, there may be downstream catch basins that accept the overland flow. The modeler must indicate how diverted flow is to be handled.

The most problematic devices include swirl concentrators, inflatable dams, leaping weirs, tilting plate regulators, and mechanical gates as there is often very little information available about their hydraulic characteristics. During model calibration, it may be necessary to prepare rating curves for these devices. The behavior of these devices may also be a function of some control strategy (e.g., when an operator opens or closes a gate or dam). Some field measurements during high flow are important for accurately capturing their performance.

Most diversions can be represented with reasonable accuracy by some type of stage-discharge relationship in hydraulic models or a flow rating curve in hydrologic models. Further difficulties arise when tailwater begins to flood the device. Hydraulic models can usually handle this type of backup, but hydrologic models cannot account for them.

Parallel Pipes and Loops

Most collection systems have a dendritic (treelike) shape with smaller pipes merging into larger downstream pipes. In some instances (such as relief sewers and inverted siphons), the pipes can be parallel. If parallel pipes are identical, then some models will handle these as multibarrel pipes. Otherwise, parallel pipes can be problematic, because the routing solution must determine how to split the flow among the multiple paths through the system.

If the sewers are truly parallel, with the same slope, length, and roughness, then an equivalent pipe can be used to represent the two pipes. Once the modeler decides on the slope and Manning's n for the equivalent pipe, the diameter of the equivalent pipe can be approximated as

$$D_e = \left[\frac{n_e}{S_e^{1/2}}\sum\frac{D_i^{8/3}S_i^{1/2}}{n_i}\right]^{3/8} \tag{3.26}$$

where D_e = diameter of the equivalent pipe (ft, m)
n_e = Manning's n for the equivalent pipe
S_e = slope of the equivalent pipe
D_i = diameter of the i-th pipe (ft, m)
S_i = slope of the i-th pipe
n_i = Manning's n for the i-th pipe

In many cases, the paths taken by the parallel pipes may be significantly different, significant loads may be placed in one parallel pipe but not the other, or the modeler simply may want to observe the behavior of each pipe individually. In such cases, modeling the pipes as parallel may not be satisfactory.

In hydrologic routing, the modeler must enter a rating table to describe the flow split between the two parallel pipes. If the two pipes have the same upstream and downstream invert elevations so that the head loss is the same, the split can be approximated based on the full-pipe characteristics of the two pipes using

$$\frac{Q_2}{Q_t} = \frac{1}{1+\left(\frac{D_1}{D_2}\right)^{8/3}\left(\frac{S_1}{S_2}\right)^{1/2}\left(\frac{n_2}{n_1}\right)} \tag{3.27}$$

where Q_2 = flow diverted into the parallel pipe (ft^3/s, m^3/s)
Q_t = total flow into the splitter node (ft^3/s, m^3/s)
D_1 = diameter of the first pipe out of the split (ft, m)
D_2 = diameter of the second pipe out of the split (ft, m)
S_1 = slope of the first pipe out of the split
S_2 = slope of the second pipe out of the split
n_1 = Manning's n for the first pipe out of the split
n_2 = Manning's n for the second pipe out of the split

If the pipes coming out of a flow split do not have the same invert elevation, then there will be some threshold flow value below which all the flow will go into the lower pipe. Equation 3.27 is valid when the inflow water surface is at the crown of the higher pipe. Between those water levels, the split in flow must be interpolated.

The methods above are appropriate when there are no significant inflows along the parallel routes. However, in some instances, the network is so complicated that it cannot be described by a parallel-pipe approximation and the system is a true looped network. In hydrologic routing, the modeler must identify how the flow is split at each diversion within the loop. If flow can reverse in a loop, hydrologic routing cannot be used and the full St. Venant equations must be solved.

Flow Reversal

The water level at the downstream end of a pipe can be so high that flow will move backward up a pipe. This can be caused by increased tailwater depth at the outlet due to flooding or tidal influence or flooding of a manhole into which the pipe discharges.

Hydrologic routing methods cannot account for flow reversals. If flow reversals are an issue in a system, then hydraulic routing methods must be used.

Dry Pipes

Pipes can have zero flow immediately downstream of force mains when the pumps feeding them are turned off or at the far upstream reaches of collection systems when there is no load coming from the customers along the line. Although dry pipes may sound like a simple problem that is easy to handle with hydrologic routing, hydraulic routing can have difficulty with zero depth.

In hydraulic modeling, the model may contain a small "virtual flow" that is added to any pipe that has no flow. This virtual flow can be subtracted out further downstream or can be negligible.

Drop Structures

In most cases, the water-surface elevation leaving the manhole is only slightly lower than the water-surface elevation entering the manhole. However, a pipe may enter the manhole much higher than the outlet (or any other pipe), as shown in Figure 3.6. This is referred to as a *drop manhole* or, more generally, a *drop structure*.

In this situation, flow at the inlet to the manhole passes through critical depth, which will serve as an internal boundary condition for the inflowing pipe. Problems occur when the manhole floods because of high flows, high tailwater, or a downstream restriction. In this case, the incoming pipe has a tailwater depth that must be accounted for in hydraulic routing. Models must switch between the two downstream boundary conditions for the incoming pipe, which is sometimes the cause of instability. In hydrologic routing, the flows are forced through the manhole regardless of depth.

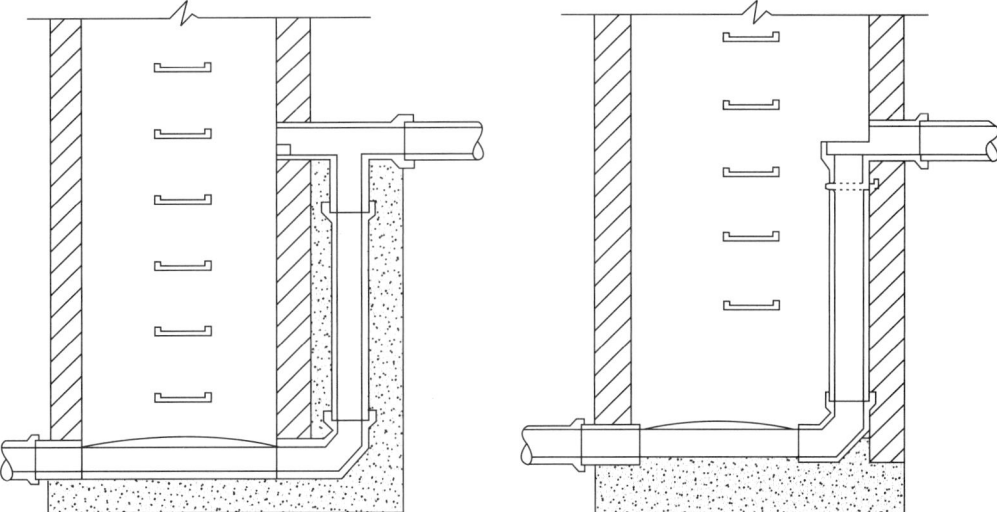

Figure 3.6 Example of drop manholes.

"Good news! Our septic tank is shot."

References

Abbott, M. B. 1979. *Computational Hydraulics: Elements of the theory of free surface flows*. London: Pitman.

Chaudhry, M. H. 1987. *Applied Hydraulic Transients*. New York: Van Nostrand Reinhold.

Chow, V. T. 1973. *Open Channel Hydraulics*. New York: McGraw Hill.

Cunge, J. A. 1969. On the subject of a flood propagation computation method (Muskingum method). *Journal of Hydraulic Research 7*, no. 2: 205–230.

Cunge, J. A., F. M. Holley, and A. Verwey. 1980. *Practical Aspects of Computational River Hydraulics*. London: Pitman.

Fread, D. L. 1993. Flow routing. In *Handbook of Hydrology*, edited by D. Maidment. New York: McGraw-Hill.

French, R. H. 1985. *Open Channel Hydraulics*. New York: McGraw-Hill.

Haestad Methods, T. M. Walski, D. V. Chase, D. A. Savic, W. Grayman, S. Beckwith, and E. Koelle. 2003. *Advanced Water Distribution Modeling and Management*. Waterbury, CT: Haestad Press.

Haestad Methods, G. Dyhouse, J. Hatchett, and J. Benn. 2003. *Floodplain Modeling Using HEC-RAS*. Waterbury, CT: Haestad Press.

Hydrologic Engineering Center (HEC). 1990. *HEC-1 Flood Hydrograph Package*. Davis, CA: US Army Corps of Engineers, Hydrologic Engineering Center.

Linsley, R. K., M. A. Kohler, and J. L. H. Paulhus. 1982. *Hydrology for Engineers*. New York: McGraw-Hill.

National Oceanic and Atmospheric Agency, National Weather Service. 2000. FLDWAV Computer Program, Version 2-0-0.

Ponce, V. M. 1986. Diffusion wave modeling of catchment dynamics. *Journal of the Hydraulics Division*, ASCE 112, no. 8: 716–727.

Ponce, V. M., R. M. Li, and D. B. Simons. 1978. Applicability of kinematic and diffusion models." *Journal of the Hydraulic Division*, ASCE 104, no. HY12: 1663.

Preissmann, A. 1960. *Propogation des intumescenes dans les canaue et rivieres*. Grenoble: First Congress de L'Association Francaise de Calcul.

Price R. K. 1973. A comparison of four numerical methods for flood routing. *Journal of the Hydraulics Division*, ASCE 100, no. 7: 879–899.

Roesner, L. A., J. A. Aldrich, and R. E. Dickinson. 1989. *Storm Water Management Model User's Manual Version 4: Extra Addendum*. EPA 600/3-88/001b. US Environmental Protection Agency.

Samani, H. M. V. and S. Jebelifard. 2003. Design of circular urban storm sewer systems using multilinear Muskingum flow routing methods. *Journal of Hydraulic Engineering* 129, vol. 11: 832.

US Soil Conservation Service. 1972. *National Engineering Handbook*. Section 4, "Hydrology." SCS/ENGNEH-4.

Weinmann, D. E., and E. M. Laurenson. 1979. Approximate flood routing methods: A review. *Journal of the Hydraulics Division*, ASCE 105, no. HY12: 1521.

Wylie, B. E., and V. L. Streeter. 1993. *Fluid Transients in Systems*. Englewood Cliffs, NJ: Prentice-Hall.

Yen, B. C. 1996. Hydraulics for excess water management. In *Water Resources Handbook*, edited by L. W. Mays. New York: McGraw-Hill.

Yen, B.C. 2001. Hydraulics of sewer systems. In *Stormwater Collection Systems Design Handbook*, edited by L. W. Mays. New York: McGraw-Hill.

Problems

3.1 Match the equation with the proper description.

Equation		Description	
1	St. Venant	a	Slide wave downstream
2	Muskingum	b	Full hydrodynamic equations
3	Kinematic wave	c	Storage routing
4	Translation	d	Based on normal depth
5	Preissmann	e	Simple storage approximation
6	Modified Puls	f	Slot for surcharged flow

3.2 Even though Muskingum routing is not considered the most appropriate routing method for sewers, it is amenable to manual calculations and spreadsheets. For this problem, route the storm with the following hydrograph through a reach of sewer with the following properties:

$K = 2000$ s

$\Delta t = 1200$ s

$x = 0.3$

In addition to the inflow hydrograph, there is a dry weather flow of 2 ft^3/s.

Time, min	Q wet, ft³/s	Time, min	Q wet, ft³/s
0	0.00	320	0.55
20	0.00	340	0.40
40	1.00	360	0.29
60	3.10	380	0.21
80	6.60	400	0.15
100	9.30	420	0.11
120	10.00	440	0.08
140	9.30	460	0.06
160	7.80	480	0.04
180	5.60	500	0.02
200	3.90	520	0.00
220	2.80	540	0.00
240	2.10	560	0.00
260	1.50	580	0.00
280	1.10	600	0.00
300	0.77		

a. Calculate the three Muskingum coefficients and verify that they sum to 1.0.

b. Calculate the inflow (add dry and wet flow) and outflow hydrographs for the reach and plot them on the same graph.

3.3 In this problem, route the flow through a gravity sewer just beyond the crest of a hill that receives water from a force main and a pump station. The gravity flow reach is shown schematically. There are numerous manholes along the way, but you are only monitoring at MH-2 and O-1. When the pump station is running, the inflow at manhole MH-1 is 20 ft³/s; when it is off, the flow is 0. There is negligible additional inflow along the pipe. The gravity pipe is circular 24-in. PVC with Manning's $n = 0.010$. At time = 0, the gravity pipe is empty (Q = 0 ft³/s) and the pump station starts.

During dry weather, the constant-speed pump runs for shorter times than in wet weather, but the discharge rate is essentially the same whenever the pump is running.

Given the inflow patterns in the following table, develop the hydrographs at the monitoring manhole (MH-2) and the outlet (O-1) for both the dry weather and wet weather conditions. Plot the dry and wet weather hydrographs on separate graphs; that is, three curves (MH-1, MH-2, and O-1) on each of two graphs. Also determine the average flow out of the reach during a 2-hour period for each condition.

Hint: There are two ways to approach this problem; one is to solve with an extended period simulation model like SewerCAD, the other is to manually calculate with a spreadsheet. With the model approach, it's safe to ignore any manhole losses. Set the outlet depth to equal the pipe crown and use a stepwise pattern for the inflow. It's suggested that a hydraulic routing time step of 0.1 hr be used with a hydrologic routing time step of 0.01 hr. With a spreadsheet, use convex routing with $c = 0.15$ for P-1 and $c = 0.06$ for P-2. Calculate flow every 0.01 hr.

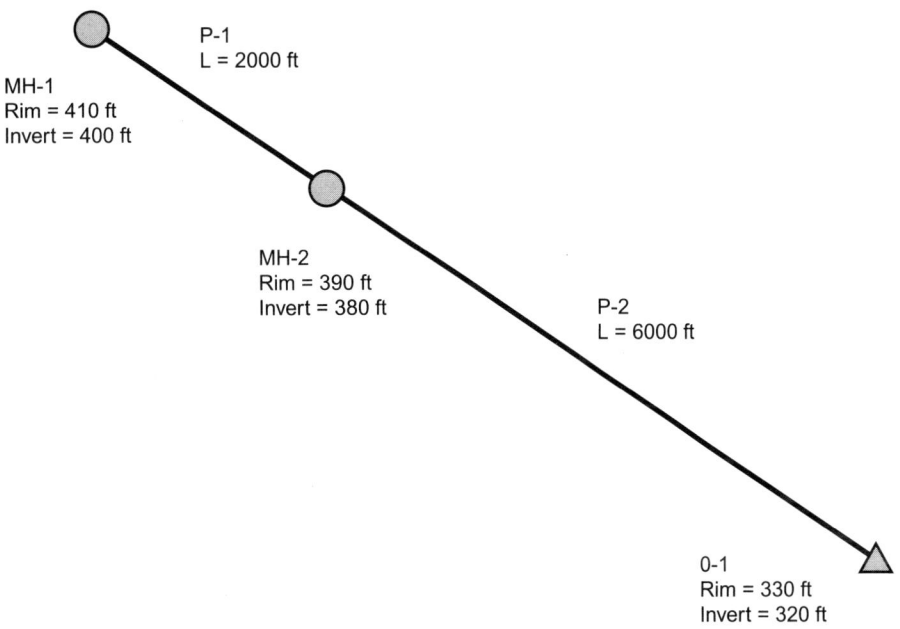

Dry Weather Pattern		Wet Weather Pattern	
Time, hr	Flow at MH-1, ft^3/s	Time, hr	Flow at MH-1, ft^3/s
0.00	20	0.00	20
0.20	0	0.30	0
0.55	20	0.45	20
0.65	0	0.60	0
0.81	20	070	20
0.90	0	0.95	0
1.15	20	1.00	20
1.22	0	1.20	0
1.45	20	1.30	20
1.50	0	1.60	0
1.72	20	1.65	20
1.80	0	1.90	0
2.00	20	2.00	20

CHAPTER

4

Force Main and Pumping Hydraulics

Recall from Chapter 1 that there are four situations in which pressure flow occurs in sewer collection systems:

- *Force mains* – Sewage is pumped along stretches where gravity flow is not feasible.
- *Pressure sewers* – Each customer has a pump that discharges to the pressure sewer.
- *Vacuum sewers* – Flow is pulled through the system by vacuum pumps.
- *Surcharged gravity sewers* – The depth of flow in a gravity pipe is above the crown because of downstream control.

Although gravity flow is generally the first choice in sewer networks, pressure flow is frequently encountered and models must be able to simulate pumping systems and the flow in pressure systems. Closed-conduit flow is governed by the continuity, energy, and momentum equations, as described in Chapter 2. With closed-conduit flow, pressure terms in the energy equations must be considered. Head losses are caused by pipe friction and also occur at pipe fixtures. Energy is added to the system by pumps.

This chapter reviews the basic principles of pressure hydraulics and pumping, which are frequently employed in sewer models.

4.1 Friction Losses

In pipe flow, shear stresses develop between the liquid and the pipe wall. The magnitude of this shear stress is dependent upon the properties of the fluid, its velocity, the internal roughness of the pipe, and the length and diameter of the pipe.

Consider, for example, the fluid segment shown in Figure 4.1. Such an element is sometimes referred to as a *control volume*. A force balance on the control volume can be used to form a general expression describing the head loss due to friction. Note the forces acting upon the element:

- The pressure difference between Sections 1 and 2.
- The weight of the fluid volume contained between Sections 1 and 2.
- The shear at the pipe walls between Sections 1 and 2.

If the flow has a constant velocity, the sum of all the forces acting on the segment must be zero, which is expressed as

$$p_1 A_1 - p_2 A_2 - \overline{A} L \gamma \sin\alpha - \tau_0 P L = 0 \tag{4.1}$$

where p_1 = pressure at section 1 (lb/ft^2, N/m^2)
A_1 = cross-sectional area of section 1 (ft^2, m^2)
p_2 = pressure at section 2 (lb/ft^2, N/m^2)
A_2 = cross-sectional area of section 2 (ft^2, m^2)
$\overline{A}$ = average area between section 1 and section 2 (ft^2, m^2)
L = distance between section 1 and section 2 (ft, m)
γ = fluid specific weight (lb/ft^3, N/m^3)
α = angle of the pipe to horizontal
τ_0 = shear stress along the pipe wall (lb/ft^2, N/m^2)
P = average perimeter of pipeline cross section (ft, m)

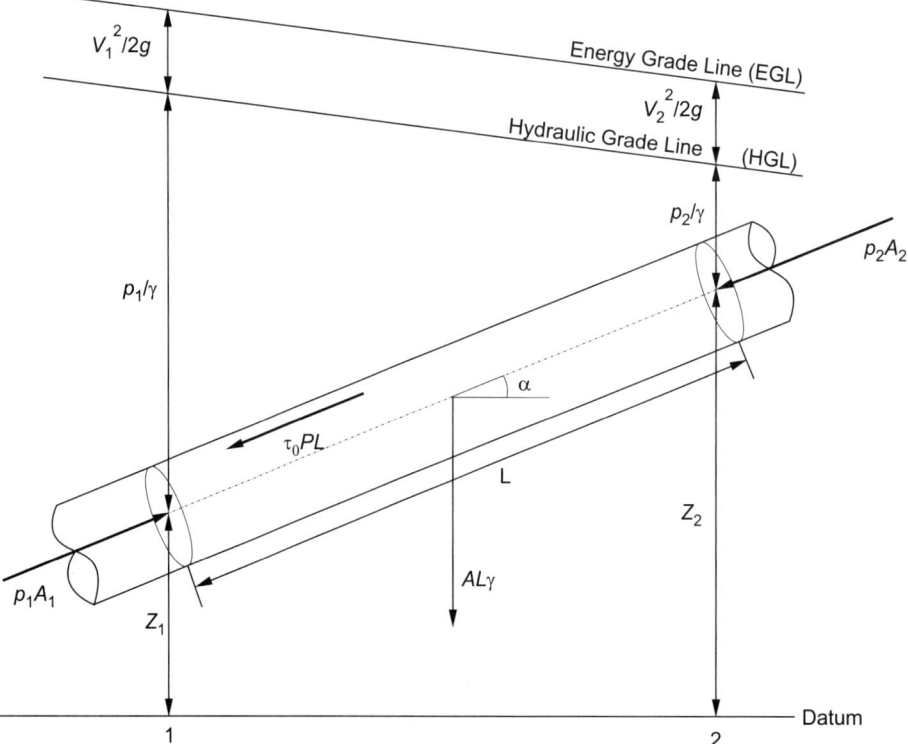

Figure 4.1 Free-body diagram of water flowing in an inclined pipe.

The last term on the left side of Equation 4.1 represents the friction losses along the pipe wall between the two sections. Figure 4.1 shows that the sine of the angle of the pipe, α, is given by

$$\sin\alpha = \frac{z_2 - z_1}{L} \qquad (4.2)$$

Substituting this result into Equation 4.1, assuming that the cross-sectional area does not change, and rearranging gives the head loss due to friction as

$$h_L = \tau_0 \frac{PL}{\gamma A} = \left(\frac{p_1}{\gamma} + z_1\right) - \left(\frac{p_2}{\gamma} + z_2\right) \qquad (4.3)$$

where h_L = head loss due to friction (ft, m)
z_1 = elevation of centroid of section 1 (ft, m)
z_2 = elevation of centroid of section 2 (ft, m)

Note that the velocity head is not considered in this case because the pipe diameter at each stage is the same, so the areas and the velocity heads are the same.

The shear stress is a function of the following parameters:

$$\tau_0 = F(\rho, \mu, V, D, \varepsilon) \qquad (4.4)$$

where ρ = fluid density (slugs/ft³, kg/m³)
μ = absolute viscosity (lb-s/ft², N-s/m²)
V = average fluid velocity (ft/s, m/s)
D = diameter (ft, m)
ε = index of internal pipe roughness (ft, m)

In turbulent flow, it is not possible to develop an analytical expression for head loss from the energy and head loss equations presented in Section 2.5. However, there are several commonly used empirical equations, including the Darcy-Weisbach and Hazen-Williams equations for closed pipes.

"I've already made arrangements to be flushed down the toilet."

Darcy-Weisbach Equation

The *Darcy-Weisbach equation* was developed using dimensional analysis and gives the head loss as

$$h_L = f\frac{LV^2}{D2g} = \frac{8fLQ^2}{gD^5\pi^2} \tag{4.5}$$

where f = Darcy-Weisbach friction factor
 g = gravitational acceleration (32.2 ft/s², 9.81 m/s²)
 Q = pipeline flow rate (ft³/s, m³/s)

A functional relationship for the Darcy-Weisbach *friction factor*, f, can be developed in the form

$$f = F\left(\text{Re}, \frac{\varepsilon}{D}\right) \tag{4.6}$$

where Re = the Reynolds number, given by

$$\text{Re} = \frac{VD\rho}{\mu} = \frac{VD}{\upsilon} \tag{4.7}$$

The pipe roughness factor, ε, divided by the pipe diameter, D, is called the *relative roughness*. Sometimes ε is called the *equivalent sand grain roughness* of the pipe. Table 4.1 provides values of ε for various materials.

Table 4.1 Equivalent sand grain pipe roughnesses (ε) for various sewer pipe materials.

Material	Equivalent Sand Grain Roughness, ε	
	ft	mm
Wrought iron, steel	$1.5 \times 10^{-4} - 8 \times 10^{-3}$	0.046–2.4
Asphalted cast iron	$4 \times 10^{-4} - 7 \times 10^{-3}$	0.1–2.1
Galvanized iron	$3.3 \times 10^{-4} - 1.5 \times 10^{-2}$	0.102–4.6
Cast iron	$8 \times 10^{-4} - 1.8 \times 10^{-2}$	0.2–5.5
Concrete	$10^{-3} - 10^{-2}$	0.3–3.0
Uncoated cast iron	7.4×10^{-4}	0.226
Coated cast iron	3.3×10^{-4}	0.102
Coated spun iron	1.8×10^{-4}	0.056
Cement	$1.3 \times 10^{-3} - 4 \times 10^{-3}$	0.4–1.2
Wrought iron	1.7×10^{-4}	0.05
Uncoated steel	9.2×10^{-5}	0.028
Coated steel	1.8×10^{-4}	0.058
PVC	5×10^{-6}	0.0015

Sources: Data from Lamont, 1981; Moody, 1944; Mays, 1999.

Colebrook-White Equation and the Moody Diagram

The best known equation relating the friction factor to the Reynolds number and relative roughness is the *Colebrook-White equation*:

$$\frac{1}{\sqrt{f}} = -0.86\left(\frac{\varepsilon}{3.7D} + \frac{2.51}{\mathrm{Re}\sqrt{f}}\right) \tag{4.8}$$

Since the Colebrook-White equation is an implicit function with f on both sides, it is difficult to use. Typically, it is solved by iterating through assumed values for f until both sides are equal.

The *Moody diagram* (Moody, 1944), shown in Figure 4.2, is a graphical solution for the Colebrook-White equation. It is interesting to note that for laminar flow (low Re) on this log-log plot, the friction factor is a straight-line function of the Reynolds number, while in the fully turbulent range (high ε/D and high Re) the friction factor is only a function of the relative roughness. Most applied water and wastewater pipeline situations fall into the low ε/D range near the "smooth" boundary for Re in the range of 10^5 to 10^6. The smooth boundary exists as a lower limit for ε/D ratios since the laminar sublayer along the wall completely covers the roughness; thus roughness no longer affects the functional resistance to flow.

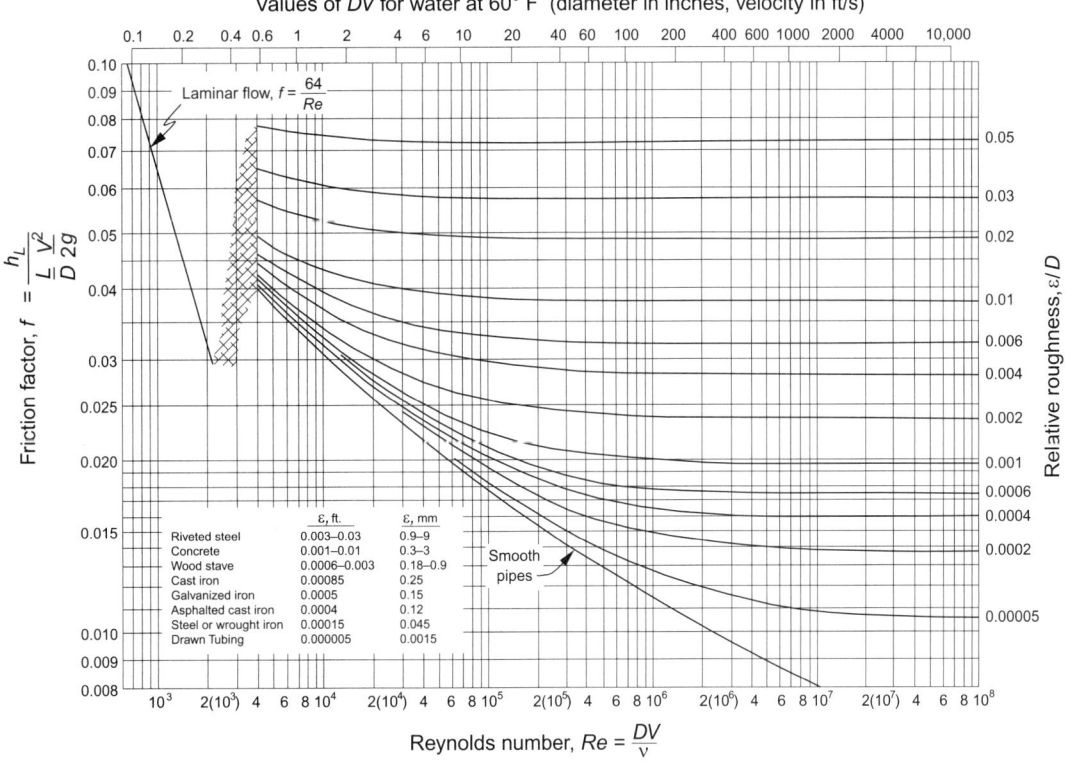

Figure 4.2 Moody diagram for solving the Colebrook-White equation (Moody, 1944).

Example 4.1 Darcy-Weisbach equation and the Moody diagram

Determine the head loss in 250 feet of 24-in. diameter concrete pipe conveying a discharge of 25 ft³/s. Assume that the water temperature is 60° F.

Solution

Table 4.1 gives the equivalent sand grain roughness for the pipe as $\varepsilon = 0.001$ ft. The relative roughness is therefore $\varepsilon/D = 0.0005$.

The cross-sectional area of the 24-in. pipe is $A = 3.14$ ft², and the velocity of flow is $V = Q/A = 7.96$ ft/s. Table C.1 on page 567 provides the kinematic viscosity for the water as $\nu = 1.217 \times 10^{-5}$ ft²/s, so the Reynolds number is

$$\mathrm{Re} = \frac{VD}{\nu} = \frac{7.96 \times 2.0}{1.217 \times 10^{-5}} = 1.31 \times 10^6$$

The Moody diagram gives the friction factor as $f = 0.017$. The Darcy-Weisbach equation gives the head loss in the pipe as

$$h_L = 0.017 \times \frac{250}{2.0} \times \frac{7.96^2}{2 \times 32.2} = 2.1 \text{ ft}$$

Hazen-Williams Equation

Another head loss expression that is frequently used, particularly in North America, is the *Hazen-Williams equation* (Williams and Hazen, 1920; American Society of Civil Engineers, 1992):

$$h_L = \frac{C_f L}{C^{1.852} D^{4.87}} Q^{1.852} \tag{4.9}$$

where
- h_L = pipe friction head loss (ft, m)
- L = pipe length (ft, m)
- C = Hazen-Williams C-factor
- D = diameter (ft, m)
- Q = flow rate (ft³/s, m³/s)
- C_f = unit conversion factor (4.73 for US customary units, 10.7 for SI)

The Hazen-Williams equation uses many of the same variables as Darcy-Weisbach, but adds a water-carrying capacity factor, C, that is assumed to be a constant for a given pipe material. Higher C-factors occur with smoother pipes (with higher carrying capacities) and lower C-factors describe rougher pipes. Table 4.2 lists typical C-factors for various pipe materials.

Table 4.2 Hazen-Williams C-factors.

Type of Pipe	Discrete Pipe Diameter, in. (cm)				
	3.0 (7.6)	6.0 (15.2)	12 (30)	24 (61)	48 (122)
Uncoated cast iron, smooth and new	121	125	130	132	134
Coated cast iron, smooth and new	129	133	138	140	141
30 years old					
Trend 1 – slight attack	100	106	112	117	120
Trend 2 – moderate attack	83	90	97	102	107
Trend 3 – appreciable attack	59	70	78	83	89
Trend 4 – severe attack	41	50	58	66	73
60 years old					
Trend 1 – slight attack	90	97	102	107	112
Trend 2 – moderate attack	69	79	85	92	96
Trend 3 – appreciable attack	49	58	66	72	78
Trend 4 – severe attack	30	39	48	56	62
100 years old					
Trend 1 – slight attack	81	89	95	100	104
Trend 2 – moderate attack	61	70	78	83	89
Trend 3 – appreciable attack	40	49	57	64	71
Trend 4 – severe attack	21	30	39	46	54
Miscellaneous					
Newly scraped mains	109	116	121	125	127
Newly brushed mains	97	104	108	112	115
Coated spun iron, smooth and new	137	142	145	148	148
Old – take as coated cast iron of same age					
Galvanized iron, smooth and new	129	133			
Wrought iron, smooth and new	137	142			
Coated steel, smooth and new	137	142	145	148	148
Uncoated steel, smooth and new	142	145	147	150	150
Coated asbestos cement, clean	147	149	150	152	
Uncoated asbestos cement, clean	142	145	147	150	
Spun cement-lined and spun bitumen-lined, clean	147	149	150	152	153
Smooth pipe (including lead, brass, copper, polyethylene, and PVC), clean	147	149	150	152	153
PVC wavy, clean	142	145	147	150	150
Concrete – Scobey					
Class 1 – Cs = 0.27; clean	69	79	84	90	95
Class 2 – Cs = 0.31; clean	95	102	106	110	113
Class 3 – Cs = 0.345; clean	109	116	121	125	127
Class 4 – Cs = 0.37; clean	121	125	130	132	134
Best – Cs = 0.40; clean	129	133	138	140	141
Tate relined pipes – clean	109	116	121	125	127
Prestressed concrete pipes – clean			147	150	150

Source: Compiled from Lamont, 1981.

Example 4.2 Hazen-Williams equation

Use the Hazen-Williams formula to determine the head loss in a 400 m section of a 300 mm PVC force main. The discharge is 100 L/s.

Solution

Table 4.2 gives the C-factor as 150. Substituting this result into Equation 4.9 gives the head loss as

$$h_L = \frac{10.7 \times 400}{150^{1.852} \times 0.30^{4.87}} 0.10^{1.852} = 1.98 \text{ m}$$

Swamee-Jain Equation

The Swamee-Jain equation (Swamee and Jain, 1976) is much easier to solve than the Colebrook-White equation. This equation is an explicit function of the Reynolds number and the relative roughness,

$$f = \frac{1.325}{\left[\ln\left(\frac{\varepsilon}{3.7D} + \frac{5.74}{\text{Re}^{0.9}}\right)\right]^2} \tag{4.10}$$

It is accurate to within about one percent of the Colebrook-White equation over the following ranges:

$$4 \times 10^3 \leq \text{Re} \leq 1 \times 10^8$$

and

$$1 \times 10^{-6} \leq \frac{\varepsilon}{D} \leq 1 \times 10^{-2}$$

Manning Equation

The *Manning equation* is commonly used for open-channel flow, but can still be used for fully rough closed pipes in the form

$$h_L = \frac{C_f L (nQ)^2}{D^{5.33}} \tag{4.11}$$

where n = Manning roughness coefficient
 C_f = unit conversion factor (4.66 for customary units, 5.29 SI)

Higher n values correspond to greater internal pipe roughness. Manning's n is also commonly assumed to be constant for a given pipe material, although this is not strictly the case (see Chapter 2). Values of n for commonly used pipe materials are presented in Table 2.3 on page 42.

Example 4.3 Manning equation

Use the Manning equation to determine head loss in a 500-ft section of an 18-in. diameter cast iron force main. The discharge is 3000 gpm.

Solution

The discharge must be first converted to ft³/s, which gives

$$Q = \frac{3000 \text{ gpm}}{448.7 \frac{\text{gpm}}{\text{ft}^3/\text{s}}} = 6.69 \text{ ft}^3/\text{s}$$

Substituting this value into Equation 4.11 gives

$$h_L = \frac{4.66 \times 500(0.012 \times 6.69)^2}{1.5^{5.33}} = 1.73 \text{ ft}$$

Pipe Roughness Changes

Wall roughness may change over time because of pipe-wall corrosion or scale deposition. In sewage pipelines, the problem is mainly one of corrosion and/or slime coating. This problem may be mitigated through the use of corrosion-resistant pipe materials or pipe coatings, with associated pipe velocities high enough to minimize slime buildup.

Comparison of Friction Loss Methods

Most hydraulic models allow the modeler to select from the Darcy-Weisbach, Hazen-Williams, or Manning head loss formulas, depending on the nature of the problem and the modeler's preferences.

The Darcy-Weisbach formula is more physically-based than the others. It is derived from the balance of forces acting on flow in pipes (although f is still found empirically). With appropriate fluid viscosities and densities, Darcy-Weisbach can be used to find the head loss in a pipe for any Newtonian fluid in any flow regime.

The Hazen-Williams and Manning formulas, however, are empirically based and generally only apply to water in turbulent flow.

The Hazen-Williams formula is the predominant equation used in the United States for pressure pipes, while the Darcy-Weisbach formula predominates in Europe. The Manning formula is not generally used for pressure flow except with inverted siphons and surcharged sewers. Table 4.3 presents these three equations in several common unit configurations. These equations solve for the friction slope, S_f, which is the head loss per unit length of pipe.

Table 4.3 Pipe friction loss equations.

Equation	Q (m³/s); D (m)	Q (ft³/s); D (ft)	Q (gpm); D (in.)
Darcy-Weisbach	$S_f = \dfrac{0.083 f Q^2}{D^5}$	$S_f = \dfrac{0.025 f Q^2}{D^5}$	$S_f = \dfrac{0.031 f Q^2}{D^5}$
Hazen-Williams	$S_f = \dfrac{10.7}{D^{4.87}} \left(\dfrac{Q}{C}\right)^{1.852}$	$S_f = \dfrac{4.73}{D^{4.87}} \left(\dfrac{Q}{C}\right)^{1.852}$	$S_f = \dfrac{10.5}{D^{4.87}} \left(\dfrac{Q}{C}\right)^{1.852}$

Table 4.3 (Continued) Pipe friction loss equations.

Equation	Q (m³/s); D (m)	Q (ft³/s); D (ft)	Q (gpm); D (in.)
Manning	$S_f = \dfrac{10.3(nQ)^2}{D^{5.33}}$	$S_f = \dfrac{4.66(nQ)^2}{D^{5.33}}$	$S_f = \dfrac{13.2(nQ)^2}{D^{5.33}}$

4.2 Minor Losses

Head losses occurring at fixtures, such as manholes, valves, tees, bends, reducers, and other appurtenances within the piping system, are called *minor losses*. These losses are the result of velocity changes and increased turbulence and eddies caused by the fixture. Although head loss might be quite high in a fixture compared to the same length in the associated pipe, most pipelines are very long, with only a few minor loss fixtures. Therefore, overall, the pipe friction losses are large compared to the fixture or minor losses.

Most minor head losses are computed by multiplying a *minor loss coefficient* by the velocity head, as given by

$$h_m = K_L \frac{V^2}{2g} = K_L \frac{Q^2}{2gA^2} \tag{4.12}$$

where
h_m = minor head loss (ft, m)
K_L = minor loss coefficient
V^2 = average fluid velocity (ft/s, m/s)
g = gravitational acceleration constant (ft/s², m/s²)
Q = pipeline flow rate (ft³/s, m³/s)
A = cross-sectional area of pipe (ft², m²)

Minor loss coefficients are determined experimentally. Table 4.4 is a list of coefficients associated with commonly used fittings.

Table 4.4 Minor loss coefficients.[1]

Fitting	K_L	Fitting	K_L
Pipe Entrance		90° Smooth Bend	
Bellmouth	0.03-0.05	Bend radius/D = 4	0.16–0.18
Rounded	0.12-0.25	Bend radius/D = 2	0.19–0.25
Sharp Edged	0.50	Bend radius/D = 1	0.35–0.40
Projecting	0.80		
		Mitered Bend	
Contraction – Sudden		θ = 15°	0.05
D_2/D_1 = 0.80	0.18	θ = 30°	0.10
D_2/D_1 = 0.50	0.37	θ = 45°	0.20
D_2/D_1 = 0.20	0.49	θ = 60°	0.35
		θ = 90°	0.80

Table 4.4 (Continued) Minor loss coefficients.[1]

Fitting	K_L	Fitting	K_L
Contraction – Conical		Tee	
$D_2/D_1 = 0.80$	0.05	Line Flow	0.30–0.40
$D_2/D_1 = 0.50$	0.07	Branch Flow	0.75–1.80
$D_2/D_1 = 0.20$	0.08		
		Cross	
Expansion – Sudden		Line Flow	0.50
$D_2/D_1 = 0.80$	0.16	Branch Flow	0.75
$D_2/D_1 = 0.50$	0.57		
$D_2/D_1 = 0.20$	0.92	45° Wye	
Expansion – Conical		Line Flow	0.30
$D_2/D_1 = 0.80$	0.03	Branch Flow	0.50
$D_2/D_1 = 0.50$	0.08		
$D_2/D_1 = 0.20$	0.13		

Source: Data from Walski, 1984

[1] D = pipe diameter, θ = downstream bend angle

Minor Loss Valve Coefficients

Most valve manufacturers provide a chart of percent opening versus *valve coefficient*, C_v, which is related to the minor loss, K_L, as

$$K_L = \frac{C_f D^4}{C_v^2} \qquad (4.13)$$

where
D = diameter of the valve (in., m)
C_v = valve coefficient (gpm/psi$^{0.5}$, m^3/s/kPa$^{0.5}$)
C_f = unit conversion factor (880 for US customary units, 1.22 for SI units)

Table 4.5 gives values of minor loss coefficients for valves that are commonly found in wastewater conveyance systems.

Table 4.5 Minor loss coefficients (K_L) for various types of fully open valves.

Valve Type	K_L
Check	
Ball	0.9–1.7
Center-guided globe style	2.6
Double door	
8 in. or smaller	2.5
10–16 in.	1.2
Foot	
Hinged disk	1–1.4
Poppert	5–14

Table 4.5 (Continued) Minor loss coefficients (K_L) for various types of fully open valves.

Valve Type	K_L
Rubber flapper	
V < 6 ft/s	2.0
V > 6 ft/s	1.1
Knife gate	
Metal seat	0.2
Resilient seat	0.3
Plug	
Lubricated	0.5–1.0
Eccentric – rectangular (80%) opening	1.0
Eccentric – full-bore opening	0.5
Slanting disk	0.25–2.0
Swing	0.6–2.2
Diaphragm or pinch	0.2–0.75

Source: Adapted from Sanks, 1998.

Example 4.4 Minor losses

The flow in an 8-in. force main is 900 gpm. The following fittings are encountered along a pipe. What is the total head loss through the junction?
- two 90° smooth bends (bend radius/D = 2)
- knife gate valve, resilient seal – open
- mitered bend, $\theta = 45°$

Solution

The flow rate is

$$Q = \frac{900 \text{ gpm}}{448.7 \frac{\text{gpm}}{\text{ft}^3/\text{s}}} = 2.01 \text{ ft}^3/\text{s}$$

The flow velocity is

$$V = \frac{Q}{A} = \frac{2.01 \text{ ft}^3/\text{s}}{\pi\left(\frac{4}{12}\right)^2} = 5.75 \text{ ft/s}$$

The minor loss coefficients for the fittings are found in Table 4.4 and 4.5 as follows:

two 90° smooth bends (bend radius/D = 2)	$K_L = 2 \times 0.25 = 0.50$
knife gate valve, resilient seal – open	$K_L = 0.30$
mitered bend, $\theta = 45°$	$K_L = 0.20$

The sum of these is the total minor loss coefficient, or

$$\Sigma K_L = 1.00$$

The minor head loss is then given by Equation 4.12 as

$$h_m = 1.0 \frac{5.75^2}{2 \times 32.2} = 0.51 \text{ ft}$$

4.3 Energy Addition – Pumps

Sanitary sewage systems sometimes include pumping stations to lift sewage from deep gravity sewers to collectors for pumping across drainage divides or for moving sewage in flat terrain. The energy added is called *pump head*. The following discussion is oriented toward centrifugal pumps, since they are the pump type most frequently used in sanitary sewage systems. In centrifugal pumps, a rotating impeller transfers the energy from the motor shaft to the water. Figure 4.3 shows an impeller for a large wastewater pump and Figure 4.4 shows a centrifugal pump in a dry well. Additional information about pumps can be found in Bosserman (2000), Hydraulic Institute (2000), Karassik et al. (2001), Sanks (1998), and Water Environment Federation (1993).

Figure 4.3 Impeller for a large wastewater pump.

Pump Head-Discharge Relationship

The relationship between energy added and pump discharge can be shown as a *head versus discharge curve* (also called a *pump head characteristic curve*), as in Figure 4.5. Empirical equations are often used to describe the relationships. *Pump head* (also called total dynamic head) is the difference in head from the suction to the discharge side of the pump. Data on this relationship are usually available from the pump manufacturer. A reasonable fit to experimental data is often obtained with a power function of the form

$$h_p = h_o - cQ_p^m \tag{4.14}$$

Figure 4.4 Centrifugal pump in a dry well.

where
h_p = pump head (ft, m)
h_o = cutoff (shutoff) head (ft, m)
Q_p = pump discharge (ft³/s, m³/s)
c, m = coefficients describing pump curve shape

System Head Curves

The purpose of a pump is to add the energy (head) necessary to overcome elevation differences and head losses. The head necessary to achieve the elevation difference is called *static head* or *static lift*. The head needed to compensate for head losses is added to the static head to obtain the *system head curve*, as illustrated in Figure 4.6.

The pump head characteristic curve shows the hydraulic capability of a given pump. The system head curve presents how the system responds to a range of flow rates introduced into or pumped through the system. The system head curve is continually sliding up and down as wet well water levels change and other pumps discharging into the force main or pressure sewer come on or off. The result is actually a family of system head curves forming a band on the graph. The band is narrow for a sewage pump station with only one pump serving the force main, since wet well depth fluctuations are not normally very large. As described further in Chapter 12, the band can be quite large for force mains with multiple pumps or pressure sewer systems.

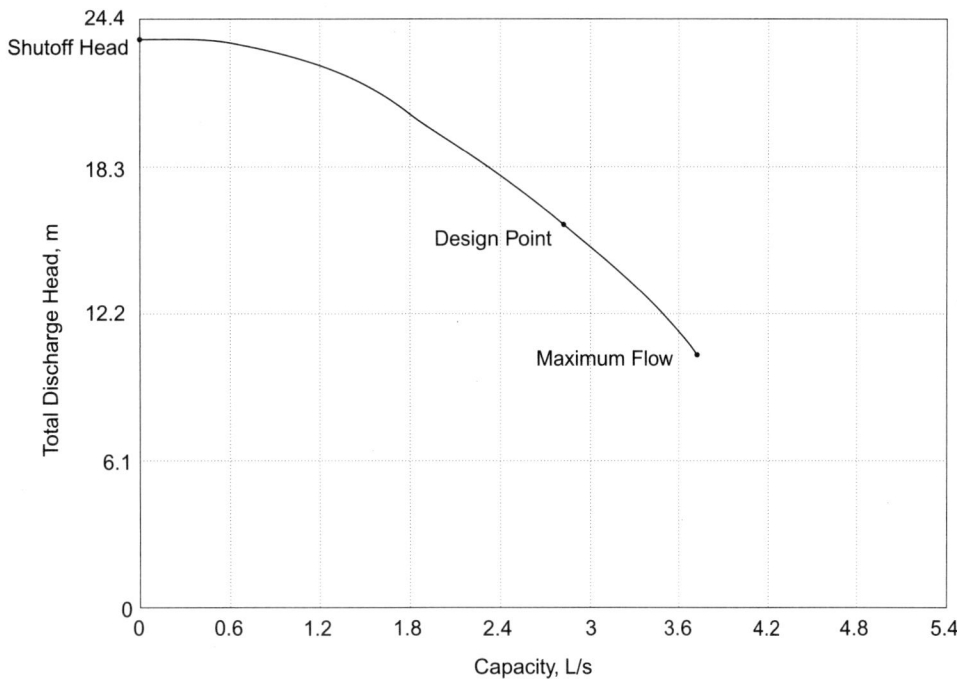

Figure 4.5 Pump head characteristic curve.

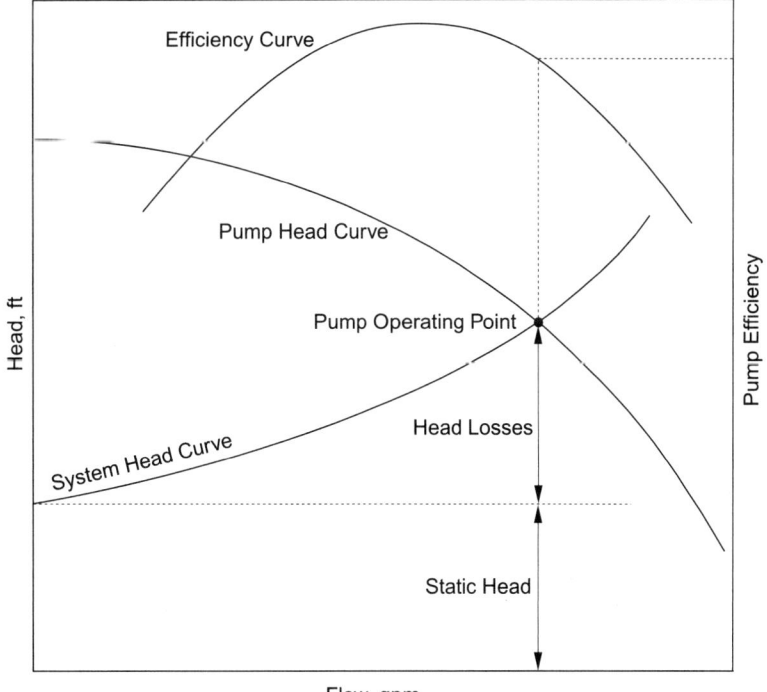

Figure 4.6 Pump curve and system head curve defining the pump operating point.

For the case of a single pipeline between two points, the system head curve is given by

$$H = h_1 + \sum K_p Q^z + \sum K_M Q^2 \qquad (4.15)$$

where
- H = total head (ft, m)
- h_1 = static lift (ft, m)
- K_p = pipe head loss coefficient (s^z/ft^{3z-1}, s^z/m^{3z-1})
- Q = pipe discharge (ft³/s, m³/s)
- z = coefficient
- K_M = minor head loss coefficient (s^2/ft^5, s^2/m^5)

Thus, the head losses and minor losses associated with each segment of pipe are summed along the total length of the pipeline, as illustrated in Figure 4.7.

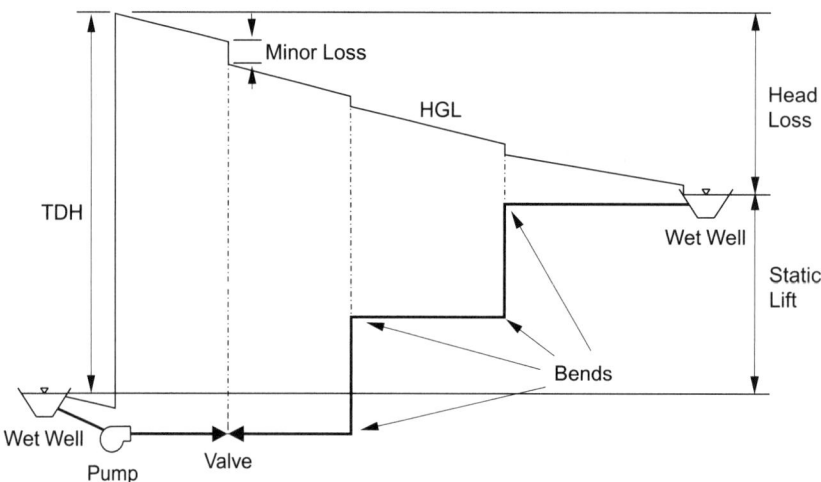

Figure 4.7 Schematic of hydraulic grade line for a pumped system.

When the pump head discharge curve and the system head curve are plotted on the same axes, as in Figure 4.6, the intersection defines the pump *operating point*, which simultaneously satisfies both the pump characteristic curve and the system curve.

Other Pump Characteristic Curves

In addition to the pump head discharge curve, other curves representing pump behavior describe brake horsepower and efficiency. The brake horsepower is the power delivered to the pump for efficient pump operation. Since utilities want to minimize the amount of energy used, the engineer should select pumps that run as efficiently as possible. Pump selection and operating costs are discussed further in Chapter 12.

Another issue to consider when designing a pump in a sewage system is the required *net positive suction head* (NPSH), which is the head at the suction side of a pump. The required NPSH generally increases with flow through the pump. The available NPSH must be greater than the required NPSH to ensure that local pressures within the pump do not drop below the vapor pressure of the fluid and cause cavitation. Cavitation is essentially a boiling and then collapse of the liquid vapor within the pump,

"Please help us reduce our garbage and improve our energy efficiency and our water quality. Help us to be eco-wise and—above all—to empower others."

which can cause damage. The required NPSH is unique for each pump model and is a function of flow rate. Manufacturers' specifications should be consulted to ensure that pumping station design has sufficient NPSH.

In manifolded pumping systems, where many sewage pumping stations may pump into a common force main network, primary design consideration is given to the conditions in the network during peak wet-weather conditions. However, during very low flow conditions, the pressure in the force main network can drop low enough to cause cavitation in an individual pump.

Fixed-Speed and Variable-Speed Pumps

A pump characteristic curve is related to the speed of the pump. The motor of a fixed-speed pump spins it at a constant speed. A variable-speed pump has a variable-speed motor or other device that changes the pump speed.

A variable-speed pump is not really a special type of pump, but rather a pump connected to a variable-speed drive or controller. The most common type of variable-speed drive controls the voltage to the pump motor, which in turn changes the speed at which the motor rotates. Differences in speed then shift the pump's characteristic curve. Variable-speed pumps are useful in locations where large system head variations occur for a given flow rate, such as in a sewer force main with multiple pumps.

Affinity Laws for Variable-Speed Pumps

A centrifugal pump's characteristic curve is fixed for a given rotational speed and impeller diameter. However, for a given model, modified curves can be determined quite accurately for any speed and any diameter by applying *affinity laws*. For variable-speed pumps, two of these affinity laws are

$$\frac{Q_{p1}}{Q_{p2}} = \frac{n_1}{n_2} \tag{4.16}$$

and

$$\frac{h_{p1}}{h_{p2}} = \left(\frac{n_1}{n_2}\right)^2 \tag{4.17}$$

where Q_{p1}, Q_{p2} = pump flow rate (ft³/s, m³/s)
n_1, n_2 = pump speed (1/s)
h_{p1}, h_p = pump discharge head (ft, m)

These relations show that pump discharge rate is directly proportional to pump speed and pump discharge head is proportional to the square of the speed. These equations allow the designer to establish pump curves for other speeds, if the curve is known for a reference speed. They must be applied to the curves and not directly to the operating point. Figure 4.8 shows how pump head curves change with changing pump speed. The line labeled "Best Efficiency Points" is a trace of the best efficiency points at each speed. The actual flow that a pump produces at each speed depends on the system head curve as well.

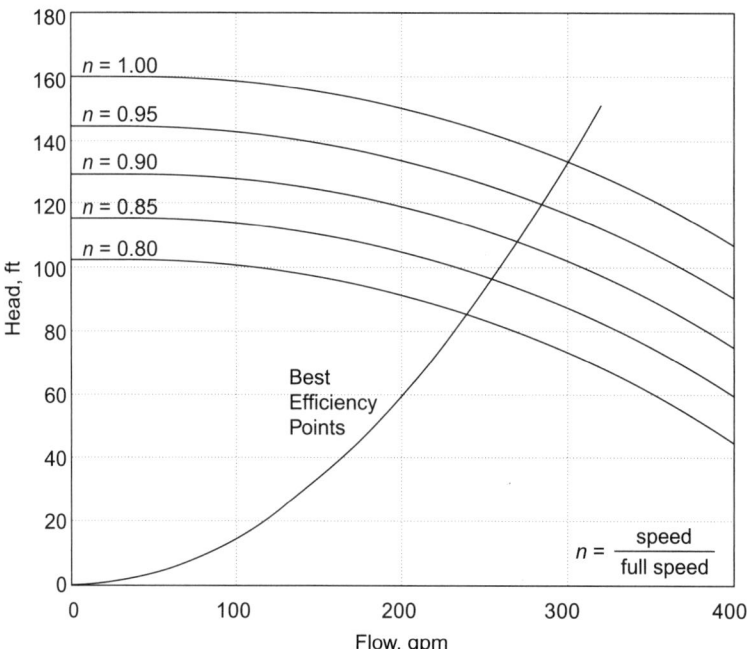

Figure 4.8 Relative speed factors (*n*) for variable-speed pumps.

Power and Efficiency

The term *power* may have one of several meanings when dealing with a pump:
- *Input power* – the power that is delivered to the motor, usually in electrical form.

- *Brake power* – the power that is delivered to the pump from the motor.
- *Water power* – the power that is delivered to the water from the pump.

Energy losses occur as energy is converted from one form to another (electrical to motor, motor to pump, pump to water), and every transfer has an *efficiency* associated with it. The efficiencies associated with these transfers may be expressed either as percentages (100 percent is perfectly efficient) or as decimal values (1.00 is perfectly efficient), and are typically defined as follows:

- *Motor efficiency* – the ratio of brake power to input power.
- *Pump efficiency* – the ratio of water power to brake power.
- *Wire-to-water (overall) efficiency* – the ratio of water power to input power.

Pump efficiency tends to vary significantly with flow, while motor efficiency remains relatively constant over the rated range. Note that there may also be an additional efficiency associated with a variable-speed drive. Some engineers refer to the combination of the motor and speed controls as the *driver*.

Figure 4.9 shows input power (horsepower curves), net positive suction head, and wire-to-water efficiency curves overlaid on typical pump head curves. For each impeller size, there is a flow rate corresponding to maximum efficiency. At higher or lower flows, the efficiency decreases. This maximum point on the efficiency curve is

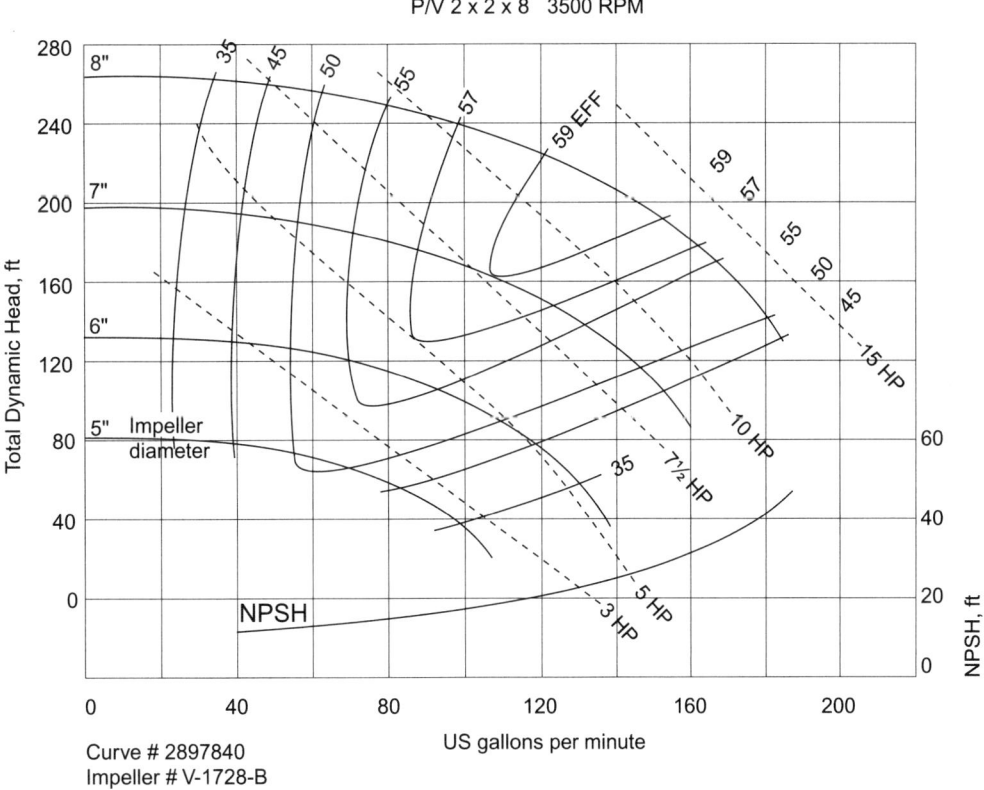

Diagram courtesy of Peerless Pump Company

Figure 4.9 Pump curves with wire-to-water efficiency, net positive suction head (NPSH), and horsepower overlays for different impeller sizes.

called the *best efficiency point* (BEP) and is the ideal operating point for the pump. For example, with a 7-in. impeller, the BEP is at a discharge of 100 gal/min and the wire-to-water efficiency is 59%.

Pump curves are available from suppliers and manufacturers. Every pump differs slightly from its catalog specifications, and normal impeller wear causes a pump's performance to change over time. Pumps should be periodically field tested to verify that the characteristic curves on record are representative of field performance. If a pump is found to be operating at relatively low efficiency, an economic analysis can help to decide among impeller, motor, or complete pump replacement.

References

American Society of Civil Engineers (ASCE). 1992. *Design and Construction of Urban Stormwater Management Systems*. ASCE Manuals and Reports of Engineering Practice No. 77, WEF Manual of Practice FD-20. Reston, VA: American Society of Civil Engineers.

Bosserman, B. E. 2000. Pump system hydraulic design. In *Water Distribution System Handbook*, edited by L. W. Mays. New York: McGraw-Hill.

Hydraulic Institute. 2000. *Pump Standards*. Parsippany, NJ: Hydraulic Institute.

Karassik, I. J., J. P. Messina, P. Cooper, and C. C Heald, eds. 2001. *Pump Handbook*, 3d ed. New York: McGraw-Hill.

Lamont, P. 1981. Common pipe flow formulas compared with the theory of roughness. *Journal of the American Water Works Association* 73, No. 5: 274.

Mays, L. W. ed. 1999. *Hydraulic Design Handbook*. New York: McGraw-Hill.

Moody, L. F. 1944. Friction factors for pipe flow." *Transactions of the American Society of Mechanical Engineers* 66.

Sanks, R. L., ed. 1998. *Pumping Station Design*. 2d ed. London: Butterworth.

Swamee, P. K. and A. K. Jain. 1976. Explicit equations for pipe flow problems. *Journal of Hydraulic Engineering*, ASCE 102, No. 5: 657.

Walski, T. M. 1984. *Analysis of Water Distribution Systems*. New York: Van Nostrand Reinhold.

Water Environment Federation (WEF). 1993. *Design of Wastewater and Stormwater Pumping Stations*. MOP FD-4. Alexandria, VA: Water Environment Federation.

Williams, G. S., and Hazen, A. (1920) *Hydraulic Tables*. New York: John Wiley and Sons.

Problems

4.1 From the following figure, estimate the water pressure (in lb/in.²) entering the pipe at the bottom of the tank.

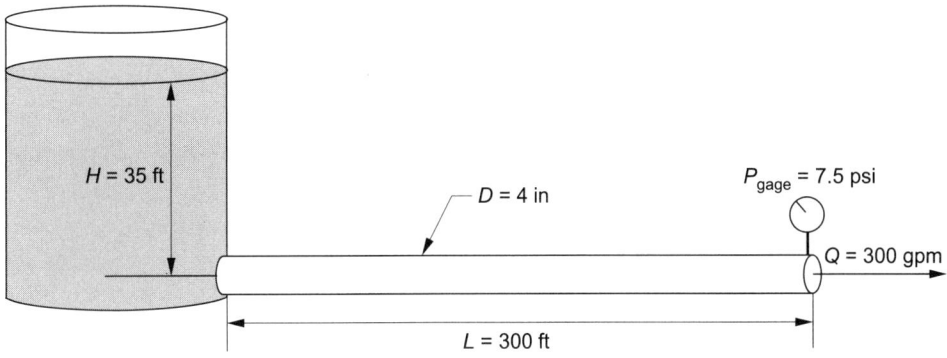

4.2 For the system in Problem 4.1, estimate the head loss due to friction in the pipe from the tank to the pressure gauge. The pipe has a sharp edged entrance.

4.3 For the system in Problem 4.1, estimate the Darcy-Weisbach friction factor (f) and the Hazen-Williams C-factor.

4.4 Determine the Reynolds number in the 4-in. pipe in the system in Problem 4.1 if the water temperature is 50° F.

   a. Is the flow laminar, transitional, or turbulent?

   b. Estimate the equivalent sand roughness height (ε) of the pipe.

4.5 Determine the flow rate in the 150-mm PVC pipe shown in the following figure, using

   a. the Darcy-Weisbach equation

   b. the Hazen-Williams equation

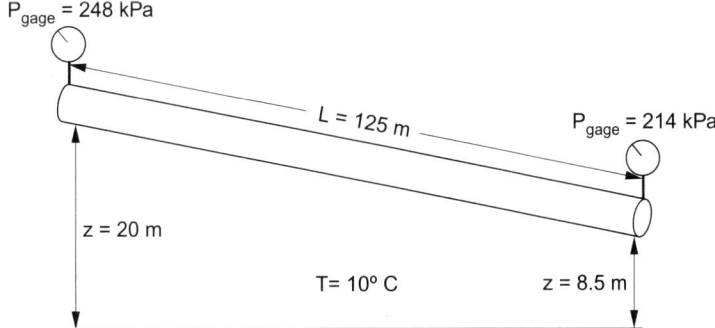

4.6 Explain why the flow rates found by the two methods in Problem 4.5 are different. What could be done to either the Darcy-Weisbach or Hazen-Williams equation to force the determined flow rates to be equal?

4.7 Estimate the minor loss coefficient for a partially closed 205-mm gate valve if the measured flow rate is 0.062 m³/s and the pressure drop is 30.3 kPa.

4.8 Estimate the discharge flow rate from the 6-in. cast iron pipe illustrated in the following figure. Use the Darcy-Weisbach equation to estimate the friction losses.

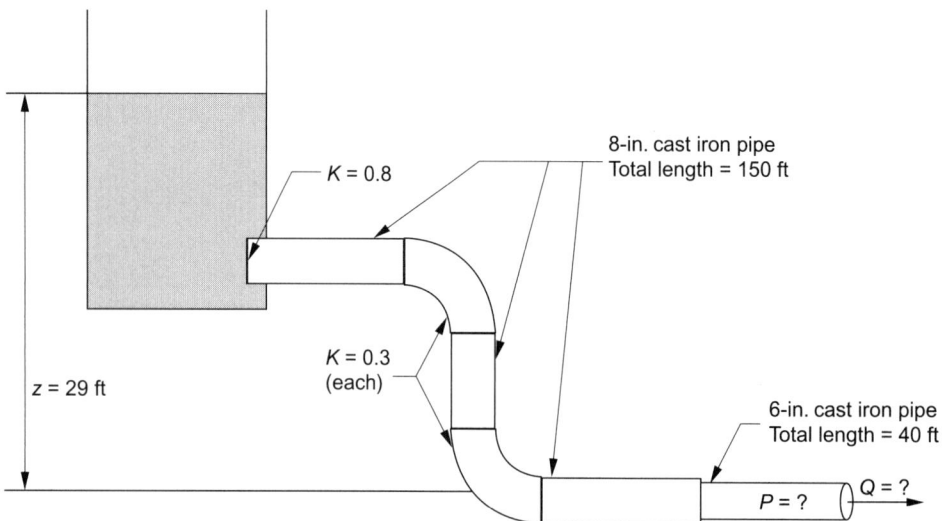

4.9 For the system in Problem 4.8, determine the gauge pressure in the 6-in. cast iron pipe located 20 ft from the discharge end.

4.10 Determine the pump head (h_p) for a centrifugal pump lifting water 9.1 m in a 180-m, 205 mm. pipe ($f = 0.019$) at a flow rate of 0.06 m³/s. The sum of the minor loss coefficients is 5.70.

4.11 Derive the system head curve to lift water 45 ft in 2500 ft of 8-in. new ductile (cast) iron pipe. The sum of the minor loss coefficients is 7.35. Clearly indicate the units of flow (Q) in the equation.

a. Use the Darcy-Weisbach equation to model friction losses. Clearly indicate how you determined the friction factor (f). Do you expect the friction factor to be constant? Why or why not?

b. Use the Hazen-Williams equation to model friction losses.

4.12 A pump system was installed to deliver water with a system curve defined as h_p (ft) $= 53.4 + 0.000097Q^2$ with Q in gpm. Use the following pump performance curve to determine the shutoff head and flow rate, total static head, and total dynamic head at the operating point.

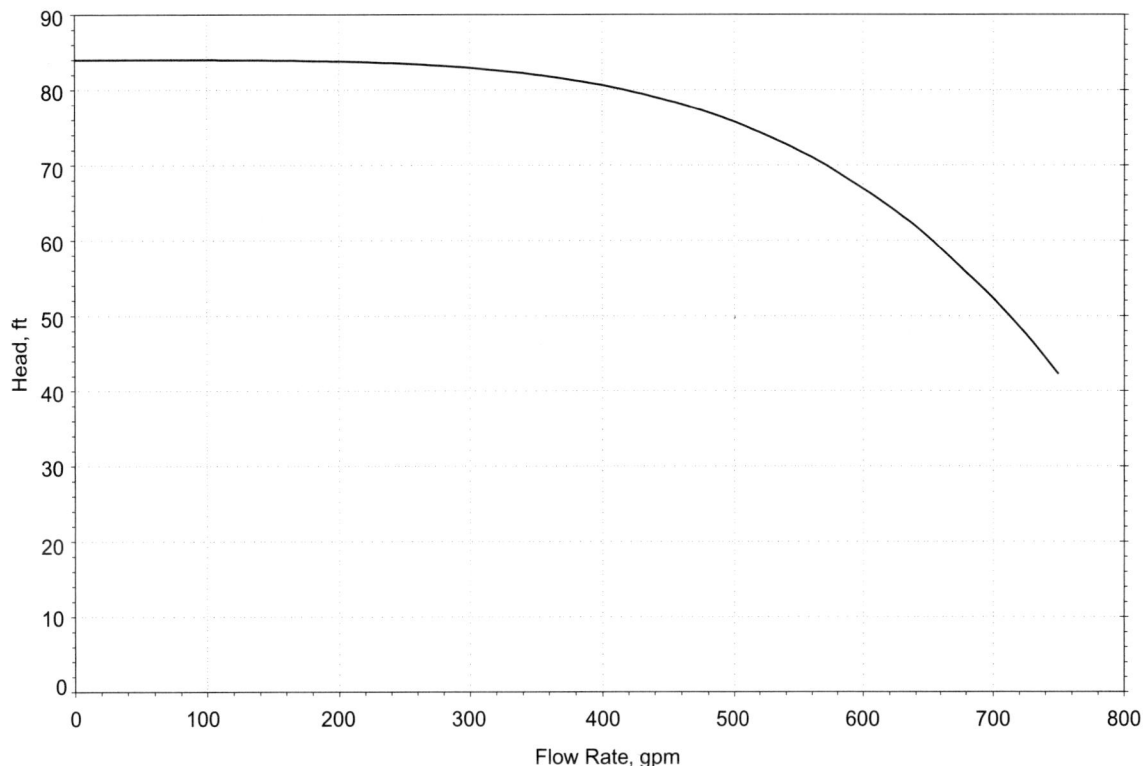

CHAPTER

5

Model Construction

A sewer network model is a mathematical description of a real sewer system. Models are used by designers, managers, and planners to simulate the performance of existing and proposed sewers under a variety of loading scenarios. They can be used to evaluate various designs in new sewer systems, expansion of existing systems, the rehabilitation of overloaded and degraded systems, and the operation of sewer networks. Simulations allow designers to evaluate the trade-offs among options and determine a cost-effective design that meets the goals of the system owner.

Recall from Chapter 1 that a *computer model* is a computer program that contains one or more mathematical models describing the flow in sewer networks. A *system model* is a computer model that contains all the data necessary to describe a particular system. Assembling a system model can be thought of as starting with a computer program and entering data so that the program can simulate the hydraulic behavior of the system.

This chapter presents an overview of the development and application of models for sewer systems. The steps required to apply a model to a particular system are described. Finally, the techniques for incorporating the elements of sewers (pipes, manholes, and pumps) into a site-specific model are described.

5.1 Developing the Modeling Plan

As with any endeavor in which the result is to be achieved efficiently and in logical order, the modeling process must begin with a plan. It is desirable that utility personnel, from upper management through engineering, operations, and maintenance, commit to the modeling effort in terms of human resources, time, and funding. Meetings with management, design engineers, and sewer system operators are needed to confirm the purpose of the modeling project. Additionally, it is important to know what is to be modeled, what data will be gathered for the model, and how the model will be calibrated to ensure that it reflects the real sewer system. Technical, schedule, budget, and resource issues must be addressed at the planning stage rather than in the middle of model assembly. The roles and responsibilities of members of the modeling team must be clearly identified.

The format of the plan and the level of detail are a matter of organizational preference. At a minimum, this plan should include

- Definition of purpose and objectives
- Criteria for the selection of the computer model
- Listing of the required data
- Plans for collecting and validating input data prior to entering it into the model
- Procedure for calibration of the model and calibration criteria
- Model validation criteria, to ensure that model calibration has not resulted in a forced fit
- Description of the applications of model results
- Schedule
- Budget
- Staff roles and responsibilities.

The plan should be flexible so it can respond to unexpected events.

5.2 The Modeling Process

In general, to successfully create and manage a sewer model, the modeler must become familiar with the basic principles of sewage system design and operation, appreciate the range of hydraulic conditions encountered in the actual system, and understand the fundamental strengths and limitations of the fluid mechanics that are programmed into the modeling software. Further, the modeler must understand the purpose of modeling the sewer network and the range of model applications. From defining the problem to developing and using a model to assist in the development of a solution, modeling can seem to be an overwhelming task. As with any large task, it is easier to break it into smaller, manageable subtasks. Figure 5.1 illustrates the sequence of tasks that make up the modeling process.

Purpose and Objectives of a Model

The six general reasons for creating a sewer model were introduced in Chapter 1. The modeling process begins with a clear definition of the objectives of the modeling project. Examples of objectives corresponding to purposes are presented in Table 5.1. It is expected that most models will have multiple purposes and hence multiple objectives.

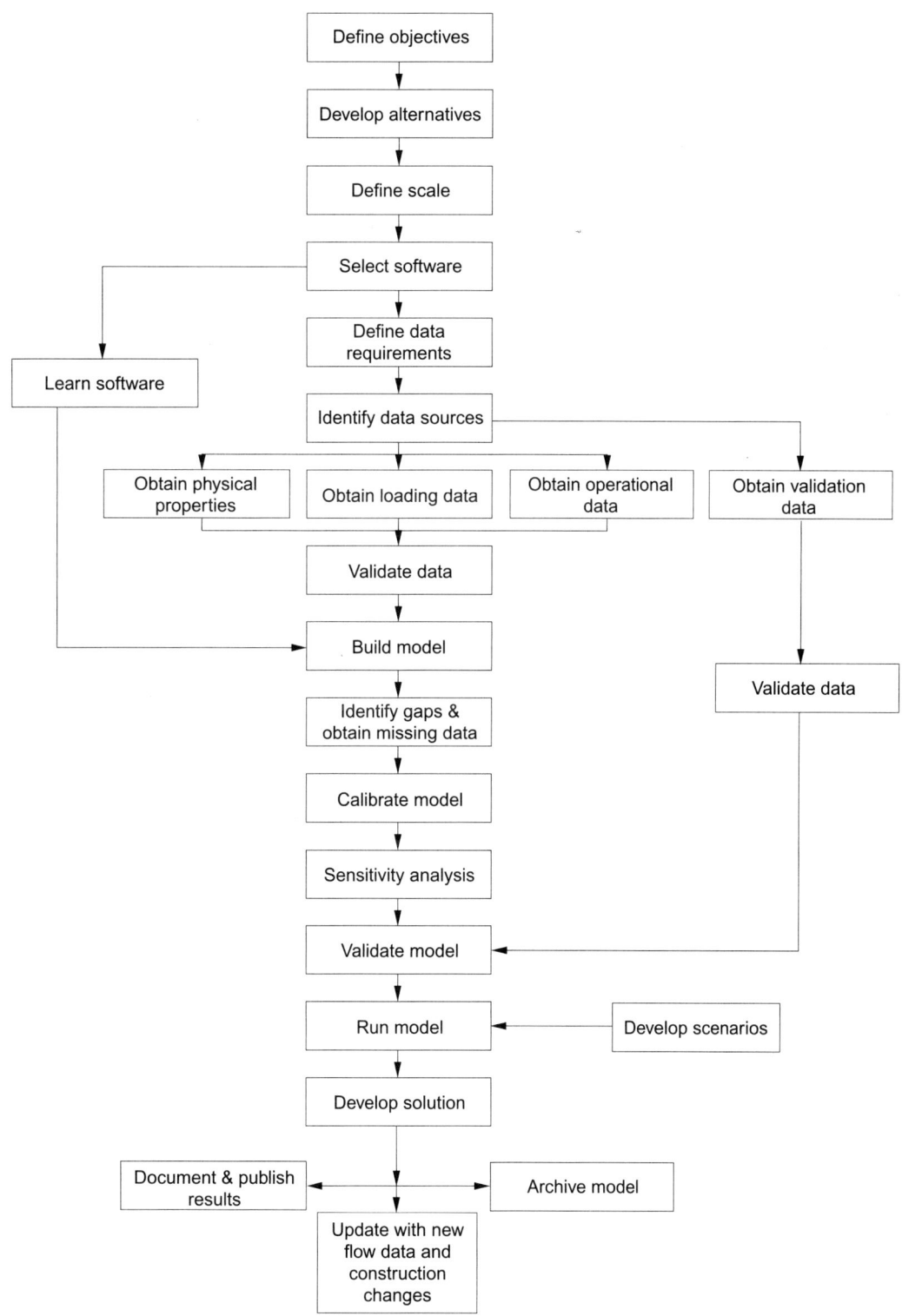

Figure 5.1 Sequence of tasks in the modeling process.

Table 5.1 Examples of sewer-modeling objectives.

Purpose of Model	Examples of Objectives
Design of new systems	• Determine optimum configuration of laterals, collectors, and force mains. • Determine required size of pipes, pumps, wet wells, and elevations.
Long-range master planning	• Identify potential problem areas resulting from growth. • Determine location and capacity of new pumping stations. • Prepare cost estimates for alternative schemes.
Rehabilitation	• Identify causes of sewer overflows. • Assess the hydraulic improvements resulting from replacement or relining of pipes.
Operation and maintenance	• Analyze downstream flows resulting from pump-control strategies. • Analyze alternative wet weather flow-control schemes. • Analyze pump station operation effectiveness. • Determine sections of the sewer system prone to siltation.
Water-quality studies	• Determine location, frequency, and water quality of sewer overflows. • Determine effect of sewer flows on treatment plant operation. • Analyze options to reduce frequency and volume of overflows.
Regulatory compliance	• CMOM[1] program – demonstrate system has adequate capacity to convey base and peak flows. • CSO Policy – demonstrate system can capture 85% of combined sewage collected.

[1] Capacity assurance, management, operations, and maintenance; see Chapter 15.

Design of New Systems. In design studies, the model is used to determine where gravity mains and force mains are required; alignments; estimated pipe, wet well, and pump sizes; and invert elevations. Hydraulic profiles are generally calculated under different flow scenarios to keep the flow contained within the conveyance system. Velocities during low flows are calculated to minimize solids deposition.

In design studies for land development, the engineer usually starts with unsewered land and must lay out a collection system that is compatible with the overall site plan and will have a minimum of high-maintenance facilities, such as pump stations and inverted siphons. In some cases, the engineer must make trade-offs between gravity systems, gravity systems with pump stations and force mains, low-pressure systems, and vacuum systems. Usually the primary known feature in design is the point where the collection system will connect to an existing sewer or a treatment facility.

Long-Range Master Planning. Master planning projects may include projecting system growth and sewer flows up to twenty years or more. A model can be used to identify potential problems (such as sanitary sewer overflow locations or inadequate flushing velocities) and to stage, size, and locate the construction of new trunk lines and pumping stations in concert with growth and development. This type of study usually involves trade-offs between size (cost) of facilities and the ability to handle future loads. During these studies, alternative configurations and cost estimates are developed.

Long-range planning usually involves projecting when sewers will be installed in a drainage basin, what flow will be generated from that basin, and when facilities should be brought on line. Analyses often involve trade-offs between small facilities needed to serve the initial customers in a basin vs. much larger facilities needed to serve that basin on full buildout.

Rehabilitation. In a rehabilitation study, a model may be used to quantify degraded hydraulic performance caused by I/I, partially blocked lines, and collapsed structures. The extent of improved hydraulics resulting from fixing or replacing degraded structures or installing relief sewers can be determined. Models can be used to identify areas where I/I reduction can lead to reduction or elimination of overflows. Model results are used both to define short-term repairs and to develop a cost-effective, long-term rehabilitation plan.

Operations and Maintenance. Models can help operations and maintenance staff identify the effects of proposed actions. With a model, it is possible to test the effects of changes to pump-on and pump-off settings in wet wells, control settings of variable-speed pumps, and the operation of flow-control structures before such actions are implemented.

Water-Quality Studies. A sewer network model may be used to provide input or be incorporated into a watershedwide water-quality model. The sewer network model quantifies the flows (quantity and frequency) and loads of contaminants discharged to surface waters. It can then be used to improve operation and reduce frequency and volume of overflows. Linkage may be dynamic or the sewer network model may be run separately and the output imported into the water-quality model.

Regulatory Compliance. In the United States, operators of sewer systems are required to demonstrate that their systems have adequate capacity, as described in Chapter 15. Utility operators may demonstrate compliance with these regulatory requirements using hydraulic sewer models.

For combined sewers or systems where overflows occur, operators may need to quantify the frequency and duration of the overflows. The network model used for this analysis must adequately quantify I/I, and may need to simulate as much as a year's operation.

Develop Alternatives

A basic list of anticipated model scenarios is developed in the initial stage of the modeling process, particularly if the sewer system owner outsources the modeling work. This not only helps in the selection of the software, but also in compensation negotiations between the system owner and the modeler.

The relative cost of making additional model runs is low compared to the cost of building the model. However, there are subsequent costs of analyzing the model results and converting the results to financial information. But the additional data often prove extremely valuable when making decisions that may involve millions of dollars of system improvements.

Scales of Models

The scale of a model and its level of detail are determined after the objectives of the model have been defined. In general, models may be classified as either macroscale or microscale. A *macroscale model* is used for general planning or evaluation of the entire sewer system or a large part of it. A *microscale model* is used for detailed analysis of specific locations within a sewer system. It is not unusual for macroscale and microscale models to be used together when assessing an entire sewer system and many of its components. For example, the results of a microscale model of a pumping station and resulting hydraulic effects could be used as input data for a macroscale model of the entire sewer system containing the pumping station.

Macroscale Models. This type of model provides a general understanding of an entire trunk sewer network or a large part thereof. These models tend to be highly simplified (skeletonized) and the results must be interpreted with the understanding that much of the sewer system detail was removed. The number of nodes per 1000 population are typically in the range of two to six (WaPUG, 1998).

Typical objectives requiring a macroscale model are to

- Identify potential hydraulic problems throughout the sewer system
- Assess the entire sewer system from a planning perspective
- Identify possible "big-picture" hydraulic updating schemes and enable holistic analysis of the interactions among various components of the system
- Establish the effects of extreme or wet weather flows and the capacity of the sewer system
- Establish the hydraulic operation of sewer overflows and bypasses, so that a broad assessment of water-quality problems can be undertaken
- Provide boundary conditions for the outlet from detailed modeling studies.

For this level of analysis, the system must be divided into fairly large areas for developing loading information.

Microscale Models. This type of model provides a detailed understanding of a small area or specific component of a sewer system. These models do not have a great degree of skeletonization or simplification. The number of nodes is likely to include most or all of the manholes within the modeled area (WaPUG, 1998). Typical objectives requiring a microscale model are

- Design or evaluation of a sewer system in a small development or local area
- Evaluation of a pumping station and nearby pipes and auxiliary structures

"How do we tell the kids that we're edible again?"

- Simulation of the hydraulic conditions for a specific localized area
- Detailed understanding of collection system performance.

The distinction between macro- and micro-level models is becoming less significant as more utilities build models that include all pipes and manholes or that exclude only the relatively small-diameter pipes. While this level of detail represents overkill for most studies, this trend has been made possible to a great extent by the ability to import data for model creation directly from CAD or GIS systems, as described in Chapter 14. Including all pipes in the model is advantageous for a wastewater utility when the need for localized problem-solving arises.

Software Selection and Training

Purchasing the software is an important early step in modeling. Available modeling software varies greatly in the ability to simulate various hydraulic conditions, handle complex loading schemes, analyze variations, and present the output in a usable format.

General-purpose software packages, such as spreadsheets, have and continue to be used to model sewer systems. However, programs with advanced graphical user interfaces and data-handling capabilities designed specifically for modeling sewer systems are now the state of the art.

Suggested criteria for selection of software include

- Applicability for the conditions to be modeled
- Direct experience or access to experienced users of the software
- Costs (acquisition, licensing, and training)
- Required skill levels
- Compatibility with the existing computer system (hardware and software)
- Ease of data input
- Data exchange capability (e.g., GIS)
- Presentation of the results
- Acceptance by the professional community
- Training and support offered by the supplier
- Long-term viability of the supplier.

Assuming that the modeler knows the basics of collection-system hydraulics and loading, one of the first steps in using the model is getting trained in the mechanics of the particular model.

Define Data Requirements

The project objectives and modeling software dictate the data requirements. Models need both spatial and temporal data that cover the expected range for which the system is to be designed. For example, if the model is being developed to redesign a pumping station within a sewer system, the collected data should include the physical design of the nearby sewer network (pipe sizes, lengths, manhole locations) and the measured and expected hydraulic loads.

In order to organize the data-collection process, data requirements are classified into the six categories in Table 5.2. Examples of specific requirements for each category are listed in the second column. Data sources are given in the third column and are discussed more fully in the following section. Where wet weather flows are significant, additional data are required, depending on the modeling approach. See Chapter 7 for additional discussion of modeling wet weather flows.

Table 5.2 Data requirements and sources.

Category	Data Requirement — Data	Data Sources
Network layout	• x & y coordinates of each pipe segment and manhole • Locations of wet wells and appurtenances • Pipe connectivity and lengths • Pipe diameters and materials • Pipe invert levels • Manhole elevations • Manhole lid types	• Construction/record drawings • Corporate GIS system • Asset-management systems • Work orders • Field survey
Hydraulic properties	• Pipe friction factors • Pump curves	• Manufacturers' specifications • Contractor submittals • Literature values • Field tests
Sanitary flows (domestic, industrial, and commercial)	• Location of each source • Min, max, mean daily flows • Diurnal patterns	• Construction/record drawings • Maps, aerial photos • Census data • Growth projections • Water billing records • Land-use data
Wet weather flows	• Infiltration rate for each pipe segment or subbasin • Locations of inflows • Quantities of inflow • Location, dates and quantities of overflows	• Field inspection • Field measurements • Analysis of treatment plant flows • Hydrologic analysis • Literature values
Operation data	• Settings for pump operation • Settings of flow-control structures • Control strategies • Flows to treatment plants • Pumped quantities	• Interviews with operations personnel • Operations records and manuals • Field inspection • Customer complaints • Maintenance records
Calibration data	• Recorded depth and rate of flow • Frequency and locations of overflows • Surface elevations • Precipitation • Rain gauge locations	• Field inspection • Field measurements • Operations records • Weather records • Flow-monitoring program

Identify Data Sources

Model data are obtained from a variety of sources and the availability of these data and their accuracy vary greatly. While the system maps and record drawings are usually readily available and generally accurate, the data needed for future planning, such as demographic changes and future land use, are fairly speculative. Once the data are located, they must be evaluated for their suitability to the needs of the model.

Any existing reports describing previously compiled analyses should be reviewed, verified, and incorporated, where applicable.

The modeler may have a choice of data sources. For example, pipe inverts may be obtained from construction or record drawings or they may be obtained from a field survey. Inflows may be estimated by hydrologic methods using precipitation and land-cover data or they may be measured in the sewer by the methods discussed in Chapter 8. The choice of data source is a trade-off between data quality (accuracy and completeness) and the cost of obtaining data. Often, data are combined from multiple sources for model input.

The accuracy of input data must also be evaluated. It may be enough to know pipe lengths to the nearest 10 ft (3 m), but pipe invert elevations should be known to the nearest 0.1 ft (0.03 m) or even 0.01 ft (0.003 m). Note that in sewer models the pipe length is usually measured to the center of the manhole.

System Maps and Record Drawings. The system maps and record drawings provide most of the information about the physical layout of an existing sewer system. The physical characteristics, location, and elevation of pipes; location and elevation of other system components such as manholes, pumping stations, and outfalls; and the sewer system boundaries are often shown on maps.

With modern models, it is possible to directly import the topology of the sewer system from digital maps. Digital maps are created or transferred into the project database with computer-aided design (CAD) or geographical information system (GIS) software. For systems that only have paper maps, digitizing those maps into a CAD or GIS system may be a worthwhile first step in modeling.

It is important that system maps be reviewed to confirm that they reflect the current state of the sewer system and that maps developed at different times use the same datum. For details of specific system components, the record drawings may be useful; this is especially true for details needed for pumping stations.

Operational Records. Many sewer utilities have records of their sewer operations. Records of pumping frequency and volumes from pumping stations, metered flows into wastewater treatment facilities, and flows from major industrial sources should be identified. Some of the most useful operational records come from SCADA and telemetry systems and field operators.

Field Surveys. Field surveys provide the most-accurate three-dimensional coordinates of sewer network features. However, survey data typically cost more than data from other sources. Surveys can be used to verify data from construction drawings and to fill in data gaps. Global positioning systems (GPS) can lower the cost of this data collection, but the modeler must know the accuracy of GPS data. Elevation data may not be as accurate as *x-y* data. However, the accuracies of today's high-end GPS systems rival those of conventional surveys.

Field Inspections. Field inspections are used to fill in missing information and to spot-check written records. Visits to pump stations can show if any equipment has been replaced since the original construction. Operators may install modified impellers or switch out pumps altogether; hence, it is important to know the actual pumps in the pumping station. Often it will be necessary to undertake field tests at pumping stations to determine the characteristic curve for each pump. Additional tests may include flow monitoring (see Chapter 8) or smoke and dye tests (see Chapter 11).

Other Data Sources. It is likely that the modeler will need to identify other data sources to create a complete model that reflects the sewer system and meets the objective requirements. The data needed depend upon the objectives of the model. The following are some of the potential sources of additional data:

- Historical reports and documents
- Manufacturers of sewer pipe and ancillary structures
- Hydrologic reports and surveys
- Land-use, cover, and building-location maps
- Census and planning projection data
- Water-consumption data, particularly for industrial/commercial sites
- Customer complaint / flooding records
- Records of major contributors to wastewater loads
- Local government agencies
- Local planning or zoning groups
- State agencies for water resources or environmental protection
- US Environmental Protection Agency (US EPA)
- US Geological Survey (USGS)
- National Weather Service (NWS)
- US Department of Agriculture (USDA) soil maps.

Collect Data

System Data. The system data for the sewer system must be gathered from sewer system maps and sewer operators. The physical data can be gathered from the system maps and record documents and include the following:

- Sewer pipe length, diameter, and material
- Invert and ground elevations
- Manhole locations
- Pump types and number
- Wet well dimensions
- Age and evidence of deterioration.

In most sewer systems, there are differences between the design specifications and the existing sewers. Deviations from the design specifications should be noted on record drawings and may also be determined from the sewer operators. The modeler must communicate with the people who work on the sewer system daily and should not overlook the knowledge that these people possess. Incomplete or out-of-date construction records must be updated by field surveys, or else assumptions will have to be made about the system to complete the connections.

Sanitary Loading Data. Obtaining sewage flow (loading) data is a fundamental step in designing a sewer system. Sanitary flows consist of wastewater from residential properties and institutional, commercial, and industrial facilities.

For a more in-depth discussion of estimating wastewater flows, see Chapters 6 and 11.

Wet Weather Flow. Most systems handle sanitary flows well, but have trouble with wet weather flows. Although there are methods to predict wet weather flow for either separate or combined systems, flow monitoring is necessary to understand the relations between sewer flow and rainfall. Chapter 7 describes how to determine wet weather flow, while Chapter 8 explains the data collection necessary for model calibration.

Operational Data. The operational data for a sewage system include information such as pump controls and regulator settings. Equipment information is available in manuals and may be programmed into the SCADA (supervisory control and data acquisition) system. In addition, system operators may have knowledge of these data. Interviewing the operators is important because operators can often provide insights different from those of the engineers and managers.

Calibration Data. Calibration data (such as flow rates, precipitation, and water elevation changes) are gathered to compare the model results to the measured values in the sewer system. If there are discrepancies between the model and the field data, the sources of the discrepancies must be identified. The model is then modified and adjusted to create results that are observed in the real sewer system.

It is good practice to use multiple calibration data sets to confirm that the model accurately simulates a variety of conditions. For example, calibration data can be gathered for dry and wet weather conditions and peak, average, and minimum flows.

Validate the Data

The modeler must establish that the data are acceptable and sufficient for model calibration. This process is referred to as *data verification and validation*. Definitions for data verification and validation have been developed for measurements of chemicals in the environment (US EPA, 2002); however, there are no standard definitions of these terms for hydraulic sewer models. In general, the modeler must determine that the data were collected and processed according to suitable methods (data verification) and meet the requirements for model calibration (data validation).

The following are examples of criteria that the modeler may use to assess the data:

- Are the data complete?
- Are the slopes, depths, and pipe sizes reasonable?
- Are the flow measurements consistent for similar days?
- Is there mass balance in the system?

Build the Model

The model-building step consists of adding data and parameters to the software. Procedures used to model specific features and components of the collection system are described in detail in Section 5.3.

Identify Data Gaps

Where existing records do not provide all the information required for the study, it is necessary to obtain the missing details, if possible, within the constraints of financial and schedule limitations. When historic and system inventory data are being gathered, efforts should include a gap analysis. Gap analysis identifies sources of missing data and where further data collection is necessary. This analysis should include determining where current data-collection activities could be improved.

Sensitivity Analysis

A sensitivity analysis should be performed to determine how model results vary in response to changes in parameters. In simple models the sensitivity is readily apparent. For example, when using the Manning equation to describe steady gravity flow in a sewer pipe, velocity is directly proportional to the square root of the slope and inversely proportional to the roughness coefficient. However, in a sophisticated sewer model, the response of the model at one location relative to changes in flows or parameters at another location may not be obvious. Combinations of parameters may have unpredictable interactive effects.

The sensitivity is analyzed by making model runs while varying more input parameters. These parameters are varied for a range of values that are expected to be encountered, and the effect to the output results are analyzed. For example, it could be observed that the model output is sensitive to the pressure in a force main leaving a pumping station but insensitive to the water level in the wet well feeding the pumping station. Interactive effects between parameters should also be analyzed. The results of the sensitivity analysis guide the calibration process (ASCE, 1992a).

Calibrate the Model

Models of existing systems should be calibrated and verified before they can be properly applied. As described in Chapter 9, model calibration consists of adjusting the sewer system attributes within reasonable limits to obtain simulated results that closely replicate actual field-monitored flows and depths and operator observations. During the calibration, the modeler should develop an appreciation of the sensitivity of the model to changes in various parameters.

Validate the Model

Model validation entails comparing results simulated by the calibrated model with information from events not used in the calibration process. This verifies that the representation of the collection system reasonably predicts monitored flows and depths and provides a robust platform for assessing system performance for a variety of events.

Once the model has been calibrated and validated, it is important to assess whether it can be used for its intended purpose. At all stages of using a hydraulic model, it is important to be aware of any limitations and inaccuracies that might influence the quality and reliability of the simulation results. The following key questions should be addressed to assess the utility of calibrated models (HR Wallingford, 1998):

- Is the model detailed enough at the points of interest?
- Did the model operate correctly over the spatial and temporal range for which it was intended?
- Did the model correctly simulate surcharge if it is going to be used to assess the performance of the system under extreme events?
- Did the pumping stations operate as expected?
- Will the model have to be altered to allow for planned changes in development area?
- Are there structures or situations that the model can not replicate?
- For which model parameters are the results sensitive or insensitive?
- What is the uncertainty in the model results?

It is important to realize that as simulated events move away from the range of data for which the model was calibrated, the accuracy of the model becomes suspect. As a result, features of the sewer system or data errors that were not thought to have a major effect may now have a significant role in the model results. For example, small errors of acceptable proportion when calibrating the model may become progressively more significant, leading to large errors for extreme conditions (e.g., a 1-in. storm in contrast to a 4-in. storm). Owing to the complexity of flow behavior in sewage systems during surcharged conditions, the model results cannot be expected to be as accurate or as consistent, unless the model has been built with sufficient detail and calibrated with a data set that includes surcharge events.

Run Simulations

Once the model has been created (and calibrated if an existing sewer system is involved), it can be used for a variety of analyses. The value of the model lies in being able to examine various "what if" scenarios. The modeler should have some idea of the kinds of scenarios that will be simulated using the model. It is usually a good idea to develop a range of scenarios in conjunction with management, engineering, and operations personnel from the utility. The modeler should not be satisfied with developing a single solution, but should examine a range of solutions so that the best one in terms of costs and benefits can be determined. It costs very little to make additional runs of a model, and the potential savings can be large.

A variety of conditions are usually simulated using the model, such as

- Wet weather loading vs. dry weather loading
- System design modifications (such as different pipe sizes, manhole locations, pumping station modifications, and locations where force mains discharge into gravity systems)
- Effects of potential problems within the system, such as pipe blockages or breaks

> ## Modeling Caveats
>
> There are many pitfalls in collection system modeling. The list below is based on Huber and Dickinson (1988).
>
> 1. Have specific project and modeling objectives and don't let modeling capabilities dictate objectives.
> 2. Use personnel who understand both the engineering fundamentals and the practical aspects of the problem.
> 3. Use the simplest model suitable for the job. For example, don't use a dynamic St. Venant equation solver when a steady-state solution will do.
> 4. Start with simple systems to get a feel for the software.
> 5. Don't use models to generate data. Use real data to verify models.
> 6. Examine results critically. Are results realistic?
> 7. Verify the model with data independent from the calibration data.
> 8. Be skeptical of results. Models can be trusted only to the extent they have been verified. For new system design, models are only are good as the data and projections used.
> 9. Modeling needs to be done in conjunction with operations and maintenance personnel. Get them involved early and develop a good relationship with them.
> 10. Garbage in = Garbage out.

- Effects of reducing the I/I wet weather flow component on pipes, pump stations, and treatment capacity
- Alternative system operating strategies
- Effects of varying tailwater conditions.

How these simulations are managed and interpreted is the key to using a model effectively. The simulations should be done in a logical and constructive way to ensure that all the objectives for the model are evaluated. The initial simulations should be simple, with minor modifications to the calibrated model. Conduct simulations by modifying the existing system or operational loads to assess the effects as the model becomes less like the existing system. This method can help in understanding the conditional limits of the real sewer system and provide greater confidence when modifying or designing the sewer system.

Develop Solutions

The results of model simulations should provide the information required to meet the project objectives. Summarizing model results and communicating them to others requires organizing the large amount of information generated. Many software packages include tools that generate customized graphs and reports, and some can generate video files showing selected behaviors of the sewer over time.

A model should be viewed as an asset of the sewer utility. During a study, files must be backed up frequently to protect against a hard disk crash or other problem. After a study, files should be saved in several places so that runs can be reconstructed or the model reused in another study.

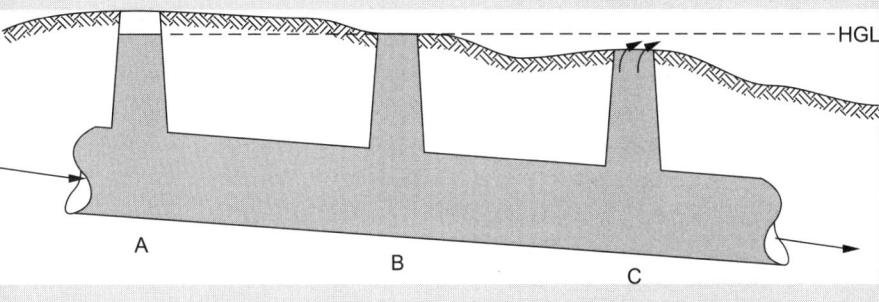

Surcharging

Sewer surcharging typically occurs in high-flow or flooding conditions when the hydraulic grade line (flow line) rises above the top of the pipe. Some sewer systems are designed to surcharge, while others are not. Surcharging occurs at low points in the system during high wet-weather loads with excess inflow and infiltration upstream, but could also occur if the sewer pipe is partially blocked by an obstruction or has collapsed.

In the model, the extent of surcharge is determined by comparing the hydraulic grade line and the pipe crown. If the hydraulic grade line falls between the top of the pipe and the ground elevation (as shown in manhole A), wastewater flows in a surcharged state. If the hydraulic grade line exceeds the rim elevation of the manhole (manhole C), an overflow occurs. Some models will calculate the overflow volume.

Bookkeeping

To complete the modeling process, the modeler must implement a series of bookkeeping activities. These activities insure that the model is properly documented and stored so that it can be retrieved and updated.

A completed model is a resource for the utility owner or operator and. A properly documented model may be used for applications beyond those of the initial intentions. For example, a model may be developed to assess the capacity and rehabilitation alternatives of an existing network. At a later date, the model may be used to design an expansion of the system.

The bookkeeping activities described here should be consistent with those of the model's owner. Standard procedures should be coordinated with model users or parties that share the data. The integration of a hydraulic sewer model into an enterprise GIS is described in Section 14.3.

Documentation. The modeler must communicate the development and the results of the model so that others can understand and evaluate them. Typically, this documentation is presented in a modeling report. Suggested contents of this report include the following:

- Names and version numbers of all commercial software used to build the model
- Source code for all customized programs developed for the model
- Identification of data sources and descriptions of field data collection activities

- Data reduction and preprocessing procedures
- Model calibration and validation procedures
- Presentation of simulation results
- Interpretation of results
- Discussion of the model's limitations

Archiving. Copies of all programs and data files used to build and run the model should be stored on archival-quality media in a secure location that is separate from where the model was developed. Instructions for running the software and loading the data must also be provided.

Updating. A wastewater collection system model should not be considered a static entity. It may require updating for the following reasons:

- Replacement or rehabilitation of the sewer pipe or manholes
- Expansion of the network
- Changes in operating procedures
- Additional monitoring data
- Update of the software

Procedures for updating the model should be established. When the model is updated, additional calibration may be required. The modeler should note whether the results from the updated model have any effect on the conclusions reached in the initial study.

5.3 Constructing the Sewer Model

A model represents the real collection system as a set of connected modeling elements that have numerical behaviors similar to the real system facilities. The model requires that certain hydraulic attributes of the system be entered so that the hydraulic calculations can be performed.

In model applications that involve designs of new systems, every new element must be modeled. In many cases, steady-state model runs for peak flow conditions are adequate, along with some runs at low- and average-flow conditions.

In models of existing systems, the issues usually center on a small portion of the system. While that portion must be modeled in detail, the modeler must decide on the level of detail needed to represent the remainder of the system. In some cases, the upstream part can be represented by a handful of large subbasins, while the downstream part can be represented by a boundary condition. However, with the ease of constructing models from GIS systems, "all-pipe" models are becoming more common, so a single model can be used for a variety of purposes. The level of simplification depends on the availability of data and the extent to which the model will be used for other purposes.

The following sections describe the modeling data used to develop the mathematical simulation of the hydraulics of a sewer system.

Level of Detail

Application of a computer model to a wastewater collection system requires defining the sewer catchment areas (subbasins, sewersheds) to be simulated. These areas become the basis for dry and wet weather flow generation within the model.

Depending <on the intended use of the hydraulic model, there are two main approaches to determining the appropriate size of model subbasins. For studies of large existing systems, including evaluating overflows and master planning, it is acceptable to simplify most of the upstream drainage and to represent large areas of the system as subbasins with single loading points. On the other hand, when sanitary sewers are designed for new land developments, or when sanitary sewer overflows can have serious receiving water, health, or regulatory consequences, then flow loading is usually parsed or distributed at closer intervals, e.g., at each manhole. The difference in these two approaches is illustrated in Figure 5.2.

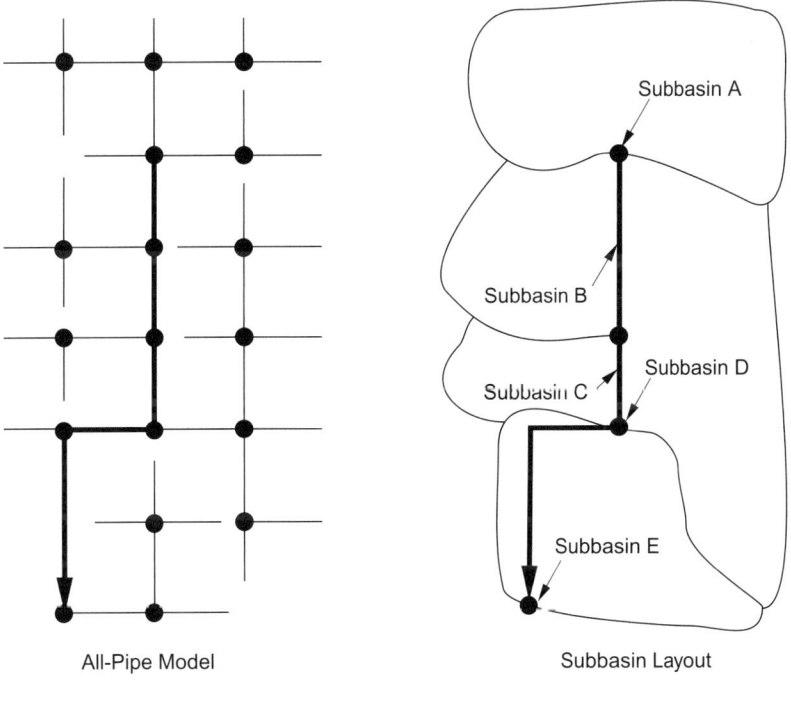

Figure 5.2 Layouts showing loading node differences between all-pipe and subbasin sewer models.

Although it is easier to work with a small number of large subbasins, it is important that when doing so, you consider the effects of peak attenuation within the subbasin. On the other hand, overland flow routing in the all-pipe model may not be needed because the area (and hence travel time) for any subbasin is so small. In addition, automated tools in GIS systems have greatly reduced the labor involved in loading all-pipe models.

Subbasin Delineation

Usually, system owners already have major subsystem boundaries delineated (e.g., to major pump stations or to one or more wastewater treatment plants). These can serve as the starting point for the collection system model. In this case, initial efforts should focus on reviewing these boundaries and making any necessary modifications to reflect changes in drainage patterns in the subsystems.

Sewer subbasins for detailed models in any type of collection system should include all hydraulically restrictive pipes and other structures. Beginning in the upstream portion of the system, the modeler should delineate subbasins based on the sewer network and land use, according to the following general guidelines:

- Subbasin areas depend on the use of the model and the availability of data. Some modelers prefer to have each subbasin correspond to a single flow meter, while others use considerably smaller areas. Subbasin areas can range from as small as 10 ac (4 ha) to as large as 300 ac (120 ha).
- Subbasin boundaries should be drawn to maintain homogenous land use within the subbasin (this is greatly simplified with GIS spatial analysis).
- Subbasin boundaries should be drawn at any hydraulic control point, such as
  - Combined sewer regulators
  - Flow diversion chambers
  - Pump stations
  - Any constructed overflow point in a separate sanitary system
  - Significant tributary junctions
  - Flow monitor locations (useful for calibration)
- Large parcels of land, such as parks, golf courses, and freeways that are not connected to the collection system should be excluded from the subbasins.
- Subbasin delineations should not cross over combined or sanitary pipes but should always end at a manhole.
- Interbasin transfers through tunnels or pumping should be noted.

Combined sewersheds typically follow ground surface contours and often include significant open spaces (such as parks) that drain to the combined sewer system, whereas sanitary sewersheds usually follow development boundaries and do not include open spaces.

For each subbasin, a load-point manhole should be identified to which the flows are assigned to best represent the effects of flows entering the system. Alternatively, flows can be distributed to all manholes in the subbasin. Figure 5.3 is an example of the level of detail in the subbasin delineation process.

Pipes

In models, pipes are links that connect nodes in a sewer network. Many pipe lengths and fittings are combined into one segment linking two nodes. The pipe links in the model should have similar pipe characteristics (diameter, pipe material, hydraulics) throughout the entire length, which are described in more detail below.

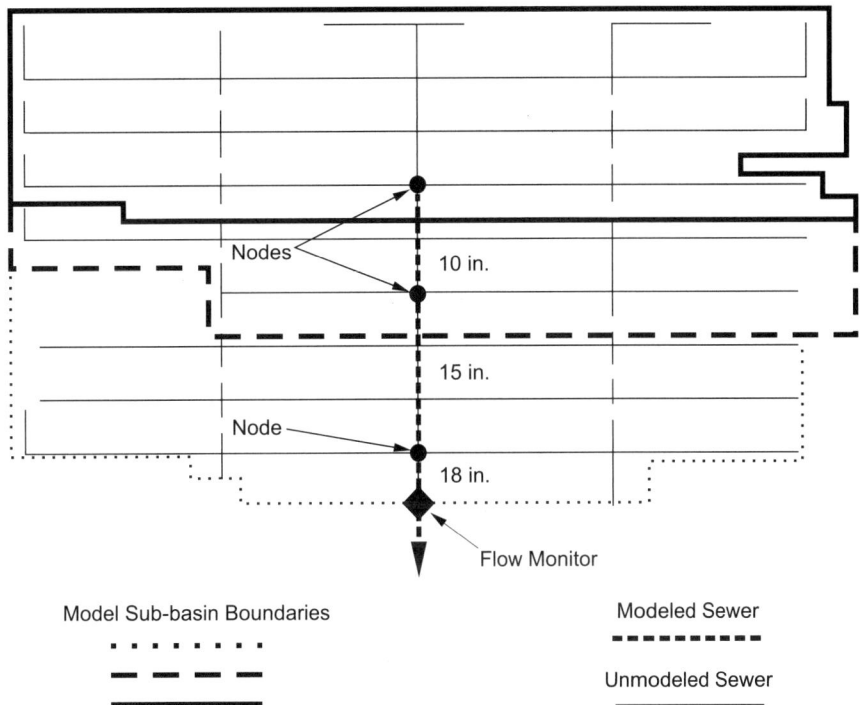

Figure 5.3 Example of a sewer subbasin delineation.

Diameter. Ideally, the diameters of pipes used in hydraulic calculations are the actual internal diameters of the pipes. However, because the actual diameters are usually not known, and the actual and nominal diameters are close enough, the nominal diameters can be used for most models. Pipes are usually described in drawings by their nominal sizes. It is important to note that pipes of the same nominal size are usually manufactured in a range of wall-crushing strengths. This is done by varying the wall thickness, which can result in different internal diameters. The pipe manufacturer will provide the exact pipe specifications, as illustrated in Figure 5.4.

The inside diameter can change as the pipe gets older. The combination of corrosion and scouring by particles and grit can slowly increase the inside pipe diameter. Alternatively, chemical deposition, sediment, roots, and grease buildup can reduce the pipe diameter. The effects of pipe blockage can be accounted for by reducing the pipe diameter or appropriately adjusting the roughness coefficient.

Length. The pipe length is the distance between the nodes (usually manholes) at each end of the pipe. There is seldom a need to model individual segments of pipe or to account for individual service connections.

Most models provide the option to use either a computer-generated scaled pipe length from digital system maps (e.g. GIS or CAD) or a user-defined pipe-segment length. Models are referred to as *scaled* if the pipes in the graphical representation are drawn to scale and *schematic* if the graphical representation is not to scale.

Material. Traditionally, pipes used in gravity flow sewer systems are made of concrete, reinforced concrete, ductile iron, or vitrified clay. PVC and HDPE plastic pipe

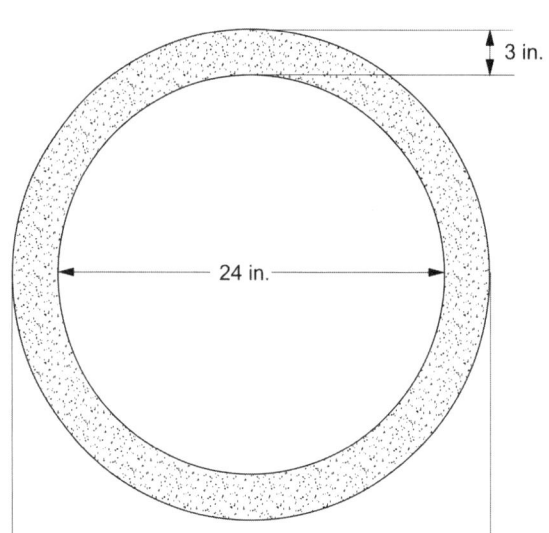

Figure 5.4 Specifications for a 24 in. ASTM C76 concrete pipe.

has become more common since the mid-1980s. Older pipe materials include unreinforced concrete (typically 24-in. and smaller), Orangeburg (cellulose fibers impregnated with coal-tar pitch), segmented clay tile pipe (used for larger-diameter sewers), brick, and asbestos-cement pipe.

Pipe material is classified as either rigid or flexible. Following is a short listing of the pipe materials in each classification. For a more complete listing of pipe material see ASCE, 1982.

Rigid Pipe

- Asbestos-cement (AC)
- Concrete
- Vitrified clay (VCP)
- Cast iron

Flexible Pipe

- Ductile iron (DI)
- Steel
- Polyethylene (PE)
- Polyvinyl chloride (PVC)
- Fiberglass-reinforced resin (FRR)
- Acrylonitrile-butadiene-styrene (ABS)

It is common for metallic sewer pipe to be lined to inhibit corrosion and reduce the pipe roughness to enhance the hydraulic flow (ASCE, 1992b). These linings can be added to the inside of the pipe during manufacture or can be added to older, existing pipes during cleaning and rehabilitation. If a pipe has been rehabilitated with a slip lining, pipe bursting, or a cured-in-place liner, the diameter in the model must reflect the new internal diameter.

Typical size ranges for commonly used sewer pipe materials are shown in Table 5.3. Pipes made from the same material may also have different standard sizes based on their use. Some manufacturers may only fabricate a limited range of sizes.

Table 5.3 Size characteristics for common sewer pipe materials.

Pipe Material	Minimum Nominal Diameter[1], in. (mm)	Maximum Nominal Diameter, in. (m)	Common Length[2], ft (m)
Asbestos-cement	4 (100)	42 (1.05)	Up to 20 (6.1)
Reinforced concrete	4 (100)	180 (4.5)	4–24 (1.2–7.4)
Vitrified clay	3 (75)	36 (0.90)	Up to 10 (3)
Ductile iron	3 (75)	64 (1.6)	Up to 20 (6.1)
PE plastic sewer	3 (75)	64 (1.6)	Long coils
PVC plastic sewer	4 (100)	48 (1.2)	Up to 20 (6.1)
FRR sewer	3 (75)	144 (3.6)	20 (6.1) standard
ABS plastic sewer	3 (75)	12 (0.30)	Up to 35 (11.2)

[1] Smaller pipe diameters are available, but are not often used for sewers.
[2] These are typical standard lengths for purchasing sewer pipe. Longer segments may be available by special order.

Roughness. Pipe friction is accounted for by Manning's n or whatever roughness coefficient is used (values for Manning's n for various pipe materials are listed in Table 2.3 on page 42). In sewer systems, the sewer pipe does not flow full most of the time. In this case, the pipe friction is also a function of the depth of flow in the pipe (ASCE, 1982). The relationship between flow depth and Manning's n is illustrated in Figure 2.13.

In sewer system models, a single Manning's n is applied to an entire pipe segment. It is common to modify Manning's n when calibrating the model so that the model replicates as closely as possible the depths and velocities that are measured.

Changes in horizontal alignment of flow typically occur at manholes in a sewer system, although a long bend consisting of a series of gradually deflected pipe is sometimes used between manholes. Such long-radius bends usually have a negligible effect on head losses.

Shape. Most sanitary sewer pipes are circular; however, older systems and major trunk lines may use egg-shaped, horseshoe, or rectangular pipes. Vertical elliptical pipe is used where the flow depth in a circular pipe would be very low. This shape increases the flow depth during low-flow conditions (when compared to circular pipe), but still allows for high-flow conditions. Horizontal elliptical pipe is used where the lateral clearance above the pipe is limited. Arch pipe is most commonly used for highway culverts. Commonly used shapes of sewer pipe are shown in Figure 5.5.

Invert Elevation. The pipe *invert* is the elevation of the inside bottom of the pipe. In some cases, the invert elevation at each end of a pipe reach can be automatically calculated by the model based on the inverts of other pipes connected to the same manhole. In most models, the slope is considered constant between any two manholes.

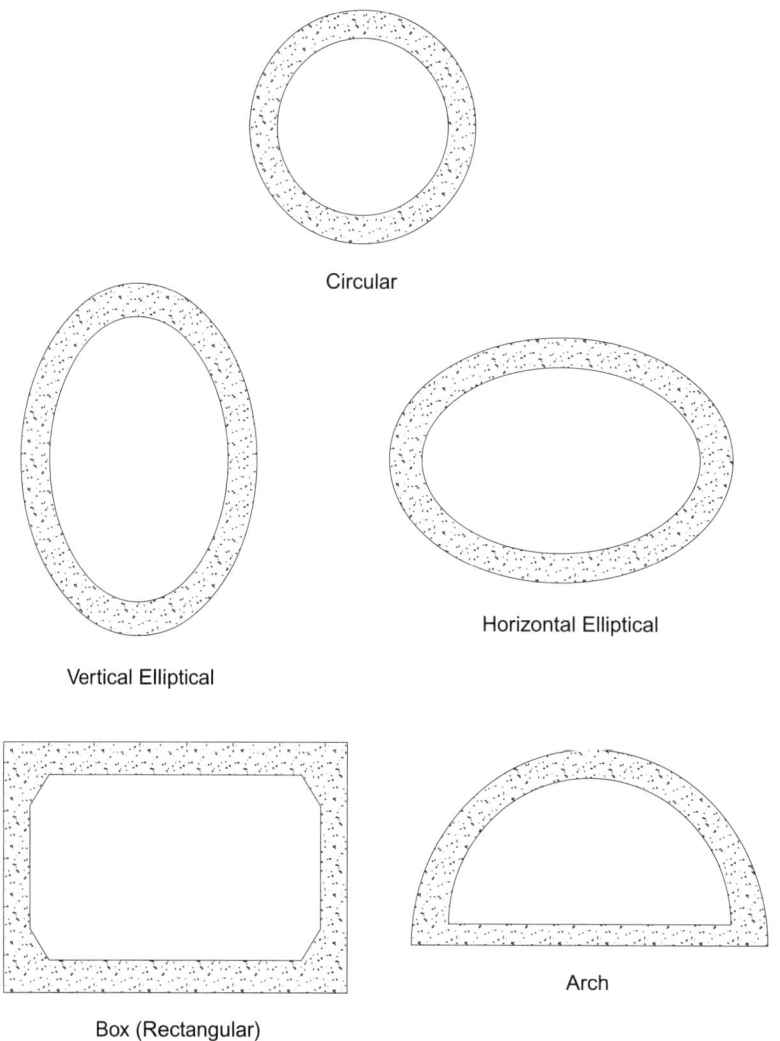

Figure 5.5 Commonly used pipe shapes.

Grease, Sediment, Roots, and Sags. Some potential hydraulic problems in sewers are caused by grease, sediment, roots, and sags. Grease from the wastewater can build up along the walls of the pipe, thereby reducing the inside diameter and area available for sewage flow. The grease can even choke the sewer pipe, causing sewer backup during high-flow conditions. Sediment can also build up in pipes, especially those carrying combined sewage containing road sand and cinders. Sedimentation is most often a problem in sewers with minimal slope because, without adequate slope and especially during dry weather, it is difficult to maintain a self-cleaning velocity (typically 2-10 ft/s [0.6-3 m/s] during peak flow conditions). Grease and sediment can be cleaned with a water jet or pipeline flusher, which should be part of the regular cleaning procedure for a sewer pipe. A nozzle (water jet) is projected into the sewer pipe, and pressurized water flushes material from the pipe walls.

Roots can penetrate into the pipe through the pipe joints and grow within the nutrient-rich sewer water. Roots have been known to almost completely plug a sewer pipe.

"One checker, two packs of cigarettes, two screws, one teapot bird, one piece of coal, three lighters, one Christmas light, one clove of garlic, four boxes of matches, two books, three pieces of broken dish, eggshells, one saltshaker peg, one pen, one cream-cheese wrapper, and one wishbone. All that stuff under the dish cabinet."

Sags are typically located at pipe joints, and are usually due to improper backfilling or bedding of the sewer pipe during installation. They create a low spot where water can pool and provide a location for sediment to collect when water velocities are low.

Some modeling software allows defining a depth of sediment in each pipe length, with the model making allowance for the reduced conveyance area and modified hydraulic radius. Other packages require the modeler to mimic the reduced conveyance capacity either by increasing the pipe roughness or by reducing the pipe diameter; this is usually done by trial and error. Usually these blockages are not considered significant until they cause surcharge during high-flow conditions. If the flow rate and extent of the surcharging and blocking location are known, the modeler can estimate the modified friction factor.

The modeler should use caution when adjusting the model because grease, roots, or similar chokes can be removed during sewer maintenance or be dislodged if flow rates become high enough. While it is better to remove the blockage instead of modeling it, the model can be a useful tool for illustrating the benefits of clearing the sewer.

Inverted Siphons. Any designed dip in a gravity sewer is referred to as an *inverted siphon* or *depressed sewer* (Figure 5.6). This occurs when the sewer must pass under structures such as other pipes, highways, or subways; a river; or across a valley. The sewer line is below the hydraulic grade line and is always filled with sewage and under pressure. An inverted siphon is modeled hydraulically by accounting for entrance losses, pressure flow through the siphon, exit losses, and a transition to open-channel flow.

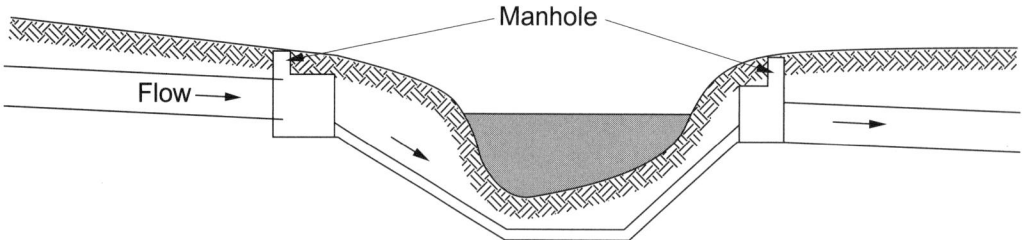

Figure 5.6 Sewer inverted siphon crossing under a stream.

Inverted siphons are typically designed using multiple smaller-size pipes (barrels) to maintain self-cleaning velocities. To avoid blockage of the sewer pipe by grit and other material collecting at the low point within the siphon, the fluid velocity in any of the inverted siphon barrels must be greater than 3 ft/s (1 m/s) at least once each day (Hammer and Hammer, 1996). However, this depends upon the slope of the outlet side of the inverted siphon and the fluid's ability to move the grit up and out of the inverted siphon. If multiple barrels are used, then the additional barrels are arranged so that the pipes are brought into service progressively as the sewage flow increases. In addition, it is common to place manholes at both ends of an inverted siphon to allow easy access for cleaning the siphon.

Manholes

Manholes (see Figure 5.7) are placed in a sewer system to provide access for inspection, maintenance, and emergency service. Manholes should be placed at sewer junctions (i.e., tees, wyes, and crosses), upstream terminal ends of sewers, and locations where there is a change in sewer grade or direction. Manholes are typically placed 300–500 ft (90–150 m) apart to provide an adequate number of entry points for maintenance. Large pipes may have greater distances between manholes. Areas with low ground elevations where stormwater can pool (e.g., flood plains), making the manhole an easy entry point for surface water, should have watertight covers. Alternatively, the manhole chimneys can be extended above the expected flood elevation.

Most manholes in sanitary sewers have only one downstream pipe. However, systems may include some locations where the flow is split into two or more pipes. Also, a single manhole at a ridgeline might be used as the upstream terminus for pipes in both directions.

Manholes should be constructed to minimize their interference with the sewer flow. To do so, the manhole floor is usually constructed with U-shaped channels separated by raised benches. Benches reduce head losses by effectively directing the path of flow through the structure (the front section shown in Figure 5.7 shows a half bench). Where a change in horizontal alignment occurs, a smooth bend is constructed in the channel. Figure 5.8 shows a typical bend in a manhole. The hydraulics of manholes is described in Chapter 2.

Invert Elevation. The manhole invert is usually defined as the elevation of the inside bottom of the pipe entering the manhole. In other instances, it represents the bottom of the pipe or trough at the center of the manhole. Invert elevations are given on

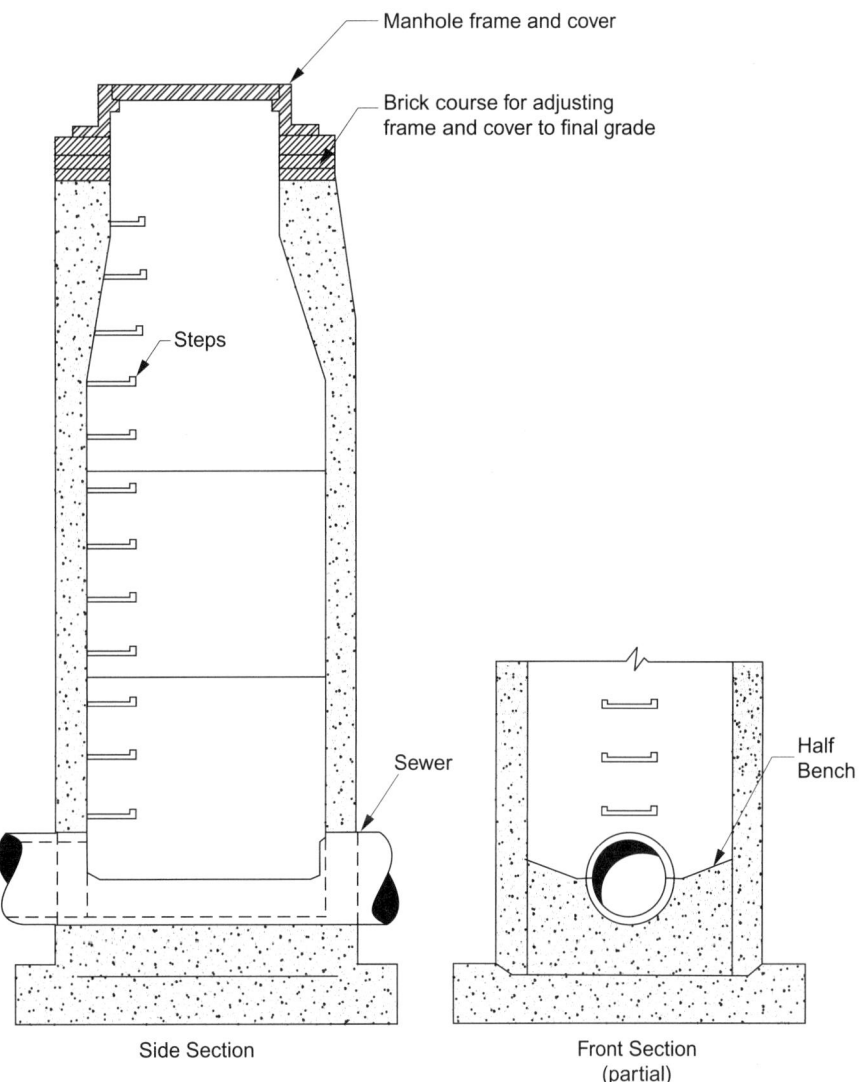

Figure 5.7 Typical manhole for a sanitary sewer.

record drawings and are usually listed on system maps. If only rim elevations are listed, the inverts can be determined by measuring the distance from the rim to the invert.

If a manhole is located where multiple sewer pipes enter, such as at a junction, it is common to have the invert elevations of the entering pipes higher than the main sewer branch leaving the manhole to avoid eddies and the accumulation of sludge and grit due to poor flow patterns.

In a gravity sewer model, small errors in elevation can lead to significant uncertainty in estimating the capacity of the sewer. Invert elevations should be known at least to the nearest 0.1 ft (33 mm), but preferably to the nearest 0.01 ft (3 mm). Data with this accuracy may only be available from record drawings or field surveys.

Rim Elevation. The rim elevation is typically at the ground elevation when the sewer is located in the street although the manhole rim may be either buried or above

Courtesy of Maria do Céu Almeida/LNEC

Figure 5.8 Manhole with a 90 degree bend.

the ground elevation. If the manhole does not need to be hidden in a grass or wooded area, the manhole rim may be above ground elevation to avoid inflow of stormwater into the manhole.

If a bolted cover is not specified and if the hydraulic grade line exceeds the manhole rim, then most models will indicate that overflow is occurring and may calculate the overflow volume. Specifying a bolted cover also allows the hydraulic grade line to rise above the manhole rim. The locations of existing bolted covers in a sewer system must be known when high-flow conditions are modeled.

Structure Size. Most manholes are cylindrical, with inside dimensions large enough to allow maintenance and inspections. In the United States, a commonly used manhole diameter for small sanitary sewers is 42 in. (1.1 m). For diameters over 24 in. (0.6 m) some sort of base is used with manhole risers. Manhole diameter for larger pipes is 48 in. (1.2 m) and, if flows are being combined, a junction chamber is used with a manhole riser. The top of the manhole usually tapers to about 2 ft (0.6 m) in diameter to allow a person to enter the manhole and to support a standard manhole cover. It is now common to taper the top of the manhole toward one side to allow the access ladder to be inlaid along a vertical wall. In some models, the diameter of the manhole is taken at the level of the outlet pipe and not at the rim, while other models allow the manhole to be defined by a number of cross-sectional areas at different elevations.

Drop Manholes. It is often necessary that a small sewer pipe enter a manhole at an invert elevation much higher than the main sewer pipe leaving the manhole. In these cases, it is undesirable to let the inflowing sewer water just pour into the manhole from above, so the incoming sewage is transported down a vertical shaft to the bottom

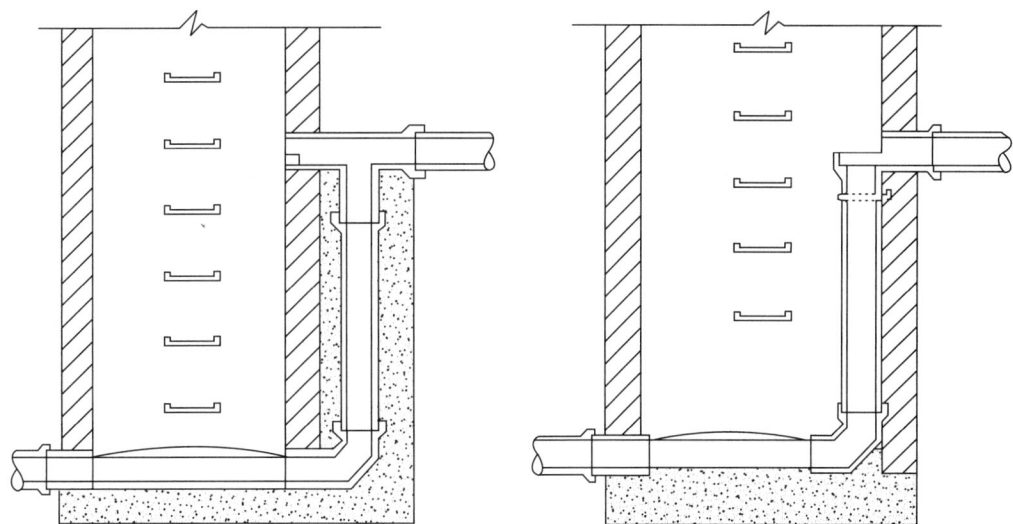

Figure 5.9 Drop manholes.

of the manhole before entering the outgoing sewer pipe, as illustrated in Figure 5.9. In some models, it is possible to have the default manhole invert elevation set to the invert level of the entering pipes. With drop manholes, it is essential that this feature not be active.

Regulators. Control structures, called *regulators*, in combined sewers divert flow and direct it to an outfall. Weirs, siphons, orifices, and gates are all examples of regulators. Figures 5.10 through 5.14 show flow in sewers that contain different types of weirs. Flow may also be split at manholes with more than one outflow pipe.

In Figure 5.10, a leaping weir is positioned transverse to the flow. Low flows fall into the interceptor but high flows "leap" over the weir and enter the overflow sewer. In Figure 5.11, side weirs allow high flows to exit the sewer and fall into the overflow sewer. Figure 5.12 shows a weir across a channel section with multiple inlets. The transverse weir in Figure 5.13 acts as a dam. Low flows drop through the orifice and enter an interceptor, while high flows spill over the transverse weir. Figure 5.14 is another example of a transverse weir. Additional descriptions of regulators may be found in Moffa (1997) and ASCE (1992a). The hydraulics of weirs and orifices is described in Section 2.11 on page 78. Additional information may be found in Metcalf and Eddy (1981), Hager (1999), and Mays (2001).

Outlet Manholes. The downstream end of a collection system model is an outlet node that represents the treatment plant, pump station, combined sewer overflows (CSO), sanitary sewer overflows (SSO), or any other place where flow exits the system or the model terminates. Depending on the system, the user can usually specify a known tailwater depth at this point or can indicate that the depth will be the full pipe, critical, or normal depth of flow in the pipe farthest downstream. The model user specifies known tailwater depth when the pipe is to be submerged at its downstream end. Usually critical depth is most appropriate when the pipe freely discharges with no tailwater effects. A free-falling outfall with a flap gate is shown in Figure 5.15. The full pipe and normal depth options are not used often.

Figure 5.10 Low flow over a leaping weir enters an interceptor.

Figure 5.11 Side weir during low flow.

Pumps

In a wastewater collection system, pumping stations are placed where the hydraulic grade line must be raised. Since sewage primarily flows by gravity, a pump transports sewage from a low elevation to a higher elevation. The sewage then flows again by gravity to the next pumping station or until it reaches its destination.

Most pumping stations within sewer systems contain centrifugal pumps, which are classified as radial-flow, mixed-flow, or axial-flow. When a low flow rate but high pumping head are needed, a radial-flow pump is used. When a high flow rate but low pumping head are needed, an axial-flow pump is used. A mixed-flow pump is used

Figure 5.12 Curved weir.

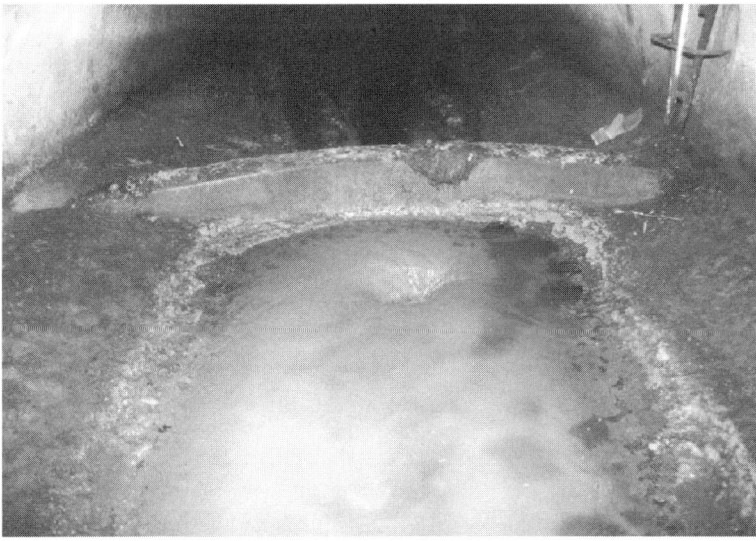

Figure 5.13 Transverse weir with a drop orifice.

for a moderate flow rate and pumping head. In general, most sewage pumps are radial- or mixed-flow.

Obtaining Pump Curves. A pump is characterized by its pumping head, efficiency, and power requirements at various flow rates. The pump head performance curve describes the pump's ability to pump sewage against a pump head at a constant impeller speed. The pump head is the difference between the total energy head before and after the pump and can be determined using the energy equation. The pump efficiency and power requirements change as the pump head changes. A set of pump head characteristic curves shows how head, efficiency, and power change as the pump flow changes (see Figure 4.9 on page 131). For further details on pump hydraulics see Chapter 4 and for the design of pump stations see Chapter 12.

Figure 5.14 Transverse weir in a combined sewer overflow (CSO).

Figure 5.15 Sewer outfall with a flap gate.

The characteristic curves for existing pumps should be available from the utility, as they are usually required in the submittals when the pumps are installed. If the pump characteristic curves are not available, they can be obtained from the pump manufacturer. However, it must be understood that an old pump may not perform as it did when it was new and so should be tested to verify that the real pump performance matches what is shown on the pump head performance curve. If the pump performance has been altered, a new pump head performance curve that reflects what the pump is actually doing should be developed.

For hydraulic modeling, the pump head performance curve and the stop and start elevations in the wet well are required. The efficiency curve is required only if energy usage is to be determined. The pump head performance curve can be entered into the model in a number of different ways. The modeler should use a method that accurately defines the pump head performance curve over the range of flows anticipated for the model and that provides results that simulate field performance.

In some cruder models, a pump is represented by a known flow rate whenever the pump status is on. This may be acceptable when there is a single pump discharging into a force main, but when there are multiple pumps, an individual pump's flow rate depends on the status of the other pumps.

In other models, the pump's flow rate may be treated as a function of wet well water level. In that case, the modeler must work out the pump operating points outside the model.

Pump Status and Controls. The pump status in a pumping station is usually controlled by the water level in the adjacent wet well on the upstream side, although it may also be controlled by some condition on the downstream system. Constant-speed pumps are off until the wet well fills to a specific water level, then turn on once the "on" level has been reached and continue to pump until the water elevation in the wet well reaches a predetermined minimum level. Variable-speed pumps are usually controlled to maintain the wet well depth within a narrow range.

Floats, pressure switches, or other water-level sensors indicate the status of the wet well. A simple float switch can be used to turn a pump on when the wet well is filled to its desired maximum elevation, and then another float turns the pump off when the wet well empties to the minimum level. Alternatively, a programmable controller could use information from a level sensor to switch the pumps on and off.

For a variable-speed pump, the speed is usually controlled to maintain a constant level in the wet. When the wet well rises above that level, the pump operates at its maximum speed until it pumps down to the desired level (or needs to call for an additional pump). If the speed is very low, the pump may shut off until the wet well rises again.

The actual control settings must be obtained from system operators. In most models, these controls are defined when information about the pump(s) is entered.

Pumped vs. Average Flow. The flow in a sewer varies daily (night vs. daytime flow), weekly (weekday vs. weekend flow), and seasonally (summer vs. winter flow), as well as in response to wet weather events. The wet well and pumping system must be designed to handle these variations. The control program for large pumping stations can be quite complicated, but, in general, the pumps pass downstream flows at a rate close to the inflow rate to the station. When sewer flow is high, the pump(s) are on more frequently. For example, during weekday mornings the average sewer flow tends to be high because people are taking their morning showers. During this time, the wet well fills more rapidly and the pumps run more often or for longer cycle times. The pumping frequency can be determined from wet well level charts or from the operations staff. Modeling of pump operation is discussed further in Chapter 12.

To model a pump station in a steady-state model, the modeler must decide whether the pump will be represented by its actual pumping flow rate when the pump is running or an average pumping flow rate for a given time of day. The piping immediately downstream of the pump station is designed to handle the peak flow of the pumps. As other pipes branch into the system downstream from the pumps, the pumping flow rate is combined with other inflowing sewage, and the effects of the peak flows introduced by the pump are diminished. In this case, the actual pumping rate should be used for modeling a pump station and nearby pipes. However, in steady-state runs of an entire sewer system or of pipes far downstream, where the pumps contribute very little to the flow, it may be more appropriate to use the average pumping flow rate.

Wet Wells

Pumping stations need wet wells to store wastewater before it is pumped. Some wet wells have bar screens or comminutors to help protect the pumps from rags and other solids that can clog a pump and increase the head loss.

The floor of a wet well usually slopes toward the suction bell of the pump to minimize the deposition of solids in the wet well. To avoid cavitation in the pump, the minimum water level in the wet well is maintained above the suction head.

Minimum, Maximum, and Initial Level. In modeling a wet well, the key inputs are the minimum (off) and maximum (on) water levels for each pump and the wet well volume. The pumps are controlled by a minimum-level control switch that turns off the pumps when the low level is reached. The minimum water level is determined from the volume of water that must be stored in the wet well to minimize wear on the pumps.

System operators usually have information on the minimum and maximum levels relative to the wet well floor that can be used as baseline elevations for calculating the levels needed by the model. A control range of at least 3.5 feet (1.07 m) is desirable between the minimum and maximum wet well levels (Metcalf & Eddy, 1981). In a model, these levels are linked to the pump controls. An initial water level in the wet well must be provided for some extended-period simulation models and depends on where the modeler wants to start the model scenario. In other models, this level is established through an initialization process. The various wet well water levels are illustrated in Figure 5.16.

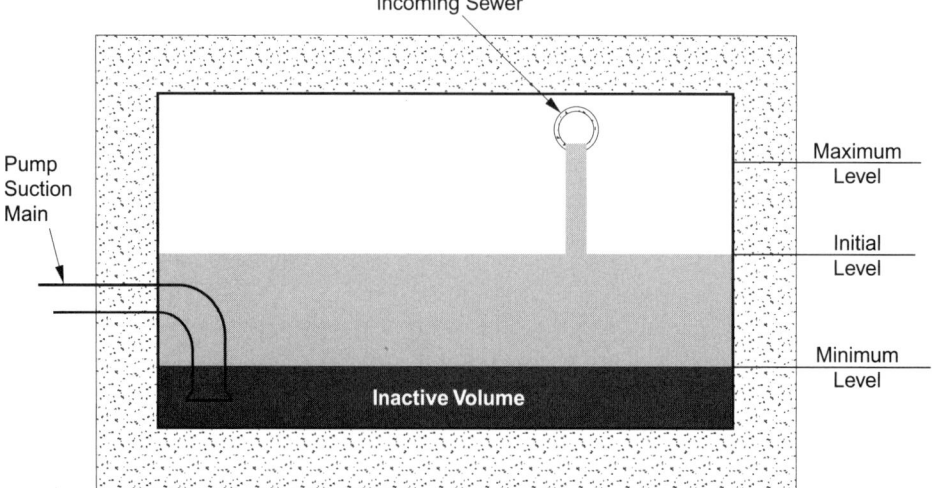

Figure 5.16 Minimum, initial, and maximum water levels in a wet well.

Volume. The active volume of the wet well is the volume of water between the minimum and maximum water levels. The active volume is automatically determined if the minimum and maximum water level and cross-sectional area of the wet well are entered into the model. The inactive volume is the volume of water below the active volume and is the remaining water in the wet well after the pump is turned off. This is the volume of water required to ensure that the suction head and submergence head are sufficient. In general, a variable-speed pump does not need as large a wet well volume as a fixed-speed pump (Metcalf & Eddy, 1981).

Irregular-Shape Wet Wells. Most wet wells have a constant cross-sectional area in the active volume. If the wet well walls are not vertical between the minimum and maximum water level, a curve relating the sewer water level and the cross-sectional area must be entered in the model.

References

American Society of Civil Engineers (ASCE). 1982. *Gravity Sanitary Sewer Design and Construction*. ASCE MOP #60 and WEF MOP #FD-5. New York: American Society Civil Engineers and Alexandria, Virginia: Water Environment Federation.

American Society of Civil Engineers (ASCE). 1992a. *Design and Construction of Urban Stormwater Management Systems*. ASCE Manuals and Reports of Engineering Practice No. 77. New York: American Society of Civil Engineers and WEF Manual of Practice FD-20. Alexandria, VA: Water Environment Federation.

American Society of Civil Engineers (ASCE). 1992b. *Pressure Pipeline Design for Water and Wastewater*. New York: American Society Civil Engineers.

Hager, W. H. 1999. *Wastewater Hydraulics: Theory and Practice*. Berlin: Springer.

Hammer, M. J., and M. J. Hammer, Jr. 1996 *Water and Wastewater Technology*. 3rd ed. Englewood Cliffs, NJ: Prentice Hall.

HR Wallingford. 1998. *The Wallingford Procedure: Volume 2 – Practical Application of the Wallingford Procedure*. Wallingford, England: HR Wallingford.

Huber, W. C., and Dickenson, R. E. 1988. *Storm Water Management Model Version 4: User's Manual*. Athens, GA: US Environmental Protection Agency

Mays, L. W. 2001. Storm and combined sewer overflow: flow regulators and control. In *Stormwater Collection Systems Handbook*, ed. by L. W. Mays. New York: McGraw-Hill.

Metcalf & Eddy, Inc. 1981. *Wastewater Engineering: Collection and Pumping of Wastewater*. ed. by G. Tchobanoglous. New York: McGraw Hill.

Moffa, P. E. 1997. "The combined sewer overflow problem: an overview." In *Control and Treatment of Combined Sewer Overflows*, ed. by P. E. Moffa. 2nd ed. New York: Van Nostrand Reinhold.

US Environmental Protection Agency (US EPA). 2002. *Guidance on Environmental Data Verification and Validation*. EPA QA/G-8, EPA/240/R-02/004. Washington D.C.: US Environmental Protection Agency.

Wastewater Planning Users Group (WaPUG). 1998. *Code of Practice for the Hydraulic Modeling of Sewer Systems*. 2nd ed. Oxfordshire, England: Wastewater Planning Users Group.

Problems

5.1 True or False: During surcharge conditions, wastewater must be flowing out of a manhole. Explain your answer.

5.2 True or False: A microscale model is most appropriate when evaluating the effect of I/I on an entire wastewater collection system after a major rain storm. Explain your answer.

5.3 Explain the difference between validating data and validating a model.

5.4 For a macroscale model of an entire wastewater collection system, identify the type of data that should be collected and indicate where that data might be found. How can a gap analysis be used to improve data gathering in the future?

5.5 You need to determine ground elevations to lay out a sewer but all you have are elevations from a digital elevation model (DEM) that was based on a contour map with 20 ft contour intervals. You need elevation data accurate to +/- 0.1 ft. Is this DEM adequate? What should you do?

5.6 The head loss in sewer models should be based on actual pipe length. Usually all that is known is the plan view of pipe length. For a 300 ft reach of sewer with a 1 percent slope, what is the actual length of the pipe? Is the difference between actual and plan length significant? What if there is a 10 percent slope?

5.7 You may use SewerCAD (contained in the CD acompanying this book) or an alternative modeling program of your choice to answer this problem. Use the schematic shown in the following figure and the data in the tables to create and run a model for a proposed sanitary sewer collection system for a small development (alternatively, you can manually perform the calculations). For the base model, all of the pipes are gravity-flow circular 12-in. concrete pipe. The infiltration into the sewer pipe is estimated to be 11 gpd per foot of pipe. The head loss for each manhole is estimated using the HEC-22 Energy Method with flat benching. The tailwater condition for the outlet is set as a free outfall.

Run the following scenarios to answer the questions.

a. Run the steady-state analysis on the average flow to determine the total flow (in gpd) at O-1 and the velocity in each pipe. Report both the upstream and downstream velocities.

b. Create a profile of the sewer that includes the pipe, ground elevation, sump elevation, manhole, outlet location, and the water profile (HGL) in the pipe from manhole MH-3 to the outlet O-1.

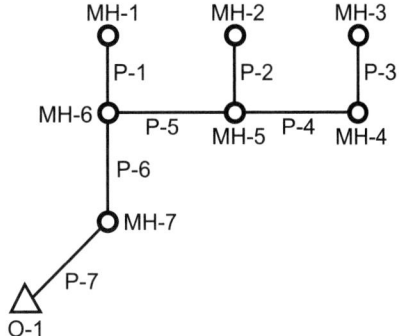

Base model pipe data.

Pipe	Length, ft	Upstream Invert Elevation, ft	Downstream Invert Elevation, ft
P-1	250	20.0	17.5
P-2	250	22.0	20.0
P-3	250	24.0	22.0
P-4	350	22.0	20.0
P-5	200	20.0	17.5
P-6	200	17.5	15.0
P-7	250	15.0	13.0

Base model node data.

Node	Ground Elevation, ft	Rim Elevation, ft	Sump Elevation, ft	Structure Diameter, ft	Average Sanitary Flow, gpm
MH-1	27.0	27.0	20.0	4.0	75
MH-2	29.0	29.0	22.0	4.0	75
MH-3	32.0	32.0	24.0	4.0	75
MH-4	31.0	31.0	22.0	4.0	75
MH-5	28.0	28.0	20.0	4.0	200
MH-6	26.0	26.0	17.5	4.0	150
MH-7	24.0	24.0	15.0	4.0	50
O-1	22.0	22.0	13.0	N/A	N/A

CHAPTER 6

Dry Weather Wastewater Flows

Accurate estimates of wastewater collection system flow rates are the foundation of hydraulic sewer models. These flow rates are sometimes referred to as *loads* or *demands*. In a model, flows are assigned to nodes (sometimes called *loading points*) that represent entry points of flow into the system or are parsed along the pipe's length. Nodes can correspond to individual manholes or large subbasins, as explained in Chapter 7. Flows may be specified as a constant rate, time versus flow (such as a hydrograph), or as a base load with a repeating pattern.

Flows in wastewater collection systems are generally divided into two categories. Wastewater (also called *sanitary* or *dry weather*) flows are the intentional discharges into the collection system. They may originate from residential, commercial, institutional, or industrial sources. Quantification of these flows is the subject of this chapter. Sanitary collection systems also collect infiltration and inflow (I/I), which principally originate as precipitation. These wet weather flows are discussed in Chapter 7.

Flow data may be developed from a variety of sources. A common procedure for estimating wastewater flow is the unit load method, where sources that generate flow are counted and multiplied by an appropriate factor to estimate flow. Another procedure uses the amount of water used (demand) corrected for consumption. The total flow in a collection system is usually measured at the influent to a wastewater treatment facility.

While there are many approaches for determining flows at loading points, they can be classified as either top down or bottom up approaches. In a top-down approach, total flow to the wastewater plant is divided among model nodes based on some rules. In a bottom-up approach, loads are determined at each customer point and other inflow points, and the aggregate should equal the total flow to the plant.

This book emphasizes a bottom-up approach to the loading of hydraulic sewer models. That is, each source of flow is identified and quantified. This is important when models are used to assess the effects of operations, maintenance, rehabilitation, and source control alternatives on the collection system. Through this method, a model may be simplified by combining contributions from a variety of users into a single flow at a node.

The methods for loading a hydraulic sewer model with dry weather flow data are summarized in Figure 6.1. In general, there are four different starting points for model loading depending on whether a system is being designed or already exists and the availability of flow metering data. All of the methods need calibration to some extent. The data sources are as follows:

1. *Wastewater flow monitoring data* – These data are taken from actual monitoring locations and are very useful for loading downstream nodes and determining time-of-day patterns. They can also be used to develop unit loads for upstream nodes by dividing the flows by the number of upstream manholes, number of customers, or land area.

2. *Unit loads from literature* – Literature values for unit loads (e.g., gallons per day per equivalent dwelling unit or fixture unit, or liters per day per kilometer of pipe) can be multiplied by the number of units at a node (e.g., number of equivalent dwelling units or fixture units or number of kilometers of pipe) to identify nodal loads.

3. *Regulatory prescribed loads* – Values for loads are given by the regulatory agency and applied to loading nodes based on population equivalents or other factors.

4. *Water use billing data* – Water consumption data are often precise and can be used to load wastewater models once they are corrected for the fraction of water delivered that does not become part of the wastewater flow.

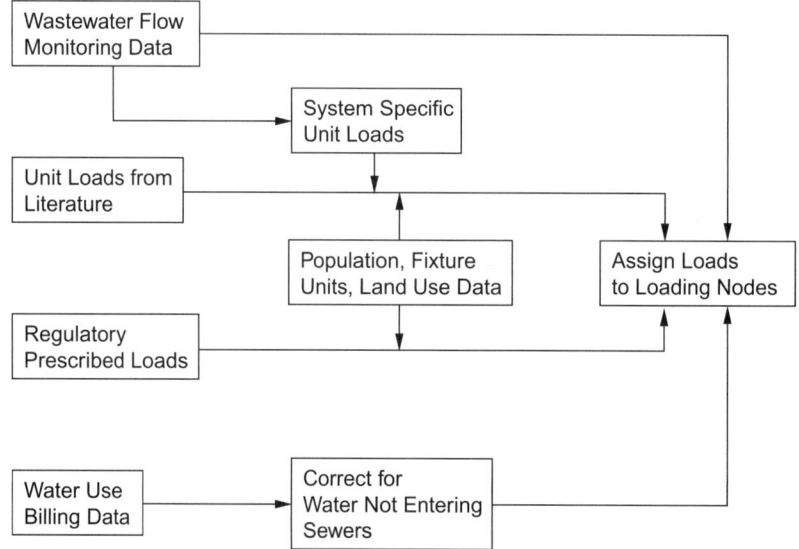

Figure 6.1 Overview of methods for determining dry weather flow rates.

6.1 Definition of Flow Rates

Hydraulic sewer models can simulate a variety of flows or combination of flows into the collection system. A modeler may develop several sets of flows that represent different times or conditions in the sewer system. As discussed in Chapter 5, the choice of flows depends on the modeling objective. The flows that are commonly used in hydraulic sewer models are listed in Table 6.1.

Table 6.1 Terms describing wastewater flows in hydraulic sewer models.

Term	Application in Hydraulic Sewer Models
Average daily	• Total flow to wastewater treatment facility in a 24-hour period. • Base flow used for peaking factors and pattern loads.
Peak hourly	• Capacity analysis of collectors, mains, and diversion structures.
Hourly time series	• Separation of wastewater flow from total flow in model calibration. • Extended-period simulation for analysis of pump station operation. • Extended-period simulation for analysis of flows to treatment facility. • Extended-period simulation for wet weather flow analysis.
Minimum	• Determine if velocities are adequate for self-cleansing.

The flow rates in Table 6.1 may be modified to represent the following conditions:

- *Present/future* – Flows change over the life of the sewer. A modeler may wish to simulate sewer hydraulics under present conditions, at the end of the design life, or at any time between.

- *Diurnal* – Sanitary flows vary over the course of a day. The pattern load technique (discussed in Section 6.4) is used to model a 24-hour cycle.

- *Weekly* – Flows from residential, commercial, and industrial sources typically vary over the course of a week. Loads may be modeled with a weekday and weekend flow or a different flow rate for each day.

- *Seasonal* – Sewers that service areas with vacation homes and hotels experience a seasonal variation in flow. Industrial sources may also produce a variation in flow due to seasonal operation.

- *Weekday versus weekend* – Peaks can be higher on weekends due to such factors as increased restaurant use, tourism, and car washing.

New Systems

For the design of a new system, gravity sections usually convey peak flows without surcharge or with some excess capacity. Generally speaking, peak hourly flows at the end of the design life of a sewer are used to simulate a worst-case scenario and provide a conservative design for the new system. In some instances, the design may be based on peak flows over a shorter period or even on instantaneous peak flows. Minimum flows are usually used to determine if velocities are adequate to prevent the buildup of solids in the sewer.

In systems in which service connections will be added over time, it may be appropriate to model the hydraulics over 5- or 10-year intervals.

For wastewater collection systems that have pump stations and force mains, storage in wet wells dampens peak flows while pump cycling tends to create a different peaking pattern. Extended-period simulation is used to design the wet wells and force mains and to determine the operating conditions of the pumps. The 24-hour pattern load occurring during a seasonal peak may also be used.

Existing Systems

Depending on the purpose of the model, a variety of loading alternatives may be used to model existing systems. In a steady-state simulation, the loading is often based on maximum or minimum flows. Design maximum flow rates are developed from estimates of maximum population and/or units in the service area.

6.2 Unit Load Factors

In the United States, an average residential flow rate value of approximately 100 gallons per capita per day (gpcd) (378 liters per capita per day [Lpcd]) has been widely used for nearly a century. This is, in fact, the design average flow specified by the GLUMRB (1997). ASCE (1982) published average sewage flow values for numerous cities in the United States. The values range from 48 gpcd (182 Lpcd) in Madison, Wisconsin, to a high of 264 gpcd (1000 Lpcd) in Boston, Massachusetts. However, these flows include varying levels of I/I.

Water use and wastewater generation rates are significantly lower in developing countries, as indicated in Table 6.2.

Table 6.2 Water consumption per capita in developing countries (Salvato, 1992).

Country or Area	gpcd	Lpcd
China	21	80
Africa	4–6	15–23
Southeast Asia	8–19	30–70
Western Pacific	8–24	30–90
Eastern Mediterranean	11–23	40–85
Algeria, Morocco, Turkey	5–17	20–65
Latin America and Caribbean	19–51	70–190
World Average	9–24	35–90

Per capita water use and wastewater generation rates must be used cautiously. In many instances, these rates include some amounts of commercial and industrial wastewater, as well as an allowance for I/I. Such rates may be adequate for initial planning studies; however, a more detailed analysis of the sources is usually required to accurately load a hydraulic sewer model.

Residential

A survey of water use in North America was conducted for the American Water Works Association Research Foundation (AWWARF), with the findings summarized in a report by Mayer et al. (1999). Water uses were determined for 1200 households in 14 cities. Residential water use was metered so that it could be assigned to one of 13 categories. For the purpose of this discussion, indoor water use is usually considered to be equivalent to wastewater flow.

Mayer et al. report that the average residential use of water was 69.3 gpcd (262 Lpcd). For individual cities, the range was from a low of 57.1 gpcd (216 Lpcd) in Seattle, Washington, to a high of 83.5 gpcd (316 Lpcd) in Eugene, Oregon. The authors attributed the differences in usage to regional variability and indicated that local data were important for quantifying water use. The average water use rate is similar to the value of 66.2 gpcd (251 Lpcd) reported by Brown and Caldwell (1984).

Mayer et al. reported that indoor water use is dependent on household size. The following first-order equation was developed to describe this relationship:

$$y = 37.2\,x + 69.2 \text{ (gpd)} \quad (6.1)$$
$$= 141\,x + 262 \text{ (Lpd)}$$

where y = indoor water use per household (gpd, Lpd)
        x = number of people per household

Residential water use may be subdivided into categories, as listed in Table 6.3. The table shows that water-conserving plumbing fixtures can effectively reduce residential water use and wastewater flows. The data also show that water use can be reduced by as much as 30 percent if water-conservation practices are followed.

Table 6.3 Residential water use in the United States with and without water-conservation practices.

Use	Flow[1], gpcd (Lpcd)		Percent of Total Water Use[2]
	Without Water Conservation	With Water Conservation	
Bathing	1.3 (5)	1.3 (5)	1.7
Shower	13.2 (50)	11.1 (42)	16.8
Dish washing	1.0 (4)	1.0 (4)	1.4
Clothes washing	16.8 (64)	11.8 (45)	21.7
Faucet	11.1 (42)	11.1 (42)	15.7
Toilets	19.3 (73)	9.3 (35)	26.7
Leaks	9.4 (36)	4.7 (18)	13.7
Other domestic	1.6 (6)	1.6 (6)	2.2
Totals	74 (281)	51.9 (197)	100.0

[1] Tchobanoglous, Burton, and Stensel, 2003
[2] Mayer et al., 1999

Commercial Sources

For commercial sources, daily average wastewater flows may be estimated by determining the unit count (e.g., the number of patrons served in a restaurant) and multiplying this value by the unit loads (usually given as gallons or liters per unit per day) shown in Table 6.4. Because of the wide variations that have been observed, every effort should be made to obtain flow data from actual or similar facilities.

Table 6.4 Wastewater generation rates for commercial establishments.

User	Flow Range	
	gal/(person or unit)/day	L/(person or unit)/day
Airport, per passenger	3–5	11–19
Assembly hall, per seat	2–3	8–11
Bowling alley, per alley	16–26	60–100
Camp		
Pioneer type	21–32	80–120
Children's, central toilet and bath	42–53	160–200
Day, no meals	11–18	40–70
Luxury, private bath	79–106	300–400
Labor	37–53	140–200
Trailer with private toilet and bath, per unit (2½ persons)	132–159	500–600
Country club		
Resident type	79–159	300–600
Transient type serving meals	16–26	60–100
Dwelling unit, residential		
Apartment house on individual well	79–106	300–400
Apartment house on public water supply, unmetered	79–132	300–500
Boardinghouse	40–58	150–220
Hotel	53–106	200–400
Lodging house and tourist home	32–53	120–200
Motel	106–159	400–600
Private dwelling on individual well or metered supply	53–159	200–600
Private dwelling on public water supply, unmetered	106–211	400–800
Factory, sanitary wastes, per shift	11–26	40–100
Fairground (based on daily attendance)	1–2	4–8
Institution		
Average type	106–159	400–600
Hospital	185–317	700–1200
Office	11–16	40–60
Picnic park, with flush toilets	5–11	20–40
Restaurant (including toilet)		
Average	7–11	25–40
Kitchen wastes only	3–5	11–19
Short order	3–5	11–19
Short order, paper service	1–2	4–8
Bar and cocktail lounge	2–3	8–12
Average type, per seat	32–48	120–180
Average type, 24 hr, per seat	42–58	160–220
Tavern, per seat	16–26	60–100
Service area, per counter seat (toll road)	264–423	1000–1600
Service area, per table seat (toll road)	159–211	600–800
School		
Day, with cafeteria or lunchroom	11–16	40–60

Table 6.4 (Continued) Wastewater generation rates for commercial establishments.

User	Flow Range	
	gal/(person or unit)/day	L/(person or unit)/day
Day, with cafeteria and showers	16–21	60–80
Boarding	53–106	200–400
Self-service laundry, per machine	264–793	1000–3000
Store		
First 7.5 m (25 ft) of frontage	423–528	1600–2000
Each additional 7.5 m of frontage	370–423	1400–1600
Swimming pool and beach, toilet and shower	11–16	40–60
Theater		
Indoor, per seat, two showings per day	3–5	10–20
Outdoor, including food stand, per car (3⅓ persons)	3–5	10–20

Source: from Ysuni, 2000, based on Metcalf & Eddy, 1981.

Industrial Wastewater Flows

Wastewater flow rates from industrial sources are highly site specific and should be based on historical data from the particular facility. For rough planning purposes, loads may be estimated from the unit flow rates presented in Table 6.5. The extent to which water use corresponds to wastewater production varies with the industry. As with commercial flows, measured flows from actual or similar facilities should be obtained. In the absence of such data, the values in Table 6.5 may serve as a guide.

Table 6.5 Average rate of water use according to Standard Industrial Classification (SIC) code.

Category	SIC Code	Use Rate, gal/employee/day	Sample Size
Construction		31	246
General building contractors	15	118	66
Heavy construction	16	20	30
Special trade contractors	17	25	150
Manufacturing		164	2790
Food and kindred products	20	469	252
Textile mill products	22	784	20
Apparel and other textile products	23	26	91
Lumber and wood products	24	49	62
Furniture and fixtures	25	36	83
Paper and allied products	26	2614	93
Printing and publishing	27	37	174
Chemicals and allied products	28	267	211
Petroleum and coal products	29	1045	23
Rubber and miscellaneous plastics products	30	119	116
Leather and leather products	31	148	10

Table 6.5 (Continued) Average rate of water use according to Standard Industrial Classification (SIC) code.

Category	SIC Code	Use Rate, gal/employee/day	Sample Size
Stone, clay, and glass products	32	202	83
Primary metal industries	33	178	80
Fabricated metal products	34	194	395
Industrial machinery and equipment	35	68	304
Electronic and other electrical equipment	36	95	409
Transportation equipment	37	84	182
Instruments and related products	38	66	147
Miscellaneous manufacturing industries	39	36	55
Transportation and public utilities		50	226
Railroad transportation	40	68	3
Local and interurban passenger transit	41	26	32
Trucking and warehousing	42	85	100
U.S. Postal Service	43	5	1
Water transportation	44	353	10
Transportation by air	45	171	17
Transportation services	47	40	13
Communications	48	55	31
Electric, gas, and sanitary services	49	51	19
Wholesale trade		53	751
Wholesale trade–durable goods	50	46	518
Wholesale trade–nondurable goods	51	87	233
Retail trade		93	1044
Building materials and garden supplies	52	35	56
General merchandise stores	53	45	50
Food stores	54	100	90
Automotive dealers and service stations	55	49	498
Apparel and accessory stores	56	68	48
Furniture and home furnishings stores	57	42	100
Eating and drinking places	58	156	341
Miscellaneous retail	59	132	161
Finance, insurance, and real estate		192	238
Depository institutions	60	62	77
Nondepository institutions	61	361	36
Security and commodity brokers	62	1240	2
Insurance carriers	63	136	9
Insurance agents, brokers, and service	64	89	24
Real estate	65	609	84
Holding and other investment offices	67	290	5
Services		137	1878
Hotels and other lodging places	70	230	197
Personal services	72	462	300
Business services	73	73	243

Table 6.5 (Continued) Average rate of water use according to Standard Industrial Classification (SIC) code.

Category	SIC Code	Use Rate, gal/employee/day	Sample Size
Auto repair, services, and parking	75	217	108
Miscellaneous repair services	76	69	42
Motion pictures	78	110	40
Amusement and recreation services	79	429	105
Health services	80	91	353
Legal services	81	821	15
Educational services	82	110	300
Social service	83	106	55
Museums, botanical, zoological gardens	84	208	9
Membership organizations	86	212	45
Engineering and management services	87	58	5
Services, NEC	89	73	60
Public administration		106	25
Executive, legislative, and general	91	155	2
Justice, public order, and safety	92	18	4
Administration of human resources	94	87	6
Environmental quality and housing	95	101	6
Administration of economic programs	96	274	5
National security and international affairs	97	445	2

Source: Dziegielewski, Opitz, and Maidment, 1996.

Fixture Unit Method

There are several methods used to estimate flows based on a count of plumbing fixtures. They are called either *fixture unit methods* or *fixture value methods,* and they can be used to determine average or peak loads for water supply or wastewater loading. Two such fixture unit methods are presented in the following sections.

Average Loading Rate. Peak wastewater flow rates may be estimated by multiplying the number of plumbing fixtures by the flow and usage rates for each fixture. Typical wastewater flows for common fixtures found in residences are listed in Table 6.6. In the United States, residential toilets manufactured after January 1, 1994, must use no more than 1.6 gal (6 L) per flush. Commercial toilets manufactured after January 1, 1997, must use no more than 1.6 gal (6 L) per flush and urinals must use no more than 1 gal (3.8 L) per flush. Additional information on wastewater flows from various plumbing fixtures may be found in ASCE (1982) and Salvato (1992).

Table 6.6 Typical rates of water use for various residential devices and appliances in the United States.

Device or Appliance	U.S. Customary Units		SI Units	
	Units	Range	Units	Range
Automatic washing machine, top loading	gal/load	34–57	L/load	130–216
Automatic washing machine, front loading	gal/load	12–15	L/load	45–60
Dishwasher	gal/load	9.5–15.5	L/load	36–60
Bathtub	gal/use	30	L/use	114
Kitchen food-waste grinder	gal/day	1–2	L/day	4–8
Shower	gal/min-use	2.5–3	L/min-use	9–11
Toilet tank, conservation type	gal/flush	1.6–3.5	L/flush	6–13
Toilet tank, standard	gal/flush	4–6	L/flush	15–23
Washbasin	gal/min-use	2–3	L/min-use	8–11

Source: Tchobanoglous, Burton, and Stensel, 2003

Peak Loading Rate. Engineers for commercial developments such as hotels and office buildings may also want to use modeling for their projects but will not have data on existing customers as a water utility would. This problem was addressed by the National Bureau of Standards during the 1920s and '30s and resulted in the *Fixture Unit Method* for estimating demands (Hunter, 1940).

This method consists of determining the number of toilets, sinks, dishwashers, and so on in a building and assigning a fixture unit value to each. Fixture unit values are shown in Table 6.7. Once the total fixture units are known, the value is converted into a peak design flow using what is called a *Hunter curve* (see Figure 6.2).

The values in Table 6.7 are based on data collected in the 1920s and 1930s. The modeler may want to reduce fixture values to reflect more modern plumbing fixtures.

Table 6.7 Fixture units for various types of commercial and residential plumbing fixtures.

Fixture Type	Fixture Units	Fixture Type	Fixture Units
Bathtub	2	Wash sink (per faucet)	2
Bedpan washer	10	Urinal flush valve	10
Combination sink & tray	3	Urinal stall	5
Dental unit	1	Urinal trough (per ft)	5
Dental lavatory	1	Dishwasher (1/2 in.)	2
Lavatory (3/8 in.)	1	Dishwasher (3/4 in.)	4
Lavatory (1/2 in.)	2	Water closet (flush valve)	10
Drinking fountain	1	Water closet (tank)	5
Laundry tray	2	Washing machine (1/2 in.)	6
Shower head (3/4 in.)	2	Washing machine (3/4 in.)	10
Shower head (1/2 in.)	4	Kitchen sink (1/2 in.)	2
Hose connection (1/2 in.)	5	Kitchen sink (3/4 in.)	4
Hose connection (3/4 in.)	10		

Source: Hunter, 1940

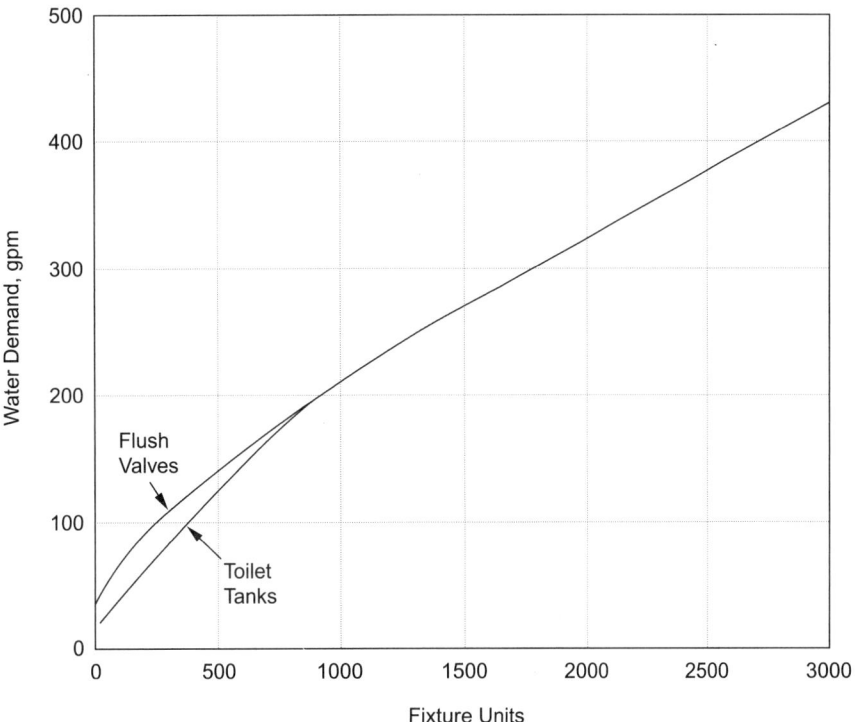

Figure 6.2 Determining peak water demand from fixture units using a Hunter curve.

The basic premise of the Hunter curve is that the more fixtures in a building, the less likely it is that they will all be used simultaneously. This assumption may not be appropriate in stadiums, arenas, theaters, and so on where extremely heavy use occurs in very short time frames, such as at halftimes or intermissions.

The values in Table 6.7 are somewhat out-of-date, as they were prepared before the days of low-flush toilets and low-flow shower heads, but a better method has not yet been developed. This technique is used in the *Uniform Plumbing Code* (International Association of Plumbing and Mechanical Officials, 1997) and a modified version is included in AWWA Manual M-22 (2004). Although the fixture unit assigned may require some adjustment to reflect modern plumbing practice, the logic behind the Hunter curve still holds true.

Land-Use Methods

Wastewater flow estimates may also be based on flow per unit area. This technique is used primarily when designing sewers for an area that will be developed in the future. For example, future flows from residential sources may be estimated by assuming a housing density equal to the maximum allowed by local zoning regulations. Typical unit-area flow rates for commercial developments range from 800 to 1500 gal/ac-day (7.5 to 14 m^3/ha-day) (Tchobanoglous, Burton, and Stensel, 2003). ASCE (1982) lists allowances for commercial wastewater flows for various cities throughout the United State. Typical examples of allowances for industrial sources

Effects of Low-Flush Toilets

At one time, toilets used 5–7 gallons of water per flush (gpf) (19–26 Lpf). With the increase in environmental awareness and water conservation in the 1970s, toilet manufacturers developed models that worked with 3.5 gpf (13 Lpf). These worked well and with increased interest on water conservation in the US, the 1992 Energy Policy Act required that all new toilets use no more than 1.6 gpf (6 Lpf). (Some manufacturers claim that their toilets use as little as 0.6 gpf (2 Lpf).)

In a study of residential water use in 14 North American cities, Mayer et al. (1999) recorded an average of 15.4 toilet flushes per household or 5.05 flushes per capita per day.

The average toilet flush volume was 3.48 gpf (13.2 Lpf) with a standard deviation of 1.19 gpf (4.50 Lpf). The majority of the flushes fell in the 3–5 gpf (11.4–18.9 LPF) range with a distinct secondary peak in the 1.5–2 gpf (5.7–7.6 Lpf) range.

The effect of low-flush toilets on water demand was also investigated. Homes that had an average flush volume of 2.0 gal (7.6 L) were classified as ultralow flush (ULF). Homes with a mixture of ULF and non-ULF toilets were classified as mixed. The remaining homes were classified as non-ULF. The toilet use per household and per capita and the number of flushes per capita per day for each group are presented in the table below.

The reduction in daily wastewater flow due to the use of ULF toilets is the difference between the per capita toilet use of the non-ULF homes (20.1 gal or 76.1 L) and the ULF only (9.6 gal or 36.3 L) homes. This value is 10.5 gal (39.7) and was determined to be significant at the 99 percent confidence level.

The often hypothesized and reported ULF problem of double flushing was not detected in this study. The average number of flushes per capita per day for the ULF homes and the non-ULF homes were not statistically different, indicating that the study homes that use only ULF toilets are not flushing more frequently than homes with no ULF toilets. It appears that double flushing of ULF toilets does not happen any more often than double flushing of non-ULF toilets.

While ULF toilets are more or less effective in moving solids out of the toilet bowl, they reduce the amount of water available to transport the solids through the service line and down the sewer, unless water is being used elsewhere by the customer.

Most sewers have sufficient flow and slope to transport solids even with low-flow toilets upstream. However, in sewers with low flows and minimal slopes, low-flush toilets can add to a sewer utility's maintenance expenses.

Water conservation has manifested itself in other ways such as low-flow showerheads and low-water-use clothes washers. Design standards, such as minimum slopes, have not been adjusted even though flush volumes have dropped from 7 to 1.6 gpf (26 to 6 Lpf). Standards for minimum slopes in small sewers may eventually need to be revisited in response to these new plumbing practices.

Category	Sample Size	Toilet Use per Household, gpd (Lpd)	Toilet Use per Capita, gpcd (Lpcd)	Flushes per Capita per Day
ULF only	101	24.2 (91.6)	9.6 (36.3)	5.06
Mixed	311	45.4 (172)	17.6 (66.6)	5.39
non-ULF	776	47.9 (181)	20.1 (76.1)	4.92
All homes	1188	45.2 (171)	18.5 (70.0)	5.05

Adapted from Mayer et al., 1999

are 13,600 gal/ac-day (130 m³/ha-day) in Santa Monica, California, and 20,000 gal/ac-day (190 m³/ha-day) in Toronto, Canada. There is a wide range of values, depending on location and type of industry or commercial enterprise.

In situations where only the total system flows are known, sanitary loads may be assigned to nodes in a sewer model by using formulas based on land-use patterns. The use of a geographic information system (GIS) to assign aerial-based land-use data to nodes in a sewer network is described in Chapter 14.

Measured-Flow Methods

Water consumption data may be used to estimate wastewater flow rates. The consumption of water by individual residences, commercial establishments, or industries may be obtained from utility billing records. Since the time interval between meter readings is typically on the order of one month, these data are suitable for developing average, but not peak, flows. It may also be possible to infer seasonal variability from monthly records. If the data record extends over a long enough time, it may be analyzed for long-term trends.

Flow rates over shorter time steps across the entire water distribution system may be obtained from the water treatment plant or the records of the water pumping stations. The analysis, which can be used to develop diurnal patterns, must account for any storage within the water distribution system. Details of this analysis are given in Haestad Methods et al. (2003).

When water-use or water-production records are used to estimate wastewater flows, the amount of water consumed for irrigation, cooling, leakage from water mains, and product water in manufacturing must be subtracted from the total demand. In the United States, approximately 60 to 90 percent of the water consumed becomes wastewater (Tchobanoglous, Burton, and Stensel, 2003). This figure varies widely with climate and season, however.

"Well, gentlemen, there's your problem."

Total flows in an existing collection system may also be obtained from the operating records of the local wastewater treatment plant. As flows are recorded over short time steps (typically 5–15 minutes), the data may be analyzed to quantify the variability on a diurnal, weekly, or seasonal basis. Remember that there may be a lag of several hours to several days between the generation of wastewater and the arrival of that wastewater at the plant flow meter. The total flow is measured at the influent to the plant. Inflow and infiltration must be subtracted to obtain estimates of sanitary flows. More accurate sanitary flow loadings will be developed if this analysis is performed on treatment plant records collected during dry weather (or from appropriately located in-sewer flow monitors, as described in Chapter 8). If there are overflows or diversions from the collection system, they must also be included in the analysis. Procedures to derive wastewater flow from total flow in a sewer are presented in Chapter 9.

When basing flow rates on literature or regulatory values, it is important to know when those numbers include an allowance for dry-weather groundwater infiltration or whether they need to be increased for infiltration.

Example 6.1 Calculation of average daily flow rates

Determine the average daily wastewater flow from a small community with the following sources:

- 250 private residences with an average of 3.5 people per household
- 140 apartment units
- 10 stores with an average of 50 feet of street frontage
- One restaurant with 125 seats
- One self-service laundry with 30 washing machines
- One school cafeteria and shower for 400 students
- One 25-acre parcel zoned for industrial development, with a projected unit load of 100 gal/ac/day (based on a nearby facility)

Solution

The wastewater from households is estimated using Equation 6.1 as

$$y = 37(3.5) + 69.2 = 198.7 \text{ gpd or approximately 200 gpd}$$

The remaining unit-load factors are obtained from the following table, which also includes the calculated flows.

Source	Unit Load Factor	Number of Units	Average Flow, gal/day
Residence	200 gal/day	250	50,000
Apartment	105 gal/day	140	14,700
Store, first 25 ft of frontage	475 gal/day	10	4750
Store, each additional 25 ft of frontage	400 gal/day	10	4000
Restaurant	40 gal/seat/day	125	5000
Laundry	530 gal/machine/day	30	15,900
School	18 gal/student/day	400	7200
Industrial park	1000 gal/ac/day	25	25,000
Total			126,500

The total wastewater flow from the community is estimated to be 127,000 gpd (480,000 Lpd). This estimate is based on average usage rates in the United States. The unit-load factors used in this example should be adjusted for local conditions. The next step is to prepare a preliminary layout of the collection system. The loads may then be assigned to nodes in the system.

Assigning Loads to a Model

Loads must be assigned to nodes in the model, but the details depend upon the modeling objective. When developing a detailed model for the design of a new system, loads from every lateral can be assigned to the manhole closest to their points of connection. In a model that focuses on the sewer trunk mains, the sum of the loads of an entire subbasin may be assigned to a single node.

If the total loads for a large area are known, they may be distributed across the model network by a variety of techniques. They may be uniformly distributed across the service area and loaded to the model at a constant g/ac-day (L/ha-day). Alternatively, the total load may be normalized by population and then assigned to the model on a population basis. Sources of population data include census data or a counting of residential units. The loading rate may also be adjusted for different land-use categories. Flows are assigned to the appropriate nodes of the collection system using the procedures described in Chapter 5.

When loads are known for individual customers, they must be aggregated to nodes or manholes in the network. The assignment may be based on the distance to the nearest node or a loading polygon assigned to each node. This loading may be done manually, by spreadsheet, or by using the tools in a geographic information system (GIS). The latter technique is described in Chapter 14.

6.3 Peaking Factors

Most sewer laterals and mains are designed to convey peak hourly flow rates (Tchobanoglous, Burton, and Stensel, 2003). A steady-state model based on peak flows may be used in the design process. In the absence of site-specific data, *peaking factors* are used to calculate design wastewater flow rates from average flow rates.

$$Q_{peak} = Q_{avg} \times PF \qquad (6.2)$$

where Q_{peak} = peak hourly flow rate (gpd, Lpd)
Q_{avg} = average daily flow rate (gpd, Lpd)
PF = peaking factor

Peaking factors can be more generically viewed as *extreme flow factors* (EFF) because they also apply to minimum flows.

Where flow records are available, at least two years of data should be analyzed to develop peak-to-average flow rate factors (Tchobanoglous, Burton, and Stensel, 2003). Site-specific peaking factors can be applied to estimated future average daily flow rates. Where commercial, institutional, or industrial users make up a significant portion of the total wastewater flow, peaking factors for the various source types or even individual customers should be estimated separately. Peak flows for each source type may not occur simultaneously; therefore, some adjustment may have to be made to the total peak flow to avoid overestimating the peak hourly flow from combined sources.

For the design of new sanitary collection systems, U.S. codes and guidelines often specify peaking factors to be used for estimating peak flows. For example, Utah specifies a factor of 4.0 for lateral and submain sewers and 2.5 for main, trunk, and outfall sewers (Utah Code R317-3, 1995). Also, the GLUMRB (1997) standards specify a peaking factor for design. These factors may be appropriate for a conservative design, but they should be used with caution in loading a hydraulic sewer model.

For system rehabilitation projects in existing systems with high I/I, the design is controlled much more by wet weather peaks than by dry weather peaks and flow monitoring is much more valuable than literature values.

Peaking Factor Charts and Equations

Nearly a century ago, progressive educators and engineers wanted to use more accurate estimates for design maximum flow rates in sewer design. They collected data from existing systems and drew envelope-bounding curves around the data. Curves completed from 1910–1940 usually present peaking factor vs. either population or flow rate. These graphs are still prominent in textbooks and design manuals used today. Most of the early curves are questionable for application to modern sewer systems because most of the data were collected from wet areas of the United States with unmetered water service, where water supply was generally abundant, and use rates were high. Also, many of these early sewers had high I/I flow. Some of the curves are for more-modern conditions and more recently constructed sewers, where I/I exclusion and control have been primary goals.

Some of the most common variable peaking factor (PF) calculation methods are as follows:

- Babbitt (Babbitt and Bauman, 1958)

$$PF = \frac{5.0}{\left(\frac{P}{1000}\right)^{0.2}} \tag{6.3}$$

where P = contributing population

- Harmon (Harmon, 1918) and Great Lakes Upper Mississippi River Board standard (GLUMRB, 1997)

$$PF = \frac{18 + \sqrt{\frac{P}{1000}}}{4 + \sqrt{\frac{P}{1000}}} \tag{6.4}$$

The GLUMRB standards indicate that Equation 6.4 should be used in conjunction with the average daily flow rate and is intended to cover normal infiltration for systems built with modern construction techniques. The graphs accompanying the standards indicate that the equation may be used for a population range of 100 to 100,000.

Data for peaking factor vs. average flow collected from various wastewater collection systems tends to yield a fairly straight line when plotted on a log-log graph. The resulting equation has the form:

$$PF = C(Q_{avg})^{-m} \tag{6.5}$$

where
C = constant (empirical coefficient)
Q_{avg} = average flow rate (ft³/s, m³/s)
m = exponent

Equations 6.2 and 6.5 are combined to calculate the design maximum flow rate as

$$Q_{peak} = C(Q_{avg})^{1-m} \tag{6.6}$$

Values of C and m for various locations are listed in Table 6.8.

Table 6.8 Coefficients for peaking factor and peak flow equations (Q in ft³/s) in several sewer systems.

Location	C	m
Los Angeles, CA[1]	2.4	0.11
Federov[2] (former Soviet Union)	1.8	0.121
Pima, County, AZ (Tucson)[3]		
$0.012 < Q_{avg} < 0.120$	1.78	0.16
$0.120 < Q_{avg} < 1.20$	1.79	0.15
$1.20 < Q_{avg} < 35.0$	1.76	0.05
Central Utah[4]		
$0.01 < Q_{avg} < 20.0$	2.60	0.16

[1] Adapted from ASCE, 1982
[2] Jakovlev et al., 1975
[3] Private correspondence, 1998
[4] Merritt, 1998

The coefficients listed in Table 6.8 represent the relationships expected in new sewers where high-quality materials and construction are coupled with typical metered water-use rates and sound I/I prevention ordinances and practices. In areas with wet climates and/or a little less rigorous control of I/I inflows, peaking factors tend to be lower, because the average flow is higher and groundwater inflow is fairly constant. Note that peaking factor equations may be applied at any point in the system; thus the design maximum flow rate can be quickly generated for every pipe in the sewer system. However, it must be remembered that these formulas were derived for a specific range of flows and should not be extrapolated, particularly to Q_{avg} flows below 0.01 cfs (~100 people).

Another example of a peaking factor curve was presented by Tchobanoglous, Burton, and Stensel (2003), as shown in Figure 6.3. It was developed from the analysis of flow records from numerous communities throughout the United States. The curve is based on average residential flow rates, exclusive of infiltration/inflow, and includes a small amount of commercial and industrial flows. Note that the peaking factor has a constant value of 4 for populations less than 5000; most node service areas in models fall into that range.

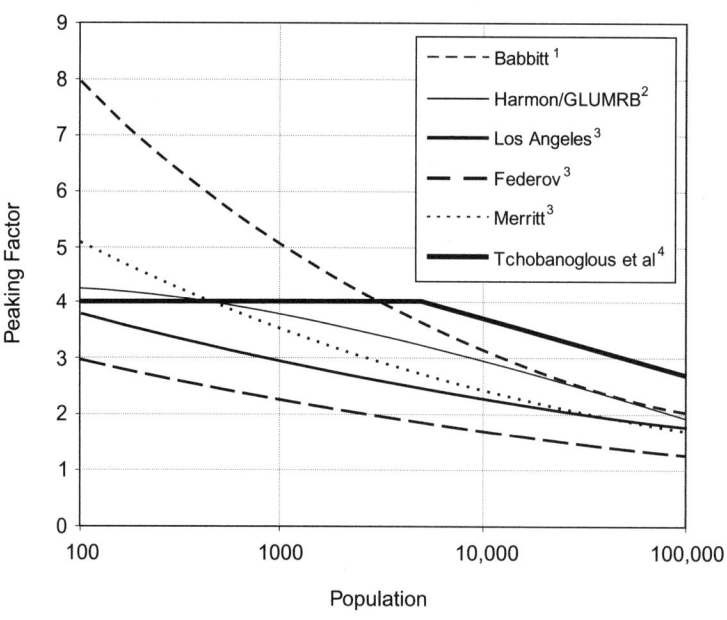

Figure 6.3 Calculated peaking factors from six formulas.

[1] Equation 6.3 [2] Equation 6.4
[3] From Table 6.8 [4] Equation 6.7

The peaking factor curve in Figure 6.3 is described by

$$PF = \begin{cases} 4, & P < 5000 \\ 7.7 - \log P, & 5000 \leq P \leq 1{,}000{,}000 \end{cases} \quad (6.7)$$

Large differences in design flows result from using higher average generation rates and the older peaking factor equations (Babbitt and Bauman, 1958; Fair and Geyer, 1954), compared to more-current rates and peaking equations. Figure 6.3 presents the peaking factors as calculated with six formulas for populations up to 100,000. Note that equations yield very high peaking factors when the population is low and should not be extrapolated into that range. A comparison of peaking factors is presented in Example 6.2.

Minimum Flows

Minimum flow factors may be used to estimate minimum expected flows from contributing populations. American Society of Civil Engineers (1982) presents graphs of two relationships. The graph of Babbitt and Bauman (1958) is described by

$$F_{min} = 0.049 \, P^{0.202} \quad (6.8)$$

and that of Gifft (1945) by

$$F_{min} = 0.065 \, P^{0.163} \quad (6.9)$$

where F_{min} = minimum flow factor
        P = contributing population

Selection of Flow Generation Rate and Peaking Factor

Selection of generation rates and peaking factors can make a large difference in the model flow rates. Their selection depends on the objective of the model and the goals or limitations of the system owner. For new sewer design, the local design codes may dictate the maximum flows. However, operating records of a water utility or of a nearby wastewater utility may allow use of alternative peaking factor formulas. For existing systems, flow data should be collected and the calibration procedures presented in Chapter 9 should be used to validate a peaking formula.

Another issue is that the peaking factor should decrease as one moves downstream. For example, where the upstream reaches of a sewer may have a peaking factor of 4, the peaking factor at the treatment plant may be on the order of 2.5 or 3. The use of different peaking factors in the same steady-state model run may result in a violation of the conservation of mass principle. More-sophisticated models handle this by keeping track of both the flow and other parameters (e.g., total upstream population) for any location in the sewer network. With this information, the model can adjust the peaking factor for the appropriate point in the network.

One approach to adjusting the peaking factor is to move loads downstream instead of flow. For each pipe, the model searches upstream to make a running count of such data as the number of houses, number of restaurant seats, and number of hospital beds for each node. This approach is useful in steady-state models used for design. For example, if two pipes meet at a manhole and one has 20 houses upstream and the other has 35 houses upstream, then the flow out of that manhole and the peaking factor would be based on 55 houses, not by simply summing the flows. Adding users instead of flows results in a decreasing peaking factor as one moves upstream through a collection system.

The peak flow at a point is given by

$$Q = \sum_{i=1}^{Types} EFF_i q_i \left(\sum_{j=1}^{Nodes} U_{ij} \right) \quad (6.10)$$

where
Q = flow at a point (gal/time, m³/time)
$Types$ = number of types of users
EFF_i = extreme flow factor for the i-th type of user
q_i = unit flow for the i-th type, (gal/unit/time, m³/unit/time)
$Nodes$ = number of upstream nodes
U_{ij} = number of units of the i-th use type at the j-th node

In its most general form, the extreme flow factor can be estimated based on population as

$$EFF = c_1 + \frac{c_2 + (m_1 + P)^{e_1}}{c_3 + (m_2 P)^{e_2}} \quad (6.11)$$

or based on flow as

$$Eff = c_1 + \frac{c_2 + (m_1 Q)^{e_1}}{c_3 + (m_2 Q)^{e_2}} \quad (6.12)$$

The c, m, and e coefficients depend on which extreme flow method is used (e.g., Harmon, GLUMRB).

Example 6.2 Peaking factors

Calculate the peak sanitary flow for a population of 10,000 using the Babbitt, GLUMRB, and modern equations (using Los Angeles and Federov data).

Solution

Use the value of 69.3 gpcd from Mayer et al. to calculate the average daily flow as

$$10{,}000 \times 69.3 \text{ gpcd} = 693{,}000 \text{ gpd}$$

The Babbitt equation gives

$$PF = \frac{5.0}{\left(\frac{10{,}000}{1000}\right)^{0.2}} = 3.15$$

The GLUMRB equation gives

$$PF = \frac{18 + \sqrt{\frac{10{,}000}{1000}}}{4 + \sqrt{\frac{10{,}000}{1000}}} = 2.95$$

The Los Angeles and Federov equations requires the average flow rate, given by

$$Q = 693{,}000 \frac{\text{gal}}{\text{day}} \times \frac{1 \text{ ft}^3}{7.48 \text{ gal}} \times \frac{1 \text{ day}}{86{,}400 \text{ s}} = 1.07 \text{ ft}^3/\text{s}$$

The peaking factor from the Los Angeles data is

$$PF = 2.4(1.07)^{-0.11} = 2.38$$

and from the Federov data is

$$PF = 1.79(1.07)^{-0.15} = 1.77$$

These results, with the corresponding flow rates, are listed in the following table.

Equation	Peaking Factor	Flow, 1000 g/d
Babbitt	3.15	2180
GLUMRB	2.95	2040
Los Angeles	2.38	1650
Federov	1.77	1230

The peak hourly flow actually used should depend on the project location and conditions at the site.

6.4 Time-Varying Flows

Wastewater flows in municipal collection systems are inherently unsteady, owing to continuously varying discharges from the sources. For an extended-period simulation to accurately reflect the dynamics of the collection system, these fluctuations must be incorporated into the model.

The temporal variations in wastewater flows for municipal wastewater systems typically follow a 24-hour cycle called a *diurnal* demand pattern. However, system flows also change weekly, monthly, and annually. As one might expect, weekend usage patterns often differ from weekday patterns. Seasonal differences in water usage have been related to climatic variables, such as temperature and precipitation, and also to the changing habits of customers, such as travel and other activities occurring in the summer. For example, sewers that service vacation residences experience higher wastewater flows during the vacation season.

Diurnal Curves

Even though each municipality has a unique flow pattern in a model, the diurnal curves may be estimated by summing the 24-hour flows of the components. Figure 6.4 illustrates a typical diurnal curve for a residential area. There is relatively little sanitary flow at night, increased flow during the early morning hours as people wake up and prepare for the day, decreased flow during the middle of the day, and, finally, increased flow again in the early evening as people return home.

As one can imagine, wastewater flow patterns are as diverse as the customers themselves. Figure 6.5 illustrates just how different diurnal flow curves for various classifications of flow can be. A broad zoning classification, such as commercial, may contain differences great enough to warrant the further definition of subcategories for the different types of businesses being served. For instance, a hotel may have a demand pattern that resembles that of a residential customer. A dinner restaurant may have its peak usage during the late afternoon and evening. A clothing store may use very little

"Yes, you may go to the bathroom."

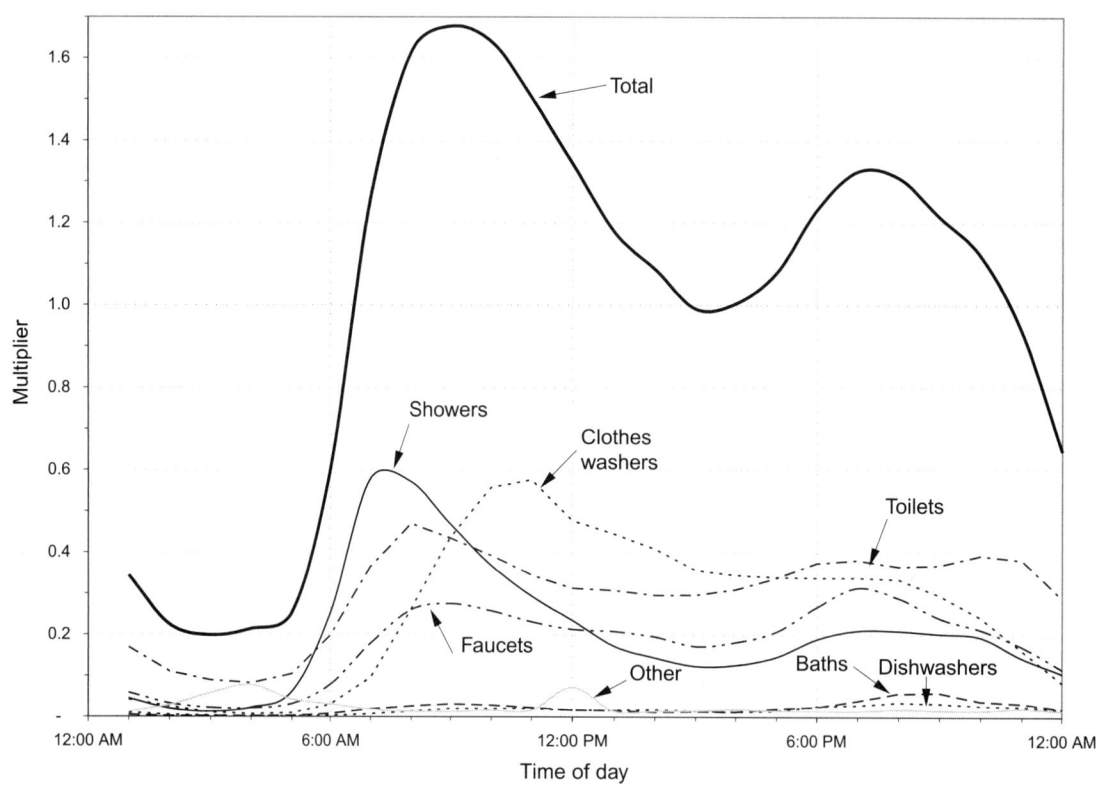

Figure 6.4 Diurnal wastewater flow pattern from a residential area.

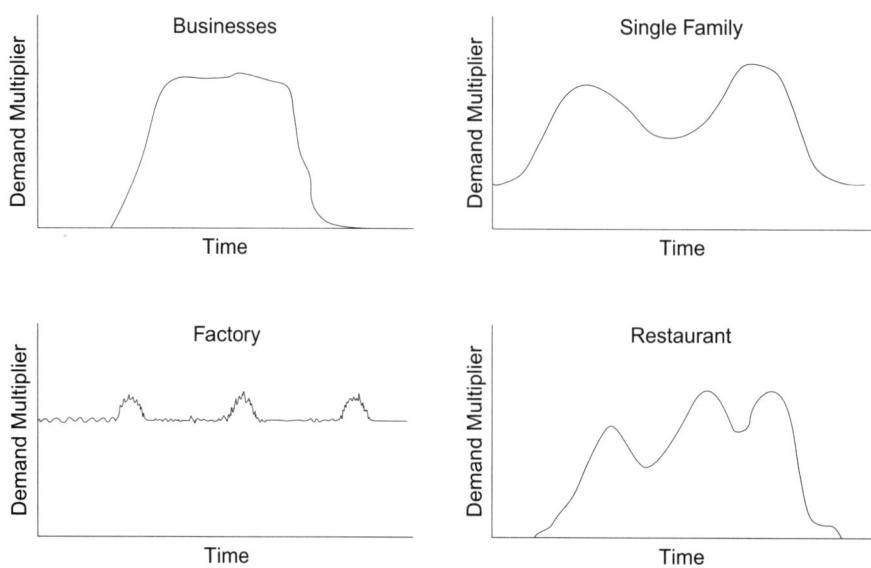

Figure 6.5 Diurnal wastewater flow curves for various sources.

water, regardless of the time of day. Water use in an office setting may coincide with coffee breaks and lunch hours.

Sometimes, sources within a demand classification have individual demand patterns that differ noticeably from the typical demand pattern. For most types of customers, the effects of such differences on the model are insignificant. For other customers, such as industrial users, errors in the use pattern may have a large effect on the model. In general, the greater the customer's use, the more important it is to ensure the accuracy of the flow data.

For commercial and industrial sources, the wastewater flow pattern may be quite different. For example, if a factory runs 24 hours a day, the overall wastewater flow pattern may appear relatively flat.

Developing Systemwide Diurnal Curves

A systemwide diurnal curve can be constructed from flow measurements collected at the wastewater treatment facility, from operating records of sewage pump stations, or in the sewer system itself by using techniques described in Chapter 8. When treatment plant influent flows are used, adjustments must be made for infiltration, travel time in the sewer, and temporary storage that may occur in wet wells of pump stations. Alternatively, wastewater flow patterns may be derived from an analysis of water use by applying the methods described by Haestad Methods et al. (2003). This procedure requires knowing the fraction of water demand that gets transformed to wastewater.

Time Increments. The time between measurements correlates directly with the resolution and precision of the constructed diurnal curve. If measurements are only available once per day, then only a daily average can be calculated. Likewise, if measurements are available in hourly increments, then hourly averages can be used to define the pattern over the entire day.

Modeling with pattern load time steps smaller than one hour is justified for specific situations, such as where wet well water levels change rapidly or there are regulatory requirements on overflows. Even if facility operations (such as pump cycling) occur frequently, it may still be acceptable for the demand-pattern time interval to be longer than the hydraulic time step, as long as the model interpolates between the larger demand-pattern time interval.

Developing Customer Diurnal Curves. Frequently, developing a diurnal curve for a specific customer requires more information than can be extracted from billing records. In these situations, more intensive data-collection methods are needed to portray the time-variant nature of the demands. This level of effort is only justified for the largest customers, such as industries that measure rate of water use or wholesale customers whose flow is metered at the tie-in point. In some instances, it may be worthwhile to install temporary flow-monitoring and data-logging equipment to determine diurnal patterns. However, it is usually easier to monitor water usage and make corrections for water that does not flow to the sewer (e.g., water that evaporates or ends up in a product).

Defining Usage Patterns Within a Model

Usage could be defined directly by describing a series of actual flow versus time points for each node in the system. One shortcoming of this type of definition is that the flow rates (in flow units) must be entered individually for each node at each time step.

Consequently, most hydraulic models express demands as a constant baseline demand multiplied at each node by a dimensionless demand pattern factor for each time increment. A demand multiplier is defined as

$$Mult_i = \frac{Q_i}{Q_{base}} \tag{6.13}$$

where $Mult_i$ = demand multiplier at the ith time step (dimensionless)
Q_i = demand in the ith time step (gpm, m³/s)
Q_{base} = base demand (gpm, m³/s)

The series of dimensionless pattern multipliers models the diurnal variation in the flow and can be reused at manholes or subbasins/subcatchments with similar loading characteristics. The baseline demand is often chosen to be the average daily demand (though peak daily demand or some other value can be used). For a baseline demand at a node of 200 gpm, Table 6.9 illustrates how nodal flows are computed using a base demand and pattern multipliers.

Table 6.9 Calculation of wastewater flows using pattern multipliers.

Time (from start)	Pattern Multiplier	Flow
0:00	0.7	200 gpm x 0.7 = 140 gpm
1:00	1.1	200 gpm x 1.1 = 220 gpm
2:00	1.8	200 gpm x 1.8 = 360 gpm

Stepwise and Continuous Patterns. In a *stepwise* flow pattern, demand multipliers are assumed to remain constant between each time step. For a *continuous* pattern, interpolation multiplier values are computed at intermediate time steps. The pattern multiplier is updated by linear interpolation between values occurring along the continuous curve at the new time-step interval. The result is a more precise curve fit that is independent of the time step specified, as shown in Figure 6.6.

Pattern Start Time and Repetition. When defining and working with patterns, it is important to understand how the pattern start time is referenced. Does pattern hour 2 refer to 2:00 A.M. or does it refer to the second hour from the beginning of a simulation? If a model simulation begins at midnight, then there is no difference between military time and time-step number. If the model is to start at some other time (such as 6:00 A.M.), then the patterns may need to be advanced or retarded.

Most modelers accept that demand patterns repeat every 24 hours with only negligible differences among weekdays and are willing to use the same pattern each day. However, owing to the change in residential and commercial water use on Saturdays and Sundays, it may be necessary to define a different pattern for weekend discharges.

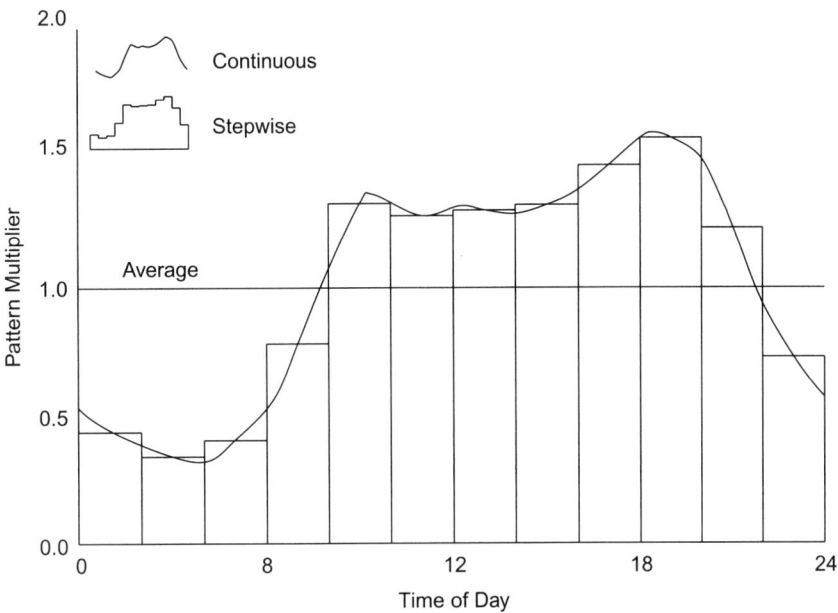

Figure 6.6 Stepwise and continuous flow pattern variations.

For a factory with three shifts, a pattern may repeat every eight hours. Other patterns may not repeat at all. Some factories may have batch processes that dump very large flows at irregular intervals. Each software package handles pattern repetition in its own way; thus, some research and experimentation may be required to produce the desired behavior for a particular application.

Example 6.3 Pattern load from a residential community

A sewage pump station is required to service a subdivision of 25 homes. The average number of people per residence is 3.1. Use the data from the AWWARF Residential Uses of Water (Mayer et al., 1999) to determine the hourly flow rate and the cumulative inflow to the pump station. Assume that all water flow goes to the sewer.

Solution

The average wastewater flow per household is determined from Equation 6.1 as

$$Q_{ave} = 37.2 \times 3.1 + 69.2 = 184.5 \text{ gal/household per day}$$

The total daily wastewater flow to the pump station is

$$Q_{base} = 184.5 \times 25 = 4613 \text{ gal/day}$$

The hourly flow rates, Q_i, are given by

$$4613 \text{ gal/d} \times Mult_i$$

The total flow per 1-hour interval is calculated as

$$\text{hourly flow (gal/d)} / 24 \text{ hr/d}$$

The following table contains the results for one day.

Interval Starting Time	Demand Multiplier	Flow rate, gpd	Hourly flow, gal
0:00	0.65	2998	125
1:00	0.34	1568	65
2:00	0.22	1015	42
3:00	0.20	923	38
4:00	0.21	969	40
5:00	0.25	1153	48
6:00	0.60	2768	115
7:00	1.26	5812	242
8:00	1.61	7427	310
9:00	1.68	7750	323
10:00	1.64	7565	315
11:00	1.50	6920	288
12:00	1.34	6181	258
13:00	1.18	5443	227
14:00	1.09	5028	210
15:00	0.99	4567	190
16:00	1.00	4613	192
17:00	1.08	4982	208
18:00	1.23	5674	236
19:00	1.33	6135	256
20:00	1.31	6043	252
21:00	1.21	5582	233
22:00	1.12	5167	215
23:00	0.94	4336	181

The following graph shows the hourly flow rates and the cumulative flow.

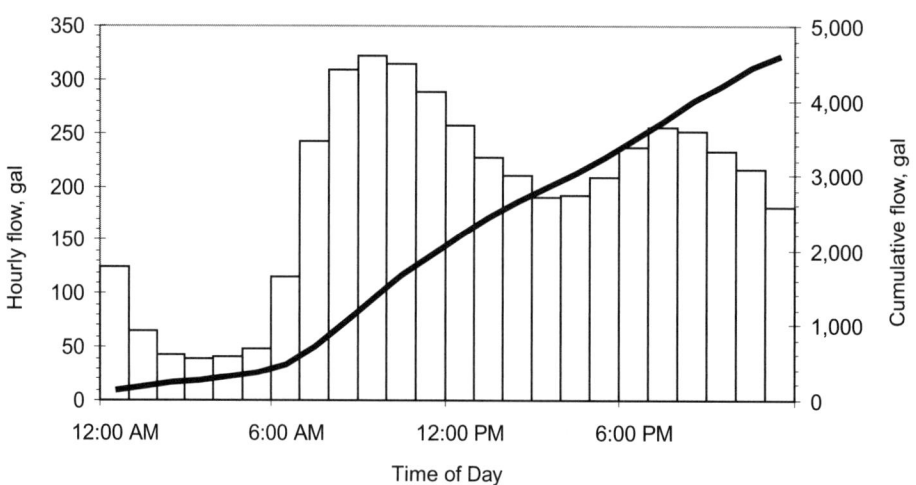

References

American Society of Civil Engineers (ASCE). 1982. *Gravity Sanitary Sewer Design and Construction.* Manual of Practice 60 (also WEF MOP FD-5). Reston, VA: American Society of Civil Engineers.

American Water Works Association (AWWA). 2004. *Sizing Service Lines and Meters.* AWWA Manual M-22. Denver, Colorado: American Water Works Association.

Babbitt, H.E., and E. R. Bauman. 1958. *Sewerage and Sewage Treatment.* 8th ed. New York: John Wiley & Sons.

Brown and Caldwell Consulting Engineers. 1984. *Residential Water Conservation Projects – Summary Report.* Washington, DC: US Department of Housing and Urban Development.

Dziegielewski, B., E. M. Opitz, and D. Maidment. 1996. "Water demand analysis," in *Water Resources Handbook*, ed. by L. W. Mays, New York: McGraw-Hill.

Fair, G. M., and J. C. Geyer. 1954. *Water Supply and Wastewater Disposal.* New York: John Wiley & Sons.

Gifft, H. M. 1945. "Estimating variations in domestic sewage." *Waterworks and Sewage* 92: 175.

Great Lakes and Upper Mississippi River Board of State Public Health and Environmental Managers (GLUMRB). 1997. *Recommended Standards for Wastewater Facilities.* Albany, NY: Health Research, Inc.

Haestad Methods, T. M. Walski, D. V. Chase, D. A. Savic, W. Grayman, S. Beckwith, and E. Koelle. 2003. *Advanced Water Distribution System Modeling.* Waterbury, CT: Haestad Methods.

Harmon, W. G. 1918. Forecasting sewage treatment at Toledo under dry weather conditions. *Engineering News-Record* 80.

Hunter, R. B. 1940. *Methods of Estimating Loads in Plumbing Systems.* Report BMS 65. Washington, DC: National Bureau of Standards.

International Association of Plumbing and Mechanical Officials. 1997. *Uniform Plumbing Code.* Los Angeles: CA. International Association of Plumbing and Mechanical Officials.

Jakovlev, S. V., J. A. A. Karlem, A. I. Zukov, and K. Siki. 1975. *Kanalizacja.* Moscow: Stroizdat.

Mayer, P. W., W. B. DeOreo, E. M. Opitz, J. C. Kiefer, W. Y. Davis, B. Dziegielewski, and J. O. Nelson. 1999. *Residential End Uses of Water.* Denver, CO: American Water Works Association Research Foundation.

Merritt, L. B. 1998. Sewage generation rates and peaking factors in central Utah. Brigham Young University. Provo, Utah: Unpublished paper presented at the 1998 Water Environment Association of Utah annual conference.

Metcalf & Eddy, Inc. 1981. *Wastewater Engineering: Collection and Pumping of Wastewater.* New York: McGraw-Hill.

Salvato, J. A. 1992. *Environmental Engineering and Sanitation.* 4th ed. New York: Wiley Interscience Publishers.

Tchobanoglous, G., F. L. Burton, and H. D. Stensel. 2003. *Wastewater Engineering, Treatment, and Reuse.* 4th ed. New York: McGraw-Hill.

Ysuni, M. A. 2000. System design: an overview. In *Water Distribution Systems Handbook*, ed. by L. W. Mays. New York: McGraw-Hill.

Problems

6.1 A sewer system is to be installed for a small lake community. The community has 38 year-round dwellings with an average of 3.4 persons per dwelling. During the summer months, an additional 57 dwellings are used, with an average of 2.8 persons per dwelling. The total land area for the community is 75 acres.

   a. Estimate the average wastewater flow during the winter months. Assume that 86% of the water used is discharged as wastewater.

   b. Estimate the average wastewater flow during the summer months. Assume that 68% of the water used is discharged as wastewater.

   c. Determine the unit area flow rate for the summer months.

6.2 Estimate the peaking factor (PF) and the peak sanitary flow (in gpd and ft^3/s) for the summer months described in Problem 6.1. Use the Babbitt method (Equation 6.3), Federov coefficients (Table 6.8), and the Tchobanoglous, et al. curve on Figure 6.3 to estimate the peaking factor.

6.3 Estimate the average daily flow rate for a city block that has the following buildings. Clearly indicate all assumptions and the estimated flow rate from each building.

   • A small church with three sets of men's and women's lavatories
   • A 200-room hotel with 35 employees and one kitchen
   • Three restaurants: a McDonald's, an
   • all-you-can-eat Chinese buffet, and a deli open from 5:00 A.M. to 3:00 P.M.
   • A public laundry facility with 22 washers and dryers
   • A beauty salon
   • A small card shop
   • A newsstand that sells magazines, refreshments, and snacks
   • A three-story office building with basement, employing 270 people with two sets of men's and women's lavatories per floor.

6.4 You are hired to upgrade the existing wastewater treatment plant for Forrest City. Use the data provided in the following table to forecast the average wastewater flows to year 2015 (create a table with the predicted wastewater flow for the years 2005, 2010, and 2015). A new industry is expected to discharge 65,000 gpd starting in year 2007. The population is expected to increase about 0.5% per year. Clearly indicate all assumptions and briefly describe the methods you used to forecast the wastewater flow when completing the following tasks.

   a. Create a plot that shows the average domestic flow, average commercial flow, and average industrial flow for each year. Take into account the additional industry water flow in 2007. Use these data to predict the average wastewater flow for each category and the total average wastewater flow for years 2005, 2010, and 2015.

   b. Determine the peaking factor (peak day/average day) for each year. From this information estimate the 2005, 2010, and 2015 peaking factors. Justify your estimates.

   c. The current wastewater treatment plant can treat 2.8 MGD at maximum capacity. Use your plots to determine whether this plant will have to be expanded and, if so, how much it should be expanded and when this expansion should be completed.

Category	Year									
	1992	1993	1994	1995	1996	1997	1998	1999	2000	2001
Total Flow										
Average	1,365,550	1,376,700	1,367,100	1,405,000	1,401,000	1,412,200	1,420,100	1,557,500	1,574,000	1,573,600
Maximum day	1,936,006	1,967,609	1,787,379	2,310,500	2,285,987	1,890,465	2,355,499	2,331,726	2,423,805	2,507,482
Domestic	834,500	843,800	854,200	837,100	828,100	858,100	861,000	987,900	992,400	986,500
Commercial	440,800	436,000	423,200	465,200	476,400	454,900	461,700	452,700	462,600	468,300
Industrial	90,250	96,900	92,700	102,700	96,900	99,200	97,400	116,900	119,000	118,800
Population Served	15,500	15,500	15,500	15,500	15,500	15,500	15,500	15,681	15,803	15,816

6.5 A pumping station serves a small subdivision of 20 homes. The metered flow into the wetwell for a typical day is shown in the following figure.

  a. Determine the total average daily flow rate and average daily flow rate per dwelling from this subdivision.

  b. Estimate the demand multipliers using 1-hour time intervals.

  c. Use the demand multipliers and total average daily flow rate to determine the volume of wastewater that is expected for each time interval.

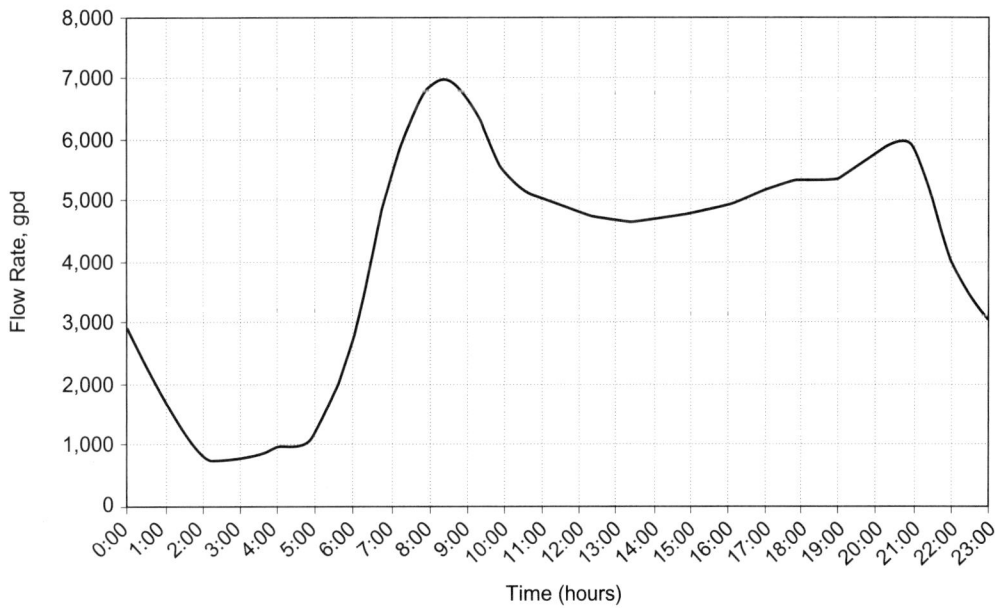

6.6 Use the model constructed for problem 5.7. Apply the pattern loads from Example 6.3 to the average sanitary flow at each manhole and run a 24-hour extended period simulation. What is the peak flow at the outlet and when does it occur?

CHAPTER

7

Wet Weather Wastewater Flows

In response to storm events, wastewater collection systems of all types receive flows in addition to the base domestic, commercial, and industrial wastewater flows that were described in Chapter 6. The effects of these wet weather flows are a major consideration in the design, operation, and management of wastewater collection systems.

Stormwater enters both combined and separate sewers via intentional and illicit connections and system imperfections. Overflows occur when loads exceed a system's hydraulic capacity. These overflows have a negative impact on environmental quality and public health. The most serious effect is high microbial concentrations in receiving waters.

With the proliferation of computers and the increase in computational power, rainfall-runoff models and other wet weather analytical techniques have become more sophisticated, allowing engineers to better understand the loads on wastewater collection systems. Rainfall-runoff models represent the transformation of precipitation into runoff for both urban and rural *catchments* (also called drainage areas or basins). In combined sewer systems, most of the runoff from contributing drainage areas is captured by the sewer. In separate sanitary systems, however, infiltration and inflow are limited by the extent of defects in the piping and appurtenances. This chapter discusses techniques used in the generation and analysis of wet weather loads in collection systems.

Depending on the purpose of the sewer model, a wide range of methods are available to calculate wet weather loading. Overall, three categories of wet weather flow modeling approaches exist:

- *Detailed hydrologic models* convert precipitation into runoff to the collection system. These models are usually needed in studies of combined sewer systems.

- For separate sanitary systems, runoff calculations are less important than for combined systems because flow is limited by pipe defects and inflows. *Empirical methods* based on numerical regression and unit hydrographs derived from flow metering data are usually most appropriate in these studies.
- For design of sanitary sewers in small land development projects, runoff should not be a significant design factor if flow monitoring data are not available. Therefore, the designer must use *rules-of-thumb* based on flow per day, flow per length of pipe, the number of manholes, or comparable data from similar systems. Instead of hydrograph routing, design can usually be based on a steady-state, peak-flow analysis.

7.1 Wet Weather Flow Definitions

Wet weather flows present special challenges to modelers. They tend to be variable in both time and space and are therefore difficult to quantify. Methods for estimating these flows vary widely due to differing local conditions. To accurately quantify wet weather flows, one must understand the nature of the flows as well as the terminology used in analysis. This section discusses basic wet weather flow terminology as applied to wastewater collection systems.

What Is Wet Weather Flow?

Stormwater runoff is generated as a result of rainfall or snowmelt. In a natural setting, runoff is not usually a problem; when it rains, most of the stormwater naturally infiltrates into the ground, is taken up by vegetation, or flows onto adjacent land or watercourses. In any modern city, however, human activities have greatly changed the way water is conveyed.

When an area is urbanized, more of its precipitation falls on impervious surfaces. Instead of infiltrating into the ground or being taken up by vegetation, a large portion of stormwater or snowmelt runs off roofs, roads, and parking lots, trickles down drainpipes, and enters drainage or sewer systems. It may then be conveyed through extensive systems of combined sewers or separate storm sewers, perhaps to treatment facilities, and finally to *outfalls* (outlet pipes) where it enters streams, rivers, and lakes. Rainfall that filters into the ground can also enter sewers, even separate sanitary sewers not intended to convey stormwater runoff.

In the context of wastewater collection systems, *wet weather flow* usually refers to the stormwater or snowmelt runoff that contributes directly to a combined sewer system, or to the flow in excess of dry weather flow that enters a separate sanitary drainage system through defects in the pipes or manholes.

Components of Flow in Wastewater Collection Systems

For modeling purposes, it is useful to further define the components of flow in wastewater collection systems. Figure 7.1 shows a typical two-day wastewater flow hydrograph. Flow rate (in ft^3/s or m^3/s) is represented on the y-axis on the left side of the plot, and precipitation intensity (in inches per hour) is given by the inverted y-axis on the right side of the plot. During a storm, the precipitation rate (in./hr or mm/hr) is plotted on a reversed secondary y-axis.

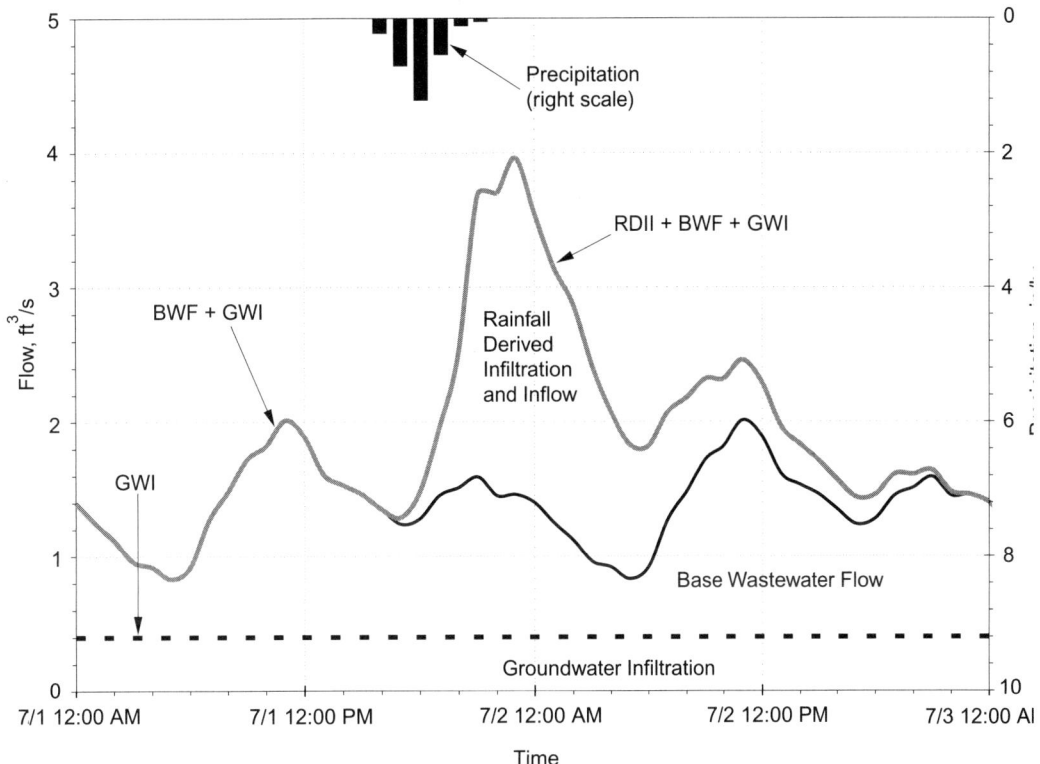

Figure 7.1 Typical wastewater hydrograph.

The sanitary sewer wastewater flow hydrograph can be divided into three basic components:

- *Groundwater infiltration (GWI)* usually enters a sewer system through sewer service connections and through defective pipes, pipe joints, connections, or manhole walls. GWI may vary seasonally, but it is usually considered to be constant over the duration of a single precipitation event.

- *Base wastewater flow (BWF)* enters the collection system through direct connections and represents the sum of domestic, commercial, and industrial flows.

- *Rainfall-derived infiltration and inflow (RDII)* is the wet weather flow portion of the sewer flow hydrograph. RDII represents the flow above the normal dry weather flow pattern; it is the sewer flow response to rainfall or snowmelt from the upstream catchment.

RDII can be further divided into inflow and infiltration:

- *Inflow* is water that enters the collection system through direct connections such as roof drains, sump pumps, catch basins, open cleanouts, stormwater inlets, or manhole vents.

- *Infiltration* is water that flows through the ground before entering the collection system through cracks and defects in pipes, joints and manholes. Infiltration is sometimes referred to as defect flow.

In combined sewers, wet weather flow is usually many times greater than sanitary flow; in some instances, sanitary flows are almost negligible during design storm events. However, in separate sanitary systems, RDII is typically a smaller portion of the precipitation, with a corresponding discharge ranging from the same order of magnitude as dry-weather flows to a rate resembling that of a combined sewer system.

Modeling Wet Weather Flows

Most wet weather modeling separates runoff into two parts: the runoff generated as a result of a precipitation (the runoff volume) and the portion of runoff that enters and is routed through the collection system (Wallingford, 1998). These processes, which are illustrated in Figure 7.2, are described in the subsections that follow.

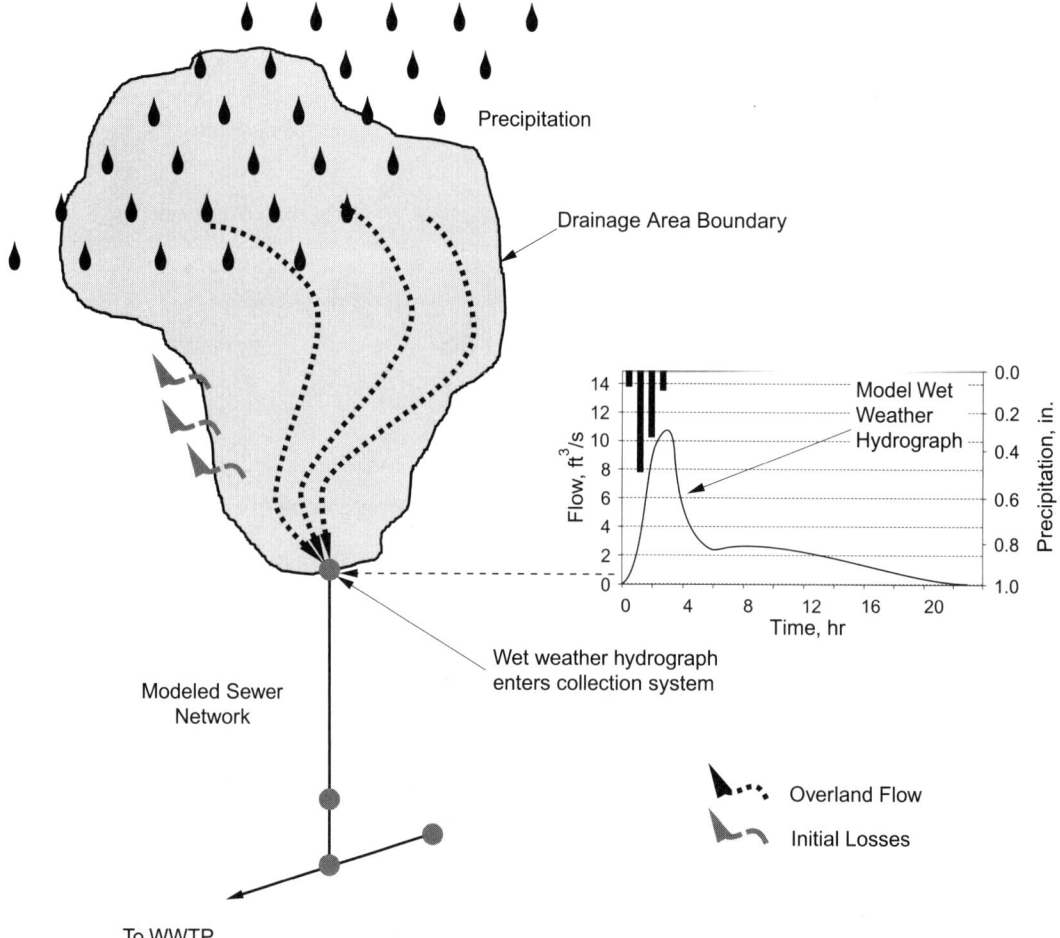

Figure 7.2 Schematic representation of wet weather flow generation in a collection system.

Runoff Generation. Runoff is generated when rainfall or snowmelt occurs. Upon reaching the ground surface, a portion of the precipitation is removed via the following processes, referred to as *rainfall abstractions*:

- *Interception* by the vegetative cover
- *Depression storage* in unconnected ground surface depressions
- *Infiltration* of water into the soil that replenishes the groundwater.

The amount of runoff generated is equal to the total precipitation minus the total rainfall *abstraction*, which is the sum of interception, depression storage, and infiltration. (Note that abstractions due to evapotranspiration and/or sublimation are ignored in most single-event runoff models.)

Runoff Collection and Intrusion. The mechanisms by which runoff enters a collection system depend on the system type:

- With combined sewers, runoff flows overland via gullies, curbs and gutters, streets, and parking lots and enters through stormwater inlets and roof connections.

- With separate sanitary sewers, most of the runoff is conveyed to the stormwater system, with only a small fraction reaching the sanitary sewer through unsealed manholes, illegal connections, or cracks in pipes and manholes.

Groundwater may enter either combined or separate sanitary sewers via cracks in pipe joints and manholes. Groundwater infiltration (GWI) may be considered part of the dry weather flow, but it can increase in response to precipitation.

The determination of wet weather flows is imprecise, and there are numerous alternative methods for developing wet weather flow to assign to model nodes. The method selected will depend on the objectives of the analysis, the type and complexity of the system being analyzed, and available hydrologic data.

The various approaches to wet weather flow modeling are summarized in Figure 7.3. As shown in the figure, loading of the sewer system model can be driven by precipitation data, hydrographs (or peak flow rates) generated external to the sewer model (and possibly adjusted by precipitation), actual flow measurements, or some combination of these.

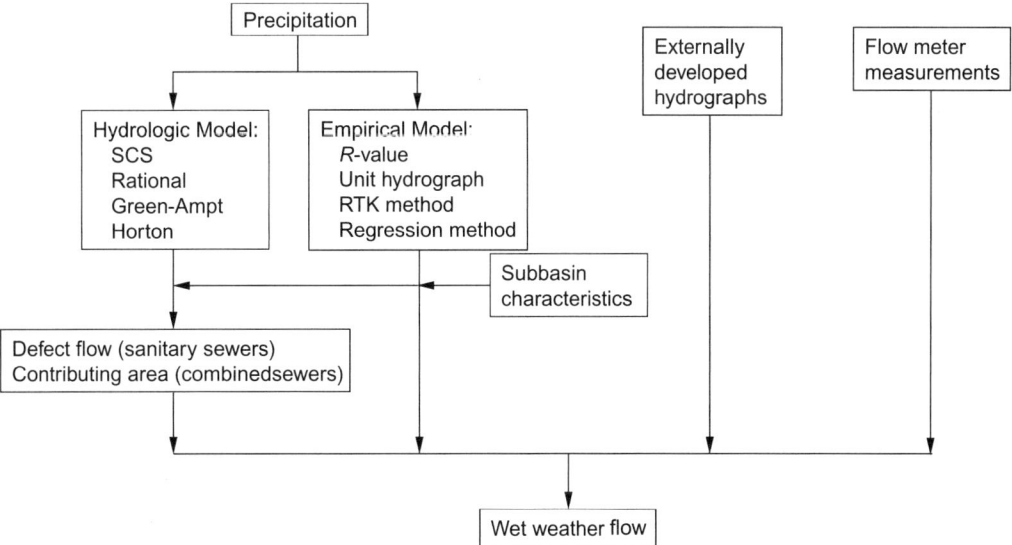

Figure 7.3 Methods used to quantify wet weather flow.

The left most path through the chart covers sewer models that adjust the precipitation using hydrologic/infiltration models such as SCS, Green Ampt or Horton to determine the water available for the sewers. In combined sewers, the resulting flows are added to the sewer. In separate sewers, the flows must be adjusted for the sewer condition to compute the defect flows entering the system. Infiltration models are covered in Section 7.4.

In the empirical models, a relation is developed between sewer flow and precipitation using one of the methods described in Section 7.6 (e.g., unit hydrograph, RTK). The methods are based on some correlation between wastewater flow and precipitation. Using precipitation data for the event being modeled, it is possible to determine wet weather flow contribution to the collection system.

The wet weather hydrographs (or peak flows) can also be determined using a technique outside of the sewer model, with the flow directly imported into the model from, for instance, a spreadsheet program. A final variation in wet weather loading is to directly use flow metering data to load the sewer model and determine hydraulic performance for those flows.

Of course, flow-monitoring data are not available when designing a new system, so unit loads (such as volume per unit of pipe length and/or diameter) are essentially the only way to account for RDII. Values for unit loadings may be specified by regulatory agencies or based on other comparable systems. These unit loadings are discussed in Chapter 9 for existing systems and in Chapter 10 for new systems.

The following section describes how the general theories behind each of these wet weather flow modeling options are applied to wastewater collection system models. The classification of wet weather flow models used here is based on reviews presented by Bennett et al. (1999), Schultz et al. (2001), and Dent (2000).

7.2 Wastewater Collection System Hydrology

In the United States, wastewater collection systems consist mainly of sanitary sewer systems for conveying household sewage and industrial wastewater, while separate storm sewers carry the surface runoff. Combined sewers are far more common elsewhere in the world, although they can also be found in older sections of many American cities. No new combined sewer systems have been designed and constructed in the US since the 1960s.

To accurately simulate the wet weather response, the modeler must have an understanding of the runoff mechanisms (hydrology) unique to combined and separate sanitary systems.

Combined Sewer System Hydrology

A combined sewer collection system conveys wastewater generated by residential, commercial, and industrial users plus stormwater generated from surface runoff. Figure 7.4 illustrates a typical combined sewer system. Note that during precipitation events, a fraction of the flow in the combined sewer may be diverted from the system directly to the receiving stream. In a typical combined sewer system, the capacity of the combined sewers is far greater than that of the interceptor sewers leading to the treatment plant or treatment systems themselves. Flows in excess of the interceptor or

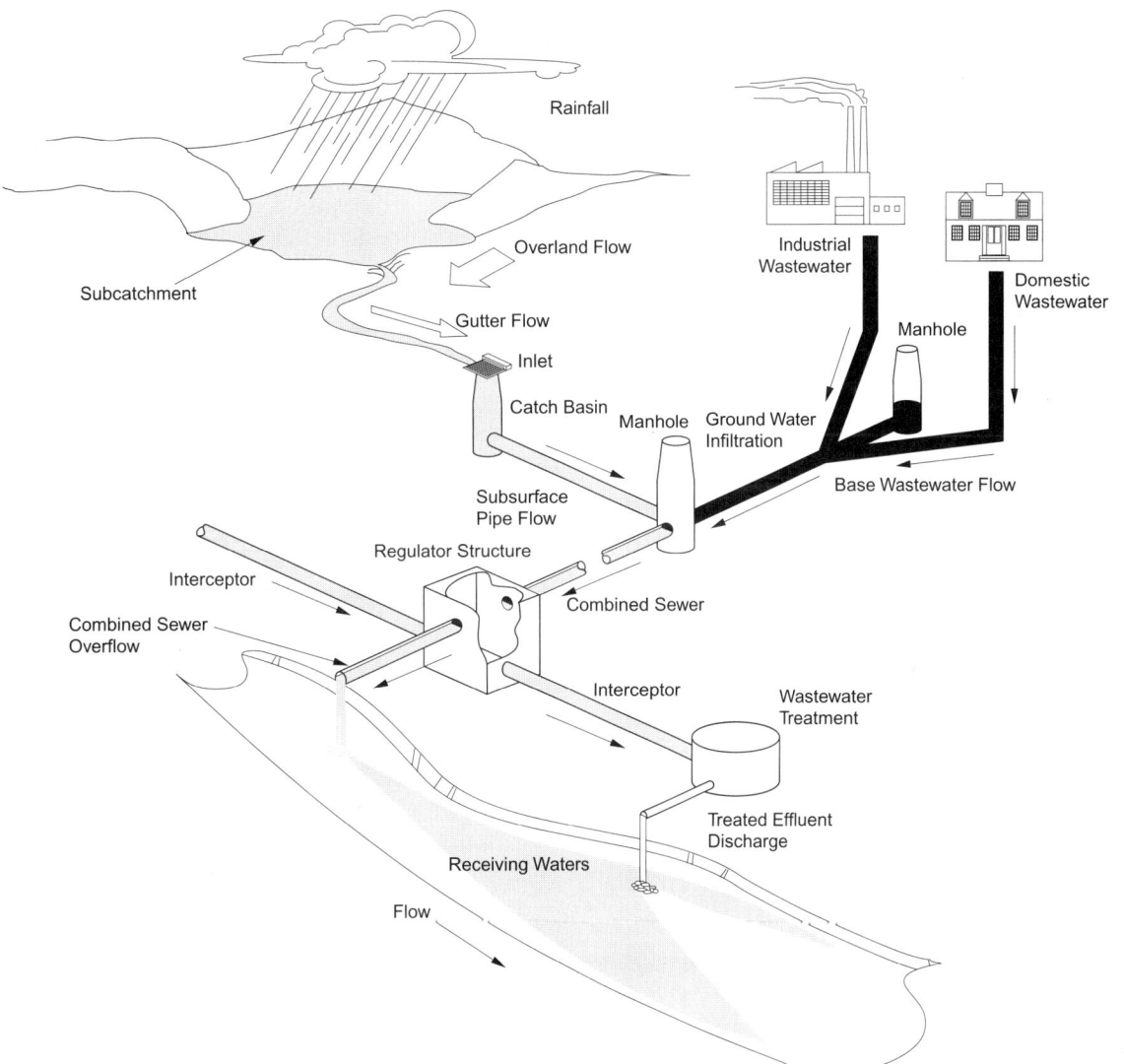

Figure 7.4 Schematic diagram of a typical combined sewer system.

treatment capacity may be released at control structures (also called regulators) or through manholes when the system surcharges. The excess flow, called *combined sewer overflow (CSO)*, may undergo partial treatment, be captured and stored for later treatment, or be released to the environment as an untreated discharge.

The critical parameter in the analysis of CSOs is wet weather capacity (total capacity less the rate of dry weather flow), with the following implications:

- Interceptor sewers, not combined sewers, control wet weather system conveyance capacity to the wastewater treatment plant.

- Relatively low interceptor capacity indicates that small, frequent rainfall are of concern in CSO analysis, in contrast to the larger, less frequent storms typically used in stormwater modeling conducted to support flood-control studies (Roesner and Burgess, 1992).

Modeling Combined Sewer Systems

The first step in the application of a computer model to a combined sewer collection system is the delineation of the sewer watershed (*sewershed*) areas to be simulated. A sewershed is the area contributing runoff to a sewer. At this point, the modeler must establish the level of detail that will be employed. In a combined sewer service area, sewersheds are generally delineated for each regulator structure in the system. Because many combined sewer systems include regulators that intercept wastewater from sewersheds of widely varying sizes, the large areas will be further delineated to develop smaller subbasins of relatively homogenous size and development conditions (land use).

Figure 7.5 illustrates the process of developing wet weather flows for a combined sewer system. Combined sewer subbasins may be modeled using two different surface types—impervious and pervious—to represent differing urban runoff response mechanisms:

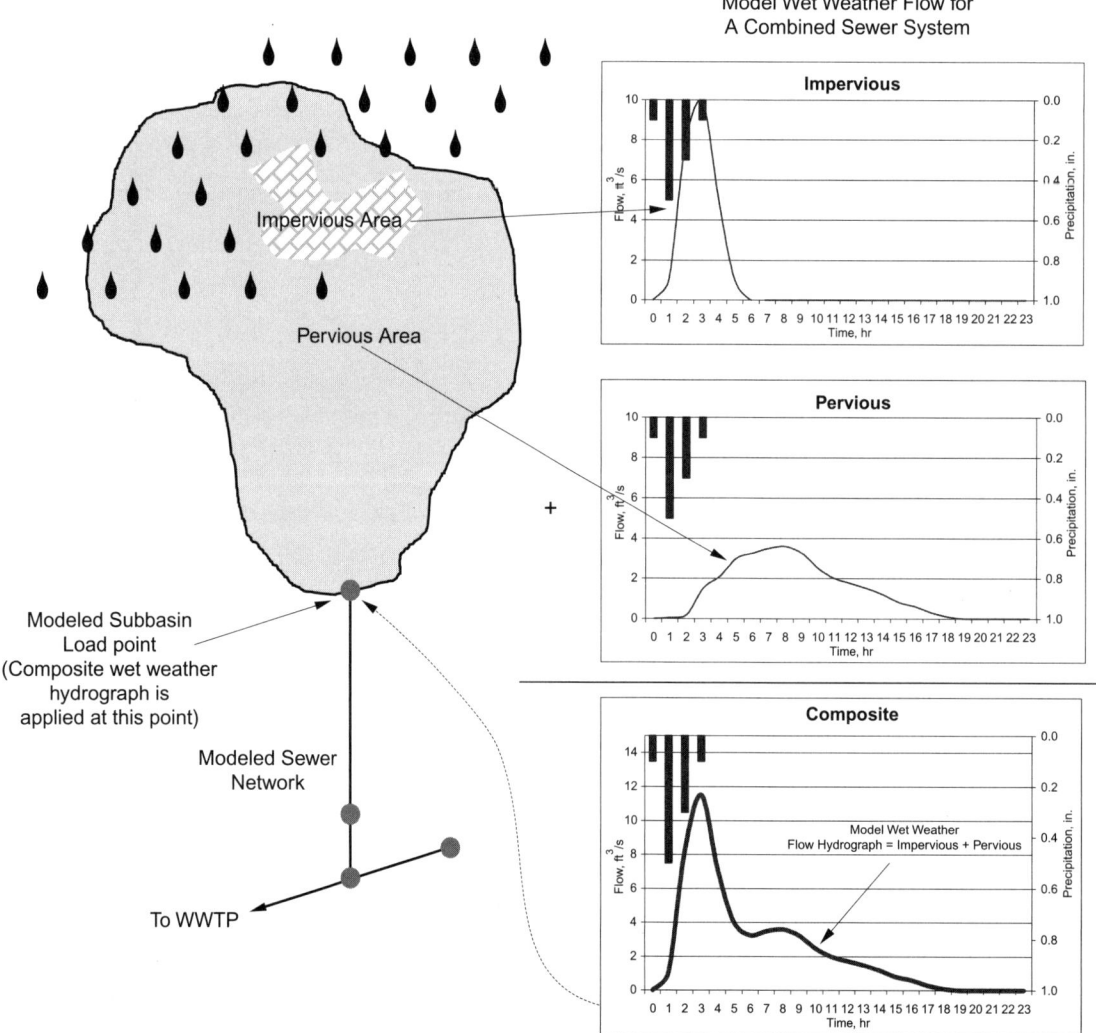

Figure 7.5 Model representation of wet weather flow for combined sewer systems.

- *Impervious response* is a relatively rapid response representing flow generated from paved surfaces (parking lots, roads, driveways) and from other connected surfaces such as roof drains. The typical resulting hydrograph has a sharp peak and duration not much longer than that of the precipitation event.

- *Pervious response* is a more delayed and attenuated response to rainfall that represents the flow generated from the open, pervious surfaces in a catchment, which do not generate runoff until the precipitation exceeds the infiltration capacity of the soil. Pervious response hydrographs are flatter than their impervious counterparts, with a later peak and longer duration.

The impervious and pervious response hydrographs are added to obtain the composite hydrograph for the sewer, as illustrated in Figure 7.5.

CSOs can be caused by relatively small rainfall events. Therefore, runoff from impervious surfaces will in most cases be the primary contributor to both peak flow rate and total runoff volume in a combined sewer collection system.

Figure 7.6 is a typical response hydrograph from a combined sewer. In this figure, the dashed line represents the average dry weather flow. The upper solid line represents the monitored storm hydrograph. The characteristic combined sewer response is extremely quick due to the directly connected impervious surfaces. In this figure, a relatively small storm (0.19 in.) generated peak flow rates nearly eight times greater than the recorded dry weather flow at that location.

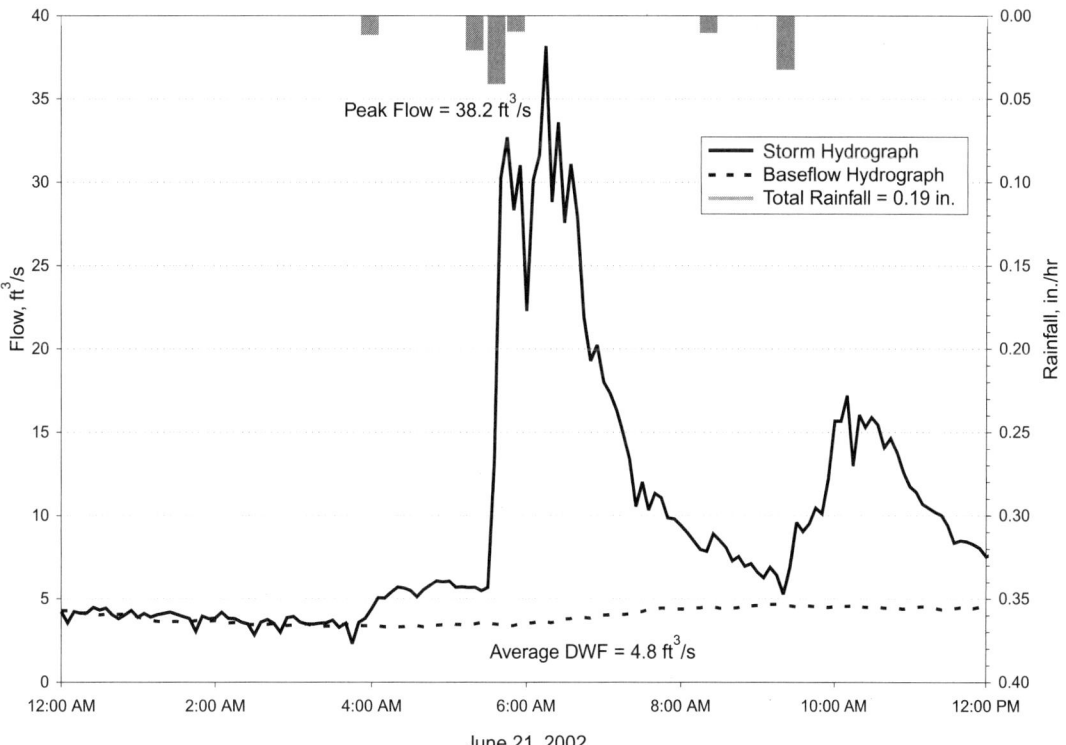

Figure 7.6 Typical combined sewer wet weather hydrograph.

Separate Sanitary Sewer System Hydrology

Separate sanitary sewer systems are designed to convey wastewater and stormwater in separate pipes. However, sanitary sewers may also collect wet weather flow via illicit connections from roof leaders, house drains, sump pumps, or storm sewers, as well as through defects in the pipes and manholes. Historically, the connection practices for house drains and sump pumps have varied widely; many such connections were not considered illicit at the time of construction. Since the 1970s, most US communities have enacted ordinances restricting the discharge of collected stormwater flow to sanitary sewers.

Figure 7.7 illustrates a separate sewer system with the illicit sources of stormwater and infiltration identified. Figure 7.8 shows infiltration of groundwater into a manhole, and Figure 7.9 shows infiltration into a sewer pipe.

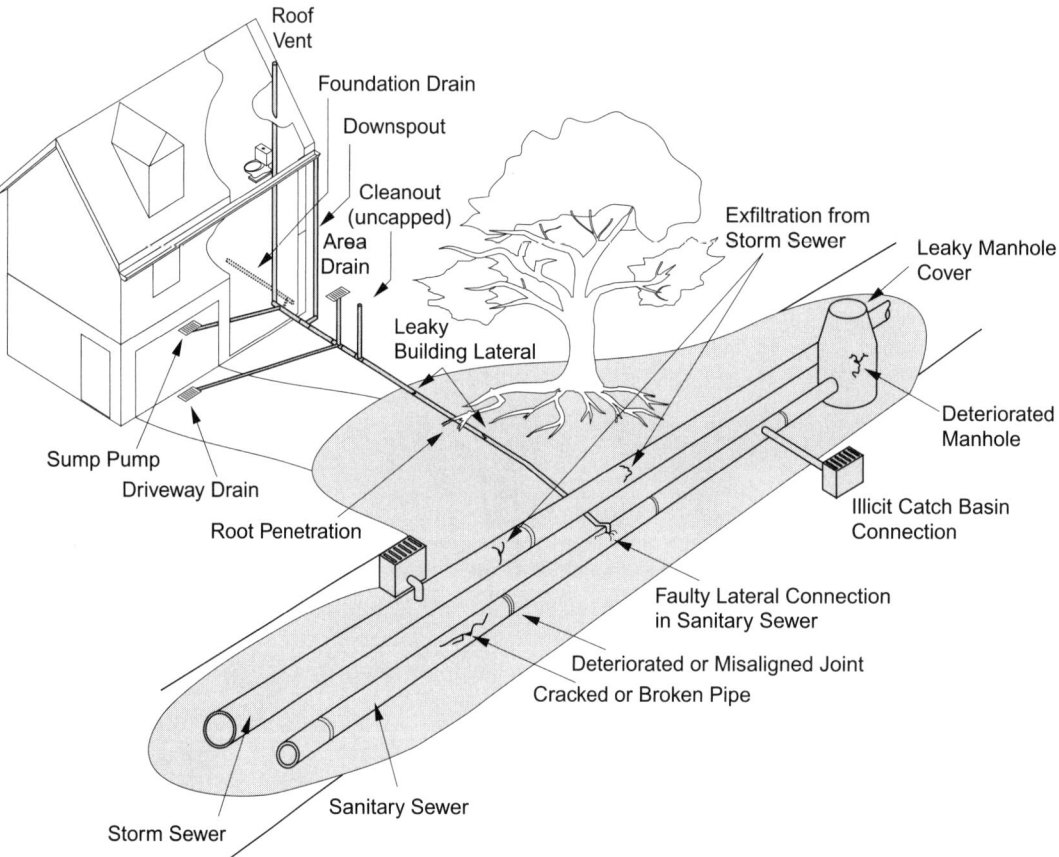

Figure 7.7 Typical separate sanitary sewer system, showing sources of infiltration and inflow.

Like combined sewers, sanitary sewer systems can experience surcharging and overflows during periods of high flow. With sanitary sewer overflows (SSOs), untreated wastewater is released to the surface through manholes. Although SSOs do not occur as frequently as CSOs, the wastewater released is more objectionable because it is less diluted by stormwater.

Section 7.2 Wastewater Collection System Hydrology   213

Figure 7.8 Infiltration of groundwater into a manhole.

Figure 7.9 Infiltration through a crack in the manhole wall near a stream.

Modeling Separate Sanitary Sewer Systems

Development of a hydraulic sewer model requires the delineation of the sewershed or catchment into smaller subbasins or subcatchments. Subbasins generally follow the development boundaries, omitting open spaces and other large "noncontributing" areas, and should be of similar size where possible. In some models, it may be desirable to designate a subbasin for each manhole.

Following delineation, the sanitary subbasins (subcatchments or sewersheds) are characterized to develop parameters that drive the runoff RDII into the sanitary sewer system. In a sanitary system, the RDII is driven less by the impervious surface of the modeled catchment, and more by factors such as

- Age of the sewer
- Condition of the sewers, manholes, and sewer service connections
- Prevalence of direct (illicit) connections of roof leaders, house drains, sump pumps, or storm sewers to the sanitary system
- Operation and maintenance of the system
- Antecedent moisture conditions (the saturation of the ground around the sewers)
- Groundwater elevation
- Construction practices at time of installation.

Figure 7.10 illustrates a process of developing wet weather flows for a separate sanitary sewer system (Montgomery Watson, 1998). Wet weather flows can be calculated either by a model or externally, as described in Section 7.1. For model-generated wet weather flows, each subbasin may have up to three different contributing area types defined to represent the following types of rainfall response:

- *Fast response* – Sewers in these areas experience a relatively rapid response to rainfall due to runoff entering through open cleanouts, illegal connections from property storm drains, and cross-connections with stormwater drains. The resulting hydrographs have short durations and high peaks, with the runoff contribution ceasing soon after the rain stops.
- *Medium response* – Sewers in these areas experience a more delayed and attenuated response to rainfall, sometimes referred to as rapid infiltration.
- *Slow response* – The hydrographs from these areas demonstrate a delayed rainfall response conceptually due to rain percolating through the ground, seeping into the less compacted trench backfill, and trickling through cracks and joints. Slow response hydrographs tend to peak well after the start of the rainfall, and flows may take many days to return to normal.

An important distinction of Figure 7.10 is that the entire modeled subbasin does not contribute runoff to the sanitary sewer system—only surfaces that contribute to defect flow do. This is in contrast to the combined sewer in Figure 7.5, where the entire modeled subbasin contributes flow to the collection system either via impervious or pervious surface runoff.

The surface areas described in Figure 7.10 are generally derived from analysis of system flow and rainfall monitoring data. The R-factor, which is described Section 7.6, represents the percentage of rainfall entering the sewer system as RDII and can be used as an initial estimate for the area of the modeled subbasin that contributes flow to the collection system (i.e., the sum of the fast, medium, and slow response areas). The R-factor can be divided between the three response areas, and then iteratively modified during the calibration process to obtain a better estimate of the actual catchment RDII response. Some modelers use all of the area in residential, commercial, and industrial areas when they are fully developed. Parks, cemeteries, and large vacant

Section 7.2 Wastewater Collection System Hydrology 215

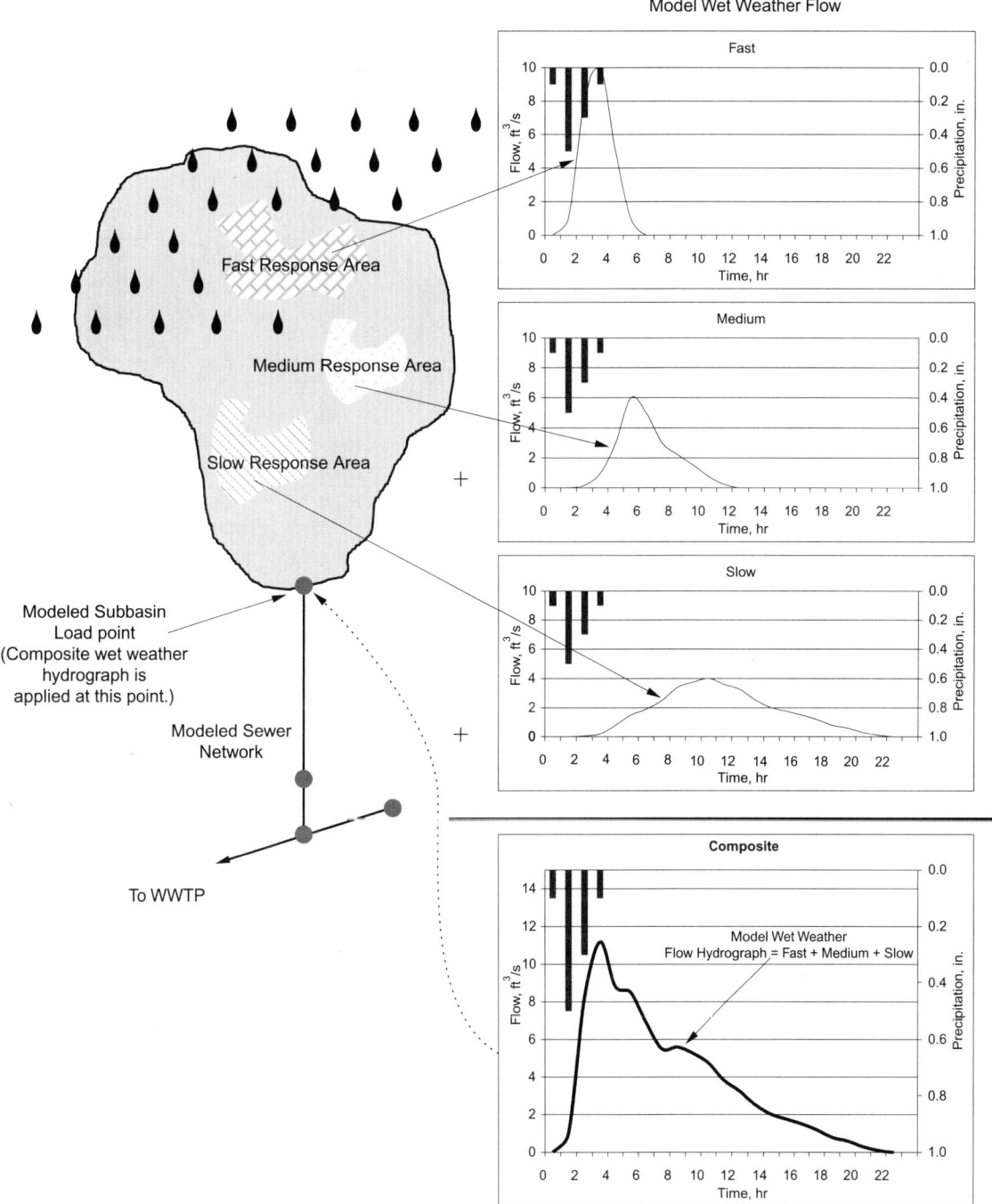

Figure 7.10 Model representation of wet weather flow for separate sanitary sewer systems.

lots are not included in the sewered areas. For long outfalls that traverse rural or uninhabited areas, it is common to select a 50–100-ft (15–30-m) strip of land running parallel to the sewer to include in the sewered area that affects infiltration calculations.

Figure 7.11 displays an example of an RDII-response hydrograph from a sanitary sewer. The dashed line represents the average dry weather flow. The solid line repre-

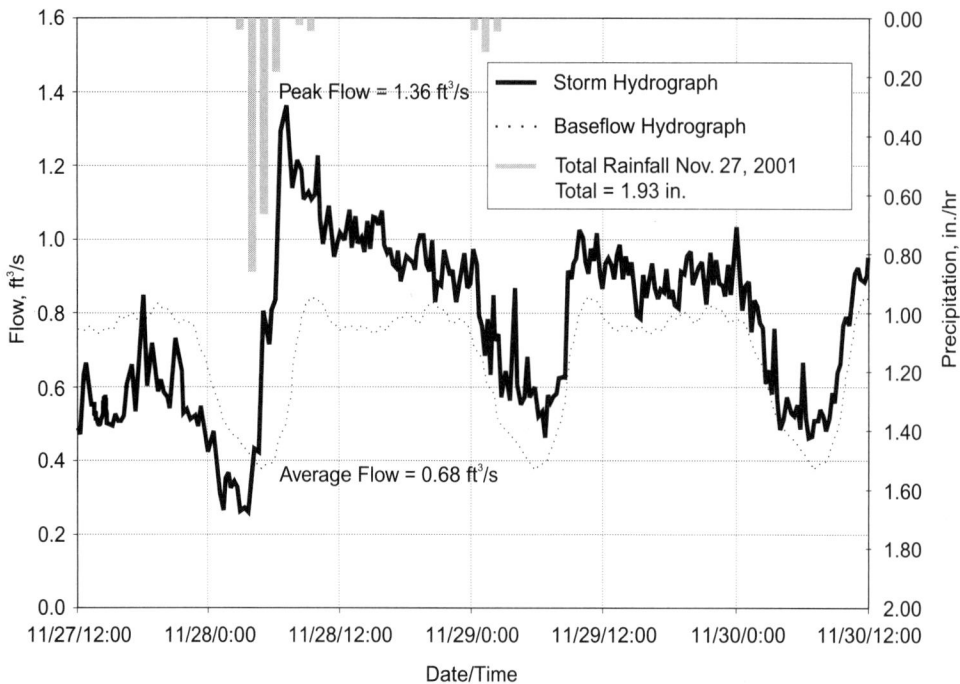

Figure 7.11 Typical sanitary sewer wet weather hydrograph.

sents the RDII hydrograph (total storm flow minus average dry weather flow). In contrast to the combined sewer hydrograph shown earlier (Figure 7.5), the response of a sanitary sewer is less dramatic, with typical peak wet weather to average dry weather flow ratios on the order of 2 to 3. Sanitary systems in extremely poor condition may have considerably higher ratios (8 to 16). The monitored basin in Figure 7.11 experienced a significant storm (a total of 1.93 in. of rainfall), yet generated peak flows only slightly more than three times the dry weather flow.

Continuous versus Event Hydrology

Wet weather flows originate as precipitation and must be converted into flows that actually enter the sewer. There are three overall approaches for determining wet weather flow:

- Determining flows external to the sewer model based on flow metering or some correlation with precipitation
- Computing flows within the sewer model using event-based hydrologic calculations
- Computing flows within the sewer model using continuous hydrologic simulations

In the first approach, the hydrologic calculations are carried out using methods such as the unit hydrograph or RTK method described Section 7.6. Only the inflow or infiltration hydrograph is imported to the model. Flow meter data can also be used to load the system.

In the event-based approach, rainfall is entered into the sewer model, which uses a hydrologic model such as SCS runoff, Horton, or the rational method, combined with some knowledge of inlets or defects, to determine water available for inflow and infiltration. Antecedent moisture conditions must be explicitly accounted for in the data entry to the extent possible with any particular method.

With continuous simulation, a long-term water budget keeps track of soil water in the unsaturated zone, snowpack depth, and depth to the water table and also accounts explicitly for processes such as evapotranspiration (which is usually ignored in event-based models). In contrast to event-based models, which stop keeping track of inflow and infiltration once the simulation moves into the tail of the hydrograph, continuous simulations keep track of moisture even during dry periods. Dent et al. (2000) argue that, although continuous simulations require a great deal more data and effort, they can provide a more accurate picture of long-term overflows and may better justify capital improvements or permit modifications. Most utilities, however, do not use continuous simulations.

While many of the processes described in this chapter are applicable to all three approaches, this chapter focuses primarily on event-based methods, whether external or internal to the sewer model. For more information about continuous hydrology, the reader is referred to hydrology texts such as Maidment (1993) and Nix (1994).

7.3 Rainfall

The rainfall data used for wet weather flow is of critical importance for sewer models in which the hydrology is explicitly calculated. However, rainfall input is often prepared as an afterthought, without proper consideration of its implications (Huber and Dickinson, 1988). This section describes sources of rainfall data as well as the types of rainfall events that should be used in typical sewer-modeling applications. Chapter 8 discusses collecting rainfall data as part of a short-term flow monitoring program.

Rainfall Data

Rainfall varies in both space and time. Depending on the characteristics of the particular storm, rainfall duration and intensity may vary so greatly that parts of the collection system may be dry while others are deluged. Therefore, collection of rainfall data at more than one location within the study catchment is important to understanding the wet weather response characteristics of the collection system. Rainfall data collected for use in sewer system models typically take two forms:

- *Intensity-Duration-Frequency (IDF) data* – The *intensity* of rainfall is the depth divided by the *duration* of the event (typically given in/hr or mm/hr). At a given location, the relationship between intensity and duration is a function of the *frequency* of occurrence. The frequency of precipitation events is also designated by the *average return interval*, which is the inverse of the frequency. Figure 7.12 is a set of IDF curves for return periods of 2 to 100 years. IDF curves are unique for each community.

- *Rainfall hyetographs* – Chow, Maidment, and Mays (1988) define a rainfall hyetograph as "…a plot of rainfall depth or intensity as a function of time…." Hyetographs may be plots of actual monitored storm events, long-term historical data from permanent meteorological stations, or simulated events. An example of a rainfall depth hyetograph is shown in Figure 7.13.

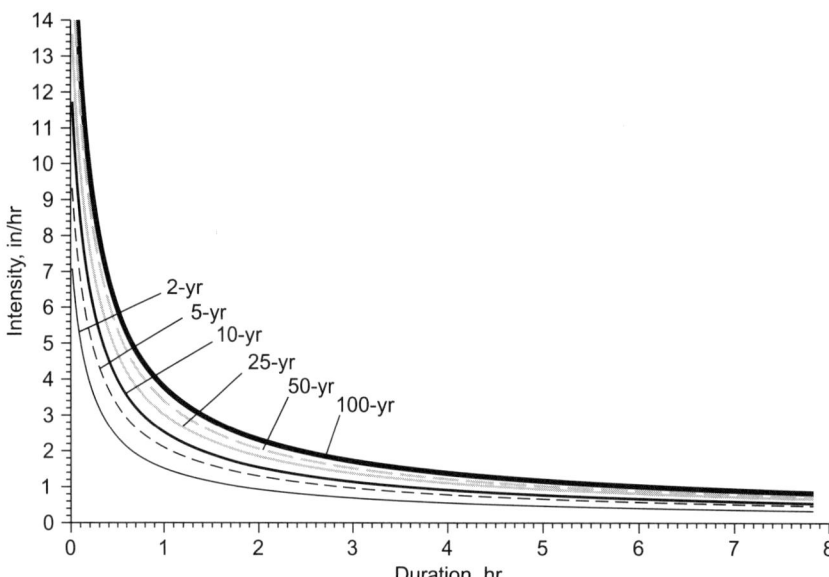

Figure 7.12 IDF curves for rainfall intensity return periods of 2 through 100 years.

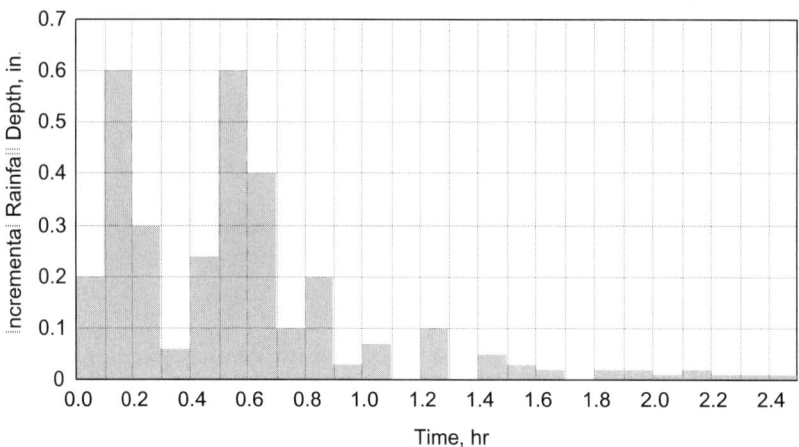

Figure 7.13 A rainfall depth hyetograph.

Selecting Model Simulation Events

The rainfall data collected as described in the previous section is processed and analyzed to select events suitable for use in the hydraulic and hydrologic analysis of the collection system. Storms can be broken down into the following categories:

- *Calibration/verification events* – These storms are monitored over a recent short-term period, generally coinciding with the collection of in-sewer flow and depth data that will be applied in developing a calibrated hydraulic model.

- *Design storms* – These events are either synthetic events developed from a locality's intensity-duration-frequency (IDF) relationships, or historical storms developed through analysis of local long-term rainfall data. They are applied after a model has been calibrated to characterize the response of the collection system to extreme events, as well as to develop conveyance-augmentation and/or overflow-mitigation alternatives.

- *Continuous records* – These long-term (one year or greater) rainfall records are used to characterize the system operation, quantify average annual overflow frequencies and volumes at CSO locations, or simulate the operation of system alternatives.

The subsections that follow cover calibration and design storms and provide guidance for the analysis of rainfall records to help select the appropriate events in each of the above categories.

Calibration Events

The purpose of wet weather calibration of a collection system model is to develop a set of hydrologic parameters that adequately predict the system response over a range of storm types. The storms selected should cover a variety of hydrologic events, but, in general, use of more events and large events will improve calibration. Calibrating for large events is especially important because most models are used to predict the response to large events (e.g., design storms) and develop system alternatives based on that predicted response. The specific storms used for calibration should be based on availability of both flow monitoring and rainfall data. Storms recorded during a flow-monitoring program should meet the following criteria to be considered suitable for use as calibration events (Wallingford, 1998):

- Total storm depth is greater than 0.2 in. (5 mm).
- Rainfall intensity is greater than 0.24 in./hr (6 mm/hr) for more than 5 minutes.
- There are at least three storms of differing duration.
- Total rainfall measured by each of the gauges is consistent with the other gauges.

Experience and judgment should be applied to these guidelines.

Design Storms

The selection of a wastewater collection system design storm has significant consequences for the community that owns the system. Not only is the capital improvements program cost a function of the design event selection, but so are the risk of regulatory noncompliance and receiving-water quality. The current emphasis by the regulatory community is to encourage system owners to use computer models to link selection of design storms and subsequent capacity sizing with the water quality standards for the receiving waters. When not explicitly mandated by the regulatory agency, the final design storm selection should balance the local community's ability to build and finance capital improvement programs with the risk of losing the beneficial use of waters for temporary periods and the risk of enforcement actions.

As design requirements for sewers are commonly set in terms of a certain return-period storm, a single-event simulation is often performed to address these requirements. There are two methods for developing design storms:

- Use of a historical hyetograph
- Generation of a synthetic hyetograph.

Design storms can be developed by analyzing long-term historical rainfall data. In the United States, the National Climate Data Center (NCDC) maintains historical rainfall records from across the nation, often for periods of 40 to 50 years. IDF curves can be developed from these data by applying frequency analysis. A commonly used distribution is the Extreme Value Type I or the Gumbel distribution (Chow, Maidment, and Mays, 1988). Once the curves have been defined, actual storms with the desired durations and return intervals can be selected for analysis.

Similarly, it may be desirable to choose a particular, well-known local rainfall event as the basis for design to make sure that a design will handle that storm (Huber and Dickinson, 1988). A benefit of using historical data is better credibility with the public.

Synthetic design storms are usually constructed with the following procedure (Arnell, 1982):

1. A storm duration is chosen, whether on an arbitrary basis or to coincide with the assumed catchment time of concentration.
2. A return period is chosen to select the total storm depth for the specified duration from local or regional intensity-duration-frequency (IDF) curves.
3. A hyetograph for the storm is created, usually on the basis of historical hyetograph shapes.

A number of procedures have been developed for synthesizing hyetographs. Some (Kiefer and Chu, 1957; Huff, 1967; Pilgrim and Cordery, 1975; Yen and Chow, 1980; US Soil Conservation Service, 1986) have developed procedures derived from an analysis of temporal distributions of naturally occurring rainfall. Pilgrim and Cordery (1975) take a quasi-probabilistic approach that tends to preserve the position in time of the periods of highest intensity. Other methods, such as the alternating-block method (Chow, Maidment, and Mays, 1988) and a similar unnamed approach for creating a probable maximum precipitation hyetograph (US Bureau of Reclamation, 1974), arrange rainfall segments so that the peak intensity is centered in the storm. Watt (1986) has published procedures for generating design storms in Canada. Following are four common methods for generating synthetic hyetographs.

Uniform Rainfall. The simplest possible design storm assumes that the intensity is uniformly distributed throughout the storm duration, as given by

$$i = i_{ave} = \frac{P_{tot}}{t_d} \tag{7.1}$$

where i_{ave} = average rainfall intensity (in./hr or mm/hr)
P_{tot} = total design storm precipitation (in. or mm)
t_d = total design storm duration (hr)

This simplified approximation is used in the rational method, with the further assumption that the storm duration is equal to the time of concentration of the catchment (AISI, 1999). This technique is seldom used in combined sewer models other than for initial estimates. It does, however, have some application where the rainfall hyetograph is visualized as a series of uniform, short-duration pulses of rainfall.

Chicago Method. Kiefer and Chu's procedure (1957) is generally known as the Chicago method. It assumes a time distribution such that if a series of ever-increasing time intervals (durations) were analyzed around the peak rainfall, the average intensity for each interval would lie on a single IDF curve (AISI, 1999). This method defines the average rainfall intensity as (Chow, Maidment, and Mays, 1988)

$$i_{ave} = \frac{c}{T_d^e + f} \qquad (7.2)$$

where i_{ave} = average intensity (in./hr or mm/hr)
T_d = total duration of rainfall (hr)
c, e, f = coefficients developed for each IDF curve; these vary with location and return period

Table 7.1 presents typical values for a 10-year return period in ten US cities.

Table 7.1 Constants for Equation 7.2 for a 10-year return period. Constants correspond to i in./hr and T_d in min (Source: Wenzel, 1982).

Location	c	e	f
Atlanta	97.5	0.83	6.88
Chicago	94.9	0.88	9.04
Cleveland	73.7	0.86	8.25
Denver	96.6	0.97	13.9
Houston	97.4	0.77	4.80
Los Angeles	20.3	0.63	2.06
Miami	124.2	0.81	6.19
New York	78.1	0.82	6.57
Santa Fe	62.5	0.89	9.10
St. Louis	104.7	0.89	9.44

T_d can be divided into t_a (time before the peak) and t_b (time after the peak), such that T_d equals $t_a + t_b$. A storm advancement coefficient, r, can then be defined as the ratio of the time before the peak t_a to the total duration (Chow, Maidment, and Mays, 1988):

$$r = \frac{t_a}{T_d} \qquad (7.3)$$

Then the recession time t_b can be defined by (Chow, Maidment, and Mays, 1988)

$$t_b = T_d - t_a = (1 - r)\, T_d \qquad (7.4)$$

Table 7.2 summarizes values of the advancement coefficient, r. The two values for Chicago are based on different studies.

Table 7.2 Values of the storm advancement coefficient (Source: Wenzel, 1982).

Location	r
Baltimore	0.399
Chicago	0.375
Chicago	0.294
Cincinnati	0.32
Cleveland	0.375
Gauhati, India	0.416
Ontario	0.480
Philadelphia	0.414

A value of $r = 0.5$ corresponds to the storm's peak intensity occurring in the middle of the storm. A value less than 0.5 places the peak earlier, while a value greater than 0.5 places the peak later than the midpoint of the storm (Chow, Maidment, and Mays, 1988). Values for r can be estimated by computing the ratio of the peak intensity time to the storm duration for a series of storms of varying duration. The value of r can then be estimated by taking the mean of the ratios, weighted according to the duration of each event (Chow, Maidment, and Mays, 1988).

The rainfall hyetograph for the Chicago method can be determined using the following equations, which are derived from Equation 7.2 above:

$$i = \frac{c\left[(1-e)\left\{\frac{t_a - t}{r}\right\}^e + f\right]}{\left[\left\{\frac{t_a - t}{r}\right\}^e + f\right]^2} \quad \text{for } t < t_a \qquad (7.5a)$$

$$i = \frac{c\left[(1-e)\left\{\frac{t - t_a}{1-r}\right\}^e + f\right]}{\left[\left\{\frac{t - t_a}{1-r}\right\}^e + f\right]^2} \quad \text{for } t > t_a \qquad (7.5b)$$

The Chicago method ignores the possibility of short-duration and long-duration rainfall intensities happening concurrently (that is, the high-intensity, short-duration rains tend to be isolated cloudburst events). As a result, the procedure produces design storms with sharp peaks. An example of hyetograph calculation using the Chicago method is presented in Example 7.1.

Example 7.1 Chicago method hyetographs

Use the Chicago method to prepare 10-year return period, 4-hour storm hyetographs using data from Table 7.1 and Table 7.2 for Chicago and New York/Philadelphia.

Solution

From Table 7.1, $c = 94.9$, $e = 0.88$, and $f = 9.04$ for Chicago. From Table 7.2, $r = 0.294$. Rearranging Equation 7.3, $t_a = rT_d = (0.294)(4) = 1.176$ hr $= 70.56$ min.

Substituting into Equation 7.5 for $t < t_a$:

$$i = \frac{94.9\left[(1-0.88)\left\{\dfrac{70.56-t}{0.294}\right\}^{0.88}+9.04\right]}{\left[\left\{\dfrac{70.56-t}{0.294}\right\}^{0.88}+9.04\right]^2}$$

and for $t > t_a$:

$$i = \frac{94.9\left[(1-0.88)\left\{\dfrac{t-70.56}{1-0.294}\right\}^{0.88}+9.04\right]}{\left[\left\{\dfrac{t-70.56}{1-0.294}\right\}^{0.88}+9.04\right]^2}$$

For New York/Philadelphia, the coefficients are $c = 78.1$, $e = 0.82$, $f = 6.57$, and $r = 0.414$. Therefore, $t_a = (0.414)(4) = 1.656$ hr $= 99.36$ min. Again substituting into Equation 7.5,

$$i = \frac{78.1\left[(1-0.82)\left\{\dfrac{99.36-t}{0.414}\right\}^{0.82}+6.57\right]}{\left[\left\{\dfrac{99.36-t}{0.414}\right\}^{0.82}+6.57\right]^2}$$

for $t < t_a$, and for $t > t_a$

$$i = \frac{78.1\left[(1-0.82)\left\{\dfrac{t-99.36}{1-0.414}\right\}^{0.82}+6.57\right]}{\left[\left\{\dfrac{t-99.36}{1-0.414}\right\}^{0.82}+6.57\right]^2}$$

Plotting these equations for values of t ranging from 0 to 240 minutes results in the hyetographs shown in the following figure.

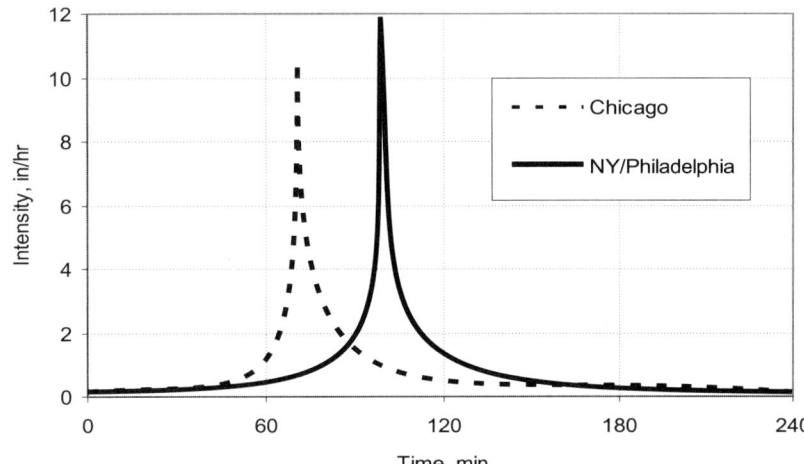

Huff and Angel. Huff and Angel (1992) analyzed data from 409 stations in nine states across the Midwest (Illinois, Indiana, Iowa, Kentucky, Michigan, Minnesota, Missouri, Ohio, and Wisconsin). They created synthetic rainfall distributions that express the ratio of the accumulated precipitation depth to the total storm depth as a function of the ratio of time to total rainfall duration. Depending on duration, each storm is placed into one of four categories differentiated by whether the peak rainfall intensity occurs in the first, second, third, or fourth quartile of the storm duration (AISI, 1999). Table 7.3 presents the median time distributions of heavy-storm rainfall at a point. Huff and Angel provided additional distributions for areas ranging from 10 to 400 square miles.

For point rainfall, the first- and second-quartile storms were found to be most prevalent (nearly two-thirds of the storms analyzed), followed by third-quartile storms (21 percent) and fourth-quartile storms (15 percent) (Huff & Angel, 1992).

Table 7.3 Dimensionless Huff and Angel storm coefficients for rainfall at a point.

Duration, hr	P_t/P_{tot}, %			
	≤6	6.1–12	12.1–24	>24
Cumulative Storm Time, %	First Quartile	Second Quartile	Third Quartile	Fourth Quartile
0	0	0	0	0
5	16	3	3	2
10	33	8	6	5
15	43	12	9	8
20	52	16	12	10
25	60	22	15	13
30	66	29	19	16
35	71	39	23	19
40	75	51	27	22
45	79	62	32	25
50	82	70	38	28
55	84	76	45	32
60	86	81	57	35
65	88	85	70	39
70	90	88	79	45
75	92	91	85	51
80	94	93	89	59
85	96	95	92	72
90	97	97	95	84
95	98	98	97	92
100	100	100	100	100

To develop the hyetograph using this method, the modeler needs the total storm depth and duration for a given design storm. The storm depth is multiplied by the dimensionless coefficient from Table 7.3 to develop a mass curve for the design storm. From this curve, a hyetograph of storm intensities can be calculated, as shown in Example 7.2.

NRCS (SCS) Storm Distributions. The US Department of Agriculture Natural Resources Conservation Service (NRCS; formerly the Soil Conservation Service) developed synthetic storm hyetographs for use in the United States for storms of 24-hour duration (US Soil Conservation Service, 1986). Figure 7.14 and Table 7.4 present the four 24-hour-duration storms that were developed (Type I, Type IA, Type II, and Type III). Type I and IA are for the Pacific maritime climate with wet winters and dry summers. Type III is for the Gulf of Mexico and the Atlantic coastal areas, where tropical storms result in large 24-hour rainfalls. Type II is for the remainder of the nation.

These distributions represent cumulative rainfall depths. A hyetograph of incremental intensities can be developed from the cumulative storm data. This process is demonstrated in Example 7.2.

Table 7.4 Dimensionless 24-hour SCS storm coefficients.

Time, hr	Percent of Total 24-Hour Storm Depth			
	Type I	Type IA	Type II	Type III
0	0.0	0.0	0.0	0.0
2	3.5	5.0	2.2	2.0
4	7.6	11.6	4.8	4.3
6	12.5	20.6	8.0	7.2
7	15.6	26.8	9.8	8.9
8	19.4	42.5	12.0	11.5
8.5	21.9	48.0	13.3	13.0
9	25.4	52.0	14.7	14.8
9.5	30.3	55.0	16.3	16.7
9.75	36.2	56.4	17.2	17.8
10	51.5	57.7	18.1	18.9
10.5	58.3	60.1	20.4	21.6
11	62.4	62.4	23.5	25.0
11.5	65.4	64.5	28.3	29.8
11.75	66.9	65.5	35.7	33.9
12	68.2	66.4	66.3	50.0
12.5	70.6	68.3	73.5	70.2
13	72.7	70.1	77.2	75.1
13.5	74.8	71.9	79.9	78.5
14	76.7	73.6	82.0	81.1
16	83.0	80.0	88.0	88.6
20	92.6	90.6	95.2	95.7
24	100.0	100.0	100.0	100.0

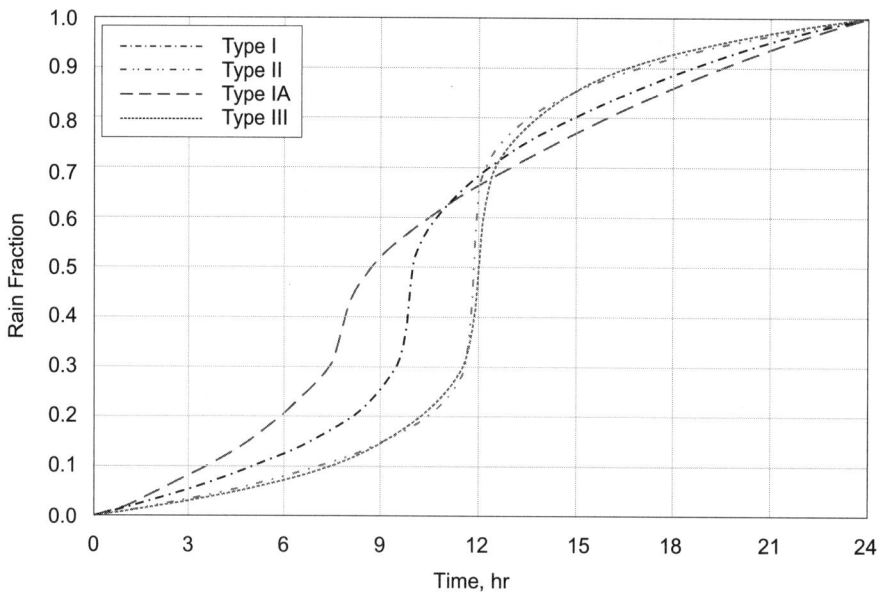

Figure 7.14 US Soil Conservation Service (SCS) storm distributions.

Example 7.2 Event hyetograph

Prepare a hyetograph for a 4.0 in., 24-hour storm in the Midwestern United States using both the Huff and Angel and the SCS Type II storm distributions.

Solution

The calculations for the Huff and Angel are listed in the following table. Column 1 is identical to the first column of Table 7.3. The values in column 2 were found with

$$\text{Time} = \text{Col 1} \times 1440 \text{ min}$$

Column 3 is obtained from the third-quartile values in Table 7.3. Column 4 values were found with

$$\text{Precipitation} = \text{Col 3} \times 4.0 \text{ in.}$$

Column 5 is the slope of Column 4. For example, at 720 minutes the slope is

$$\text{Intensity} = \frac{1.52 - 1.28}{720 - 648} \times 60 \text{ min/hr} = 0.20 \text{ in./hr}$$

Cumulative Storm Time, %	Time, min	P_t/P_{tot}, %	Cumulative Depth, in.	Intensity, in./hr
0	0	0	0.00	0.00
5	72	3	0.12	0.10
10	144	6	0.24	0.10
15	216	9	0.36	0.10
20	288	12	0.48	0.10
25	360	15	0.60	0.10
30	432	19	0.76	0.13

Cumulative Storm Time, %	Time, min	P_t/P_{tot}, %	Cumulative Depth, in.	Intensity, in./hr
35	504	23	0.92	0.13
40	576	27	1.08	0.13
45	648	32	1.28	0.17
50	720	38	1.52	0.20
55	792	45	1.80	0.23
60	864	57	2.28	0.40
65	936	70	2.80	0.43
70	1008	79	3.16	0.30
75	1080	85	3.40	0.20
80	1152	89	3.56	0.13
85	1224	92	3.68	0.10
90	1296	95	3.80	0.10
95	1368	97	3.88	0.07
100	1440	100	4.00	0.10

The calculations for the SCS distribution are similar and are presented in the following table.

Time, hr	Time, min	P_t/P_{tot}, %	Cumulative Depth, in.	Intensity, in./hr
0	0	0	0.00	0.00
2	120	2	0.09	0.04
4	240	5	0.19	0.05
6	360	8	0.32	0.06
7	420	10	0.39	0.07
8	480	12	0.48	0.09
8.5	510	13	0.53	0.10
9	540	15	0.59	0.11
9.5	570	16	0.65	0.13
9.75	585	17	0.69	0.14
10	600	18	0.72	0.14
10.5	630	20	0.82	0.18
11	660	24	0.94	0.25
11.5	690	28	1.13	0.38
11.75	705	36	1.43	1.18
12	720	66	2.65	4.90
12.5	750	74	2.94	0.58
13	780	77	3.09	0.30
13.5	810	80	3.20	0.22
14	840	82	3.28	0.17
16	960	88	3.52	0.12
20	1200	95	3.81	0.07
24	1440	100	4.00	0.05

The following figure displays the calculation results. It clearly illustrates the large differences that can be obtained, depending on which method is applied. The SCS method yields a peak storm intensity of nearly 5 in./hr, compared to a peak of less than 0.5 in./hr using the Huff and Angel approach. Further, the SCS distribution allocates nearly 50 percent of the total storm volume in two hours of the 24-hour event.

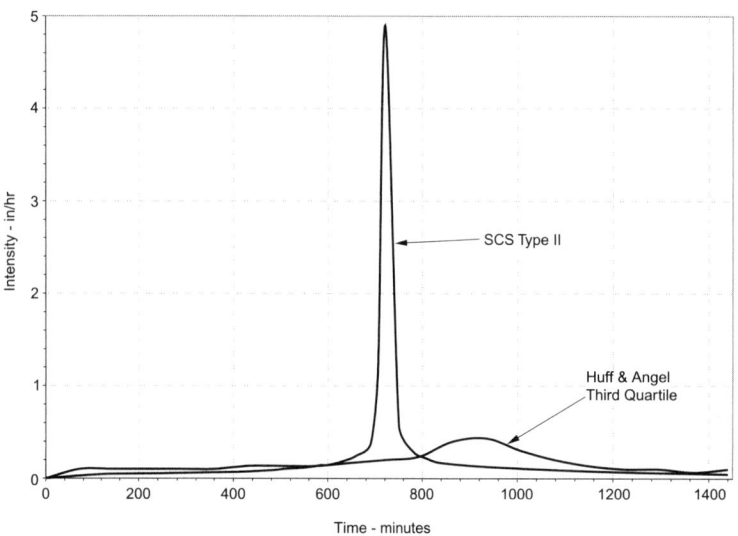

Figure 7.15 compares a synthetic 5-year, 24-hour storm distribution with an actual monitored storm. Note that historical patterns vary greatly; the one in this figure was chosen for display only. The figure highlights the fact that historical storms may have hyetographs much different from those predicted using standard rainfall distributions. This can become an issue in model calibration (see Chapter 9) if one tries to calibrate flow measurements based on typical synthetic rainfall distributions. Most synthetic hyetographs are based on a unimodal (single peak) storm and cannot be expected to accurately represent the multimodal (two or more peaks) rainfall distribution shown in the figure. The time history assigned to synthetic storms generally represents an average of many storms, not a single event (Huber and Dickinson, 1988).

Continuous Records

While design work is driven by large storm events, analysis of CSOs and compliance with CSO regulations relate to the occurrence of overflows on an average annual basis. Also, sanitary sewer master planning may require comparing the annual average SSO frequency and volume before and after proposed capital improvements.

Current US policy on CSOs supports the use of continuous-simulation modeling (use of long-term rainfall records rather than individual storm events). Under the presumptive approach to CSO control, the US EPA has established the objective of water quality as the elimination or capture for treatment of 85 percent (by volume) of the combined sewage collected in the combined sewer system during the precipitation event on a system-wide annual basis. Therefore, continuous simulation of long-term historical rainfall data addresses these criteria (WEF, 1999). Further discussion on the CSO policy is found in Chapter 15.

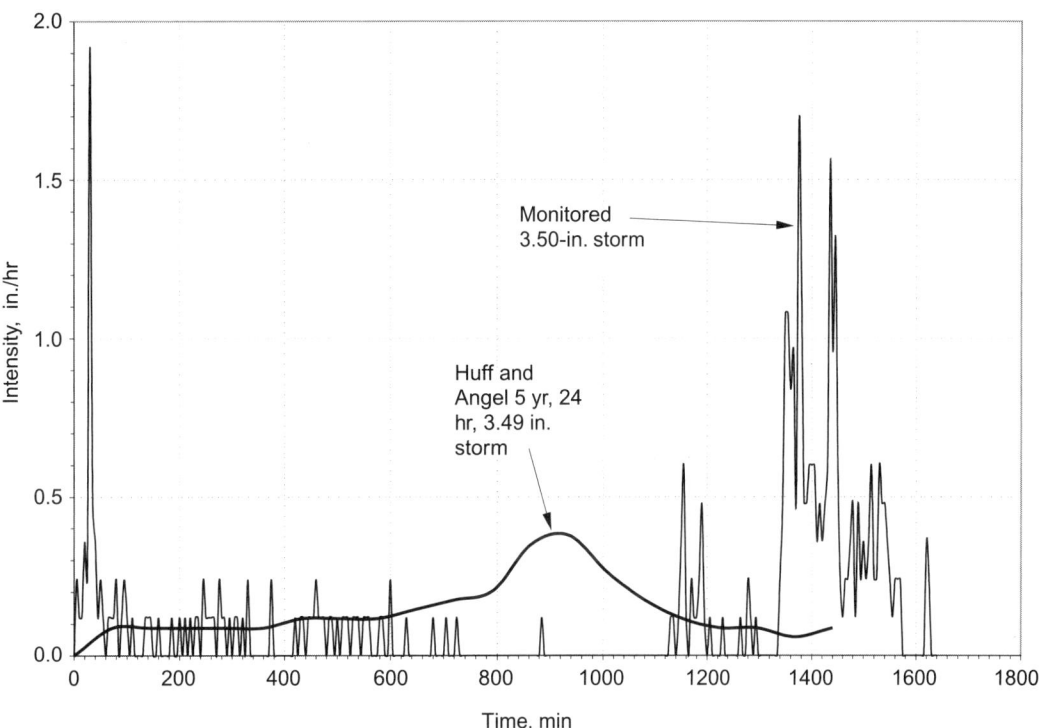

Figure 7.15 Comparison of synthetic and historical design storm hyetographs.

Long-term rainfall records enable simulations to be based on a sequence of storms, so that the additive effect of storms' occurring close together can be examined. They also allow inclusion of storms with a range of characteristics (US Environmental Protection Agency, 1999). A continuous period of data can be selected as representative of average conditions or of extreme conditions of interest. For example, rainfall data for each year of a historical record at a location can be compared, and the year that conforms most closely to the historical mean can be selected as the representative average year (Water Environment Federation, 1999). In some models, simulation techniques allow the modeler to concentrate on the periods that matter to sewer system analysis without having to run the model over the long dry spells between storms.

7.4 Modeling Runoff

To perform hydraulic calculations, a model needs a way to determine wet weather flow to a collection system. As stated earlier, there are numerous methods to determine the wet weather contribution to a collection system. The subsections that follow present some of the more commonly used techniques.

There is no single "best" method for loading wet weather flows into a model. Rather, the choice of the method depends on the following:

- Nature of the problem being solved with the model
- Status of the collection system (existing or planned)

- Type of collection system (combined or sanitary)
- Availability of flow monitoring and precipitation data
- Familiarity of the modeler with various methods
- Resources available for the study.

There are usually several acceptable ways to model any problem. However, many unacceptable ways also exist. Using a hydrologic model based on Horton's method would be inappropriate when designing a new sanitary sewer; using a simple gallon/day/mile (liter/day/km) value would be inappropriate for a combined system with large overflows.

Rainfall Abstractions

Only a portion of the rain that falls on a basin contributes to the wet weather flow in the sewer system. Many methods for estimating wet weather flow to sewers, particularly to combined sewers, start with the amount of precipitation or snowmelt and subtract the *rainfall abstraction*, which is the portion of the precipitation that does not contribute to runoff. Instead, this water returns to the atmosphere through evaporation or transpiration following interception by vegetation or storage in depressions, infiltrates the soil and contributes to groundwater, or else contributes to stream flow. The quantity of rainfall must exceed the total abstraction for there to be overland flow (runoff). Of the various types of abstraction described, only three—interception, depression storage, and infiltration—need to be considered in event-based analysis of wastewater collection systems. In a long-term continuous simulation, transpiration and evaporation may be important.

Interception. Interception covers a variety of processes that result from the capture of rainfall on vegetation or man-made cover before it reaches the ground (Chow, Maidment, and Mays, 1988). Intercepted rainfall either returns to the atmosphere via evaporation or is ultimately transmitted to the ground surface. Interception loss by vegetation depends on both the characteristics of the rainfall and the vegetations' characteristics. It is greatest at the beginning of a storm when the vegetation is dry (Chow, Maidment, and Mays, 1988).

On an annual basis, interception can be quite considerable and in some areas may approach 20 to 30 percent of the total rainfall (Haestad Methods and Durrans, 2003). The percentage is often much smaller during the relatively short and intense storms of interest to urban collection system studies. Therefore, interception is often ignored in the analysis of collection systems or is lumped together with the depression storage parameter.

Depression Storage. Depression storage is the volume of precipitation that must fall before runoff can occur. It includes initial losses from surface ponding, surface wetting, interception, and evaporation (Huber and Dickinson, 1988). Depression storage depends on surface type and slope, and it can be calculated using a regression equation or specified as an absolute value. Although paved surfaces are dominated by depression storage, other losses such as surface wetting, infiltration, and evapotranspiration (although not in the short term) also have an effect on the initial loss.

Depression storage may be derived from rainfall and runoff field data for impervious areas by plotting runoff volume (as depth) against rainfall volume for several storms.

The rainfall intercept at zero runoff represents the depression storage (Huber and Dickinson, 1988). However, depression storage is often treated as a calibration parameter, particularly in the modeling of sanitary sewer systems. In these cases, extensive preliminary work to determine the "real" depression storage may be meaningless because the value changes during calibration.

Table 7.5 provides a summary of depression storage data from a study of eighteen European catchments (Huber and Dickinson, 1988). The small catchments (less than 1 ac or 0.4 ha) were primarily roadway tributaries. These data were aggregated to develop a relationship between depression storage and slope. Figure 7.16 shows these data as a graph, with the best-fit equation given by

$$D = k S^{-0.49} \tag{7.6}$$

where k = a coefficient equal to 0.0303 for D in in. or 0.77 for D in mm
D = depression storage (in., mm)
S = catchment slope (%)

Table 7.5 European depression storage data (Huber and Dickson, 1988).

Catchment Name	Country	Paved Area, ac	Impervious Area, %	Depression Storage, in.	Number of Events
Lelystad Housing Area	Netherlands	0.5	44	0.059	10
Lelystad Parking lot	Netherlands	0.5	100	0.035	10
Ennerdale Two	U.K.	3.1	89	0.02	6
Ennerdale Three	U.K.	3	100	0.016	9
Bishopdale Two	U.K.	2.4	76	0.018	11
Hyde Green One	U.K.	2.2	71	0.019	7
Hyde Green Two	U.K.	2	49	0.02	8
School Close One	U.K.	1.7	65	0.009	11
School Close Two	U.K.	0.9	55	0.026	11
Lund 1:75	Sweden	2.1	100	0.005	11
Klostergarden:76	Sweden	0.9	100	0.041	11
Klostergarden 1:77	Sweden	2.3	100	0.02	13
Klostergarden 2:76	Sweden	3.3	100	0.019	11
Klostergarden 2:77	Sweden	4.1	100	0.013	12
Klostergarden 3:76	Sweden	3.1	100	0.022	11
Klostergarden 3:77	Sweden	2.3	100	0.022	13
Klostergarden 4:76	Sweden	1.6	100	0.022	10
Klostergarden 4:77	Sweden	1.9	100	0.022	11

Experimental studies have shown that initial losses also depend on surface type, with variation within each surface type dependent on the surface slope, as given by (Wallingford, 2001)

$$D = k/S^{1/2} \tag{7.7}$$

where D = average depth of depression storage (in., m)
k = a coefficient (in., m)
S = slope (in./in., m/m)

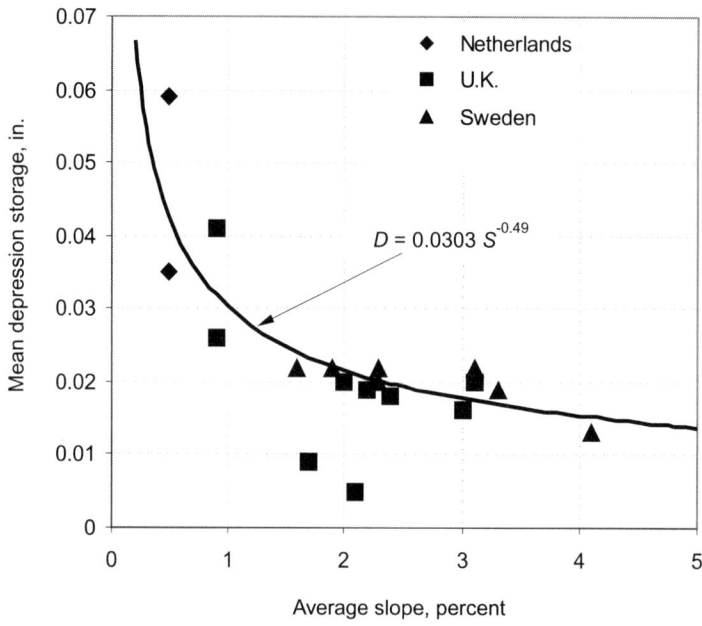

Figure 7.16 Depression storage versus catchment slope.

The value of k reflects such factors as the surface microtopography and layout. Typical values for k are 0.0028 in. (0.000071 m) for paved and roof surfaces and 0.0011 in. (0.000028 m) for pervious surfaces. Pitched roof surfaces have the same coefficient as road surfaces but use a slope of 0.05 (Wallingford, 2001).

In general, depression storage is inversely correlated with land slope; however, values used for depression storage will vary greatly based on topography and land use. When using hydrologic approaches to load a collection system model, values used for depression storage will usually need to be checked during calibration and may vary over a study area.

Infiltration. Factors that influence the process of infiltration into the soil (as opposed to infiltration from the groundwater into the sewer system) include (Chow, Maidment, and Mays, 1988):

- Soil surface condition
- Vegetative cover
- Soil properties (such as porosity and hydraulic conductivity)
- Soil moisture content at the time of the storm
- Slope
- Compaction

The rate of infiltration is often greater than the rainfall rate. When this happens, all rainfall is lost to infiltration. If the rainfall is greater than the infiltration capacity of the soil, however, surface ponding and/or surface runoff will occur (Haestad Methods and Durrans, 2003). Sandy and gravelly soils tend to have higher infiltration capacities than do silts and clays (Haestad Methods and Durrans, 2003). For all soils, the infiltration rate decreases with time and approaches a constant rate as the soil becomes wetter.

There are several approaches for determining infiltration in models. Models may explicitly calculate infiltration rate versus time, compare total infiltration with some maximum value, or calculate runoff without explicitly determining infiltration. Two methods that explicitly calculate infiltration are Horton and Green-Ampt. The rational method and percent of rainfall do not directly calculate infiltration. The SCS method keeps track of cumulative retention.

Horton Equation

Horton's infiltration equation describes the infiltration capacity of pervious or semipervious surfaces as a function of time (Horton, 1933 and 1939).

$$f_p = f_c + (f_o - f_c)e^{-k(t - t_0)} \tag{7.8}$$

where f_p = infiltration capacity of the soil (ft/s, m/s)
f_c = minimum or ultimate value of f_p (ft/s, m/s)
f_o = maximum or initial value of f_p (ft/s, m/s)
t_0 = beginning time of storm (s)
k = decay coefficient (s^{-1})

Equation 7.8 describes the familiar exponential decay of infiltration capacity evident in heavy storms (Huber and Dickinson, 1988). Different values for Horton's infiltration model are available in the literature. It should be noted that values of f_c as determined by infiltrometer studies are highly variable and can show an order of magnitude of variation for seemingly similar soil types. Furthermore, the direct transfer of values measured on rural catchments to urban catchments is not advised due to the differences in soil compaction and vegetation (Wallingford, 2001).

The parameter f_o is always greater than f_c. The range for f_c is from 300 mm/hr (12 in./hr) to low values on the order of 1 mm/hr (0.04 in./hr) as one moves from sands to clays. The parameter k is on the order of 0.01 to 0.03 per second (Rawls, Ahuja, Brakensiek, and Shirmohammadi, 1993). Infiltration is zero for paved surfaces and roofs.

Green-Ampt Equation

In contrast to the empirically developed Horton equation, the Green-Ampt method is based on a theoretical application of Darcy's law (which relates flow velocity to the permeability of the soil) and conservation of mass. The resulting equation inversely relates the infiltration rate f to the total accumulated infiltration F as (Chow, Maidment, and Mays, 1988)

$$f = K_s \left(\frac{\psi(\theta_s - \theta_i)}{F} + 1 \right) \tag{7.9}$$

where f = infiltration rate (in./hr, cm/hr)
K_s = saturated hydraulic conductivity (permeability) (in./hr, cm/hr)
ψ = capillary suction (in., cm)

θ_s = volumetric moisture content (water volume per unit soil volume) under saturated conditions
θ_i = volumetric moisture content under initial conditions
F = total accumulated infiltration (in., cm)

The benefit of the Green-Ampt method is that the calculated infiltration rate is based on measurable soil parameters, rather than the empirical coefficients of Horton. As one moves from sands to clays, values of capillary suction range from 5 to 40 cm (2 to 16 in.), while values of saturated hydraulic conductivity range from 25 to 0.06 cm/hr (10 to 0.025 in./hr) (Rawls, Ahuja, Brakensiek and Shirmohammadi, 1993). For more information on these parameters, see Chow, Maidment, and Mays (1988).

To calculate the infiltration rate at a given time, the total infiltration up to that time must be calculated. This value can be determined by integrating the following equation with respect to time (starting at $t = 0$) and solving for F:

$$F = FK_s t + \psi(\theta_s - \theta_i)\ln\left(1 + \frac{F}{\psi(\theta_s - \theta_i)}\right) \quad (7.10)$$

where t = time (hr)

Equation 7.10 cannot be explicitly solved and requires a numerical method, such as the Newton-Raphson or bisection method, to solve for F. Also, the derivation of Equation 7.10 assumes that the rainfall intensity is always greater than the infiltration rate at a given time step. If the intensity is less than the associated infiltration rate, then the infiltration is equal to the rainfall amount for that time step.

Rational Method

The rational method for estimating peak runoff dates to the work of Mulvaney (1851) in the mid-eighteenth century and was introduced to the United States by Kuichling (1889). It is probably the most widely used method for the design of stormwater conveyance systems (Chow, Maidment, and Mays, 1988). Although the method is much criticized, it continues to be used in collection system design, primarily because of its simplicity. It is often applied in combined collection system models for which runoff from impervious surfaces dominates the system inflow. Because the runoff coefficient from pervious surfaces is known to vary significantly with antecedent moisture conditions, the fixed-percentage model is typically not applied to systems dominated by permeable-surface runoff (Wallingford, 1998). In highly urbanized settings with mostly impervious surfaces, there is little reason to use methods more complex than the rational method. It is also very useful in small land development designs where peak-flow, steady-state modeling is adequate.

The hypothesis behind the rational method is that the duration of the rainfall event resulting in the highest peak storm discharge from any watershed is equal to the watershed's *time of concentration*. The time of concentration is the time it takes runoff to travel from the most hydraulically remote point to the basin outlet. For example, for a basin in which stormwater requires 30 minutes to travel from the most distant point to the sewer manhole, the designer would refer to local intensity-duration-frequency data for the design event and use the intensity corresponding to a 30-minute storm to compute the peak RDII.

The peak flow is calculated with

$$Q = C_f CIA \tag{7.11}$$

where Q = peak runoff rate (ft³/s, m³/s)
   C_f = a conversion factor (1.008 for U.S. units; 2.78 × 10⁻³ for SI)
   C = runoff coefficient (dimensionless)
   I = precipitation intensity (in./hr, mm/hr)
   A = area (ac, ha)

Because the conversion factor C_f for US customary units is approximately equal to 1, it is often omitted from the calculation.

Numerous methods exist for computing time of concentration (Haestad Methods and Durrans, 2003). Two of the more commonly used equations are from Hathaway (1945):

$$t_c = \left(\frac{2Ln}{3\sqrt{S}}\right)^{0.47} \tag{7.12}$$

and from Kirpich (1940):

$$t_c = \frac{KL^{0.77}}{S^m} \tag{7.13}$$

where t_c = time of concentration (min)
   L = length of overland flow (ft)
   n = Manning's coefficient of friction
   S = slope of overland flow (ft/ft)
   K, m = factors adjusted for the specific location

Equation 7.12 is applicable to drainage basins with areas of less that 10 ac and slopes of less than 0.01. Equation 7.13 was developed for small drainage basins (1–112 ac) in Tennessee and Pennsylvania, where K = 0.0078 and m = 0.385 in Tennessee and K = 0.0013 and m = 0.5 for Pennsylvania. The estimated t_c should be multiplied by 0.4 if the overland flow path is concrete or asphalt or by 0.2 if the channel is concrete lined. Additional models for time of concentration are presented by Haestad Methods and Durrans (2003).

A SURE SIGN OF RAIN

The runoff coefficient C quantifies the fraction of rainfall that becomes runoff. Table 7.6 summarizes typical runoff coefficients for different development types. Table 7.7 provides the same information for different types of land cover.

Table 7.6 Runoff coefficients of different types of development for use in the rational method (Schaake, Geyer, and Knapp, 1967).

Type of Development	C
Urban business	0.70–0.90
Commercial office	0.50–0.70
Residential development	
Single-family homes	0.30–0.50
Condominiums	0.40–0.60
Apartments	0.60–0.80
Suburban residential	0.25–0.40
Industrial development	
Light industry	0.50–0.80
Heavy industry	0.60–0.90
Parks, greenbelts, cemeteries	0.10–0.30
Railroad yards, playgrounds	0.20–0.40
Unimproved grassland or pasture	0.10–0.30

Table 7.7 Runoff coefficients of different types of surface areas for use in the rational method (Schaake, Geyer, and Knapp, 1967).

Type of Surface Area	C
Asphalt or concrete pavement	0.70–0.95
Brick paving	0.70–0.80
Roofs of buildings	0.80–0.95
Grass-covered sandy soils	
Slopes of 2% or less	0.05–0.10
Slopes of 2–8%	0.10–0.16
Slopes over 8%	0.16–0.20
Grass-covered clay soils	
Slopes of 2% or less	0.10–0.16
Slopes of 2–8%	0.17–0.25
Slopes over 8%	0.26–0.36

The rational method is described in Haestad Methods and Durrans (2003); Chow, Maidment, and Mays (1989); and Veissman, Lewis, and Knapp (1989). In its original form, the rational method predicts a single peak discharge for a subbasin.

NRCS (SCS) Method

In the United States, the Natural Resources Conservation Service (NRCS; formerly the Soil Conservation Service or SCS) developed a method for the prediction of runoff from rural catchments. The method is widely used in the United States as well as in France, Germany, Australia and other parts of the world (SCS, 1969, 1985, 1997).

The subbasin response is modeled using two parameters:

- *Retention* refers to the continuing rainfall losses following the initiation of surface runoff. These losses are predominantly due to infiltration.
- *Initial abstraction* refers to water that fills depressions or wets surfaces before runoff can begin. It consists of all rainfall losses that occur before the beginning of runoff, including interception, infiltration, and depression storage.

All precipitation either is captured as part of the initial abstraction, is retained by infiltrating into the soil, or becomes surface runoff. There is an upper limit (S) on the amount of precipitation that can be stored in the soil. The basis of the method is the continuity equation:

$$P = I_a + F + P_e \qquad (7.14)$$

where
I_a = initial abstractions (initial losses) (in., mm)
F = cumulative actual retention (in., mm)
P_e = total runoff (in., mm)
P = total rainfall (in., mm)

together with a relationship between rainfall, runoff and actual retention of the form

$$\frac{F}{S} = \frac{P_e}{P - I_a} \qquad (7.15)$$

where S = maximum potential retention (storage) (in., mm)

These equations combine to give the SCS model

$$P_e = \frac{(P - I_a)^2}{(P - I_a) + S} \qquad (7.16)$$

for values of $P > I_a$. Data analyzed from many small experimental watersheds yielded the following empirical relationship:

$$I_a = 0.2S \qquad (7.17)$$

Thus, equation 7.16 becomes:

$$P_e = \frac{(P - 0.2S)^2}{P + 0.8S} \qquad (7.18)$$

when $P > 0.2S$ ($P_e = 0$ when $P < 0.2S$). It may be appropriate in some applications to modify I_a to assume that $I_a = 0.1S$ or $I_a = 0.3S$. For instance, in heavily urbanized areas where there is little opportunity for initial abstractions to occur, $I_a = 0.1S$ may be appropriate. Equation 7.18 must be modified when the relationship between I_a and S is assumed to be different (Haestad and Durrans, 2003).

The storage parameter S is related to an index known as the runoff curve number CN. CN represents the combined influence of soil type, land management practices, vegetation, urban development and antecedent moisture conditions on hydrologic response. CN varies between 0 and 100, with 0 corresponding to no runoff and 100 to 100 percent runoff. The storage parameter is related to CN by:

$$S = \frac{1000}{CN} - 10 \quad \text{for } S \text{ in in.} \tag{7.19}$$

$$S = \frac{25400}{CN} - 254 \quad \text{for } S \text{ in mm} \tag{7.20}$$

Practical values of CN range from about 30 to 98, where larger values are associated with more impervious land surfaces (Durrans, 2003). CN values for urban areas are presented in Table 7.8. The SCS model, however, is rarely applied to the modeling of combined sewer systems. It does, however, see some use in the modeling of infiltration and inflow responses in separate sanitary sewer systems.

Table 7.8 Runoff curve numbers for urban areas (SCS, 1986)[a].

Cover Type and Hydrologic Condition	Average Percent Impervious Area[b]	Curve Numbers for Hydrologic Soil Group:			
		A	B	C	D
Fully developed urban areas (vegetation established)					
Open space (lawns, parks, golf courses, cemeteries, etc.)[c]:					
Poor condition (grass cover < 50%)		68	79	86	89
Fair condition (grass cover 50% to 75%)		49	69	79	84
Good condition (grass cover > 75%)		39	61	74	80
Impervious areas:					
Paved parking lots, roofs, driveways, etc. (excluding right-of-way)		98	98	98	98
Streets and roads:					
Paved; curbs and storm sewers (excluding right-of-way)		98	98	98	98
Paved; open ditches (including right-of-way)		83	89	92	93
Gravel (including right-of-way)		76	85	89	91
Dirt (including right-of-way)		72	82	87	89
Western desert urban areas:					
Natural desert landscaping (pervious area only)[d]		63	77	85	88
Artificial desert landscaping (impervious weed barrier, desert shrub with 1 to 2 in. sand or gravel mulch and basin borders)		96	96	96	96
Urban districts:					
Commercial and business	85	89	92	94	95
Industrial	72	81	88	91	93
Residential districts by average lot size:					
1/8 acre or less (town houses)	65	77	85	90	92
1/4 acre	38	61	75	83	87
1/3 acre	30	57	72	81	86
1/2 acre	25	54	70	80	85
1 acre	20	51	68	79	84
2 acres	12	46	65	77	82

Table 7.8 (continued) Runoff curve numbers for urban areas (SCS, 1986)[a].

Cover Type and Hydrologic Condition	Average Percent Impervious Area[b]	Curve Numbers for Hydrologic Soil Group:			
		A	B	C	D
Developing urban areas					
Newly graded area (pervious areas only, no vegetation)[e]		77	86	91	94
Idle lands (CNs are determined using cover types for cultivated agricultural lands. See Mockus, 1969.)					

a. Average runoff condition, and $I_a = 0.2S$.
b. The average percent impervious area shown was used to develop the composite CNs. Other assumptions are as follows: impervious areas are directly connected to the drainage system, impervious areas have a CN of 98, and pervious areas are considered equivalent to open space in good hydrologic condition.
c. CNs shown are equivalent to those of pasture. Composite CNs may be computed for other combinations of open space cover type.
d. Composite CNs for natural desert landscaping should be computed using Figure 2.3 or 2.4 (in TR-55) based on the impervious area percentage (CN = 98) and the pervious area CN. The pervious area CNs are assumed equivalent to desert shrub in poor hydrologic condition.
e. Composite CNs to use for the design of temporary measures during grading and construction should be computed using Figure 2.3 or 2.4 (in TR-55) based on the degree of development (impervious area percentage) and the CNs for the newly graded pervious areas.

As noted above, P_e in this section is the cumulative depth of runoff and must be converted to volume units by multiplying the drainage area contributing to the sewer by the depth of runoff.

7.5 Determining Hydrographs from Runoff Volumes

While steady state design models require only a single value for wet weather flow, most wet weather analysis is based on unsteady flow (i.e., dynamic or extended period simulation) modeling. The input for an unsteady flow model includes hydrograph loads assigned to nodes. The methods described in the previous section are useful in determining infiltration, runoff volume or runoff peak flow, but those values must be converted to hydrographs in order to be useful.

The rational method uses rainfall intensity information to generate peak flows. Even though it is very useful in storm and sanitary sewer piping design based on peak flow, in itself, it is not a method for hydrograph generation. There have been some approaches proposed to modify the method so that it can be used as the basis for hydrographs. The modified rational method, as described in Chow, Maidment and Mays (1988), is an example of one such method that can be used in small drainage areas.

As was the case in determining runoff, there are numerous methods for developing hydrographs. They break down into overland flow routing, standard unit hydrographs and triangular hydrographs. Some methods require that the user determine the peak flow and time to peak as a first step, while others use cumulative rainfall without the need to explicitly determine these peaks.

Determining Peak Flow and Time to Peak

With the rational method for computing runoff, peak flow is computed directly, but most other methods solve for only the total volume or depth of runoff. The volume of runoff can be computed from runoff depth as

$$V_r = P_e A \qquad (7.21)$$

where
- V_r = volume of runoff (ft³, m³)
- P_e = total runoff depth (ft, m)
- A = drainage area (ft², m²)

Note that most runoff methods give runoff in millimeters or inches, and these values must be converted to meters or feet for use with Equation 7.21.

The volume of runoff that actually enters the collection system depends on the type of system (combined or separate) and the extent of defects and inflows if it is a separate sanitary system. This volume can be given by

$$V = rV_r \qquad (7.22)$$

where
- V = volume of water entering a collection system (m³, ft³)
- r = fraction of runoff that enters collection system

A simple method for generating a hydrograph given the depth of runoff involves using a triangular hydrograph. The shape of the hydrograph depends primarily on the time to peak, which can be approximated by (Pilgrim and Cordery, 1993)

$$T_p = 0.5D + 0.6t_c \qquad (7.23)$$

where
- T_p = time to peak (s)
- D = precipitation duration (s)
- t_c = time of concentration (s)

The total time of runoff consists of $T_p(1+K)$, where K is the ratio of time of the recession leg of the hydrograph to time to peak, as shown in Figure 7.17. Knowing the times and the volume of runoff (V_r), the peak runoff can be given by

$$Q_p = 2V_r/[T_p(1+K)] \qquad (7.24)$$

where
- Q_p = peak runoff (ft³/s, m³/s)
- K = ratio of recession time to time to peak

The values of T_p and K will vary depending on the mechanism through which flow enters the collection system. It will tend to be lower when direct inflow predominates and higher when there is significant groundwater infiltration into the sewers.

Snider Triangular Hydrograph

A variation on Equation 7.24 for determining peak flow is given by Snider (1972) who gives peak flow as

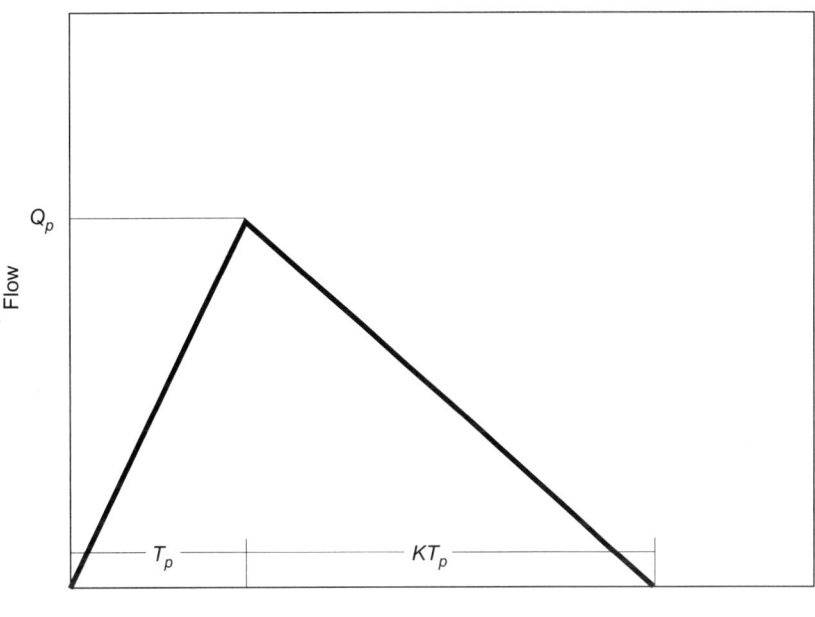

Figure 7.17 Triangular hydrograph constructed from three runoff parameters.

$$Q_p = \frac{kV_r}{T_p} = \frac{kAP_e}{T_p} \qquad (7.25)$$

where k is a coefficient that combines unit conversions and accounts for the nature of the drainage basin. A range of values for k for use with various units is given in Table 7.9:

Table 7.9 Values of k for use with Equation 7.25.

	k		
Condition	Any consistent units	P_e in cm, A in km^2, T_p in hr	P_e in in., A in mi^2, T_p in hr
Flat, swampy basin	0.62	1.29	300
Typical basin	0.75	2.08	484
Steep basin	1.2	2.58	600

Runoff during the rising and falling legs of the hydrograph is given by:

$$Q = Q_p \frac{t}{T_p} \text{ for } t < T_p \qquad (7.26a)$$

$$Q = Q_p\left(1 - \frac{t - T_p}{KT_p}\right) \text{ for } T_p \leq t \leq KT_p \qquad (7.26b)$$

Triangular hydrographs are simple to create using Snider's method and can be used with peak flows developed from many of the runoff methods. They work well with unimodal precipitation events that one would normally obtain from synthetic hyetographs (e.g. Chicago method, Huff and Angel), but do not work as well with multimodal storms or snowmelt.

This triangular hydrograph approach is applicable to determining surface runoff from combined sewer system drainage areas contributing to loading nodes. The method is analogous to the RTK method for sanitary sewer I/I presented on page 254; however, with the RTK method, an additional factor R is used to account for the fraction of water that enters the sewer. Storm runoff can be divided into multiple triangular hydrographs to account for fast inflow and slow infiltration, and these hydrographs can be fit to actual flow-monitoring data.

Unit Hydrograph Approach

The concept of the *unit hydrograph* was introduced by Sherman (1932). A unit hydrograph is a hydrograph that represents the response of a drainage area to a specified amount of excess rainfall (runoff) occurring over some duration. Unit hydrographs may be developed synthetically using a method such as the SCS Unit Hydrograph technique (see page 243-250), or from field measurements (see page 249).

Unit hydrograph theory rests on the assumption that the runoff response of a drainage basin to an effective rainfall input is linear (that is, it may be described by a linear differential equation). Practically speaking, this means that the concepts of proportionality and superposition can be applied. For example, it means that the volume and discharge rates resulting from 2 in. of effective rainfall in a given time interval are four times as great as those caused by 0.5 in. of effective rainfall in the same interval. It also means that the total time for the basin to respond to each of these rainfall depths would be the same, and thus the base length of each of the direct runoff hydrographs would be the same. For easier application to a variety of runoff depths, unit hydrographs are typically developed for 1 in. or 1 cm of rainfall excess.

The unit hydrograph approach to collection system flow contribution estimation is *spatially lumped*, meaning that it assumes no spatial variability in the effective rainfall input into a drainage basin. In cases where the basin is so large that the effective rainfall input varies from one location to another within a basin, the unit hydrograph approach requires the division of the basin into subbasins, with routing of the runoff from each subbasin to obtain the integrated basin response.

Hinks and Mays (1996) describe the calculation of a hydrograph from a unit hydrograph as a process of convolution in which the excess precipitation (runoff) at a given time step is multiplied by the coefficient of the unit hydrograph to determine the flow. If the unit hydrograph is developed for say a 1-hour storm with a runoff depth of 1 in. as shown in Figure 7.18, then the hydrograph for a storm of the same duration that produced 0.5 in. of runoff can be found by multiplying the flow values by 0.5.

Unfortunately, the rainfall durations and intensities for most storms are not uniform. Therefore, it is necessary to break the rainfall into multiple intervals and superimpose hydrographs to arrive at the final runoff hydrograph.

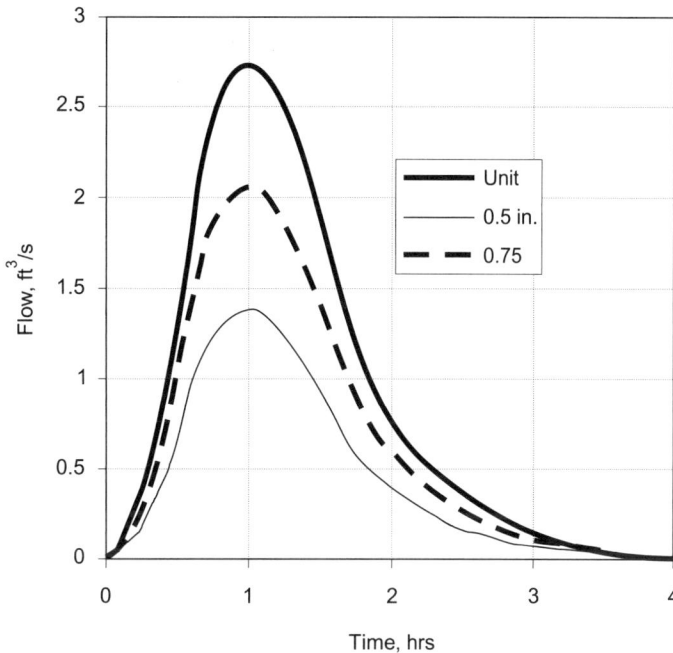

Figure 7.18 Unit hydrographs for storms of varying depth.

The runoff at time step 1 becomes

$$Q_1 = P_{e1}U_1 \tag{7.27}$$

And at time 2 it becomes

$$Q_2 = P_{e1}U_2 + P_{e2}U_1 \tag{7.28}$$

Additional time increments are computed similarly. This equation for this approach can be generalized as

$$Q_t = \sum_{i=1}^{t} P_{e(i)} U_{(t-i+1)} \tag{7.29}$$

where Q_t = hydrograph value at time t (ft³/s, m³/s)
P_e = excess precipitation (runoff) (in., mm)
U = unit hydrograph discharge ordinate (ft³/s/in., m³/s/in.)

NRCS (SCS) Dimensionless Unit Hydrograph

The NRCS (SCS) analyzed a large number of unit hydrographs derived from rainfall and runoff records for a wide range of basins and basin locations and developed the average *dimensionless unit hydrograph,* the ordinates of which are given in Table 7.10 and Figure 7.19 (Snider, 1972). The times on the horizontal axis are expressed in terms of the ratio of time to time of peak discharge (t/T_p), and the discharges on the vertical axis are expressed in terms of the ratio of discharge to peak discharge (Q/Q_p).

Application of the dimensionless unit hydrograph involves estimating the lag time t_L of the drainage basin. The lag time can be estimated by relating it to an estimate of the time of concentration (typically $t_L = 0.6t_c$), or it can be estimated directly. The time to peak of the synthetic unit hydrograph of duration Δt is then computed as

$$T_p = (\Delta t/2) + t_L \quad (7.30)$$

The NRCS recommends that Δt be equal to $0.133t_c$, or equal to $0.222t_L$ (Snider, 1972). A small variation from this value is acceptable.

Similar to the calculation of Q_p for the Snider triangular unit hydrograph (see Equation 7.25), the peak discharge Q_p for the synthetic unit hydrograph for 1 in. (or 1 cm) of runoff is calculated as

$$Q_p = \frac{C_f k A Q}{T_p} \quad (7.31)$$

where Q_p = peak discharge (cfs, m³/s)

C_f = conversion factor (645.33 US, 2.778 SI)

k = 0.75 [a constant based on geometric shape of dimensionless unit hydrograph (Snider, 1972; see Table 7.9)]

Q = runoff depth for unit hydrograph calculation (1 in. US, 1 cm SI)

A = drainage basin area (mi², km²)

T_p = time to peak (hr)

Simplifying Equation 7.31 yields

$$Q_p = \frac{484 A}{T_p} \quad \text{(for U.S. units)} \quad (7.32)$$

or

$$Q_p = \frac{2.08 A}{T_p} \quad \text{(for SI units)} \quad (7.33)$$

The coefficients 484 and 2.08 appearing in the numerators of Equation 7.32 and Equation 7.33 include a unit conversion factor and are average values for many drainage basins. These values may be reduced to about 300 and 1.29, respectively, for flat or swampy basins, or increased to about 600 and 2.58, respectively, for steep or mountainous basins. Care should be taken when changing this coefficient, as the base length and/or shape of the synthetic unit hydrograph must also be changed to ensure that it represents a volume of water equivalent to 1 in. or 1 cm of effective rainfall over the drainage basin area.

After T_p and Q_p are estimated using Equation 7.32 and Equation 7.33, the desired synthetic unit hydrograph may be graphed or tabulated using the dimensionless unit hydrograph shown in Table 7.10 and Figure 7.19. The complete hydrograph for a particular rainfall event can then be computed using the convolution technique described in the previous subsection.

Table 7.10 Ordinates of the NRCS (SCS) Dimensionless Unit Hydrograph (SCS, 1969).

t/T_p	Q/Q_p	t/T_p	Q/Q_p
0	0.000	1.7	0.460
0.1	0.030	1.8	0.390
0.2	0.100	1.9	0.330
0.3	0.190	2.0	0.280
0.4	0.310	2.2	0.207
0.5	0.470	2.4	0.147
0.6	0.660	2.6	0.107
0.7	0.820	2.8	0.077
0.8	0.930	3.0	0.055
0.9	0.990	3.2	0.040
1.0	1.000	3.4	0.029
1.1	0.990	3.6	0.021
1.2	0.930	3.8	0.015
1.3	0.860	4.0	0.011
1.4	0.780	4.5	0.005
1.5	0.680	5.0	0.000
1.6	0.560		

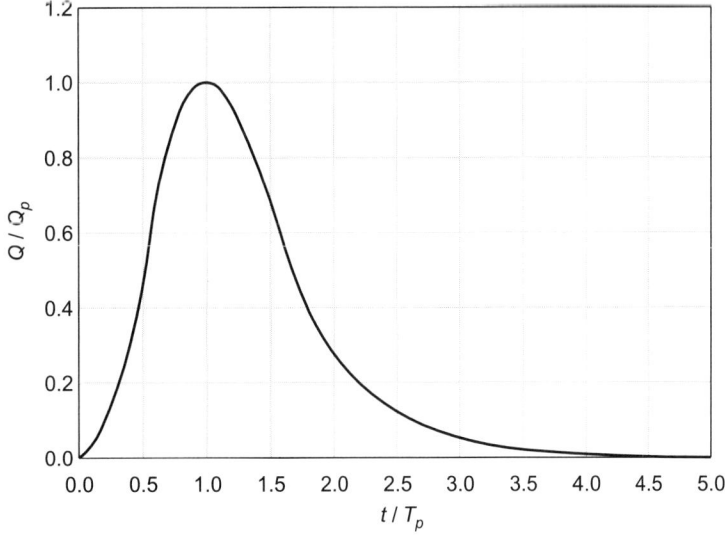

Figure 7.19 NRCS (SCS) dimensionless unit hydrograph ordinates.

Example 7.3 Snider and SCS unit hydrograph calculation

A precipitation event with 4 mm of runoff occurs on a 4000 m² area contributing to a catch basin in a combined sewer system. The time to peak is 90 minutes and the average drainage basin k is 0.75. Determine the peak flow and draw the hydrograph using both the Snider triangular unit hydrograph and the SCS standard unit hydrograph methods. Assume the runoff rate is constant.

The peak flow is calculated the same way for both methods:

$$Q_p = 0.75(0.004 \text{ m})(4000 \text{ m}^2)/[(90 \text{ min})(60 \text{ s/min})] = 0.0022 \text{ m}^3/\text{s}$$

The rising limb of the Snider triangular hydrograph is constructed by drawing a line from the origin to the point (90 min, 0.0022 m³/s). Because the area of the triangular hydrograph must equal the runoff volume, the duration (base) of the hydrograph is computed as

$$T_d = (2)(0.004 \text{ m})(4000 \text{ m}^2)/0.0022 \text{ m}^3/\text{s} = 14{,}545 \text{ s} = 242.4 \text{ min}$$

This point can then be connected to the hydrograph peak.

The SCS hydrograph is constructed by multiplying the unit hydrograph ordinates in Table 7.10 by T_p and Q_p.

The hydrographs are shown in the figure below.

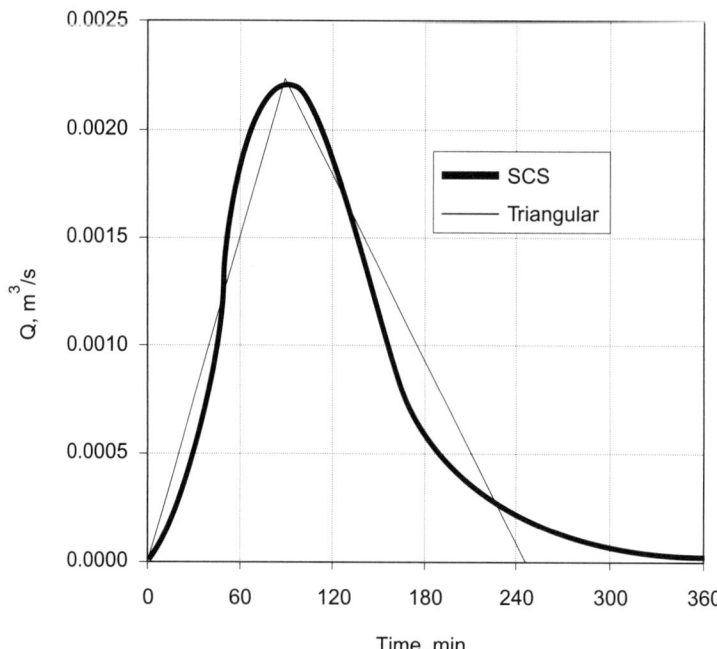

Nonlinear Reservoir

When the subbasins contributing flow to the sewer are large, it may be necessary to route the overland flow to the loading node. Excess rainfall can be imagined as a depth of water on the surface contributing directly to surface runoff. *Overland flow routing* is the process by which excess rain is transformed into surface flow (Dawdy, Schaake and Alley, 1978). The subbasin size and length of overland flow, the catchment roughness and slope characteristics, the volume and intensity of rainfall, and the percent imperviousness are the most significant factors affecting the shape and magnitude of the runoff hydrograph.

Overland runoff is often represented using the kinematic wave equation. However, direct solution of this equation, in combination with the continuity equation, is time consuming in models that contain a large number of subbasins. Simple reservoir-based models represent the physical processes as accurately as the complex physically-based approaches (Wallingford, 1998).

Many runoff models use either the nonlinear or the double-linear reservoir approach. Each subcatchment can be divided into subareas with defined properties (pervious/impervious areas and depression storage) (Huber and Dickenson, 1988). The outflow from the subcatchment is given by

$$Q = w\frac{1.49}{n}(d - d_p)^{5/3}s^{1/2} \qquad (7.34)$$

Where
- Q = subcatchment outflow (ft³/s, m³/s)
- w = subcatchment width (ft, m)
- n = Manning's roughness coefficient
- d = water depth (ft, m)
- d_p = depression storage (ft, m)
- s = slope (ft/ft, m/m)

As can be seen, the outflow is computed as the product of velocity (from Manning's equation, based on the difference between total depth and depression storage), depth, and subcatchment width.

The subcatchment slope, s, should reflect the average along the pathway of overland flow to the inlet locations. For simple geometry, the slope is simply the elevation difference divided by the length of flow. For more complex geometries, several overland flow paths may be delineated and their slopes determined. The subcatchment slope can then be determined using a path-length weighted average (Huber and Dickinson, 1988).

Values of Manning's roughness coefficient n are not as well known for overland flow as for channel or pipe flow because of factors such as the considerable variability in ground cover, transitions between laminar and turbulent flow, and very small flow depths (Huber and Dickinson, 1988). Table 7.11 lists typical Manning's n values for overland flow. Note that overland flow roughness is typically viewed as a calibration parameter that can be modified (within reasonable limits) to match predicted hydrographs with monitored hydrographs.

Table 7.11 Estimates of Manning's roughness coefficient, n, for overland flow (from Huber and Dickinson, 1988).

Source	Ground Cover	n	Range
Crawford and Linsley, 1966	Smooth asphalt	0.012	
	Asphalt of concrete paving	0.014	
	Packed clay	0.030	
	Light turf	0.200	
	Dense turf	0.350	
	Dense shrubbery and forest litter	0.400	
Engman, 1986	Concrete or asphalt	0.011	0.010–0.013
	Bare sand	0.010	0.010–0.016
	Graveled surface	0.020	0.012–0.030
	Bare clay-loam (eroded)	0.020	0.012–0.033
	Range (natural)	0.130	0.010–0.320
	Bluegrass sod	0.450	0.390–0.630
	Short grass prairie	0.150	0.100–0.200
	Bermuda grass	0.410	0.300–0.480

Overland routing performed using a double-linear reservoir approach transforms the net resulting rainfall for each subcatchment into an inflow hydrograph at each node using two notional linear reservoirs in series to represent the storage that is available on the ground and in minor drains and the delay induced between the peak rainfall and peak runoff. In this way, a reduced peak runoff is generated with a lag after the peak rainfall. The flow-routing coefficient depends on the rainfall intensity, contributing area, and slope (Wallingford, 2001).

7.6 Empirical Methods for Generating Hydrographs

The methods presented in Sections 7.4 and 7.5 can be used to generate wet weather hydrographs without flow monitoring data. (Of course, models using these methods should be calibrated, as discussed in Chapter 9.) The methods presented in this section rely on empirical correlation of measured wet weather flow with rainfall amounts and other parameters to derive a hydrograph or peak flow value.

In terms of sophistication, the methods described in this section range from the theoretically correct unit hydrograph approach to some crude empirical relationships. The modeler must choose an appropriate method based on the level of detail required from the model, difficulty of implementation, and availability of data.

While the methods described in Section 7.4 are appropriate for combined sewer systems, the methods in this section are oriented toward determining RDII in sanitary systems. Because they are based on actual flow monitoring, the methods described in this section circumvent the obstacle of not knowing the exact location and magnitude of defects or inflow points.

The starting point for these methods is a wet weather hydrograph. The wet weather hydrograph is developed by subtracting sanitary flow and groundwater infiltration from the measured flow during a storm. Methods for collecting flow data and determining the hydrograph are described in detail in Chapter 8. Using the methods described in the following sections, this measured wet weather hydrograph can be extended to storms of different magnitudes and durations.

Percentage of Rainfall Volume (R-Factor)

The portion of precipitation that actually enters the collection system is an important parameter in many of the methods described in this section. It is based on the assumption that the fraction of precipitation that enters the collection system is relatively constant over a fairly wide range of events and is described by

$$V = RV_p \qquad (7.35)$$

where
V = volume of inflow/infiltration entering sewer (ft^3, m^3)
V_p = volume of precipitation (ft^3, m^3)
R = fraction of precipitation that enters sewers

Equation 7.35 can also be divided by the drainage area to give an equation in terms of depth instead of volume units. Also, R is frequently expressed as a percentage rather than the decimal form used in the equation.

V_p is the product of the average depth of precipitation over the subbasin and the area of the subbasin. Where continuous precipitation data are available, V_p is equal to the area under the storm hyetograph multiplied by the area of the subbasin. R-values are determined from field monitoring of rainfall and flow. Once R is known, V can be determined for other rainfall events (other values of V_p) and used as a starting point for developing hydrographs.

R-values are developed on a storm-event basis. RDII is highly dependent on antecedent soil-moisture conditions and will be affected by the shape of the hyetograph for a given storm (Bennett et al., 1999). If the soil is saturated before a storm, the R-value for that event will be high, whereas it is lower if the soil is dry. Because this method requires judgment, it is frequently applied inconsistently. It may serve as a useful tool for comparing subbasins experiencing the same storm with the same antecedent moisture conditions. See "RTK Hydrograph Method" on page 254 for typical values of R.

Unit Hydrographs from Flow Measurements

Unit hydrographs were described in "Unit Hydrograph Approach" on page 242. As mentioned in that section, unit hydrographs can be developed using field measurements as well as synthetic unit hydrograph techniques. The process for developing the unit hydrograph from measured data [i.e., determining the $U(t)$ function for Equation 7.29] is referred to as *deconvolution*. In that process, one needs to solve the equations backwards for $U(t)$ given measured values for Q and P. For instance, the unit hydrograph for the 1-in. (25 mm) storm Figure 7.18 may have been developed using the measured hydrograph for a 0.75-in. (19.0mm) storm shown as the dashed line.

Although deconvolution can sometimes be done manually, it usually involves computerized regression analysis. The process is beyond the scope of this book but is addressed in sources such as Collins (Johnstone and Cross, 1949), Hinks and Mays (1996), Snyder (1955) and Westphal (2001).

Simplifications to Unit Hydrograph

Developing unit hydrographs is workable for streams with a long period of record and many storms, but collection system monitoring is often a short-term exercise with only a handful of significant storms occurring during the monitoring program. The data may not support standard unit hydrographs. It may be necessary to normalize the handful of hydrographs measured based on the duration of the storm and the total runoff.

Once hydrographs for the storms have been collected, the time can be normalized using

$$t^* = t/T_d \qquad (7.36)$$

where t^* = unit hydrograph dimensionless time
  t = hydrograph time (hr)
  T_d = storm duration (hr)

The flow values can then be normalized by dividing by the depth of precipitation

$$Q^*(t^*) = \frac{Q(t)}{P} \qquad (7.37)$$

where $Q^*(t^*)$ = flow at t^* per unit of precipitation (ft³/s/in., m³/s/mm)
  $Q(t)$ = flow at time t corresponding to t^* per Equation 7.36 (ft³/s, m³/s)
  P = precipitation depth (in., mm)

Given the hydrographs for three storms shown in Figure 7.20a, the flows can be normalized using the equations above to give the unit hydrographs shown in Figure 7.20b. While these hydrographs will not lie on top of one another, they will be reasonably close if the storms are not too different. Some average of these hydrographs can be used in modeling. The time can also be scaled using time to peak instead of storm duration.

To the extent that the monitored drainage basin is similar to other drainage basins, the vertical axis can be normalized by dividing by the area to produce an axis with units of flow per unit area per unit rainfall depth, and the resulting unit hydrograph can be used in other basins.

Inflow Coefficient Method

A modification of the rational method is the inflow coefficient method (Nelson, 1987). The peak inflow from each subbasin is determined with:

$$Q = C_f KIA \qquad (7.38)$$

where Q = peak inflow rate (ft³/s, m³/s)
  C_f = a conversion factor (1.008 for U.S. units; 2.78 × 10⁻³ for SI)
  K = inflow coefficient
  I = precipitation intensity (in./hr, mm/hr)
  A = area (ac, ha)

Section 7.6 Empirical Methods for Generating Hydrographs 251

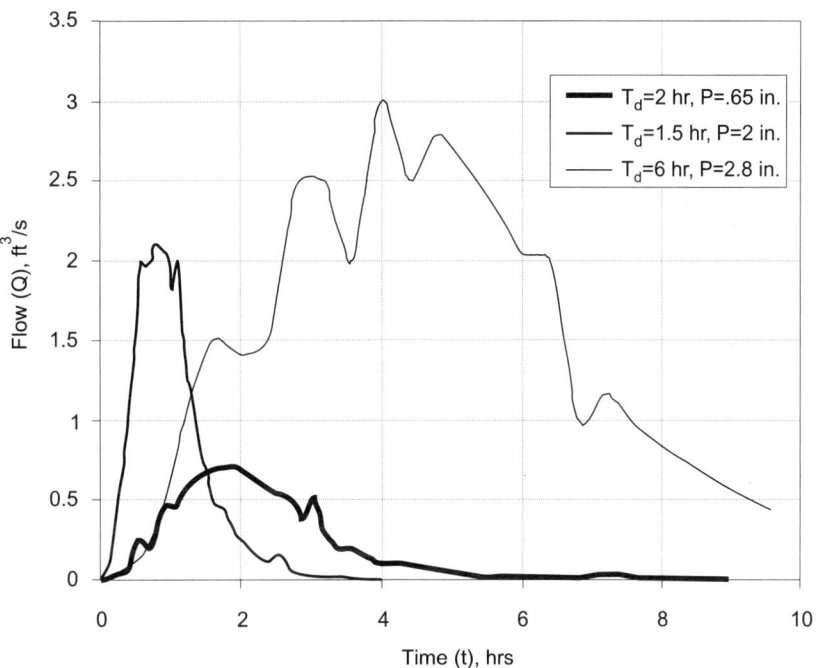

Figure 7.20a Actual hydrographs from events.

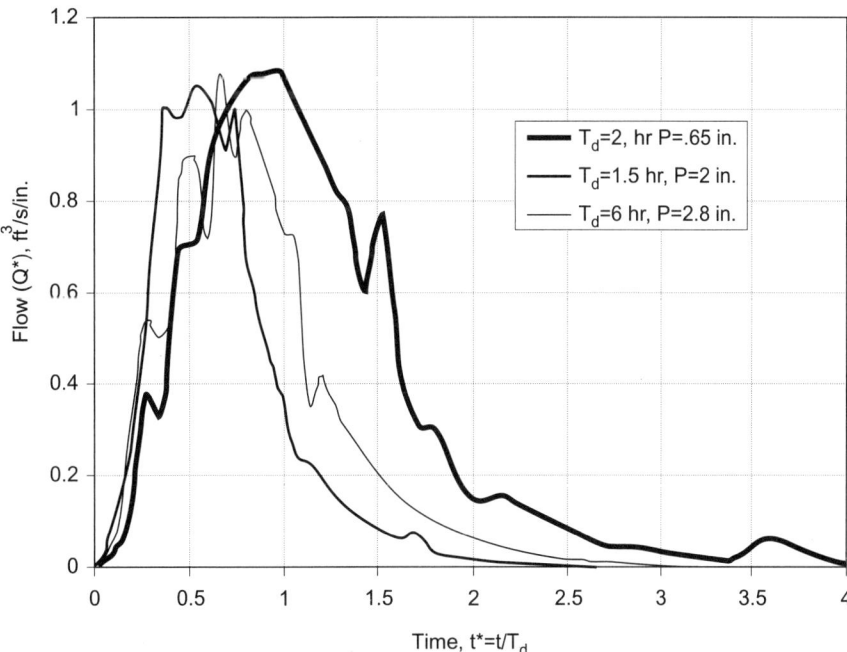

Figure 7.20b Hydrographs normalized for flow and time.

The I and A terms are identical to those in Equation 7.11. The values for the time of concentration, I and K are determined from field data. Note that K is a measure of the runoff that enters the sewer system and not the total runoff. Unlike the R-value, K is based on peak flow and intensity rather than volume.

In a study in Olathe, KS, Nelson (1987) reported a range of inflow coefficients from 0.001 for new interceptor lines to 0.085 for the oldest area of the city. For design purposes, a value of 0.01 was used for a sewer at the end of its design life. Once the K value has been determined, one of the methods described earlier for developing a hydrograph, such as triangular or SCS dimensionless hydrograph, can be use to generate the corresponding hydrograph. The area under the hydrograph should be checked to make sure it is reasonably close to the total volume of inflow to the collection system. This method is most appropriate where peak flow rather than storm volume is the primary concern. Peak flows can also be used in steady state runs for design of new systems, as described in the section "Unit Loads for Design Studies" on page 261.

Rainfall/Flow Regression

Once sewer flows and the corresponding rainfall have been measured, it is possible to develop regression equations relating rainfall and runoff. In most cases, multiple linear regression is used such that the wet weather flow at any time can be given by

$$Q(t) = \sum_{i=0}^{t} C_i P_{t-i} \tag{7.39}$$

where $Q(t)$ = wet weather flow (ft^3/s, m^3/s)
P_{t-i} = precipitation at i-th time step before time t (in., mm)
C_i = regression coefficient relating flow to precipitation at i-th time step before t

The most important coefficients are usually those immediately preceding time t. They will have the largest coefficients, while earlier time steps have less impact on the flow at time t and hence smaller coefficients. The time steps used do not necessarily need to be the same increment, but can be, for example, one hour for the time steps immediately preceding t and several hours long for hours during previous days. There is no rule as to the number of hours prior to time t that the regression must cover. To the extent that long-term infiltration is covered as RDII as opposed to base groundwater flow, it may be necessary to begin the regression analysis several days before the precipitation event. The unit hydrograph method described earlier can be viewed as a special case of regression methods.

One of the key advantages of this method is that it can be derived for one set of precipitation events and used for precipitation events with a somewhat different rainfall pattern.

This method requires continuous flow and rainfall data. An example of a regression equation developed from the RDII analysis in the Portland, OR, study is

$$Q(t) = C_1 P_{0-1} + C_2 P_{2-3} + C_3 P_{4-6} + C_4 P_{7-12} + C_5 P_{13-24} + C_6 P_{25-48} + C_7 P_{49-96} + C_8 P_{97-168} + C_9 P_{169-360} \tag{7.40}$$

where C_i = coefficient estimated from regression
P_{t-i} = cumulative rainfall for the specified range of hours; for example, P_{0-1} is the total depth of rainfall between hours 0 and 1 before time t (in.)

A separate set of C_i values was developed for each of the seven subbasins in the study. A similar approach was reported by Wright et al. (2000).

Example 7.4

Given the measured flow and precipitation data for a single event in the table below, develop the regression coefficients so that to regenerate the hydrograph and plot that hydrograph. Use data from the current time and the previous 5 hours to generate the coefficients. Use 1-hr time steps.

t, hrs	Flow, m³/s	Precipitation, mm
0	0	0
1	0	0
2	0	0
3	0	0
4	0	0
5	0	0
6	0	0
7	0	0
8	0.02	0.5
9	0.06	0.8
10	0.075	1.6
11	0.12	2
12	0.14	1.2
13	0.1	0.2
14	0.08	0
15	0.07	0
16	0.028	0
17	0.03	0
18	0.01	0
19	0.02	0
20	0	0

Using the regression analysis from a spreadsheet program, the regression coefficients were determined as

i	C_i
1	0.0264
2	0.0455
3	-0.0113
4	0.0343
5	0.0022
6	0.0146

Thus, the equation for $Q(t)$ is

$$Q(t) = 0.0264 P_t + 0.0455 P_{t-1} - 0.0113 P_{t-2} + 0.0343 P_{t-3} + 0.0022 P_{t-4} + 0.0146 P_{t-5}$$

In general, regression coefficients should not be negative. If data from more storms had been used, there would most likely not be any negative coefficients. The figure below shows the goodness of fit which has a linear regression index of determination value of 0.971.

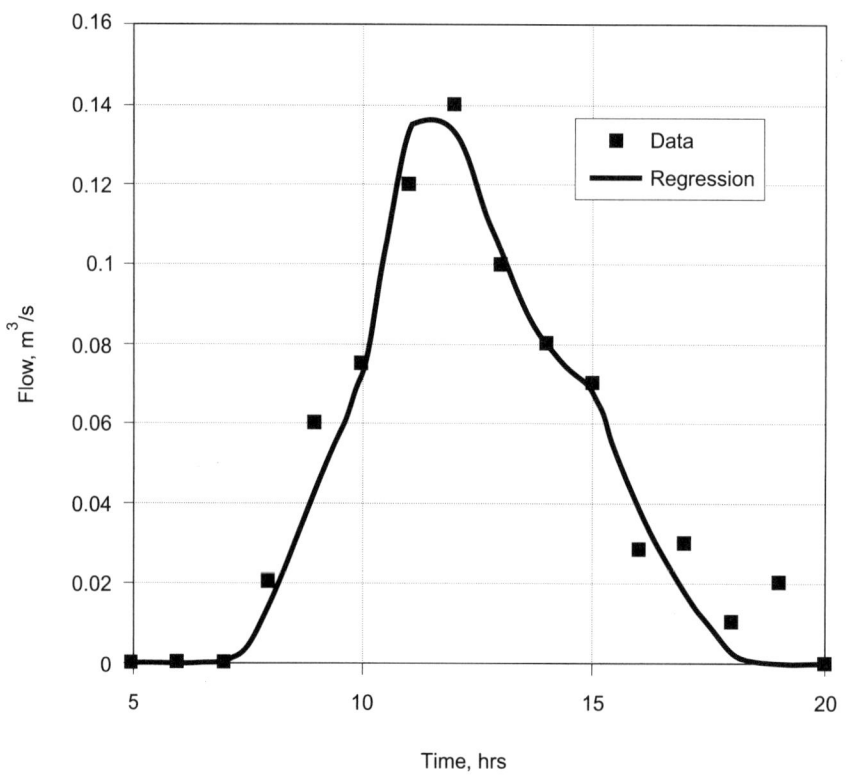

RTK Hydrograph Method

What is referred to as the *RTK* method is simply a special case of generating triangular hydrographs based on sewer flow monitoring and precipitation data. It involves fitting a triangular hydrograph with three parameters: *R, T,* and *K*. Some investigators found that trying to fit a single triangular hydrograph to flow monitoring data did not work well because they were really modeling three different processes: rapid inflow, intermediate infiltration and inflow, and long-term infiltration. They determined that by breaking the wet weather hydrograph into three separate hydrographs, each with its own values of *R, T,* and *K*, the triangular hydrographs fit each component well. The three hydrographs can be summed by the principle of superposition to model the overall system response to rainfall (Bennett et al., 1999).

Examples of the use of the *RTK* method are provided by Miralles, Miles, and Perez, (2001) and Vallabhaneni et al. (2002). The *RTK* method can be applied when there is a need to either create the flow hydrograph from rainfall records or to use the curve-fitting results to make inferences about the relative contributions of inflow and direct infiltration versus longer-term infiltration.

"Wow! That was a classic nor'easter."

There are actually two approaches to apply the RTK method:

1. Determine the RTK values for an entire storm based on the total precipitation. This is easy to do manually and is the approach illustrated in this section. The disadvantage of this approach is that the hydrographs are only applicable for storms with similar precipitation durations and patterns. The method can be used to account for different precipitation magnitudes.

2. Determine the RTK parameters as a unit hydrograph based on a precipitation hyetograph. Determining the RTK parameters is considerably more difficult with this method and involves trial-and-error, but because the resulting hydrographs are unit hydrographs, they can be applied to different rainfall events.

Regardless of which approach is used, the RTK method is a curve fitting approach and it should not be extrapolated to events which significantly differ from those for which the coefficients were determined.

In the RTK method, the shape of each of the three triangles is represented by three parameters:

R: the fraction of the rainfall over the watershed that enters the sanitary sewer system.

T: the time to peak in hours.

K: the ratio of the time to recession to the time to peak.

The sum of the three R-values equals the total fraction of rainfall over the sewershed that enters the sanitary sewer system:

$$R = R_1 + R_2 + R_3 \tag{7.41}$$

where R_1, R_2, R_3 = fraction of rainfall entering the sewer system from the fast, intermediate, and slow components

The total R value is identical to the R described in the percentage of rainfall volume method, as in Equation 7.35. It provides an indication of the total amount of rainfall-produced inflow and infiltration that enters the sanitary sewer system. This rate varies with such factors as the specific soil conditions and topography. The total R is less than 0.01 for sanitary sewers in good condition. Typical values range from 0.02 to 0.04 for sanitary sewer systems. Values of total R as high as 0.2 have been found in sanitary sewer systems that are in very poor condition.

This procedure provides nine parameters that can be adjusted to estimate observed wastewater flows from rainfall (R, T, and K for each of the three unit hydrographs). The fitting of unit hydrographs can be time consuming, depending on the number of flow meters and the number of events. Bennett et al. (1999) reported that it took approximately 100 hours to determine the coefficients for five basins using this approach.

As shown in Figure 7.21, the three hydrographs are summed to produce the total RDII hydrograph.

- The first triangle represents rapid infiltration and inflow. This is the rainfall that more or less immediately enters the sewer during the rainfall event. This typically produces high peak flows in the sanitary sewer system.

- The second triangle represents intermediate-term infiltration and inflow response.

- The third triangle represents long term infiltration response. These parameters represent the recession curve of the observed wastewater flows.

It is not always necessary to develop three hydrographs. For example, in a basin where rapid inflow represents almost all RDII, it may be possible to adequately model wet weather flow with only a single hydrograph. Examples of values for the R, T, and K parameters used in two studies are presented in Table 7.12.

Table 7.12 Examples of values of parameters in the RTK unit hydrograph method.

Reference	Description	Hydrograph	R, %	T, hr	K
Bennett et al., 1999	Portland, OR: five subbasins, 11 monitored events	Rapid	0.15–7.33	1	0.25–3.0
		Intermediate	0.76–18.5	4–24	1.0–7.0
		Slow	0.91–21.6	12–132	0.45–15
Vallabhaneni et al., 2002	Cincinnati, OH: one pilot area (130 ac), 19 events	Rapid	0.4–4.0	1	1.0–2.0
		Intermediate	0.03–4.0	3	2.0–3.0
		Slow	0.03–4.0	5–7	3.0–7.0

The R-values vary among RDII events, generally being higher for wet antecedent moisture conditions and lower for dryer antecedent conditions. The first step in determining the parameters should be to adjust the R, T, and K values of the default curve to obtain a reasonable fit for all events for a given meter. Then, R-values can be adjusted for individual events to obtain the best reproduction of the observed RDII flows.

As shown in Figure 7.21, the unit hydrograph is modeled as a triangle with a duration $T + TK$ and a peak flow Q_p. The area under each hydrograph is equal to R times the volume of rainfall, or

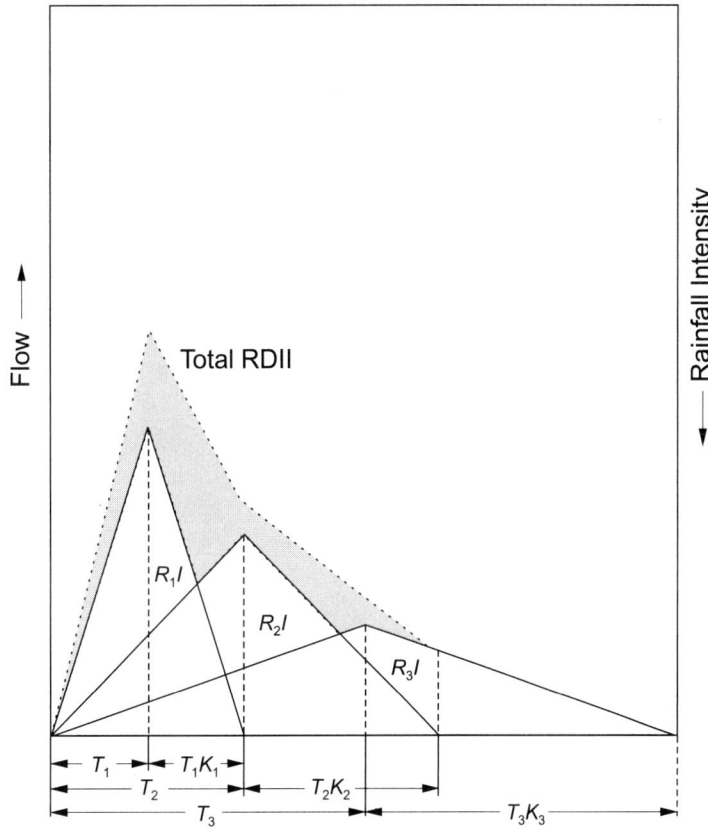

Figure 7.21 Definition of parameters for the RTK unit hydrograph method.

$$\frac{1}{2}(T_i + T_i K_i) Q_{pi} = \frac{R_i P A}{3600 \text{ s/hr}} \tag{7.42}$$

where
- T_i = time to peak (hr)
- K_i = ratio of the time to recession to the time to peak
- Q_{pi} = peak discharge (ft^3/s, m^3/s)
- R_i = volumetric runoff coefficient
- P = rainfall (ft, m)
- A = area of subbasin (ft^2, m^2)

When used with the first approach above, P is the total precipitation, while when used with the unit hydrograph approach, P is the precipitation during the time step (usually an hour).

The parameter K should be constant for all events for a given subbasin. The T values should be relatively constant when used with the unit hydrograph approach but will depend on the duration of the event if used with total precipitation.

If the values of T and K must be changed significantly to match the observed flows for a particular event, this is often a sign that the rainfall data used to calculate the parameters are not representative of the rainfall that fell over the basin for that particular event.

R-values vary among RDII events, generally being higher for wet antecedent moisture conditions and lower for dryer antecedent conditions. The first step in determining the parameters should be to adjust the *R*, *T*, and *K* values of the default curve to obtain a reasonable fit for all events for a given meter. Then, *R*-values can be adjusted for individual events to obtain the best reproduction of the observed RDII flows.

Determining R, T, and K from Field Data. The steps in developing the RTK parameters are

1. Collect rainfall and flow data
2. Separate the hydrograph into one to three triangular hydrographs
3. Determine the coefficients for each of the individual hydrographs
4. Repeat for other events to determine values to be used for modeling.

Example 7.5 Determining *R*, *T*, and *K* parameters

Given a 50 ac drainage area, which receives a 2 in. precipitation event over 75 minutes, the resulting hydrograph is shown in the Figure below. The average dry weather flow pattern for that time of day is shown in that graph also.

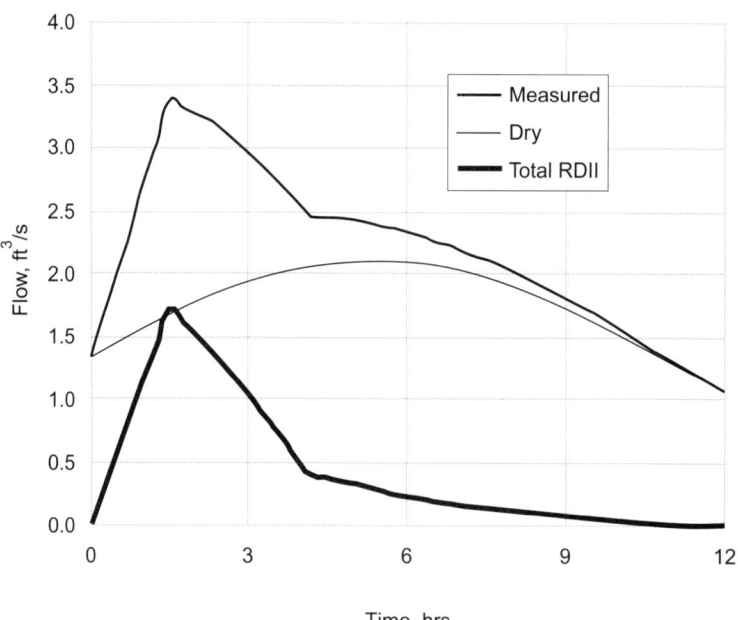

The first step is to subtract the two curves to determine the RDII hydrograph which is shown as the heavy line in the figure.

The RDII hydrograph is then manually divided into three triangular hydrographs to cover the rapid, intermediate and slow I/I. In this problem, the slow and the intermediate hydrographs were comparable and small, and it may have been possible to use only two triangular hydrographs.

Section 7.6 Empirical Methods for Generating Hydrographs 259

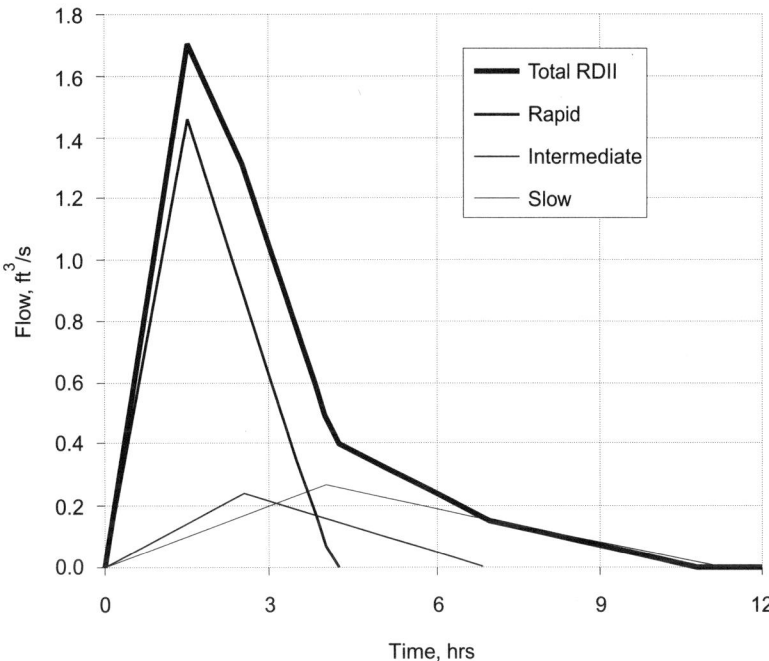

By observation, the K values are 1.75. The time to peak and peak flows for each hydrograph are shown in the table below. Given these values, it is possible to determine R for each by solving Equation 7.42 for R. For the rapid hydrograph, the calculation is

$$R = \frac{(1.5+(1.75*1.5))\text{hr}(3600\text{s/hr})1.47\text{ft}^3/\text{s}}{2(43560\text{ft}^2/\text{ac})(50\text{ac})(2\text{in.}/12\text{in.}/\text{ft})} = 0.03 = 3\%$$

Response	Q_p, ft³/s	K	T, hr	R, %
Rapid	1.47	1.75	1.5	3
Intermediate	0.24	1.75	2.5	0.8
Slow	0.27	1.75	4.0	1.4

Calculate Flows Using R, T, and K. The RDII occurring during the event is modeled using the following equations. For $t \leq T_i$, the flow is

$$Q = Q_{pi}\frac{t}{T_i} \tag{7.43}$$

For $T_i \leq t \leq T_i K_i + T_i$, the flow is

$$Q = Q_{pi}\left(1 - \frac{t - T_i}{T_i K_i}\right) \tag{7.44}$$

where t = time from start of storm event (hr)

The RTK method can be used for storm of various magnitude in terms of volume but does not work as well for storms of different duration than those for which the R, T and K values were determined. For storms of different duration, the modeler must use judgment in adjusting T and possibly even K if the hyetograph is significantly different.

Example 7.6 Calculation of RTK hydrograph.

Calculate the RDII hydrograph resulting from a 1.5-in. storm event with a duration of 1 hour. The subbasin has an area of 75 ac, and the R, T, and K parameters are listed in the following table.

Parameter	Rapid	Intermediate	Slow
T, hr	2	3	8
K	2	3	6
R	0.0061	0.0102	0.031

Solution

The peak flows for each hydrograph are

$$Q_{p1} = \frac{2 \times 0.0061 \times \left(1.5 \text{ in/hr} \times \frac{1 \text{ ft}}{12 \text{ in}}\right) \times (75 \text{ ac} \times 43{,}560 \text{ ft}^2/\text{ac})}{(2 + 2 \times 2) \times 3600 \text{ s/hr}} = 0.231 \text{ ft}^3/\text{s}$$

$$Q_{p2} = \frac{2 \times 0.0102 \times \left(1.5 \text{ in/hr} \times \frac{1 \text{ ft}}{12 \text{ in}}\right) \times (75 \text{ ac} \times 43{,}560 \text{ ft}^2/\text{ac})}{(3 + 3 \times 3) \times 3600 \text{ s/hr}} = 0.193 \text{ ft}^3/\text{s}$$

and

$$Q_{p3} = \frac{2 \times 0.031 \times \left(1.5 \text{ in/hr} \times \frac{1 \text{ ft}}{12 \text{ in}}\right) \times (75 \text{ ac} \times 43{,}560 \text{ ft}^2/\text{ac})}{(8 + 8 \times 6) \times 3600 \text{ s/hr}} = 0.126 \text{ ft}^3/\text{s}$$

The hydrographs are calculated using Equation 7.43 before the peak and Equation 7.44 after the peak. The hydrograph stops when $t = T_i + T_i K_i$. The total RDII is the sum of the three hydrographs. Calculations for the first 7 hours and other selected intervals are presented in the following table. The contributing and total hydrographs are shown in the figure. The peak RDII of 0.41 ft³/s occurs 3.0 hours after the beginning of the storm event.

Time, hr	Discharge, ft³/s			
	Rapid	Intermed.	Slow	Total
0.0	0.00	0.00	0.00	0.00
0.5	0.06	0.03	0.01	0.10
1.0	0.12	0.06	0.02	0.20
1.5	0.17	0.10	0.02	0.29
2.0	0.23	0.13	0.03	0.39
2.5	0.20	0.16	0.04	0.40
3.0	0.17	0.19	0.05	0.41
3.5	0.14	0.18	0.05	0.38
4.0	0.12	0.17	0.06	0.35

Time, hr	Discharge, ft³/s			
	Rapid	Intermed.	Slow	Total
4.5	0.09	0.16	0.07	0.32
5.0	0.06	0.15	0.08	0.29
5.5	0.03	0.14	0.09	0.25
6.0	0.00	0.13	0.09	0.22
6.5		0.12	0.10	0.22
7.0		0.11	0.11	0.22
7.5		0.20	0.16	0.26
8.0		0.09	0.18	0.26
8.5		0.07	0.17	0.25
39.0			0.01	0.01
40.0			0.00	0.00

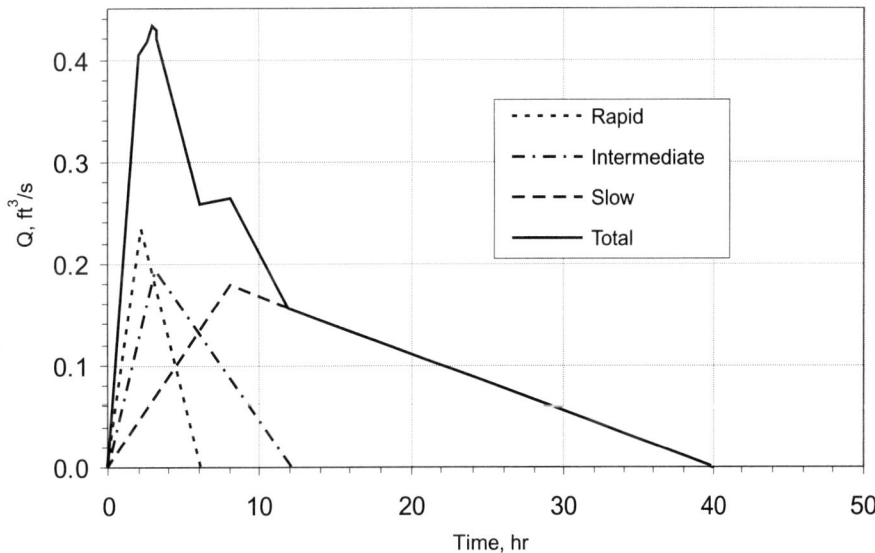

Unit Loads for Design Studies

For a new sanitary system, RDII should be minimal. Nonetheless, some allowance for wet weather inflows should be made during design. In this case, wet weather loadings may be specified by the regulatory agency, or the design engineer may be required to determine values from the literature or from studies in comparable areas. These loading rates are useful for peak hour model runs used in small sewer designs where hydrograph routing is not necessary.

In some situations, design loadings such as a peak flow of 400 gpcd (1500 Lpcd) may already include an allowance for wet weather inflow. In other cases, allowances are explicitly added based on unit length, length and diameter, drainage area, or number of manholes. The American Society Civil Engineers (1982) gravity sewer manual provides some guidance on infiltration allowances, which is summarized in Table 7.13.

(Inches and millimeters in the table refer to diameter not depth.) Some cities report using values as low as 50 gpd/mi/in. (4.6 Lpd/km/mm).

Table 7.13 Infiltration allowances (based on American Society Civil Engineers, 1982).

Diameter, in. (mm)	gpd/mi	Lpd/km	gpd/mi/in.	Lpd/km/mm
8 (200)	3500-5000	8225-11,750	450-625	42-58
12 (300)	4500-6000	10,575-14,100	375-500	35-46
24 (600)	10,000-12,000	23,500-28200	420-500	39-46

Other municipalities reported using infiltration allowances ranging from 140 to 2000 gpd/acre (1300 to 18,500 Lpd/ha), although that value was based on data collected during the 1960s and newer sewer installation should result in lower values.

The design values above do not account for rainfall depth or intensity. In order to develop such values, RDII measurements must be coupled with precipitation data to yield unit loadings in terms of inflow rate or volume per unit per depth of rain. Such values must be determined through calibration, and they are discussed in more detail in Chapter 9.

7.7 Snowmelt

In many parts of the world, snow is the dominant form of precipitation. Water produced by melting snow supplies reservoirs, lakes, and rivers, and infiltrating meltwater recharges soil moisture and groundwater (Gray and Prowse, 1993). Because snowmelt is an additional mechanism by which wet weather flow may be generated, it affects sewer design.

Although runoff flow rates from snowmelt are usually low, they may be sustained over several days. Rainfall superimposed on snowmelt base flow produce higher runoff peak flows and volumes, while increasing the melt rate of snow (Huber and Dickinson, 1988). Semadeni-Davies (2000) reports that Swedish towns have experienced snowmelt flows four to five times as great as wastewater. Simulation of snowmelt effects is more critical for facilities affected by an increase in runoff volume (as opposed to peak flow), such as pump stations and detention facilities.

Most of the techniques for modeling runoff generated by melting snow were developed for mountainous, rural, and agricultural watersheds (US Army Corps of Engineers, 1998). These same models have recently been applied to urban watersheds. This section describes, in general terms, the models for forecasting runoff from snowmelt in urban environments.

Runoff Potential

The physical properties of interest to modelers are depth, density, and water equivalent (Gray and Prowse, 1993). The potential quantity of runoff in snowpack is the *snow water equivalent*, which is the equivalent depth of water in snow cover, given by

$$SWE = d_s \rho_s / \rho_w \tag{7.45}$$

where SWE = snow water equivalent (in, mm)
 d_s = depth of snow (in, mm)
 ρ_s = density of snow (slugs/ft³, kg/m³)
 ρ_w = density of water (1.94 slugs/ft³, 1000 kg/m³)

The density of freshly fallen snow varies widely, depending on the amount of air contained within the lattice of the snow crystals, but is commonly 3–7.5 lb/ft³ (50–120 kg/m³) (Gray and Prowse, 1993). The density of fallen snow increases due to *metamorphism*, which is a change in the size, shape, and bonding of snow crystals with temperature and water-vapor gradients, settling, and wind packing. Typical densities for settled snow are 12–19 lb/ft³ (200–300 kg/m³), but may be as high as 22 lb/ft³ (350 kg/m³) for hard wind slab (Gray and Prowse, 1993).

Snowmelt Models

The temperature-index and degree-day methods are described in numerous references, including the *National Engineering Handbook* (US Soil Conservation Service, 1971), Huber and Dickinson (1988), and Semadeni-Davies (2000). The *meltwater rate*, M, is a function of daily average air temperature as

$$M = \begin{cases} 0, & T_a < T_m \\ C(T_a - T_m), & T_a \geq T_m \end{cases} \quad (7.46)$$

where M = meltwater rate, (in/day, mm/day)
 C = melt rate factor (in/°F/day, mm/°C/day)
 T_a = daily average air temperature (°F, °C)
 T_m = threshold temperature, (32°F, 0°C)

Values of C for rural areas are in the range 0.72–3.6 in/°F/day (1.4–6.9 mm/°C/day) and 1.7–4.1 in/°F/day (3–8 mm/°C/day) for urban areas (Huber and Dickenson, 1988). Gray and Prowse (1993) presented the following empirical equation for C:

$$C = K\rho_s \quad (7.47)$$

where C = melt rate factor, mm/°C/day
 K = 0.124 for U.S. Customary units or 0.011 for SI units
 ρ_s = snow density (slugs/ft³, kg/m³)

Equation 7.46 gives the meltwater rate on a daily basis. The air temperature data typically available are the minimum and maximum values for each day, so T_a is commonly taken as the average of these values. Incorporation of meltwater into continuous-simulation hydrologic models requires temperature data for more frequent time steps. Procedures for developing hourly meltwater rates from this type of data are given by Huber and Dickinson (1988).

More-detailed models for forecasting snowmelt runoff are most often based on the energy-balance method described by Anderson (1976). The units for each energy budget term are energy/area-time (for instance, langleys/day, where 1 langley = 1 cal/cm²). The energy balance is (Huber and Dickinson, 1988)

$$\Delta H = H_{rs} + H_g + H_{rl} + H_c + H_e + H_p \quad (7.48)$$

where ΔH = change in heat storage in snowpack

H_{rs} = net (incoming minus outgoing) shortwave radiation entering snowpack

H_g = conduction of heat to snowpack from underlying ground

H_{rl} = net longwave radiation entering snowpack

H_c = conductive exchange of sensible heat between air and snowpack

H_e = release of latent heat of vaporization by condensation of atmospheric water vapor

H_p = advection of heat to snowpack by rain

It requires 80 calories to melt 1 gram of snow (latent heat of fusion), or 80 langleys per cm (8 langleys per mm) of snow depth. The meltwater rate is given by

$$M = \Delta H/8 \qquad (7.49)$$

where M = meltwater rate (mm/day)

ΔH = change in heat storage in snowpack (langleys/day)

Procedures for estimating each term in Equation 7.48 are described by Huber and Dickinson (1988) and Gray and Prowse (1992).

The rate of snowmelt is calculated by multiplying the meltwater rate times the area of the watershed. However, production of meltwater is not necessarily equivalent to runoff, as snowpack is a porous medium and free water moves downward through the snowpack before runoff is generated. Huber and Dickinson (1988) use a simple reservoir-type routing procedure to simulate this process. The free-water holding capacity of snowpack is modeled as fraction of the snow depth, usually between 0.2 and 0.5. In a continuous simulation, this depth is filled with meltwater before runoff occurs.

Snow tends to insulate the soil beneath it. If the ground is frozen before snow falls, it tends to remain frozen. Unfrozen soil tends to remain unfrozen underneath a snowpack. Therefore, the soil properties related to runoff (such as infiltration and detention storage) are assumed to remain unchanged by snow. Infiltration into the soil is reduced if the ground if frozen.

The energy-balance method offers the advantage of accounting for factors such as solar radiation, wind speed, and *albedo* (the reflectance integrated over visible wavelengths of solar radiation) that affect the meltwater rates. It can also account for rain-induced melting. However, the application of this method to urban environments has been limited. Part of the difficulty is that the energy-balance method has extensive data requirements. Also, urban snow data are sparse, which limits the possibility of assessing or improving model performance.

Huber and Dickinson (1988) showed that the energy-balance equation can be reduced to the degree-day equation with appropriate substitutions and assumptions. Anderson (1976) reported that, under many conditions, results obtained using the energy-balance model were not significantly better than those obtained using the degree-day method. However, Matheussen and Thorolfsson (2001) stated that the energy fluxes related to snowmelt are significantly altered in the urban environment, and degree-day models are not suitable for urban areas.

References

American Iron and Steel Institute (AISI). 1999. *Modern Sewer Design*. 3d ed. Washington, DC: American Iron and Steel Institute.

Anderson E. A. 1976. *A Point Energy and Mass Balance Model of Snow Cover*. Report NWS 19. Washington, DC: US Department of Commerce.

Arnell, V. 1982. *Rainfall Data for the Design of Sewer Pipe Systems*. Report Series A:8. Göteborg, Sweden: Chalmers University of Technology, Dept. of Hydraulics.

American Society of Civil Engineers. 1982. "Gravity Sanitary Sewer Design and Construction." *Manual of Practice* No. 60 (WEF MOP FD-5) Alexandria, VA: American Society of Civil Engineers.

Bennett, D., R. Rowe, M. Strum, D. Wood, N. Schultz, K. Roach, M. Spence, Adderly. 1999. *Using Flow Prediction Technologies to Control Sanitary Sewer Overflows*. WERF, 97-CTS-8. Alexandria, VA: Water Environment Research Foundation.

Chow, V. T., D. R. Maidment, and L. W. Mays. 1988. *Applied Hydrology*. New York: McGraw-Hill.

Dawdy, D. R., J. C. Schaake, and W. M. Alley. 1978. *Distributed Routing Runoff Models*. US Geological Survey Water Resources Investigation Report. 78-90. Reston, VA: US Geological Survey.

Dent, S. 2000. Continuous simulations vs. design storms comparison with wet weather flow prediction methods. In *Collection Systems Wet Weather Pollution Control: Looking into Public, Private and Industrial Issues*. Alexandria, VA: Water Environment Research Foundation.

Dent, S., L. Wright, C. Mosley, and V. Housen. 2000. "Continuous Simulation versus Design Storms Comparison with Wet Weather Flow Prediction Methods." *Collection Systems Wet Weather Pollution Control*. Rochester, NY: Water Environment Federation.

Gray, D. M., and T. D. Prowse. 1993. "Snow and Floating Ice." In *Handbook of Hydrology*, ed. by D. R. Maidment. New York: McGraw-Hill.

Haestad Methods and S. R. Durrans. 2003. *Stormwater Conveyance Modeling and Design*. Waterbury, CT: Haestad Press.

Hathaway, G. A. 1945. Design of drainage facilities. *Transactions, American Society of Civil Engineers* 110: 697–730.

Hinks, R. W., and L. W. Mays. 1996. Hydrology for excess-water management. In Mays, L.W., *Water Resources Handbook*. New York: McGraw-Hill.

Horton, R. 1933. Separate roughness coefficients for channel bottom and sides. *Engineering News-Record* 111, no. 22: 652–653.

Horton, R. 1939. Analysis of runoff plot experiments with varying infiltration capacity." *Transactions, American Geophysical Union* 20: 693–711.

Huber, W. C., and R. E. Dickinson. 1988. *Storm Water Management Model User's Manual, Version 4*. EPA-600/3-88-001a. Athens, GA: US Environmental Protection Agency.

Huff, F. A. 1967. Time distribution of rainfall in heavy storms. *Water Resources Research* 3, no. 4: 1007–1019.

Huff, F. A. and J. R. Angel. 1992. *Rainfall Frequency Atlas of the Midwest*. Bulletin 71. Champaign, IL: Illinois State Water Survey.

Johnstone, D., and W. P. Cross. 1949. *Elements of Applied Hydrology.* New York: Ronald Press.

Kuichling, E. 1889. The relation between rainfall and the discharge in sewers in populous districts. *Transactions American Society of Civil Engineers* 20: 1.

Maidment, D. R. 1993. *Handbook of Hydrology.* New York. McGraw-Hill.

Matheussen, B. R., and S. T. Thorolfsson. 2001. Urban snow surveys in Risvollan-Norway. In *Urban Drainage Modeling*, Proceedings of the Specialty Symposium of the World and Water Environmental Resources Conference. Alexandria, VA: American Society of Civil Engineers.

Mays, L. W. 2001. *Water Resources Engineering.* New York: John Wiley & Sons.

Miralles, F., S. W. Miles, and A. I. Perez. 2001. A methodology for the evaluation and design of improvements in wet weather sanitary sewer system in the municipality of Luquillo, Puerto Rico: A pilot case study. *WEFTEC Latin America 2001.* Alexandria, VA: Water Environment Federation.

Mockus, V. 1969. Hydrologic soil-cover complexes. *National Engineering Handbook*, Section 4: Hydrology: Chapter 9. Washington, DC: US Soil Conservation Service.

Montgomery Watson. 1998. *City of Baton Rouge/Parish of East Baton Rouge Sanitary Sewer Overflow (SSO) Corrective Action Plan.* Baton Rouge, LA: Montgomery Watson.

Mulvaney, T. J. 1851. On the use of self-registering rain and flood gauges in making observations of the relation of rainfall and of flood discharges in a given catchment. *Transactions Institute Civil Engineers, Ireland* 4, Part 2: 18.

Natural Resources Conservation Service (NRCS). 1997. *National Engineering Handbook.* Washington, DC: US Department of Agriculture. http://www.info.usda.gov/CED/ (accessed 6/16/04).

Nelson, R.E. 1987. Sanitary sewer modeling. Paper presented at the *37th Kansas University Environmental Engineering Conference.* Lawrence, KS: Kansas University.

Nix, S. J. 1994. *Urban Stormwater Modeling and Simulation.* Boca Raton, FL: CRC Press.

Novotny, V., K. R. Imhoff, M. Olthof, and P. A. Krenkel. 1989. *Karl Imhoff's Handbook of Urban Drainage and Wastewater Disposal.* New York: John Wiley & Sons.

Pilgrim, D. H., and I. Cordery. 1975. Rainfall temporal patterns for design floods. *Journal of the Hydraulic Division, American Society of Civil Engineers* 101, no. HY1: 81–95.

Rawls, W. J., L. R. Ahuja, D. L. Brackensiek, and A. Shirmohammadi. 1993. Infiltration and soil water movement. Chapter 5 *Handbook of Hydrology.* D. R. Maidment, ed. New York: McGraw-Hill.

Roesner, L. A., and E. H. Burgess. 1992. The role of computer modeling in combined sewer overflow abatement planning. In *Proceedings of the Symposium on Water Resources and River Basin Management of the International Association on Water Pollution Research and Control* (16th Biennial Conference and Exposition). Washington, DC: International Association on Water Pollution Research and Control.

Schaake, J. C. Jr., J. C. Geyer, and J. W. Knapp. 1967. Experimental examination of the rational method. *Journal of the Hydraulics Division, American Society of Civil Engineers* 93, No. HY6.

Schultz, N. U., D. M. Wood, V. Adderly, and D. Bennett. 2001. RDI/I quantification research results. Helsingør, Denmark: 4th DHI Software Conference. http://www.dhisoftware.com/uc2001/Abstracts_Proceedigs/Proceedings/Conference_Proceedings.htm (accessed 6/16/04).

Semadeni-Davies, A. 2000. Representation of snow in urban drainage models. *Journal of Hydrologic Engineering* 5, No. 4: 363–370.

Sherman, L. K. 1932. Stream flow from rainfall by the unit graph method. *Engineering News Record*. No. 108: 501.

Snider, D. 1972. Hydrographs. *Hydrology,* National Engineering Handbook, Section 4. Washington, DC: US Soil Conservation Service.

Snyder, W. M. 1955. Hydrograph analysis by method of least squares. *Proceedings of American Society of Civil Engineers*. No. 81: 73

US Army Corps of Engineers. 1998. *Engineering Design Runoff and Snowmelt*. Manual No. 1110-2-1406. Washington, DC: US Army Corps of Engineers.

US Environmental Protection Agency (US EPA). 1999. *Combined Sewer Overflows: Guidance Monitoring and Modeling.* EPA 832-B-99-002. Washington DC: US Environmental Protection Agency.

US Soil Conversation Service. 1971. Estimation of direct runoff from snowmelt. In *National Engineering Handbook,* Part 630 Hydrology, Chapter 4. Washington, DC: Natural Resources Conservation Service.

US Soil Conservation Service. 1986. *Urban Hydrology for Small Watersheds.* Technical Release 55. Washington, DC: US Department of Agriculture.

Vallabaneni, S., J. M. Koran, S. E. Moisio, and C. I. Moore. 2002. SSO evaluations: infiltration and inflow using SWMM RUNOFF and EXTRAN. In *Best Modeling Practices for Urban Water Systems, Monograph 10,* ed. by W. James. Guelph, ON: CHI Publications.

Veissman, W. Jr., G. L. Lewis, and J. W. Knapp. 1989. *Introduction to Hydrology.* New York: Harper-Collins.

Wallingford. 1998. *The Wallingford Procedure: Volume 2 Practical Application of the Wallingford Procedure.* Wallingford, England: Wallingford.

Wallingford. 2001. *HydroWorks, v7.0* (Build 42). Wallingford, England: Wallingford.

Water Environment Federation (WEF). 1999. *Prevention and Control of Sewer System Overflows,* 2d ed. Manual of Practice FD-17. Alexandria, VA: Water Environment Federation.

Water Research Centre (WRc). 1987. *A Guide to Short Term Flow Surveys of Sewer Systems.* Swindon, UK: WRc Engineering.

Watt, W. E. 1989. *Hydrology of Floods in Canada: A Guide to Planning and Design.* Ottawa: National Research Council of Canada.

Wenzel, H. G. 1982. Rainfall for urban stormwater design. In *Urban Stormwater Hydrology.* Water Resources Monograph 7. ed. by D. F. Kibler. Washington, DC: American Geophysical Union.

Westphal, J. A. 2001. Hydrology for drainage system design and analysis. in L. W. Mays, *Stormwater Collection Systems Design Handbook*. New York: McGraw-Hill.

Wright, L., S. Dent, C. Mosley, P. Mosley, P. Kadota, and Y. Djebbar. 2000. Computing rainfall dependent inflow and infiltration simulation methods. In *Models and*

Applications to Urban Water Systems Monograph 9, ed. by W. James. Guelph, ON: CHI Publications.

Yen B. C., and V. T. Chow. 1980. Design hyetographs for small drainage structures. *Journal of the Hydraulic Division, American Society of Civil Engineers* 106, No. HY6: 1055–1076.

Problems

7.1 Use the rational method to determine the peak RDII in the pipe segment downstream of each inlet in the combined sewer shown in the schematic. The 10-yr storm in Figure 7.12 may be used to determine the rainfall intensity. Use the Hathaway equation to determine the time of concentration. Each pipe segment has a length of 300 ft and an average velocity of 4 ft/s.

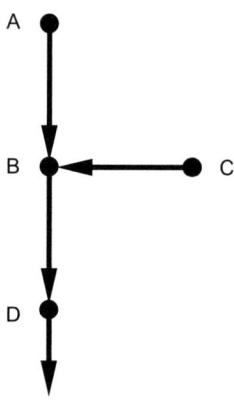

Inlet	Land use	Area, ac	Slope	n	Flow path length, ft
A	Condominiums	0.8	0.001	0.045	450
B	Single-family homes	1.2	0.002	0.055	480
C	Single-family homes	0.9	0.001	0.055	360
D	Commercial office	0.6	0.0008	0.024	390

7.2 Construct the RDII hydrograph resulting from a 2 in. storm event with a duration of 1 hour. The subbasin has an area of 50 ac. The R, T, and K parameters are listed in the following table. Determine the time to peak and the total volume of runoff.

Parameter	Rapid	Intermediate	Slow
T (hr)	1.5	3	10
K	2	4	8
R	0.0055	0.0094	0.014

7.3 Develop a 2-hour design storm hyetograph for a 10-year return period storm using the Chicago method. Use the constants for Houston from Table 7.1 and the advancement coefficient, $r = 0.4$.

7.4 Prepare a 4-hour hyetograph for a 70 mm rainfall event using the Huff and Angel dimensionless coefficients.

7.5 Prepare a 24-hour hyetograph for a 40 mm rainfall event using the Type II SCS distribution.

7.6 Determine the total volume of runoff that is available in a 20-in. snowpack overlaying a 25-acre subbasin. The density of the snow is 15 lb/ft^3.

CHAPTER

8

Data Collection and Flow Measurement

Data relating to the physical characteristics of a sewer system are fairly static. For example, changes resulting from physical deterioration, sediment buildup, rehabilitation, or expansion typically occur over years. The variations in flow, however, are more challenging to account for because they are dynamically changing.

A wastewater collection system model must be able to simulate the flow in the sewer network at all locations and times. In an ideal world, the modeler would be able to measure the flow at each point of entry into the system and apply the principles of mass balance and hydraulics to calculate the flow throughout the system. Unfortunately, this is not practical. The pragmatic approach is to load the model with the best information available, using measurements of the sewage flow at selected points in the system to calibrate. The engineer then adjusts the model inputs until the results agree with the observed flows.

Calibration requires an in-depth understanding of the components of flow and the factors that affect their variability. This can best be achieved through a sound data-collection plan that describes the locations where measurements need to be taken, the frequency of the measurements, the flow measurement instrumentation, the duration of flow monitoring, and the required data management system for storing and retrieving that data. This chapter describes the techniques and instrumentation for measuring flow, depth, and precipitation as they relate to sanitary sewer modeling.

8.1 Flow Measurement Considerations

The project objectives and the data requirements of the model (discussed in Chapter 5) provide the basis for the design of the flow monitoring program. There are three types of flow measurements:

- Continuous flow measurements collected by recording instruments
- Point measurements of flow or precipitation collected by manual methods
- Measurements of peak flows occurring during a defined interval

Continuous flow data are the most desirable for model calibration, because such data can be used to generate full hydrographs and help separate infiltration and inflow from dry weather flow. Point and peak-flow measurements can be used to fill in data gaps.

A flow monitoring program typically consists of a network of gaging stations that continuously monitor and record flow, depth, or precipitation. Stations may be fixed for the duration of the program, or they may collect data for a short time and then be moved to another location.

Components of Flow

The design of a flow monitoring program begins with an understanding of the components of flow in a collection system, their point of entry, and an assessment of the variability of each component, as shown in Table 8.1. Locations of the largest sources of flow should be placed on a skeleton layout of the system, and factors that affect their variability should be noted (for example, schools generate flow primarily during school hours). Commercial sources that experience seasonal peaks along with preliminary estimates of industrial sources should also be considered. Regions of the network that are older or are located in areas of high groundwater should be identified as areas of potential high infiltration and known overflows should be located.

Table 8.1 Components of flow in sanitary sewers.

Component	Description	Point of Entry/Exit	Variability
Base wastewater flow (sanitary)	Discharge from residential, commercial, or institutional sources	Tee or wye connection into collector line from a service or lateral	Typically a 24-hour pattern, may vary according to day of week; commercial sources may have seasonal or weekend versus weekday pattern
Base wastewater flow (industrial)	Wastewater from industrial process	Tee or wye connection or manhole; may have dedicated line	Source specific
Groundwater infiltration	Groundwater	Joints or cracks in pipes or at manholes	With season according to groundwater elevation
Rainfall derived infiltration and inflow (RDII)	Stormwater runoff, roof drains, or snowmelt	Catch basins, inlets, or direct connections to sewer; defects in sewer pipes, manholes, or pump stations	Driven by precipitation event, antecedent conditions, or temperature
Overflow	Intentional or unintentional discharge from sewer system; may reenter system at a downstream location	Controlled discharge with regulators or overflow at manholes	According to flow in sewer; may be mechanically controlled; varies with rainfall intensity and duration

Ideally, each of the flows described in Table 8.1 can be estimated beforehand using the procedures presented in Chapter 6 and will agree with the values measured in the flow monitoring program. However, the agreement is usually not perfect, and adjustments must be made in the model calibration process.

Review of Existing Information

The next step is to collect and review available flow information, which is used to develop preliminary estimates of range and variability of flows. For existing systems, operating records of treatment plants and pump stations are a valuable resource. Flows observed at these locations are a composite of base wastewater flow and groundwater infiltration during dry weather, and also include RDII following storm or snowmelt events. Procedures for separating RDII from the total flow hydrograph are described in Chapter 9. While these data describe only the total flow collected by the sewage network upstream of the measurement point, they can yield useful information on the range and variability of flows and may help identify long-term trends.

Continuous flow measurements are collected at the headworks of most wastewater treatment plants. Flow data can also be obtained or derived from pumping station operation records. If flows are not directly measured, they can be calculated using pump-head characteristic curves, the wet well elevations, the head on the discharge side of the pump, the wet well volume, and the pump run times (WEF, 1994). For example, the flow rate can be determined from the suction and discharge heads and the pump-head characteristic curve. The pump run times can also give the volume pumped during a given time interval. The underlying assumption is that the incoming flow does not vary widely in the measurement interval. However, to minimize error, the measurement intervals must be kept small.

Flows from industrial sources may be estimated from pretreatment permits or interviews with managers. Logging of flow rates at the water meter, minus any water that is used in the product being manufactured or for irrigation, can also be used to estimate the wastewater flow rate. Average industrial water use rates according to Standard Industrial Classification code are tabulated in Table 6.5 on page 179.

Selection of Metering Locations

The selection of flow metering locations is fundamental to assuring accurate representation of flows throughout the system. Flow metering locations are generally selected to support a master planning effort or a specific study such as identifying sources and amounts of defect flow.

In the design of a flow metering program to support modeling for master planning, the primary focus should be on defining land-use flow generation quantities and demand patterns. Areas of homogenous land use should be identified and used to develop flow generation rates. These rates can then be applied to unmetered areas and to future developments with similar land uses to predict future flows. Figure 8.1 shows a typical layout of flow meters in areas where sewers serve a specific land use.

An additional consideration in flow measurement to support master planning efforts is measuring the existing capacity of the major interceptor system. Flow meters are typically located along interceptors near major confluences and can be used to identify basins that may need additional capacity to handle future flows.

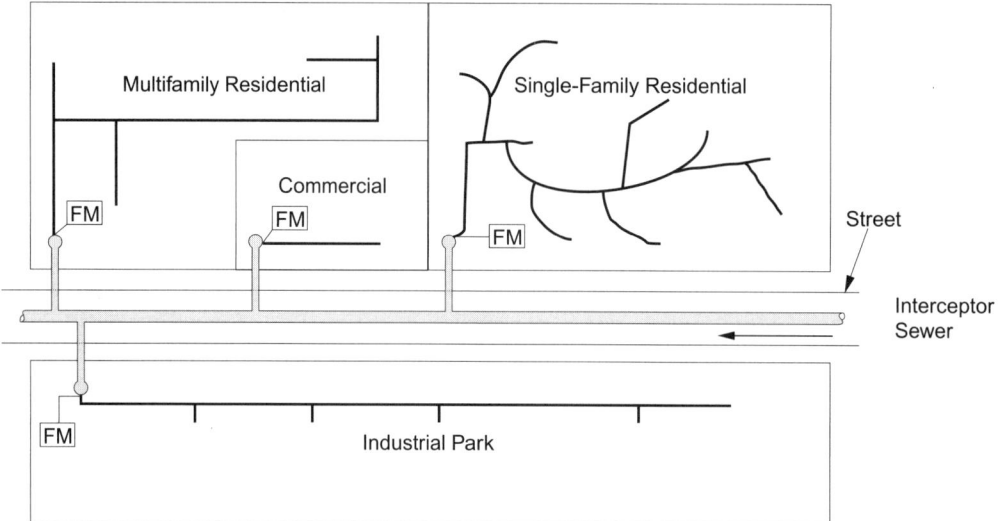

Figure 8.1 Typical flow metering locations.

Flow measurement programs for identifying sources and amounts of defect flows focus on identifying areas in greatest need of physical inspection and provide guidance on the type of physical inspection that is needed. Flow metering programs supporting RDII studies are highly detailed, have more flow meters installed per unit area, and are conducted in both wet and dry seasons. The objective is to limit the amount of sewer system affected by unknown inflows between metering locations. The usual basin size for RDII analysis is 25,000–50,000 ft (7500–15,000 m) of upstream pipe for each flow meter, but depends on the system and the nature of the problem.

Other factors that can influence the selection of meter locations regardless of the application are:

- Areas where previous studies have indicated numerous defects
- Age of the collection system
- Areas where there have been a high number of complaints about backups or overflows
- Areas where there are a high number of operational and maintenance problems

With all flow meters, it is important to adhere to the manufacturer's recommendations for lengths of straight pipe upstream or downstream of a meter or the distance to the nearest manhole for open-channel measuring devices. Failure to follow these guidelines can yield poor results from even the most expensive meter.

Safety Considerations

Working in sewer environments is quite dangerous, with hazards from toxic and explosive gases, microbes, engulfment, lifting of equipment in and out of manholes, and traffic. Workers die in sewer accidents every year. Individuals should not attempt to work in sewer environments without receiving adequate training and complying with applicable rules. In the United States, these rules are provided by the Occupational Safety and Health Administration (OSHA).

Work inside a sewer often meets the definition of "confined space entry." A *confined space* is any enclosed area that meets the following requirements:

- It is not designed for human occupancy.
- It has restricted entry and exit.
- It is not designed for continuous employee occupancy.

Atmospheric testing, safety equipment, and ventilation are required for confined space entry. OSHA confined-space entry standards are listed in 29 CFR 1910.146.

8.2 Flow Measurement

A variety of manual and automated techniques are available for measuring sewage flow; the most common are listed in Table 8.2. Selection of the appropriate flow measurement method depends on the type of conduit and the range of expected flows. Although it is possible to measure velocities at selected points in an open channel or pressure pipe and use the continuity equation to calculate discharge, this may require a large number of measurements, which can be impractical.

Alternate approaches include establishing *control sections* by manipulating the geometry of the channel or pipe, and using temporary flow and depth meters. The former method establishes a unique and well-established relationship such that flow is a function of a single parameter, such as depth. In open-channel flow, this technique involves constructing a weir or flume. Control sections are well suited for placement in sewer pipes but are very expensive to retrofit into an existing sewage system. The other common approach is to use a temporary meter that can measure or estimate average velocity and depth in a pipe, from which flow can be calculated for a given installation. Most temporary flow surveys use velocity-area meters.

Hydraulic Control Sections in Open Channels

In open-channel flow, measurement structures are designed to produce a hydraulic *control section*—any feature that produces a hydraulic condition in which there is a reliable, one-to-one relation between depth and discharge. For example, flumes and weirs provide a single depth-to-discharge relation. This means that for a measured depth at a given location relative to the control, a flow rate, Q, can be calculated if certain conditions on the downstream side are met.

Flow-measuring devices, such as flumes and weirs are called primary devices since they provide the unique relation between flow and water-surface elevation. To produce a flow measurement with one of these devices, however, the water-surface elevation must be measured with some secondary device, such as an ultrasonic transducer, bubbler, or ruler. This section describes the primary devices, while a later section on depth measurement describes the secondary devices.

Table 8.2 Open-channel flow measurement techniques.

Method	Description	Advantages	Disadvantages
Manual			
Timed flow	Timing of how long it takes to fill a container with a known volume.	• Simple to implement • Used when physical access to sewer is limited	• Labor intensive • Suitable only for low flows
Dilution method	Injection of dye or saline solution at an upstream location and monitoring the concentration at a downstream location.	• Accurate for instantaneous flows or temporary monitoring	• Labor intensive • Impractical for continuous flow monitoring
Velocity area	A velocity meter and surveying are used to manually measure velocity and depth. Discharge is calculated by numerical integration.	• Best method for natural stream channels	• Impractical in piped systems
Control Section			
Broad-crested weir	Device is placed across the flow such that the flow over the crest can be related to depth. Flow is determined by the depth upstream of the weir.	• Often found in diversion chambers for CSOs • Less likely to have sediment build up as compared with sharp-crested weirs	• Cannot be used in full pipes • Often improperly installed or maintained • Invalid if approach conditions are not satisfied
Sharp-crested weir	Device is placed across the flow such that the flow over the crest can be related to depth. Flow is determined by the depth beyond the weir.	• Used in sewers with existing weirs • Reasonably accurate technique	• Subject to clogging or siltation • Cannot be used in full pipes • Often improperly installed or maintained • Invalid if approach conditions are not satisfied
Flume	Specially designed sections that provide a restriction in area and produce an increase in velocity. Flow is related to upstream depth.	• Less prone to clogging than weirs • Accurate technique • Require little maintenance	• Invalid under high-tailwater conditions • More expensive than weirs to retrofit
In Pipe or Channel with Sensors			
Velocity area	Sensors measure both depth and average velocity in cross section. Flow calculated as $Q = A \times V$.	• Can be used in open channels, full or partially full pipes • Submerged or reversed flow	• Require regular maintenance • Two sensors must be accurate to get correct results.
Computation	Measurements are made of depth, slope, roughness, and channel geometry. Flow is calculated with Manning's or similar equations.	• Requires normal depth	• Invalid with any backwater effects or surcharge

Weirs. Figure 8.2 illustrates the types of weirs that are commonly placed in manholes to measure flow. The hydraulics of weirs are discussed in Chapter 2. In general, sharp-crested weirs, which can be any of the weir types shown in Figure 8.2, are only used in temporary flow monitoring locations because they tend to trap solids behind them, which reduces their accuracy as flow meters and causes maintenance problems. Broad-crested weirs, which can be rectangular or trapezoidal, may be used to monitor combined sewer overflows when the hydraulics of the diversion can be arranged to not trap solids.

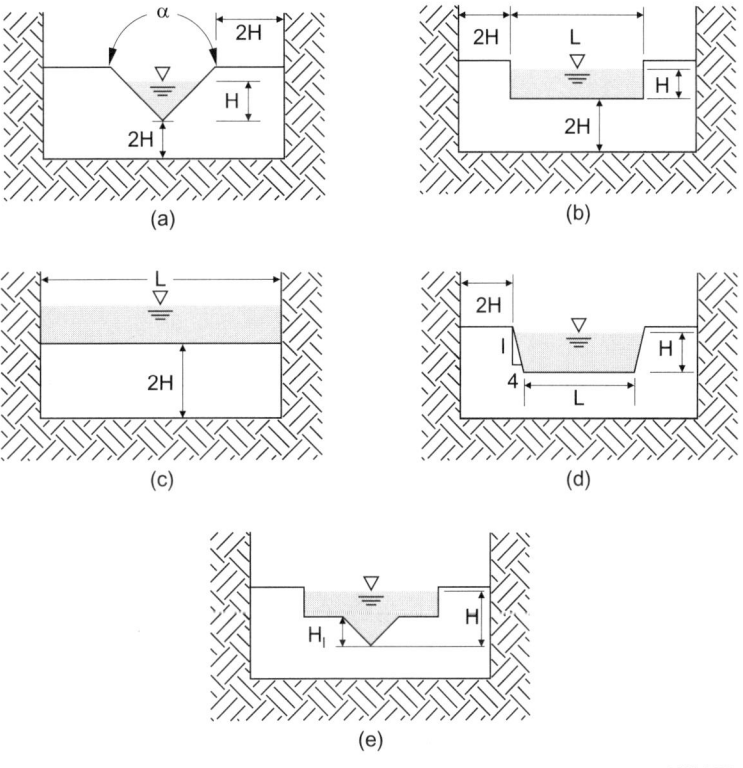

WEF, 1994

Figure 8.2 Flow monitoring weirs: (a) V-notch, (b) rectangular contracted, (c) rectangular suppressed, (d) trapezoidal, (e) compound.

Portable Weirs. Portable weirs can be placed anywhere in a pipe to measure flow rates. An example is for a plug-and-weir study where the upstream end of a pipe is blocked and the weir is placed at a downstream section to measure any additional contributions to the flow between the block and the weir.

Depth measurements are made upstream or downstream of the weir plate to calculate the flow rate. Some manufacturers engrave a scale on the face of the weir to allow direct reading of the flow rate. However, this approach is intended for very low flow rates as reading the face of the weir means looking directly into the wastewater flow. Measurements can also be taken by other manual methods or they can be obtained and continuously recorded using more sophisticated instruments described in Section 8.3.

The approach velocity upstream of the weir should not generally exceed 0.5 ft/s (0.15m/s). For each weir there is a maximum depth of flow corresponding to an upper limit of accurate results. Operating the weir with the downstream side submerged is not recommended, because one must then apply additional formulas to correct for the submerged conditions. Manufacturers of weirs for insertion into sewers provide rating curves or tables for their weirs, an assessment of their accuracies, and instructions for installation. Figure 8.3 shows a weir that can be temporarily installed in a sewer pipe.

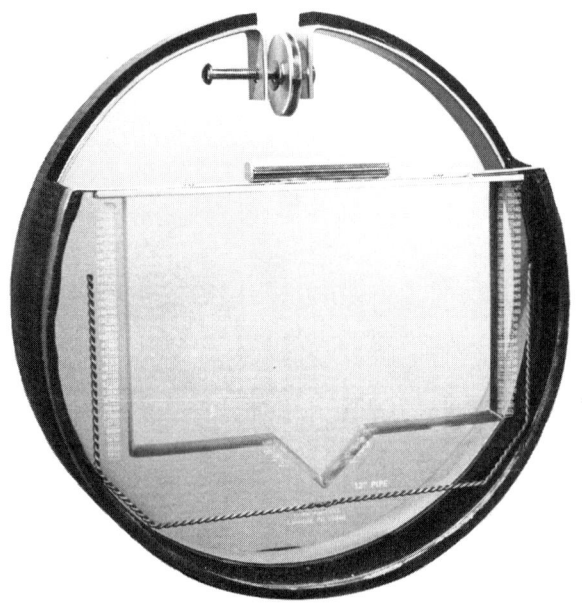

Courtesy of the Thel-Mar Co., Brevard, NC

Figure 8.3 Temporary insertable weir.

Flumes. Critical flow is an instance in which there is a unique definitive relationship between the depth of flow and the discharge in an open channel. If one can cause a flow to pass through critical depth, then measurement of that depth can be used to determine the discharge. This is the principle behind flumes.

Flumes are specially designed open channel flow sections that cause critical flow to occur in the throat of the flume (Bos, 1989). They are often located at the inlet to wastewater treatment plants and are able to overcome the siltation and head-loss problems found with weirs.

While Parshall flumes are the most commonly used configuration for wastewater applications, Palmer-Bowlus flumes, H-flumes, Leopold-Lagco flumes, and trapezoidal flumes are also used, each with its own advantages and disadvantages (Grant, 1989). Figure 8.4 shows a large Parshall flume with an ultrasonic depth sensor located above the channel. Palmer-Bowlus flumes are especially useful in sewer flow monitoring because they can be constructed in existing circular pipes.

An insertable, self-instrumented flume has also been developed for use in pipes (Figure 8.5). Typical dimensions for flumes can be found in hydraulic references

Figure 8.4 Parshall flume with an ultrasonic depth sensor.

(French, 1985; Grant, 1989) and from manufacturers that make prefab fiberglass or plastic flume inserts.

Flumes are accurate over a wide range of flows and a properly installed and instrumented flume can yield accuracy that is limited only by that of the depth sensor. For example, a Parshall flume with a 12-in. (0.30-m) throat can measure flows ranging from 0.12 to 16.1 ft^3/s (0.0034 to 0.46 m^3/s). No other device is as accurate over two orders of magnitude.

In reality however, some flumes are poorly constructed, with inadequate attention to the sensitivity of the device to such factors as approach velocity. As a result, it is not unusual to find inactive, inaccurate, or uncalibrated flumes installed in a system.

For a flume to be accurate, flow must pass through critical depth in the throat section. If the flow downstream of the flume backs up and prevents critical depth, then the unique discharge-to-depth relation no longer holds and more complicated formulas for submerged flow (French, 1985) must be used.

When there is free discharge through a Parshall flume, there are simple formulas to determine flow (French, 1985) based on throat width. For example, for a flume with a throat width of 1–3 ft (0.3–2.4 m), the flow is given by

$$Q = \begin{cases} 4WH^{1.522W^{0.026}}, & \text{U.S. customary units} \\ 1.22W(0.305H)^{1.476W^{0.026}}, & \text{SI units} \end{cases} \quad (8.1)$$

where Q = flow (ft³/s, m³/s)
W = throat width (ft, m)
H = upstream head (ft, m)

The exact location of the point at which to measure upstream head is provided in the flume dimensions and is critical to accurate measurement.

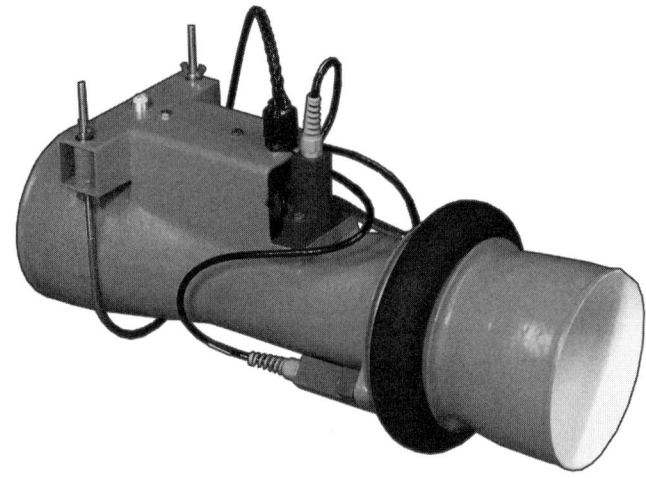

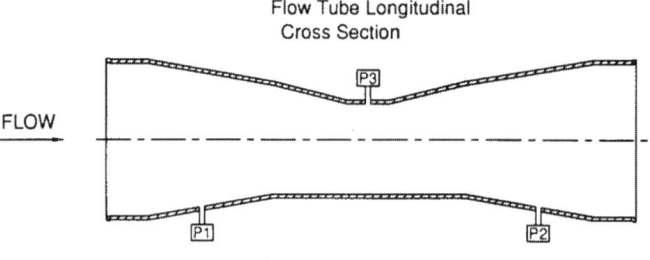

P1, P2, P3 = Submersible Pressure Transducers

Courtesy of Renaissance Instruments.

Figure 8.5 Insertable instrumented flume.

In-Pipe Methods

There are several methods for measuring flow in a pipe or channel that do not require constructing a control section. In open-channel flow, these methods involve measuring the average velocity and depth of flow, which can be converted into a cross-sectional area if the geometry of the pipe is known. In the case of full-pipe flow, only the average velocity must be measured, since the cross-sectional area remains constant for a given pipe.

Correctly calculating the flow through an open channel requires measuring both velocity and depth. Depth-velocity or area-velocity meters use the continuity equation to derive flow, given as

$$Q = VA \tag{8.2}$$

where Q = flow rate (ft³/s, m³/s)
        V = average velocity (ft/s, m/s)
        A = area of flow (ft², m²)

Measuring depth of flow in a pipe and then calculating the flow with an equation such as the Manning formula only yields accurate results when the flow in the pipe is uniform. This method yields significant error when there are small errors in any parameter used in the equation.

Where normal flow exists, the depth always increases as the velocity increases. However, backwater conditions, in which the average velocity may actually decrease as depth increases, occur frequently in sanitary sewer systems, especially during high-flow events. Using the depth and Manning's equation to calculate velocity and flow under these conditions is invalid and yields velocities and flow rates that are too high.

Depth-only measurements should be used only when there are no other options. If at all possible, a depth-to-velocity relation (i.e., rating curve) should be defined for the site. If there are no clear relations between the depth and velocity, then another measurement site should be investigated.

In some instances, there may have been a significant investment made in depth-only measurements at a site. Occasionally the data can be revived by installing a velocity-measuring device at the site. If a good relationship can be developed between the existing depth-only measurements and the velocity measurements, then the modified depth-velocity relation can be used to calculate the non-Manning flow at that site. However, such a relation often cannot be developed, owing to the flow characteristics in a manhole.

Manual Methods

While most sewer flow monitoring is accomplished with electronic sensors, flow and maximum depth of water in a surcharged manhole can also be determined using manual methods.

Timed Flow. Small flows may be calculated by determining the time required to collect a known volume of flow as it moves from an elevated pipe into a container. An average flow rate is obtained by measuring the time that it takes to fill the known volume. A variation of this technique is to allow the flow to enter the container for a predetermined time and then measure its volume. This method is limited to extremely low flows and is most often used in the measurement of flow from a single defect, such as a crack or opening in a pipe.

A more common use of this technique lies in approximating the flow into a wet well. Given the active volume of the wet well (i.e., the volume between the pump-on and pump-off levels) and the time to fill the wet well, the average inflow during a fill cycle is given by

$$Q = Vol(active)/t \qquad (8.3)$$

where Q = discharge (ft³/s, m³/s)
        $Vol(active)$ = fill volume (ft³, m³)
        t = time required to fill (s)

Dilution-Gauging Method. In the dilution-gauging method, a dye or chemical tracer of known concentration is introduced at an upstream location, and the concentration is monitored at a downstream location. The downstream monitoring point must allow complete mixing of the tracer in the sewer. Kilpatrick and Cobb (1985) give a complete discussion of this method.

The injection and monitoring stations are placed as shown in Figure 8.6. When the tracer concentration reaches equilibrium at the measuring station, the discharge is calculated with Equation 8.4.

$$Q_s = Q_t \frac{(C_t - C_{eq})}{(C_{eq} - C_s)} \tag{8.4}$$

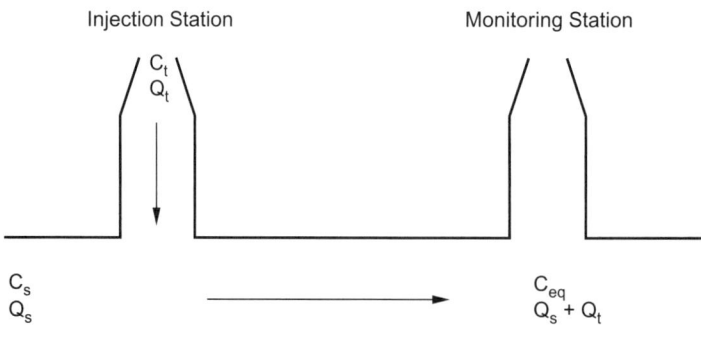

Figure 8.6 Locations of stations for the dilution method.

Where
- Q_s = wastewater flow (ft³/s, m³/s)
- Q_t = tracer injection rate (ft³/s, m³/s)
- C_t = concentration of tracer in the injection station (mg/L)
- C_{eq} = equilibrium concentration of tracer at the downstream monitoring station (mg/L)
- C_s = concentration of tracer in the wastewater (mg/L)

The tracer chemical selected should be conservative (i.e., does not react or break down in the pipe). If a dye is used, a sample should be tested to see if it is adsorbed or breaks down in the sewage. If it does, the decay is usually modeled with a first-order term, and downstream readings are corrected for the decay. Salt makes a good tracer because it can be detected with a simple conductivity probe, whereas a dye usually requires a fluorometer. The dilution-gauging method requires that Q_s and C_s remain constant during the test and no major tributary sewers enter the flow between the injection and measuring points.

Manual Velocity-Area Method. In the velocity-area method, a cross section is divided into segments and a point-velocity probe is used to measure the velocity at various depths in each segment. The discharge is calculated as the product of the vertically averaged velocity and the area of each segment. The total flow in the cross section is then computed by summing the flows from all segments. This method is widely used for measuring flow in streams with a handheld current meter (Rantz, 1982). It is most frequently used in sewer studies for in situ calibration of installed depth-area-velocity meters. In this process, the velocity is measured with a point-velocity meter, such as an electromagnetic or propeller meter.

High Water Marks. While not specifically a method for determining the flow rate, the recording of high water marks provides insight into the performance of a sewer system. In pipes and manholes that have recently experienced high water, the levels may be noted by the color of the interior surface. High water marks can also be easily identified from sanitary debris on the manhole steps.

A common practice is *chalking* the manhole, in which a vertical line is drawn up the side with chalk. The manhole is then inspected after a storm to determine the depth of flow by observing where the chalk was washed away.

Tea Cups. With this approach, a series of cups is attached to the manhole wall or a central pole hung from the manhole cover frame. After an event, the manhole is inspected and the level determined by the highest filled cup. This method is useful in situations where chalk is erased over time in a sweating manhole or the surcharge is so rapid that chalk is not erased.

8.3 Instrumentation

A variety of instruments and sensors may be used to measure depth and/or velocity, as summarized in Table 8.3. The depth sensors are usually located upstream of a control section and are typically installed with a mechanical or electronic recording device. Velocity sensors can be located anywhere in a sewer pipe and their measurements are multiplied by the cross-sectional area to obtain the discharge. Combination units measure both the depth of flow and velocity.

"The machine then selects the likely equations from a complicated pattern of theoretical probables. It calculates these, and the correct answer is printed on a card. Then our Miss Swenson files them God knows where, and we can never find the damn things again."

Depth

The depth of flow may be measured manually with a staff gauge, which is simply a ruler that is attached to a vertical surface. Staff gauges are graduated such that they can be easily viewed from a convenient location in units of 0.01 ft for U.S. customary units and 0.01 m for SI units. A staff gauge may be used to check the calibration of an electronic sensor or serve as a backup depth measurement.

Several technologies are available today to generate accurate and reliable depth data. These devices can collect and store data for long periods and then electronically transmit the data to a central database. The three technologies that are commonly used in sewer monitoring are pressure transducers, bubbler systems, and ultrasound.

Mechanical devices that are rarely used today include floats and probe recorders. Floats are connected to strip chart recorders, which have to be manually analyzed to produce digital data. A probe recorder measures the wastewater surface from a probe attached to a thin electrical wire that is lowered to the surface. When the probe makes contact with the water surface, a circuit is completed and the level of the probe recorded. Both of these devices are susceptible to fouling and mechanical failure.

Table 8.3 Depth and velocity sensors.

Type	Operating Principle
Depth Sensors	
Staff gauge	Gauge with graduations that is vertically mounted on the side of the channel. Readings are manual.
Mechanical float	Typically located in a side chamber to dampen waves. It is connected to a pen and marks paper on a rolling drum.
Ultrasonic	Mounted above the channel and sends an ultrasonic signal to the water surface. Depth computations are based on the time the reflected signal takes to return to the sensor.
Pressure transducer	Pressure transducers are sited at the bottom of the wastewater stream and measure pressure, which is converted to depth. Must be calibrated.
Bubbler	Emits a continuous stream of bubbles. A pressure transducer located in the gas supply line away from the wastewater stream senses the resistance to bubble formation, converting it to depth.
Velocity Sensors	
Mechanical current meter	Propeller or screw type, measures velocity by counting the revolutions over time (30 to 60 seconds). Hand held in the stream.
Electromagnetic current meter	Flow around a magnet induces a current. Instrument display readout is in ft/s or m/s. Hand held in the stream. Measures point (not average) velocity.
Transit time ultrasonic	Measures velocity by comparing reflected sonic wave speed upstream and downstream. Valid only at full flow.
Doppler ultrasonic	Measures velocity by examining the reflected sonic waves from particles or bubbles. Typically measures peak velocity, which is then converted to average velocity.
Radar	Measures reflected waves from the surface of the flow. Measures surface velocity, which is then converted to average velocity.
Combination units	Depth is measured with a pressure transducer, flow area is calculated from channel geometry. Average velocity is measured by Doppler ultrasonic.

Pressure Transducers. Pressure transducers measure the hydrostatic pressure of the wastewater above the sensor (Figure 8.7) and convert it to depth. These devices are mounted directly in the flow at the bottom of the pipe and provide a resistance or voltage that is proportional to the height of the fluid above the sensor. They are generally inexpensive but are also prone to measurement drift. A pressure transducer can be calibrated by placing it in a constant-level tank or bucket and measuring the output. Some newer sensors automatically calculate drift and are self-calibrated.

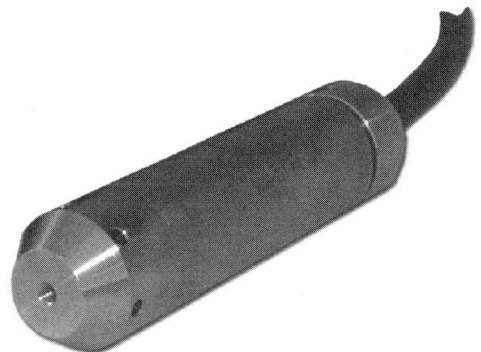

Courtesy of Campbell Scientific, Inc. Logan, Utah

Figure 8.7 Pressure depth sensor.

When silt or gravel collects in the pipe, the measuring device may be offset from the bottom. As a consequence, low-flow depths may not be measured accurately, if at all.

Bubblers. Bubbler systems operate by measuring the pressure required to produce bubbles, compared to an atmospheric reference. As illustrated in Figure 8.8, pressurized gas is supplied by an air compressor or a compressed gas tank (air or nitrogen) and the control valve (pressure regulator) is adjusted until bubbles form in the flow.

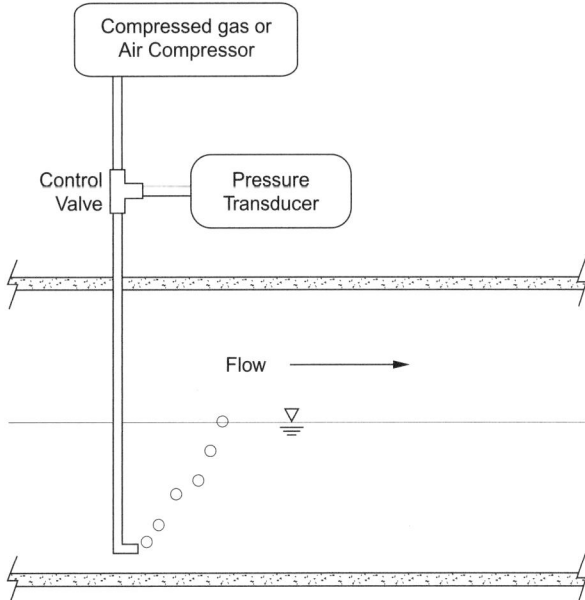

Figure 8.8 Bubbler depth measurement.

The pressure transducer measures the pressure required to form the bubbles, which is translated into the depth of the water and stored in a data logger. Bubblers have the advantage of self purging, eliminating some of the concerns of silt accumulation.

Compressed gas is used less frequently today because the small pumps that are often used to deliver compressed air are more reliable. However, in remote locations where the period between required pump inspections is lengthy and/or power for an air compressor is not available, then compressed gas supplied from a tank is more desirable. Bubblers are as dependable as the pump or pressure supply used to produce the bubbles.

Ultrasonic Devices. Since the early 1970s, range or distance measurements have been commonly made with ultrasonic devices, like those found on some cameras. Ultrasonic devices are usually mounted on top of a pipe, where they measure the distance to the top of the flow. The sensors emit an ultrasonic pulse to the water surface and measure the time for the reflected signal (echo) to return, as illustrated in Figure 8.9. The time it takes the sound wave to propagate through the air is proportional to the temperature. Thus based on the time and temperature, the distance to the surface can be calculated. Since the internal diameter of the pipe and the offset of the sending unit from the top of the pipe are known, the depth can be easily calculated. Figure 8.10 shows a typical ultrasonic depth meter installation.

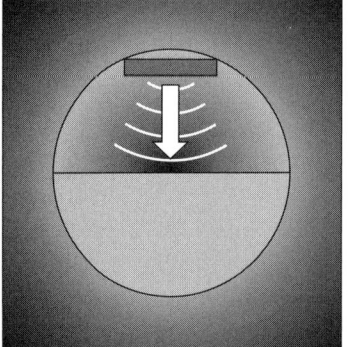
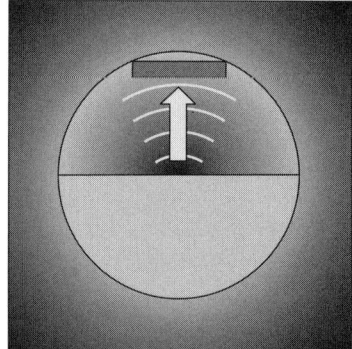

Figure 8.9 Depth measurement with an ultrasonic device.

Maria do Céu Almeida/LNEC

Figure 8.10 Ultrasonic depth meter installed in a pipe.

Velocity Meters

There are many types of velocity measuring devices such as Pitot tubes and propellers, but most become inoperative in a sewer environment. Therefore, most sewer-flow velocity measurements are made with electromagnetic, ultrasonic, or radar meters, as described in the following sections. Each type of meter, is further classified as to whether it is full pipe or open channel; and these categories can be subdivided according to how the signals are processed. Most flow meters contain some sort of data-logging capability so that information can be loaded into a portable computer in the field.

Electromagnetic Meters. Electromagnetic (EM) velocity meters (mag meters) operate according to Faraday's law of induction, which states that when a voltage is induced in a conductor passing through a magnetic field, the voltage is proportional to the average velocity. Mag meters are widely accepted for measuring the flow in full-pipe flow systems containing solids, where devices such as venturi meters, propellers, and orifices would fail.

Mag meters for pressure-pipe flow are usually purchased as a spool piece. In this case, a short segment of pipe is cut out and replaced with a pipe segment containing the mag meter. These meters are durable, will not clog, and are relatively insensitive to solids and grease.

For open-channel flow, as illustrated in Figure 8.11, a mag meter sensor is placed on the bottom of the pipe. The sensor and associated software use measurements of depth, area, and velocity to calculate flow rate. A typical installation of a flow metering station in a manhole is show in Figure 8.12. Note that the data recording module is located above the water.

Another common application of mag meter technology for wastewater systems is the portable velocity probe. These probes, known as EM probes, are often used to measure the point velocities at representative points throughout a cross section. The mea-

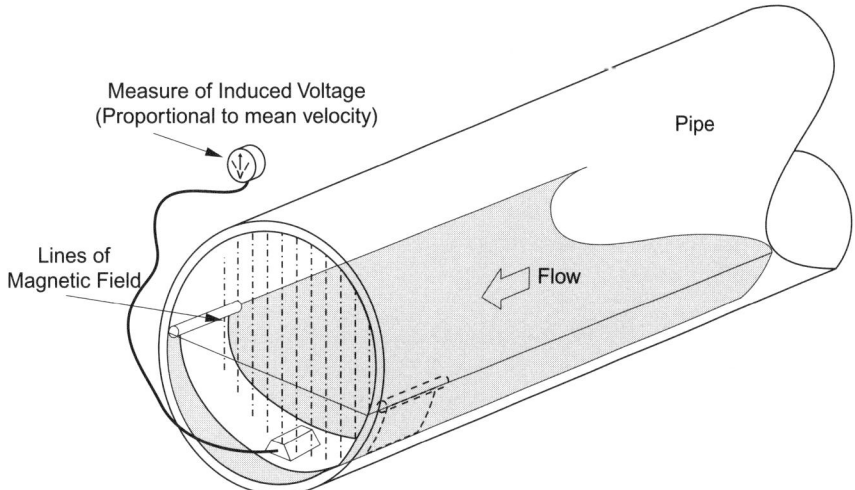

Figure 8.11 Open-channel mag meter.

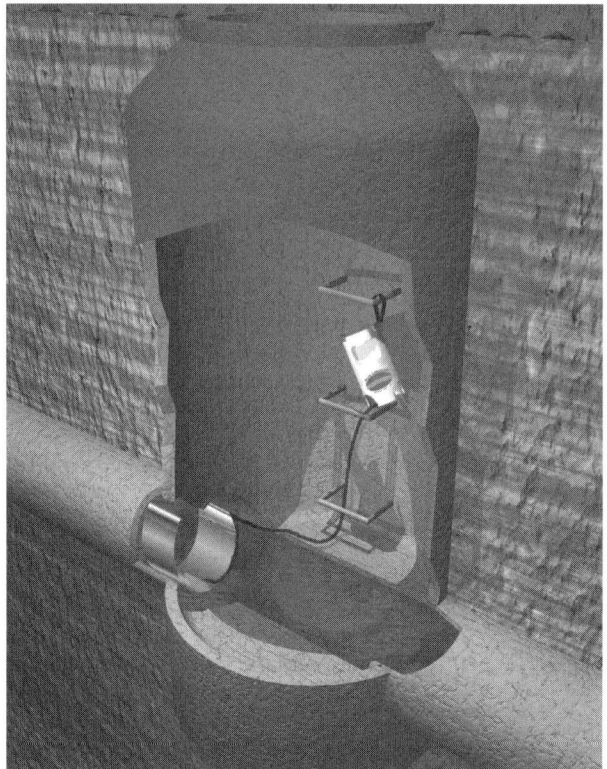

Courtesy of Marsh-McBirney

Figure 8.12 Portable flow meter with electromagnetic sensor installed in a manhole.

surements are compiled to obtain an average velocity. Hand-held EM probes may be used to collect single point measurements or to calibrate other velocity meters.

Ultrasonic Meters. Ultrasonic devices are frequently used to measure the velocity with either of two techniques: Doppler or transit-time. Doppler flow meters use the reflection of sonic energy to determine the flow velocity. Transit-time meters rely on the relation between the change in wave speed and the fluid velocity.

Random Doppler Meters – The most common type of ultrasonic meter for wastewater collection systems depends on the application of the Doppler principle. The principle states that when a pulse of energy (acoustic or electromagnetic) with a precise frequency is sent toward an object, the shift in frequency of the reflected signal is proportional to the object's velocity. This principle is also used in police radar guns and weather radar.

In most wastewater applications, a velocity probe mounted on or near the bottom of the pipe emits ultrasonic (0.5 MHz) signals upstream into the flow. The probe listens (constantly) for the return signal created when the signal hits a solid particle or an air bubble. The probe detects the frequencies that are related to the velocity of the particles within the flow. The signals must be processed within the measuring instrument to determine the maximum or average velocity. Figure 8.13 illustrates an ultrasonic flow meter.

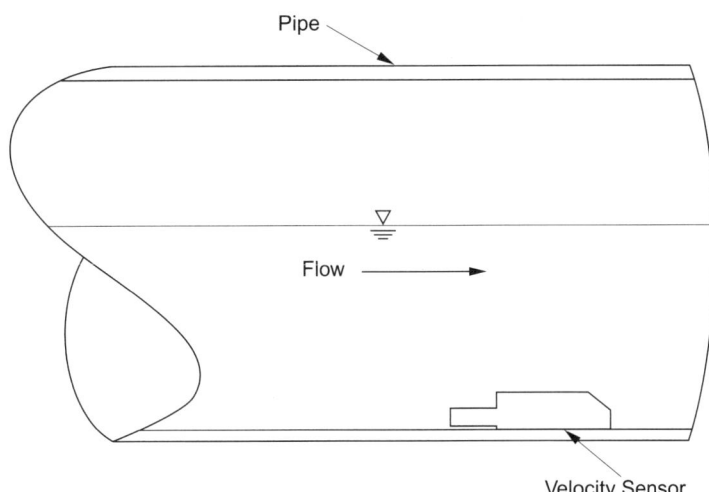

Figure 8.13 Ultrasonic flow meter in cross section.

Coherent Doppler Meters – Another variation of Doppler velocity measurement has evolved from ocean-current meters that propagate an ultrasonic pulse in several directions from a probe resting on the ocean floor. For sewer measurements, the probe listens only at preset intervals rather than continuously. Thus, the signal is at a known distance and the flow velocity is calculated by considering the whole spectrum. This is referred to as *coherent* or *gated* Doppler and it provides the first practical method of directly measuring the distribution of velocities throughout the flow.

An example of a sensor using this technology is shown in Figure 8.14. A transducer assembly is mounted on the invert of the pipe or channel. Short pulses are emitted in different directions along narrow acoustic beams and echoes of these pulses are back-scattered by the suspended material or bubbles in the flow. Because the material and bubbles have motion relative to the transducer, the frequency of the echoes is adjusted (Doppler shifted). Measurement of the frequency allows the calculation of the flow speed. A fifth source is mounted in the center of the transducer assembly and aimed vertically to measure depth.

Transit Time Meters – Transit-time ultrasonic flowmeters are based on the principle that the transit time of an acoustic signal along a known path is altered by the fluid velocity (Bureau of Reclamation, 2001 and Day, 2000). A high frequency acoustic signal sent upstream travels slower than a signal sent downstream. By measuring the transit times of signals sent in both directions along a diagonal path, the average path velocity of the fluid can be calculated. Knowing the path angle with respect to the direction of flow, the average velocity in the channel can be computed.

Transit time meters are installed with pairs of acoustic sensors that send and/or receive signals and may be used for both open channels and full pipes. In Figure 8.15a, a pair of transducers is mounted in a diametrically opposed configuration and an average axial velocity is measured along the acoustical path. This configuration is suitable for measuring flow in a full pipe.

Figure 8.15b shows a chordal path configuration that is used for open channels. In this case, each pair of transducers measures the average axial velocity corresponding to its chordal path and the velocity profile is numerically integrated over the cross-sectional flow area to determine the volumetric flow rate. Note that a depth sensor is also required for this installation. Transit time meters are suitable for irregular shaped channels. The accuracy of the measurements depends on the number and locations of the sensors.

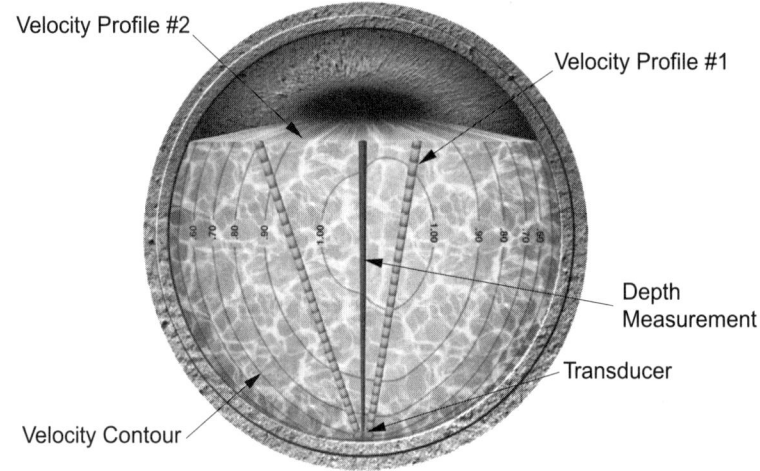

Figure 8.14 Coherent Doppler sensor operation.

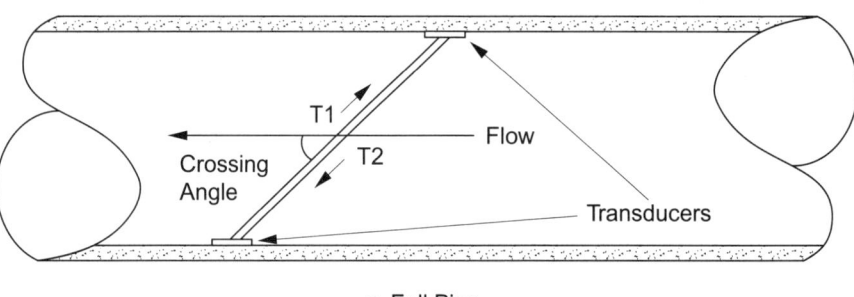

a. Full Pipe

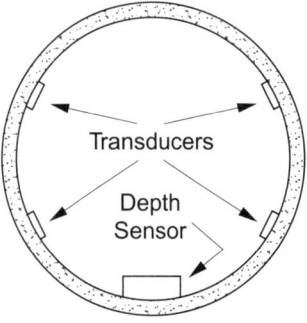

b. Open Channel

Figure 8.15 Transit-time meter in full pipe and open channel.

Full-Pipe Ultrasonic Meters – Both Doppler and transit-time meters can also be used in full-pipe flow. In these applications, there is no need for any depth measurement. The key issue in selecting the meter is whether a spool piece, insertion, or clamp-on (strap-on) installation is used.

Spool-piece installations are commonly used with transit-time meters because alignment is so important. An insertion probe is usually adequate for Doppler meters; however, these probes are subject to fouling by grease and debris.

Clamp-on ultrasonic meter installations are frequently used in temporary installations for the measurement of flow in force mains. These installations require full-pipe flow and may be compromised by excessive vibration or electrical noise in the pump station. Their primary benefits are the convenience of installation and the avoidance of contact with materials that can foul the sensors. The disadvantage of these meters is that irregularities in the pipe wall from corrosion, grease, or solid deposits can affect accuracy.

Radar Meters. Radar meters depend on the Doppler Method, but instead of sending ultrasonic signals, they send radio-frequency signals. As radio frequencies are not appreciably affected by the local temperature, one complication of the use of ultrasonics is eliminated. In the past, the high frequencies used by radar systems increased power demands and shortened battery life, but the new miniaturized radar systems are more energy efficient making them more practical.

When monitoring sewers with radar meters, surface waves provide the target or point of reflection. The radar measures the surface velocity of an open channel, which then needs to be converted to the average velocity. This conversion is usually calibrated with measurements of surface and average velocities from hand-held point velocity probes. Figure 8.16 shows a radar-based sensor connected to a portable computer for data logging in the field. Figure 8.17 shows a typical flow-metering installation with such a device.

Because the sensor is placed above the fluid rather than submerged, installation is easier and there is no sensor fouling. Radar meters can measure caustic, hot, or solids-laden flow.

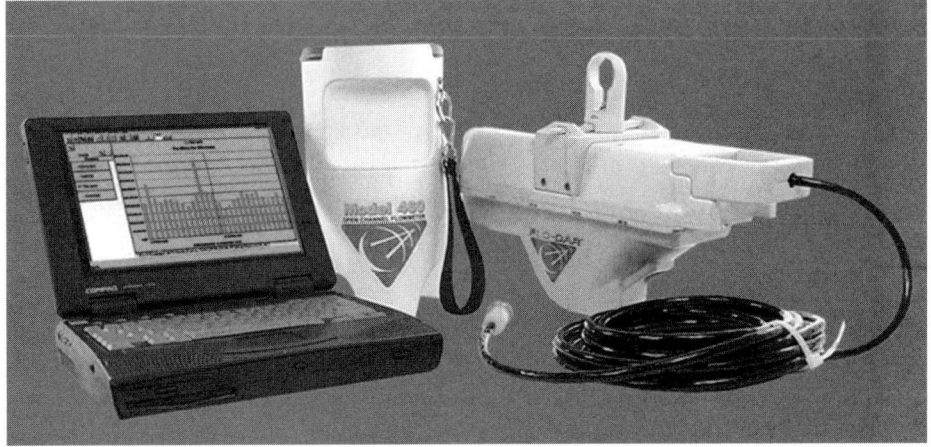

Courtesy of Marsh-McBirney

Figure 8.16 Doppler radar flow meter components.

Figure 8.17 Installation of a radar sensor in a sewer.

8.4 Precipitation Measurement

Because wet weather conditions are usually the most critical situation for sewer modeling, it is important to calibrate the model under these conditions. Depending on the model, precipitation values in one form or another are needed.

Some modelers attempt to use rainfall data collected at a weather station a considerable distance from the basin under study. However, depending on the nature of the storm, values from distant stations can be misleading. In general, if there are no permanent rainfall stations in the basin, it is worthwhile to install several temporary rainfall gauges during the time that wastewater flow data are being collected. Ideally, the modeler would have a temporary rain gauge in each subbasin where RDII is being quantified.

When rainfall is significantly different between rain gauges, graphical techniques can be used to distribute point rainfall quantities over the basin (Burton and Pitt, 2002). The US Environmental Protection Agency (1999) recommends the inverse-distance weighting method. Other techniques include Thiessen polygons and the isohyetal method. It is important to note that every method of conversion from point to area measurements has its limitations.

Precipitation Data Acquisition

In many parts of the world, precipitation is measured through weather data collection networks. In the United States, the National Oceanic and Atmospheric Administration, National Climatic Data Center Climatic Services Branch is responsible for the collection of precipitation data. These data are available on an hourly, daily, and monthly frequency for a large number of stations and may be purchased in electronic format.

Measurement of Rainfall

Rainfall is measured with either nonrecording or recording gauges. Nonrecording gauges only measure the total rainfall depth for a single event. They do not supply any information about the storm duration or intensity making them insufficient when an event hyetograph is required. Recording rain gauges measure the amount, duration, and time distribution of rain throughout the storm. Rainfall intensities can also be determined from these data.

Nonrecording Rain Gauges. Any vertical-sided container can be used as a rain gauge. However, measurements of rain within different containers are not necessarily comparable, due to differences in size, shape, and exposure. The United States standard 8-in. nonrecording rain gauge has been used throughout the life of the National Weather Service (Yang, Goodison, and Metcalfe, 1998). It consists of a support framework; a 24-in. (610-mm) high, 8-in. (200-mm) diameter overflow can; a 20-in. (510-mm) high, 2.53-in. (64-mm) inside diameter measuring tube; a 20-in. (510-mm) long wooden measuring stick; and an 8-in. (200-mm) diameter collector or receiver.

The collector has a beveled, machined edge and its area is exactly ten times that of the measuring tube. Thus, the rainfall depth captured by the gauge is magnified ten times in the measuring tube. The measuring stick is marked in 0.1-in. (2.54 mm) increments, so rainfall can be measured to the nearest 0.01 in. (0.25 mm). If the rainfall depth is greater than 2 in. (50 mm), the excess rain is stored in the overflow can.

Inexpensive nonrecording rain gauges of various sizes are available and can be placed throughout the watershed to measure rainfall variations, especially for short, localized thunderstorms (Burton and Pitt, 2002).

Recording Rain Gauges. There are three types of recording rain gauges used in the United States: tipping-bucket, weighing, and float. A tipping-bucket gauge, illustrated in Figure 8.18, operates by means of a two-compartment bucket. When a certain quantity (depth) of rainfall fills one compartment (via funnel), the weight of the water causes it to tip and empty, and the second compartment moves into position for filling. Similarly, the second bucket tips when full and moves the first compartment back into position. This process continues indefinitely. As the buckets are tipped, they actuate an electrical circuit, causing a pen to mark a revolving drum (or the tipping may be recorded digitally). With some tipping-bucket models, the precipitation is discharged from the buckets into a graduated cylinder and manual readings of total volume at defined intervals can be used to verify data from the tipping-bucket.

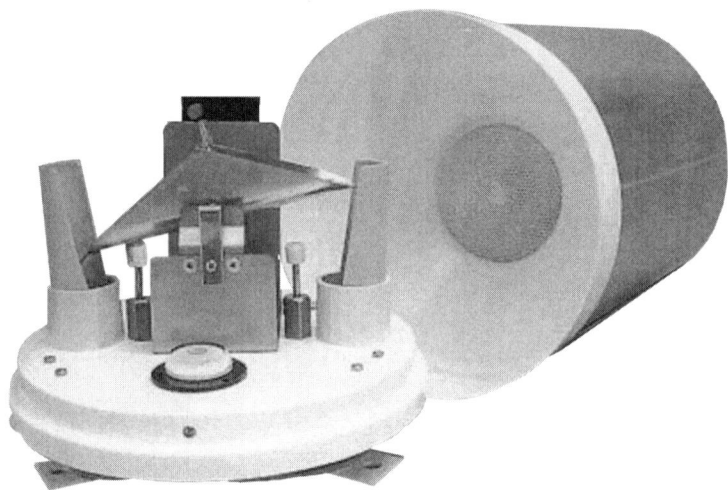

Model 6506A Tipping bucket Rainfall Gauge. Photo courtesy of Unidata.

Figure 8.18 Tipping-bucket precipitation gauge.

A weighing gauge measures the rain or snow that falls into a pail set on a platform of a spring or lever balance. The increasing weight of the bucket and its contents is recorded on a chart, which correlates to the accumulation of precipitation.

There are several types of float recording gauges. In most, the float is placed in a collector and as the rainfall depth increases, the rise of the float is recorded on a chart. In others, the collector rests in a bath of oil or mercury and as its weight increases from the accumulated rainfall, the float measures the rise of the oil or mercury.

With some newer recording gauges, the collector must be emptied manually. However, many consumer gauges are emptied automatically by self-starting syphons. These gauges operate by filling a small reservoir that is drained by a siphon when the reservoir capacity is reached. Each fill/drain cycle is recorded digitally at the electronic weather station.

Older recording gauges record a pen trace on a chart. The punched-tape recorder punches the amount of precipitation accumulated in the collector on a tape in digital code, which later can be run through a translator for computer evaluation of the record.

Gauge Operation Considerations

Measurement errors can occur in both nonrecording and recording gauges. These errors, in almost all cases, tend to underestimate the actual amount of rain that fell. The four main types of errors are observer error, rain gauge location, rain gauge density, and wind effects.

The location of the rain gauge in relation to its surroundings is important. Gauges should be located in open spaces away from immediate shielding effects of trees or buildings (US Environmental Protection Agency, 1999).

Sufficient gauge density for the accurate measurement of rainfall depth, intensity, and volume is highly dependent on local conditions. These conditions include seasonal differences, with summer storms generally including spatially small, intense convective events, and winter storms including broad frontal storms with less spatial variability. Bosch and Davis (1999) studied the spatial correlation of rain gauges in a watershed located in the coastal plain of Georgia. The authors reported that gauges separated by 1.3 mi (2.1 km) or less are likely to yield a correlation coefficient of 0.9 for summer storms. The distance increases to 5.5 mi (8.9 km) for the same correlation coefficient for winter storms. The Natural Resources Conservation Service (1993) presents graphical methods for estimating the accuracy of precipitation measurements based on the distance between stations. The procedures are based on data collected in the midwestern United States.

The effects of wind during a storm have the greatest impact on the accuracy of rain gauge measurements and they always result in capture of a smaller quantity of rain than what actually fell. The vertical acceleration of air forced upward over a gauge imparts an upward acceleration of rain, resulting in a deficient catch. This effect is greater for small raindrops and thus results in more significant measurement error for lighter rainfalls (Linsley, Kohler, and Paulhus, 1982). To mitigate these wind effects, several types of shields have been developed. The higher the gauge is located, the greater the wind effect, so locations on rooftops and wind swept hillsides should be avoided.

Radar Imagery

In 1980, the National Weather Service's Next Generation Weather Radar (NEXRAD) Program was established. As of 2004, there are 158 NEXRAD radar systems (called WSR-88D) deployed throughout the United States and at selected overseas locations and each has a maximum range of 290 miles (470 km). Each WSR-88D system contains a computer processing system for converting radar data to meteorological data products and displaying it graphically (Smith, 1993). Vendors have developed systems that process and calibrate NEXRAD data to produce high-resolution, short-duration estimates of rainfall.

"When we're right, we're right."

Nearly everyone is familiar with the images shown on nightly televised weather reports, where varying colors indicate the relative intensity of rainfall. Each pixel size represents approximately 1.2 mi^2 (3.1 km^2), which provides sufficient coverage in areas where the storms are concentrated or exhibit high spatial variability. These images display the returned signal strength; generally, the higher the return signal, the more intense the rainfall.

When interpreting these images, it is important to consider that occasionally, precipitation is circulating in the cloud formation rather than actually falling to the ground. To properly correlate the return signal strength to actual rainfall, rain gauges are required in the study area. This technique is called *ground-truthing* and correlates the return signal strength to the actual rainfall measured on the ground. This allows development of individual hyetographs for each cell in the study area. The advantage of this process is that spatial variability is accurately measured and displayed for the entire area. Depending on the study-area size, this may represent a significant cost savings, as the cells may provide information that would have required hundreds of rain gauges. Figure 8.19 is an example of gauge-adjusted radar measurements.

Stevens, Lopez, and Jacquet (2002) evaluated the use of gauge-adjusted radar rainfall measurements in a RDII program in King County, Washington. The system consisted of approximately 17 million linear ft (5.2 million m) of sanitary sewers and has a service area of 1100 mi^2 (2800 km^2). A commercial system provided radar data with 0.6 mi^2 (1.6 km^2) geographic resolution (pixel size) and a 5-minute temporal resolution. The radar data for each storm were calibrated with 72 recording rain gauges.

The service area was divided into eight calibration zones. The accuracy of the calibration was assessed by determining the number of pixels in each zone with a predicted accumulation within 20% of the accumulation measured with the associated rain gauges. For 10 storms, 70% of the radar predictions were with 20% of the rain gauge measurements. For the largest storm, the total accumulation ranged from 1.36 to 5.74

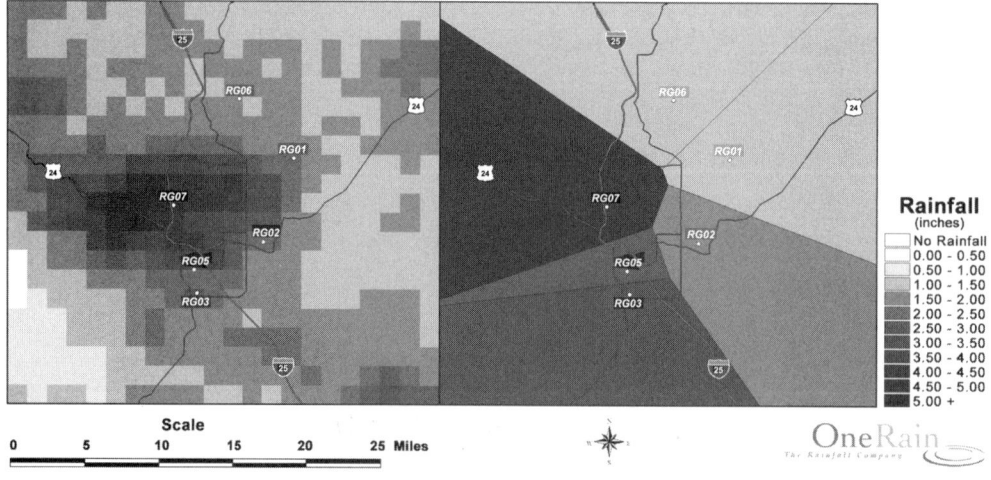

Figure 8.19 Radar-derived rainfall distribution.

in. (35 to 146 mm) and 100% of the predicted values were within 20% of the rain gauge data. Storms with a total accumulation of less than 1 in. (25 mm) resulted in less-accurate predictions. The utility of the radar systems was demonstrated by observation of a localized storm that had large accumulations at the 0.6 mile^2 (1.6 km^2) resolution. This storm was not observed in two rain gauges that were located in the vicinity, approximately 3 miles (5 km) apart.

In another study, Jacquet, Piatyszek, and Lyard (2002) reviewed the use of radar-based rainfall data in Dade County, Florida and Allegheny County, Pennsylvania. The 0.38 mi^2 (1 km^2) resolution used in Allegheny County resulted in greater accuracy than the 1.2 mi-by-1.2 mi (2 km-by-2 km) resolution used in Dade County. The Allegheny County study used advection processing to replace pixels contaminated by shadows and ground clutter to improve predictions. *Advection processing* is an automatic step which replaces ground clutter pixels with the sum of the pixels that will be passing over that pixel during the next five or six minutes or even up to 12 minutes if a radar image is missing. Meeneghan et al. (2002) describe the process of using radar data to model RDII. Several firms offer services of calibrating NEXRAD data to local gauges and delivering data in the formats needed by the modeler.

References

Bureau of Reclamation. 2001. *Water Measurement Manual, A Water Resources Technical Publication*. Washington, DC: United Stated Department of the Interior, Bureau of Reclamation.

Bos, M. G. 1989. *Discharge Measurement Structures*. 3rd rev. ed. Wageningen, The Netherlands: International Institute for Land Reclamation (ILLR).

Bosch, D. D. and F. M. Davis. 1999. *Rainfall Variability and Spatial Patterns for the Southeast*. Tifton, GA: Southeast Watershed Research laboratory, United States Department of Agriculture - Agricultural Research Service. http://www.cpes.peachnet.edu/sewrl/Papers/Paper001.PDF. (Accessed 5/04).

Burton, G. A. and R. E. Pitt. 2002. *Stormwater Effects Handbook A Toolbox for Watershed Managers, Scientists, and Engineers*. Boca Raton, FL: Lewis Publishers.

Day, T. J. 200. *Sewer Management Systems*. New York: John Wiley & Sons.

French, R. H. 1985. *Open Channel Hydraulics*. New York: McGraw-Hill.

Grant, D. M. 1989. *ISCO Open Channel Flow Measurement Handbook*. Lincoln, NB: ISCO Environmental Division.

Jacquet, C., E. Piatyszek, and S. Lyard. 2002. "Radar-based rainfall input requirements synthesis of US and French 10 years experience." In *Proceedings of the Ninth International Conference on Urban Drainage*. Reston, VA: American Society of Civil Engineers.

Kilpatrick, F. A and E. D. Cobb. 1985. "Measurement of discharge using tracers." In *Techniques of Water-Resources Investigations of the United States Geological Survey*, Book 3, Chapter A16. Washington, DC: US Government Printing Office.

Linsley, R. K. Jr., M. A. Kohler, and J. L. Paulhus. 1982. *Hydrology for Engineers*. 3rd ed. New York: McGraw-Hill.

Meeneghan, T. J., M. D. Loehlein, R. E., Dickinson, R. D. Myers, and T. Prevost. 2002. "Impacts of rainfall data on model refinements in the greater Pittsburgh area." In

Proceedings of the Ninth International Conference on Urban Drainage. Reston, VA: American Society of Civil Engineers.

Natural Resources Conservation Service (NRCS). 1993. *National Engineering Handbook*. Part 630 "Hydrology." Chapter 4: "Storm Runoff Depth." Washington, DC: US Department of Agriculture.

Rantz, R. E. 1982. *Measurement and Computation of Stream Flow*. Vol. 1: *Measurement of Stage and Discharge*; Vol. 2: *Computation of Discharge*. US Geological Survey Water Supply Paper 2175. Reston, VA: US Geological Survey.

Smith, J. A. 1993. "Precipitation." In *Handbook of Hydrology*, ed. by D. R. Maidment. New York: McGraw-Hill.

Stevens, P., M. Lopez, and G. Jacquet. 2002. "Evaluation of gauge adjusted radar for rainfall measurements in RDII programs." In *Proceedings of the Ninth International Conference on Urban Drainage*. Reston, VA: American Society of Civil Engineers.

US Environmental Protection Agency (US EPA). 1999. *Combined Sewer Overflows Guidance for Monitoring and Modeling*. Washington, DC: Environmental Protection Agency 832-B-99-002.

Water Environment Federation and American Society of Civil Engineers (WEF). 1994. *Existing Sewer Evaluation and Rehabilitation*. Alexandria, VA: Water Environment Federation.

Yang, D., B. E. Goodison, and J. R. Metcalfe. 1998. "Accuracy of NWS 8" standard nonrecording precipitation gauge: Results and application of WMO intercomparison." *Journal Atmospheric and Oceanic Technology* 15 (Feb): 54–68.

Problems

8.1 What are the pros and cons of a flume compared to a velocity-area measuring device?

8.2 Why are weirs not advisable for long-term flow measurement in sewers?

8.3 You want to know the flow in a sewer by a dilution method. You introduce salt water with a total dissolved solids concentration of 50,000 mg/L at a flow of 2 L/s. The background TDS concentration upstream of the injection point is 550 mg/L and you measure the TDS downstream of injection at 820 mg/L. What is the sewer flow rate?

8.4 You have installed a Parshall flume with a 2-ft wide throat. Given the depth hydrograph in the following table, determine the flow hydrograph.

t, hr	h, ft	Q, ft³/s
0	1.21	
1	1.60	
2	1.63	
3	1.45	
4	1.38	
5	1.15	

8.5 In a separate sewer system, you have measured the hydrograph at an upstream point, A, and a downstream point, B, in a drainage area as shown in the following table. You would like to know the contribution from the drainage area between the two points. Develop a hydrograph, called B–A. Based on the shape of the hydrograph, would you expect that there is more I/I in the upstream or downstream drainage areas?

t, hr	Q_A, L/s	Q_B, L/s	Q_{B-A}, L/s
0	212	391	
1	212	391	
2	254	448	
3	341	567	
4	487	765	
5	600	918	
6	629	958	
7	600	918	
8	537	833	
9	446	709	
10	375	612	
11	329	550	
12	275	476	
13	245	436	
14	229	414	
15	216	397	
16	212	391	

CHAPTER

9

Model Calibration

Hydraulic sewer models contain many parameters that describe the physical properties, hydraulic properties, loads, boundary conditions, and operating conditions of the collection system. The physical (e.g., system layout, pipe sizes) and hydraulic (e.g., pipe roughness) properties usually do not change from one run to the next. However, loading, boundary, and operating conditions typically do change, both between model runs and over time. Steady-state models reflect a snapshot view of system conditions for a particular time of interest. In contrast, extended-period simulations model the variation of conditions through time.

Many of the model parameters are quantified during the initial data collection phase (described in Chapter 5) and are assigned to the model as it is constructed. However, many other parameters cannot be measured, or otherwise obtained directly, and must initially be estimated using values from literature or professional judgment. Once the model is running, these estimated parameters should be adjusted to bring model-predicted values into agreement with observed values. This process is called calibration.

After a model has been calibrated, the modeler and other decision makers can feel confident that the representations and assumptions about the system reflect actual system conditions and operations. The calibration procedures and the data required to support calibration should be part of the modeling plan described in Chapter 5. However, data collection frequently yields unexpected results, and the number and magnitude of events that are actually monitored cannot be controlled. Standards for calibration are difficult to define for hydraulic sewer models. Rather, the goal is to minimize, within reason, the differences between measured and predicted results. Accordingly, calibration is as much art as science.

9.1 Basic Calibration Concepts

Calibration is the process of running a model using a set of input data, comparing the results to actual measurements, and then making the necessary adjustments so that the model results and the actual measurements agree (US Environmental Protection Agency, 1999). Calibration seeks to minimize the deviation between measured field conditions and model output by adjusting the parameters of the model (Jewell, Nunno, and Adrian, 1978).

There is considerable disagreement in the literature about the use of the words "validation" and "verification." The US Environmental Protection Agency (1995) defines *verification* as "the process of testing the calibrated model using one or more independent data sets." However, another EPA report (1999) in the same series defines *validation* as "the process of testing the calibrated model using one or more independent data sets."

Regardless of which term is used, models should be tested against independent data sets. If the model performs well in the tests, the user can feel more confident in applying it. If the model does not work well, it may be an indication that the model was forced to fit the calibration data set but does not accurately represent the physical processes occurring. Using rainfall patterns different from those for which the model was calibrated can lead to difficulty matching data during verification.

Overview of Calibration

In general, calibration of hydraulic sewer models focuses on minimizing differences between predicted and measured flows. At critical points in a network, such as diversion structures and overflow locations, the ability of the model to predict hydraulic grade elevation may also be evaluated. Ultimately, the selection of calibration criteria depends on the purpose of the model.

The steps in model calibration are summarized as follows (3-Waters, 2001; Ormsbee and Lingireddy, 1997):

1. Determine purpose for the modeling effort (see Chapter 5).
2. Collect model calibration data.
3. Make comparisons between model and field data.
4. Identify source of discrepancies between model and field data.
5. Correct model data or discard invalid field data.
6. Verify model using independent data.

This process is based on the premise that much of the data collection follows the initial development of the model. That is, only the data required to represent the physical system were initially available. Loads were estimated from demographic data. Later, flows were measured at a few selected points in the system to begin the calibration process. With the advent of widely available SCADA data and/or temporary flow measurements, it has become more feasible to collect considerable flow and depth data before or during the model-building process. The calibration procedure would be modified in such cases.

The calibration process can only be applied to the model if a sufficient number of measurements were taken throughout the system. A model is said to be calibrated when measured and model values are within some acceptable range. For example, if the measured and modeled peak flow rates are within 5 percent of each other, then the model may be considered calibrated for peak events. Criteria such as matching peak flow rate, minimum flow rate, average daily flow volume, and time of predicted diurnal variations are used. The WAPUG (1989) provides some standards for judging the acceptability of a model. More rigorous parameters for error measurement in hydraulic models have been developed (Yen, 1982; ASCE Task Committee, 1993); however, these rarely apply to sewer models.

Initial calibration runs often point out features of the system, such as a connection or bypass, that may not have been evident from the available maps. The modeler makes corrections and repeats the calibration runs until satisfied that the model produces reasonable simulations of the overflows. Wet weather models are usually calibrated for more than one storm to ensure appropriate performance for a range of conditions.

Wherever there is a great difference between the estimated and measured values, the modeler must consider the potential sources of error. Such errors can arise from the meter installation itself or misrepresentation of the collection system.

Calibration Parameters

Before beginning model calibration, three questions should be addressed:

1. What are the model parameters that will be adjusted during calibration?

2. What data will the model be calibrated against?

3. What is a reasonable range for each parameter?

Table 9.1 contains a list of typical model parameters. For dry weather calibration, the modeler adjusts the hydraulic properties and the dry weather loads to calibrate the model to the monitoring data. If adjustments to the physical properties beyond the range of reasonable measurement errors are required for model calibration, then the revised properties should be verified with additional field observations.

Hydraulic sewer models are nearly always calibrated to match known flows at locations throughout the system, including overflows. Depending on the purpose of the model, it may also be calibrated to match the measured water surface elevations or velocities in the system. Attempting to model complex hydrologic and inflow issues with only a few adjustment parameters involves a great deal of simplification and approximation. In some cases, it may be possible to match the flow but not the water surface elevation. A meter just upstream of the blockage shown in Figure 9.1 would match model flows but would show a higher depth than the model because of the debris in the sewer.

The magnitude of parameter adjustment depends on the sensitivity of the model output to the parameters and on the discrepancy between the model and the field data. The results of a sensitivity analysis show which parameters have the greatest effect on model results. Predicted flows are usually highly sensitive to loads and insensitive to Manning's n and minor loss coefficients. Predicted hydraulic grade lines are sensitive to both flows and hydraulic properties.

Photo courtesy of R. D. Zande and Associates

Figure 9.1 Obstructions in pipes make it difficult to match the measured and modeled water levels.

Table 9.1 Model parameters.

Group		Description
Physical properties		Pipe length Pipe diameter Pipe slope Vertical alignment Horizontal alignment Manhole geometry Defects
Hydraulic properties		Manning's n Minor loss coefficients
Wastewater loads (BWF)		Constant flows Pattern loads Hydrograph
Groundwater infiltration (GWI)		Unit loads for pipes Unit loads for manholes
Rainfall-derived infiltration and inflow (RDII)	Runoff[1]	Soil properties Antecedent conditions Land use/land cover parameters Depression storage depth Slope RTK parameters
	Flow to sewer	Inlet hydraulics Direct connections Overland flow parameters
Operations	Pump Station	Pump curves On/off set points Wet well geometry
	Diversions	Hydraulic properties Open/close settings

1 Runoff parameters are dependent on the runoff model used. See Chapter 7.

Building-Block Approach

The calibration of a hydraulic sewer model begins with the identification of the components of flow. Since a flow gauge measures total flow, the components must be determined by subtraction. As defined in Chapter 7, the components of flow are as follows:

- *Sanitary* or *base wastewater flow (BWF)* enters the collection system through direct connections and represents the sum of domestic, commercial, and industrial flows.
- *Groundwater infiltration (GWI)* typically enters a sewer system through poorly constructed sewer service connections and from the ground through defective pipes, pipe joints, connections, or manhole walls. GWI may vary seasonally, but is usually constant over the duration a single precipitation event.
- *Rainfall-derived infiltration and inflow (RDII)* is the wet weather flow portion of the sewer flow hydrograph. RDII represents the flow above the normal dry weather flow pattern; it is the sewer flow response to rainfall or snowmelt in the upstream catchment.

At any point in the sewer, a flow meter measures the total flow, which is equal to BWF + GWI during dry weather and the sum of all three components during a storm. The approach presented in this chapter is to calibrate a model by loading it with parameters that describes each component of flow. The model sums the components and calculates the total flow through the collection system.

Steady-State and Extended-Period Simulations

Both steady-state and extended-period simulation models require calibration. For steady-state models, individual flows are compared between the model and the field measurements, whereas in extended period models, model and measured hydrographs are compared. Steady-state models are typically calibrated for minimum or average dry weather flows and for peak dry and peak wet weather flows. A common approach is to begin calibration with average sanitary and groundwater infiltration flows representative of the average dry weather condition. Once the average flows have been determined for all nodes, they serve as the base for the calculation of peaking factors or pattern load multipliers.

Once the dry weather flows are calibrated, the modeler attempts to match the wet weather flows. This is usually much more difficult because of the complexity of the processes affecting wet weather flow, especially the extent of defects in the collection system.

9.2 Dry Weather Flows

During dry weather, only sanitary discharges and groundwater infiltration are expected to contribute to the total flow, or

$$Q_t = Q_s + Q_{GWI} \tag{9.1}$$

where Q_t = total flow in sewer (ft^3/s or gpd, m^3/s)
Q_s = flow from sanitary sources (ft^3/s or gpd, m^3/s)
Q_{GWI} = groundwater infiltration (ft^3/s or gpd, m^3/s)

Depending on the generating source, sanitary flow may be modeled as a constant flow rate or as a pattern load in which an average baseline demand is multiplied at each time step by a demand multiplier, given by

$$Mult_i = \frac{Q_i}{Q_{base}} \qquad (9.2)$$

where $Mult_i$ = demand multiplier at the ith time step (dimensionless)
Q_i = demand in the ith time step (ft³/s or gpd, m³/s)
Q_{base} = base demand (ft³/s or gpd, m³/s)

Figure 9.2 is a graph of typical flow data for dry weather conditions in a representative community for a number of days. In some communities, there are significant differences between weekdays and weekends.

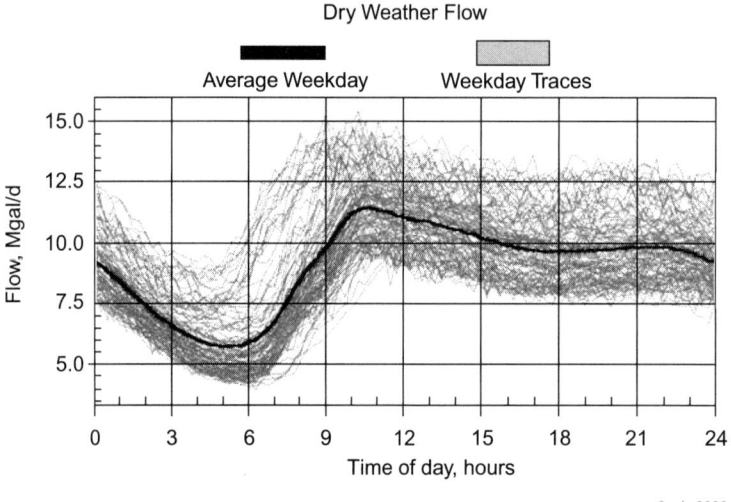

Figure 9.2 Example of a dry weather flow pattern.

Even during dry weather, there may be unusual flow events, such as dumping of batch tanks by an industrial customer or halftime restroom use at stadiums or arenas. The modeler can either remove these effects from the field data before calibration or include these events in the model.

To solve Equation 9.1, either Q_s or Q_{GWI} can be estimated independently. Average sanitary flow may be estimated from the unit-load factors described in Chapter 6. The sanitary flow is subtracted from the average flow measured over a 24-hour period (Q_t) to obtain Q_{GWI}. The $Mult_i$ terms for the sanitary pattern loads are determined by substituting the average sanitary load for the Q_{base} term in Equation 9.2 for each time step. Example 9.1 demonstrates the use of this calibration procedure. Alternatively, the modeler can use $Q_s + Q_{GWI}$ as the dry weather flow and not try to separate them.

Q_{GWI} is normalized to a characteristic of the collection system, such as pipe diameter, pipe length, service area, number of manholes, or some combination of these factors. Q_{GWI} may be estimated using a constant unit rate (such as volume/day/length of pipe). Table 9.2 lists ranges of these unit rates. The ranges in this table are large, and little guidance is available for selecting the appropriate value for a given sewer system, beyond the fact that the unit rate will increase with the age of the sewer. Site-specific estimates of Q_{GWI} may be developed and normalized to a unit, and then applied to the unmetered portion of the collection system. Q_{GWI} may also be estimated from a sewer evaluation program, as described in Chapter 11.

Table 9.2 Infiltration unit rates.[1]

Unit Rate		Value	
		SI	U.S. Customary
flow/pipe length:	8 in. (205 mm)	8230–11,750 L/day/km	3500–5000 gpd/mi
	12 in. (305 mm)	10,600–14,100 L/day/km	4500–6000 gpd/mi
	24 in. (610 mm)	23,500–28,200 L/day/km	10,000–12,000 gpd/mi
flow/pipe dia x pipe length		4.6–140 L/day-mm dia/km	50–1500 gpd/in.-dia/mile
flow/service area		1.3–187 m³/day/ha	140–2000 gpd/ac

[1] Source: American Society of Civil Engineers (1982)

In large systems, owing to travel time and attenuation in the collection system, the flow at the plant generally shows less variation than the flow in the upper reaches of the system. Caution must be used in applying a diurnal pattern at the plant to the rest of the system. Flow metering for smaller areas provides a more accurate picture of loading patterns.

Example 9.1 Dry weather flow calibration.

Wastewater flows were collected in a sewer over a 24-hour period during dry weather, as shown in the following figure. The monitoring location is 7200 ft downstream of the centroid of the community described in Example 6.1 on page 186. The average velocity in the sewer is 2 ft/s. Determine the groundwater infiltration and demand multipliers needed to model the sanitary flow.

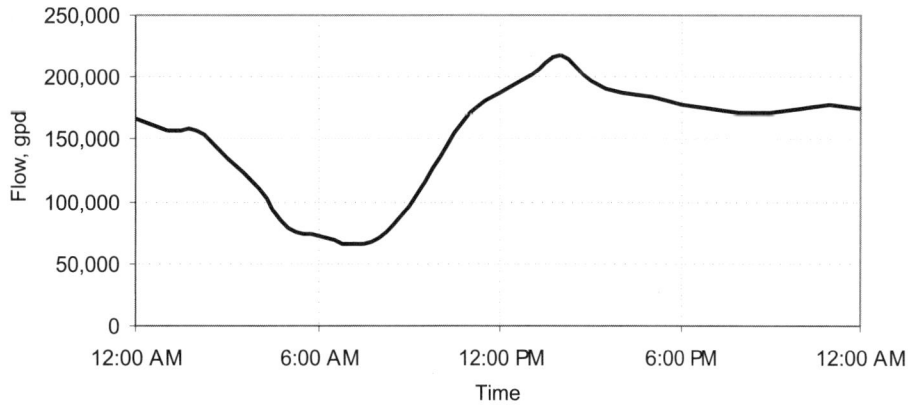

Solution

The results are listed in the following table. Columns 1 and 2 are the measured flow data corresponding to the preceding hydrograph. An explanation of the steps used to develop the data in the remaining columns follows the table.

1	2	3	4	5
Hour	Measured Flow, 1000 gpd	Sanitary Flow, 1000 gpd	Demand Multiplier	Adjusted Demand Multiplier
0	167	142	1.12	1.04
1	157	132	1.04	0.86
2	157	132	1.04	0.68
3	134	109	0.86	0.41
4	111	86	0.68	0.37
5	78	53	0.41	0.31
6	73	48	0.37	0.35
7	65	40	0.31	0.55
8	70	45	0.35	0.88
9	96	71	0.55	1.16
10	137	111	0.88	1.29
11	172	147	1.16	1.40
12	188	163	1.29	1.53
13	202	177	1.40	1.36
14	219	193	1.53	1.28
15	198	172	1.36	1.26
16	187	162	1.28	1.20
17	185	160	1.26	1.18
18	177	152	1.20	1.16
19	175	149	1.18	1.16
20	172	147	1.16	1.18
21	172	147	1.16	1.20
22	175	149	1.18	1.12
23	177	152	1.20	1.04

The average flow in the 24-hr period is the sum of Column 2 divided by 24, or 151,858 gpd. From Example 6.1, the average sanitary flow is 126,550 gpd. The infiltration, Q_{GWI}, is

$$151,858 - 126,550 = 25,308 \text{ gpd}$$

This GWI flow is assumed to be constant over the 24 hr period. For each time step, the sanitary flow, Q_S, is calculated in Column 3 by subtracting the 25,308 from the total flow.

The demand multiplier is calculated in Column 4 by dividing the hourly flow by the average flow of 126,500 gpd.

The travel time between the centroid of the source and the monitoring station is

$$\frac{7200 \text{ ft}}{2 \text{ ft/s}} \times \frac{1 \text{ hr}}{3600 \text{ sec}} = 2 \text{ hr}$$

The demand multipliers in Column 4 are adjusted to account for the travel time in the sewer by subtracting 2 hours from each time step. For example, the Adjusted Demand

Multiplier (column 5) at 8 hours is equal to the Demand Multiplier (column 4) at 10 hours.

The components of flow are shown in the following figure.

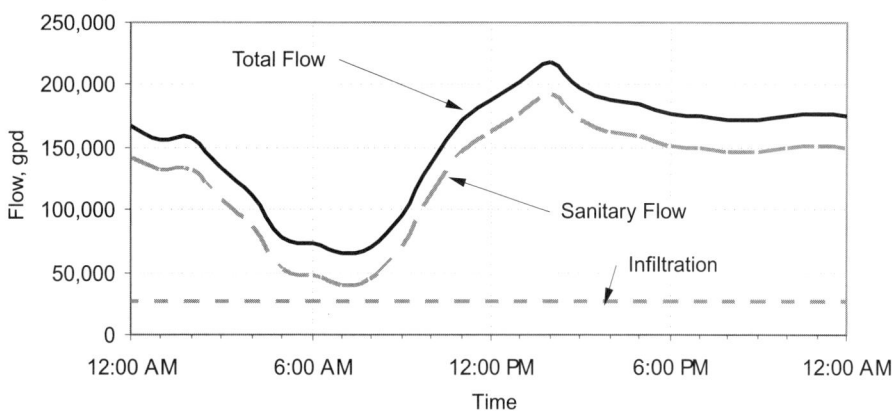

9.3 Wet Weather Flows

During a rainfall and for some time afterward, an additional component of flow enters the wastewater collection system. Rainfall-derived infiltration and inflow (RDII) was introduced in Chapter 7 and is defined as the portion of flow in a sewer hydrograph above the normal dry weather pattern (Bennett et al., 1999). When RDII occurs, Equation 9.1 is expanded to

$$Q_t = Q_s + Q_{GWI} + Q_{RDII} \tag{9.3}$$

where
Q_t = total flow in sewer (ft³/s or gpd, m³/s)
Q_s = flow from sanitary sources (ft³/s or gpd, m³/s)
Q_{GWI} = groundwater infiltration (ft³/s or gpd, m³/s)
Q_{RDII} = rainfall derived infiltration and inflow (ft³/s or gpd, m³/s)

Figure 9.3 shows the contributions of the three components to the sewer hydrograph. Initially the flow consists of $Q_s + Q_{GWI}$. Precipitation begins at 1:00 PM on July 1 and continues until 11:00 PM. Q_{RDII} appears at approximately 2:00 PM and continues until 11:00 PM on July 2. After that time, the flow contains only $Q_s + Q_{GWI}$.

The general procedure for quantifying Q_{RDII} from monitoring data is to determine Q_s and Q_{GWI} using the methods presented in Section 9.2, and then determine Q_{RDII} using Equation 9.3. This procedure is demonstrated in Example 9.2 on page 318.

In a large network, it is often necessary to determine Q_{RDII} for model locations where monitoring data do not exist, as well as for a range of storm durations and intensities. There are a number of methods for estimating peak Q_{RDII}, the volume of RDII, or the Q_{RDII} hydrograph for all locations in a collection system. The commonly used methods described in the subsections that follow are appropriate for sanitary-only systems. These methods must be calibrated for local conditions based on flow measurements. For combined systems, hydrologically-based methods (Chapter 7) are more appropriate. Hydrologic methods do not work as well for sanitary-only systems because they

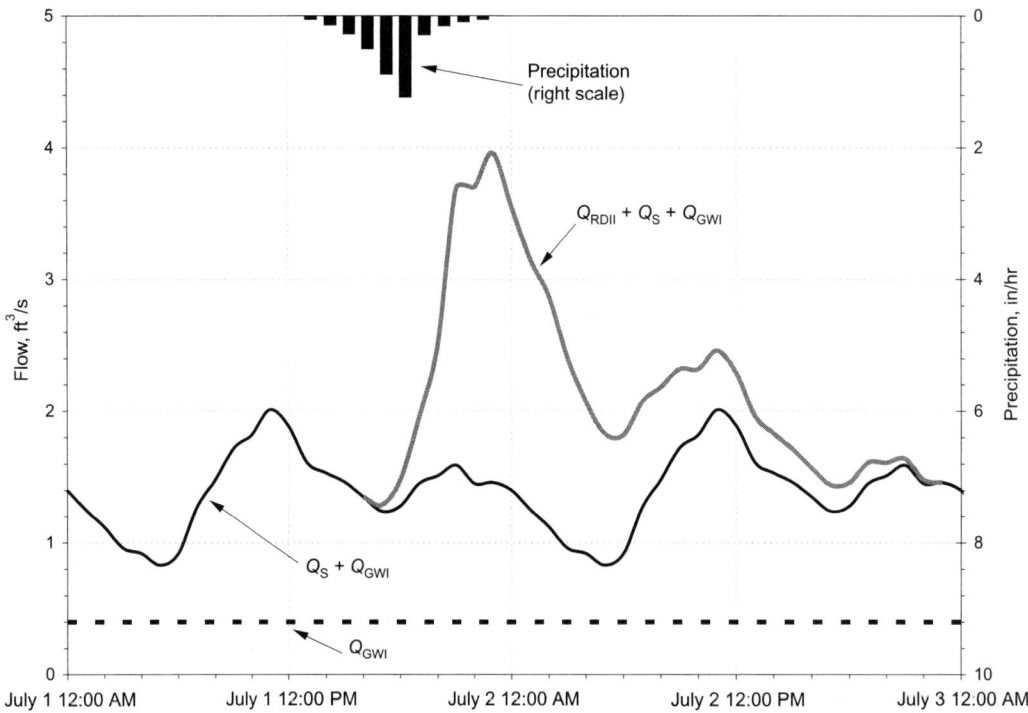

Figure 9.3 Sewer hydrograph consisting of Q_s, Q_{GWI}, and Q_{RDII}.

do not explicitly account for defect flows, and because most of the stormwater flow is captured by the parallel stormwater system rather than entering the sanitary sewer.

Constant Unit Rate Method

In addition to simply comparing hydrographs at points in the collection system, wet weather inflow to collection systems can be characterized in terms of volume per time per some independent variable. The independent variable could be depth of precipitation, drainage area, length and diameter of pipe, number of manholes or laterals, or some combination of these parameters. Once these parameters have been identified for a monitored location, they may be assigned to other loading nodes having similar characteristics. The resulting flow volumes must still be converted into peak flows or hydrographs using the techniques described in Chapter 7.

In a study in Portland, Oregon, Bennett et al. (1999) monitored flows in seven subbasins of the sanitary sewer system. The monitoring period extended from January 1996 to March 1997, and eleven rainfalls were used to estimate RDII parameters. The constant rate method was applied to the data by dividing the RDII storm volumes by each subbasin's characteristics. The results are summarized in Table 9.3.

Table 9.3 shows that there can be considerable variation within these unit loading rates. Much of this variation can be attributed to such factors as differing land use, sewer age, and sewer condition. These unit rates should only be applied in areas with similar characteristics.

Table 9.3 Constant rate method applied in Portland, Oregon.[1]

Parameter	Vol/rain, Mgal/in.	Vol/rain/acre service area, Mgal/in./ac	Vol/rain/ manhole, gal/in./MH	Vol/rain/ lateral, gal/in./lateral	Vol/rain/ length-pipe, gal/in./foot	Vol/rain/in.- mile pipe, gal/in./in.-mi
mean	3.698	4194	7867	1653	31.2	17,462
median	1.422	2608	8576	1149	26.9	13,307
standard deviation	4.995	4180	6292	1736	26.4	15,680
coefficient of variation	135.1%	99.7%	80.0%	105.0%	84.4%	89.8

[1] Source: Bennett et al. (1999)

Figure 9.4 shows, for seven locations, the average values ±1 standard deviation for RDII normalized by the number of manholes. For any given site, these unit rates do not vary much. Figure 9.4 shows that there are three groups of RDII responses, as defined by the RDII volume per inch of rainfall per number of manholes:

- Low – 3000 gal/in/manhole
- Medium – 7700 gal/in/manhole
- High – 20,000 gal/in/manhole

These values primarily provide a numerical basis for categorizing the extent of RDII in a subbasin and serve as a tool for estimating RDII in other subbasins in the project area. The constant unit rate, when calibrated with data from the local sewer system, may be a useful technique for determining RDII. These RDII values can be determined for each subbasin. The available precipitation may need to be adjusted for the initial abstraction. Similar correlations can be performed for peak flow rate instead of volume.

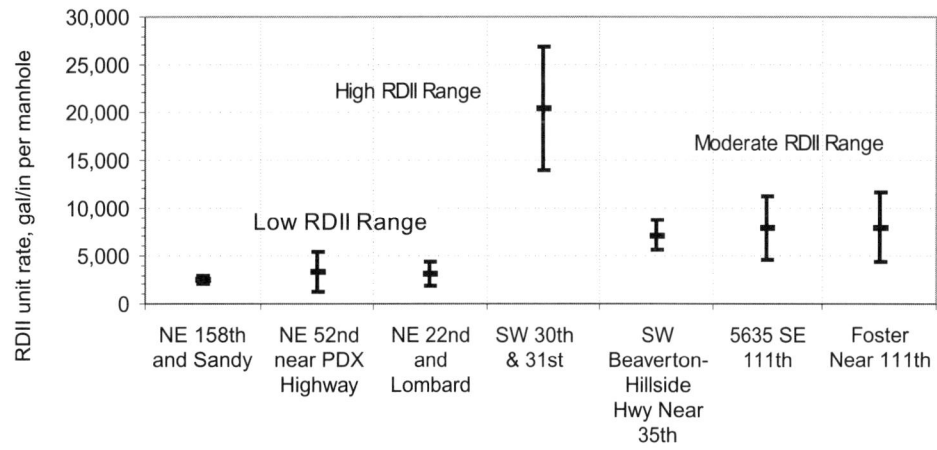

Reprinted with permission from the Environment Research Foundation

Figure 9.4 Range of values (mean ±1 standard deviation) for the constant unit rate divided by the number of manholes.

Percentage of Rainfall Volume (R-Value)

The R-value method for predicting peak runoff rates is described in Chapter 7. For each subwatershed, the ratio of volume of RDII to total rainfall is given by (Wright et al., 2001)

$$R = \frac{V_{RDII}}{V_{rain}} \qquad (9.4)$$

where
- R = RDII ratio
- V_{RDII} = volume of RDII (ft^3 or gal, m^3)
- V_{Rain} = volume of rainfall (ft^3 or gal, m^3)

For a simple model, R is calculated for one or more storms and assumed to be constant for all storms. However, R does vary due to differences in hyetographs, storm depth and/or antecedent moisture conditions. For example, Ohlemutz and Walkowik (2002) reported different measured R values for wet and dry years in Vallejo, California.

In a variation of the R-value method, Bennett et al. (1999) plotted the following sets of rainfall and RDII parameters from a sewer monitoring program in Portland, Oregon:

- RDII volume vs. total rainfall (Equation 9.4)
- Peak flow vs. total rainfall
- Peak flow vs. peak intensity

Linear relations can be developed between pairs of parameters, such as correlating volume of runoff with storm depth or basin area. Statistical tools may be used to assess the strengths of the correlations and the standard errors of the predictions of peak flow and volume. The regression model used by Bennett et al. (1999) included a slope and intercept. In the example shown in Figure 9.5, the regression of RDII volume vs. total rainfall has an intercept of 0, so Equation 9.4 is valid for this station.

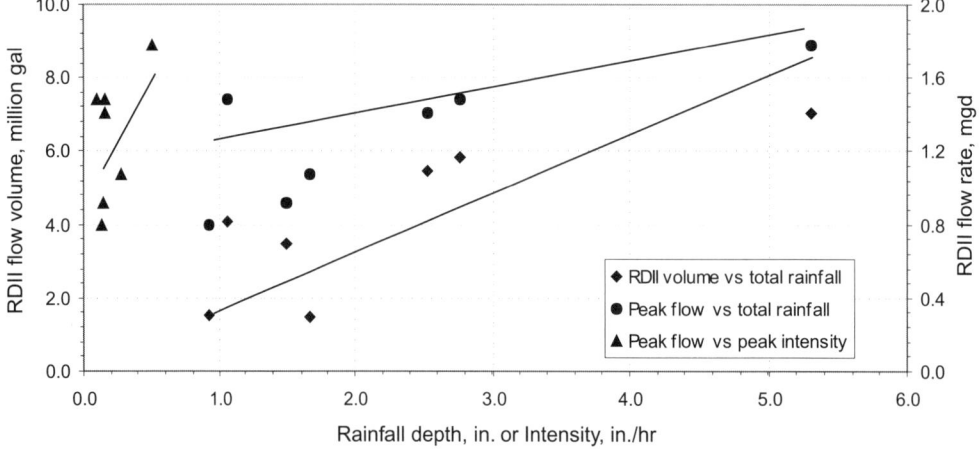

Reprinted with permission from the Environment Research Foundation

Figure 9.5 Plot of RDII volume or peak flow vs. rainfall depth or intensity for a station in Portland, Oregon.

The results of three case studies in which the R-value method was assessed are summarized in Table 9.4. The results were mixed. In the Portland study, the R-value method was a good predictor of both peak flow and runoff volume for individual and multiple storms, whereas in Minneapolis-St. Paul it was not. The Montgomery study had intermediate results. All three studies showed that the R-value method was not a good predictor of RDII volumes or peak flows over extended periods. In sanitary systems, high values of R correspond to areas with large defect flows.

Table 9.4 Summary of the evaluation of the R-value method.[1]

Criterion	Minneapolis-St. Paul, MN	Portland, OR	Montgomery, AL
Predict peak flow for individual storms	N/A	Good	Poor to fair, depending on amount of data available
Predict volume for individual storms	Poor	Good	Good, depending on amount of data available to develop trend
Predict peak flow for multiple storms	N/A	Good: average 13% absolute error	Fair to poor, depending on amount of data available to develop trend
Predict volume for multiple storms	Fair to poor	Good: average 24% error	Good, depending on amount of data available to develop trend
Predict volume for 24-hour, 7-day, and 30-day periods	Not able to predict over extended periods	Able to predict over storm duration but not over extended period	Not able to predict over extended periods
Most required data are commonly available	Yes	Yes	Yes
Other required data can feasibly be obtained in 3–6 months	Yes, provided hourly data are used. Several years of daily data needed	Yes	Yes

[1] Bennett et al. (1999)

Percentage of Stream Flow

Some studies have shown that local stream flow can be a reliable predictor of RDII, since the hydrologic conditions that increase stream flow are similar to those that affect RDII entering a sewer system. Either daily peak flows (Figure 9.6) or continuous flow data (Figure 9.7) can be used to develop a relation between sewer flow and stream flow. This approach is valid to the extent that the collection system responds to a precipitation event in the same way as the stream drainage system. It is most applicable where the stream and collection system drainage areas coincide.

The major advantage of this method is that stream-flow records often extending over several decades are readily available from the US Geological Survey (USGS). If a correlation between stream and sewer flow is developed for a system, the frequency distribution of the stream flow can be used to predict the frequency of corresponding flows in the sewer. However, this method is not widely used because of the importance of selecting a stream with a drainage area similar to that of the sewer system (sewersheds are typically much smaller than gauged watersheds. In addition, during large events, sewers may stop admitting RDII once they surcharge.

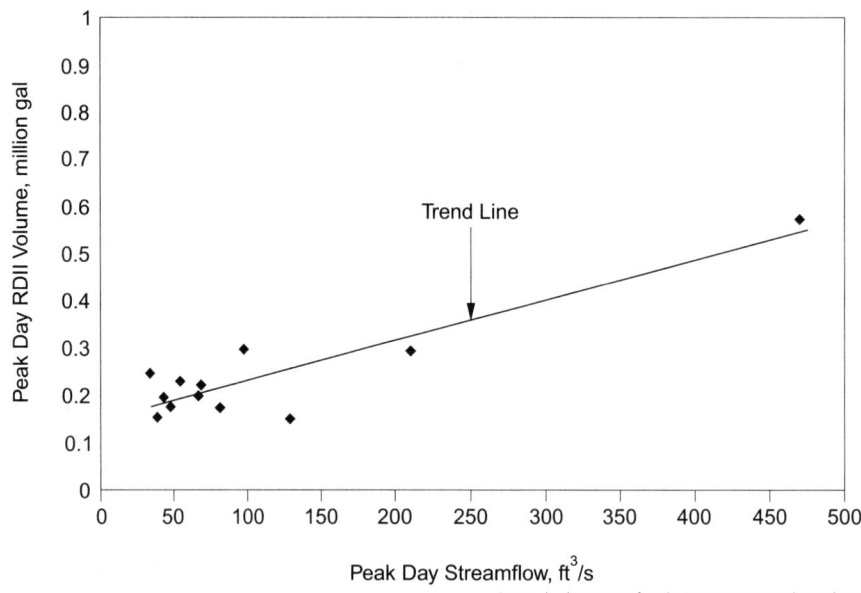

Figure 9.6 Plot of peak day RDII volume vs. peak day stream flow.

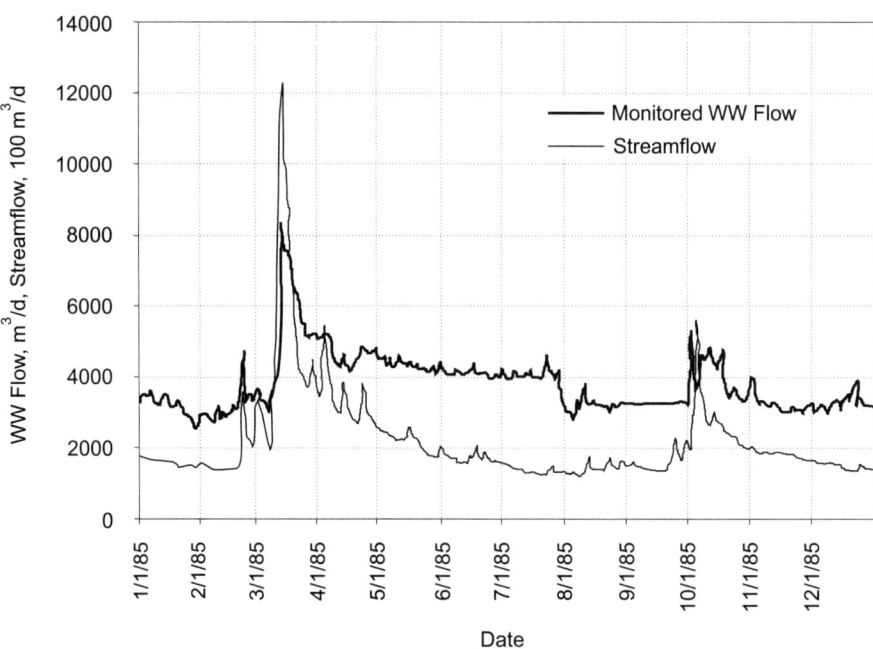

Figure 9.7 Simultaneous time series of continuous sewer flow and flow in Vermillion River, MN.

Two case studies described by Bennett et al. (1999) are summarized in Table 9.5. The percentage-of-stream-flow method was not a good predictor of peak flow or volume in Minneapolis-St. Paul. It was a good predictor for peak volume for multiple storms in Montgomery.

Table 9.5 Summary of the evaluation of the percentage of stream flow method.[1]

Criterion	Minneapolis-St. Paul, MN	Montgomery, AL
Predict peak flow for individual storms	Poor	Poor
Predict volume for individual storms	Poor	Fair
Predict peak flow for multiple storms	Poor	Fair
Predict volume for multiple storms	Poor	Good
Predict volume for 24-hour, 7-day, and 30-day periods	Poor	No
Most required data are commonly available	Yes, if stream gauge average daily flows are available	Yes, if stream gauge average daily flows are available
Other required data can feasibly be obtained in 3 to 6 months	Yes, provided hourly data are used. Several years of daily data needed	No

[1] Source: Bennett et al. (1999)

RTK Hydrograph

The RTK hydrograph method for predicting RDII (see "RTK Hydrograph Method" on page 254) was evaluated in studies in Bend, Oregon, and Montgomery, Alabama (Bennett et al., 1999), the results of which are summarized in Table 9.6. In the Portland study, the method was able to predict peak flow and volume for single and multiple storms and predict volume for extended periods. In the Montgomery study, the method was fair to good for predicting peak flow and volume for single and multiple storms, but it was unable to predict RDII volume for extended periods.

Table 9.6 Summary of the evaluation of the RTK hydrograph method.[1]

Criterion	Portland, OR	Montgomery, AL
Predict peak flow for individual storms	Good, ranges from –32 to 32% error	Good, depending on amount of data used to develop synthetic hydrograph
Predict volume for individual storms	Good, ranges from –23 to 247% error	Fair, depending on amount of data used to develop synthetic hydrograph
Predict peak flow for multiple storms	Good, average of 12% absolute error	Good, depending on amount of data used to develop synthetic hydrograph
Predict volume for multiple storms	Good, average of 11% absolute error	Good, depending on amount of data used to develop synthetic hydrograph
Predict volume for 24-hour period	Good, –18% to 20% error	Not able to predict over extended periods.
Predict volume for 7-day period	Good, –19% to 21% error	
Predict volume for 30-day period	Good, –23% to 19% error	
Most required data are commonly available	Yes	Yes
Other required data can feasibly be obtained in 3–6 months	N/A	N/A

[1] Source: Bennett et al. (1999)

> ## Probabilistic Method
>
> The probabilistic method is a frequency analysis of peak RDII flows. The method differs from the traditional hydrologic frequency analysis in that a peak value (flow or volume) is identified for each month over a period of record that is representative of wet and dry seasons. A statistical analysis is performed to determine recurrence intervals for peak flows or volumes. Bennett et al. (1999) suggest that a minimum record of 2 years is required.
>
> In an evaluation of the Minneapolis-St. Paul sewer system (Bennett et al., 1999), the method was applied by selecting the peak flow for each month at each monitoring location for a 2-year period. The frequency distributions were determined by plotting the calculated monthly exceedance probability on log-probability graphs. Because of the limited data, the authors were not able to verify the accuracy of the method. The method is useful for assessment of existing conditions but cannot be used to evaluate rehabilitation alternatives.

For each event, there are nine parameters (three for each hydrograph) in the RTK unit hydrograph model. Most modelers hold T_{1-3} and K_{1-3} constant while allowing R_{1-3} to vary according to antecedent conditions. There is little guidance available for calibrating these parameters.

Predictive Equation Based on Rainfall-Flow Regression

As described in "Rainfall/Flow Regression" on page 252, the rainfall-flow multiple-regression method uses rainfall and flow-monitoring data to derive a relationship between rainfall and the RDII hydrograph. This relationship, expressed as an equation, is then used to estimate RDII flows resulting from rainfall that is quantified over specific time intervals. Once a satisfactory fit between measured and estimated flow is obtained, the regression equations can be used to characterize and quantify RDII flows.

The method requires continuous flow and rainfall data. The following equation was developed from the RDII analysis in the Portland, Oregon, study:

$$RDII\ Flow\ (t) = C_1 Rain_{0-1} + C_2 Rain_{2-3} + C_3 Rain_{4-6} + C_4 Rain_{7-12} + C_5 Rain_{13-24} + C_6 Rain_{25-48} + C_7 Rain_{49-96} + C_8 Rain_{97-168} + C_9 Rain_{196-360} \qquad (9.5)$$

where

$RDII\ Flow\ (t)$ = RDII flow at time t (ft³/s)
C_i = coefficient estimated from regression (ft³/s/in.)
$Rain_{i-j}$ = cumulative rainfall for the specified range of hours; for example, $Rain_{0-1}$ is the rainfall between hours 0 and 1 before time t (in.)

A separate set of C_i values was developed for each of the seven subbasins in the Portland study. The higher coefficients correspond to basins with a great deal of I/I. The coefficients generally decrease over time (that is, $C_i > C_{i+1}$). In basins with more inflow, the initial C values are much larger than the later ones, while in basins with more infiltration, the values do not drop as rapidly. Coefficient values for one basin in the Portland study are listed in Table 9.7. A similar approach was reported by Wright et al. (2001).

Table 9.7 Values of regression coefficients (C_i) for one subbasin, in Equation 9.5, Portland, Oregon.

i	C_i, ft^3/s/in.
1	3.5
2	2.0
3	1.5
4	0.0
5	1.0
6	1.08
7	0.49
8	0.0
9	0.0

The predictive-equation method was evaluated in the Portland and Montgomery studies. The results, as shown in Table 9.8, were generally good. The prediction errors in the Portland study were considered acceptable. The Montgomery study indicated the need to develop regression equations using storms with characteristics similar to those used in applying the model.

Table 9.8 Summary of the evaluation of Equation 9.5 based on the rainfall/RDII flow regression method.[1]

Criterion	Portland, OR	Montgomery, AL
Predict peak flow for individual storms	Good, −15 to 13% error	Good if storm for which regression equation was developed had similar peaking characteristics as individual storm
Predict volume for individual storms	Good, −10 to 347% error	Good if storm for which regression equation was developed had similar peaking characteristics as individual storm
Predict peak flow for multiple storms	Good, average of 14% absolute error	Good if storm for which regression equation was developed had similar peaking characteristics to multiple storms being tested
Predict volume for multiple storms	Good, average of 11% error	Good if storm for which regression equation was developed had similar peaking characteristics to multiple storms being tested
Predict volume for 24-hour period	Good, 0% to 26% error	Good if storm for which regression equation was developed had similar peaking characteristics to multiple storms being tested and baseflow component holds steady over extended period
Predict volume for 7-day period	Good, −1% to 26% error	
Predict volume for 30-day period	Good, −4% to 23% error	
Most required data are commonly available	Yes	Yes
Other required data can feasibly be obtained in 3–6 months	N/A	Yes

[1] Source: Bennett et al. (1999)

Example 9.2 Wet weather calculations.

A wastewater collection system has a base sanitary flow of 0.75 m³/s. The dry weather calibration results indicate that Q_{GWI} is 0.1 m³/s. The demand multipliers are shown in the following table. Data from a storm are presented in the second table. Determine the RDII hydrograph, the volume of RDII, and the time from the onset of the rainfall to the peak RDII.

Time	Multiplier	Time	Multiplier	Time	Multiplier	Time	Multiplier
1:00 A.M.	0.85	7:00 A.M.	0.87	1:00 P.M.	1.21	7:00 P.M.	1.05
2:00 A.M.	0.72	8:00 A.M.	1.08	2:00 P.M.	1.13	8:00 P.M.	1.11
3:00 A.M.	0.56	9:00 A.M.	1.32	3:00 P.M.	1.06	9:00 P.M.	1.19
4:00 A.M.	0.52	10:00 A.M.	1.42	4:00 P.M.	0.95	10:00 P.M.	1.05
5:00 A.M.	0.43	11:00 A.M.	1.61	5:00 P.M.	0.84	11:00 P.M.	1.06
6:00 A.M.	0.52	12:00 P.M.	1.49	6:00 P.M.	0.88	12:00 A.M.	1.00

Date and Time	Q_t, m³/s	Precipitation, mm/hr
8/11/02 12:00 A.M.	0.85	
8/11/02 1:00 A.M.	0.74	0.10
8/11/02 2:00 A.M.	0.64	0.45
8/11/02 3:00 A.M.	0.52	0.69
8/11/02 4:00 A.M.	0.49	2.40
8/11/02 5:00 A.M.	0.47	3.74
8/11/02 6:00 A.M.	0.69	4.51
8/11/02 7:00 A.M.	1.25	4.22
8/11/02 8:00 A.M.	1.91	3.81
8/11/02 9:00 A.M.	3.19	2.46
8/11/02 10:00 A.M.	3.42	1.89
8/11/02 11:00 A.M.	3.81	0.72
8/11/02 12:00 P.M.	3.37	0.00
8/11/02 1:00 P.M.	2.91	
8/11/02 2:00 P.M.	2.70	
8/11/02 3:00 P.M.	2.35	
8/11/02 4:00 P.M.	1.96	
8/11/02 5:00 P.M.	1.73	
8/11/02 6:00 P.M.	1.61	
8/11/02 7:00 P.M.	1.59	
8/11/02 8:00 P.M.	1.48	
8/11/02 9:00 P.M.	1.39	
8/11/02 10:00 P.M.	1.19	
8/11/02 11:00 P.M.	1.15	
8/12/02 12:00 A.M.	1.03	
8/14/02 1:00 A.M.	0.83	
8/15/02 2:00 A.M.	0.69	
8/16/02 3:00 A.M.	0.54	
8/17/02 4:00 A.M.	0.49	

Solution

The results are listed in the following table. For each time step, the RDII flow is given by

$$Q_{RDII} = Q_t - Q_{GWI} - Mult_i \times 0.75 \text{ m}^3/\text{s}$$

RDII begins at 5:00 A.M. The volume of RDII is calculated by numerically integrating the area under the RDII hydrograph or

$$V_{RDII\,i} = 1 \text{ hr} \times 3600 \text{ s/hr} \times \tfrac{1}{2} (Q_{RDII\,i-1} + Q_{RDII\,i})$$

The total volume of RDII is the sum of the sixth column or 77,000 m^3.

The peak RDII is 2.50 m^3/s at 11:00 A.M. or 10 hours after the onset of the storm.

The values in column 5 are the RDII flows that are used as a starting point for regression methods and other methods to predict wet weather flows.

1	2	3	4	5	6
Time	Q_t, m^3/s	Q_{GWI}, m^3/s	Multiplier	Q_{RDII}, m^3/s	RDII, m^3
12:00 A.M.	0.85	0.1	1.00	0.00	
1:00 A.M.	0.74	0.1	0.85	0.00	
2:00 A.M.	0.64	0.1	0.72	0.00	
3:00 A.M.	0.52	0.1	0.56	0.00	
4:00 A.M.	0.49	0.1	0.52	0.00	
5:00 A.M.	0.47	0.1	0.43	0.05	90
6:00 A.M.	0.69	0.1	0.52	0.20	450
7:00 A.M.	1.25	0.1	0.87	0.50	1260
8:00 A.M.	1.91	0.1	1.08	1.00	2700
9:00 A.M.	3.19	0.1	1.32	2.10	5580
10:00 A.M.	3.42	0.1	1.42	2.25	7830
11:00 A.M.	3.81	0.1	1.61	2.50	8550
12:00 P.M.	3.37	0.1	1.49	2.15	8370
1:00 P.M.	2.91	0.1	1.21	1.90	7290
2:00 P.M.	2.70	0.1	1.13	1.75	6570
3:00 P.M.	2.35	0.1	1.06	1.45	5760
4:00 P.M.	1.96	0.1	0.95	1.15	4680
5:00 P.M.	1.73	0.1	0.84	1.00	3870
6:00 P.M.	1.61	0.1	0.88	0.85	3330
7:00 P.M.	1.59	0.1	1.05	0.70	2790
8:00 P.M.	1.48	0.1	1.11	0.55	2250
9:00 P.M.	1.39	0.1	1.19	0.40	1710
10:00 P.M.	1.19	0.1	1.05	0.30	1260
11:00 P.M.	1.15	0.1	1.06	0.25	990
12:00 A.M.	1.03	0.1	1.00	0.18	774
1:00 A.M.	0.83	0.1	0.85	0.09	486
2:00 A.M.	0.69	0.1	0.72	0.05	252
3:00 A.M.	0.54	0.1	0.56	0.02	126
4:00 A.M.	0.49	0.1	0.52	0.00	36

Regardless of the methods used to model wet weather flows, modelers should be careful in applying coefficients, whether unit loads, *R*-factors, or regression coefficients, from one basin to another. Two basins may appear similar, but one may have poorly installed structures, resulting in high RDII, or there may be a storm sewer illegally or mistakenly tied into a sanitary sewer system. The flow from one or two catch basins can cause significant problems in calibrating wet weather flow.

Additionally, modelers must be aware of the difficulties in simulating wet weather flows in response to rainfall events beyond the calibration range. The variability in the data presented in this chapter indicates the difficulties in modeling the complex rainfall/runoff/inflow process with a few parameters.

9.4 Special Considerations in Calibration

Despite the best efforts of the modeler, differences between the model and the field observations will occur. It is the modeler's job to determine where and why these variations occur and to correct them. If there is a high level of confidence in the flow metering data but the modeled and metered data do not match, then the problem with the model is that it misrepresents the physical system. This is generally a topological error, such as a previously unrecorded overflow or a relief sewer. Similarly, if the physical model is based on field-surveyed data and the metered and modeled flows do not agree, the modeler should question the flow-metering data. Is it accurate, was the site suitable, did the data analyst and field crew have to make numerous adjustments? Much time has been spent attempting to calibrate models before close scrutiny showed that there was an instrument error.

Flow is the primary parameter used to evaluate calibration. The metered data and the predicted flows are plotted versus time. If the model flows match the metered flows, then the model is considered to be well calibrated. Models are fairly easy to calibrate for dry weather flow conditions. Calibration for wet weather flow is much more difficult, however, because of uncertainty in the location and nature of defects in the collection system and spatial and temporal variations in precipitation and snowmelt patterns.

Even when model flows match field-measured flows, there may still be errors in the depth of flow. Depending on the use of the model, these differences may be less important than flow differences. They usually stem from incorrect slopes or pipe roughness coefficients in the model. If the flows are correct but the depth of flow is significantly higher in the field, then there may be a partial blockage in the downstream pipes from roots or debris.

When a monitored reach of gravity sewer is fed from a pump station, the model usually predicts the correct flow rates if the pump curves are correct, but it may have trouble matching the on/off levels. This is usually caused by errors in the pump on/off settings or in the geometry of the pump station wet well.

Some general types of errors and their corrections are discussed in the subsections that follow. The discussion in this chapter is qualitative. For specific models, acceptable levels of variance between meter and model data may be quantified.

Volume Differences

Often, there is a good match in the overall shape and timing of the modeled and metered hydrographs, yet there is a significant difference in the total volume under the curve. If meter data were used to create the original estimates of flow per capita, then there should be a good correlation of volumes during dry weather.

In Figure 9.8, the volume of the flow generated by the model is approximately 1.5 times the metered flow, which is an unacceptable variance. A bit of detective work is required to determine why this difference occurred.

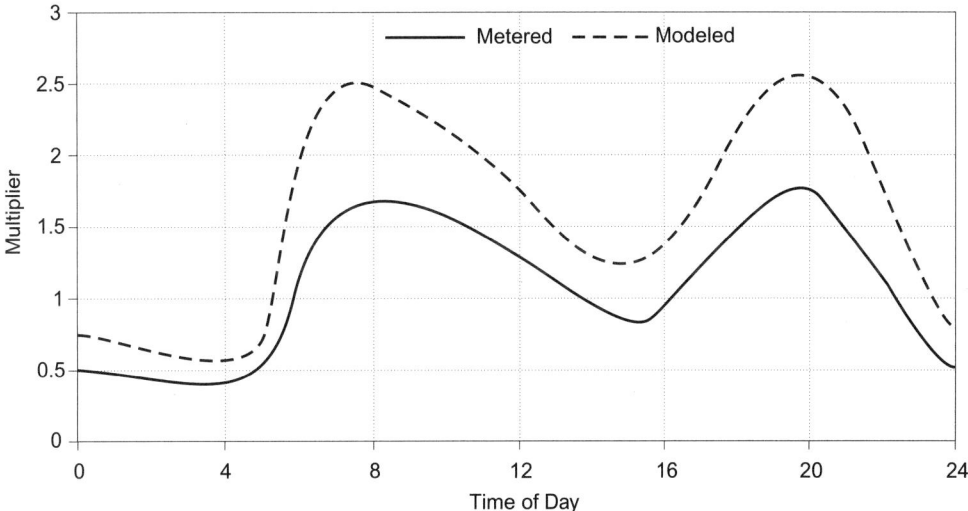

Figure 9.8 Volume mismatch between modeled and metered flows.

If the measured flows are significantly higher than the estimates based on population and unit demands, then further investigation is warranted. Always confirm that the meter was in proper operating condition. If the meter was working properly, then an investigation of the major flow producers in that metered basin should be conducted. If the measured flow is uniformly greater than the model flow, then groundwater infiltration may be larger than originally estimated. Also, one large wastewater producer can have a noticeable effect on a small basin. Examples of this are a hospital, linen service, or any other "wet" industry. However, these users generally have different diurnal curves with appreciable differences in the shapes of the hydrographs, as illustrated in Figure 9.9. It may be worthwhile to monitor actual water use at some large commercial and industrial facilities (taking into account the fact that water does not necessarily equate to wastewater production).

If variations in the demand pattern cannot explain the discrepancies between the model and monitoring data, there may be errors in the layout of the system. A measured flow higher than what is indicated by normal flow-generation factors may be due to additional connections to the system not included in the model. On occasion, a modeler may observe an upstream basin with lower flows than predicted, while an adjacent basin has more flow than expected. In such a situation, there is almost always an undocumented connection between the two systems. The modeler must review the basin boundaries for potential points where the customers and piping may actually belong in a different basin.

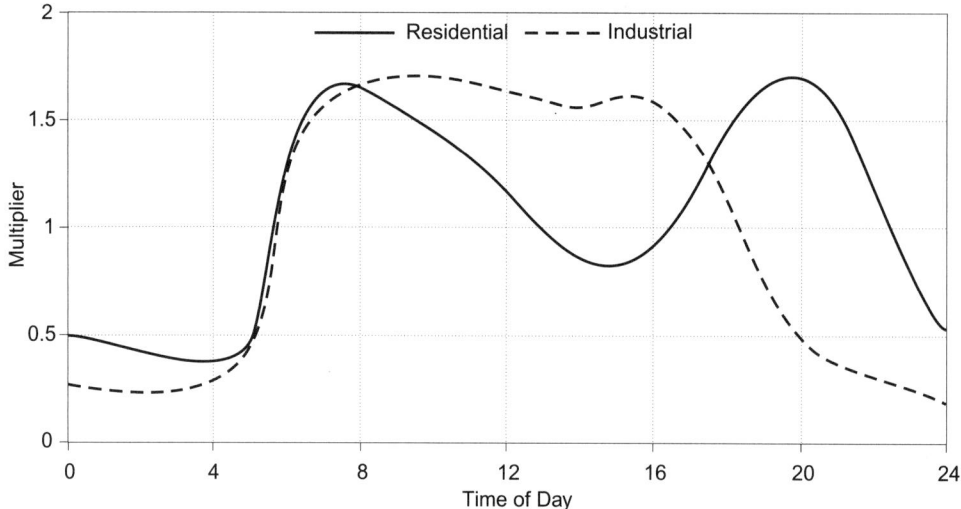

Figure 9.9 Typical residential and industrial sanitary flows.

In Figure 9.10, the dotted line indicates a diversion or overflow from basin D to E. During dry weather, flows from D go only into basin C. During wet weather events, excess flows are diverted to E. If the diversion is not modeled correctly, the flow at E may be higher than anticipated during wet weather, and the flow at C lower. This weather-related shift in the flow must be considered during the calibration process.

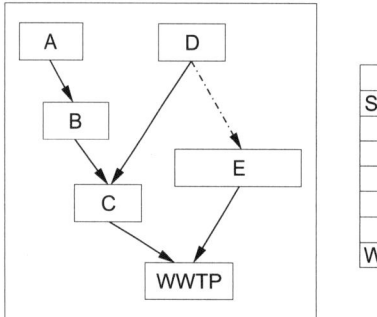

	Basin Isolation	
Site ID	Gross	Net
A	A	A
B	A+B	B+A
C	A+B+C+D	A+B+C
D	D	D
E	E	D+E
WWTP	WWTP	A+B+C+D+E

Figure 9.10 Changes in flow patterns caused by overflow.

Shape Considerations

It is also possible for the model to predict peak flow rates higher than those observed in the system. This generally occurs when large pipes act as reservoirs and significantly attenuate the injected flows. Some models shift the timing of the hydrograph by considering the velocity and the length of pipe but do not attenuate the flow based on the volume of the pipe.

Other explanations for this type of discrepancy include operational problems, such as an accumulation of roots, fats, oils, and greases in the line. Any large obstruction may have a dampening effect on the peak flow in the system.

There is no standard diurnal curve shape that is universally applicable. Thus, if there are differences that cannot be explained, the modeler should not be afraid to adjust the diurnal curve. As discussed earlier, flow peaks tend to be attenuated as they move through the system. Especially in large systems, the diurnal pattern at the treatment plant will be much flatter than patterns at upstream locations, which are closer to customers.

If the measured downstream diurnal curve is used to define upstream flows and the model is capable of attenuating hydrographs, the modeler may find that the resulting model flows at the metered location are less than those measured. It may be necessary to adjust the overall shape of the upstream hydrograph to calibrate against the downstream meter if the initial calibration unsatisfactory. This should be within reasonable tolerances, as illustrated in Figure 9.11.

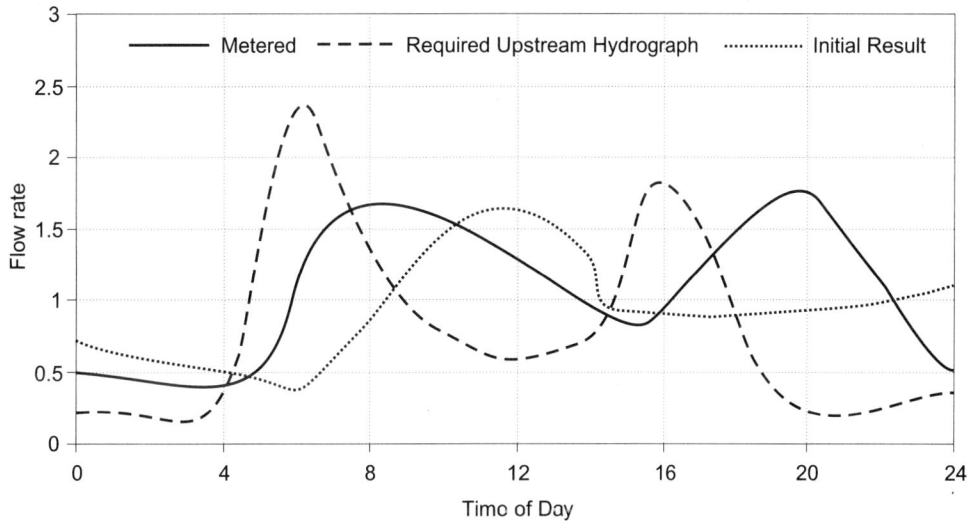

Figure 9.11 Calibration of downstream flow resulting from upstream peak.

Timing Shifts

Another common consideration is a shift in the diurnal curve. These time-shifted hydrographs or demand patterns may not be a problem. If the goal of the project is to determine the peak flow rate in the pipes, then the timing of that rate may be irrelevant. If, on the other hand, there are considerations for storage and pump stations, then the timing of the curve becomes more important. Figure 9.12 contains a time-shifted hydrograph. To correct a time shift, confirm the proper operation of the flow meter that is being used in the calibration and change the definition of the diurnal curve until a match is achieved.

In this example, the modeled flow has been shifted. To correct this, the definitions of the hourly demand multipliers (Equation 9.2) are rolled back several hours. However, the adjustments should be reasonable. For example, the demand pattern may have to slide back several hours for weekend days because customers generally wake up latter on weekends. In the case of wet weather peaks, a storm may have struck the sewer basin earlier than it reached the local rain gauge.

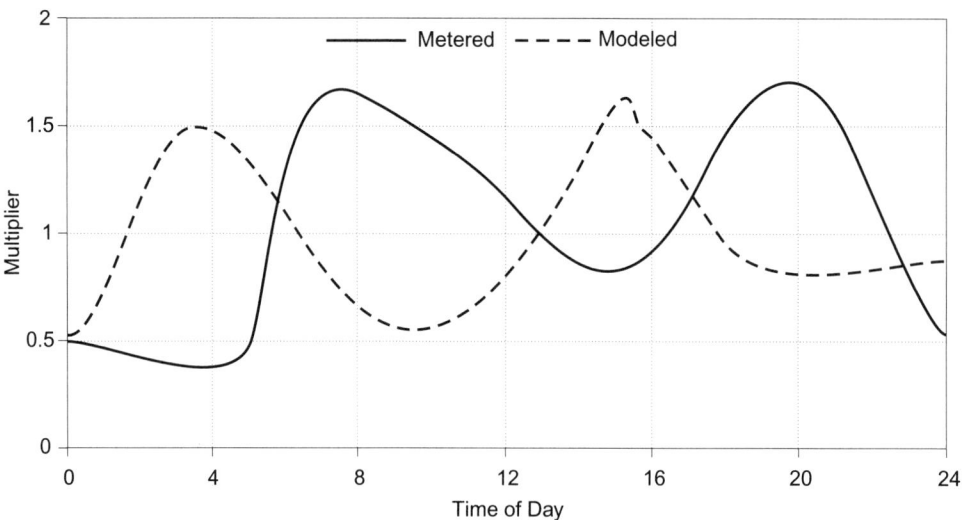

Figure 9.12 Time-shifted diurnal curve.

9.5 Understanding Overflows

In the previous discussion of volume errors, it was noted that if the volume predicted by the model (based on reasonable parameters) is substantially higher than the measured volume, the problem may be caused by instrument error or a physical representation that does not include an existing diversion or overflow from the system. Collection system overflows often cause problems in model calibration because they are not usually metered or even recognized.

Wastewater collection system overflows fall into one of three categories:

- *Engineered overflows* – Combined sewers commonly have constructed diversions that allow excess storm and sanitary flows to be diverted to receiving waters during a high-flow event. These structures may consist of weirs, orifices, tilting plate regulators, and/or valves that are designed to overflow at a certain inflow rate. Some are permanently fixed, while others can be adjusted. Engineered overflows are usually "permitted" (i.e., listed in an NPDES permit in the U.S.) and metered.

- *Capacity overflows* – These are usually manholes (or catch basins in combined systems) that overflow because there is not enough pipe capacity (diameter or slope) downstream.

- *Maintenance overflows* – These overflows do not occur if pipes have sufficient capacity and the sewers are in good condition. They are the result of a pipe being blocked by roots, grease, sediment, lumber, or debris, or a collapsed pipe. As with capacity overflows, these overflows typically occur through manholes.

A calibrated sewer model must be able to simulate the overflows in a system. The calibration process is a useful tool for distinguishing between capacity and maintenance overflows. The procedures described in the subsections that follow are useful for identifying the locations and quantity of overflows during the early stages of modeling.

Estimating Combined Sewer Overflow

An undocumented or forgotten diversion from the system creates a unique signature in the calibration process. Figure 9.13 shows this identifier. Comparing the modeled and metered flows during dry weather reveals a good match, and the model calibrates within the predefined tolerance. However, wet weather flows are always lower than predicted. Usually, the magnitude of the error is large enough to be a clear indicator of an upstream overflow.

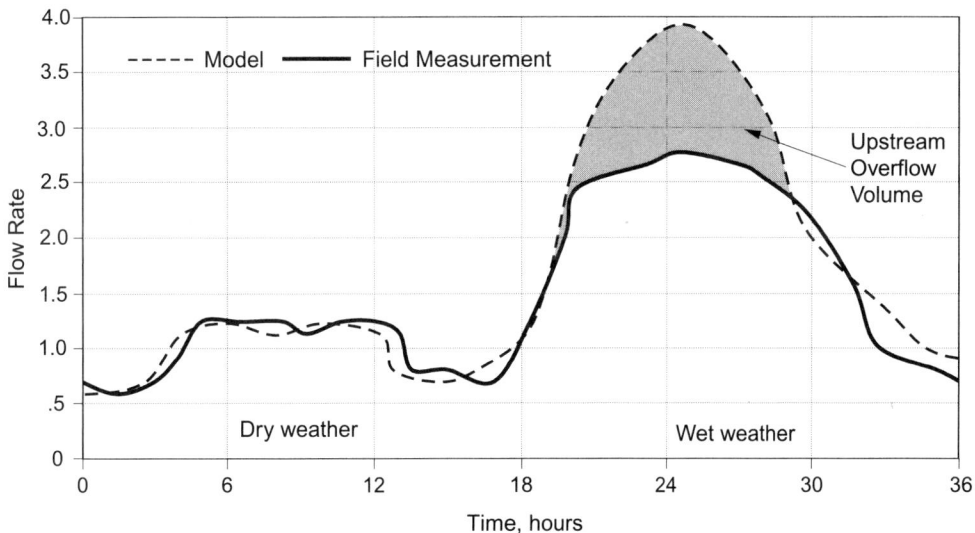

Figure 9.13 Dry and wet weather calibration results indicating an overflow.

If the CSO is small, the temptation is to revise the stormwater contribution calculations and effectively mask the overflow. However, if the predicted wet weather flow entering the storm system would have to be greatly altered to bring the model into agreement, then unexpected overflows are a more likely culprit. Most permitted CSOs require some kind of flow measurement or an indication of when overflows occur as part of the permit conditions.

By comparing the reasonable prediction of flows at a metering location with the measured flows, the modeler can estimate flow leaving the system. This estimate can be confirmed further by inspecting the location and revising the model to include the diversion structure. Once the geometry of the overflow is known, realistic estimates of its wet weather performance can be included in the model. If the flow losses still exceed the capacity of the documented structure, then additional overflow locations may be present. Locating additional overflows in the combined sewer system can be difficult, as old and forgotten overflows may exist in difficult-to-inspect areas along overgrown creeks and waterways. It is best to ask the most experienced field crews if they are aware of any old or abandoned facilities. Such relief connections may have been installed without formal documentation.

Estimating SSOs

Sanitary sewer overflows (SSOs) are overflows that occur in sanitary-only systems due to excessive I/I, undersized pipes, or obstructions that reduce the capacity of system components. SSOs may be elusive (Stevens and Sands, 1995), since they occur infrequently and are difficult to witness or document.

If SSOs are present, modeled and observed flows will typically match during dry weather periods, but observed wet weather flows will be lower than those predicted by the model. The modeler first checks the meter to ensure that it was operating properly during the wet weather event and establish a high level of confidence in its measurements. Flow meters may fail in wet weather when their readings are most critical.

To assess the relative amount of overflow, the modeler can perform the same comparisons as described in the previous section. The difference between the estimated flows and the measured flows is an approximation of flow lost from the system. The modeler must not attempt to predict the overflow *rates* based on insufficient data points. The mechanisms that create a hydraulic condition sufficient to raise a manhole cover and the ensuing unpredictable nature of the resulting opening make estimates of flow rates imprecise.

Detecting Overflows with Scattergraphs

The hydraulic element chart for normal flow in circular cross sections was introduced in Section 2.2 on page 47. The relation between velocity and depth is reproduced in Figure 9.14. If the flow in a sewer pipe is normal, a meter that records both depth of flow and velocity should report values that align with the curve in Figure 9.14. Deviations from this trend suggest nonnormal flow or other unusual conditions. Stevens and Sands (1995) and Nelson, Habibian and Andrews (2000) described signature scattergraphs that indicate possible SSOs upstream or downstream of a monitoring location.

As flow increases in a sewer, the hydraulic grade line (HGL) may increase to levels above the top of the pipe, causing a pressurized condition. An overflow occurs whenever the HGL rises to the lowest manhole rim elevation in the system, as illustrated in Figure 9.15a. An obstruction has developed downstream of the monitoring location, causing an overflow. Note that in Figure 9.15b there is an increase in velocity when the HGL reaches 120 in. The overflow at the downstream manhole produces the additional velocity detected at the monitoring location.

Figure 9.16a shows an overflow occurring upstream of a monitoring location. The volume of water passing the flow meter remains steady during the overflow. Hence, the scattergraph shows constant velocity when the HGL is greater than the pipe diameter, as shown in Figure 9.16b.

In summary, good calibration in dry weather with poor calibration in wet weather may indicate a loss of flow from the collection system or poor representation of RDII. Calibration relies on accurate flow metering, good demographic or customer information for flow-generation verification, and the correct physical description of the system. Models consist of flows and the pipes that convey them. A misrepresentation of either can affect the calibration process.

Section 9.5   Understanding Overflows   327

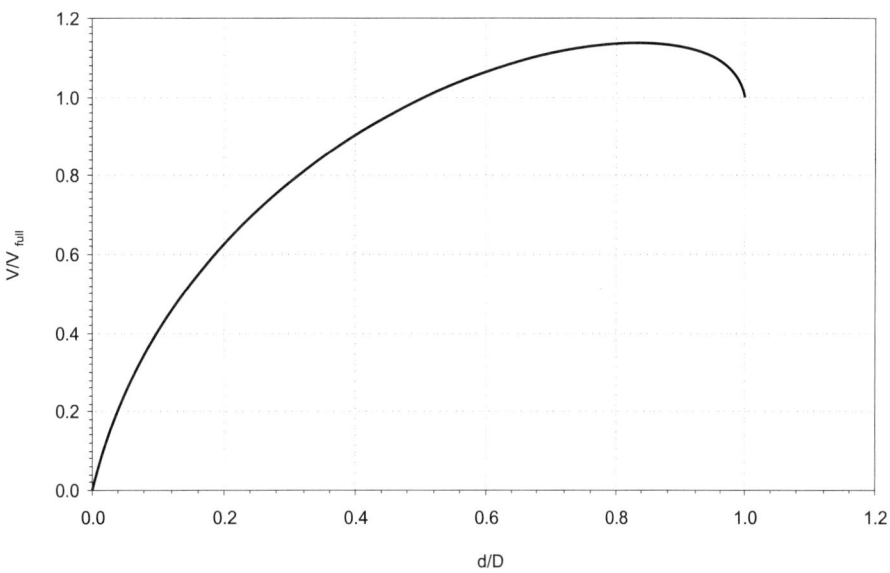

Figure 9.14 Idealized relationship between depth and velocity in an open channel.

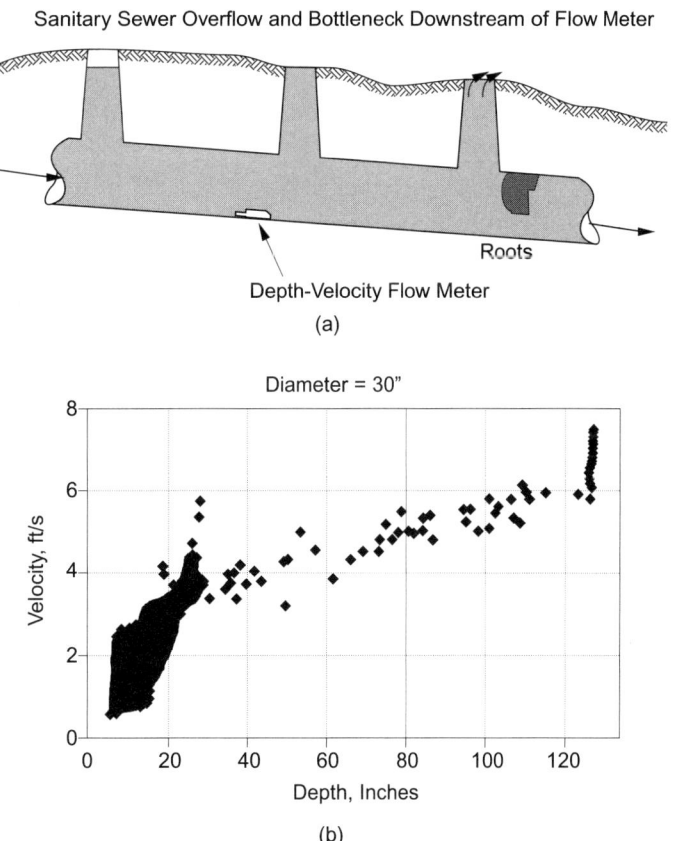

Stevens and Sands, 1995

Figure 9.15 Overflow downstream of a monitoring location: (a) hydraulic profile and (b) depth velocity scattergraph.

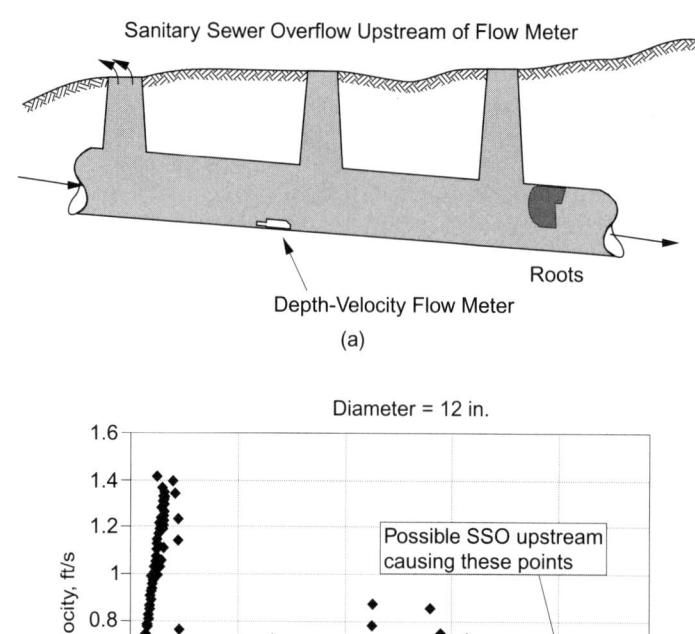

Figure 9.16 Overflow upstream of a monitoring location: (a) hydraulic profile and (b) depth-velocity scattergraph.

References

American Society of Civil Engineers (ASCE). 1982. *Gravity Sanitary Sewer Design and Construction.* Manual of Practice 60 (also WEF MOP FD-5). Reston, VA: American Society of Civil Engineers.

American Society of Civil Engineers (ASCE), Task Committee on the Definition of Criteria for Evaluation of Watershed Models of the Watershed Management Committee. 1993. Criteria for evaluation of watershed models. *Journal of Irrigation Drainage Engineering.* ASCE 119, no. 3: 429-443.

Bennett, D., R. Rowe, M. Strum, D. Wood, N. Schultz, K. Roach, M. Spence, and V. Adderly. 1999. *Using Flow Prediction Technologies to Control Sanitary Sewer Overflows.* Alexandria, VA: Water Environment Research Foundation.

Jewell, T. K., T. J. Nunno, and D. D. Adrian. 1978. Methodology for calibrating sewer models. *J. Environmental Engineering* 104: 485.

Nelson, R. E., A. Habibian and H. O. Andrews. 2000. *Protocols for Identifying Sanitary Sewer Overflows*. ASCE/EPA Cooperative Agreement CX 826097-01-0. Reston, VA: American Society of Civil Engineers.

Ohlemutz, R. and M. Walkowiak. 2002. A case study at Vallejo Sanitation and Flood Control District: A methodology for assessing the effectiveness of sanitary sewer rehabilitation on reducing infiltration and inflow. In *Pipelines 2002: Proceedings of the Pipeline Division Specialty Conference*. Reston, VA: American Society of Civil Engineers.

Ormsbee, L. E. and S. Lingireddy. 1997. "Calibrating Hydraulic Network Models." *Journal of the American Water Works Association* 89, no. 2: 44. Denver, CO: American Water Works Association.

Sinak, D. 2002. "O&M capacity assurance: Case studies in flow data." In *Pipelines 2002: Proceedings of the Pipeline Division Specialty Conference*. Reston, VA: American Society of Civil Engineers.

Stevens, P. L. and H. M. Sands. 1995. Sanitary sewer overflows leave telltale signs in depth-velocity scatttergraphs. *National Conference on Sanitary Sewer Overflows (SSOs)*. EPA 625-R-96-007. Washington, DC: U.S. Environmental Protection Agency.

3-Waters Technical Services. 1996-2004. *Hydraulic Modeling for Improved Collection System Management Training Documents*. Salana Beach, CA.

US Environmental Protection Agency (US EPA). 1995. *Combined sewer overflows: Guidance for Long-Term Control Plan*. EPA 832-B-95-002. Washington, DC: US Environmental Protection Agency.

US Environmental Protection Agency (US EPA). 1999. *Combined sewer overflows: Guidance for monitoring and modeling*. EPA 822-B-99-002. Washington, DC: US Environmental Protection Agency.

Wastewater Planning Users Group (WAPUG). 1998. *Code of Practice for the Hydraulic Modelling of Sewer Systems*, version 2. City: Wastewater Users Planning Group.

Wright, L., S. Dent, C. Moosley, P. Kadota, and Y. Djebbar. 2001. In *Models and Applications to Urban Water Systems*, Monograph 9, ed. by W. James. Guelph, ON: CHI Publications.

Yen, B. C. 1982. Some measure for evaluation and comparison of simulation models. In *Urban Stormwater Hydraulics and Hydrology*; ed. by B. C. Yen. Highlands Ranch, CO: Water Resources Publications.

Problems

9.1 Would you expect dry weather flow to be more important in a separate or combined sewer system? Why?

9.2 In calibrating a model, if you can match the flow at a monitoring station but the water level measured in the pipe is significantly greater than the model calculation, what do you suspect is wrong?

9.3 Rainfall data from a nearby weather station shows a brief afternoon thundershower, but the flow monitor in the sewer shows little or no increase in flow. What could explain this?

9.4 During a major storm, the flow at a monitor increases significantly, and then levels off at a high value for a considerable period of time before dropping off. What would explain that?

9.5 You measure an infiltration rate of 80,000 gpd in a basin. That basin drains an area of 450 ac and has the distribution of pipes in the following table.

Diameter, in.	Length, mi
8	6.21
12	2.44
15	0.82

Determine the unit infiltration rate in units of:

a. gpd/mile

b. gpd/in-mi

c. gpd/acre

9.6 You have a measured hydrograph at the downstream end of a long reach of sewer, but you need to load the model at the upstream end. Given the downstream hydrograph (Q) in the following table, calculate the upstream inflow hydrograph (I) using the convex routing method (with $c = 0.7$) described in Chapter 3.

t, hr	Q, m³/s	I, m³/s
0.0	1.13	
0.5	2.57	
1.0	3.31	
1.5	2.80	
2.0	5.51	
2.5	6.07	
3.0	7.97	
3.5	7.00	
4.0	5.17	
4.5	3.92	
5.0	3.12	
5.5	2.43	
6.0	2.78	
6.5	2.23	
7.0	2.40	
7.5	2.55	
8.0	1.95	

Plot both hydrographs on the same graph.

9.7 Determine Manning's n for some old brick sewers. Flow can be measured to within about 4 ft³/s, and depth can be measured to within 0.2 ft. Measure depth at a point where the flow is at normal depth.

Develop the following curves relating flow, normal depth, and n using a program like FlowMaster, or manually from hydraulic elements charts.

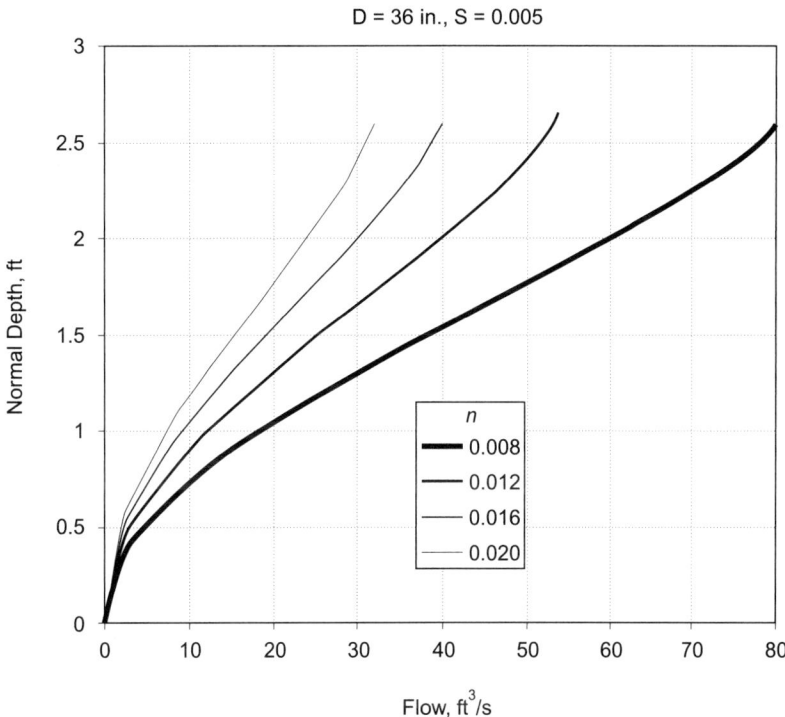

Given the raw data points in the following table, determine the most likely value of n. Then, perform an error analysis. Using a high value for depth and a low value for flow based on the error in measurement, find a high-end estimate of n. Then, using a low depth and high flow, find a low-end estimate of n. (It helps to actually draw the points on the graph.) The first row in the table is completed as an example. The observed flow and depth are 10 ft^3/s and 0.8 ft which correspond to an n of roughly 0.012 from the graph. With a low value for flow (Q_{low}=10 - 4 = 6) and a high value for Depth (D_{high} = 0.8 +0.2 = 1.0), the correct Manning n would be 0.020 from the graph.

Observations		From Graph	Error Analysis					
Q, ft³/s	D, ft	n	Q_{low}	D_{high}	n_{high}	Q_{high}	D_{low}	n_{low}
10	0.8	0.012	6	1.0	0.020	14	0.6	0.004
25	1.5							
30	2.0							
60	2.5							

What do the results tell you about the conditions under which you should collect data to measure n? Should it be under low depths or high depths? Why?

Why didn't we work with the pipe virtually full?

CHAPTER

10

Design of New Gravity Wastewater Collection Systems

Engineers have designed gravity wastewater collection systems for over a century without the aid of computer models. Why then has the use of computerized models become standard practice in sanitary sewer design?

First, computerized models relieve engineers of tedious, iterative calculations, allowing them to focus on design decisions. Second, because models can account for much more of the complexity of real-world systems than manual calculations, they give the engineer, and the sewer utility, increased confidence that the design will function properly when it is installed. Third, the ease and speed of modeling gives engineers the ability to explore many more options under a wide range of conditions, resulting in a more cost-effective and robust design. Finally, models can be integrated with computer-aided drafting (CAD) and geographic information systems (GIS) software, facilitating the production of construction drawings and making better use of the available data.

The following is a list of steps for the design of gravity sewer systems.

1. Identify the area(s) to be served.
2. Obtain regulatory codes and design guidelines and set system design criteria.
3. Collect geologic, geographic, and topographic data.
4. Collect information on roads, railroads, population, industry, other utilities and community planning.
5. Undertake field investigations, including feature surveys and ground truthing at sites that potentially conflict with other services.
6. Identify the natural drainages, streets, and existing or planned wastewater inflow points at the boundaries of the area to be sewered. Locate all proposed sources of wastewater. Identify likely elevations of customer laterals.

7. Design the horizontal layout of the sewer, including manholes and possible pumping station locations. If necessary, prepare alternate layouts.
8. Divide the total area into logical subareas, as needed, and develop design flow rates for each section in the system.
9. Select pipe sizes, slopes, and inverts. Perform the hydraulic design of the system. Revise selections until the design criteria are met.
10. Complete cost estimate(s) for the design and alternate designs.
11. Carefully review all designs, along with assumptions, alternates, and costs.
12. Modify the design or develop alternate designs, or even alternate layouts. This cycles the designer back to the appropriate earlier step.
13. Complete the plan and profile construction drawings and prepare the specifications and other bid documents.

The primary focus of this chapter is the hydraulic design of the sewer, including information on obtaining the data needed to perform the hydraulic design and a discussion of how models are used in the design process. Hydraulic analysis is critical, since it is used to select sewer pipe sizes, invert elevations, and sometimes pipe routes. Additional details regarding sewer design may be found in references such as ASCE (1982) and Metcalf and Eddy (1981).

10.1 Materials

Although this chapter centers on hydraulic design, other factors, such as pipe material and manhole construction, must also be considered. This section provides a brief overview of the physical components of sewer systems.

Pipes

Gravity sewer pipes are available in a variety of materials, including cast and ductile iron, PVC (polyvinyl chloride; see Figure 10.1), concrete, asbestos cement, HDPE (high density polyethylene), ABS (acrilonitrile butadiene styrene), FRP (fiber reinforced plastic), brick, and vitrified clay. Most pipe has solid walls, although there are some truss or profile wall pipes available. Most new sewer pipe has a circular cross section; however, many older sewers, especially those made from brick, have different cross-sectional shapes.

A wide array of ANSI, ASTM and AWWA standards are available for specification of pipe. Manufacturers and suppliers are another source of design handbooks and other information on pipe materials. Manufacturers also specify how pipes should be bedded. Figure 10.2 shows a typical trench box and excavator used for pipe installation.

The weak links in most piping systems are the pipe joints and service connections. Currently, most joints are made of a flexible elastomeric seals or rings. Many older pipes have cement mortar or bituminous material for joints. Some pipe materials, such as polyethylene, rely on thermally fused pipe ends.

It is best to install wye or tee service connections when the main is installed so that the quality of the workmanship is maintained. Such lines should be run to the edge of the pavement and plugged if customers are not immediately ready to connect. Later connections need to be made with proper quality control and inspection.

Figure 10.1 PVC pipe ready for installation.

Figure 10.2 Excavator and trench box for sewer installation project.

Manholes

Manholes are structures designed to provide access to a sewer. Access is required for visual inspection of sewers, placement and maintenance of flow or water quality monitoring instruments, and cleaning and repair of the sewer. According to ASCE (1982), a manhole design must pass four major tests:

- Provide convenient access to sewers for observation and maintenance operations

- Cause a minimum of interference with the hydraulics of the sewer
- Be durable and generally watertight
- Be strong enough to support applied loads.

In the past, manholes were constructed of brick, concrete block, or poured concrete. Today, most manholes are constructed with a precast or poured-in-place concrete base and precast concrete rings up to the surface, where a tapered segment holds the cover. Covers (see Figure 10.3) are typically 21–24 in. (500–600 mm) in diameter. The use of lined, coated manholes or plastic manholes is increasing for economic reasons and to provide corrosion resistance and reduce infiltration through the manhole walls.

Shape and Dimensions. Most manholes are round and 4–6 ft (1.2–1.8 m) in diameter, with larger sizes for larger sewers. In small sewers, the manhole is generally centered over the pipe. For large-diameter sewers, the manhole entrance is often offset, with a work platform to the side of the sewer. The rungs or ladders used for entering manholes should be corrosion resistant to provide the long-term durability and strength needed to prevent failure.

Figure 10.3 Manhole covers.

Other Appurtenances

Gravity sewers typically contain very few special appurtenances. Devices such as inverted siphons (see Section 10.8) and permanent flow meters such as Parshall flumes (page 278) may be used in some instances.

In combined sewer systems, it is sometimes permissible to have some type of flow diversion structure for flows in excess of the system capacity. These structures range from simple, passive devices such as weirs and orifices, to more dynamic devices such as vortex separators and tilting plate regulators, to remotely controlled gates and inflatable dams. Outlets to receiving streams will usually have a flap gate or duck-billed valve to prevent surface water from entering the collection system.

Pipe junctions usually occur at manholes; however, other junction types may exist in a system. Examples are blind connections and underground box structures with no direct access to the surface.

10.2 Initial Planning

Before a new gravity sewer system is designed, a planning study should be undertaken to address the issues of whether to provide sewer service, the type of conveyance wanted (gravity and/or pressure), and the pros and cons of separate versus combined systems.

Decision to Provide Sewer Service to an Area

Wastewater disposal in an area may take the form of on-site treatment and disposal, small decentralized treatment systems, or a large centralized treatment system. Some of the factors that must be analyzed when considering the construction of a wastewater collection system are:

- Population growth and housing density
- Amenability to on-site disposal systems
- Environmental impact of habitation
- Pollution problems in the area
- Accessibility to and cost of collection systems and sewage treatment
- Regulatory requirements
- Ease of construction, including the extent of rock excavation required.

An onsite wastewater treatment system that is properly designed, manufactured, constructed, operated, and maintained and that has a suitable effluent-receiving body may be an appropriate means of wastewater disposal, especially when a development is far from a regional system. However, wastewater collection and centralized treatment systems usually prove to be the most cost-effective solution to providing sewage services. Public health authorities generally favor collection and centralized treatment systems over on-site systems because they are much easier to inspect, monitor, and regulate.

A preliminary investigation is generally conducted to determine the potential area to be served, the consequences of not serving the area, how the area will be served, and the economic feasibility of such a project. There is usually some break-even population above which a centralized sewage collection and treatment system is desirable, although the exact break-even point varies widely, according to site-specific considerations.

A common problem is determining how to serve the first areas to be developed in a drainage basin. In the short term, construction of treatment at the downstream end of the development is the least expensive option. However, construction of a large regional treatment system with larger sewers sized for full buildout may be more economical in the long run.

Types of Conveyance

Wastewater collection systems use gravity, pressure, vacuum, or some combination of these methods to convey wastewater. In most cases, lower total life-cycle costs (construction, operation, and maintenance) favor gravity sewers over pressure or vacuum systems. In gravity systems, pumping may be required to move flows in areas of flat or uneven topography. In these systems, sewage flows by gravity into a wet well and is pumped through a force main. The hydraulic analysis of pump stations and force mains is described in Chapter 12.

Low-pressure sewers differ from force mains in that the pumps are located on the property of each customer. These systems are used either where direct gravity flow is not possible or where excavation depths, extensive shallow rock, obstacles, and alignments make the smaller and shallower pressure lines more economical. The pressurized lines may discharge into a wet well or into a gravity sewer. These systems are discussed further in Chapter 13.

Vacuum systems operate on the basis of differential air pressure created by a central vacuum station. Wastewater from each connection is discharged to a sump that is isolated from the main line by a valve. When the level in the sump reaches a designated limit, an actuator opens the valve and the vacuum propels the wastewater to the central vacuum station. In a good vacuum system, the maximum water-level differential in each vacuum zone is about 25 ft (7.6 m). This means that vacuum systems are relegated to rather flat areas. Multiple vacuum zones may be placed in series, but operating complexity and costs increase rapidly. More information on these systems may be found in US EPA (1991) and Crites and Tchobanoglous (1998).

Separate versus Combined Systems

In the past, conveyance of sanitary flows and storm drainage in the same conduits (combined sewers) made economic sense. Today, with expensive mandatory treatment requirements in place, the cost of control and treatment for new systems is almost always lower if the two types of flow are conveyed and treated in completely separate sewer systems. Currently, most pollution control agencies specifically prohibit combining storm drainage and wastewaters in their regulations governing new sanitary sewer design, construction, and operation (e.g., GLUMRB, 1997).

However, it is conceivable that future treatment requirements for storm waters in urban and industrial settings may become so stringent that combined system conveyance and treatment may again be the more economical solution. The practice of integrated watershed management, which considers the combined effect on receiving waters of stormwater and treated wastewater, may result in some portion (such as the first flush) of stormwater being directed into the sanitary system.

"My name is Ozymandias, king of kings: Look on my works, ye Mighty, and despair!"

10.3 Preliminary Design Considerations

Design codes and criteria are promulgated by various public environmental and pollution-control agencies. Codes give information on location and clearances relative to other utilities, flow-generation rates, peaking factors, and hydraulic guidelines. In the United States, design codes commonly come from a state or county/regional agency. Most of these codes can be traced back to the Ten State Standards (GLUMRB, 1997), which were first published in 1951. Codes may reflect the effects of local conditions, such as soil and weather, on the design of sewers. Current codes tend to make more use of such terms as "recommended" or "guidelines," rather than "required" or "mandatory." Some regulatory agencies have adopted a more performance-based approach to establish system regulations. Design engineers need to be well-versed in these codes.

Depending on the regulatory agency evaluating the design, either the sewers must be able to carry the design flow while flowing full or at some given fraction of the full *depth*, or the design flow must be some percentage of the full-pipe *capacity* (e.g., 75 percent of capacity at design flow). The engineer must determine which is the better approach for a given case, as the two requirements can produce different pipe sizes. For example, a 12-in. (300-mm) sewer with $n = 0.013$ and a 1-percent slope can carry 3.56 ft^3/s (0.101 m^3/s) when full. Seventy-five percent of the capacity is 2.67 ft^3/s (0.075 m^3/s), while the capacity at 75 percent of full depth is 3.25 ft^3/s (0.092 m^3/s). Minimum slopes to prevent sedimentation and minimum cover to prevent traffic impacts must also be considered.

Where local codes do not exist or do not address a specific issue, widely adopted standards, such as the Recommended Standards for Wastewater Facilities (GLUMRB, 1997), should be consulted. References such as Metcalf and Eddy (1981), ASCE (1982), and Hammer and Hammer (2001) also provide guidance for sewer design.

In addition to technical design criteria and the hydraulic loads, other pertinent considerations include the following:

- *Costs* – The planning, design, construction, operation, and maintenance costs should all be considered in assessing the long-term sustainability of the project.

- *Schedule* – The time between the initial planning and the operation of a sewer may be as long as a decade, and the project may need to be constructed in phases.

- *Operation and maintenance* – Gravity sewers are not maintenance free. They require periodic inspections and cleaning, and some components may require repair or replacement. An organization to operate the system must be in place.

- *Environment* – Construction of the sewer results in both temporary disruption of and long-term effects on the environment. Short-term effects include temporary lowering of the groundwater table and release of sediments. Over its design life, the sewer system will affect the performance of the wastewater treatment facility and the water quality of the receiving water body.

- *Regulatory compliance* – The sewer project must comply with all applicable laws and regulations.

The design criteria should be developed in consultation with the sewer utility and the financing and regulatory agencies. Consensus on the design criteria before the start of the design is essential.

Data Requirements

The data requirements for building a hydraulic sewer model are discussed in Chapter 5. Additional physical data, beyond that necessary for hydraulic analysis, is required for the design of new sewers. The following list of data requirements has been adapted from American Society of Civil Engineers (1982):

- Topography, surface and subsurface conditions, details of paving to be disturbed, underground utilities and structures, subsoil conditions, water table elevations, traffic control needs, and elevations of structure basements or connection points

- Locations of streets, alleys, or unusual structures; required rights of way; and similar data necessary to define the physical features of a proposed sanitary sewer project, including preliminary horizontal and vertical alignment

- Details of existing sanitary sewers to which a proposed sewer may connect

- Information pertinent to possible future expansion of the proposed project

- Locations of historical and archeological sites, significant plant or animal communities, or other environmentally sensitive areas.

The data may be obtained from a variety of sources. Maps, aerial photographs, construction drawings, and ground surveys may be queried. Typically, no single data source is complete, so one must identify inconsistencies and fill in gaps.

Instrument surveys are the most accurate method of obtaining high quality spatial data. Many vertical-elevation reference and control points should be established systematically along the route and be accurate to within about 0.01 ft (3 mm) (ASCE,

1982). These rather prominent and durable control points are used later as reliable reference points for the crucial elevation control needed during sewer construction.

Alternatives

Alternate system configurations, alignments, and pipe sizes must be explored during the design of new sewers. Each alternate design should be considered until it is apparent that it is infeasible or inferior to another design. The point at which an alternative is dropped from consideration will vary. In some cases, a simple calculation will show that an alternative does not meet one or more design criteria. In other cases, an alternative design must be completed, with a detailed cost estimate, before its economic ranking is known.

It may be necessary to document alternate designs dropped from consideration and the reasons for those decisions. Such decisions are made at various levels. The design engineer will typically make decisions regarding pipe sizes, invert elevations, and manhole details. However, decisions regarding alignments, stream crossings, and locations of pump stations often require input from sewer utility management and permitting authorities.

Hydraulic sewer models are invaluable for managing design alternatives. Most modeling packages have capabilities that facilitate the analysis of multiple alternatives without building separate models. A final design report usually should include results of alternate designs that were considered and the justifications for rejecting them.

10.4 Initial System Layout

Sanitary sewers are almost always laid out in a dendritic (treelike) pattern. Unlike water distribution systems, which have pressurized flow in all directions, gravity sewers normally allow flow in only one direction and are rarely looped. Some of the more prominent factors that affect the layout of the final wastewater collection network serving a designated area are political jurisdictions and boundaries, development types and patterns, street and right-of-way patterns, alignment of existing underground services (particularly stormwater conveyance), land topography, and geology. When large cost savings are involved, some of these factors can be modified or changed, most notably the political boundaries. Political boundaries may change through cooperative agreements, formation of an overlapping special service district, or establishing service authorities based on basin rather than political boundaries. Armed with good information, designers can delineate major drainage areas and begin the process of laying out the wastewater collection system network.

Developers should consider the location of all utilities when laying out new streets. Substantial cost savings can be realized from simultaneous construction of all underground utilities. When new sewers are proposed for an existing development, the locations of all underground utilities should be determined before beginning the layout of the sewage collection system.

Generally speaking, it is most economical to plan the network and design pipes for the service and flows expected at full buildout of the drainage areas. However, the cost of such piping in areas that remain sparsely populated can be significant, and much of the loading may not be realized for many years. This results in tradeoffs between budget limitations and the desire to provide ultimate capacity. Modeling can assist with evaluating various options to arrive at rational, feasible decisions about the extent and capacity of the system.

Gravity Sewer Layout

The layout of a gravity sewer system begins with a topographic map of the service area. The drainage divide lines and natural drainage paths for a new service area should be drawn on the map. Then, the locations of the sewer outlet(s) and elevations of the highest services should be identified. The highest manhole is located where it can provide a connection to a lateral from the highest service. The highest possible invert is determined either from the elevation of the basement (or lowest plumbing fixture) minus an adequate drop along the lateral, or the minimum depth that would give a lower elevation.

The sewer should continue along streets or other public rights-of-way at the flattest acceptable slope, as determined by capacity needs, self-cleansing requirements, minimum depth, or service lateral depths.

When localized high points in the sewer alignment are encountered, a downhill slope may be maintained by either deeper excavation or an alternate path. Crossing depressions of streams may require an inverted siphon (see Section 10.8). Ultimately, the line ends at a connection to a trunk sewer, a wastewater treatment facility, or a pumping station. Sometimes service areas include drainage divides, such that only part of the development can flow by gravity into downstream sewers. Other parts drain by gravity to a pump station that either lifts the flow to the minimum elevation necessary to continue by gravity or pushes the flow through a force main (pressure pipe) to the desired location.

Manhole Location and Spacing

Manholes are generally placed at every change in slope, pipe size, or alignment; where two or more incoming lines are joined; at the upstream end of lines; and at distances not greater than about 300 ft (90 m) for diameters less than 6 in. (150 mm), about 400 ft (120 m) for diameters of 6–15 in. (150–400 mm), and about 500 ft (150 m) for diameters of 18 in. (450 mm) or greater. These distances are dictated by regulations and by the reach of cleaning and maintenance equipment. Manhole spacing greater than 500 ft has sometimes been used for sewers large enough to allow a person to work and walk in the sewer if needed (Hammer and Hammer, 2001). Additional manholes may be required to drop the hydraulic grade line, as described in Section 10.7 on page 358.

The following are some additional considerations related to manhole location:

- Street intersections are common locations for manholes (American Society Civil Engineers, 1982).
- A terminal manhole should be located at the upper end of a sanitary sewer to provide access for maintenance.
- Manholes should not be placed in a location that allows surface water to enter.
- Inserts may be used to limit infiltration through pick holes.
- Manholes in cross-country settings usually have chimneys raised above the ground to prevent surface water intrusion, as shown in Figure 10.4.

Figure 10.4 Typical manhole in a cross country setting.

Location of Pumping Facilities

Pumping facilities are logically placed at low points to collect gravity flow from an area and pump it to a desired point. Pumping facilities are best placed on public land, where they are readily accessible but also as isolated as possible to minimize odor and noise complaints. Aesthetic or other local considerations may require putting a pumping station some distance from the ideal location as determined from an initial hydraulic and cost-efficiency point of view.

Sewer Easements

To the extent possible, sewers should be laid in public rights-of-way to avoid easements across private land. In most cases, placing sewers under public streets is best because of construction and maintenance issues. A slight modification in the road network in a subdivision can sometimes result in significant cost savings.

Nevertheless, system economy and design feasibility sometimes make it necessary to consider non-street routes. If not already in place, easements must be obtained early in the planning and design process. Although obtaining easements may be easy in most cases, the process can take a long time and cause project delays. Easements must be sufficiently wide to allow access for construction, inspection, maintenance, and repair (ASCE, 1982). Designers should also be fully informed about utility prohibitions and restrictions for sewers that run along or across railroads, highways, major arterial roads, streams, ponds, or lakes.

Example of a Sewer Network Layout

The depth of the upstream end of a gravity sewer is typically governed by the types of structures to be served. There are several rules of thumb, such as placing the invert at least 3 ft (1 m) below the foundation slab. This results in relatively shallow minimum sewer depths where there are no basements and deep sewers where structures have basement drains. Additional factors influencing manhole depth are described in Section 10.6.

If structure elevations are lower than the street, it is usually necessary to either install sump pumps to convey the wastewater to the gravity sewer or run the sewer lateral through the back of the property to a lower street.

In new land developments, sites can be graded or sewer lines can be installed so that flow is directed by gravity to the sewer under the street. In areas with existing structures, a survey of the existing facilities should be conducted to determine the typical location of the lowest plumbing fixture in the homes.

If extensive rock excavation is necessary for sewer installation, increasing the depth of a sewer can greatly increase costs. In new land developments with no rock and a low water table, cost is less sensitive to depth.

The layout of a sewer system is illustrated in Figures 10.5 through 10.7. The existing contours, roads, and sewer line and the boundary of the proposed subdivision are shown in Figure 10.5. The drainage divide and natural drainage paths are shown in

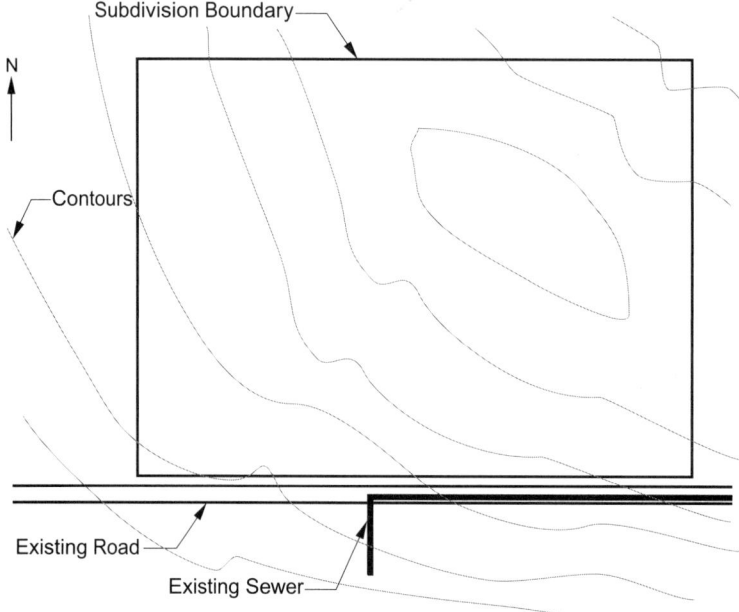

Figure 10.5 Location of subdivision boundary, existing road, and existing sewer with topographic contours prior to development.

Section 10.4　　　　　　　　　　　　　　　　　　　　　　　Initial System Layout　345

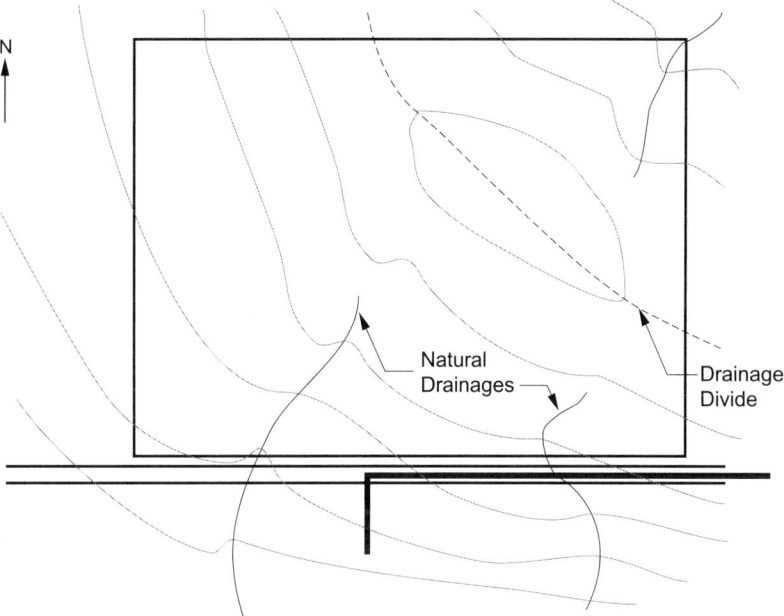

Figure 10.6 Location of subdivision boundary, drainage divide, and natural drainageways prior to development and installation of new sewers.

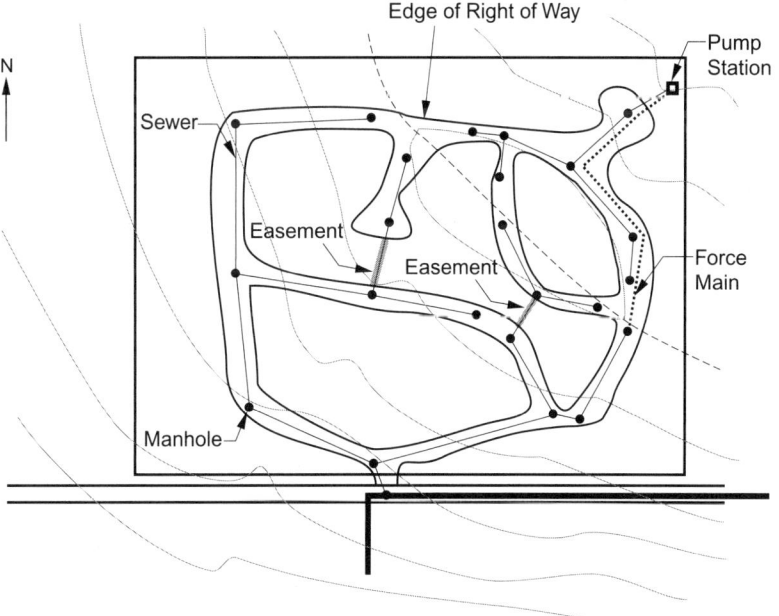

Figure 10.7 Location of subdivision boundary with proposed roads, right-of-way, sewer manholes, and force main for installing new sewers.

Figure 10.6. Note that the divide runs through the subdivision and it is impractical to service the entire project with a single gravity sewer.

The proposed roadways and the sewer layout are shown in Figure 10.7. The network consists of two separate sewer lines. The northeast portion of the subdivision will be served by a gravity sewer that flows to a pump station. This station will discharge into a force main (dotted line) that runs parallel to the gravity sewer but in the opposite direction, until it discharges into a manhole in a second sewer line. This second system ties into the sewer main south of the property.nt. The layout requires easements in two locations.

10.5 Flows in Sanitary Sewers

Chapter 6 discussed sanitary design flows in detail. One approach to formulating design loads is to follow the values recommended in the appropriate code with regard to flow per household or commercial building. The values found in codes that can be used to generate average and peak flows are generally conservative and, in most cases, provide some excess capacity. Nevertheless, the designer must be alert for the rare situations where these normally conservative values are still not adequate; in particular, for commercial and industrial areas. The recommended approach is to follow the method described in Chapter 6. Usually, average flows at loading nodes are determined based on population or a population equivalent, and these flows are adjusted for design purposes using extreme flow factors (peak and minimum multipliers). Peak design flow is most critical for pipe sizing, while minimum flows are most important for insuring that slopes are adequate for self cleansing.

As described in Chapter 6, the initial design minimum flow rate is not the smallest flow rate expected in the pipe, but rather the smallest flow rate for which self-cleansing is expected. Since the absolute minimum flow in some small sewers is zero, the minimum design flow rate is actually the largest flow rate during the lowest flow period for the line, perhaps using the lowest flow week for the time period. Chapter 6 and the sidebar on page 347 contain additional information on design flow rates.

The design maximum flow rate is the discharge for which capacity must be available. The initial and final average flow rates are needed if peaking factors are used to generate the design minimum and maximum flow rates, which are needed for self-cleansing and capacity considerations during design or analysis.

Low Flows in Early Years

Solids buildup can be a significant problem in sewers when the flows are extremely small, particularly in areas with very flat slopes. This problem is often found in the upper reaches of sewers in developing areas with few connections when the sewer is first placed in service. If increasing slopes (and thus velocities) in these small flow sections would result in unacceptable depths and/or costs, a more practical solution might be to use periodic flushing or cleaning until area flows have increased enough for the sewers to be self-cleansing.

Allowances for Infiltration and Inflow

Non-wastewater flows that enter a wastewater collection system come from *groundwater infiltration* or *rainfall-derived inflow and infiltration,* as described in Chapter 7. Collec-

What Are Minimum Flow and Velocity?

Most sewer design is based on providing enough slope to achieve a minimum velocity of 2 ft/s (0.6 m/s) at full flow. However, in the upper reaches of most sewer systems, flows are very low and are frequently zero (intermittent flow). With such low flows, the minimum velocity necessary for the pipes to be self cleansing is rarely achieved.

With one or two houses at the end of a sewer branch, it is unlikely that flows will exceed 20 gpm (1.3 L/s), yet most sewers in these situations perform adequately. This is possible because velocity does not decrease proportionally with flow. For example, for an 8-in. (400-mm) sewer at a slope of 0.4/100 (GLUMRB, 1997), it only takes 12 gpm (0.76 l/s) to reach 1 ft/s (0.3 m/s), but it takes 120 gpm (7.6 l/s) to reach 2 ft/s (0.6 m/s). This relationship is illustrated in the figure below.

The question remains of what flow an engineer should use when determining whether the velocity will be high enough to prevent solids deposition. Standard references (ASCE, 1982) provide a curve for the ratio between minimum and average flows, with the minimum flow being checked for minimum velocity. However, the lowest value on that curve, 0.2, corresponds to a population of 1000, whereas there are many sewers serving much smaller populations. While such a value is probably not correct, the true minimum velocity in small sewers is zero, and there is a statistical distribution of flow such that 0.2 times the average flow would be extremely small.

In small sewers, it may be best to think of self-cleaning as an event that occurs only once or twice a day, especially during the early years of a pipe's life. The concept of a minimum-to-average flow ratio is meaningless in small sewers with intermittent flow, so basing slopes on minimum velocity may be impractical. The engineer is then faced with either adopting minimum slopes from the standards without explicitly basing the design on velocity or, for important sewers, using a tractive force approach as described in Chapter 2.

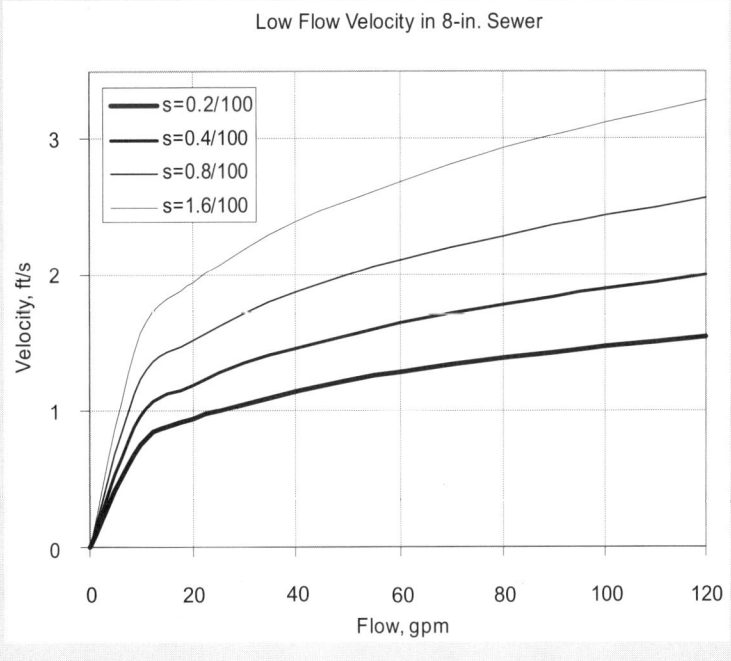

tively, these flows are called inflow and infiltration (I/I). Sources of I/I are illustrated in Figure 7.7 on page 212.

In modern codes, allowances for I/I are specified by applying a constant unit rate (e.g., volume/day/length of pipe, volume/day/length of pipe × pipe diameter, or volume/day/service area) as described in Chapter 9 on page 301. Designers should review regulations and guidance in their local areas. The consensus is that good sewer design and construction, along with tight ordinances and codes and good enforcement, can keep I/I at very low levels.

Phased/Staged Construction

A service area may have defined boundaries, with an expected rapid buildout and plans to complete the full system in a single project. However, when development will take place over decades, completion of the long-term system through a series of smaller subprojects may save money or make expensive projects financially feasible.

Sewers are often sized for ultimate upstream buildout if the probability is high that full development will occur within a few decades, since this is almost always more cost effective than laying parallel pipes in future years to handle upstream growth. When new services are added over a long period of time, the model can be used to analyze several projected loading scenarios.

10.6 Horizontal and Vertical Alignment

Section 10.4 presented guidance for the general layout of the sanitary sewer system that must be performed early in the design process. Once the design flows for these pipes have been determined, the engineer can proceed with designing the vertical sewer alignment and sizing the pipes. Issues related to vertical alignment are presented in this section, and hydraulic design and pipe sizing are covered in Section 10.7. However, because pipe size can affect invert elevations (due to cover requirements), and pipe slope affects pipe capacity and thus pipe size, the two tasks must be performed concurrently in many cases.

Pipe Slopes

A minimum velocity must be maintained to prevent solids buildup during low flows and is determined by the tractive force method described in Section 2.9. Alternatively, the minimum slopes specified in Table 2.2 may be used. These minimum slopes vary according to pipe diameter.

ASCE (1982) recommends that flow velocities be less than 10 ft/s (3.5 m/s) at peak flow. Higher velocities may be tolerated if proper consideration is given to the pipe material, abrasive characteristics of the wastewater, turbulence, and thrust at changes in direction. GLUMRB (1997) states that if velocities are greater than 15 ft/s (4.6 m/s), special provisions shall be made to protect against displacement by erosion and impact.

Minimum slopes for house connections are often specified in local codes. In addition to the real need for somewhat steeper slopes for self-cleansing given the small flow rates in most laterals, the steeper minimum slopes cover a multitude of shortcomings commonly encountered with laterals, such as poor slope control, alignment, bedding, placement, and backfill, leading to pipe differential settlement and joint separation. ASCE (1982) recommends a minimum slope of 0.01, while Metcalf and Eddy (1981) recommend 0.02.

Curved Sewer Alignment

Typically, sewer piping is installed in straight segments, with changes in the vertical or horizontal alignment occurring at manholes. However, in some cases, a good solution may be to use a curved sewer alignment to change direction. For example, a vertically curved alignment might be used to maintain a reasonable depth without the need for additional manholes where the ground surface makes a fairly large change in slope over a few hundred feet. A horizontal or vertical curve may be used to avoid obstructions or give future access for lateral connections or repair. Curved vertical and horizontal alignments are shown in Figure 10.8

Hydraulically, there is little to prohibit curved alignment as long as the minimum slope meets capacity and self-cleansing needs. The main objections to curved alignment are the extra effort and cost for field survey staking and construction, as well as the extra location information needed to avoid damage during future digging, connect laterals, or provide maintenance. When the cost savings resulting from fewer manholes and shallower construction outweighs these problems, curved sewers should be considered. Vertical curvature is probably of less concern than horizontal curvature, since future crews may not have immediate access to detailed information for locating the alignment. Universal use of metallic location tape placed above the sewer line during construction helps to alleviate reservations about curved alignment.

Burton (1996) generally recommends straight alignment for pipes 24 in. (600 mm) and smaller. For larger sewers, curvature should have a radius of not less than 100 ft (30 m). Rigid pipe may be installed in a curve by putting a deflection at each joint. The maximum permissible deflection depends on the type of joint and the pipe diameter. Flexible pipe is simply forced into the desired curvature. In either case, the pipe manufacturer should be consulted regarding allowable limits for deflection. The geometry of curved alignments is described by ASCE (1982).

An example of a curved segment of sewer pipe is shown in Figure 10.8. The radius of curvature, R, is given by

$$R = \frac{L}{2\tan\left(\frac{\Delta}{2N}\right)} \qquad (10.1)$$

where R = radius of curvature (ft, m)
L = length of sewer pipe segment (ft, m)
Δ = total deflection angle of curve (degrees or radians)
N = number of sewer pipe deflections

Minimum Depth of Cover

Sewer pipe should be placed as shallow as possible while still being located
- Deep enough to provide gravity service whenever feasible

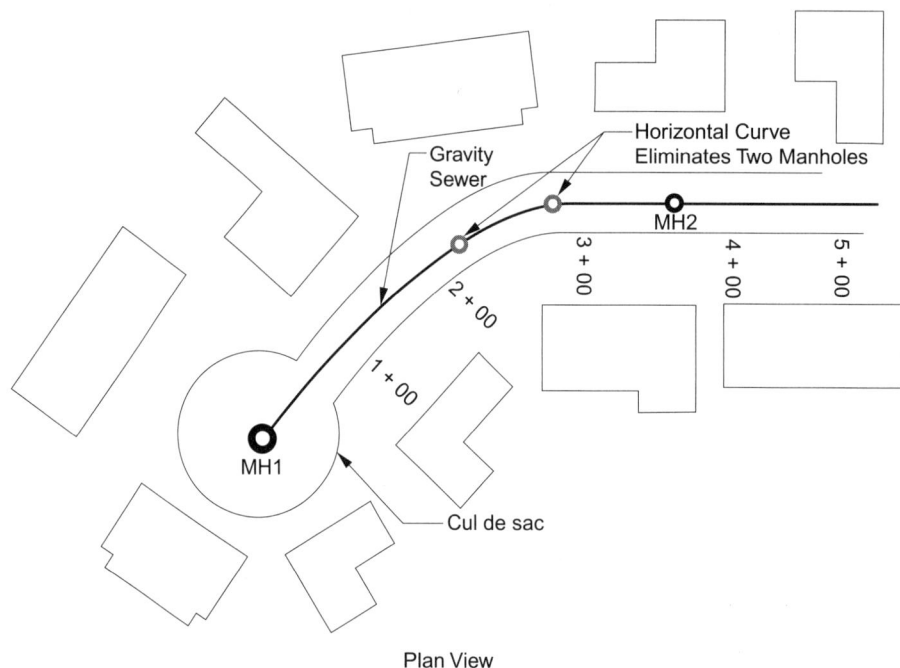

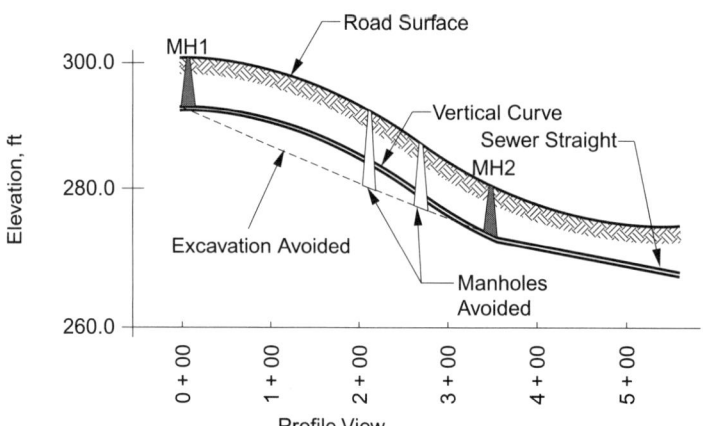

Figure 10.8 Horizontal alignment (plan view) and vertical alignment (profile view) of curved sewers.

- Below the frost line (in permafrost areas, the sewer must be insulated, perhaps even heated)

- A reasonable distance below other utilities, especially potable water lines, unless special features are used to protect against contamination

- Deep enough to adequately distribute traffic and other moving surface loads without causing loading stress breaks in pipes or connections

The *cover depth* is the distance from the soil surface to the top of the outside surface of the pipe. Minimum cover in nontrafficked areas is generally 1.5–2 ft (0.45–600 m) and in trafficked areas is 4–5 ft (1.2–1.5m), depending on the pipe type. In areas with base-

ments needing gravity sewer service, minimum depths have traditionally been 8–9 ft (2.4–2.7 m). Modern basements are often used as living areas and may be several feet deeper than they were in the past. Sewers serving these deeper basements may need to be 11–12 ft (3.4–3.7 m) deep or more. Utilities may have a specification such as "top of sewer must be at least 3 ft (1 m) below basement floor," although requiring a service line slope of 1 to 2 percent may be a more appropriate way of specifying minimum depth. If very few buildings have significantly deeper basements, individual or local-area pumps that discharge to the street sewer might be a more economical life-cycle solution.

A significant cost issue relative to minimum depth sometimes occurs in relatively flat service areas, where the required pipe slope is greater than the slope of the ground surface. As the gravity sewer proceeds downstream, it is forced deeper. An alternative approach, especially where the water table is high or shallow rock is encountered, is to raise the upstream end of the sewer and service buildings with pumps. In such cases, the cost of pumped lateral services on the upstream end should be weighed against the increased construction cost of the deeper system.

A rough approximation of the costs of raising the upstream end of a sewer can be made by multiplying the difference in depth by the incremental estimated excavation and pipe placement cost, adding the incremental cost of manholes in the deeper alternative, and comparing this value with the construction and operation costs of the pressurized service line. Situations sometimes occur in which an isolated deep gravity service can result in several hundred thousand dollars in incremental sewer construction costs, as compared to pumping to a shallower street main.

For streets that run along contours on the side of a hill as shown in Figure 10.9, it will be difficult to convey wastewater from buildings on the downhill side of the street to a main with a typical burial depth. Options include a very deep main, pumping to a relatively shallow main, or running the lateral through an easement to the main in the next street downhill. The steepness of the area, extent of rock excavation, and distance between streets will determine which option is best.

Most codes require that the top of the sewer be at least 1.5 ft (0.45 m) below the bottom of any nearby water main, unless special sewer pipe and/or joints are used (GLUMRB, 1997). The required horizontal separation is often at least 10 ft (3 m) without special pipe and joint features.

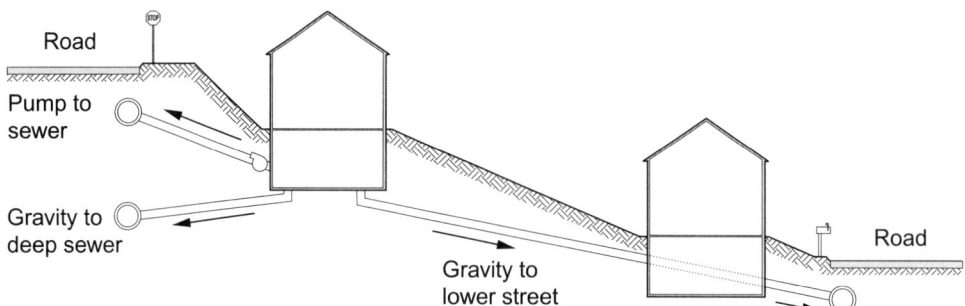

Figure 10.9 Alternatives for providing sewer service to structures below road level.

Maximum Depth

Maximum sewer depths are often set at 20–25 ft (6–8 m). Common factors that have historically limited depth are as follows:

- Groundwater makes construction more expensive and hazardous, and makes high-quality pipe bedding and pipe placement more difficult.
- Soil layers, rock layers, or other subsurface conditions make excavation very difficult, the cave-in hazard high, or pipe structural loadings too high.
- Trench stability is more difficult to manage with greater depth. Often extreme (costly) measures are needed for deep sewers, such as special cutoff walls and piling support walls.
- Maximum depth capability of excavation and other maintenance equipment available to the owner may be exceeded.

Relatively new construction techniques, such as microtunneling with laser-guided boring or pipe jacking, are becoming particularly economical for deep sewers in the 1–3 ft (300–900 mm) diameter range.

A limitation on maximum depth can be viewed primarily as a cost issue, to be weighed against the cost of increased pumping or alternative horizontal alignment. Since the cost of pumping, including construction and O&M, is very high, even deep sewer placement may cost less than additional pumping stations. Chapter 13 covers economic aspects of pumping.

In areas where few or no service laterals are needed, trenchless sewer construction using horizontal directional drilling or boring and jacking may prove cost effective. Trenchless construction can also be used (and is often required) for service laterals where they cross railroads, streams, or major highways.

10.7 Hydraulic Design

After the proposed sewer network layout has been determined, including structure locations and initial elevations, and the design flows have been computed, the next major task is the hydraulic design. Hydraulic design primarily consists of determining what the pipe sizes will be, but, as discussed in Section 10.6, the tasks of setting invert elevations and determining pipe sizes are interrelated. Therefore, some adjustment of structure elevations will likely take place during the hydraulic design.

Life-Cycle Cost

A typical example of when a life-cycle cost analysis should be performed is the case in which a utility can lay either a very deep sewer in a flat area with a very high initial cost or a series of shallow sewers connected by a force main and pump station.

The estimated initial cost for the deep-sewer alternative is $825,000, with annual O&M (operation and maintenance) costs of $10,000. The shallow sewer is estimated to cost $300,000, the force main $125,000, and the pump station $225,000. The design life of the project is 50 years, but the pump station will need to be rehabilitated in 25 years at $50,000. The annual O&M cost is $5000 for the shallow sewers and $20,000 for the pump station.

The interest rate for the analysis is 6 percent. To convert the O&M cost to a present worth for comparison, the series present-worth factor is calculated as 15.7. To determine the present worth of the pump station rehab, a present-worth factor of 0.233 is used. The calculation is summarized in the table.

In this case, the deep-sewer alternative has the lowest life-cycle cost and is also likely to be more reliable. However, environmental, financing, social, and political considerations can also factor into the design selection.

Item	Cost, $	Factor	Present Worth, $
Deep sewer	825,000	1	825,000
Deep sewer O&M	10,000/yr	15.7	157,000
TOTAL: Deep sewer project			$982,000
Shallow sewer	300,00	1	300,000
Force main	125,000	1	125,000
Pump station	225,000	1	225,000
Sewer O&M	5000/yr	15.7	78,500
Pump station O&M	20,000/yr	15.7	314,000
Pump station rehab	50,000	0.233	11,650
TOTAL: Shallow sewer project			$1,054,150

The following summarizes the basic steps in the hydraulic design process:

1. Make an initial estimate of diameter.

2. Run the hydraulic analysis and check results against design criteria.

3. Make adjustments to pipe sizes, elevations, etc. as needed to meet the design criteria.

4. Check along the pipeline to ensure that minimum cover is maintained and burial depths are not excessive.

5. Check the minimum velocity at the design minimum flow rate and the maximum velocity at the design maximum flow rate.

6. Check situations where the pipe size decreases downstream and determine if this is acceptable; change the diameter if it is not. Maintain the same diameter if impacts are not acceptable.

7. Check where the pipe is shallow or above ground and determine whether deeper burial, an inverted siphon, or an elevated pipe (see Section 10.8) is the best solution. Check for conflicts with other buried utilities and structures.

8. Check areas with high velocity or slope and determine if a drop manhole is desirable.

9. Where the slope is minimal, check if lowering downstream manholes relative to upstream manholes is desirable to reduce pipe size.

10. Where excavation costs and pipe sizes are uneconomical, investigate pressure sewers or pumping stations and force mains.

11. When planning an addition to an existing system, the capacity of all existing downstream piping and pumping to the treatment facility must be checked to determine if bottlenecks exist. If downstream sewers have insufficient capacity, sewer rerouting or design of a parallel relief sewer may be needed to carry the new flows.

12. Develop cost estimates.

13. Repeat the hydraulic calculations and cost estimates, and perhaps investigate alternate routes, until an optimal design is achieved.

This section describes the hydraulic design of sewer piping and manholes. It also discusses the use of computer models for design and types of hydraulic analysis.

Pipe Sizing

Pipe sizes are selected to convey the peak flow. According to ASCE (1982), it is customary to design pipes having diameters of 15 in. (357 mm) and smaller to flow half full, while larger-diameter pipes are designed to flow three-quarters full. Actual criteria vary among jurisdictions. Commercially available pipe sizes were discussed in Chapter 5.

Some regulatory agencies are allowing sewers to be designed with little to no excess capacity such that they will surcharge during design flow events. Surcharging tends to increase the amount of in-system storage that occurs, and less conservative designs lower construction costs. However, because such systems have very little safety allowance built in, having an accurate hydraulic model becomes even more important.

Small-Diameter Sewers. The smallest pipe diameter traditionally specified in the U.S. for gravity sewer mains is 8 in. (200 mm). This requirement was based on difficulties associated with cleaning and connecting laterals to smaller-diameter pipes, as well as the propensity of small sewers to clog more frequently. However, smaller diameter sewers are often desirable because they posses higher velocities for a given slope and flow rate, allowing for better self-cleansing at low flows. Because good connectors and inspection and cleaning equipment are now readily available for diameters 6 in. (150 mm) and smaller, the use of 6-in. or even 4-in. (100-mm) pipe may be allowed in some cases.

Pipe Size Reduction Downstream. Sewer pipe sizes usually increase in the downstream direction due to an increasing flow rate. However, if the ground slope of a sewer route increases significantly in the downstream direction, the pipe size in a sewer run may actually be able to decrease without decreasing capacity. If the steep portion of the sewer run is long, significant cost savings may result from using a smaller pipe.

For smaller sewer sizes, prohibition of sewer-size reduction downstream is common, with the reasoning that small-diameter pipes have a higher probability of large debris lodging where the size reduces. For sewers larger than about 18 in. (450 mm), such clogging is much less likely, and pipe-size reduction is a viable option if an appropriate hydraulic transition is provided. The designer should not switch back and forth between larger and smaller sizes if the slopes undulate over the route. Increased costs associated with manholes having different-size connectors and greater pipe ordering and delivery complexity may negate the anticipated cost savings. However, if size reduction is possible for a distance of several thousand feet or more, then it should be considered as a cost-saving feature.

Manholes

A smooth, U-shaped channel should be formed in the manhole base to convey the wastewater through the manhole with minimal head loss. This practice is referred to as manhole *benching* or *shaping*. If the manhole has multiple inflow pipes, the U-shaped channels from each inflow should be curved to merge and provide a smooth transition through the manhole. A small elevation drop is common through manholes to allow for slight vertical misalignment and compensate for head loss. For manholes with smooth and smooth-curvature channels, the energy loss should only be about 0.02 ft (6 mm) for manholes on straight pipe runs, with another 0.02 ft (6 mm) for each additional inflow pipe due to changes in flow direction and increased turbulence. Figure 10.10 shows a benched manhole with smooth transitions for three inflow pipes.

Photo courtesy of R. D. Zande and Associates

Figure 10.10 Looking down into a benched manhole with three inflow pipes.

Some codes call for matching the crown elevations of all the pipes at a manhole, while other codes, such as the GLUMRB (1997), call for matching the 80 percent of maximum depth point of the pipes. Manholes may occasionally be designed to surcharge at maximum design flows, usually to dissipate energy.

Computer Modeling for System Design

Hydraulic design calculations can be performed manually, with a computer spreadsheet program, or with a sewer system model with a graphical user interface. However, the design process usually involves many iterations, which makes manual calculations impractical for all but the simplest systems. The ability of sewer system models to display plan and profile views with color coding and annotation makes them more desirable than spreadsheet models. In addition, spreadsheet and manual calculations are insufficient for handling the unsteady flow and gradually varied flow calculations that are required in many cases.

Although engineering judgment cannot, and should not, be removed from the design process, some software applications provide constraint-based design facilities that can produce a design that will meet a set of constraints specified by the user (Haestad Methods, 2001). The factors that are considered by the automated design algorithm include

- Percent full at design flow
- Range of pipe sizes considered
- Matching of pipe inverts or crowns at manholes
- Use of a drop structure if the maximum slope is exceeded
- Placement of pipe crown below the top of existing structures
- Placement of pipe invert below the bottom of an existing invert
- Ensuring downstream pipe not smaller than the upstream pipe
- Ensuring slope is less than the maximum allowable
- Ensuring minimum cover is provided at each structure.

The design engineer should not simply accept an automated design, but rather should carefully review it to ensure that it meets design criteria and determine if some adjustments in parameters can yield a better-functioning or lower-cost design.

Steady Flow versus Extended-Period Simulation (EPS) Analysis

As discussed in Chapter 1, modeling can be useful for evaluating system design. Models can range in complexity from simple spreadsheets to sophisticated dynamic solvers. The engineer should choose the appropriate model for the task at hand. Depending on the problem and complexity of proposed solutions, a steady-state model, an unsteady (extended-period simulation) model, or a fully dynamic model with real-time control capability may be the appropriate design tool.

In a steady-state model, flows and boundary conditions are constant in time at any point in the system, and the steady-state gravity-flow equations described in Chapter 2 apply. In reality, flows are constantly changing throughout the day, but for many analysis and design situations only a specific, single flow rate, such as the peak or minimum, is needed. This snapshot of the flow at the desired time (e.g., time corresponding to design maximum flow rates) is then analyzed; in this case, to determine needed pipe capacity.

Extended-period simulation (EPS) models show how a sewer network will behave over time. This type of analysis can be used to examine how wet wells fill and drain; how pumps toggle on and off; and how pressures, hydraulic grades, and flow rates change in response to variable loading conditions and automatic control strategies. EPS is a useful tool for assessing the hydraulic performance of different pump and wet well sizes.

In wastewater collection systems, unsteady flow is often the result of wet weather events. Stormwater is supposed to be excluded from new sewer systems, and flow routing may not be required for new sewer design. Instead, the peak hourly flows are generally used to determine the sizes of the laterals and smaller sewers (Metcalf & Eddy, Inc., 1981), and a steady-state simulation with peak hourly flows may be performed to assess the capacity of a designed or existing line. A second steady-state run with minimum design flow rates can determine if the velocities at these low flow rates are adequate to prevent solids buildup.

For long-term planning studies, it is unrealistic to try to establish short-term inflow hydrographs for future conditions. Therefore, steady-state runs are usually conducted for several different future times to assess the effects of increased flows and new areas coming into service. These steady-state runs represent the worst-case conditions expected in the system.

EPS may be used in the design of new gravity sewers to analyze the effects of the following conditions:

- Wet weather peaks as they move downstream in large systems
- Draining of batch tanks by industrial customers
- New sewers tying into existing areas with inflow and infiltration (I/I) problems
- Worst-case I/I projections for planned sewers
- Effect of wet well level fluctuations on gravity sewers flowing into wet wells
- Fluctuations of flow and depth in sewers downstream of a force main as a result of pump cycling
- Adequacy of sizing and cycle time for pump station wet wells.

When EPS is used, sanitary loads are typically simulated using 24-hour pattern loads, as described in Chapter 6. Hydrographs or pattern loads for industrial customers should be based on site-specific flows. Wet weather flows are assigned to the model with hydrographs developed using the techniques described in Chapter 7. The hydraulic time step is typically one hour for diurnal fluctuations, but shorter time steps may be required when flows are highly variable, such as for short-duration storms or pump cycling. The sensitivity of the model to changes in the time step can be explored by comparing the results of the analysis using different increments. The time step for the input hydrographs (hydrologic time step) used for flow routing should be less than or equal to the hydraulic time step used for depth calculation. For cyclic events, the length of the simulation should be at least several loading cycles.

The duration of the analysis should be long enough that results do not vary between cycles.

Design Maximum Flow Rates with Pumping

The design of gravity sewers downstream of a pumping station is challenging because the design maximum flow is not the flow upstream of the station, but rather the maximum pumping flow. Instead of a smooth hydrograph, the pipe experiences a step flow, as shown in Figure 10.11. In this case, the pump discharge is 500 gpm (32 L/s), while the average inflow is 150 gpm (9.5 L/s). For open-channel pipes immediately downstream of a lift station or at the end of a force main, the peak pump discharge should be used as the design maximum flow rate. However, as the flow proceeds downstream, pump cycling becomes less of an influence, and the hydrograph is dampened until the peak flow rate approaches that of the inflow to the pumping station (flattest line in Figure 10.11). The most conservative design practice is therefore to use the peak pump discharge to size downstream mains; however, an unsteady flow routing model (described in Chapter 3) can account for downsteam dampening effects and may be a more appropriate analysis tool in many instances.

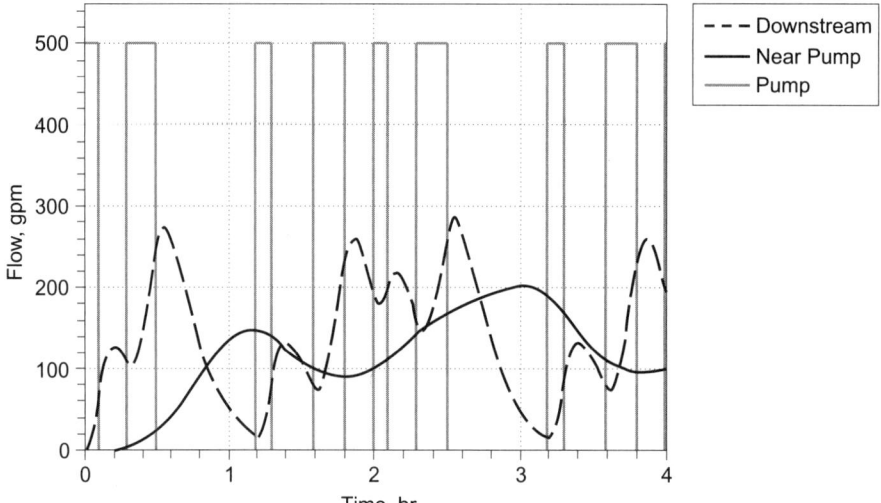

Figure 10.11 Example of pump station flow attenuated at downstream points in a sewer.

10.8 Special Installations

Sewers must sometimes be installed in steep terrain or along or across streams or other obstructions. The subsections that follow describe some special installation types.

Sewers in Steep Terrain

If steep terrain results in velocities in excess of 15 ft/s (4.6 m/s), the engineer should consider using more durable pipe materials such as ductile iron and an energy-dissipation manhole at the end of the steep slope. Alternatively, flatter slopes can be maintained through the use of drop manholes, as illustrated in Figure 10.12. With a drop-manhole configuration, pipes are commonly sloped to prevent velocities in excess of approximately 10 ft/s (3 m/s). The water drop in the manhole dissipates energy without causing extremely high velocities, which are both a hazard to workers in the manhole and abrasive to the pipes. However, drop manholes do cause turbulence, which can release hydrogen sulfide from the wastewater, resulting in odor and corrosion problems. ASCE (1982) provides additional guidance on drop manholes.

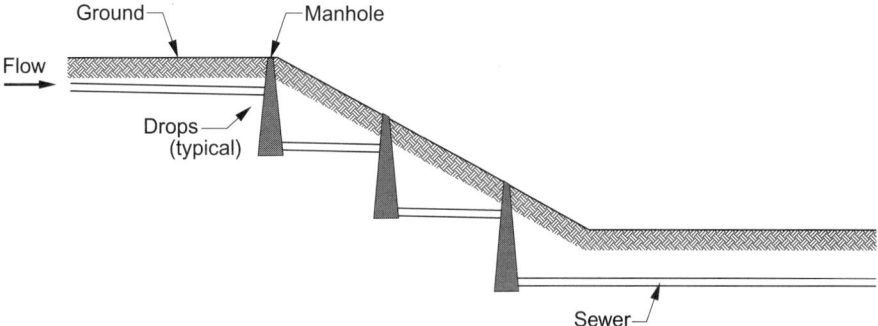

Figure 10.12 Application of drop manholes in a sewer crossing steep terrain.

Sewers Along Streams

When sewers must be routed along waterways, extra care is needed to protect the sewer from erosion and breakage. Sewers placed parallel to streams or drainage channels are typically constructed of lined ductile iron or plastic pipe. The sewer is normally still designed as an open-channel flow conduit, but an inverted siphon may be required when crossing under a waterway. If the probability of breakage and spills is deemed significant, the streambank may need to be stabilized to prevent washout of the pipe. Stabilization is preferably achieved using a method based on the stream's natural geomorphology. Manholes along streams often have their chimneys extended above the level of expected flooding to prevent flood waters from entering through the top of the manhole. In larger streams in cold climates, extended chimneys may need to be protected from ice floes.

Elevated Crossings

Sometimes the best solution to crossing an obstruction such as a canal, stream, or gully is use an elevated, above-grade structure, as shown in Figure 10.13. In some cases, open-channel flow can be maintained. If the flow must be pressurized at the crossing (i.e., there is a sag in the pipe), then it is an inverted siphon (see next subsection).

A true elevated sewer will have the same slope as the upstream and downstream pipes. The designer should examine the ground profile to identify the segment of pipe that is above grade. Special pipe materials and construction techniques may be required for the exposed pipe. For example, some plastic pipes may be damaged by ultraviolet light, while metal pipe may need a wrap or coating.

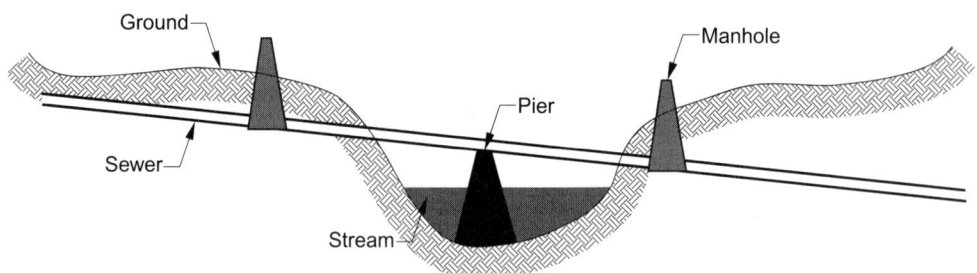

Figure 10.13 Profile of an elevated stream crossing.

Inverted Siphons (Depressed Sewers)

An *inverted siphon* is a sag in a sewer used to avoid an obstruction such as a gulley, stream, canal, depressed railway, or roadway. However, this type of structure is not really a siphon, and the term *depressed sewer* has been suggested as more appropriate (Metcalf and Eddy, 1981). Because the pipe(s) comprising the inverted siphon are below the hydraulic grade line, it always contains sewage, and its hydraulic behavior is that of a pressure-flow conduit. An example of a depressed sewer is shown in Figure 10.14.

Minimum diameters for depressed sewers are the same as for gravity sewers: 6 or 8 inches (150 or 200 mm). Depressed sewers require a larger sediment carrying capacity for self-cleansing than do normal, open-channel sewers, because it is desirable to scour larger particles out of the siphon to avoid buildup and clogging, and also because particles must be suspended in the turbulent flow to be successfully

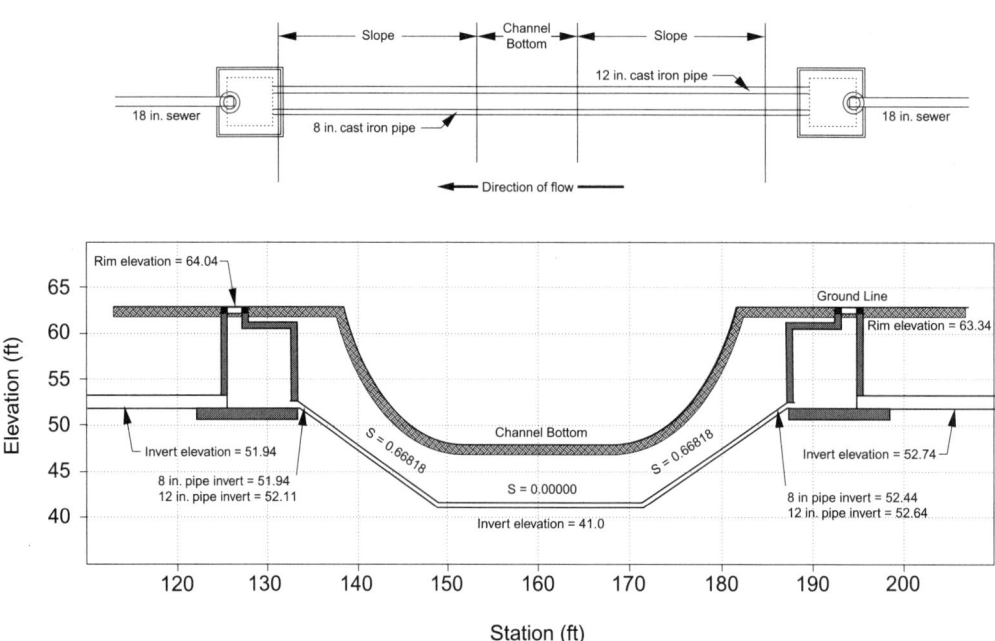

Graphic reprinted with permission from Pearson Education

Figure 10.14 Plan and profile of a depressed sewer (inverted siphon) used to avoid obstructions.

removed. To make them as maintenance free as possible, velocities of at least 3 ft/s (0.9 m/s) need to be achieved at a minimum of every few days. Higher velocities can be induced by placing a splitter box with different weir levels at the inlet and using two or more parallel pipes in the siphon section. All flow goes into the smaller pipe until it surcharges, then the overflow spills into the next pipe, and so on. Depressed sewers are usually constructed using lined ductile iron or plastic pressure pipe.

The hydraulic design is best handled by applying the energy equation from the inflow section at the entrance to the depressed section, through the transitions (bends), to the outlet where flow enters the open-channel pipe. Head loss resulting from changes in velocity at the entrance must be accounted for. If bends in the pipe are greater than 10 to 20 degrees, allowances must be made for losses at the bends (Metcalf & Eddy, Inc., 1981).

To model depressed sewers and obtain good profile maps, it may be necessary to insert nodes or imaginary manholes along the siphon corresponding to points where the slope of the pipe changes. The invert elevation at the manhole would be the same as at the siphon, but manholes would have no or minimal minor loss associated with them, and the top of the manhole would extend above the expected maximum hydraulic grade line.

Based on both theoretical and laboratory analyses, May (2003) determined that the rising leg of the siphon could either be too steep or too shallow, which could result in accelerated deposition of solids. He recommended slopes between 22.5 and 45 degrees to prevent deposition.

10.9 Wastewater Collection System Optimization

Engineers must constantly weigh the cost implications of project decisions with the goal of providing a fully functional, high-quality project at the lowest cost. This is done by analyzing wide range of alternative layouts, pipe sizes, and invert elevations. Optimization consists of using a computerized method to automatically analyze a range of alternatives and find the one that accomplishes the project objectives for the least cost.

Sewer system design is not readily amenable to mathematical programming optimization techniques such as gradient search, linear programming, or dynamic programming. Most optimization methods applied to sewer system design are a combination of some mathematical programming technique and a heuristic algorithm to arrive at the least-cost design.

A great deal of research on the application of optimization to collection systems occurred in the 1970s, with papers by Argaman, Shamir, and Spivak (1973); Barlow (1972); Dajani and Hasit (1974); Deb (1974); Deininger (1970); Liebman (1967); Mays (1975); Mays and Yen (1975); Meredith (1971); Merritt and Bogan (1973); Tang, Mays, and Yen (1975); and Yen and Sevuk (1975). The most promising of these was Mays' approach, which used discrete dynamic programming to trade off pipe costs and excavation costs. However, it required data on the sensitivity of costs to excavation depth, which were not usually available.

Early optimization models were not widely adopted by practicing engineers for several reasons, including lack of user-friendly interfaces and difficulties with handling nonlinear cost and hydraulic equations. In addition, practicing engineers often are not interested in the least-cost solution as much as they are in providing conservative safety factors in their design. Optimization tends to remove any conservatism from design.

Walters (1985) and Tekeli and Belkaya (1986) developed models for sewer system layout which were expanded upon by Lui and Matthew (1990) to include hydraulics as well as layout. Greene, Agbenowosi, and Loganathan (1999) produced a GIS-based method to identify the optimal route for sewers given manhole locations in a GIS.

Desher and Davis (1986) published one of the early microcomputer models of a collection system and showed that costs could be reduced by 20 percent through a sensitivity analysis of design criteria. Kulkarni and Khanna (1985) developed an algorithm to optimize force mains. Elimam, Charalambous and Ghobrial (1989) produced a heuristic algorithm to design sewers and used a digitizer to build the network. Charalambous and Elimam (1991) extended this work to include force mains.

More recently, Swamee (2001) proposed a method based on Lagrangian multipliers, while Vollertsen, Hvitveld-Jacobsen and Talib (2002) developed an approach which purported to account for water quality transformations in sewers. Gill, Parker, Savic and Walters (2001) developed a model that minimizes pollution from combined sewer overflows.

Genetic and evolutionary algorithms have been applied to the optimization of sewer and drainage systems. Cembrowicz and Krauter (1987) applied the evolutionary strategy to optimize pipe sizes and dendritic layout for a gravity sewer system. Parker et al. (2000) coupled a genetic algorithm with an artificial neural network (ANN) trained with a hydrodynamic model and applied it to minimizing combined sewer overflow. Diogo et al. (2000) developed a fairly comprehensive model integrating a genetic algorithm for general system layout with a dynamic programming and knowledge-based approach for further optimizing the detailed design of the optimal layout. Savic and Walters (2001) developed a genetic algorithm optimization that used simplified routing based on the kinematic wave method to speed the solution, as compared with solving the Saint-Venant equations.

While automated design procedures (Haestad Methods, 2003) are, strictly speaking, not optimization models, the results from such procedures can serve as a starting point for trial-and-error adjustments of pipe sizes and invert elevations to minimize costs. That is, the engineer

1. Performs the initial constraint-based design

2. Estimates the cost for the initial design

3. Modifies or further constrains the diameters, invert elevations, or other parameter and checks hydraulic feasibility with the model

4. Performs another cost estimate

This process continues until the engineer is satisfied that the design cannot be substantially improved.

Even though optimization models have shown promise, they have yet to reach the level of being widely accepted in engineering practice.

Example of Optimization/Sensitivity Analysis

Formal optimization to minimize sewer construction costs has not been practiced widely for a variety of reasons (Merritt, 1999). However, case studies have shown that optimization cost savings of 5 to 10 percent are often achievable, compared to good designs that were not optimized. In addition, cost-sensitivity studies on design parameters such as flow rate, Manning's n-value, minimum depth, and self-cleansing particle size often lead to much larger cost savings. The latter case is actually similar to a value-engineering sensitivity analysis. A sewer design model is used to determine the impact of adjustments in design parameters on project costs. Curves can be prepared relating cost and any design parameter. Designers and decision makers then consider these results to decide whether changes in the design criteria and constraints are desirable in light of the changes in costs associated with different values.

A sewer project designed in 1998 and constructed in 1999 consisted of replacing a smaller sewer main with a new 48-in. (1200-mm) interceptor sewer, along a 3.1-mi (5-km) route. Two additional 24-in. (600-mm) replacement mains, each about 0.5 mi (0.8 km) long, joined the new trunk line along its route and were part of the project. The project design was done in a "standard" fashion by a capable and experienced engineering firm. The completed sewer was built in accordance with appropriate codes and will serve the area well.

An optimization and cost-sensitivity study was performed for this project to provide information for value engineering considerations. The study was conducted using the Merritt Optimizing Design System (MODS) (Merritt, 2000). This sewer project appeared to be rather straightforward, but the optimized design, based on essentially the same design values and constraints as the original design, was priced about 17 percent lower—about one million dollars. This 17-percent cost differential resulted from the optimization model's ability to select the best (least-cost) combination of pipe sizes and slopes that met all constraints and criteria established for the design. In this case, nearly all of the savings resulted from pipe-size reductions.

The optimal design placed the lines at slightly steeper slopes in some reaches to allow smaller-diameter pipes to carry the design flows. The cost of the increased depths were far smaller than the pipe cost savings, yielding a large net cost reduction. This 17-percent reduction due to optimization was rather large in this case, but similar case studies typically show a 5 to 10 percent savings from optimization.

Next, the sensitivity of costs to values of Manning's n were determined, and a curve of cost versus n was developed. The figure below shows that costs could be reduced by 5 percent by reducing Manning's n from 0.013 to 0.011.

Even larger savings were made possible by removing some of the conservatism from projected flow rates. By preparing curves relating values such as design flow to cost, the owner can gain an appreciation of the cost for reduction of risk. For example, a 20-percent increase in the design flow resulted in only a 9-percent increase in cost, while a 20-percent reduction would result in a savings of 13 percent. Optimization and cost-sensitivity plots clarify the situation and provide accurate information from which to make final design decisions.

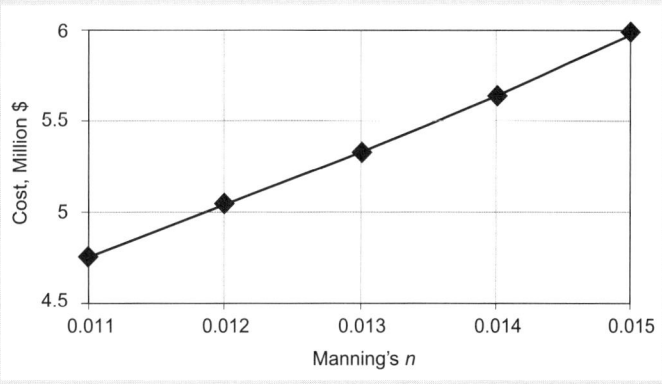

References

American Society of Civil Engineers (ASCE). 1982. *Gravity Sanitary Sewer Design and Construction.* Manual of Practice 60 (also WEF MOP FD-5). Reston, VA: American Society of Civil Engineers.

Argaman, Y., U. Shamir, and E. Spivak. 1973. Design of optimal sewerage systems. *Journal of Environmental Engineering Division*, ASCE 99, EE6, 703.

Barlow, J. F. 1972. Cost optimization of pipe sewerage systems. *Proceedings of the Institution of Civil Engineers* (London), no. 2: 57.

Burton, F. L. 1996. Wastewater collection systems. In *Water Resources Handbook*, edited by L. W. Mays. New York: McGraw-Hill.

Cembrowicz, P. G., and G. E. Krauter. 1987. Design of cost optimal sewer networks. *Proceedings of the Fourth International Conference on Urban Storm Drainage* (Lausanne, Switzerland), 367–72.

Crites, R. and G. Tchobanoglous. 1998. *Small and Decentralized Wastewater Treatment Systems.* New York: McGraw-Hill.

Dajani, J. S., and Y. Hasit. 1974. Capital cost minimum drainage networks. *Journal of Environmental Engineering Division*, ASCE 100, EE2, 325.

Deb, A. K. 1974. Least cost design of branched pipe network system. *Journal of Environmental Engineering Division*, ASCE 100, EE4, 821.

Deininger, R. 1970. Systems analysis for water supply and pollution control. In *Natural Resource Systems Models in Decision Making*, edited by G. H. Toebes. Water Resources Center, Purdue University.

Diogo, A. F., G. A. Walter, E. R. de Sousa, and V. M. Graveto. 2000. Three-dimensional optimization of urban drainage systems. *Computer-Aided Civil and Infrastructure Engineering* 15, 409–426.

Elimam, A. A., C. Charalambous, and F. H. Ghobrial. 1989. Optimum design of large sewer networks. *Journal of Environmental Engineering* 115, no. 6: 1171.

Gill, E., M. A. Parker, D. A. Savic, and G. A. Walters. 2001. Cougar: A genetic algorithm and rapid integrated catchment modeling application for optimizing capital investment in combined sewer systems. *World Water & Environmental Resources Congress* (Orlando, Florida).

Greene, R., N. Agenowosi, and G. V. Loganathan. 1999. GIS-based approach to sewer system design. *Journal of Surveying Engineering* 125, no. 1: 36.

Great Lakes and Upper Mississippi River Board of State Public Health and Environmental Manager (GLUMRB). 1997. *Recommended Standards for Wastewater Facilities.* Albany, NY: Great Lakes Upper Mississippi River Board.

Haestad Methods. 2001. *SewerCAD Sanitary Sewer Modeling Software.* Waterbury, CT: Haestad Methods.

Haestad Methods. 2003. *SewerCAD Sanitary Sewer Modeling Software.* Waterbury, CT: Haestad Methods.

Hammer, M. J., and M. J. Hammer, Jr. 2001. *Water and Wastewater Technology*, 4th ed. Upper Saddle River, NJ: Prentice-Hall.

Liebman, J. C. 1967. A heuristic aid for the design of sewer networks. *Journal of Sanitary Engineering Division*, ASCE 93, SA 4, 81.

Lui, G., and R. G. S. Matthew. 1990. New approach for optimization of urban drainage systems. *Journal of Environmental Engineering* 116, no. 5: 927.

May, R. P. 2003. Preventing sediment deposition in inverted sewer siphon. *Journal of Hydraulic Engineering* 129, no. 4: 283

Mays, L. W. 1975. Optimal layout and design of storm sewer systems. Ph.D. Diss., University of Illinois, Urbana.

Mays, L. W., and B. C. Yen. 1975. Optimal cost design of branched sewer systems. *Water Resources Research* 11, no. 1: 37-47.

Meredith, D. D., 1971. Dynamic programming with case study on planning and design of urban water facilities. In *Treatise on Urban Water Systems*. Colorado State University.

Merritt, L. B. 1999. Obstacles to lower cost sewer systems. Sewer Design Paper #99-1. Provo, UT: Civil and Environmental Engineering Department, Brigham Young University.

Merritt, L. B. 2000. Example cost sensitivity curves from case studies. In *Proceedings of WEAU Annual Conference*. Salt Lake City, UT: Water Environment Association of Utah.

Merritt, L. B., and R. H. Bogan. 1973. Computer-based optimal design of sewer systems." *Journal of Environmental Division*, ASCE 99, EE1, Proc. Paper 9578.

Metcalf & Eddy, Inc. 1981. *Wastewater Engineering: Collection and Pumping of Wastewater*. New York: McGraw-Hill.

Parker, M. A., D. A. Savic, G. A. Walter, and Z. Kappelan. 2000. SewerNet: A genetic algorithm application for optimizing urban drainage systems. *International Conference on Urban Drainage*.

Savic, D. A., and G. A. Walters. 2001. Evolutionary computing in water distribution and wastewater systems. *World Water and Environmental Resources Congress* (Orlando, Florida).

Tang, W. H., L. W. Mays, and B. C. Yen. 1975. Optimal risk-based design of storm sewer networks. *Journal of Environmental Engineering Division*, ASCE 101, EE3, 381.

Tekeli, S., and H. Belkaya. 1986. Computerized layout generation for sanitary sewers. *Journal of Water Resource Planning and Management* 112, no. 4: 500.

US Environmental Protection Agency (US EPA). 1991. *Alternative Wastewater Collection Systems*. EPA 625/1-91/024. Washington, DC: US Environmental Protection Agency.

Walters, G. A. 1985. The design of the optimal layout for a sewer network. *Engineering Optimization*, no. 9: 37.

Yen, B. C., and A. S. Sevuk. 1975. Design of storm sewer networks. *Journal of Environmental Engineering Division*, ASCE 101, EE4, 535.

Problems

10.1 You are trying to decide between using 21- or 24-in. pipes for a sewer that will be laid at a slope of 0.004 with a Darcy-Weisbach roughness height of 0.0002 ft. Your design standards require that it be able to carry a peak flow of 14 ft^3/s, but the average flow will be about 5 ft^3/s and the minimum flow will be 2 ft^3/s.

First, determine the full pipe capacity for each diameter. To do this, you will need to assume a flow, calculate the Reynolds number, determine f, and check if the hydraulic gradient slope is 0.004. You can use the Moody diagram, Colebrook-White equation, or Swamee-Jain equation. Iterate until you reach a solution. Use a kinematic viscosity of 1.0×10^{-5} ft^2/s. (Alternatively, you can use a program such as FlowMaster or SewerCAD.)

Parameter	21 in.	24 in.
Velocity, ft/s		
Relative roughness		
Reynolds Number		
Friction factor		
Slope		
Flow, ft^3/s		

From the answers in the previous table, you might think that a 21-in. pipe would not work. But remember that a pipe's peak carrying capacity occurs when it is approximately 95 percent full. Using a hydraulic elements chart or a computer program, find the velocity and depth of flow at each of the flow rates given below. Assume that you can ignore any gradually varied flow effects (i.e., assume normal flow exists).

Flow, ft^3/s	Velocity (21), ft/s	Depth (21), in	Velocity (24), ft/s	Depth (24), in
2				
5				
14				

Given the points from the previous table (and the full pipe value), draw a graph with depth on the vertical axis and flow and velocity (for both pipe sizes) on the horizontal axis.

At the lower flow rate, is there a significant difference in the velocity?

Which size pipe would you recommend and why?

10.2 You are required to size a single-barrel inverted siphon (depressed sewer) under a small stream. The inverted siphon is 75 m long with a Hazen-Williams C-factor of 120. You would like to maintain a velocity of at least 0.6 m/s even at low flow. Important elevations are shown in the following figure.

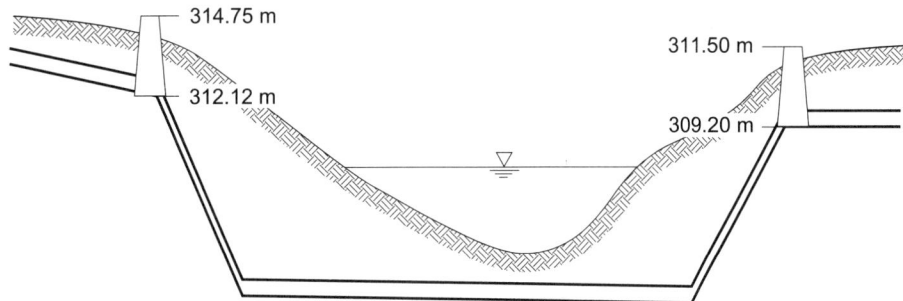

Try diameters of 600, 750, and 900 mm. You would like to select a pipe that will not surcharge the upstream manhole, yet will carry a minimum flow of 300 L/s at a velocity of 0.6 m/s and a maximum flow of 2000 L/s. The downstream gravity sewer has enough capacity to set the water level in the downstream manhole to 310.00 m.

For each diameter pipe, draw a curve of flow vs. upstream head and flow vs. velocity. Using the graphs, select the optimal pipe size and justify your decision.

10.3 You must lay out the sanitary sewer system for a new subdivision. You have been given the road layout and topographic map shown in the figure. Lay out the sewer system by drawing each pipe with an arrow beside each gravity pipe showing the direction of flow. Make sure that all gravity sewers flow downhill. If you must pump, show the pump station and use a dashed line to show the force main.

Some considerations for design:

- Keep the sewers in the road as much as possible
- Minimize the use of pump stations and force mains
- House laterals must drain to the front of the house
- New sewers must end at the existing sewer in the southwest corner of the map.

It is suggested that you photocopy the attached map and draw the lines in color.

An important feature in this design is a greenbelt along a stream in the development. The land developer wants you to create two sets of plans:

a. The first set is for the existing land-use ordinances, which allow sewers to cross a greenbelt but not run along the greenbelt.

b. The second set of plans is for use if the developer receives a variance from the zoning ordinance enabling him to locate the sewer along the length of the greenbelt.

[Zoning ordinances are laws that restrict the construction activities that can occur in each zone. Land owners can request variances which enable them to not comply with a provision in an ordinance.]

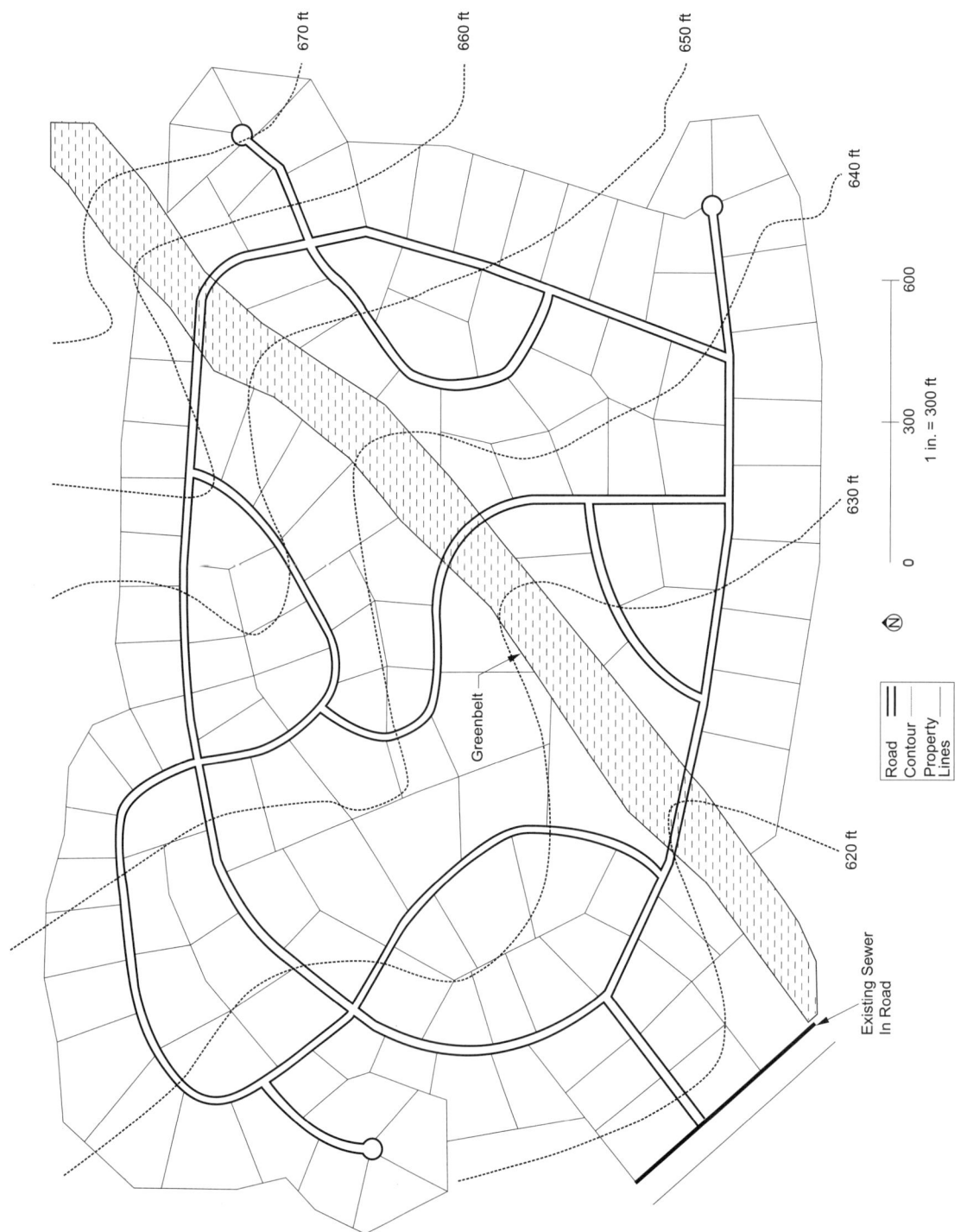

10.4 You are designing a sanitary sewer to flow across a fairly flat floodplain. The manhole spacing is 400 ft and the ground profile is shown in the following table.

Station, ft	Ground Elevation, ft
0	784.25
400	783.88
800	780.65
1200	781.85

Use a PVC pipe with a 12 in. diameter. The sewer will have Manning's $n = 0.010$, and there is 0.1 ft of head loss in each manhole. The tailwater elevation is 776.85 ft, and the manhole invert matches the inverts of the incoming and outgoing pipes. You want at least 3 ft of cover above the top of the pipe. Pick invert elevations and check to see if the pipe is surcharged at a maximum flow of 2.0 ft^3/s and the velocity is still reasonable at a minimum flow of 0.2 ft^3/s. Complete the following tables. If you are using manual calculations or a computer program based on normal flow, use the normal depth in the pipe table. If you are using an approach that calculates backwater curves using a gradually varied flow analysis, give both the upstream and downstream depths and the average velocity.

Manhole data

Station, ft	Invert Elevation, ft
0	
400	
800	
1200	

Pipe data

Up Station, ft	Down Station, ft	Slope	Depth at 2 ft^3/s, ft	Velocity at 2 ft^3/s, ft/s	Depth at 0.2 ft^3/s, ft	Velocity at 0.2 ft^3/s, ft/s
0	400					
400	800					
800	1200					

When you have performed the hydraulic calculations, draw a profile of the sewer showing the ground elevation and top and bottom of the pipe. Annotate the drawing so that it can be understood. It may be drawn manually, with a hydraulic analysis program, or using CAD.

CHAPTER

11

Wastewater Collection System Evaluation and Rehabilitation

The wastewater collection systems of some major cities were constructed beginning in the late 1800s or early 1900s. Many of the cities built combined sewer systems, which convey wastewater resulting from residential, commercial, and industrial usage, as well as stormwater runoff. As the drawbacks of combined sewer discharges came to be better understood, cities began separating the sewer systems used to convey wastewater to the treatment plant from those carrying stormwater to receiving water bodies. Both combined and separate systems present distinct challenges to designers and operators.

Combined sewer systems deliver highly variable flows to the treatment plant or even directly to receiving waters when flows exceed the capacities of the regulators, interceptor sewers, and treatment plants. Both combined and sanitary sewer collection systems deteriorate and incur defects, such as collapsed and cracked pipes, offset joints, and cracked manholes. Groundwater may infiltrate any system through these defects, even during dry weather. Additionally, during periods of wet weather, defective components and illicit connections of stormwater drains allow the entry of surface runoff (rainfall-derived infiltration/inflow or RDII).

The combination of wastewater, groundwater infiltration, and RDII can even exceed the capacity of segments of the sanitary sewer collection system. The result is surcharges or overflows from manholes upstream of the pipe segments whose capacities are exceeded. In areas with basements, collection system capacity problems may show up as basement flooding complaints rather than overflows. If the total flow exceeds the capacity of the wastewater treatment plant, the bypass of untreated wastewater into receiving waters can result. Wastewater overflows and bypasses have the potential to impair human health and the environment and lead to permit violations, with associated fines and adverse publicity.

During the last half of the twentieth century, environment professionals have struggled with identifying optimal solutions to minimize sewer system overflows and adequately operate and maintain the aging infrastructure. Mathematical modeling techniques, coupled with receiving-water quality analyses, sediment analyses, and biological sampling, have provided the best perspective to date into the nature and extent of the problems associated with collection systems (Water Environment Federation, 1999). This chapter discusses several methods for evaluating wastewater collection systems and managing excess flows within these systems, with a particular emphasis on the application of mathematical models to the understanding of wastewater collection system operation.

Modeling can be used in two general ways in system evaluation and rehabilitation:

- The model can be used to simulate existing conditions and, in conjunction with field data, aid the engineer in understanding the sources of problems such as overflows and surcharging.
- The model can be used to simulate alternative rehabilitation approaches to determine the effectiveness of each. This information can be combined with cost estimates to select the best approach.

11.1 Planning for System Characterization

Before a collection system and various rehabilitation schemes can be evaluated, the engineer must have good knowledge of how the system currently functions. Present performance demands on the system may differ greatly from original design assumptions and protocols developed with significantly different water-pollution-control objectives (Water Environment Federation, 1999). A lack of knowledge of one's system can lead to less-than-optimal design, which often leads to greater operational and maintenance (O&M) expenses. *System characterization* is the process of acquiring and interpreting information about a collection system in order to understand its current physical and operating conditions.

System characterization is a complex, multistep process; therefore, some basic planning should occur before the investigation begins. The three steps in the planning stage of system characterization are as follows (Water Reasearch Centre, 2000):

1. *Determine the performance requirements* – What do you need the system to do?
2. *Assess the current performance* – How is the system currently falling short of performance requirements?
3. *Select the approach and set priorities* – What level of investigation is warranted? Where are the most serious problems?

Additionally, because data requirements are in part driven by hydraulic model input requirements, an appropriate modeling tool should be selected before system characterization begins. For more information on model selection, see "Software Selection and Training" on page 143.

The planning procedure for system characterization described here can normally be applied to small- or medium-size systems. In larger systems, it may be appropriate to subdivide investigations into smaller, more manageable units, usually into separate drainage basins. Similarly, in small suburban systems, a modified and perhaps less-detailed approach may be appropriate.

Performance Requirements

Collection system managers throughout the United States have expressed the need for performance indicators that provide criteria for evaluating their systems (Arbour and Kerri, 1998). Recently, a technique known as *benchmarking* has been used to obtain and analyze collection system O&M data. The benchmarking process involves "...gathering information on the productivity and performance of other collection system agencies, and then comparing actual information from an agency that wishes to improve its levels of production and performance" (Arbour and Kerri, 1998).

Where rehabilitation is required, the performance requirements are also used to evaluate potential solutions against the relevant standards. It is important that all rehabilitation needs (hydraulic, environmental, structural, and operational) be considered together, because integrated solutions are the most cost-effective.

A work group consisting of major stakeholders involved in Combined Sewer Overflow (CSO) policy development identified and recommended 24 measures of performance to track and quantify results of CSO control (American Metropolitan Sewerage Agencies, 1996). These measures are presented in Table 11.1. All are not appropriate for every collection system, so common sense, local conditions, and cost-effectiveness should drive the selection of suitable measures of performance.

Table 11.1 Summary of recommended measures of performance (AMSA, 1996).

Administrative	End of Pipe		Receiving Water	Ecological, Human Health, Resource Use
	Flow Measurement	Pollutant Load Reduction		
• Documented implementation of Nine minimum controls[1, 2] • Status of the long-term control plan[1] • Waste reduction	• Wet weather flow budget • CSO frequency[1] • CSO frequency in sensitive areas[1] • CSO volume • CSO volume in sensitive areas • Dry weather overflows	• BOD load • TSS load • Nutrient load • Floatables	• Dissolved oxygen trend • Fecal coliform trend • Floatables trend • Sediment oxygen demand trend • Trend of metals in bottom sediments	• Shellfish bed closures • Benthic organism index • Biological diversity index • Recreational activities • Beach closures • Commercial activities

[1] Appropriate for national tracking.
[2] See Chapter 15 for a listing of the nine minimum controls

Another list of performance standards was developed for European collection systems. European Standard EN 752-2: 1997, Clause 6 provides a list of basic performance requirements as follows:

- The pipework operates without blocking.
- The flooding frequencies are limited to prescribed values.
- Public health and life are safeguarded.
- Sewer surcharge frequencies are limited to prescribed values.
- The health and safety of the operator personnel are safeguarded.
- Receiving waters are protected from pollution within prescribed limits.

- Drains and sewers do not endanger existing adjacent structures and utility services.
- The required design life and structural integrity are achieved.
- Drains and sewers are watertight, in accordance with testing requirements.
- Odor, nuisance, and toxicity do not arise.
- Appropriate access is provided for maintenance purposes.

Current Performance

An initial assessment should be made of the current performance of the system. The aim of this step is to gain an appreciation of the nature and scale of the problems in each drainage area so that

- A precise scope of the diagnostic study can be drawn up
- A program for completion of all drainage-area studies can be produced and priorities assigned against each study (Water Research Centre, 2000).

The assessment should be conducted using performance indicators. Where performance indicators are not available, the current performance should initially be assessed using reports of incidents such as sewer collapses, flooding, and pollution of watercourses. Records of past incidents, together with any other relevant local knowledge of the system (e.g., recurring maintenance problems), should be collated and an initial assessment carried out to compare current performance with the specified performance criteria.

European Standard EN 752-2: 1997, Clause 8 recommends that the following information be collated and compared with performance requirements:

- Flooding incidents
- Pipe blockage incidents
- Sewer collapse incidents
- Disease, injury, or fatal incidents to operators
- Disease, injury, or fatal incidents to members of the public
- Sewer damage incidents
- Compliance with discharge permits into and out of the system
- Closed-circuit television (CCTV) survey and visual inspection data
- Complaints of sewage-related odor
- Hydraulic performance analysis
- Performance of mechanical and electrical equipment
- Results of testing and monitoring
- Performance and condition of flow-control structures
- Sewer surcharge incidents.

Arbour and Kerri (1998) used the following general "core components" of a collection system to compare several collection system agencies' O&M programs:

- Sewer maintenance
- Pump station and force main maintenance
- Emergency response
- Planning, scheduling, and work-order control
- Level of service provided to users
- Control of infiltration/inflow and sanitary sewer overflows (SSOs) and/or minimizing combined sewer overflows (CSOs)
- Equipment
- Finance
- Personnel
- Safety
- Regulatory compliance.

In general, system performance should be considered using four major categories, as follows:

1. **Hydraulic** – All records of past flooding incidents should be collected and, where possible, followed up on to establish the extent and frequency of problems, the reasons for problems, and the magnitudes of the storms causing them. This information can be extrapolated using modeling.

2. **Environmental** – Combined or sanitary sewer overflows suspected of causing unacceptable pollution should be documented. Other available environmental data should also be collated, including the following:
   - Pollution incident records/reports
   - Complaint records
   - Permit requirements and regulatory interpretation
   - Long-term water quality data
   - Sewer use ordinances/industrial waste pretreatment requirements
   - Water quality data for receiving water body or sewage treatment plant
   - Existing models and results
   - Any reported details of illicit connections.

   A systematic visual survey of the receiving water may be necessary at this stage in order to identify aesthetic impacts of discharges.

3. **Structural** – Records of sewer collapses and previous inspections should be collated to establish whether there is any evidence of need for rehabilitation.

4. **Operational** – Records of operational problems, including incident reports (such as sewer blockages, odor complaints, and pumping station failures) and planned maintenance records (such as sewer-cleaning programs) should be reviewed.

The nature and severity of all performance problems should be described.

Approach to System Characterization

Following the initial assessment of the current performance of the system, it is necessary to decide on the level of investigation required. In the majority of drainage areas, a detailed diagnostic study is appropriate, including an environmental assessment. In drainage areas that have been previously studied or where few problems exist, an abbreviated investigation may be sufficient. Similarly, in small suburban catchments, it may acceptable to concentrate solely on known or suspected problems, rather than performing detailed investigations.

System characterization should be conducted for dry weather and wet weather conditions. There are three types of problems that can occur during wet weather (many systems experience all of these):

- Wastewater backs up into customer basements and property.
- Raw sewage spills into the environment before reaching the treatment plant.
- Wet weather flows reach the treatment plant and cause operational problems.

Where there are a large number of sewershed areas requiring detailed investigation, it is necessary to prioritize perceived problems and refer to these rankings when drawing up a comprehensive program for investigation. In this way, areas with the most serious problems can be dealt with first. The rankings assigned can depend largely on outside pressures from sources such as the environmental regulator.

The relative severity of the problems in a drainage area versus the cost to correct them should also be considered when prioritizing. For example, if the problems in an area are primarily structural, the total length of critical sewer and the collapse rate can be useful measures of the cumulative risk of collapse in a catchment. Also, special consideration should be given to environmental investigations that must be undertaken for a wide area, such as the catchment area for a river.

The characterization must account for flow increases that will occur in the future. Increases in flow may occur because of growth or because of expansion of the collection system to areas currently served by on-site disposal.

11.2 System Characterization

As stated previously, system characterization is necessary to evaluate the performance of an existing system and plan rehabilitation efforts. This section describes components of a typical system-characterization process. The components used for a particular area will depend on available sources of information and the characterization approach outlined for the area.

In the United States, additional motivators for performing system characterization are the existing CSO regulations and the proposed SSO regulations (collectively described as capacity, management, operation, and maintenance or CMOM) described in Chapter 15. The regulations require each municipality to collect and manage information about their collection system, understand system operational and hydraulic characteristics, and develop a capacity assurance plan. System characterization is a necessary part of fulfilling these requirements.

Review Existing Records

The first task in system characterization is to compile all existing information describing the physical attributes of the system. Most county or municipal collection system agencies have large amounts of collection system data, much of which is stored digitally (for example, in a GIS). Typically, however, most of the initial information on the system is gathered from paper maps such as drainage plans and construction drawings. The digital and paper maps are used to inventory and locate key facilities in the study area, and unique identifiers are assigned to each of the manholes, sewer segments, and other facilities (Water Environment Federation, 1999).

Facilities that must be inventoried include the following:

- Treatment plants (water and wastewater)
- Intercepting sewer networks (combined and separate sanitary)
- Primary trunk sewer networks
- Pump stations (stormwater and sanitary)
- Force mains
- CSO regulators and diversion structures
- Constructed SSOs and/or bypasses
- Hydraulic control points (flow dividers, gates, siphons, separate/combined system junctions)
- In-line storage/treatment facilities
- Off-line storage/treatment facilities.

An initial goal of the data-collection phase is the generation of a digital pipe and manhole database for the existing system. The selected hydraulic model will define the specific attribute data required. The data collection task should build on existing databases, if available, to further develop the system representation and incorporate data on

- Water usage (current and future)
- O&M work orders
- Flooding and surcharge incidents (customer complaints)
- City/county/regional planning
- Demographics (census)
- Ground elevations
- Soils
- Flow and rainfall amounts
- Pump station operations
- Treatment plant plans and operations
- Storage facility plans and operations.

When collecting data, it is important to consider the level of accuracy required. The necessary precision of input data depends on the required accuracy of the results, the level of detail required by regulators, and the purpose of the project(s). Often, the detail and accuracy needed for hydraulic modeling can be used to establish the requirements. For example, manhole and pipe invert elevations may need to be known to the nearest 0.1 ft for modeling, while manhole lid elevations need not be as accurate, since they are only used to check if overflow will occur.

Efforts to clean up existing imprecise data can potentially absorb a large portion of the project budget. Excessive emphasis on either data cleanup or data collection is not usually cost effective. If the accuracy of existing data does not meet requirements, confining the collection of additional field data to problem areas that will undergo detailed study is often preferable to checking or cleaning up all of the data.

Design Criteria. Familiarity with original design criteria can aid the engineer in understanding the existing system. Of particular importance in CSO/SSO abatement planning is original design information for treatment plants and the sewer system. This information is compared with current system conditions to help identify system capacity deficiencies. Unfortunately, this information is not available for many older sewer systems.

Construction Methods. Methods and materials used in the construction of sewage systems can give clues to parts of the system that may experience high I/I or excessive wastewater spills. Improving and enforcing mainline sewer construction standards can limit long-term future problems resulting from improper bedding and backfilling, inadequate support at junctions, or improper manhole construction.

Plumbing standards should also be reviewed. Jurisdictions that enforce more strict plumbing inspections typically have less RDII in the system. Conversely, where there is token or no inspection (or self-regulation), systems tend to have a higher proportion of "expedient" connections to the public sewer and poorly constructed house drains.

Finally, the location and extent of stormwater drainage can affect collection system RDII. Good street and easement stormwater drains limit the need for illicit stormwater connections to the sanitary sewer. Areas that rely on open drainage ditches tend to have higher levels of RDII (Moody, 2001).

Operation & Maintenance History. A collection system's operation and maintenance history provides insight into system operations, including chronic problem areas, the nature of typical maintenance issues (such as roots, grease, and collapsed pipes), and typical pump station operational issues. Developing an understanding of system operations involves reviewing current maintenance practices, scheduled maintenance activities, past incidents, and customer-complaint records. Water research Centre (2000) suggests that:

> "Some of the tools used in this investigation can also be used for other parts of the study. For example, a hydraulic model may be used to establish the cause of sedimentation in a sewer, and a visual inspection using CCTV may be used to identify the cause of repeated blockages in sewers. The operations and maintenance investigation will therefore need to be coordinated closely with the hydraulic, environmental, and structural investigations."

Update System Inventory

Where existing records do not provide all of the information required for the study, it is necessary to set up a program to obtain details. The regional priority for investigation within each system, as established at the initial planning stage, indicates when the investigation phases are likely to begin and, hence, when the information will be required.

Information collection should be coordinated with any program for upgrading the general sewer records for the area. Because such a program is likely to be long term, it may be necessary to selectively upgrade records for certain sewers in advance of the general records upgrading to avoid delaying the collection system studies.

The following spatial data represent the minimum information that should be compiled during a collection system study:

- Basin topography, including watershed and sewershed boundaries
- Land use, land cover, and impervious cover
- Facility (such as pipes, manholes, pump stations, and regulators) and outfall locations
- Hydrologic features
- Demographic data (population, employment)
- Industrial user inventory
- Field screening of flow-monitoring locations

Requirements are developed for each data type, which may include

- Spatial range
- Temporal range
- Frequency of measurements
- Accuracy and precision

To a large extent, the data requirements for system characterization consist of the data requirements of the hydraulic sewer model selected.

Data Sources. The next step is to identify sources for each data requirement, as listed in Table 5.2 on page 144. In practice, data are obtained from multiple sources; for example, pipe materials, sizes, and inverts may be found in as-built drawings and work orders. A field survey may be required where data is missing, incomplete, or suspect.

Sources for data must be scrutinized for their suitability to the needs of the study. Any existing reports describing drainage areas, previous studies, or existing compilations of drawings should be reviewed and incorporated, where applicable. City and regional planning commissions are typically good sources for local spatial data (Water Environment Federation, 1999).

Identify Data Gaps. These historic data-processing and system-inventory-update efforts should include a gap analysis. A gap analysis identifies data sources and areas where further data collection is necessary. It includes determining where current activities can be improved through the collection of additional information that provides links to other sources of data in the information system. During this analysis, the need to collect sewer-attribute information outside of the model network is defined.

Quality Assurance/Quality Control (QA/QC). The initial phase of QA/QC involves developing and documenting workplace practices and methods for the collection and storage of system data. The Standard Operating Procedures (SOPs) developed during this phase help to ensure that future data are collected, purified, and stored effectively, and that the results of the study are accepted by regulatory agencies.

Collection System Condition Investigation

Any plan for detecting and correcting problems in existing wastewater collection systems must include field investigations. Regular inspection programs are conducted to determine current system conditions and to plan required maintenance and repairs.

Traditionally, systems experiencing problems with overflows and flooding have been required by regulatory agencies to perform a Sewer System Evaluation Survey (SSES) (American Society of Civil Engineers, 2004). These studies usually involve some combination of inspections, flow monitoring, CCTV studies, and modeling. The US Environmental Protection Agency (2004) has published a capacity management and operations and maintenance checklist to provide guidance for system assessments, and the American Public Works Association (2003) has published a guidebook for sewer system overflows. Additional information on collection system assessment may be found in Water Environment Federation (1994; 1999) and Read and Vickridge (1997).

Internal Condition Inspection. Physical inspection of the sewer pipes and manholes is often necessary to identify sources of RDII or flow monitoring/modeling anomalies. Investigations should target elements of the collection system with conflicting information, locations where field modifications have been made, and locations where information is lacking. Some of the problems found during these inspections include cross-connections between separate sewers and combined or storm sewers, connections to outfalls or storm lines by private developers, blockages causing unplanned diversions or flooding, and structural failures in areas of past collapses or areas of street or surface failure (WEF, 1999).

Manhole Location and Inspection. Sewer manholes can be important sources of infiltration through joints and cracks in their walls. Also, the manhole/pipe connection is a prime location for defective construction and the accompanying infiltration.

"Topside" inspections, which do not require confined-space entry, can be a cost-effective method for quickly identifying defects and infiltration sources in manholes. Cameras can also be lowered into the manhole, allowing photographing or videotaping of the inside of the inlet and outlet sewers to a distance of about 20 ft. This type of inspection is best conducted when the water table is high, making leaks more visible. Figure 11.1 shows a manhole with signs of infiltration, and Figure 11.2 shows roots growing into a manhole with a poorly constructed drop inlet on the left side. Note the roots below the inlet.

CCTV. Currently, the most frequently used and satisfactory method of sewer inspection is the use of *closed-circuit TV (CCTV)* cameras. The camera is pulled or crawls through sewers, continuously recording tape for later review or "before and after" comparisons. The person monitoring the camera's progress can record a running commentary on the tape.

The inspection should be slow enough that all features can be observed. Pan-and-tilt cameras are moved along the pipe only when the lens is pointing in the direction of the sewer's axis, as defects can otherwise be missed. If the camera is moved while the lens is turned to inspect a specific defect, it should later be returned to the point where the lens was first moved to obtain a normal (forward-looking) view of the same section of sewer.

CCTV is useful for finding roots, grease accumulation, collapsed pipes, sags, illegal taps in the main, and cracks, but not for identifying locations where sediment tends to be deposited (since the pipe is usually cleaned before inspection) or where illegal connections exist on customer property. Figure 11.3 shows partial blockage of a sewer by roots.

An interesting improvement in CCTV is *sewer scanning and evolution technology (SSET)*, which can produce a single image of a sewer reach, rather than a moving video.

Figure 11.1 Manhole with staining due to infiltration.

Figure 11.2 Manhole with roots.

Smoke Investigations. With smoke testing, smoke is introduced to the collection system to identify locations of physical defects and direct inflows. Smoke investigations are especially useful for finding illegal inflow to sanitary sewer systems; for example, smoke is emitted from the rain gutters of properties having connected roof drains. Similarly, smoke rises from pervious surfaces overlying defective lateral connections that may be contributing to excessive infiltration in the sewer system. Prior to

Figure 11.3 Partial blockage of a sewer by roots.

conducting a smoke investigation, local residents, as well as emergency responders, should be notified. Smoke testing is best performed when the water table is low.

Figure 11.4 shows a blower used to force smoke into a manhole. The smoke rises out of the sewer through any opening that can allow inflow and infiltration into the sewer. Figure 11.5 shows smoke rising out of vents in the manhole covers, although smoke can also exit through roof leaders, catch basins, and building roof vents.

Alternative Investigative Technologies. Plug-and-weir techniques, also referred to as "flow isolation," can identify sewer segments with excessive flows due to I/I. The upstream end of a sewer reach is blocked while the downstream flow is measured with a weir to look for inflows between the two locations. The sewer can only be blocked for a short time. Sharp-crested V-notch weirs, as shown in Figure 11.6, are usually employed for these measurements.

In separate systems with suspected problems, dye testing can identify anomalies if catch basins and downspouts are connected to the sanitary sewer system. Dye is introduced at the suspected inflow, and the downstream sanitary and storm lines are monitored to see if the dye appears.

Inspection of the Condition of Controls and Ancillary Structures

Field inspections should be conducted for all hydraulic control facilities, including

- Pump stations
- Siphons
- Regulators and flow diversions
- Overflows
- Outfalls.

Figure 11.4 Blower forcing smoke into an open manhole.

Figure 11.5 Smoke escaping through manhole covers during a smoke test.

Figure 11.6 Sharp-crested V-notch weir inserted into a gravity sewer.

Considering that most CSO and SSO abatement technologies are centered around maximizing the use of existing collection and treatment facilities, verification of their actual hydraulic performance is often a good idea. In particular, the operability of these facilities under high flow and surcharge should be evaluated. Qualitative data, such as photographs of an outfall during an overflow event, as well as quantitative information (geometry, pipe and pump sizes, etc.) should be recorded.

11.3 Hydraulic Investigations

The hydraulic investigation establishes the actual performance of the system as well as any upgrading requirements. It often involves comparing the system's actual performance with that predicted by the model. In some cases, it may be appropriate to concentrate the investigation on those parts of the system where detailed information is required, reducing the scale of the investigation in other parts of the system. The hydraulic investigation involves the following four steps:

1. Collect field data
   - Flow/rainfall monitoring
   - Pump station testing
   - Overflow monitoring
   - Delineation of areas with separate and combined sewers
   - Review of CCTV, smoke testing, flow monitoring, and related data
2. Analyze data
3. Build and verify hydraulic model
4. Assess hydraulic performance
   - Compare with performance criteria

- Identify hydraulic deficiencies
- Identify causes of deficiencies
- Analyze corrective measures based on hydraulic performance and cost.

The aim of this investigation is to study the hydraulic performance of the system and to identify the locations and causes of any substandard performance. Examples of unacceptable performance include

- Flooding of buildings or open spaces
- Nonpermitted discharges to receiving waters
- Frequent surcharging of flows in sewers
- Flow conditions leading to a buildup of sediments.

The main elements of the investigation are developing a verified hydraulic model of the existing system and assessing its hydraulic performance under existing, design, and future conditions.

Field Data Collection

Field investigations provide the primary means for determining the operational status and condition of the collection system. While the data-collection effort described in Section 11.2 provides insight into how the system was designed to work, field data collection reveals how the system actually works.

Precipitation-measurement and flow-monitoring techniques have been commonly applied to wastewater collection systems and are useful for characterizing system conveyance. Analysis of the data collected can provide an overall assessment of the system's physical condition. Chapter 8 described in detail the techniques and equipment available for quantifying flow rates in combined or separate sanitary sewer systems. This section briefly describes some analytical procedures that can be applied to the flow data to characterize wastewater system response to dry weather and wet weather conditions.

Analysis of flow-monitoring data requires a continuous data stream to determine flow volumes. Intermittent data loss creates gaps in the time series and thus prevents accurate determination of flow volumes. The flow and rainfall data for each monitor should be reviewed during the monitoring period to assess the completeness of the data.

Because every storm is unique, data loss during wet weather periods is of much greater significance than dry weather data loss. Unfortunately, data loss generally increases during storm events due to factors such as

- Surcharging due to downstream constriction, resulting in flow velocities below the range of the velocity sensor
- Fouling or damage of the sensors located in the sewer flow
- Sensor malfunction or installation instability
- Loss of power.

A further complication occurs when the loss of data from one site affects not only the upstream catchment, but also the analysis of flows generated in the catchment immediately downstream. If backwater conditions are not occurring, it is possible to reconstruct depth or velocity measurements if one of those signals is lost, as discussed in Chapter 9.

A final point to consider in the analysis of flow-monitoring data is that, even under ideal conditions, a flow monitor provides accuracy in the range of ±10–20 percent. The comparison of upstream and downstream monitors will be skewed if the upstream monitors record flows a few percent higher than the actual value, while the downstream monitor records flows a few percent lower, or vice versa.

Data Analysis

As described in Chapter 7, wastewater flow hydrographs can be characterized by three components:

- Groundwater infiltration (GWI)
- Base wastewater flow (BWF)
- Rainfall-dependent inflow and infiltration (RDII).

Dry weather flows (BWF + GWI) at a particular site can be estimated by analyzing both the flow-monitor record and the rainfall record. Flow hydrographs and rainfall hyetographs are plotted together for each monitoring location and reviewed to select the periods free from rainfall. Weekdays from this selection set are then combined and averaged to produce a representative weekday diurnal pattern and estimates of the average, maximum, and minimum dry weather flows. The same procedure is implemented for weekend days. Procedures for separately quantifying GWI and BWF are described in detail in Section 9.2. Figure 11.7 displays typical weekday and weekend average diurnal flow patterns.

After the base sanitary flow and groundwater components of the hydrograph have been determined, the rainfall-dependent portion of the hydrograph can be estimated. Figure 11.8 is an example of how an RDII hydrograph is computed. The uppermost hydrograph is the total storm flow as taken from flow monitor data, with the total storm volume (area under the hydrograph) given in the legend in millions of gallons. The average dry weather flow hydrograph (the lowest hydrograph shown) has been superimposed onto this period of wet weather flow. The middle hydrograph represents the RDII for this storm event and was obtained by subtracting the average dry weather hydrograph from the total storm flow.

Once this cursory dry and wet weather analysis has been performed, the flow-monitoring data can be further summarized to assist in the characterization of the collection system response. The following statistics can be computed from the monitoring data (at least three monitored storm events should be used):

- *RDII volumes for each flow-monitored basin.* This includes the total monitored RDII volume (storm volume minus dry weather flow volume) for the storms selected for analysis, as well as the incremental RDII volumes. Incremental volumes represent the RDII volume contributed by the tributary area between the upstream meter(s) and the downstream meter. RDII volumes are calculated by numerical integration of the flow data.

- *RDII percentages.* RDII percentages represent the portion of the total rainfall that entered the sewer system as inflow/infiltration. It is computed by dividing the estimated RDII volume by the recorded rainfall volume for a

Section 11.3 Hydraulic Investigations 387

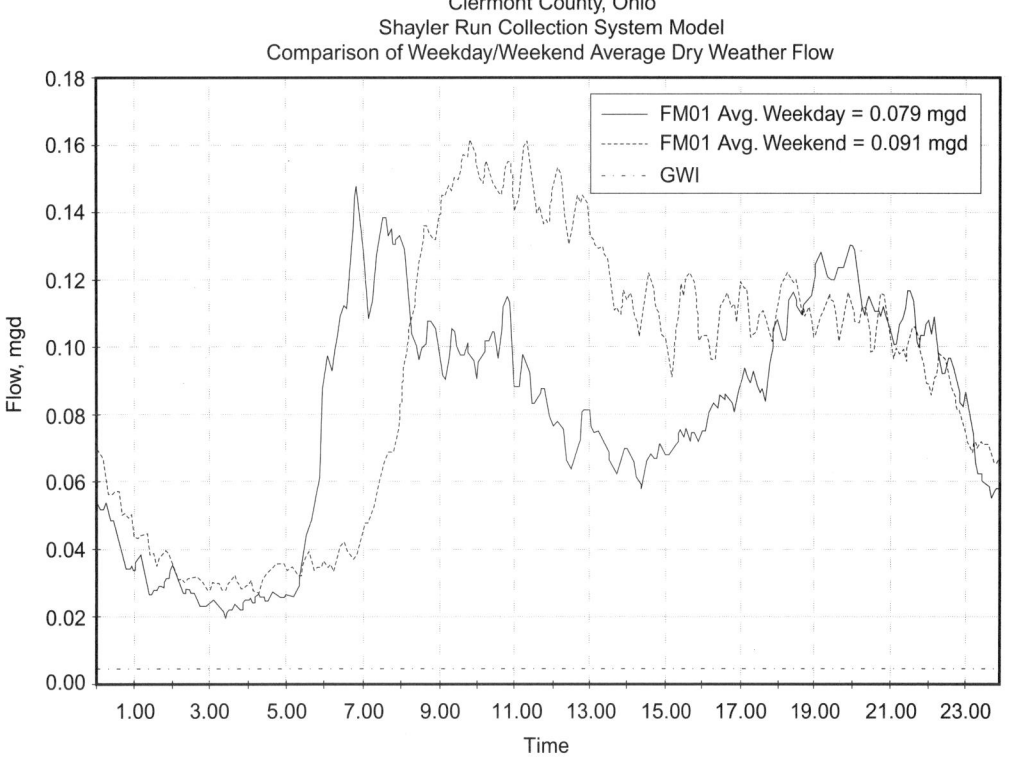

Figure 11.7 Typical weekday and weekend flow patterns.

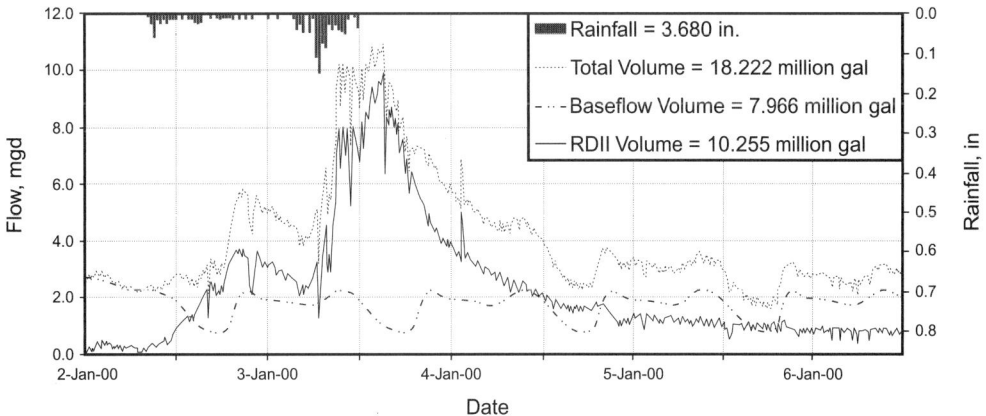

Figure 11.8 Typical RDII analysis hydrograph.

particular monitoring basin. This percentage, which is discussed in more detail in Chapters 7 and 9, is often referred to as the *R*-factor. It is given by (Wright et al., 2001)

$$R = \frac{V_{RDII}}{V_{rain}} \times 100\% \qquad (11.1)$$

where V_{RDII} = volume of RDII (ft³, m³)
V_{rain} = volume of rainfall (ft³, m³)

This normalization of RDII volume using *R*-factors provides a better way of comparing monitored basins. A high *R*-value in a sanitary system indicates that there is a good deal of potential for reducing RDII through field activities to detect and remedy I/I sources. Some use a value on the order of 7 percent as a cutoff for deciding if a basin is a candidate for I/I reduction, but such values are site specific.

R is often expressed as a decimal fraction rather than a percentage. In this form, *R* is analogous to the rational method runoff coefficient in a combined system, and thus is typically used to determine initial percent-impervious values for the model subcatchments.

In order to further assess the sources of RDII, variants of *R* may be calculated as follows:

- *Peak R* – the highest RDII percentage from an individual storm monitored at a particular meter
- *Total R* – the RDII percentage calculated from the total RDII volume over the selected storms
- *Incremental R* – the RDII percentage over the analyzed storms allocated to the tributary area between the upstream meter(s) and the downstream meter.

Additional ratios that may be developed from monitoring data include:

- *Peak flow/average DWF ratio* – instantaneous wet weather peak flow divided by the average daily dry weather flow.
- *Peak depth/diameter ratio* – instantaneous peak wet weather depth divided by the pipe diameter at the flow-monitor location (d_{max}/D).

Peak depth/diameter ratios and peak flow/average DWF ratios help to identify basins with potential capacity problems and basins which may have inflow sources contributing excess wet weather flow to the collection system. Peak flow/average DWF ratios greater than about 4 in a separate sanitary sewer system can indicate significant inflow sources in the monitored basin. Peak depth/diameter ratios greater than 1 indicate that the pipes at the flow-monitoring location are surcharged and capacity problems may exist.

Note that peak ratios for flow and depth in combined systems are much higher than those in separate sanitary sewers. For example, peak flow/average DWF ratios of 10 or higher are not uncommon in combined systems and generally can be conveyed without surcharging the sewer trunk system. In highly urbanized areas, combined system *R*-values can approach 100 percent.

The various indices can be somewhat misleading if an overflow occurs upstream of the measurement point. Overflows should be monitored, but this can be difficult if there are many unpermitted manhole overflows.

Figure 11.9 is a graphical display of typical flow-monitoring results showing R values by flow monitor subcatchment. This type of mapping is a powerful method of presenting statistics and analyzing flow-monitoring data. This particular map is also a good example of the data-loss difficulties that may be encountered with flow monitoring. Rigorous numerical analysis of flow-monitoring data requires a continuous data stream. Gaps in the time series due to intermittent data loss affect the analyses for both the upstream and downstream basins. The basins identified by the hatch pattern for "Data Loss" display this effect; R-values could not be determined due to anomalies encountered in the data monitoring.

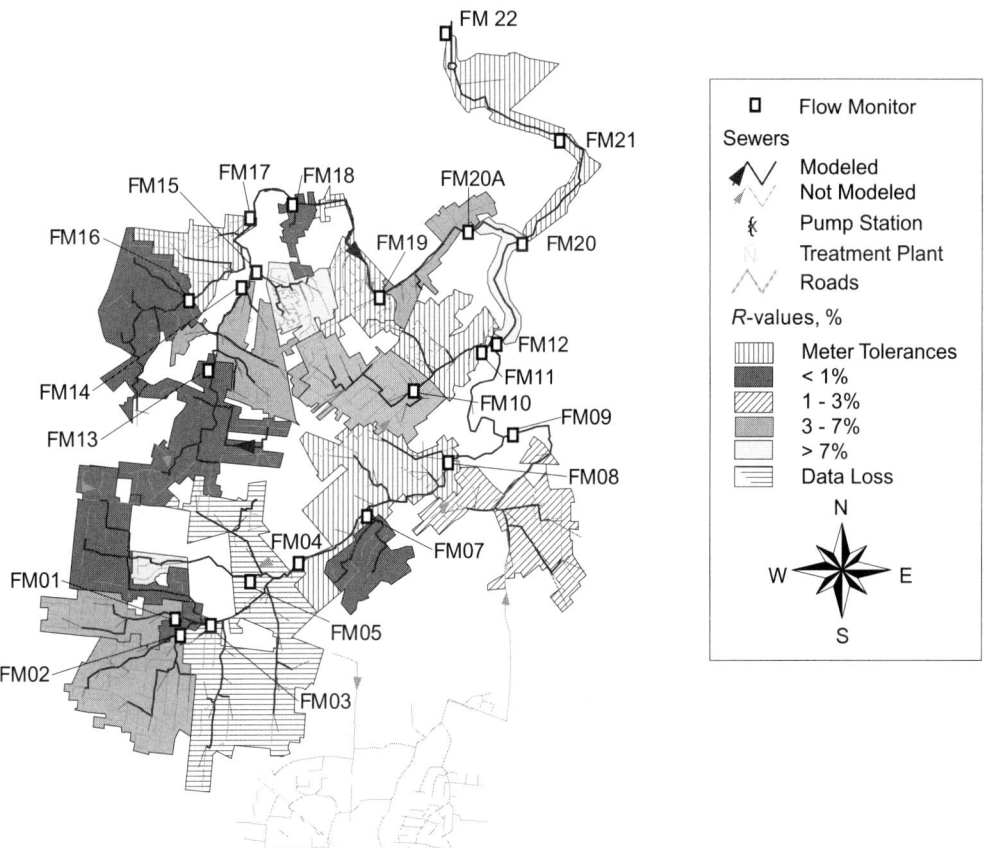

Figure 11.9 R-values in a collection network.

Note that the flow-monitoring statistics represent a static analysis of the collection system: they describe the collection system at fixed points (the flow monitor locations) and do not indicate the cause(s) of problem(s), or even if there is a problem within that monitored basin. The interpretation of these statistics is complicated by the interaction of the variables that affect the volume and rate of RDII entering a collection system. These variables include

- Infrastructure variables
  - Soil type and geology of the area
  - Age and construction of the sewer
  - Sewer material

- Storm event variables
  - Storm cell speed and direction
  - Antecedent moisture conditions
  - Intensity and duration of rainfall.

It is impossible to factor these variables into an RDII analysis based solely on flow-monitoring data. However, they can be evaluated to account for variability of the data and to develop a more informed assessment of the condition and operation of the collection system. Modeling provides the ability to extrapolate from field data to new situations.

RDII hydrographs and statistics can be used to determine initial model parameters for each subbasin (e.g., fraction of precipitation that enters the system for sanitary sewer systems; percent impervious surface for contributing areas in combined sewer systems). During the modeling phase, the RDII is further differentiated, and suitable factors are applied to simulate the shape of the response. The resulting robust, calibrated model can then be used to simulate the wet weather flows resulting from storms with characteristics similar to those of the monitored events. Chapter 9 discusses in more detail the specific steps for calibrating a model and developing RDII parameters.

Figure 11.10 presents the refined R-values for each subbasin, based on the calibrated sanitary sewer model, for the same sewershed shown in Figure 11.9. The hydraulic model was calibrated by adjusting R-values and other parameters so that the model predicts flows and depths similar to those recorded at the flow meters. As can be seen, the model calibration filled in the gaps where flow monitor data loss occurred. Model calibration also allowed the R-values to be refined for a number of subcatchments, leading to I/I percentages that are somewhat different from those developed using the flow-monitoring data alone.

Application of Hydraulic Modeling

The intended purpose of a model and the information required from it determine the type of model that is appropriate. Therefore, the objectives of the model must be defined at the outset. In general, the objectives are to

- Develop a model to accurately simulate the operation of the existing wastewater collection system and its ancillary structures
- Develop a model that will become an operational and planning tool. Specifically, the model will be used to assess the ability of the system to convey flows resulting from design events and to evaluate the performance of rehabilitation alternatives (discussed in Section 11.4).

Modeling projects are typically classified as either macroscale or microscale; this classification of models was described in Section 5.2. Macroscale models usually have specific objectives that could be either basinwide or more localized. Macroscale modeling efforts can provide the following:

- A simulation of the flows and conditions at one or more specific locations, such as a pumping station
- A simulation of the boundary conditions in trunk or interceptor sewers so that more detailed (microscale) models of connecting sewer systems can be modeled with, for instance, the correct tailwater conditions

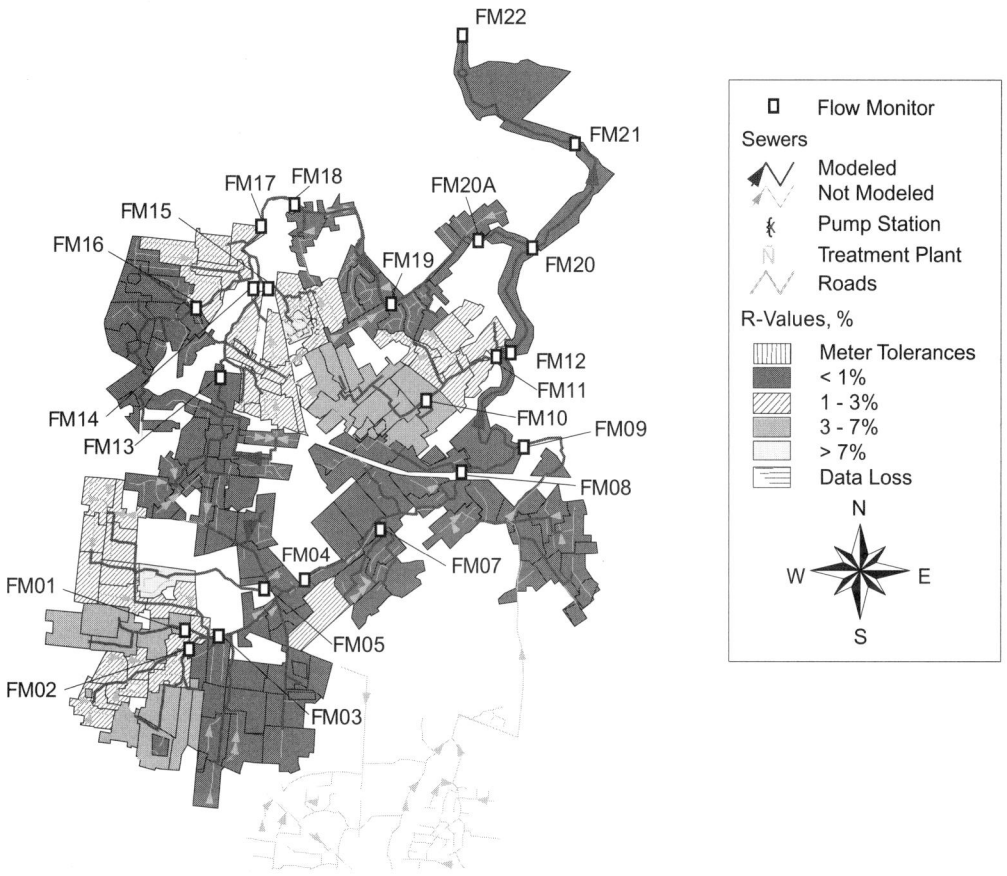

Figure 11.10 R values based on a calibrated model.

- A simple framework model of a network into which a detailed model can be incorporated, eliminating the need for boundary conditions

- An overall assessment of a whole basin

- An initial step in evaluating options for major changes in the collection system

- A quick means of gaining an understanding of the operation of specific sections of a sewer or ancillaries, or the downstream end of a large sewer system where there may be reverse flows or other phenomena that can be better quantified with modeling

- A reasonably accurate representation of a trunk or interceptor sewer system, without needing to exactly model the layout of the sewer systems that connect into them.

Macroscale models are characterized by considerable simplification, usually including only pipes larger than 15 or 18 inches in diameter. Due to their considerable simplification, macroscale models are not adequate for detailed modeling of flooding within a basin or for SSO mitigation in that basin, both of which require more detailed models (WAPUG, 1998).

Microscale models provide a detailed analysis of the problems within a specific drainage area, which may be a discrete catchment or part of a larger basin. The purposes of such models are primarily to

- Identify hydraulic problems within a drainage area, including identification of flooding areas, surcharged pipes, throttles, reverse flows, and combined sewer or sanitary sewer overflows and other ancillaries with poor performance
- Identify the need for possible hydraulic upgrading schemes and carry out initial appraisals
- Establish the hydraulic operation of sewer overflows and bypasses for a broad assessment of water quality problems
- Identify interactions of competing pump stations in complicated force mains to find bottlenecks and causes for wet well flooding
- Identify location and quantity of RDII.

A microscale model includes ancillary structures such as overflows, pump stations, and diversion structures, as well as known problem areas, particularly those with flooding and surcharge. The simplification of sewer networks for microscale models should be carried out carefully, with particular attention to low-lying manholes or gullies and the heads of branches. Microscale models generally extend well into the system, often including pipes smaller than 12 inches in diameter (WAPUG, 1998).

In an ideal situation, with data organized and management centralized through the application of GIS-based tools and interfaces, models can be constructed to any level of detail. Further, microscale models are frequently developed for specific investigations and integrated into macroscale models covering larger areas. For instance, problems and development pressures in certain basins may warrant modeling to a microlevel. If mitigation measures in these basins rely on interbasin transfers and overall system-capacity management, a macroscale model of the surrounding collection system is necessary to determine the downstream effects of any mitigation strategies.

Regardless of whether the model is macroscale or microscale, it must be calibrated and verified upon completion of the model-building phase. As described in Chapter 9, model calibration consists of adjusting drainage basin and collection system attributes within reasonable ranges to obtain simulated results that closely replicate actual field-monitored flows and depths for a set of monitored storm events. This process ensures that the representation of the collection system accurately predicts monitored flows and depths, as well as system performance under both long-term hydrologic conditions and design storms.

After model calibration, a series of historical storms are simulated to verify the hydraulic and hydrologic representation of the modeled system. The model results from these "blind" tests indicate whether the calibrated hydraulic and hydrologic parameters of the model provide a good representation of actual system performance. The verification process assesses whether the model retains its generality.

Once the model is sufficiently calibrated and verified, it is important to assess whether it can be used for the purpose it was intended. The following key questions should be addressed to assess the utility of calibrated models (Wallingford, 1998):

- Is the model detailed enough at the points of interest?
- Did the model operate correctly under surcharge if it is going to be used to assess the performance of the system under extreme events?

"I've always felt that my role as a beaver transcends any political changes at E.P.A."

- Did the overflow structures operate, or were the loads too low in that run?
- Are the modeled representations of the overflows suitable for the flows that will be applied?
- Did the pumping stations operate properly and as expected?
- Will the model have to be altered to allow for planned changes in the development area?
- Are there structures and/or situations that the model can not replicate?
- How much uncertainty is there in the runoff model?

At all stages of using a hydraulic model, it is important to be aware of any limitations and inaccuracies that might influence the quality and reliability of the simulation results. The accuracy of the model decreases as the severity of the rainfall increases for the following reasons (Water Research Centre, 2000):

- The model will usually be run using storms of significantly greater return periods than those for which it was calibrated and verified. With increasing storm severity, the model is moving further away from the range of data for which it was calibrated. As a result, the following can occur:
  - Unknown features of the sewer system may come into play, such as high-level overflows or cross-connections between storm and sanitary systems.
  - Due to slight inaccuracies in quantifying input parameters, errors of acceptable proportion at low flow rates may become much larger as the flow rate is increases.
  - At very high intensities of rainfall, the verified rainfall/runoff/pipe flow relationship may cease to apply. The difference often results from runoff contributions from additional sources when intensity increases. For example, flow can enter through cleanouts with missing caps once ponding becomes high enough, and illegally connected sump pumps may only activate during more intense rainfall events.
- Due to the complexity of sewer-flow behavior in surcharged conditions, the prediction of depth (and hence the onset and volume of flooding) cannot be

expected to be as accurate or consistent unless the model is sufficiently detailed and calibrated to a series of storms that *included* surcharge events.

- The increasing tendency for surcharge to be experienced in the subcatchments of the model, where the simplified modeling techniques are necessarily less effective in reflecting the true situation, will tend to distort the overall picture.

Despite the likely shortcomings of the model in predicting flooding associated with extreme storms, the model should be run for the wide range of storm frequencies described.

Assess Hydraulic Performance

Dry and wet weather calibration ensure that a model provides a robust platform to predict flow and surcharge depth for a variety of simulated conditions. The performance of the wastewater collection system can then be assessed using a series of design storms. For combined sewer systems, dry weather modeling can identify pipes with very low velocities that may require flushing to minimize odor problems. Models can also be used to identify locations likely to experience problems with dry weather overflow in either separate or combined systems.

To investigate the quantitative aspects of collection system performance, the model is run using design storms for a range of return periods to ascertain if and when each pipe length begins to surcharge and subsequently flood. The performance defined in this way can then be related to the criteria for *trigger* (rehabilitation action needed) and *target* (expected performance after rehabilitation) levels of performance and the deficiencies clearly identified.

Design storm durations should be selected to assess a variety of conditions. Short-duration, high-intensity storms, such as 1-hour storms, result in high peak inflows and are useful for highlighting local capacity issues. Long-duration storms, because of their large flow volumes, are better suited to applications such as trunk sewer planning and design, which tends to be more affected by flow volume than inflow rates. Usually, the time of concentration in a basin is a good indicator of the storm duration that is the most significant for design. Long-duration storms are also important for evaluating the performance of storage facilities and their effect on treatment plant loading.

The specific objectives in assessing the quantitative performance of a sewer system are

- To establish the return period of the storm event for which each pipe length of the model begins to surcharge

- To establish the return period of the storm event for which each pipe length begins to flood

- To establish the performance characteristics of ancillary structures in the sewer system that only operate fully for design events (that is, larger events than those used to assess water quality impacts)

- To assess health and environmental impacts by determining overflow volumes.

In some regions, an additional factor affecting system performance is runoff generated from snowmelt. Procedures used to model this component of RDII are presented in Section 7.7.

Figure 11.11 displays the results of a typical design storm analysis of a collection system. In this system, design storms ranging from a 2-month, 30-minute storm to a 10-year, 12-hour storm were run. For each storm simulation, the number of pipes with a predicted surcharge higher than 2 ft above the crown of the pipe is plotted in Figure 11.11a, and the number of pipes in which the maximum flow exceeded the design capacity is plotted in Figure 11.11b.

Figure 11.11a shows a consistent increase in the number of surcharged pipes in the system from the 2-month storm to the 5-year storm. The increase in surcharge from the 5-year storm to the 10-year storm is negligible (generally less than 10 percent). In fact, the 5-year, short-duration storms (30 min, 1 hr, and 3 hr) surcharge nearly the entire system. Approximately 540 of the 591 pipes are surcharged during a 5-year storm, and almost 550 of the 591 pipes during a 10-year storm. A similar conclusion can be drawn from the pipe-capacity graph in Figure 11.11b.

Further review of these graphs reveals that this collection system is most severely affected by the short-duration, intense storms. Peak surcharging typically occurs during the 3-hour storm, regardless of the return period of the storm. It appears that the system can convey peak flows associated with the lower-intensity 6-and 12-hour storms. Thus, the 5-year storm should be a reasonable cutoff for analysis and design of capacity-augmentation measures. This conclusion can change, however, once costs are assigned; for instance, the incremental cost of increased capacity going from, for example, a 5-year storm to a 10-year storm may be very small relative to the benefits received. Such situations may lead clients to select the larger design storm as a more conservative basis for design of systemwide improvements.

Capacity Analysis. One of the primary goals of hydraulic modeling is the assessment of the conveyance capacity of the collection system. Conveyance capacity can be assessed by looking at both simulated peak flows in comparison to design capacities and the extent of system surcharge. Model results typically provide peak flow rates for each pipe, from which comparisons such as peak-flow-to-design-flow ratios can be made. Surcharge depths are also reported, either as a node depth or as an HGL for each pipe. Figure 11.12 shows a typical graphical display of modeled peak-flow-to-pipe-capacity ratios. The dark line segments indicate pipes with peak flows predicted to be substantially higher than the existing pipe capacity. These areas need to be investigated for potential capacity augmentation measures, such as increased pipe size or relief pipe construction. The capacity investigation should be compared with RDII reduction strategies to develop a plan of action.

If the sewer capacity is adequate in the model but overflows or backups occur in actuality, blockages may be to blame. For example, sewers can be blocked by roots, lumber, sediment, or pipe collapses. Possible remedies are facility maintenance, rehabilitation, or replacement.

11.4 Evaluating Rehabilitation Strategies

Comprehensive sanitary sewer upgrade and SSO control plans are typically built on system operation and maintenance strategies for system optimization, with the goal of minimizing collection system overflows. Beyond optimizing the existing system, the primary methods for controlling overflows from the sanitary collection system include augmentating capacity, providing storage, and implementing cost-effective I/I

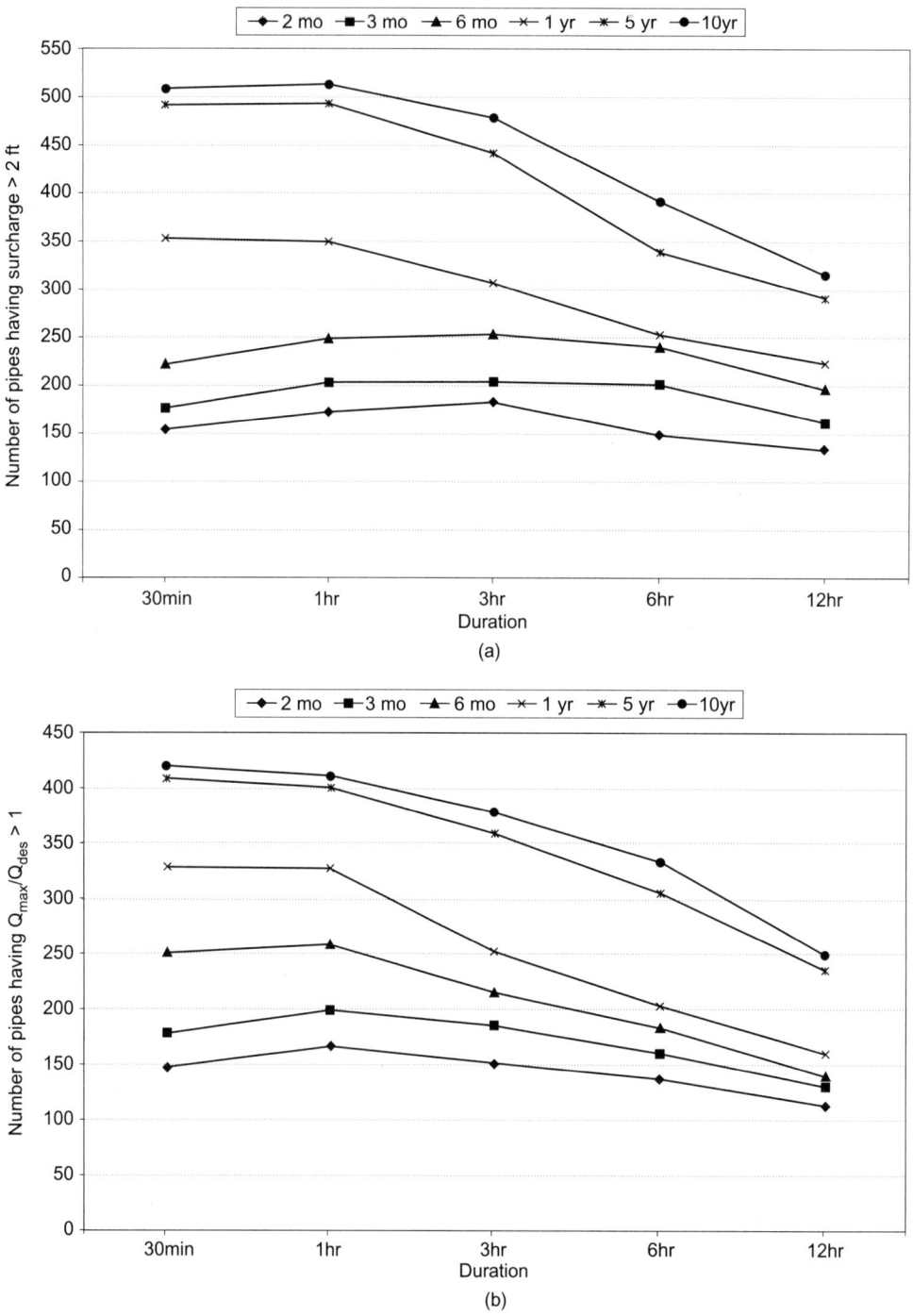

Figure 11.11 Capacity analysis of a sewer system.

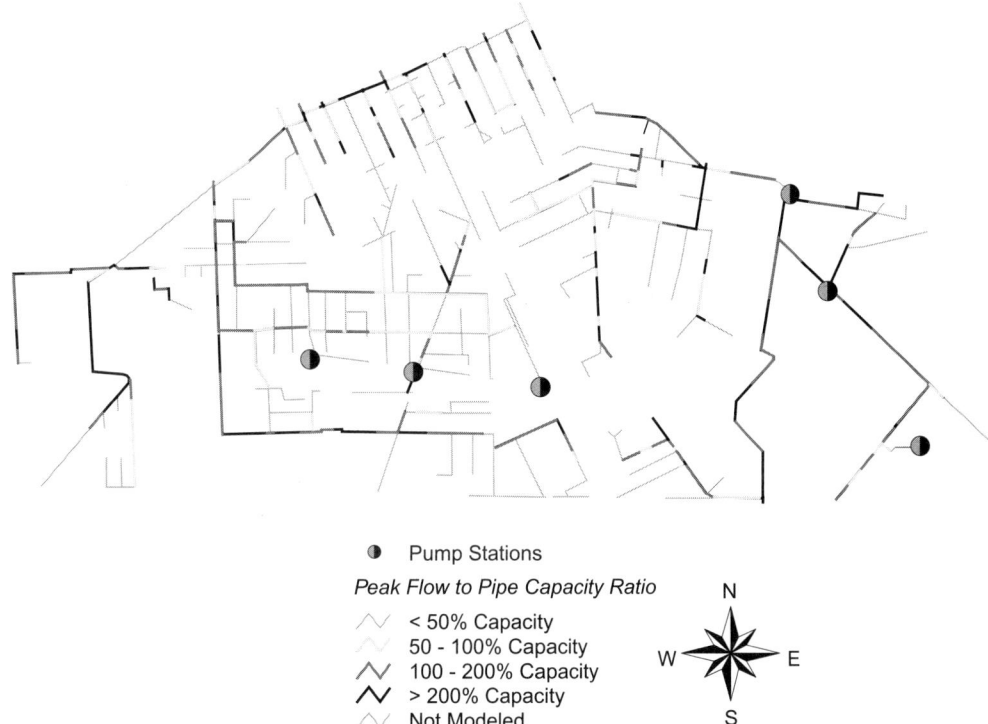

Figure 11.12 Collection system capacity analysis: peak-flow-to-pipe-capacity ratios for a 10-year, 6-hour design storm.

reduction measures. Wet weather treatment facilities may also be looked at as part of an overall watershed/water-quality-based program.

Figure 11.13 illustrates the recommended approach to developing strategies for controlling RDII and SSOs. Options falling within the categories near the bottom of the figure should be a greater component of mitigation measures. These low-cost, non-capital-intensive programs can be most effective in mitigating I/I.

The evaluation of rehabilitation options consists of three basic steps:

- Screening of options to eliminate those that are not appropriate or infeasible
- Evaluating in detail the options remaining after the screening process
- Selecting the most environmentally sound, cost-effective, and publicly acceptable option (i.e., "the recommended plan").

It is essential to understand the type of system for which options are being developed: combined, sanitary, or some combination. The type of system and related overflow types (CSOs or SSOs) will determine the applicable water quality objectives, regulatory compliance requirements, and potential mitigation approaches. Some control strategies, such as in-system storage, may be applicable to either type of system, while others may not. For example, sewer rehabilitation to reduce RDII can be a cost-effective way to prevent SSOs, but similar rehabilitation techniques would not typically be applied to a combined sewer system unless there were structural problems with the sewer (Water Environment Foundation, 1999).

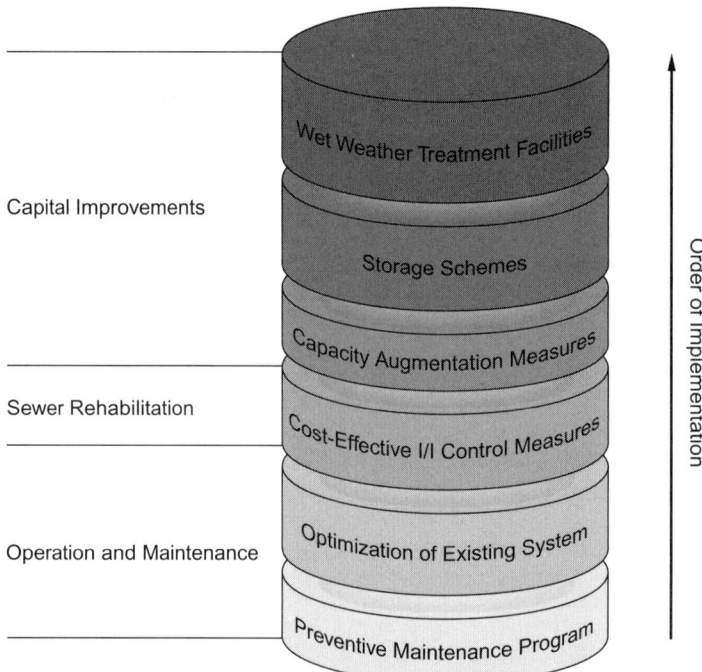

Figure 11.13 Strategies for mitigation of RDII and SSO.

For combined systems, mitigation options generally include
- Modification of sewer operations
- Storage of wet weather flow
- Use of realtime controls
- Treatment of overflows
- Blending of wet weather flows at treatment plant.

For sanitary-only systems (Field and O'Connor, 1997), the options usually include
- Removing RDII
- Cost-effective rehabilitation
- Inspection and maintenance of collection systems and pump stations to ensure proper operation
- Storage of wet weather flow
- Maximizing treatment plant capacity.

One or more sets of options should be developed that meet all the identified needs of the system. Further, in the United States, any solutions for I/I and SSO control must be analyzed within the context of the proposed CMOM regulations (see Chapter 15). Wherever possible, integrated solutions, which solve more than one problem, should be considered. For example, increased hydraulic capacity can be provided by replacing a sewer in poor condition with an upsized sewer, rather than paralleling another sewer in good condition.

The solutions considered should aim to satisfy the following criteria (Water Research Centre, 2000):

- Economy of direct costs
- Minimum disruption during construction
- Phasing of the solutions according to the priorities assigned to the problems.

These criteria are most readily met by retaining as much of the existing system as practicable. Maximize the use of existing assets by

- Using renovation in preference to replacement where there are structural problems
- Using flow-reduction or attenuation measures to relieve hydraulic overload, in preference to replacement or reinforcement (Water Research Centre, 2000).

The subsections that follow primarily discuss the analysis of structural control and treatment strategies such as sewer rehabilitation, sewer separation, and inflatable dams. Brief discussions of nonstructural strategies (public education, land use control, litter control) are also provided, with more detail available in Water Environment Foundation (1999), Moffa (1990), and Water Pollution Control Federation (1989).

Preventive Maintenance Program

In cases where the model predicts adequate capacity but field data indicate a lack of capacity (e.g., overflow and surcharging occur), the problem usually lies in a collapsed sewer, a sag filled with sediment, grease blockage, or root penetration. Some of these problems can be verified with CCTV. Preventive maintenance techniques such as flushing, high velocity cleaning, root cutting and, in some cases, replacement or lining, may eliminate overflows.

Source Controls

Source controls attempt to reduce the quantity of runoff entering the sewer system by reducing the runoff volume at the source (Water Environment Foundation, 1999). They range from nonstructural strategies involving relatively low-cost operational or functional modifications of existing facilities, to structurally intensive strategies involving substantial construction of new facilities. The effects of these measures can be simulated by altering coefficients in the hydrographs used to drive the models.

Low-cost alternatives may include *best management practices (BMPs)* such as

- Public education
- Erosion control
- Street cleaning
- Litter control
- Pesticide application control
- High-velocity cleaning and flushing
- Catch basin cleaning
- Land-use regulations.

"I can't decide whether to turn pro first or go directly into rehab."

These alternatives are somewhat effective but limited in attacking the source of stormwater pollution problems in combined systems. Industrial-waste pretreatment can reduce the pollution effects of overflows.

Structurally intensive alternatives include sewer separation in combined systems and infiltration control in separate sanitary systems. These controls are discussed in more detail in the sections that follow.

Sewer Separation

Separation is the conversion of a combined sewer system into separate stormwater and sanitary sewage collection systems. This alternative, historically considered the ultimate answer to CSO pollution control, has been reconsidered in recent years because of cost and the major disruptions to traffic and other daily community activities associated with separation. Although less hazardous than combined sewage, separate stormwater runoff still contains pollutants such as sediments, organic matter, bacteria, metals, oils, and floatables, which will be discharged to receiving waters.

Several potential benefits of sewer separation might warrant its consideration in specific cases, including the following:

- Eliminating CSOs and preventing untreated sanitary sewage from entering the receiving waters during wet weather periods. Sanitary sewage is a more objectionable source of some pollutants, such as TSS, sanitary floatables, and bacteria.

- Reducing the volume of flow to be treated at the wastewater treatment plant, thus reducing O&M costs by eliminating surface runoff inflows during wet weather periods.

- Reducing I/I to the wastewater treatment plant if new sanitary sewers are constructed to replace old combined sewers.

- Reducing upstream flooding and overflows in systems with undersized combined sewers that back up frequently during storms.

Combined sewer separation is generally more effective and economical than building treatment facilities for remote segments of a combined sewer system serving relatively small areas.

While sewer separation, which eliminates CSOs, will dramatically improve receiving water quality and treatment plant performance, separation alone may be insufficient to achieve water quality objectives unless accompanied by some form of stormwater control. Nonpoint-source modeling conducted following sewer separation as part of the Rouge River National Wet Weather Demonstration Project (Detroit, Michigan metropolitan area) demonstrated a reduction in total annual pollutant loadings when compared to previous conditions with no CSO controls. In general, the greatest reduction of annual pollutant loading occurs when CSO controls are integrated with stormwater controls (Cave, Harold, and Quasebarth, 1996).

The modeling of sewer separation can be tricky. Even though sewer separation effectively removes the intentional inflow component from the modeled system, the newly separated sewers still exhibit some wet weather response due to RDII. Further, the extent of the separation needs to be understood before developing the model, including

- How much area will be separate
- Where the separation occurs relative to the overflow and/or flow monitor
- Whether there will be a full separation that includes all house connections, roof leaders, and subdrains, or a partial separation that disconnects only road and/or parking lot surfaces from the combined system.

In the case of full separation, the modeler needs to convert combined sewer basins, represented by areas with percent impervious values, to sanitary sewer areas represented by a percent contribution analogous to the *R*-factor, or percentage of rainfall that enters the sewer as RDII.

Combined sewer separation is usually too big a job to be undertaken all at once. Instead, it is usually done one subbasin at a time, in conjunction with street repaving. The old combined sewer is usually kept as the storm sewer, and a new, watertight sanitary sewer is constructed. With the current emphasis on "daylighting" urban streams to restore them to their natural channels, funding may become available to separate sewers and restore natural channel flow.

Pipe Rehabilitation/Replacement

Rehabilitation of the system, including private laterals, can increase system carrying capacity and reduce I/I. The technologies include the following:

- Replacing a sewer with watertight pipe of the correct size
- Paralleling a sewer of inadequate capacity with a relief sewer
- Rehabilitating an existing sewer with one of several trenchless methods, which include
    - Inversion liners (cured-in-place soft liners)
    - Sliplining with thin-walled pipe
    - Pipe bursting (a mole breaks the old pipe and a new one is pulled in behind it).

Models are helpful for evaluating the expected performance of the rehabilitation and replacement options. They can accurately estimate the post-rehabilitation carrying capacity of the sewer, but are less accurate at calculating the post-rehabilitation I/I, as discussed in the following section. Models are excellent for finding answers to "what-if" questions. It is much less expensive to find, for instance, that a 12-in. (300-mm) pipe is too small in a model run than to install the pipe and find that it is inadequate.

In general, rehabilitation techniques are usually less expensive than installing new pipes, but they only work if the carrying capacity needs only a slight increase. If a major increase in capacity is needed, a relief sewer is usually less expensive. Replacement is usually only justified where there is a combination of structural and hydraulic problems. Models are especially useful for evaluating these site-specific alternatives.

Inflow/Infiltration Control

RDII control practices restrict the rate and/or volume of stormwater runoff entering the combined or separate sanitary sewer system. Both infiltration of groundwater into a sewer system and direct inflow of surface stormwater runoff can significantly influence the magnitude and frequency of CSOs and SSOs, along with the size and cost of control technologies. Reducing the quantity of RDII makes additional system capacity available to contain wet weather flows and reduces the magnitude and frequency of the CSOs and SSOs reaching receiving waters.

Typical RDII control practices are

- *Groundwater infiltration control* – Sources of infiltration include groundwater entering the collection system through defective pipe joints, cracked or broken pipes, manholes, footing drains, and springs. Infiltration flow rates tend to be relatively constant and do not affect peak flow as much as indirect inflows. Infiltration problems are usually not isolated and often reflect more general sewer system deterioration. Extensive sewer rehabilitation is often needed to remove infiltration effectively. The rehabilitation effort often must include house laterals, which are normally a significant infiltration source. Infiltration control generally reduces overflows to a lesser extent than control of wet weather inflow.

- *RDII control* – Combined sewer systems were designed to effectively drain stormwater and convey sanitary sewage. For a large percentage of storm events, the runoff flows are much greater than sanitary flows in the combined system. CSO control efforts can be assisted by diverting some of the surface runoff inflow to an alternate surface drainage system or to groundwater via infiltration devices, or by retarding the rate at which these flows are permitted to enter the system. Inflow control in separate systems usually involves identifying and eliminating discharge from catch basins, roof leaders, and sump pumps.

These points highlight the importance of separating groundwater infiltration from RDII during the modeling analysis. Other flow-control practices are described by Water Pollution Control Federation (1989).

The implementation (retrofit) of combined-system RDII controls in developed areas on the scale necessary to substantially control CSOs is difficult and may be impractical. Flow-control techniques, however, may be useful and practical for addressing problems in specific portions of an overall system. Control measures that avoid increasing stormwater flows in a combined system are most effectively implemented in areas currently being developed, where their use can be required as a condition for development or reconstruction. Examples of control measures include porous pavement for parking surfaces, "green roofs" (planting of grasses and plants on roofs to absorb rainfall), and rain barrels or cisterns that capture rainfall for subsequent use in watering gardens.

For the long-term resolution of wet weather overflows in sanitary systems, however, the first option to investigate is preventing water from entering the system. To achieve this aim, it is necessary to investigate the sources of RDII entering the system, and then implement a program of rehabilitation and remediation works to prevent the ingress of stormwater into the system. The effectiveness of large-scale I/I reduction on sewer overflows is highly variable. In one study, Montgomery Watson (1998) found that large-scale RDII problems (e.g., large SSOs or impacts on wastewater treatment plants) could not be effectively controlled by upstream sewer rehabilitation projects. A problem potentially encountered with rehabilitation projects is that of "chasing infiltration," where eliminating one defect raises the water table and thus the amount of infiltration at another defect.

Others argue that such projects are cost-effective and point to studies such as those done in done in the US in Johnson County, KS; Nashville, TN; Oklahoma City, OK; and Fairfax County, VA. The probability of success depends to a great extent on the local conditions. The Johnson County study (US Environmental Protection Agency, 1999) focuses primarily on private laterals and reduced inflow from a 10-year, 1-hour storm from 494 to 214 mgd (1857 to 804 ML/d). In Oklahoma City, a comprehensive program of maintenance and sewer line replacement reduced customer backup complaints from 173 in 1983 to 20 in 2000 (US Environmental Protection Agency, 2001). In Fairfax County (US Environmental Protection Agency, 2002), the goal was to decrease wet weather flows to the Alexandria Sewage Authority treatment plant from 85 to 65 mgd (320 to 244 ML/d). With the exception of one hurricane, flow has not exceeded 50 mgd (188 ML/d).

There has been much debate on the most effective way to document the effects of sanitary sewer rehabilitation activities in reducing RDII. Review of the literature and collected agency questionnaires indicates the following general methodologies for prediction of RDII reduction (Lukas et al., 2001):

- *Local experience* – The determination of expected flow removal should be based on results from pilot studies or full-scale rehabilitation projects. However, the reliability of local experience depends on the accuracy with which the results are measured.

- *Assignment of RDII rates to observed defects* – This method assigns flow rates (either by direct observation or from an experiential database) to defects observed in CCTV or smoke-testing investigations. Predictions are made by calculating the remaining RDII assuming that all or a portion of these defects are eliminated. This methodology depends on a database of experience, but it can overestimate expected benefits if infiltration migrates to another defect.

- *Assignment of a quantity of RDII removed by rehabilitation of a specific component of the sewerage system* – In this method, a removal amount is assigned for a specific component type. For example, the quantity of RDII assigned by engineering calculation for rehabilitation of a manhole is X gpm. Removal attributed to manhole rehabilitation is then the product of the assigned rate X and the number of manholes to be rehabilitated. The weaknesses of this method are the potential for overly optimistic calculation of the rate assigned to each component and the assumption that each item is a similar RDII contributor.

- *Estimation of removal based on simulation models* – In this method, a hydrologic model is constructed, including parameters intended to estimate infiltration and/or inflow. Reduction of these parameters in the model is used to estimate the results of rehabilitation. This method is only as accurate as the conclusions drawn about the source of RDII. For example, consider the case where the modeler assumes that most of the I/I occurs through manhole lids and therefore estimates that there will be a dramatic decrease in I/I with lid inserts. If the real source of I/I in that system is a catch basin connected to the sanitary sewer, the model would seriously overestimate the reduction in flow.

- *Assignment of an RDII rate after project implementation* – In this method, a base rate of RDII is assumed after rehabilitation. The base rate is typically a result of local experience or pilot programs where pre- and post-rehabilitation flows are measured. For example, one city assigned a remaining RDII rate of 5000 gpd for a two-year storm after completion of "limited comprehensive rehabilitation." Analysis of several projects may yield a range of expectations.

Another approach is to perform statistical analyses on peak flows predicted from continuous model simulations. This type of analysis is performed with a model calibrated to pre-rehabilitation (existing) conditions and with parameters estimated for post-rehabilitation conditions. A series of storms can be applied to each model (pre- and post-rehabilitation) in order to generate predicted peak flows and volumes on each system. With sufficient model runs, it may be possible to fit a smooth regression line to the relationship between return period and flow to simplify comparisons of the pre- and post-rehabilitation conditions shown in Figure 11.14. It is important to monitor the collection system after the rehabilitation has been completed, with these data used to recalibrate the hydraulic or hydrologic model.

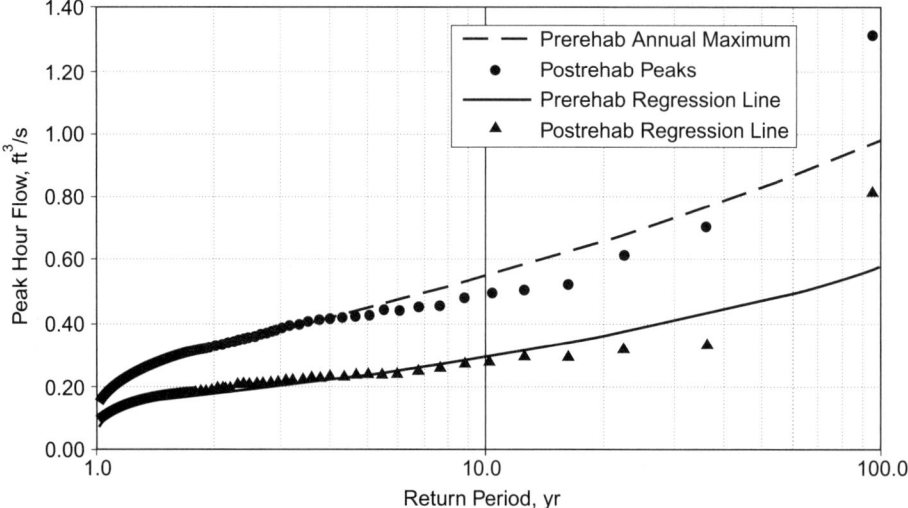

Figure 11.14 Return periods for peak flows under pre- and postrehabilitation conditions.

Interbasin Transfers

Interbasin transfers convey excess flows from one collection system or treatment plant service area to another via either a new gravity sewer, a conveyance tunnel (discussed in more detail in the storage section below), or a pump station. These transfers can be used all the time or only during peak wet weather conditions. A calibrated hydraulic model that is fully integrated with the entire service area can be a useful tool for determining the most effective methods and conveyance routes. Real-time control modeling, discussed in more detail in the next subsection, can be used to determine appropriate operational algorithms for pumps, gates, and other structures that control flows between basins.

The modeling of interbasin transfers begins with an analysis of the existing system with a calibrated model. This analysis identifies the locations and areas with limited capacity where diversion to another system may be viable. Initially, the analysis consists of simply adding an outfall pipe to the model at the selected location, with the elevation of the pipe set at the critical elevation above which the transfer is activated. This configuration provides the initial estimate of the peak flow for sizing the pump station or gravity sewer that will be used to convey the excess flows. The model can then be used to determine the operating scheme for the diversion and the effect of the increased flows on the downstream system to which it will discharge.

Real-Time Controls

A real-time control (RTC) system can be used to manage the wastewater collection system. A collection system is controlled in realtime if flows within the system are governed by movable regulators that operate based on the behavior of the system, either at the regulator site or at a group of sites. In contrast with traditional static systems having fixed control structures, RTC systems can actively manage flows (Wallingford, 1998).

The city of Seattle uses real-time control modeling to operate its system of combined-sewer regulators (Speer et al., 1992). The city of Philadelphia used RTC modeling to design the operation of an inflatable dam system. A real-time control system enabled maximum utilization of the storage available within the combined sewer network of the regional municipality of Hamilton-Wentworth (Canada) and helped reduce the frequency and volume of combined sewer overflows. This system was developed with sophisticated RTC elements in conjunction with detailed hydraulic and hydrologic modeling (Stirrup, Vitasovic, and Strand, 1997).

RTC systems require continuous data collection of system-flow and rainfall characteristics. Data are transferred to a central location, where decisions are made about operation of regulators, pump stations, or other control elements, based on the current and anticipated states of the entire system.

Although RTC potentially offers considerable advantages over a passive system, there are several limitations in applying it successfully (Wallingford, 1998):

- *Regulatory* – RTC may present some problems to regulators, in that the operators have more freedom than they do in passive systems. This type of operation means that the regulatory agency must agree to control rules rather than relying on the hydraulics of a structure to achieve a certain performance. Once control rules are agreed upon, a stringent set of monitoring procedures must be put in place to prove that the agreed-on control rules were actually being implemented in the event of a failure.

- *Technical* – RTC requires monitoring information so that decisions to be made in "real-time." There is always some risk that monitoring systems can fail or report incorrect values. Further, the system as a whole (theoretically the total interaction among the sewers, treatment plants, and receiving waters) must be properly understood in order to predict that the effects of any action will be beneficial. RTC is made more complex by the need for different operating rules to achieve different ends, such as dealing with dry weather conditions, pollution effects, or flooding. Decisions must be made about which set of rules apply at any given time. A great deal of knowledge of the system must be available to decision-makers, necessitating the implementation of some form of SCADA (supervisory control and data acquisition) system if RTC is to form a significant part of the strategy for running a network.

- *Investment* – Investment is needed to provide a safe and efficient method of running the system. It is also necessary for training and integrating the operators to run a more complex system. Finally, investment is necessary to provide the control systems and telemetry and to cover the long-term costs of operating an RTC system.

The modeling process involves creating an RTC file containing rules, logic statements, and parameters that control the operation of the structures according to the sequence of rules specified by the modeler. There are several models available that can handle RTC systems.

Storage Facilities

Because of the variability and high flow rates associated with wet weather flows in collection systems, storage facilities become important control alternatives. These facilities capture and store wet weather flows in excess of the downstream system capacity, releasing the water back into the system when capacity becomes available. The construction of storage high in a system that experiences flooding can obviate the need for extensive trunk-main augmentation and treatment-plant expansion.

Storage can be configured as either an in-line or off-line facility. Alternatives to traditional storage facilities include deep tunnels and wet weather treatment facilities. This section briefly describes each of these storage options, along with modeling procedures for analyzing storage facilities.

In-Line Storage. *In-line storage* uses the existing volume of primary combined or sanitary sewer trunks and interceptors available during storm events to temporarily store the flow generated by a wet weather event. The stored flow is later released at a controlled rate when interceptor conveyance and treatment capacity become available. In its most basic arrangement, in-line storage can be implemented through the construction of oversized pipes with some form of flow restriction on the downstream end. Such a facility can be emptied according to the available downstream capacity. Sewers with a relatively flat slope actually perform some of this function automatically.

Off-Line Storage. *Off-line storage* consists of tanks and tunnels connected to the sewer system that start filling when the water reaches a trigger level. These tanks then empty when downstream capacity becomes available. The flow into the tank is usually controlled by an overflow device incorporated into a diversion structure. Stored flows return to the system either by gravity (where the site allows) or by pumping. While there is often a reluctance to accept the need for pumping, it does offer the advantage of flexibility in facility location and control options.

Tunnels. An alternative method of providing significant off-line storage in congested urban areas is the mining of tunnels or reservoirs in bedrock (deep-tunnel storage). Deep tunnels combine both conveyance upgrades and storage requirements. During dry weather, the tunnel can transfer flow from an overloaded service basin to a less-taxed basin, while during wet weather the tunnel can provide storage for flows in excess of treatment plant capacity. Chicago and Milwaukee are two examples of systems with deep-tunnel storage.

Rapid filling of deep tunnels can result in significant oscillations in water levels in drop shafts to the extent that overflows may occur due to hydraulic transients. Such situations must to be modeled using specialized transient analysis software that can solve for mass oscillations.

Modeling System Storage. The modeling of system storage begins with an analysis of the existing system using a calibrated model. This analysis identifies the locations and areas of concern where storage may be viable. Initially, a storage analysis consists of simply adding an outfall pipe to the model at the selected location, with the elevation of the pipe set at the critical elevation above which the storage is activated. The flow through that pipe provides the initial estimate of the volume for which the tank should be sized.

Storage facilities have the effect of reducing the sewer hydrograph peak flow. Hydraulic models provide a way to evaluate this reduction. A large storage facility can essentially eliminate overflows, while a small facility only eliminates overflows for smaller events. Different sizes and configurations of facilities can be modeled until the dimensions of a cost-effective storage basin are determined. The facility can then be simulated for a variety of storms to determine the frequency of overflows.

After the storage volume has been determined, the hydraulic model can be used to simulate the filling, storage, and emptying cycles for wet-weather design events. Figure 11.15 is a schematic of a typical model configuration for a simple off-line storage tank with gravity inflow to fill the tank and a pump to drain the tank after the wet weather event. The system topography, the location of the tank, and whether the tank is above or below ground will determine whether the tank is emptied by a gravity pipe or by a pump. The storage tank itself can be simulated as a wet well or storage node used in conjunction with one or more pumps to model a pumping station. To simulate the operation rules, it is necessary to closely simulate both the flows and surcharge depths in the main sewer. RTC capabilities are particularly useful for this type of simulation.

Wet Weather Treatment Facilities

The US Environmental Protection Agency (Field, Sullivan, and Tafuri, 2004) has conducted a great deal of research oriented toward more management of overflows, as

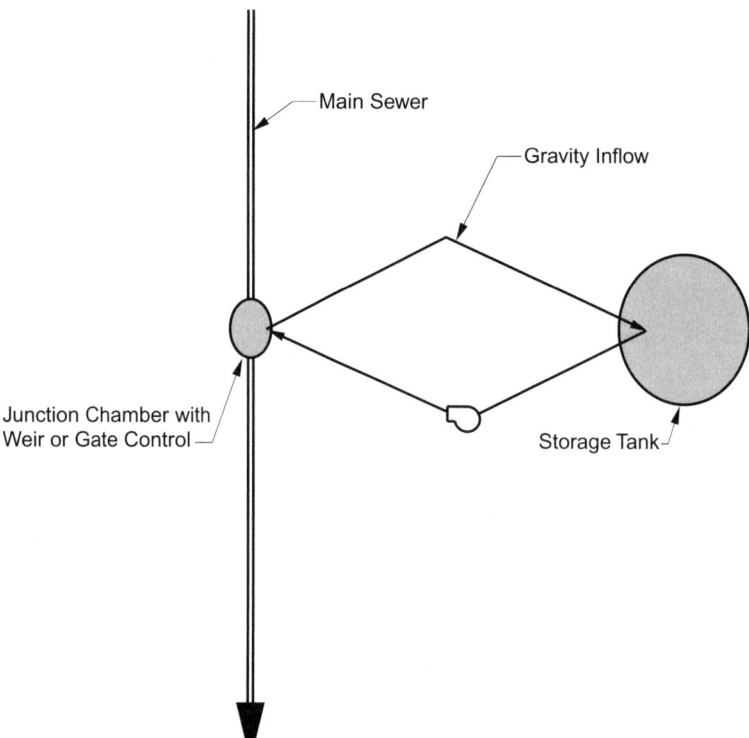

Figure 11.15 Flow diagram of an off-line storage system.

opposed to their elimination. An alternative to traditional storage or deep tunnels is a wet weather treatment facility, with disinfection as minimum treatment.

A wet weather facility provides storage and a primary level of treatment for excess flows that would otherwise be discharged through an SSO or CSO without treatment. Wet weather treatment facilities can be installed at overflow locations or as part of the wastewater treatment plant. The location depends on land availability and the capacity of the collection system to transport wet weather flows to the central plant.

Wet weather treatment facilities installed at overflow locations should have sufficient storage capacity to capture and return excess flows to the system for most wet weather events. For large, infrequent events, the facilities provide primary treatment for sewage before it is discharged into adjacent waterways. The treatment generally consists of some combination of screening, primary sedimentation, and disinfection, with no biological or advanced treatment.

Even if the system capacity is such that wet weather flows can reach the treatment facility without overflows, these flows can still be problematic. Wet weather flows can hydraulically overload secondary treatment processes to the extent that it may take a long time for the process to recover from the upset. Bypassing of treatment units has generally not been allowed under US regulations. Proposed changes to regulations allow excess flows to bypass secondary treatment processes under certain conditions. The bypassed flow undergoes primary treatment in wet weather treatment facilities, and is then blended back in with flow that has received secondary treatment (US Federal Register, 2003).

Even with primary treatment, wet weather treatment facilities still carry the stigma of discharging sewage into waterways and may not be acceptable to the public. Despite these concerns, wet weather treatment facilities have been permitted in Houston, TX, and Johnson County, KS.

References

American Public Works Association. 2003. *Preparing Sewer Overflow Response Plans: A Guidebook for Local Governments*. Kansas City: American Public Works Association.

American Society of Civil Engineers. 2004. "Sanitary sewer overflow solutions." Washington, DC: US Environmental Protection Agency. www.epa.gov/npds/pubs/sso_solutions_final_report.pdf.

Arbour, R. and K. Kerri. 1998. *Collection Systems: Methods for Evaluating and Improving Performance*. USEPA Grant No. CX924908-01-0. Sacramento, CA: California State University.

Association of Metropolitan Sewerage Agencies (AMSA). 1996. *Performance Measures for the National CSO Control Program*. Washington, DC: Association of Metropolitan Sewerage Agencies.

Cave, K., E. Harold, and T. Quasebarth. 1996. *Preliminary Pollution Loading Projections for Rouge River Watershed and Interim Nonpoint Source Pollution Control Plan*, RPO-NPS-TR07.00. Detroit, MI: Rouge River National Wet Weather Demonstration Program

Field, R., and T. P. O'Connor. 1997. Control strategy for storm-generating sanitary sewer overflows. *Journal of Environmental Engineering*. 12391: 41.

Field, R., D. Sullivan, and A. N. Tafuri. 2004. *Management of Combined Sewer Overflows*. Boca Raton: Lewis Publishers.

HR Wallingford. 1998. *The Wallingford Procedure: Volume 2 Practical Application of the Wallingford Procedure*. Wallingford, England: HR Wallingford.

Haestad Methods. 2001. *SewerCAD v5.0*. Waterbury, CT: Haestad Methods, Inc.

Harold, E. M. 2001. "System evaluation and capacity assurance." *Ecoletter* (Water and Waste Operators Association of Maryland, Delaware and the District of Columbia; and the Chesapeake Water Environment Association), Summer 2001.

Lukas, A., M. S. Merrill, R. Palmer, and N. Van Rheenan. 2001. Search of Valid I/I Removal Data: The Holy Grail of Sewer Rehab? *Conference Proceedings, Water Environment Federation 74th Annual Conference and Exposition*. Alexandria, VA. Water Environment Foundation.

Moffa, P. E. 1990. *Control and Treatment of Combined Sewer Overflows*. New York: Van Nostrand Reinhold.

Montgomery Watson. 1998. *City of Baton Rouge/Parish of East Baton Rouge Sanitary Sewer Overflow (SSO) Corrective Action Plan*. Baton Rouge, LA: City of Baton Rouge.

Moody, N. R. 2001. Water Environment Federation Collection Systems Technical Discussion. Group posting, October 2.

Read, G. F., and I. G. Vickridge. 1997. *Sewers – Rehabilitation and New Construction*. London: Arnold.

Speer, E., R. Swarner, Z. Vitasovic, M. S. Gelormino, and N. L. Ricker. 1992. Real-time control for CSO reduction. Paper presented at Water Environment Federation Conference, New Orleans, LA.

Stirrup, M., Z. Vitasovic, and E. Strand. 1997. Real-Time Control of Combined Sewer Overflows in Hamilton-Wentworth Region. *Water Quality Research Journal of Canada* 32, No. 1: 155–168.

US Environmental Protection Agency. 1999. Private Inflow/Infiltration source control program helps reduce SSOs. Washington, DC: US Environmental Protection Agency Fact Sheet.

US Environmental Protection Agency. 2001. Affordable large scale sewer line replacement. Washington, DC: US Environmental Protection Agency Fact Sheet.

US Environmental Protection Agency. 2002. Implementing Integrated CMOM. Washington, DC: US Environmental Protection Agency Fact Sheet.

US Environmental Protection Agency. 2004. CMOM Program Self Assessment Checklist. US Environmental Protection Agency. www.epa.gov/npdes/pubs/cmomselfreview.pdf (accessed 5/26/04).

US Federal Register. 2003. National pollutant discharge elimination system permit requirements for municipal treatment discharges during wet weather conditions. 68 no. 216: 63042.

Wastewater Planning Users Group (WAPUG). 1998. *Code Of Practice For The Hydraulic Modelling Of Sewer Systems Version 2*. Wallingford: Wastewater Planning Users Group.

Water Environment Federation (WEF). 1999. *Prevention and Control of Sewer System Overflows*, 2d ed. Manual of Practice FD-17. Alexandria, Virginia: Water Environment Federation.

Water Environment Federation (WEF). 1994. *Existing Sewer Evaluation and Rehabilitation*. WEF Manual of Practice FD-6. Alexandria, Virginia: Water Environment Federation.

Water Research Centre (WRc). 2000. *Sewerage Rehabilitation Manual* 4th ed. Wiltshire, England: Water Research Centre.

Wright, L., S. Dent, C. Mosley, P. Kadota, and Y. Djebbar. 2001. "Comparing rainfall dependent inflow and infiltration simulation methods." In *Models and Applications to Urban Water Systems Monograph 9*, ed. by W. James, Guelph, Ontario: CHI.

Problems

11.1 Define each of the following acronyms.

a. CCTV
b. CSO
c. SCADA
d. RDII
e. SSO
f. RTC
g. WEF
h. GWI
i. CMOM

11.2 Pipe blockages are best found using what technique?

11.3 Smoke testing is best used to locate _____.

11.4 Which rehab technique can result in a larger-diameter pipe?

11.5 Given a hydrograph flow (Q), plus GWI and BWF, write an equation to determine RDII.

11.6 When is the flow at a flow-monitoring point not a good indication of the total flow in the upstream basin?

11.7 Would you expect a higher R-factor in a sanitary or combined sewer? Why?

11.8 What are the pros and cons of combined sewer separation?

11.9 What is the difference between in-line and off-line storage? What are the relative benefits of each?

11.10 Wet weather hydrographs for a 2-hour rainfall event in three different systems (a, b, and c) are provided in the following table. A dry weather flow (DWF) hydrograph from the same location is also provided, and is the same for all three systems. Plot the four hydrographs and try to draw conclusions about whether the wet weather flow in each system is driven more by inflow or infiltration, and whether upstream overflows exist.

Time, hr	DWF, ft³/s	Q(a), ft³/s	Q(b), ft³/s	Q(c), ft³/s	RDII(a), ft³/s	RDII(b), ft³/s	RDII(c), ft³/s
0	1.1	1.1	1.1	1.1			
1	1.2	1.2	1.2	1.2			
2	1.1	1.6	1.2	1.1			
3	1.3	2.4	1.8	2.4			
4	1.2	2.9	2.2	2.7			
5	1.3	3.5	2.5	2.8			
6	1.5	3.7	2.8	2.8			
7	1.8	3.8	2.7	2.7			
8	2.1	3.5	2.7	2.8			
9	2.0	3.1	2.5	2.8			
10	1.9	2.7	2.6	2.7			
11	2.0	2.4	2.3	2.6			
12	1.9	2.0	2.3	2.0			
13	1.8	1.8	2.4	1.9			
14	1.7	2.0	2.2	2.0			
15	1.9	2.0	2.3	2.0			
16	1.8	1.9	2.3	1.9			
17	2.0	2.1	2.3	2.1			
18	1.8	2.0	2.2	2.0			
19	1.6	1.9	2.0	1.9			
20	1.5	1.6	2.0	1.6			
21	1.3	1.3	1.8	1.3			
22	1.2	1.3	1.6	1.3			
23	1.1	1.2	1.5	1.2			
24	1.2	1.2	1.4	1.2			

11.11 A simplified system is shown in the following figure, and system data on dry weather loads (which are constant in time), wet weather inflow hydrographs, structure elevations, and pipe lengths are provided in the accompanying tables. All pipes are 8-in. PVC with a Manning's n of 0.010. The wet weather infiltration rate for the pipes is 50 gpd/ft. The manhole inverts are the same as the pipe inverts, and the manhole rim elevations are the same as the ground elevations. The invert, tailwater elevation, and ground elevation at the outlet are 450.0 ft, 450.3 ft, and 460.0 ft, respectively.

Perform an initial hydraulic analysis using the dry weather and wet weather infiltration and inflow rates provided. Route the flows using a simple routing method such as convex routing with 1-hr time steps if using a software model. If performing the calculations by hand, simply translate the flows downstream with a 2-hr time step. (The results will be slightly different depending on the method used.) Compute the outflow hydrograph for a 10-hr period.

Next, simulate two rehabilitation options:

- *Reduced Infiltration* – Simulate flows for the case in which the infiltration rate in the pipes is reduced from 50 gpd/ft to 5 gpd/ft using an inversion liner. Calculate the outlet hydrograph for that case.

- *Reduced Inflow* – Simulate flows for the case where the inflow hydrographs at manholes MH-1 and MH-4 were reduced to 10 percent of the original inflow hydrographs by eliminating catch basins (these values have already been provided in table). Use the original infiltration rate of 50 gpm/ft.

Answer the questions at the end of the problem.

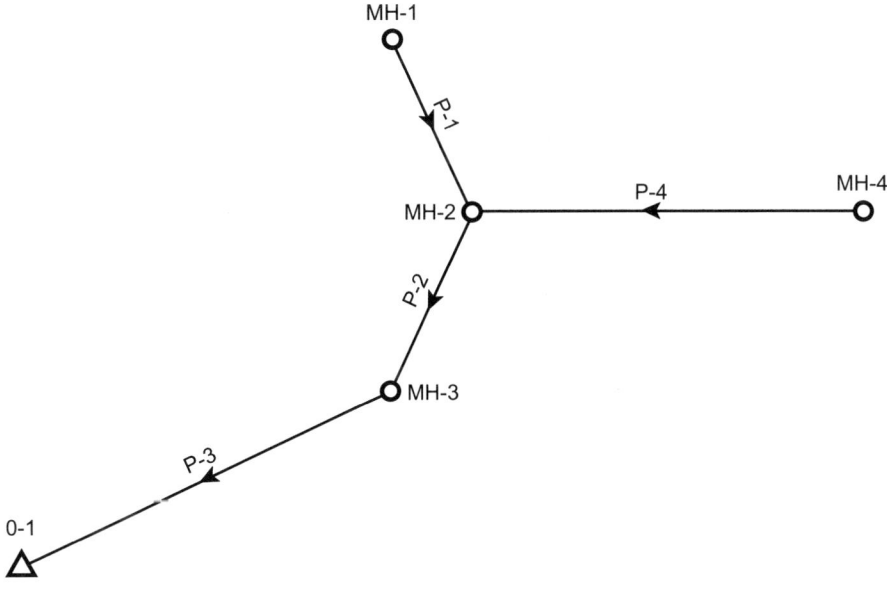

Manhole	Ground Elevation, ft	Invert Elevation, ft	Dry Weather Flow, 1000 gpd
MH-1	462.0	455.3	50
MH-2	461.5	454.0	10
MH-3	457.5	452.7	10
MH-4	462.0	455.4	30

	Flow, 1000 gpd			
Time, hr	MH-1 before rehab	MH-1 after rehab	MH-4 before rehab	MH-4 after rehab
0	0	0	0	0
2	60	6	200	20
4	90	9	350	35
6	70	7	300	30
8	20	2	100	10
10	0	0	0	0

Pipe	Upstream Node	Upstream Invert Elevation, ft	Downstream Node	Downstream Invert Elevation, ft	Constructed Slope, ft/1000 ft	Length, ft
P-4	MH-4	455.4	MH-2	454.0	2.33	600
P-1	MH-1	455.3	MH-2	454.0	3.25	400
P-2	MH-2	454.0	MH-3	452.7	2.60	500
P-3	MH-3	452.7	O-1	450.0	2.70	1000

a. Plot all three downstream hydrographs on a single graph. Use either gpd or ft^3/s.

b. If the full pipe flow for the most downstream pipe is 527,000 gpd (0.82 ft^3/s), for which of the three cases will the flow exceed the capacity for at least some of the time.

c. What time corresponds to the highest flow?

d. What is the depth of flow at the downstream end of P-2 at hour 4? Given a diameter of 8 in., in which case will the pipe be surcharged? Use Manning's equation and assume normal depth if doing a hand calculation.

e. At the peak of the event, determine the hydraulic grade line at manhole MH-3 for each of the three cases. Given that the manhole invert elevation is 452.7 ft, the crown elevation is 453.4 ft, and the rim elevation is 457.5 ft, will the manhole be surcharged or overflowing in any of the cases?

f. If, in this greatly simplified problem, the costs of the "reduced infiltration" and "reduced inflow" alternatives are identical, which would you recommend and why?

g. If part b. indicated that the flow in the "reduced infiltration" case exceeds the downstream full pipe capacity, why was it not shown to be surcharged in part e?

11.12 A computer model predicts a reach of sewer should be able to convey 250 L/s when full, yet it backs up and overflows when the flow is measured at 170 L/s?. What are the possible causes? (Check all that are applicable.)

__ Root blockage

__ Excessive upstream filtration

__ Grease coating of pipes

__ Upstream pump not running on curve

What steps can be taken to confirm the problem? What steps can be taken to correct the problem?

11.13 During wet weather metering, flows past a metering point in a sanitary sewer increase dramatically as soon as it begins to rain and decrease fairly quickly afterward. What is the likely cause of the problem?

__ Infiltration

__ Inflow

__ Blockage due to roots

What steps can be taken to confirm the problem? What steps can be taken to correct the problem?

11.14 In a combined sewer system, an outfall continues to discharge wastewater during dry weather. What are the likely causes of this problem? How can the problem be diagnosed and corrected?

11.15 Consider the large trunk sewers receiving flow from an east and west drainage basin and delivering it to a treatment plant at the downstream end. East basin contains some older sewers while west basin has relatively little I&I. The wet weather flows to the treatment plant are excessive and interfering with plant operation. They need to be reduced.

The characteristics of the piping are shown in the following figure and the hydrographs for a major storm are listed in the table. The monitoring program was able to separate the flow into wastewater (WW), infiltration and inflow. Route the flow through the system preferably using a computer model (although manual calculation are acceptable—use some very simple routing).

416 Wastewater Collection System Evaluation and Rehabilitation

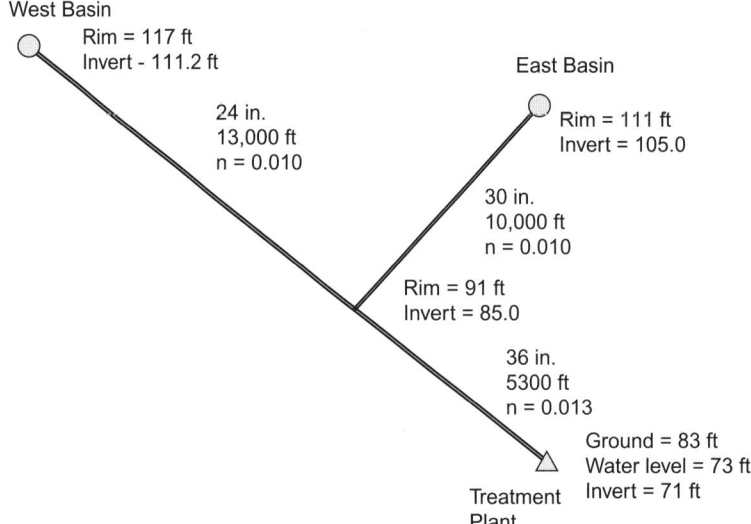

Time, hrs	WW East	Infiltration, East	Inflow, East	WW West	Infiltration, West	Inflow, West
0	3.00	0.00	0.00	3.50	0.00	0.00
1	3.60	0.00	0.00	4.20	0.00	0.00
2	3.90	0.12	0.90	4.55	0.04	0.19
3	4.20	0.37	2.70	4.90	0.12	0.56
4	3.90	0.79	2.90	4.55	0.26	0.60
5	3.90	1.12	2.26	4.55	0.37	0.47
6	3.60	1.20	1.13	4.20	0.40	0.23
7	3.00	1.12	0.44	3.50	0.37	0.09
8	2.40	0.94	0.12	2.80	0.31	0.02
9	2.10	0.67	0.03	2.45	0.22	0.01
10	2.10	0.47	0.00	2.45	0.16	0.00
11	1.80	0.34	0.00	2.10	0.11	0.00
12	1.20	0.18	0.00	1.40	0.06	0.00
13	1.50	0.10	0.00	1.75	0.03	0.00
14	2.10	0.05	0.00	2.45	0.02	0.00
15	2.40	0.36	0.00	2.80	0.12	0.00
16	2.70	0.24	0.00	3.15	0.08	0.00

Determine the inflow hydrograph to the treatment plant. Plot that hydrograph. It is probably easiest to combine the three components of flow into a single hydrograph for the east and west basin. Load the model with those hydrographs and run through a model (or manual calculation).

Now consider that there are two plans:

Plan A will consist of the relining of major portions of both collection systems. It is expected to reduce the infiltration to one third of its current value and the inflow to one half of its current value. Simulate those new hydrographs and determine the hydrograph at the plant. plot it on the same graph as the original hydrograph.

Plan B will consist of smoke testing the entire older East basin to eliminate old combined sewers and catch basins. This is expected to reduce the inflow to one fourth. But this will not affect the infiltration anywhere, nor the inflow in the more modern West basin. Simulate the hydrograph at the plant and plot.

What are the peak flows in each of the three scenarios and at what time do they occur?

	Time to peak, hrs	peak flow, ft^3/s
Original	5	12.6
Plan A	5	9.2
Plan B	6	10.7

Given that Plan B is simpler and less expensive, would you recommend plan A or B?

Plan A begins to resemble the original solution after about 10 hours. Why?

11.16 Given a 120 m long, 600 mm sanitary sewer with upstream invert at elevation 50.48 m and downstream invert at 50.00 m, you suspect that grease has reduced the capacity of the sewer. Using a chalk mark, you determine that when the flow is 0.30 m3/s, the water level in the upstream manhole is at 52.85 m while the downstream manhole water level is at 50.40 m.

Calculate the value of Manning's n that you would need to have that much head loss in the sewer.

Estimate the normal depth you can expect to attain in the sewer at the same flow rate after you have cleaned the sewer and restored the Manning n value to 0.013.

CHAPTER

12

Force Mains and Pump Stations

Ideally, all wastewater would flow downhill by gravity to a treatment plant. In some cases, however, so little slope is available that sewers cannot carry the wastewater by gravity and the sewage must be pumped. In other cases, it is necessary to pump sewage across high points in the topography. In both situations, use of a pump station that discharges into a force main (also referred to as a *rising main*) is the most effective way to transport sewage.

This chapter applies the fundamentals of pumps and pressurized flow covered in Chapter 4 to the hydraulic design of pump stations and force mains. Another application of pressurized flow is the use of pressure sewers with individual pumps on each customer's property. Pressure sewer systems are addressed in Chapter 13.

There are many issues that must be considered in the design of a pump station and force main. They include the following:

- Need for pumping
- Force main sizing
- Type of pumping (constant speed, variable speed)
- Energy efficiency
- Type of station (submersible, wet well/dry well)
- Number of pumps
- Pump type (axial flow, radial flow)
- Pump orientation (vertical, horizontal)
- Pump selection (flow, head, horsepower)
- Wet well sizing

- Hydraulic transients
- Power
- Controls
- Siting and access
- Odor control.

Design of a force main system consists of choosing pipe sizes, developing system head curves for each station, and finding pumps that work well with those curves. This chapter concentrates on the hydraulic aspects of design, rather than on structural, electrical, and control issues. See Sanks (1998) and WEF (1993) for comprehensive presentations of these aspects.

Hydraulic design is relatively simple for force mains that are fed from a single pump station, but becomes much more complicated for force mains fed by several pump stations or force mains with multiple high points. The issues are further complicated when the loads on the pump stations are expected to change significantly over time. Each of these issues is addressed in this chapter.

12.1 Need for Pump Stations

In general, wastewater collection utilities prefer to minimize the number of pump stations and force mains in their systems. In addition to the ongoing cost of energy to run the pumps, pump stations tend to require more maintenance than any other component of the collection system. Two arguments in favor of force mains are that they are usually smaller than gravity pipes carrying the same flow and, in contrast to gravity pipes, the slope at which they are laid is not as critical, allowing for shallower burial depths.

The boundaries of most wastewater collection utilities do not usually correspond to a single drainage basin. For utilities that cover several drainage basins, the layout of the system initially consists of an analysis of the tradeoffs between constructing wastewater treatment plants at the downstream end of each drainage basin versus pumping water across divides to a centralized plant. There are significant economies of scale in constructing and operating a single treatment plant rather than many smaller plants. Therefore, pump stations and force mains are generally constructed when the distances between drainage basins are not too large. In some cases, gravity flow between basins is more economical, but force mains are preferred because they can be smaller and follow a shorter, more-direct route or be routed to avoid areas where obtaining easements may be problematic (see Figure 12.1).

Another application of force mains occurs in treatment plant regionalization, in which an old, obsolete plant is abandoned in favor of a new or regional treatment plant. When the old plant is abandoned, all of the sewers in the area still run to the old plant, so a pump station must usually be built at the plant site to send wastewater to the new or regional treatment plant.

Force mains are also needed within a drainage basin when a land-development project is too far away from an existing sewer to connect economically with a gravity line. Figure 12.2 illustrates a situation in which the route for a gravity sewer is much longer than for a force main. In addition, it may be difficult to lay the gravity sewer due to land ownership/right-of-way issues, wetlands, or difficult excavation along the gravity route.

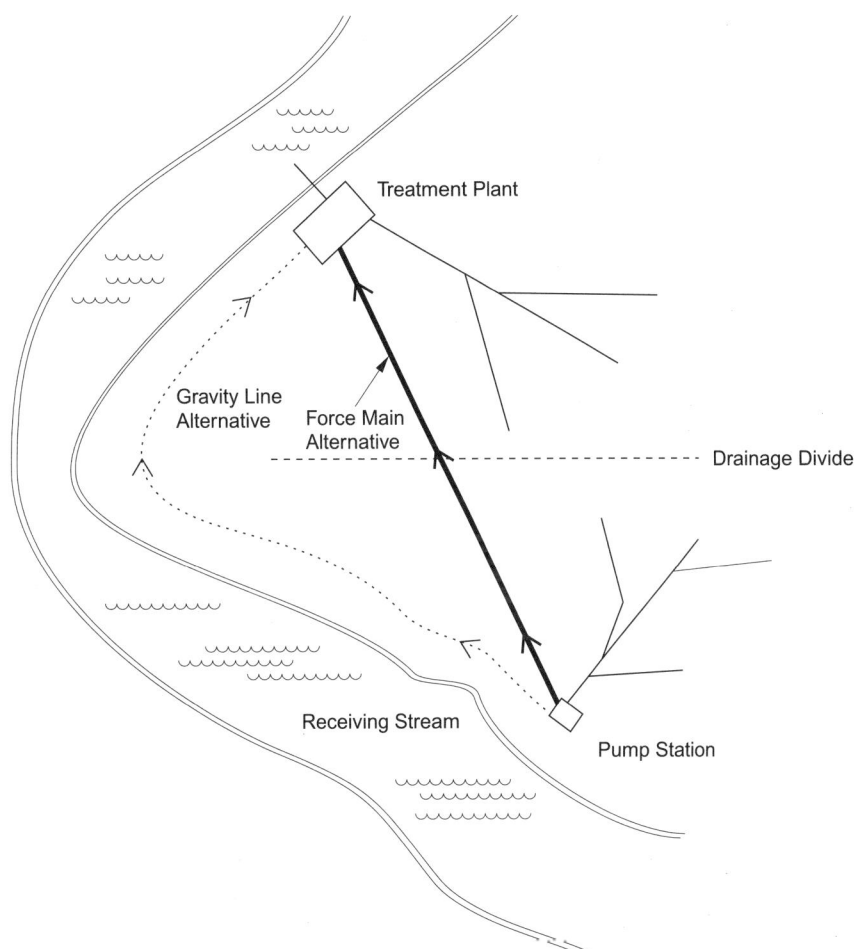

Figure 12.1 Force main and gravity flow alternatives for connecting a gravity collection system to a central treatment plant across a drainage divide.

Even within an individual land development project, some of the land may lie on opposite sides of a small ridge. There may only be a single interceptor sewer or wastewater treatment plant into which the project can discharge. Therefore, a force main and pump station are required to collect the sewage at a single point, as illustrated in Figure 12.3.

Force mains and pump stations are also used in areas where the slope of the land is so small that the downstream end of the sewer would need to be very deep with a gravity system. For example, if the minimum slope for a 12-in. (300 mm) diameter sewer is 0.005 and the ground is fairly flat, a sewer that is only 4 ft (1.2 m) deep at the upstream end would be nearly 20 ft (6.5 m) deep after a run of 3000 ft (900 m) at the minimum slope pumps. A 20 ft (6.5 m) excavation, especially in a coastal area with high groundwater and sandy soil, is extremely costly and encourages infiltration. Installation of one or even two pump stations along the way is likely to be the more economical alternative.

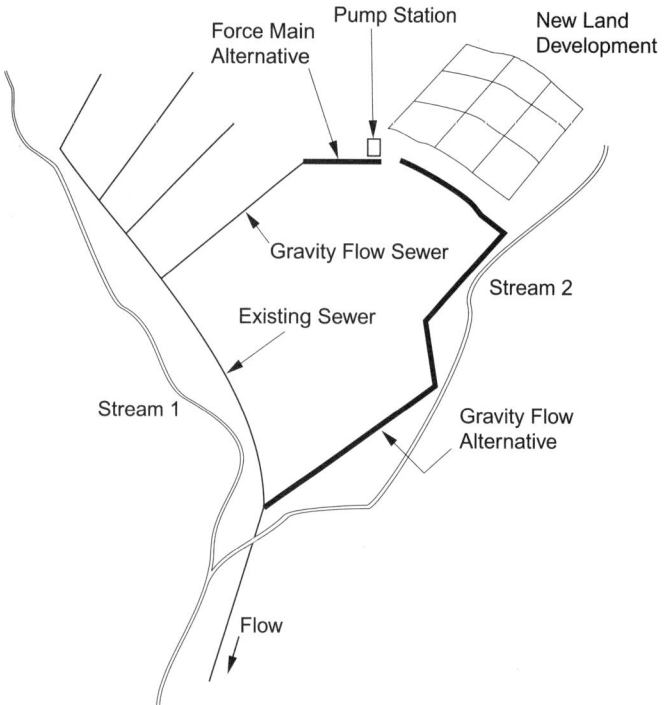

Figure 12.2 Force main alternative used to shorten the route of a sewer within a drainage basin.

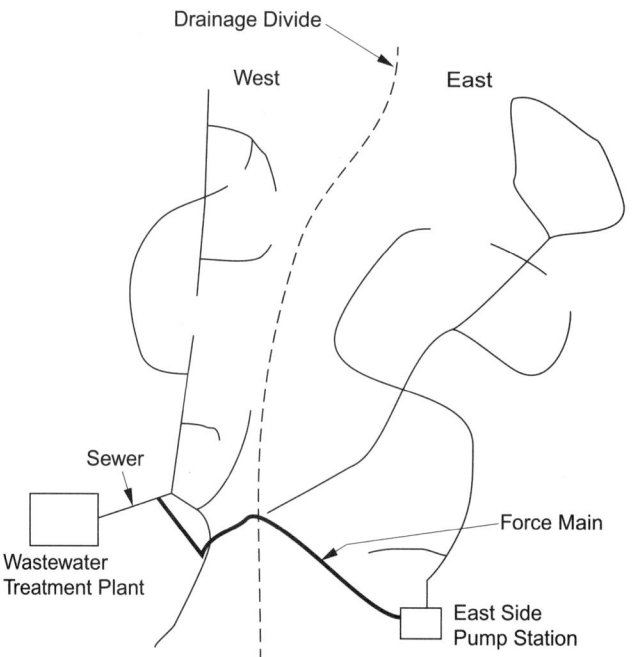

Figure 12.3 Force main pumping across a divide in a development.

12.2 Pump Station Overview and Design Considerations

This section briefly discusses the various pump station configurations, components, and design considerations. Section 12.4 presents information on hydraulic modeling of pump stations, which can aid the design process.

Components

The basic components of a pump station are incoming piping from an upstream gravity or pressure sewer, a subsurface wet well for collecting and storing inflow, suction piping to connect the wet well storage to the pumps, pump motors, pump on/off or speed controllers, and discharge piping to connect the pumps to the downstream force main. As shown in Figure 12.4, pumps and motors may be located in the wet well, in an adjacent dry well, or, in some cases, on the ground surface. Figure 12.5 is a cut-away view of a typical large pump station with submersible pumps.

Additional pump station components include valves, flow meters, access hatches, ladders, enclosures, and equipment for removing pumps in need of service. Many pump stations are buried underground or hidden behind landscaping with only the access hatch and control panel visible, as shown in Figure 12.6.

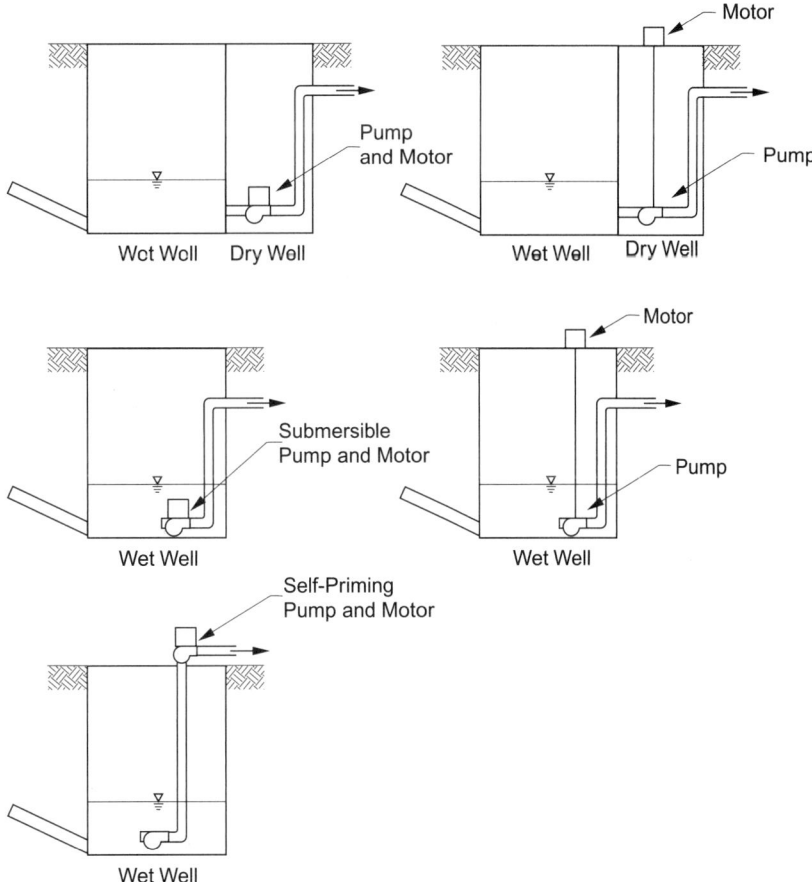

Figure 12.4 Various pump station configurations.

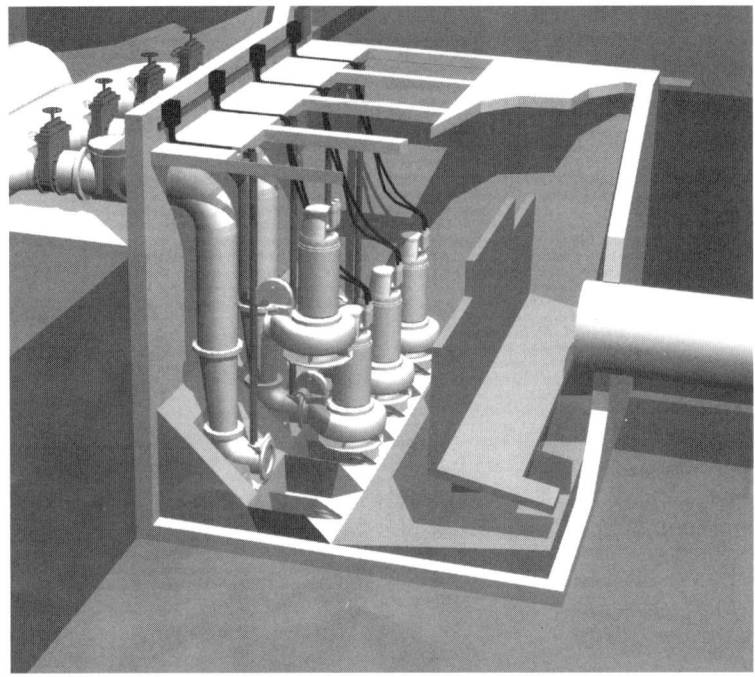
Figure 12.5 Cut-away view of a large pump station.

Figure 12.6 Access hatch and controls for an underground pump station.

Design Decisions

Pumps and pump stations are characterized in a number of ways, as listed in Table 12.1. Many of the design decisions in this table are described in more detail in the subsections that follow. For additional details on pump station design, the reader is referred to Burton (1996), GLUMRB (1997), Hydraulic Institute (2000, 2001), Karassik et al. (2000), Sanks (2000), Submersible Wastewater Pumps Association (1997), Tchobanoglous (1981), and WEF (1993), plus the relevant local, state, provincial, or national design standard.

Table 12.1 Pump and pump station characteristics.

Pump/Station Characteristic	Typical Selections
Pump orientation	Vertical, horizontal
Suction	End suction, radial suction
Discharge orientation	Radial, axial, turbine
Type of motor	Dry pit, submersible, dry pit/submersible
Coupling	Close coupled, separately coupled, long shaft
Drive	Constant speed, variable speed
Structure	Wet well, wet well/dry well
Pump Type	Centrifugal, progressive cavity, diaphragm, screw
Intake	Submerged, in-line booster
Staging	Single stage, multistage

An additional consideration in the case of smaller pump stations is the purchase of a pre-engineered, packaged pump station. These stations are assembled at the factory and shipped in one or two pieces to the site. They are available in a variety of configurations and typically include the pumps, motors, controls, pump enclosure, and other accessories.

Pump Capacity

The design flow for the pump station should be greater than the maximum projected inflow to the pump station. At this flow, the pump must supply enough head to provide the necessary lift and overcome downstream head losses at the design flow. If a candidate pump does not meet this flow and head requirement, then it will be necessary to use a different (or an additional) pump or reduce system head losses by increasing the size of the force main.

Almost all pump stations have multiple pumps. A common configuration is a duplex system, which has two identical pumps. The pumps are selected so that a single pump running alone can keep up with the design flow. Larger stations and stations with highly variable flows (for example, due to high RDII) may use three or more pumps, often with a smaller pump for use during periods when loads are small. A pump station should be designed so that, even if the largest unit is out of service, the remaining pumps can meet the design flow.

Pump Station Configuration

As Figure 12.4 showed, pump stations can be configured several ways. This section describes the various options.

Wet Well and Dry Well. A configuration with separate wet and dry wells for storing wastewater and housing pumping equipment, respectively, is most desirable from the standpoint of easy maintenance. Personnel can service pumps without first pulling them out of the wet well and cleaning them. These stations are usually the most costly to construct and thus are only used for larger systems. However, even dry wells can flood due to a pipe break or stormwater intrusion (pump stations are usually at low points). Thus, the motors for pumps in dry wells may be located above the flood level and connected with long shafts. Alternatively, dry well submersible pumps, which can withstand flooding, can be used. Sump pumps should be installed in dry wells to keep them dry. A large dry well pump station is shown in Figure 12.7.

Wet Well Only. For pump stations without a separate dry well, there are three types of pump:

- Submersible pumps
- Wet-pit pumps with above-grade motors
- Above-grade self-priming pumps.

Figure 12.7 Pumps and motors in a large dry well pump station.

The first two pump types are installed so that they are always submerged. Submersible pump motors are also submerged, while motors for wet-pit pumps are located at an elevation that will not be flooded and are connected by a shaft to the pumps below. Figure 12.8 shows a large submersible pump being installed, and Figure 12.9 shows four submersible pumps in a wet well. Above-grade motors in a station with wet-pit pumps are shown in Figure 12.10.

With self-priming pumps, both the motor and pump are located above grade. The self-priming pump is the easiest to maintain, but can also be less reliable because the prime can be lost, and there are limitations to the maximum lift that can be provided by the pump (usually about 25 ft [7 m]).

Courtesy of ITT Flygt

Figure 12.8 Large submersible pumps being installed in a wet-well pump station.

Pump Types and Selection

Wastewater pump selection is complicated by the fact that wastewater is laden with a variety of solids. A particular pump may be efficient from a hydraulics standpoint but unable to handle wastewater. Usually, when specifying wastewater pumps, the engineer will call for pumps that can pass a specific-size solid (for example, 3 in. [75 mm]). Screening or comminution before the pumps can reduce the importance of this

Figure 12.9 Submersible pumps in a wet well.

Figure 12.10 Above grade motors for wet-pit pumps.

requirement, but the engineer needs to work closely with manufacturers to ensure that a pump is appropriate for the application.

Positive-displacement pumps are capable of pumping wastewater, but centrifugal pumps are usually the more economical choice. Positive-displacement pumps are usually reserved for handling sludges and industrial wastes that can be heavily solids laden, gritty, or viscous. Screw pumps are useful when wastewater must be lifted but not discharged into a force main. Screw pumps are usually efficient and handle solids well, but are fairly expensive to install and maintain.

Centrifugal pumps are classified by the orientation of flow from the shaft as radial, axial, or mixed. Radial-flow pumps discharge perpendicular to the shaft, axial-flow pumps discharge parallel to the shaft, and mixed-flow pumps discharge at an angle to the shaft. In general, radial-flow pumps are most efficient for high-head conditions, while axial-flow pumps are most efficient for lower-head applications (e.g., pumping stormwater over a levee).

A concern with axial-flow pumps is that, unlike radial-flow pumps, they can have an extremely high power draw as the flow drops below the design flow. Typical dimensionless pump-characteristic curves for radial- and axial-flow pumps are shown in Figures 12.11 and 12.12.

An additional consideration is whether constant-speed or variable-speed pumps will be used. A variable-speed pump is simply a constant-speed pump with a variable-speed drive that can adjust the speed based on a control setting, such as to maintain a constant wet well level.

Wastewater pumps are nearly always vertically mounted because this orientation is more efficient from the standpoint of saving space, thereby minimizing excavation.

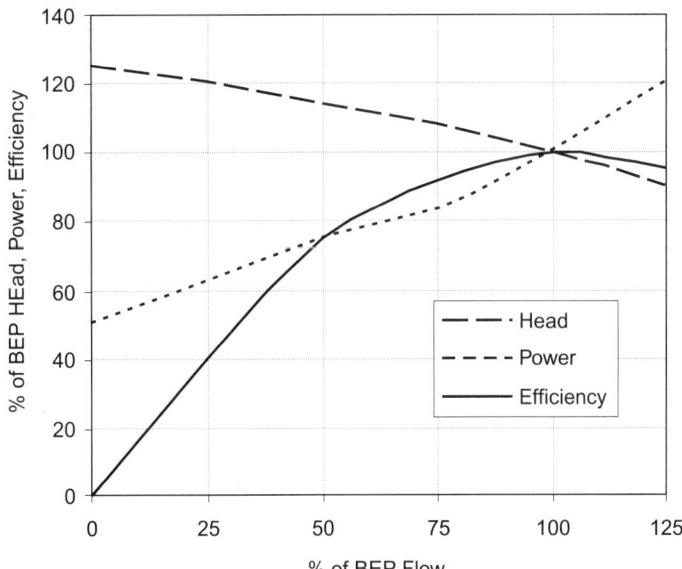

Figure 12.11 Dimensionless pump characteristic curves for head, power and efficiency expressed as a percentage of these values at a radial-flow pump's best efficiency point (BEP) (based on Sanks, 1998).

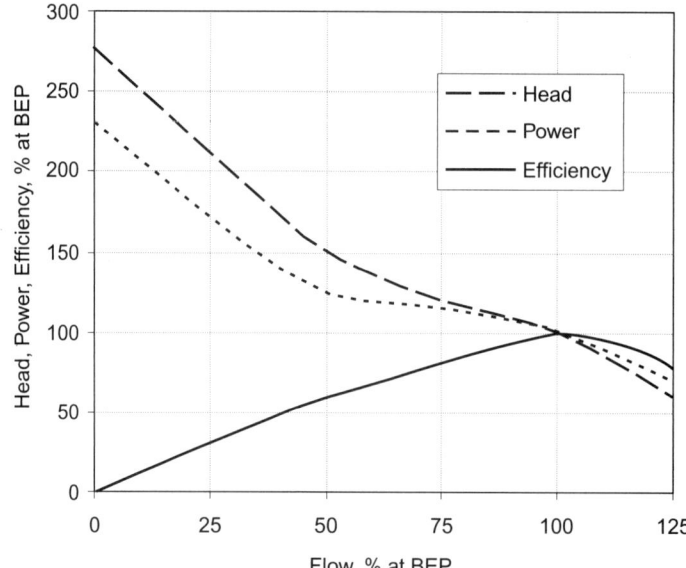

Figure 12.12 Dimensionless pump characteristic curves for head, power, and efficiency expressed as a percentage these values at an axial-flow pump's best efficiency point (BEP) (based on Sanks, 1998).

Because wastewater pumping usually does not involve a high head, single-stage pumping (i.e., a single impeller on the pump shaft) is usually adequate. When higher heads are required, it is usually easier to select a higher-speed motor to bring the head into range than to use multistage pumps.

Pump Type and Specific Speed. A pump characteristic called *specific speed* can help to ensure that the best type of pump is used for a particular installation. In the US, the specific speed is calculated as

$$N_s = \frac{NQ^{0.5}}{h^{0.75}} \tag{12.1}$$

where N_s = specific speed
 N = rotational speed of the pump (rpm)
 Q = pumping rate (gpm)
 h = energy head produced by the pump (ft)

Outside of the US, specific speed is typically defined as

$$N_s = \frac{NQ^{0.5}}{(gh)^{0.75}} \tag{12.2}$$

where N = angular speed of the pump (rad/s)
 Q = pumping rate (m³/s)
 g = gravitational acceleration, 9.81 m/s²
 h = energy head produced by the pump (m)

The flow and head are taken at the best efficiency point (BEP) of the desired pump. Specific speed has units, but they are cumbersome and are usually not explicitly stated. Typical ranges of N_s for efficient operation of different pump types are given in Table 12.2.

Table 12.2 Typical specific speeds for wastewater pumps.

Pump Type	U.S. Customary	SI
Radial	500–4000	10–80
Mixed	3000–6500	60–125
Axial	4000–9000	75–175

Although Table 12.2 provides some overall guidance in pump selection, the engineer must specify a specific pump and not just a type of pump. It is therefore important to consult catalogs and discuss the situation with pump manufacturers so that they can provide the best pump for the job.

Pump Coverage Charts and Performance Curves. Selecting the pump can be an intimidating process, given the number of pump models and manufacturers available. Most manufacturers provide a "pump coverage chart" for choosing the pump model given the desired flow and head. A typical chart is shown in Figure 12.13. As one moves to the right in this chart, the pump suction and discharge flanges and openings in the casing become larger, while moving upward corresponds to larger casing diameters and higher-speed pumps.

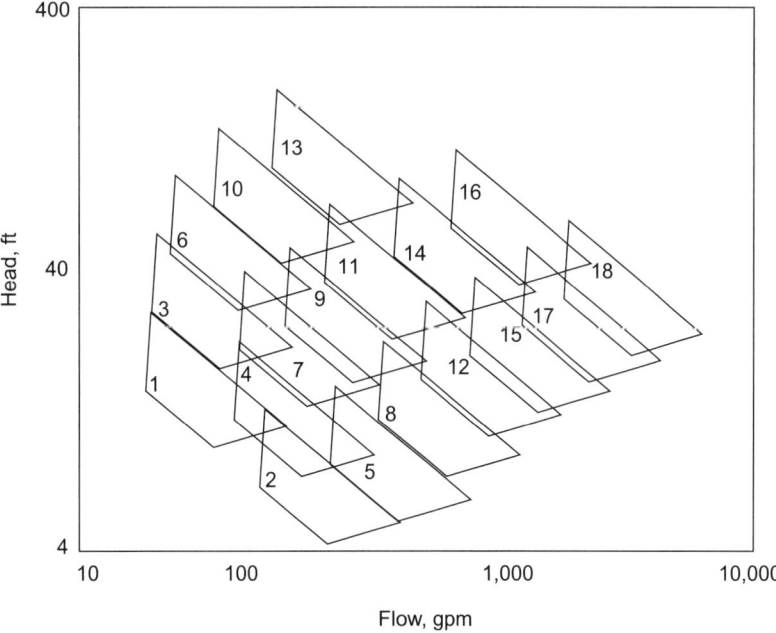

Figure 12.13 Typical pump selection coverage chart. (Numbered areas correspond to different pump models).

After the sizes of the casing and flanges have been selected, the designer should refer to the individual pump curves to determine the impeller diameter that best matches the system head curve (see "Developing System Head Curves" on page 437). After the candidate pump has been selected, it is advisable to insert it into the hydraulic model of the system and verify that the design flow rate, pump operating point, and best efficiency point are all close over the range of pump operating conditions. (Section 12.4 covers modeling of pumped systems.) The model should also be used to check performance when multiple pumps are running.

It is essential to select pumps that will operate as close as possible to their best efficiency points. Running a pump at a point away from its best efficiency point wastes energy, increases load and wear on the shaft bearings and seals, and may hasten motor burnout if running at a point with a high brake horsepower requirement (Bachus, 2004; Mackay, 2004). Model runs for a wide range of conditions are an easy way to identify actual operating points and compare them with the best efficiency point.

Wet Well Sizing

A wet well provides head so that suction piping can remain full of water and not entrain air. A wet well also provides storage so that the pumps do not need to exactly match inflow rates to the station. The *pump cycle time* is defined as the time between successive pump starts. The recommended minimum cycle time is a function of the type of motor and is longer for larger pumps. WEF (1993) recommends no more than six starts per hour for 25 hp (20 kW) pumps, with two starts per hour for 137–270 hp (100–200 kW) pumps.

Constant-Speed Pumps. The actual cycle time for a constant-speed pump is directly related to the volume of the wet well. The minimum pump cycle time corresponds to inflow rates to the station of one-half the pump's design flow rate. At that inflow rate, half of the cycle is spent pumping down the wet well and the other half is spent filling it back up. This gives a minimum wet well volume of

$$V = \frac{Qt}{4} \qquad (12.3)$$

where V = volume (gal, m^3)
Q = design flow (gpm, m^3/min)
t = minimum pump cycle time (min)

This volume is the active volume between the "pump on" and "pump off" levels in the wet well. The volume below the "pump off" level keeps the suction head flooded, and some freeboard volume above the "pump on" level provides a margin of safety.

Variable-Speed Pumps. Wet wells can be smaller if variable-speed pumps are used, because, if the speed controls are set to match the pump rate to the inflow rate, a wet well only needs to be large enough to keep the suction-side piping submerged and prevent vortices and air entrainment. At very low flows, however, it is more efficient to turn the pump off for a time and let the wet well fill before turning it on again. Moreover, the variable-speed drive may fail from time to time. A sufficiently large wet well can enable the pump to be run at a constant speed until the variable-speed drive is repaired.

Additional Considerations. Wet wells can be too large for the flow. This is often the case early in the life of a pump station designed to serve a land-development project, but which must be brought on line when the flows are only a fraction of those at full buildout. In such cases, the on and off levels may be set closer than they will be at buildout, chemicals (such as permanganate or peroxide) may be added to control odors, and it may even be necessary to add water to the inflow so that the time of travel through the wet well and force main do not become excessive.

Water level in a wet well is monitored through a variety of devices, including floats, bubblers, ultrasonic gauges, and pressure transducers such as the one shown in Figure 12.14. Remote stations usually have a control panel with an alarm, as shown in Figure 12.15.

In all but the smallest stations, wet wells should be divided into sections that can be isolated and cleaned without taking the station out of service.

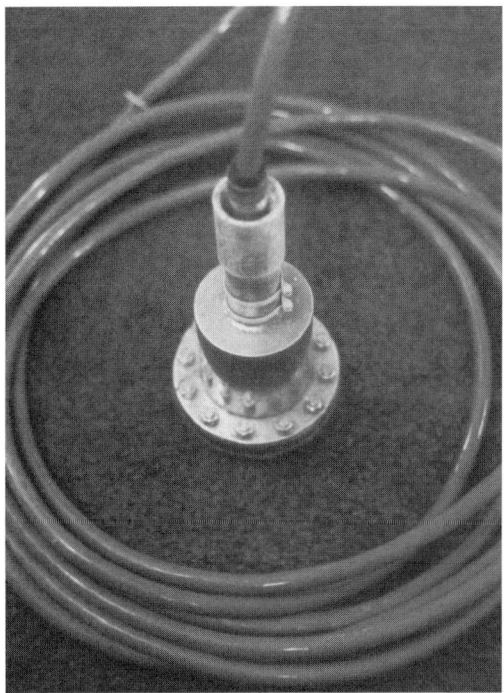

Figure 12.14 Pressure transducer for installation in the bottom of a wet well.

Net Positive Suction Head

When the actual pressure at a point in the fluid drops below the vapor pressure of the fluid, the fluid vaporizes. When the pressure increases, the vapor pocket collapses in a process known as cavitation. Cavitation is the vaporization of water in the pump, not the release of air bubbles, which is a common misconception.

In submerged wet well pumps, cavitation usually is not an issue, as the pump is located in the wastewater; providing the required minimum submergence is all that is needed. However, cavitation can occur in dry well and self-priming pumps. It initially manifests as a rumbling noise in the pump, as if gravel were passing through the pump, and it can increase to a roar as the cavitation pockets actually damage the pump.

Figure 12.15 Control panel with alarm for a remote pump station.

Pumps are likely places for cavitation because high velocities lead to low pressures. The potential for cavitation is usually evaluated by comparing the *net positive suction head required by the pump* ($NPSH_r$) with the *net positive suction available in the system* ($NPSH_a$). $NPSH_r$ is a property of the pump and usually increases with increasing flow.

$NPSH_a$ depends on the system and is equal to the sum of atmospheric pressure at the pump and the static head (gauge pressure) measured on the suction side of the pump minus the sum of the vapor pressure of the fluid and the head loss between the wet well and the pump suction (velocity head is usually negligible). For a typical situation in which the pump pulls water from a wet well, the $NPSH_a$ can be calculated with the following equation (Sanks, 1998):

$$NPSH_a = H_{bar} + H_s - H_{vap} - h_l \quad (12.4)$$

where $NPSH_a$ = net positive suction head available (ft, m)
H_{bar} = barometric pressure at the elevation of the pump (ft, m)
H_s = static head (i.e., wet well water level − pump elevation) (ft, m)
H_{vap} = vapor pressure of water (ft, m)
h_l = head loss between the wet well and pump (ft, m)

Values for the barometric pressure as a function of altitude and vapor pressure as a function of temperature are given in Appendix C. The head loss can be calculated using a hydraulic model of the suction-side piping. The static head term is positive if the wet well water level is located above the pump inlet and negative if the wet well water level is below the pump (suction lift).

If $NPSH_a$ is less than $NPSH_r$, cavitation is likely to occur. Engineers are encouraged to add some safety factor to ensure that available NPSH is adequate. If meeting the net positive suction head requirement is problematic at a station, some of the possible solutions are

- Lower the pump
- Raise the minimum wet well water level
- Increase the diameter of the suction-side pumping
- Select a pump with a lower $NPSH_r$
- Reduce the pump rotational speed.

Appurtenances

For pumps in a wet well, there is very little suction-side piping because the pumps are submerged in the wastewater. Self-priming pumps require a foot valve or check valve to prevent the suction line from draining when the turned off. Dry-well pumps require an isolating valve whenever it is possible for the suction water level to be higher than the pump.

A check valve and an isolating valve should be placed on the discharge side of all pumps. The check valve prevents water from flowing back through the pump when it is off, and the isolating valve allows the pump to be maintained in place or removed. The check valve should be located between the isolating valve and the pump discharge. Each check valve should have an external position indicator. It should be possible to operate isolating valves without entering the dry well. Gate valves and plug valves are usually used for wastewater isolation.

Metering the flow from each pump station is good practice. This can be done by metering either the force main leaving the station or each of the individual pump lines. The single station meter may seem less costly but, because it is on the discharge line, it is usually larger and more costly than any individual line meter. In addition, it needs its own set of isolating valves, while the individual pump meters can be placed between the pump and the discharge valve. Noninvasive electromagnetic or ultrasonic meters are usually preferred for wastewater pumping stations; however, they can be difficult to locate given the ideal required length of straight pipe before the meter.

Another approach to monitoring flow rates at constant-speed stations is to time the cycle of the pump. The rate at which the wet well fills gives the inflow rate, and the time to draw down gives the net discharge rate. An accurate measurement of wet well volume is needed for this method.

12.3 Force Main Sizing with a Single Pump Station

When a pump station is served by a single force main, there is usually a narrow band of system head curves against which the pumps must run. (The concept of system head curves was introduced in Chapter 4.) In such a situation, constant-speed pumps are economical for most cases, especially for those with nearly flat system head curves.

The key design parameter for force mains is an acceptable design velocity in the range of 2–8 ft/s (0.6–2.6 m/s), with a desired value of about 5 ft/s (1.5 m/s). Even with a limited number of available pipe sizes to choose from, achieving this velocity is not usually difficult. In the case of variable-speed pumps, flows can vary significantly, so it is more difficult to get all possible flow rates in the correct range. However, this can usually be accomplished if the pumps are set to shut off at very low a flow rates.

The engineer should not be overly conservative in pipe sizing, as the design for peak flows can lead to very low velocities early in the life of the force main. In some cases, he or she might consider an additional facility for storing some wet-weather flow upstream of the pump station, thus allowing the force main to be smaller and pumped flow to the treatment plant steadier.

Although estimating the domestic and industrial loads on a pump station is not simple, it can usually be done with some certainty. A more difficult component of estimating loads for design is accounting for infiltration and inflow (I/I). For new wastewater collection systems, the assumption of a fairly low I/I is usually justifiable, but a pump station serving an older system with high existing I/I, or even combined sewers, presents the design engineer with the problem of estimating how much the I/I will increase or decrease in the future. (Determination of system loading was described in considerable detail in Chapters 6 and 7.) Modeling flows in the upstream collection system, combined with flow monitoring, provides a way to determine design loads at the pump station. Stations with variable-speed pumps or more than two pumps are the usual solution if dry- and wet-weather flows differ greatly.

Determining Pipe Sizes

An initial estimate of the diameter of the force main can be obtained with

$$D = k\sqrt{\frac{Q}{V}} \qquad (12.5)$$

where D = diameter (in, mm)

Q = design flow (gpm, L/s)

V = desired velocity (ft/s, m/s)

k = 0.64 for US customary units or 35.7 for SI units

The result is usually rounded to the nearest (not necessarily the larger) commercially available diameter.

For example, if the design flow is 3000 gpm (190 L/s) and the desired velocity is 5 ft/s (1.5 m/s), then the diameter given by Equation 12.5 is 15.7 in. (401 mm). Based on this formula, the engineer can use a nominal 16-in. (400-mm) pipe as a starting point, but try other diameters to arrive at the best solution over the full range of flows to be encountered. For example, if the average flow is on the order of 750 gpm (48 L/s), then a smaller main may be desirable. If the average flow is 2500 gpm (160 L/s), a larger main may pay for itself in energy savings.

Developing System Head Curves

Once the range of reasonable diameters and flows for the force main is known, the engineer can construct a system head curve. As described in Chapter 4, the vertical axis of the system head curve is the head needed to move a fluid from the suction to the discharge side of the pump. In a simple case with a single pump station and no diversions of flow along the force main, the system head curve is simply the sum of the head needed to lift the water from the suction-side wet well or manhole to the discharge-side manhole (where the flow changes back to gravity flow) and the head needed to overcome friction. This can be written as

$$h = h_l + h_f \tag{12.6}$$

where h = system head (ft, m)
h_l = lift head (ft, m)
h_f = head loss due to friction (ft, m)

The lift head is independent of flow for any single system head curve, but friction loss is a function of flow rate and includes both pipe head loss and minor (form) losses. If pumping along relatively flat terrain, friction head losses predominate, yielding a steep system head curve. For pumping over a hill, lift head predominates, yielding a relatively flat system head curve.

System head curves are illustrated in Figure 12.16. The friction head loss can be calculated using a head loss equation such as the Darcy-Weisbach, Hazen-Williams, or Manning equation (see Chapter 2).

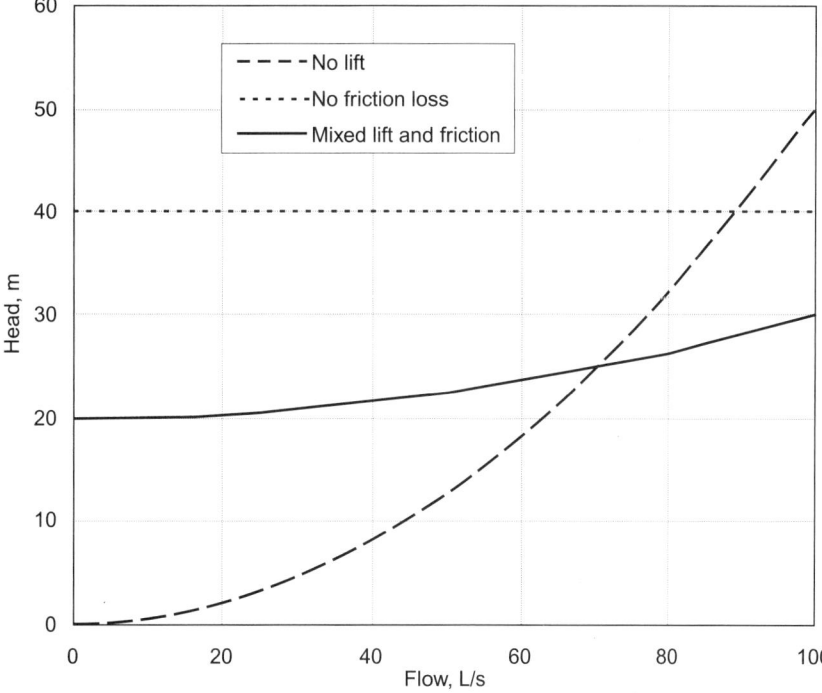

Figure 12.16 System head curves for no lift, no friction losses, and a combination of both head losses.

Hydraulic models of the force main system can be used to simplify the development of system head curves. With a model, it is easy to try different pipe sizes or check how the system head curve changes with varying wet well levels. Models are especially helpful with multiple pump stations serving a single force main.

A particular pump station and force main configuration will have a band of system head curves covering the range of heads experienced on the suction and discharge sides of the pump. Usually, fluctuations in wet well level are fairly small—on the order of 3–6 ft (1–2 m)— and thus do not significantly impact the pumping rate. However, as described in "Identifying Potential Problems" on page 443, the effect of wet well level can be more pronounced if the wet well is submerged (i.e., the water surface rises above the intended maximum level).

Typical system head curves for a 3000-gpm (190-L/s) pump with the wet well fluctuating between 110 and 115 ft (33.5 and 35.0 m) and the water level in the discharge manhole at 145 ft (44.2 m) are shown in Figure 12.17 for a 2000-ft (610 m) pipeline with Hazen-Williams C factor of 130 and possible diameters of 14, 16, and 20 in. (350, 400, and 500 mm).

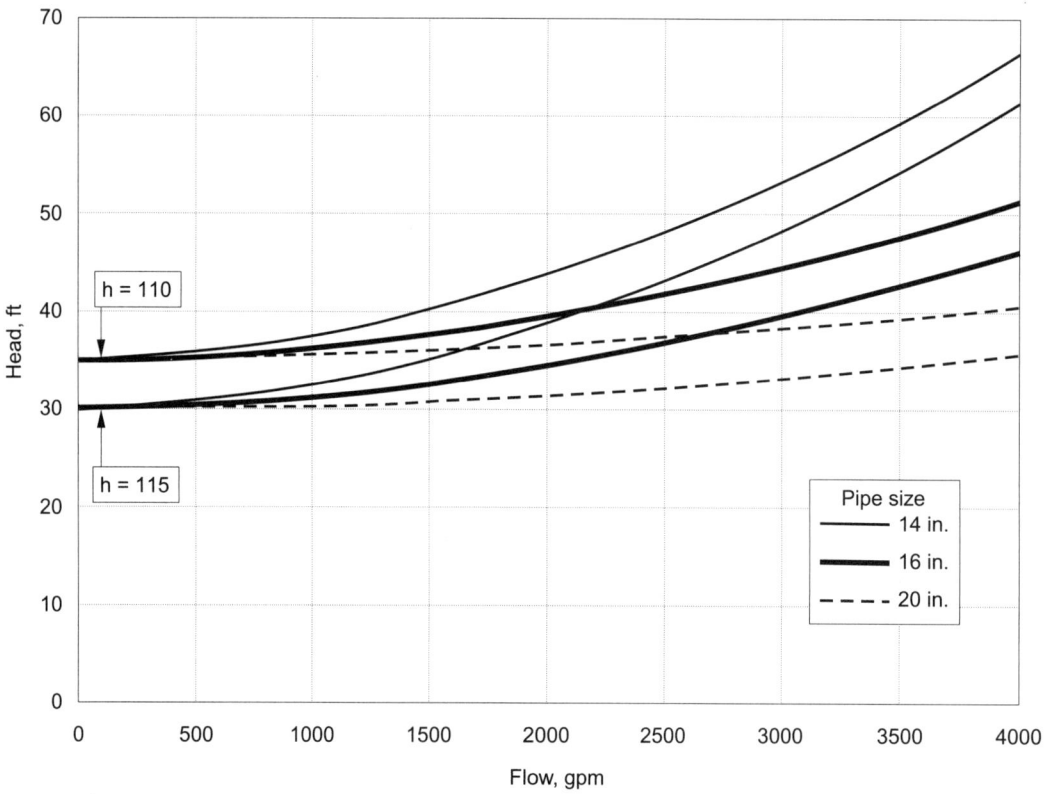

Figure 12.17 System head curves for various wet well water levels and pipe diameters.

Selecting Economical Pipe Size

For a force main with a single constant-speed pump station, it is possible to arrive at a design that minimizes total life-cycle costs. The two primary cost components that are sensitive to pipe diameter are force main construction cost and energy cost. Pipe

> ### Pump vs. Pump Station System Head Curves
>
> System head curves are usually developed for a pump station rather than for individual pump slots in the station. This approach is sufficiently accurate for most applications, but there is a slight error, since the losses in the piping between the suction header and discharge header are usually overestimated when multiple pumps are operating. Head loss is overestimated because the real flow is split between parallel pumps, while most methods for calculating system head do not reduce the flow in this area. For example, if two pumps, running in parallel, each producing 400 gpm, the flow in the piping and the head loss is based on 800 gpm. However, the flow in the individual pump suction and discharge lines is 400 gpm. The error caused by this is usually negligible because the head loss and lift outside the pump station are much greater than any loss in the indi-

diameter typically affects the cost of pumping equipment only slightly. It does not significantly affect pump station structural and control equipment costs.

The problem can therefore be considered to consist of finding the commercially available diameter that minimizes the sum of pipe construction costs and pump energy costs. If the annual pumping cost is relatively constant, the cost equation is

$$C_{PW} = C_{pipe} + SPWF \times C_{energy} \tag{12.7}$$

where
C_{PW} = present worth of pipe and energy cost ($)
C_{pipe} = cost of pipe installation ($)
$SPWF$ = series present worth factor (yr)
C_{energy} = annual pumping energy cost ($)

The series present worth factor is given by

$$SWPF = \frac{(1+i)^N - 1}{i(1+i)^N} \tag{12.8}$$

where
i = interest rate (decimal)
N = amortization period (yr)

The cost of energy is given by

$$C_{energy} = \frac{kQ_p hpt}{e_p e_m} \tag{12.9}$$

where
Q_p = pump flow at operating point (gpm, L/s)
h = pump head at operating point (ft, m)
p = price of energy (cents/kW-hr)
t = total duration pump runs at operating point during the year (hr)
e_p = pump efficiency at operating point (%)
e_m = motor efficiency (%)
k = 0.0189 for US customary units or 1.019 for SI units

For a pump station where only one pump runs at a time, t can be approximated as

$$t = 8760 Q_a/Q_p \tag{12.10}$$

where Q_a = average flow rate to pump station (gpm, L/s)

To use Equation 12.9, the engineer must first estimate average annual pumping flow rate, develop a set of system head curves corresponding to different pipe diameters, and select a group of candidate pumps whose pump head and efficiency characteristic curves are known. The values of flow, head, and efficiency should be calculated at the typical operating point. Additional information on computing efficiency is provided in Section 12.5.

Example 12.1 Economical pipe size.

Determine the most economical diameter for a 2000-m pipe with a Manning's n of 0.013 and a lift of 40 m, with pumps selected to give a pump efficiency of 70% and a motor efficiency of 95%. The pumps are selected to pump at 100 L/s, and the average flow rate to the station is 40 L/s. The cost of power is $0.08/kW-hr, the interest rate is 8% (0.08), and the amortization period is 20 years ($SWPF$ = 9.818).

Solution

For the pipeline, the system head loss can be computed using Equation 12.6 and the Manning equation (Equation 4.11) to compute head loss due to friction (h_f):

$$h_f = 40 + \frac{0.0348}{\left(\frac{D}{1000}\right)^{5.33}}$$

where D is in mm. The total duration the pump runs per year is given by

$$t = 8760\frac{40}{100} = 3504 \text{ hr}$$

The diameter can be estimated from Equation 12.5 for a velocity of 1.6 m/s as

$$D = 35.7\sqrt{\frac{100}{1.6}} = 290 \text{ mm}$$

Therefore, diameters of 200, 250, 300, 350, and 400 mm will be considered. The results are listed in the following table and plotted in the figure. In this case, the 300-mm pipe has the lowest life-cycle costs. All but the 400-mm pipe provide reasonable velocities. This type of analysis for energy costs is described further in WEF (1997) and in Walski, Chase, and Savic (2001). Even though the second reference deals with water distribution, the principles are the same.

Diameter, mm	Unit Cost, $/m	Pipe Cost, $1000	Head, m	Annual Energy Cost, $1000	Present Worth of Energy Cost, $1000	Present Worth, $1000	Velocity, m/s
200	82	163	225	97	949	1112	3.2
250	117	233	96	41	406	639	2.0
300	156	314	61	26	259	573	1.4
350	200	400	49	21	208	608	1.0
400	248	495	45	19	188	683	0.8

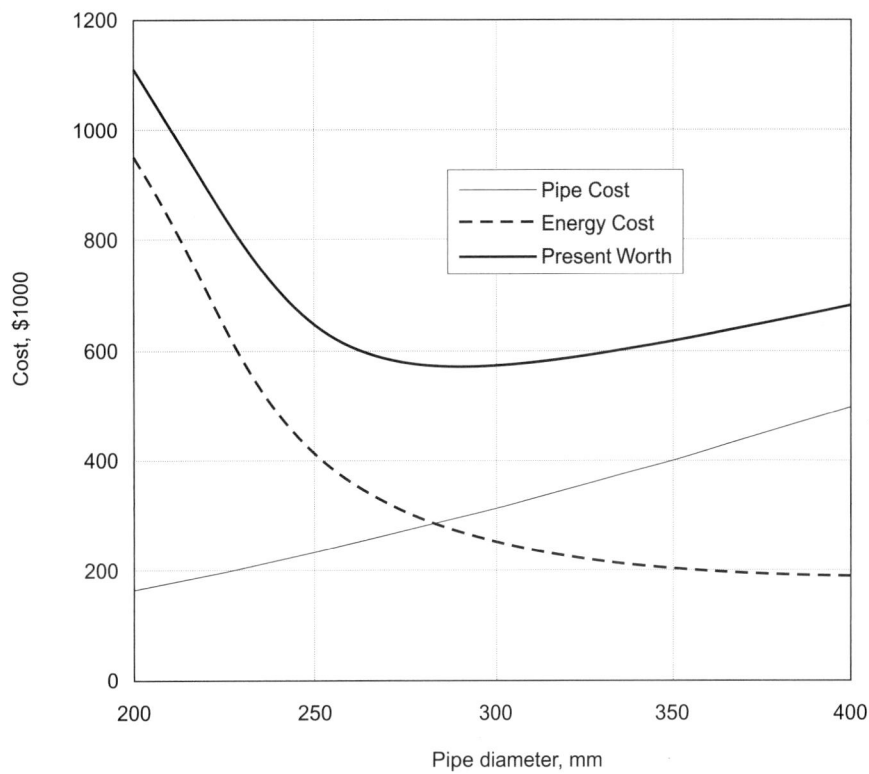

When the actual flow changes dramatically over the life of a project, for instance, as a land development builds out, it may be necessary to do the present worth calculations for separate time periods. Walski (1984) showed that for a linearly increasing flow rate, the flow rate one-third of the way through the project life yields the most accurate estimate of the average operating costs for most projects.

12.4 Modeling Pumped Systems

As described previously, two basic model types are steady-state (static) models and unsteady flow models. Systems with pump stations can be modeled using either approach, but an unsteady flow model (either an EPS with hydrologic routing or a dynamic model) has advantages in that it can:

- Provide information on how the system performs over time, including wet well level fluctuations and pump cycle times
- Be used to perform accurate energy cost analyses
- Provide information on wastewater volumes, not just flow rates
- Account for flow attenuation
- Show the range of flow rates experienced over time, helping to ensure that the piping is sized correctly.

Steady-state (static) model runs may not be adequate for analyzing pumping stations that are subject to flooding. Issues involving wet well sizing and flooding are best analyzed with extended-period simulation (EPS) model runs.

A model of a system with a single pump station typically consists of:
- Inflow to the wet well, either as a single design flow (in the case of steady-state models) or an inflow hydrograph
- Wet well volume (only necessary with unsteady models) and elevation data
- Pump performance characteristics and control settings
- Force main characteristics
- Downstream boundary condition (e.g., water elevation at discharge manhole)

The subsections that follow present information on various aspects of modeling wastewater pumping systems.

Modeling Pumps

The most accurate way to model a particular pump is to enter a number of points (usually three or more) from the pump head characteristic curve into the model and let the model determine the operating point. Some models allow specification of a single design point from which the model approximates a typical curve for a radial discharge pump. Other models allow specification of the power provided by the pump. This is usually a poor approximation to the actual pump performance, and the modeler must remember that this value is the power added to the water, not the rated horsepower of the pump motor. Some models simply transfer flow from the wet well to the end of the force main without truly modeling force main hydraulics.

Control settings for pumps usually consist of a low wet well level at which the pump turns off and a high level at which the pump turns on. If there are multiple pumps, there are multiple on/off settings.

As stated in "Pump Capacity" on page 425, pumps should be selected to provide sufficient head at the design flow rate, which typically corresponds to the anticipated maximum inflow. In a model, if the pump can keep up with the inflow, then the performance of the system is adequate. If the wet well level in the model rises when the pump is running, then either the force main or the pump must be modified to develop a system that will work.

In systems with variable-speed pumps, the modeler must specify how pump speed will be controlled. The most typical control scheme is some form of *flow matching*, in which the pump speed is regulated maintain a constant level in the wet well. The result is that the pumping rate matches the inflow rate as long as the inflow to the wet well does not exceed the pump capacity. Different software models have different ways of representing this type of pumping system, such as a relationship between wet well level and discharge rate. For more efficient operation, variable-speed pumps are typically set to shut off when the inflow rate is very small.

Downstream Flow Attenuation

The hydrographs for pipes immediately downstream of a pump station have sharp peaks due to the abrupt on/off cycles of the pumps. These pipes must be sized based on the peak flow from the pump. Moving downstream, however, these peaks are attenuated due to the fact that, when the pump cycles on, some of the water goes toward increasing downstream flow, while some fills "horizontal storage." For systems in flat terrain, the attenuation effect can be significant.

Flow attenuation is illustrated in Figure 12.18, which shows the effect of changes in pumping rates on a downstream pipe. (Q_{pump} is the actual pumping flow rate; Q_{down} is the flow downstream due to that pumping, and Q_{ave} is the average flow rate.) Even though the pump discharges 520 gpm (33 L/s), the downstream flow on this day would not exceed 370 gpm (23 L/s). Using the peak flow (520 gpm) for steady-state model runs on dry-weather days could give excessive flow rates for pipes far downstream of the pumping station. With a single pump station, this difference should not be significant, but in a system with many lift stations, using the peak pumping rate for dry-weather flow can significantly overstate the flow downstream. These effects can be investigated using an EPS or dynamic model that routes flows. Steady-state models typically provide the option to use the actual pumped flow downstream or to use a flow rate based on the inflow to the pump station. During wet weather, the pumps are more likely to remain on all the time, so the effects of cycling are reduced.

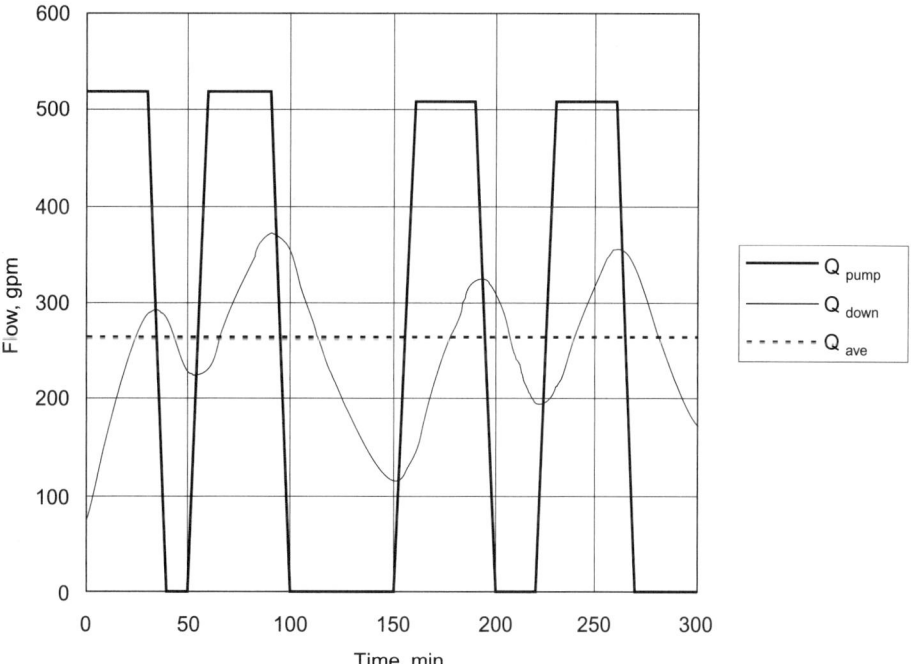

Figure 12.18 Flow attenuation in downstream sewer pipe caused by pump cycling.

Identifying Potential Problems

An important application of models is identification of potential problems in system operations. Two situations that can be assessed with the aid of a model are the effect of wet well flooding on pump performance and the potential for downstream flooding due to flows in excess of the design flow.

"Scotch and toilet water?"

When the water level in a wet well rises above the normal high level, the wet well is said to be "flooded" or submerged. This situation occurs when the inflow to the pump station exceeds the design pump rate, most often during wet weather. Apart from the obvious concern of wet well overtopping, high wet well levels can lead to problems with pump performance.

Because wastewater pumps do not usually pump against a very high head, an increase in wet well depth of a only a few feet (1–2 m) can significantly affect the system head curve, causing the pump to convey a higher flow than the rated design. Some pumping stations will pump 30 to 70 percent above their rated capacity when the wet well is submerged. Since power in excess of the pump's design power is drawn as the operating point shifts to the right on the pump curve, it is possible to overload the motor so that it fails or shuts off just when it is needed most.

In the situation illustrated in Figure 12.19, a pump designed to operate at 4000 gpm (253 L/s) for normal wet well levels will actually pump 5000 gpm (316 L/s) when the wet well is flooded by 10 ft.

The increase in pumping rates due to wet well flooding just described can result in downstream flooding. Another situation that can occur during wet-weather events is that a pump station designed to have only one pump running at a time may call for a second pump. The additional flow can contribute to flooding in the downstream gravity system, as illustrated in Figure 12.20, in which a second pump is added to the example of Figure 12.19. The flow does not double because of the additional head losses in the force main, but nevertheless flows significantly increase when two pumps are run in a station sized for a single pump. In the example, with two pumps running, the flow increases to nearly 6000 gpm (380 L/s).

Modeling a Pipeline with Multiple High Points

Modeling a system with a force main is more complicated if multiple high points exist along a pipe run, as illustrated in Figure 12.21. There are three options for constructing the pipeline:

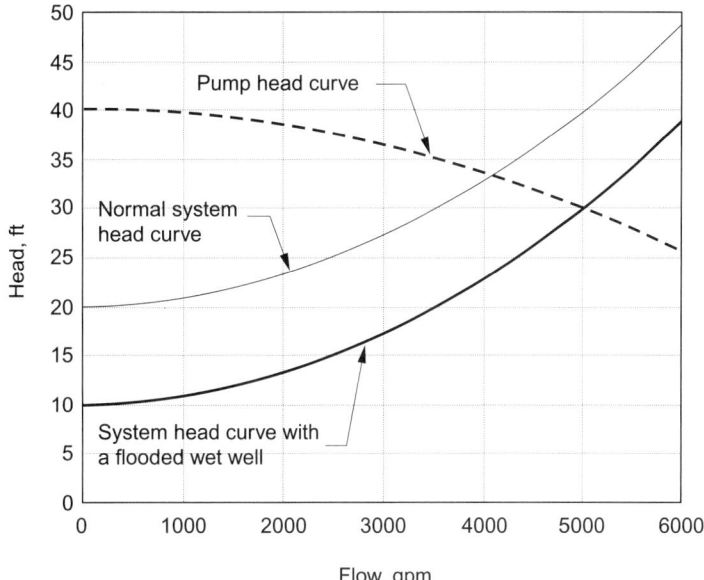

Figure 12.19 Effect of a flooded wet well on system head curve.

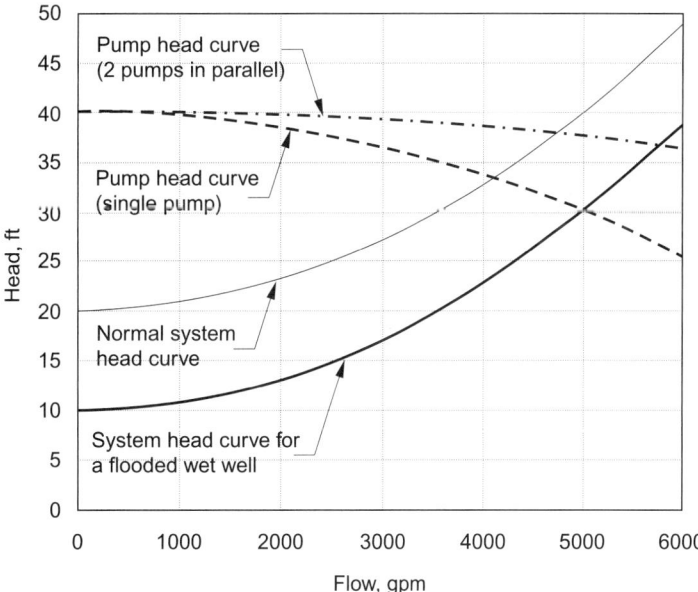

Figure 12.20 Effect of a flooded well on the discharge of a pump station with two pumps in parallel.

1. The force main has a combination air/vacuum valve at A. Gravity flow is possible between A and B.
2. The force main is sealed at A and operates as siphon.
3. The force main from the pump station discharges to a manhole at A. A gravity pipe runs from A to B, and an additional pump station is constructed at B.

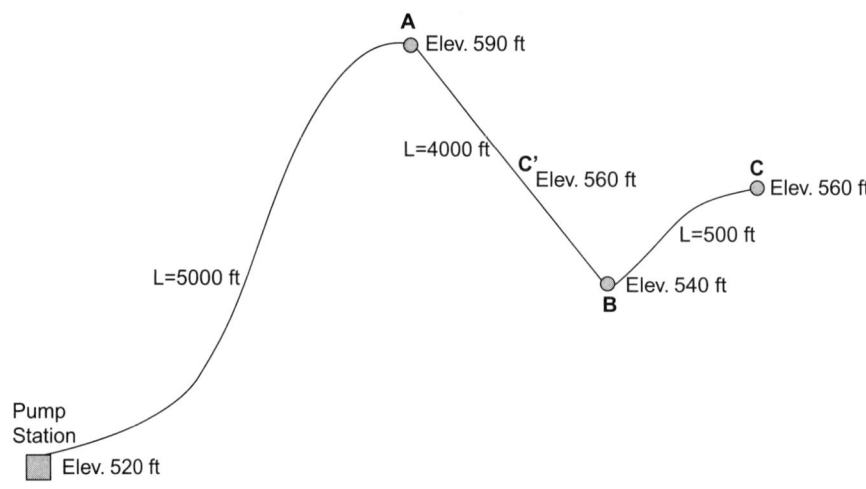

Figure 12.21 Profile of pipeline with multiple high points.

Option 3 is usually the most expensive, but is the best option if there are any service connections between A and B. Constructing two separate force mains makes the analysis easier. Moreover, it is easier to make the system work with more-economical constant-speed pumps.

Option 2 appears attractive at first because it uses the least pumping energy. However, there are usually operational problems because gas pockets form at A and restrict the capacity of the pipeline.

Option 1 is the most common approach, although it is the most complicated to analyze. For low flow rates, the system acts as a force main from the pump station to point A and as an inverted siphon from point A to point C. However, at a higher flow rate, the pipe becomes full, and the pipeline must be analyzed as flowing from the pump station to point C. The transition between the two types of flow occurs at a flow rate corresponding to the full-flow capacity of the pipe between A and B, which can be calculated using a gravity-flow model such as FlowMaster or SewerCAD. For the simple case of constant slope, diameter, and Manning's n, the flow rate is

$$Q = \frac{kD^{8/3}S^{1/2}}{n} \qquad (12.11)$$

where Q = full-flow capacity (gpm, ft³/s, m³/s)
    D = diameter (in., mm)
    S = slope (ft/ft, m/m)
    n = Manning's n
    k = 0.275 for Q in gpm and D in in., 0.463 for Q in ft³/s and D in ft, or 0.312 for SI units

■ **Example 12.2** Discontinuous system head curve.

Plot the system head curve for the pipeline in Figure 12.21. There is a single pump station to point C, so water must flow over the intermediate high point at A. For a 12-in. pipe, the flow from the variable-speed pump varies from 800 to 3200 gpm.

Solution

The full-flow capacity of the pipe from A to B is

$$Q = \frac{0.275(12)^{8/3}\left(\frac{50}{4000}\right)^{1/2}}{0.011} = 2100 \text{ gpm}$$

For flows below 2100 gpm, gravity flow exists between points A and C', and the system head curve can be calculated from the pump station to point A using the Manning equation for friction loss:

$$h = 590 - 520 + \frac{13.2(5000)(0.011Q)^2}{12^{5.33}}$$

For flows greater than 2100 gpm (154 L/s), the system head curve between the pump station and point C is

$$h = 560 - 520 + \frac{13.2(9500)(0.011Q)^2}{12^{5.33}}$$

These system head curves are shown in the following figure. As the flow increases to greater than 2100 gpm, the pipe behaves as if there were gravity flow until the pipe section from A to C' fills with water. Once it fills and shuts off the air-release valve at A, the system switches to the higher curve. As flows decrease, system performance switches back to gravity flow as soon as the head at A drops to atmospheric pressure. If the pipe slope from A to B is steep enough for gravity flow, the condition may be referred to as *flow away from the high point*.

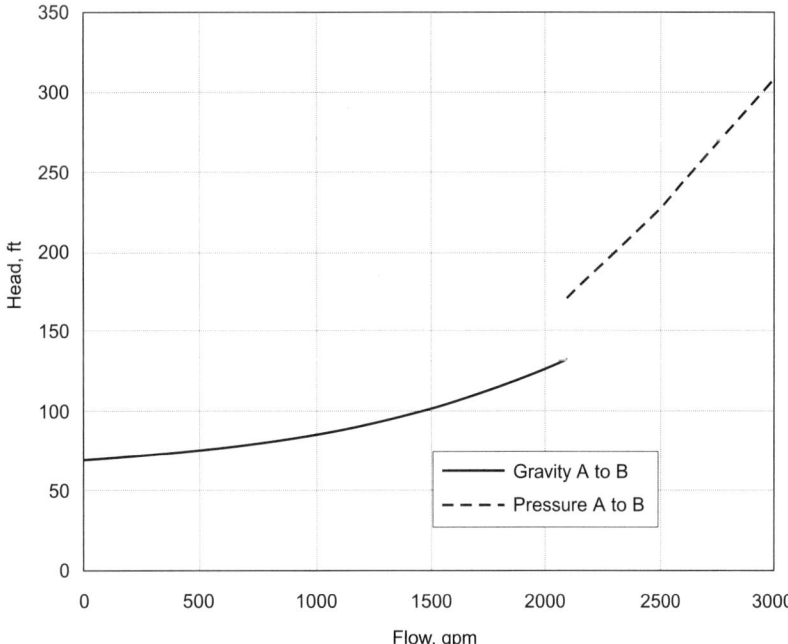

In Example 12.2, it would be more economical to pump at a rate less than 2100 gpm (133 L/s) whenever feasible. If point A were much higher than point C, it would be more economical to pump at a higher rate. Each situation must be evaluated individually.

In modeling flow through a force main with multiple high points, any pipes that can flow partly full should be modeled as gravity pipes, even though they will be flowing full in some cases. In Figure 12.21, only the pipe from the pump station to point A should be modeled as a pressure pipe, while the pipes from A to C should be modeled as gravity pipes, even though they will usually flow full. In Example 12.2, the pipe from A to B has a constant slope. If the slope were not constant, it would be easier to analyze the flow with a model than with a manual calculation.

Pockets of hydrogen sulfide and other corrosive gases tend to form at high points in force mains. Whether these pockets remain trapped on the downward-sloping pipe depends primarily on the slope of the pipe and the velocity. Gas pockets will tend to move downstream when P', given by the following equation, is greater than 1 (Walski et al., 1994):

$$P' = \frac{0.88 V^2}{g D S^{0.32}} \qquad (12.12)$$

where
V = velocity (ft/s, m/s)
g = gravitational acceleration (ft/s^2, m/s^2)
D = diameter (ft, m)
S = slope

More thorough discussions of corrosive gases in sewers are given in American Society of Civil Engineers (1989) and Pomeroy (1974).

12.5 Efficiency Considerations

Pump selection should be based on an analysis of overall life-cycle costs for the pump station. One of the more difficult quantities to determine is the energy cost, which was described in "Selecting Economical Pipe Size" on page 438. To compute the energy cost, it is necessary to estimate the actual efficiency of the pump(s). The following sections describe methods for determining efficiency for both constant- and variable-speed pumps. Some modeling software can automatically perform energy cost calculations.

Constant-Speed Pumping

Manufacturers usually provide pump-characteristic data in the form of graphs that must be converted to equations in order to perform calculations. The head characteristic curve can usually be approximated by a power function as

$$h = h_o - aQ^b \qquad (12.13)$$

or a polynomial as

$$h = a_0 + a_1 Q + a_2 Q^2 + a_3 Q^3 \qquad (12.14)$$

where
h = total dynamic head (ft, m)
Q = pump flow (gpm, ft^3/s, m^3/hr, m^3/s)
h_o = pump shutoff head (ft, m)

a, b = power regression coefficients

a_0, a_1, a_2, a_3 = polynomial regression coefficients

Although h_0 can be read directly from the pump curve, a and b must be calculated. A simple approach is to pick two points, (Q_1, h_1) and (Q_2, h_2), from the head characteristic curve. These points should be fairly far from each other and cover the range of flows expected. Coefficients a and b can be determined with

$$b = \frac{\log\left(\frac{h_0 - h_2}{h_0 - h_1}\right)}{\log\left(\frac{Q_2}{Q_1}\right)} \tag{12.15}$$

and

$$a = \frac{h_0 - h_1}{Q_1^b} \tag{12.16}$$

The logarithms can be base 10 or base e as long as they are consistent. The coefficients for the polynomial curves can be determined using a polynomial regression computer program.

Brake power curves are approximated by

$$P = P_0 + AQ^B \tag{12.17}$$

where P = brake horsepower (hp, kW)
P_0 = power when $Q = 0$
Q = pump flow (ft³/s, gpm, m³/s, m³/hr)
A, B = regression coefficients

A and B can be estimated using two points, (Q_1, P_1) and (Q_2, P_2), as

$$B = \frac{\log\left(\frac{P_2 - P_0}{P_1 - P_0}\right)}{\log\left(\frac{Q_2}{Q_1}\right)} \tag{12.18}$$

and

$$A = \frac{P_1 - P_0}{Q_1^B} \tag{12.19}$$

The efficiency curve is usually approximated by a parabola of the form

$$e_p = xQ^2 + yQ + z \tag{12.20}$$

where e_p = pump efficiency (%)

Although pump efficiency is used in Equation 12.20, in some cases, especially for close-coupled pumps, the manufacturer will provide wire-to-water efficiency instead.

In theory, the efficiency curve should pass through the origin, so that z can usually be taken as zero. With that approximation, x and y can be calculated from two values (Q_1, e_1) and (Q_2, e_2) as

$$x = \frac{e_2 - e_1 \frac{Q_2}{Q_1}}{Q_2^2 - Q_1^2 \frac{Q_2}{Q_1}} \tag{12.21}$$

$$y = \frac{e_1 - xQ_1^2}{Q_1} \tag{12.22}$$

and

$$z = 0 \tag{12.23}$$

As stated in Chapter 4 (page 130), pump efficiency is the ratio of water power out of the pump to brake horsepower in and wire-to-water efficiency is the ratio of water power out to electric power in. Thus, the efficiency for water (wastewater) pumping can be calculated from the flow, head, and power as

$$e = K\frac{Qh}{P} \tag{12.24}$$

where
- e = efficiency (%)
- Q = pump flow (ft^3/s, gpm, m^3/hr, m^3/s)
- h = head (ft, m)
- P = power (hp, kW)
- K = 0.025 for Q in gpm, h in ft, power in hp
- = 0.272 for Q in m^3/hr, h in m, power in kW
- = 11.3 for Q in ft^3/s, h in ft, power in hp

Efficiency data are not provided for a range of flows as large as that of the brake horsepower data. In such cases, it may be better to calculate the efficiency curve using Equation 12.25 instead of Equation 12.20.

$$e = K\frac{Q(h_o - aQ^b)}{P_o + AQ^B} \tag{12.25}$$

Example 12.3 Curve-fitting pump performance data.

Use Equations 12.15 through 12.23 to determine the coefficients for a typical wastewater pump (4-in. nonclog vertical pump at 1160 rpm) with data from the following table and figure.

Q, gpm	h, ft	P, hp	e, %
0	70	5.0	0
300	56	7.8	57
550	38	9.5	62

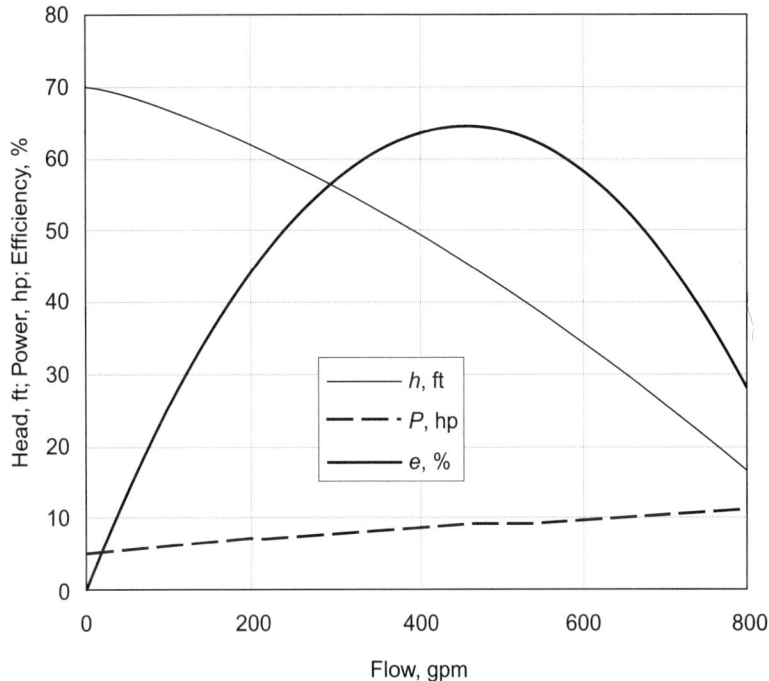

Solution

Equations 12.15 through 12.23 give the values of the coefficients as follows:

Coefficient	Value
a	0.00586
b	1.36
A	0.0322
B	0.783
x	−0.000309
y	0.283

With Equations 12.15 through 12.23, it is possible to calculate pump efficiency, head, and power for any flow rate for a constant-speed pump. For simple systems with a single pump (i.e., only one operating point), there is usually no need to use the equations. However, they are useful when there are several pump stations or several pumps operating in a given station.

Variable-Speed Pumping

While constant-speed pumps usually operate over a fairly narrow band of flow rates, variable-speed pumps can operate over a wider band of flow rates. Adjustments for variable-speed pumps can be made using the pump affinity laws introduced in Chapter 4. For a given point on a pump characteristic curve, the flow, head, and power can be related to the speed by arranging the affinity laws as:

$$\frac{Q}{Q_f} = \frac{N}{N_f} = n \tag{12.26}$$

$$\frac{h}{h_f} = \left(\frac{N}{N_f}\right)^2 = n^2 \tag{12.27}$$

$$\frac{P}{P_f} = \left(\frac{N}{N_f}\right)^3 = n^3 \tag{12.28}$$

where Q = pump flow (gpm, ft³/s, m³/s)
Q_f = flow at full speed (gpm, ft³/s, m³/s)
N = rotational speed of the pump (rpm)
N_f = rotational speed of the at full speed (rpm)
n = ratio of pump speed to full speed
h = pump head (ft, m)
h_f = pump head at full speed (ft, m)
P = power (hp, kW)
P_f = power at full speed (hp, kW)

Substituting the affinity law into Equations 12.13, 12.17, 12.20, and 12.24 gives the following equations for interpolating values for head, power, and efficiency:

$$h = n^2 h_o - an^{2-b} Q^b \tag{12.29}$$

$$P = n^3 P_o + A n^{3-B} Q^B \tag{12.30}$$

$$e = x\left(\frac{Q}{n}\right)^2 + y\left(\frac{Q}{n}\right) + z \tag{12.31}$$

and

$$e = K \frac{Q n h_o - a n^{1-b} Q^{1+b}}{n^3 P_o + A n^{3-B} Q^B} \tag{12.32}$$

The value of these equations is that once the coefficients have been developed for the pump operating at full speed, there is no need to recalculate the coefficients for that pump if it is operated as a variable-speed pump. The pump curves at 70 percent (n = 0.7) and 40 percent (n = 0.4) of full speed are shown in Figure 12.22.

There are some shortcomings with using the pump affinity laws as presented above. First, data from real pumps do not precisely follow the relationships derived from the affinity laws. Second, while the pump efficiency curves should simply slide to the left for lower-speed operation, the variable-speed drive itself introduces some inefficiency, so the overall (wire-to-water) efficiency drops as the speed slows. Finally, the affinity laws cannot be used to move from one operating point to the next. For example, if a pump produces 300 gpm at full speed, one cannot simply use the affinity law directly to calculate the flow at another speed (say 70 percent) as Q = 300(0.7/1.0) = 210 gpm. Instead, the actual operating point must be determined using the system head curve.

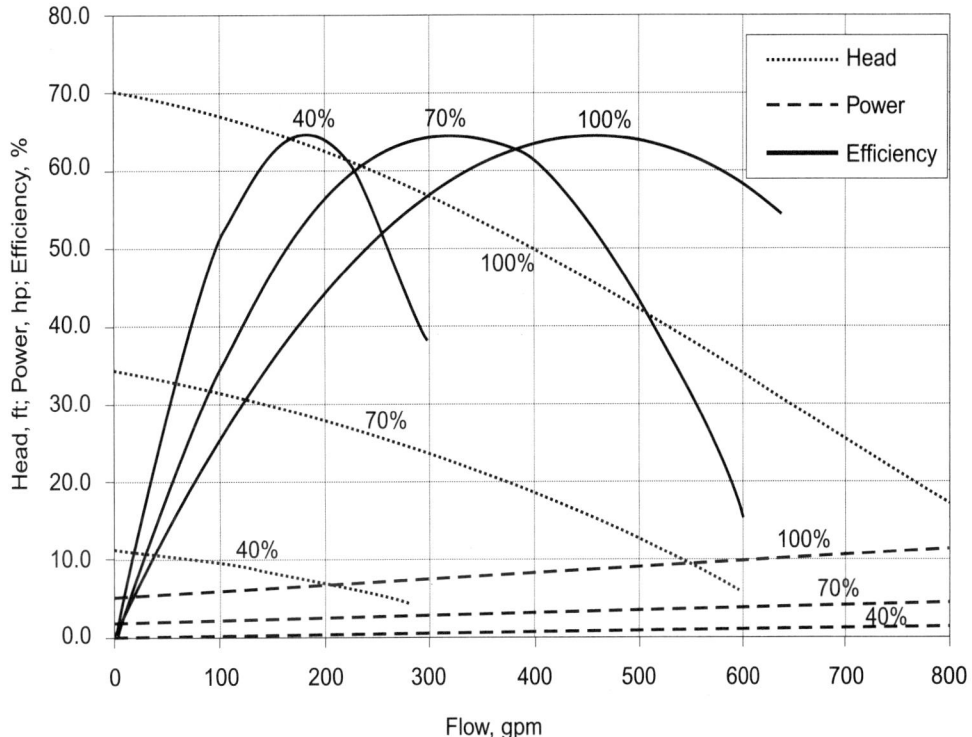

Figure 12.22 Pump characteristic curves (head, power, and efficiency) for variable-speed pumps.

The system head curve intersects the family of pump head curves at many different speeds. The actual operating point depends on the logic used to control the pump. Typical logical controls include:

- Maintain constant wet well level
- Maintain constant discharge pressure
- Maintain constant discharge
- Manually set pump speed.

It is this control logic that determines the operating point of the pump. For wastewater pumps set to maintain a constant wet well level (i.e., match the inflow rate to the wet well), the operating point will be the intersection of the system head curve and a vertical line equal to the flow rate, and the speed will be that of the pump curve that intersects that point.

This type of operation is illustrated in Figure 12.23 for the pump characteristics shown in Figure 12.22. When the inflow is 440 gpm, the pump runs at full speed and meets that inflow. As the flow drops to 300 gpm, the pump speed drops to 90 percent of full speed to match that flow. If the flow drops to 100 gpm, the speed can drop to 79 percent. However, at this point, the velocity in the force main may be so low and the pump may be running so inefficiently that it is better to stop the pump and allow the wet well level to rise. When the wet well hits a high level, the pump comes on again at full speed and pumps the wet well down to the desired level, while maintaining a good flushing velocity. If the speed drops below 75 percent of full speed, the pump is

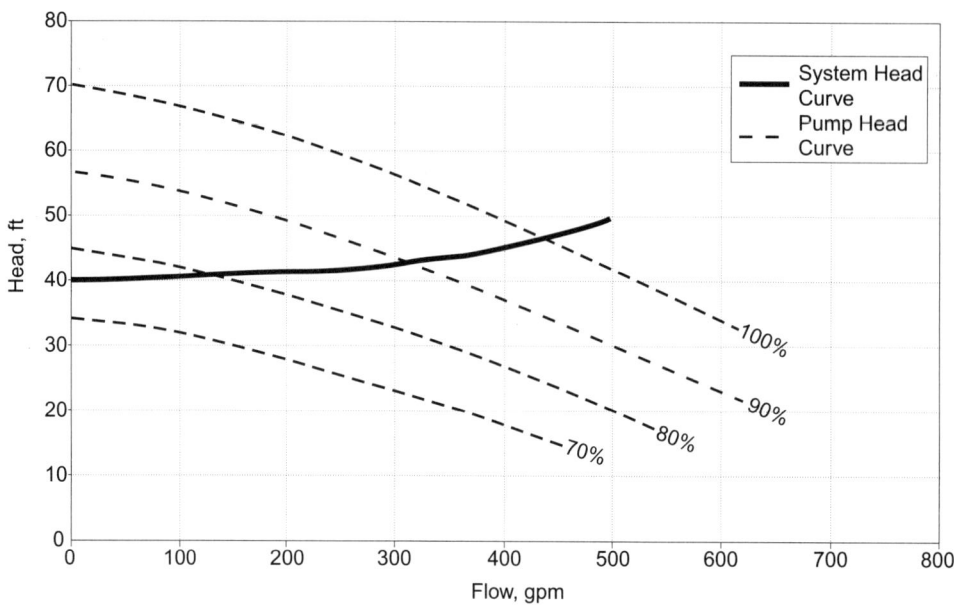

Figure 12.23 Operating points on system head curve of a variable-speed pump at different speeds expressed as a fraction of full speed.

no longer able to produce any flow and the impeller simply turns ineffectively, unless it is shut off by the pump control. (The at operating speeds of less than 75 percent is zero.) The results are summarized in Table 12.3. If the inflow exceeds 440 gpm, the pump will not be able to keep up with the flow and the wet well level will rise. Another pump, if available, is usually turned on when the level hits a set point.

Table 12.3 also illustrates that the efficiency of variable-speed pumps drops off as the operating point deviates from the pump's full-speed best-efficiency point. While the drop is less than for a constant-speed pump, the loss of efficiency is still significant. This reduction in efficiency highlights the need for multiple pumps in stations that experience a wide range of flows, such as in systems with combined sewers or significant infiltration or inflow.

Table 12.3 Efficiencies of a variable-speed pump.

Flow, gpm	Speed, rpm	Head, ft	Efficiency, %
0	<75	40.0	0
100	79	40.3	30.8
200	84	41.2	49.8
300	90	42.7	59.9
400	96	44.8	64.1
440	100	45.8	64.0

The loss of efficiency with decreasing flow is less dramatic for steeper system head curves. Because of this, variable-speed pumps are more attractive in situations in which most of the energy is used to overcome friction rather than elevation.

Automated Energy Calculations

Some hydraulic models can be used to determine pumping power usage and energy costs by simulating a period of time using extended-period simulation runs. This capability is helpful for making comparisons between different pumps or different types of pump stations. It is especially useful for variable-speed pumps, which have continuously changing flow rate, head, and efficiency.

Figure 12.24 shows a comparison of pump efficiencies between a constant-speed pump and a corresponding variable-speed pump calculated by the WaterCAD model (Haestad Methods, 2003). The constant-speed pump can operate near its best efficiency point whenever it cycles on, whereas the efficiency of the variable-speed pump fluctuates as the flow changes.

In addition to calculating efficiency and rates of energy use, models can calculate cumulative energy use, which can be used in life-cycle cost analyses.

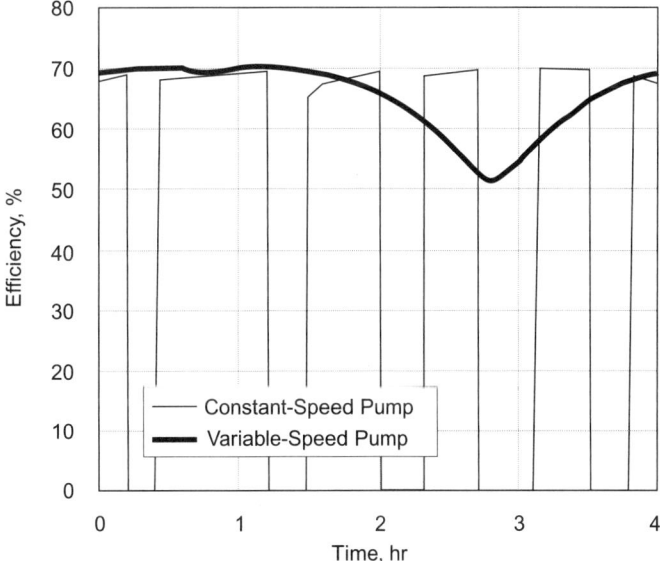

Figure 12.24 Comparison of pump efficiencies over time for a constant-speed pump and a variable-speed pump computed by the WaterCAD model (Haestad Methods, 2003).

12.6 Force Mains with Multiple Pump Stations

Developing system head curves and selecting pumps for force mains with multiple pump stations is a more difficult task than for force mains with a single pump station. A single pump station sees a narrow band of system head curves, whereas a pump station working with several other stations can be faced with a wide range of system head curves, depending on which other pumps in the system are operating along the force main. These complications make manual calculation of system head curves difficult, so it is especially important to use a model to generate system head curves.

The problem of calculating head curves is further complicated when construction of pump stations along the force main is staggered over time. In these cases, flows during the early years of the force main's life barely reach scouring velocity and/or pumps are shut off for a very long time between pump cycles, while in later years capacity is limited. In these cases it may even be necessary to initially install a small force main with plans to install a parallel line as growth occurs and development reaches buildout.

Figure 12.25 shows a typical layout of a force main with three pump stations along it. The system head curve experienced by Pump Station 2 (PS2) varies depending upon whether Pump Station 1 (PS1) and Pump Station (PS3) are running. Models can be used to generate the hydraulic grade line (HGL) downstream of PS2 for all combinations of pump operation. The wet well water level can be subtracted from the calculated hydraulic grade at the discharge of the pumps to develop the set of system head curves. Some software can automatically generate these system head curves. The curves in Figure 12.26 show that PS2 may be required to operate against a wide range of heads at any flow rate. Similar sets of curves could be created for PS1 and PS3.

When a pump station must operate against a wide range of heads, it may be impossible for a single constant-speed pump to run efficiently at all the heads encountered. There are several options, including the following:

- Several different-sized pumps to cover the range of heads
- A large variable-speed pump
- A large constant-speed pump with a control valve

If the head required is primarily for overcoming friction losses ($h_f > h_l$), a variable-speed pump will usually have the lowest life-cycle costs, but multiple constant-speed pumps will be more economical if friction losses are small and most of the energy goes into overcoming lift ($h_l > h_f$).

The pump farthest from the discharge end of the force main will experience the widest range of fluctuations of system head, while pumps nearer the discharge point will experience fairly constant system heads. In some cases, the diameter of the entire force main may be constant, but more typically the pipe size increases as one moves downstream in the direction of flow due to additional loads entering the system.

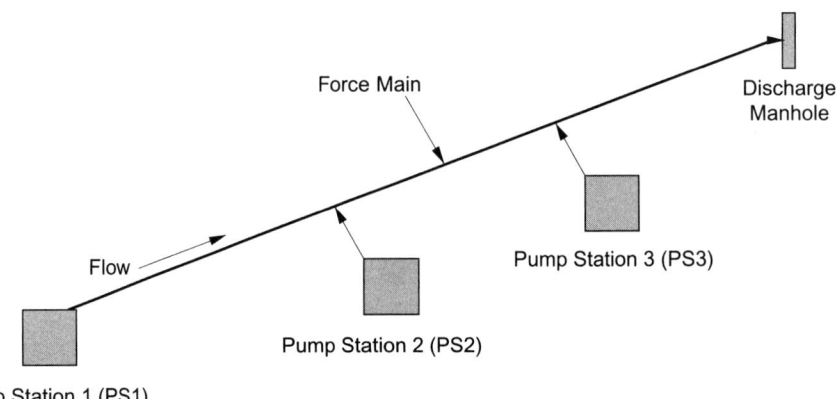

Figure 12.25 Force main with three pump stations.

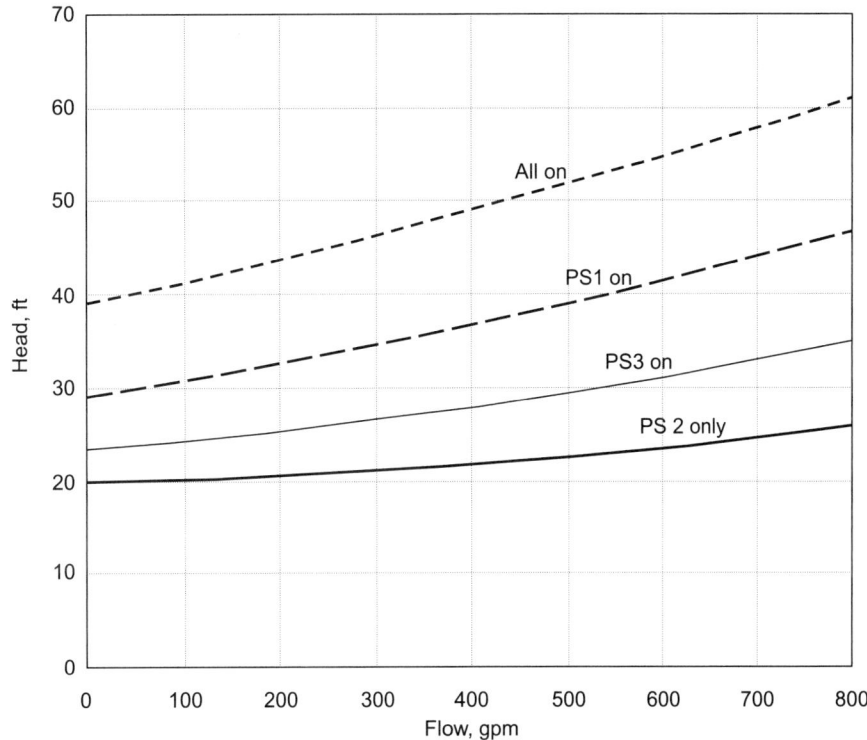

Figure 12.26 System head curves at pump station PS2 as a function of the operation of pump station PS2 only, PS3, PS1, and all pump stations on.

Pump selection for multiple pump stations is complicated by the fact that the number of combinations of possible pumps is very large. A common approach is to initially model the pump stations as known inflows (instead of using pump curves) and try a variety of pipe sizes to achieve a reasonable range of velocities. When all pumps are running, the velocity should stay below 8 ft/s (2.5 m/s), and a reasonable velocity should still be achieved when only one pump is running. Once pipe sizes are known, it is possible to determine the range of HGLs at the outlet of each pump station. Knowing the HGLs, wet well water levels, and pump flow rates, initial pump selection can occur. The actual pump curves can then be inserted into the model, and the system can be simulated for the full range of pump combinations. A life-cycle cost analysis as described in Section 12.5 can then be performed.

When variable-speed pumps are used, the process is similar. However, instead of having distinct lines, as in Figure 12.26, the system head curves fill the entire area from the top line (all pumps running) to the bottom line (only PS2 running). Variable-speed pumps are not a cure-all, as they tend to be maintenance intensive and have a tendency to "hunt" for a correct speed.

12.7 Hydraulic Transients

Hydraulic transients occur whenever a fluid accelerates or decelerates. The magnitude of the pressure change resulting from the change in velocity is

$$dh = \frac{a}{g} dv \quad (12.33)$$

where dh = change in head (ft, m)
   a = speed of the pressure wave (ft/s, m/s)
   g = gravitational acceleration (32.2 ft/s^2, 9.81 m/s^2)
   dv = change in velocity (ft/s, m/s)

The speed of a pressure wave depends on the type of pipe and joint and the presence of dissolved gases in the fluid; it typically varies from 4000-1000 ft/s (1200–300 m/s). The higher values correspond to fairly rigid pipes and joints with no entrained gases.

From Equation 12.33, if flow with a velocity of 5 ft/s (1.5 m/s) suddenly stops in a force main, perhaps due to a pump shutting off unexpectedly, the change in head will be 500 ft (150 m) for a pipe with a = 3200 ft/s (1000 m/s). This shows up as an abrupt 215-psi (1400 kPa) drop in pressure on the discharge side of the pump and a corresponding increase on the suction side. This drop in pressure could cause the fluid in the pipe to briefly vaporize and then condense in a process called *column separation*, sometimes with catastrophic results. The pressure wave from this transient event moves back and forth through the pipe until it is dampened by friction, outflow of water, or surge-control devices.

Because of the potential for high pressures that can damage the system, engineers must consider transients when designing pumping stations. Unfortunately, some of the devices for controlling surges in clean water (e.g., standpipes and air chambers) do not work as well for wastewater and require more maintenance.

For smaller force mains, there is usually enough surge allowance built into the pipe to handle most normal transient events if the velocity is less than 8 ft/s (2.4 m/s). A pipe with a thick-enough wall can contain most events. Other control mechanisms include:

- Adjusting pump check valves so that they close by the time the pressure wave reflects, but not so quickly that they slam as soon as the pump kicks off

- Using pumps with a long run-down time, so that the magnitude of the surge is small

- Installing air release/vacuum breaker valves at high points to prevent column separation.

Surge devices must be maintained regularly, which can be difficult with wastewater, as grease can clog air and vacuum valves.

For long, large-diameter force mains, the risk of damage due to transients is sufficiently high that an analysis of the pipeline with a transient analysis model is justifiable.

Most transient analysis is done with computerized solutions using the method of characteristics. Figure 12.27 shows a profile of a force main and transient pressures from a pump shutdown computed using the Hammer transient analysis model (Haestad Methods, 2003). The upper line shows the maximum head experienced at any point along the pipe, and the lower line shows the minimum head. The shaded area is the portion of the pipeline that will experience negative pressure (hydraulic grade line below pipe) and possible cavitation or pipe collapse. With a model, the engineer can, for example, evaluate the effectiveness of a vacuum breaker valve at the intermediate high point in Figure 12.27 for relieving negative pressures. Figure 12.28 shows a typical pressure trace on the downstream side of the pump in the previous figure.

Numerous texts address transients in more detail than can be covered here, including ASCE (1992), Betamio de Almendia and Koelle (1992), Chaudhry (1979), Sanks (1998), Watters (1984) and Wylie, Streeter, and Suo (1993).

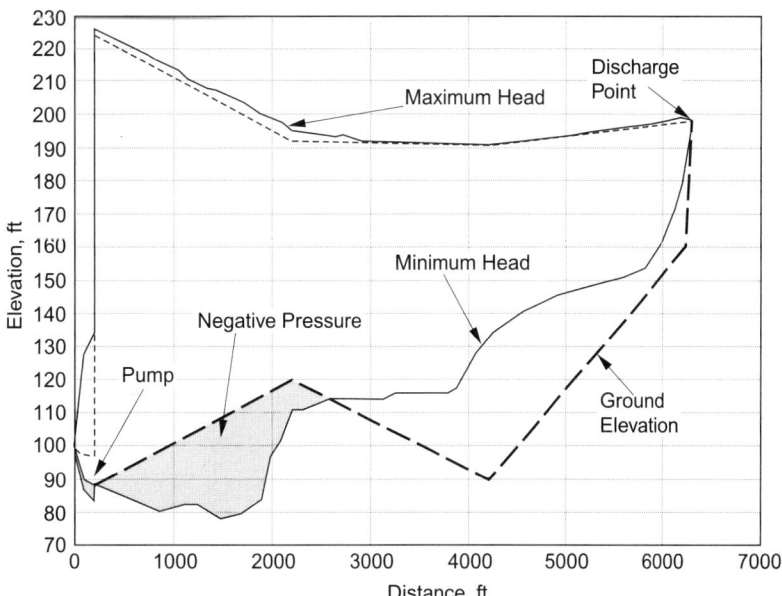

Figure 12.27 Profile of transient pressures and maximum and minimum heads along a force main after a pump shutdown — calculated by the Hammer transient analysis model (Haestad Methods, 2003).

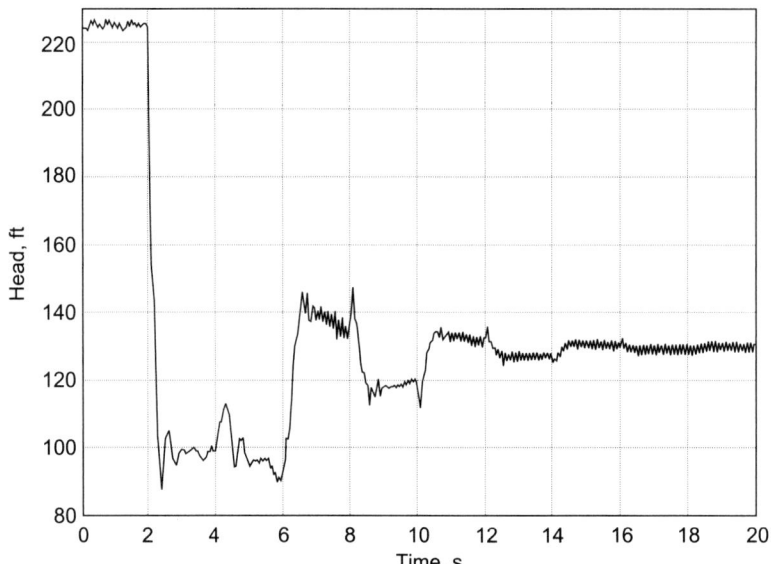

Figure 12.28 Pressure trace on the downstream side of the pump at station 0 in Figure 12.27.

References

American Society of Civil Engineers (ASCE). 1989. *Sulfide in Wastewater Collection and Treatment Systems*. ASCE MOP 69. American Society of Civil Engineers.

American Society of Civil Engineers (ASCE). 1992. *Pressure Pipeline Design for Water and Wastewater*. New York: American Society of Civil Engineers.

Bachus, L. 2004. The mechanical seal game. *World Pumps*, no. 449: 38.

Betamio de Almendia, A., and E. Koelle. 1992. *Fluid Transients in Pipe Networks*. London: Elsevier Applied Science.

Burton, F. L. 1996. Wastewater collection systems. In *Water Resources Handbook,* edited by L. W. Mays. New York: McGraw-Hill.

Chaudhry, M. H. 1979. *Applied Hydraulic Transients*. New York: Van Nostrand Reinhold.

Great Lakes and Upper Mississippi River Board of State Public Health and Environmental Managers (GLUMRB). 1997. *Recommended Standards for Wastewater Facilities*. Albany, NY: Great Lakes Mississippi River Board.

Haestad Methods. 2003. *HAMMER Transient Analysis Model*. Waterbury, CT: Haestad Methods.

Haestad Methods. 2003. *WaterCAD Water Distribution Modeling*. Waterbury, CT: Haestad Methods.

Hydraulic Institute. 2000. *Hydraulic Institute Standards*. Parsippany, NJ: Hydraulic Institute.

Hydraulic Institute. 2001. *Pump Life Cycle Costs: A Guide to LCC Analysis for Pumping Systems.* Parsippany, NJ: Hydraulic Institute.

Karassik, I. J., J. P. Messina, P. Cooper, and C. C. Heald. 2000. *Pump Handbook.* New York: McGraw-Hill.

Mackay, R. C. 2004. ANSI vs. API? *Pumps and Systems* 12, no. 3: 36.

Pomeroy, R. D. 1974. *Process Design Manual for Sulfide Control in Sanitary Sewage Systems.* EPA 625/1-7-005. US Environmental Protection Agency.

Sanks, R. L. 1998. *Pumping Station Design.* Butterworth-Heinemann.

Submersible Wastewater Pump Association. 1997. *Submersible Pumping Systems Handbook.* Highland Park, IL: Submersible Wastewater Pump Association.

Tchobanoglous, G. 1981. *Wastewater Engineering: Collection and Pumping of Wastewater.* New York: McGraw-Hill.

Walski, T. M. 1984. Estimating O&M costs when costs vary with flow. *Journal of Water Resources Planning and Management* 110, no. 3: 355.

Walski, T. M., D. V. Chase, and D. A. Savic. 2001. *Water Distribution Modeling.* Waterbury, CT: Haestad Press.

Walski, T. M., T. S. Barnhart, J. M. Driscoll, and R. M. Yencha. 1994. Hydraulics of corrosive gas pockets in force mains. *Water Environment Research* 66, no. 6: 772.

Water Environment Federation (WEF). 1993. *Design of Wastewater and Stormwater Pumping Stations.* WEF MOP FD-4. Alexandria, VA: Water Environment Federation.

Water Environment Federation (WEF). 1997. *Energy Conservation in Wastewater Treatment Facilities.* WEF MOP MFD-2. Alexandria, VA: Water Environment Federation.

Watters, G. Z. 1984. *Analysis and Control of Unsteady Flow in Pipelines.* Stoneham, MA: Butterworth.

Wylie, E. B., V. L. Streeter, and L. Suo. 1993. *Fluid Transients in Systems.* Englewood Cliffs, NJ: Prentice Hall.

Problems

12.1 Specify the all nominal sizes for PVC pipe that could be used to carry 750 gpm. The velocity in the pipe should be within the typical velocity range for a force main.

12.2 Use the sketch of the pumping station in the figure to determine the system head (in feet) to lift water to the gravity sewer at a flow rate of 500 gpm when the water level in the wet well is at the high and low water elevations. The force main is 150 ft of 6 in. ductile iron pipe. The pump inlet is 2 ft below the wet well low-water elevation. Assume that minor losses are negligible.

  a. Use the Darcy-Weisbach equation to find the friction head.

  b. Use the Hazen-Williams equation to find the friction head.

  c. Use the Manning equation to find the friction head.

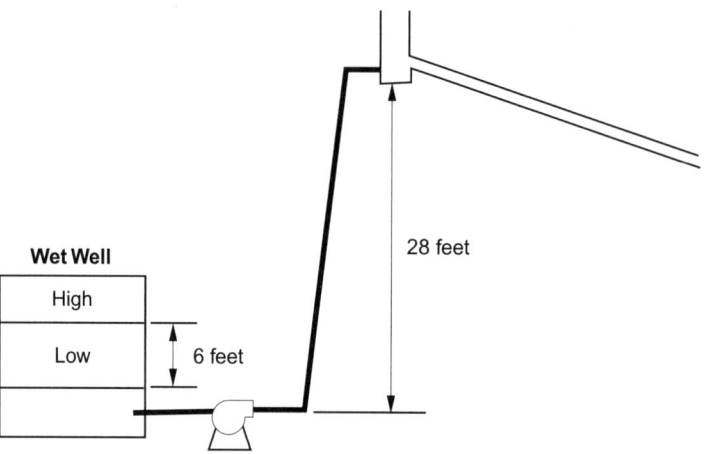

12.3 Create a system head curve for a 350 ft, 12 in. force main designed to lift water 55 ft. The pipe C-factor is 110 and the sum of the minor loss coefficients (K) is 5.5.

12.4 Use the sketch in the figure to create a system head curve for the pipeline leaving the pumping station. The pumping station must pump water over the intermediate high point A. The pipeline is 15 in. with Manning's $n = 0.013$. The flow from the variable-speed pump in the pumping station ranges from 1100 to 3500 gpm.

a. Determine the full pipe capacity for the pipe connecting A and B.

b. Develop the discontinuous head system head curve for the flow rate range from the pumping station.

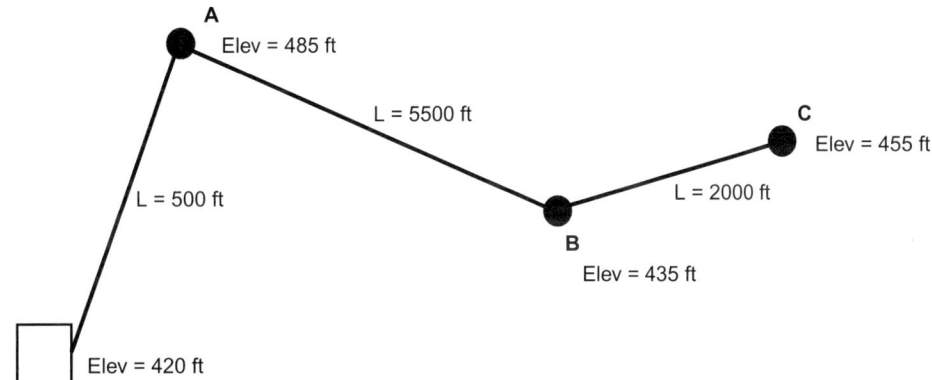

12.5 Estimate the annual pumping cost for a pumping station using the system curve and pump performance curve in the following figure. The average flow into the pumping station is 250 gpm. The motor efficiency is 95% and the power cost is 8.3 cents per kWh.

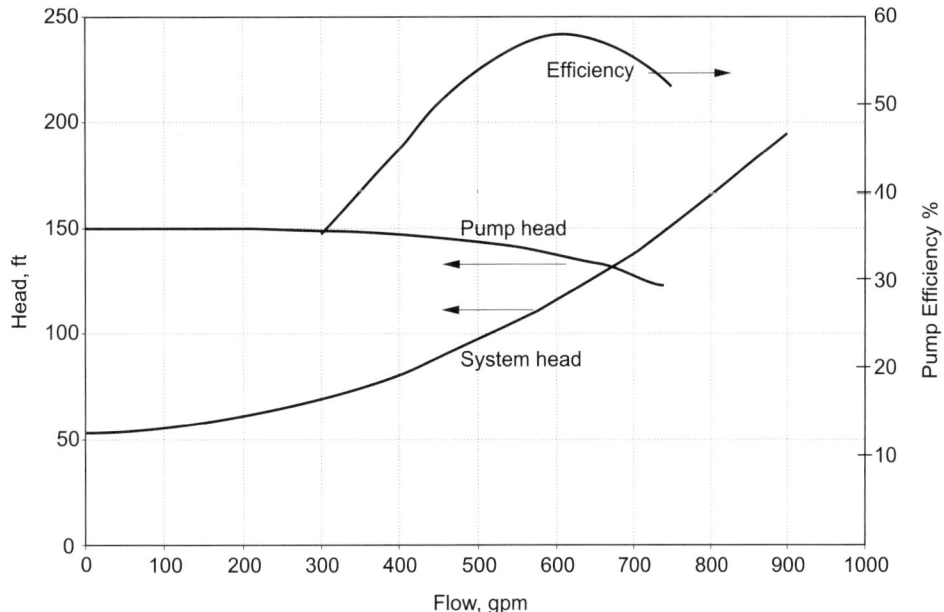

12.6 You are assigned to design a pumping station with the most economical pipe diameter. The length of pipe for the pumping station is 1500 ft with Manning's $n = 0.011$ and is to lift water 65 feet at a flow rate of 1100 gpm. The pump and motor efficiency are 72% and 93%, respectively. The average flow into the pumping station is 450 gpm. The pumping station cost is amortized over 15 years at an 8.7% interest rate. The power cost in the area is 7.9 cents per kWh. The table contains the unit costs for purchasing and connecting pipe to the pumping station.

Nominal Size, in.	Cost per Linear Foot, $
6	20
8	26
10	37
12	52

12.7 A junior engineer told you that a centrifugal pump is rated at 0.55 m^3/s when operating at 1170 rpm against a head of 17 m. He calculated that the expected applied power to the shaft is 98 kW. Determine if this is possible if the best efficiency rating for this pump is 85%. Support your conclusion.

12.8 A variable-speed centrifugal pump is rated at 72 BHP at a flow rate of 3500 gpm with 48 ft of head feet and an impeller rotational speed of 850 rpm.

a. Determine the pump efficiency, specific speed, and impeller type of the centrifugal pump.

b. What are the power, head, discharge capacity, and specific speed for the pump at 1170 rpm?

c. What is observed when comparing the specific speed values for this pump attached to different motors, and why is this observed?

12.9 Using the pump performance curve in the figure, estimate the pump coefficients to describe the pumping head (a and b), power (A and B), and pumping efficiency (x, y, and z).

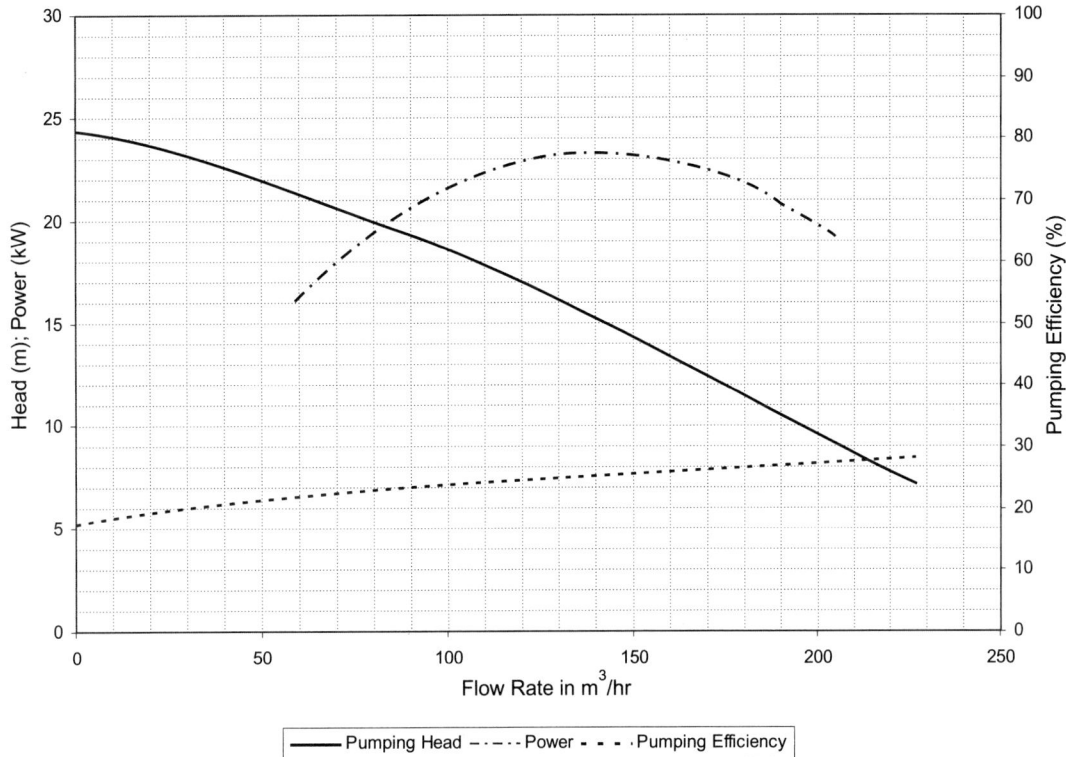

CHAPTER

13

Low-Pressure Sewers

Pressure sewers (also called *low-pressure sewers*) are similar to force mains (Chapter 4), but differ in that individual sewer pumping systems are located on the property of each customer. Low-pressure systems are usually installed where excavation is difficult because of rock, the ground surface is flat or nearly so, or there are long distances between customers. Any of these factors can make gravity sewers difficult and costly to install.

Low-pressure sewers have both advantages and disadvantages compared to gravity sewers. The primary advantages are

- Lower cost of pipe network installation due to smaller piping and lowered excavation costs
- Greater flexibility in routing of piping
- Fewer manholes
- Reduced potential for infiltration and inflow.

The primary disadvantages include

- Higher operation and maintenance costs for power, repair, and replacement of pumps
- Failure during power outages
- Maintenance of air-release/vacuum-breaker valves.

Pressure sewers have become a popular solution for areas that lack the population density to support a traditional gravity sewer system and are also unsuitable for septic systems. They are especially attractive as a means of reducing both excavation costs and infiltration in areas with high water tables.

13.1 Description of Pressure Sewers

The first pressure sewers in the United States were installed in Radcliff, Kentucky in the late 1960s. Although the system was eventually abandoned, it demonstrated that the concept could work (Clift, 1968). Fair had earlier proposed a system for hanging pressure sanitary sewers inside large storm or combined sewers (US Environmental Protection Agency, 1991).

The technology in pressure sewers has improved, and they have become a reliable alternative to septic systems and conventional gravity sewers. The primary improvement was in the reliability of the small grinder pumps installed at each customer location. Rezek and Cooper (1985) reported that there were 78 pressure sewer systems in operation by the mid-1980s. Hundreds of pressure systems are currently in operation, including some that serve more 1000 customers (Feuss, Farrell, and Rynkiewicz, 1994; Farrell and Darrah, 1994).

Pressure sewer systems consist of the following components, which are described in more detail in the sections that follow:

- *Pumps* – move wastewater from the customer's premises to the main
- *Storage tanks* – hold wastewater when the pump is not running and provide submergence for the pump
- *Service lines* – connect the grinder pumps to the main
- *Pressure sewer main* – a larger pipe in the street or right of way
- *Air-release valve* – releases trapped air from accumulation points in the network
- *Discharge point* – transition point from pressure to gravity flow at the end of the pressure system.

All pressure-system pumps collect water from a suction storage tank. The primary distinction is whether the tank is used for solids removal as well as providing suction head. *Grinder pumps* have a grinder, similar to a garbage disposal, to grind whatever is received in the storage tank before it is pumped. General Electric Company developed the first grinder pump in 1967 (Carcich, Hetling, and Farrell, 1972).

Alternatively, pumps may be preceded by some type of solids-removal process, usually called *septic tank effluent pump (STEP) systems*. The earliest septic tank effluent pumping systems were documented by Langford (1977).

Pumps

Depending on the manufacturer, the pump mechanism in pressure sewer systems is either centrifugal or progressive cavity. Pumps for pressure sewer systems usually have a grinder reduce the size of solids. Some systems can use solids-handling pumps, which are designed to pass fairly large solids.

The system head that the pump must overcome to discharge wastewater into the pressure sewer main can vary widely from low to high points in the system and from high- to low-flow periods. Installers do not want to keep a large inventory of pumps for different heads. Therefore, it is desirable to use pumps with a fairly steep pump-head characteristic curve (see Chapter 4 for a description of pump-head curves).

Progressive-cavity pumps (also referred to as semipositive-displacement pumps) produce roughly the same discharge regardless of the head against which they pump (i.e., they have very steep head characteristic curves). The head in the main affects the discharge from centrifugal pumps to a much greater extent. Progressive-cavity pumps can typically function with 1 to $1^{1}/_{2}$ hp (0.75–1.2 kW) motors. Centrifugal pumps function best with 2 hp (1.5 kW) motors so that they will work when the head in the main is high. Typical head characteristic curves for progressive-cavity and centrifugal pumps are shown in Figure 13.1.

Single-family dwellings and small apartments use a single pump in the pump vault, referred to as a simplex unit. Large apartments, commercial buildings, and trailer parks use duplex units containing two pumps.

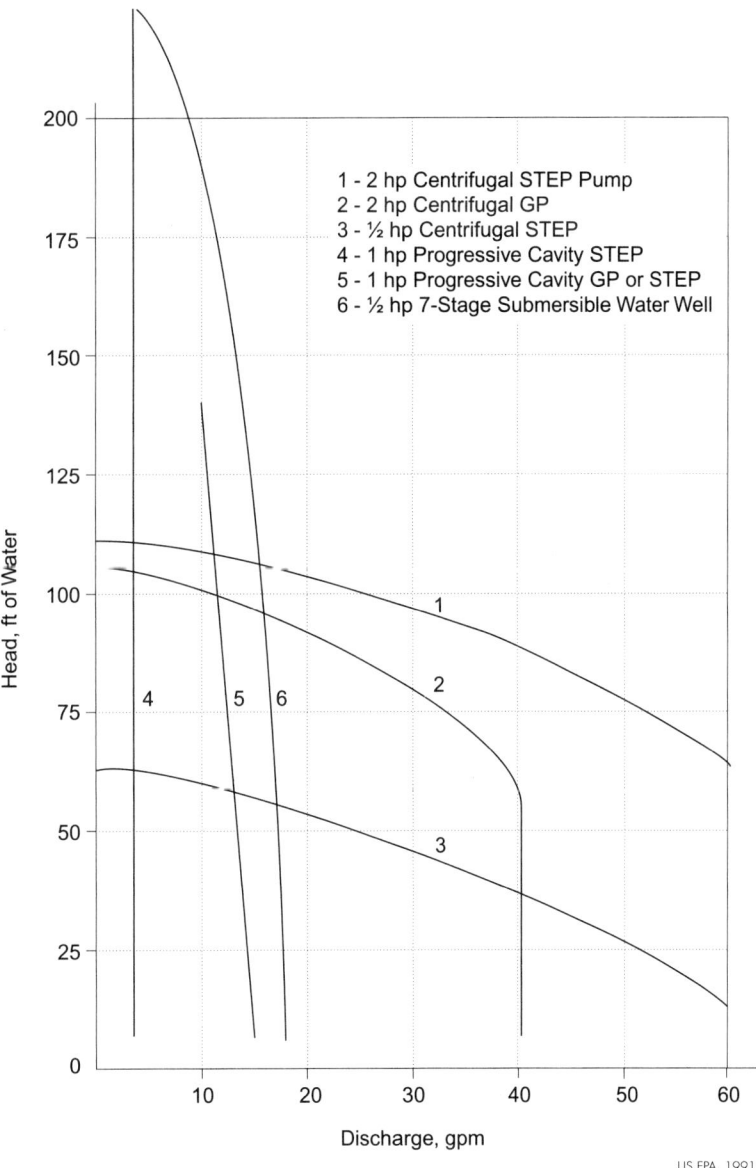

Figure 13.1 Typical head characteristic curves for various types of sewer pumps.

Storage Tanks

Storage or holding tanks are usually located just outside the footprint of the structure being served, although in some instances they are placed in the basement or crawl space. The tanks are generally made of HDPE, fiberglass, or treated concrete. A typical home tank has a storage volume of about 47 gal (179 L) below the alarm level (the point at which a warning is sent that the tank is getting full). The pump is activated when sewage in the tank reaches a volume of 32 gal (121 L) and is turned off when the volume reaches 24 gal (91 L). This yields a volume of roughly 8 gal (30 L) to be pumped each cycle, leaving about 24 gal (91 L) in the bottom of the tank (e/one, 2001). This configuration allows for some submergence of the pump intake at the low level, as well as some freeboard to prevent flooding during power outages and malfunctions. A typical tank with pump is shown in Figure 13.2. A pump vault in a STEP system is shown in Figure 13.3.

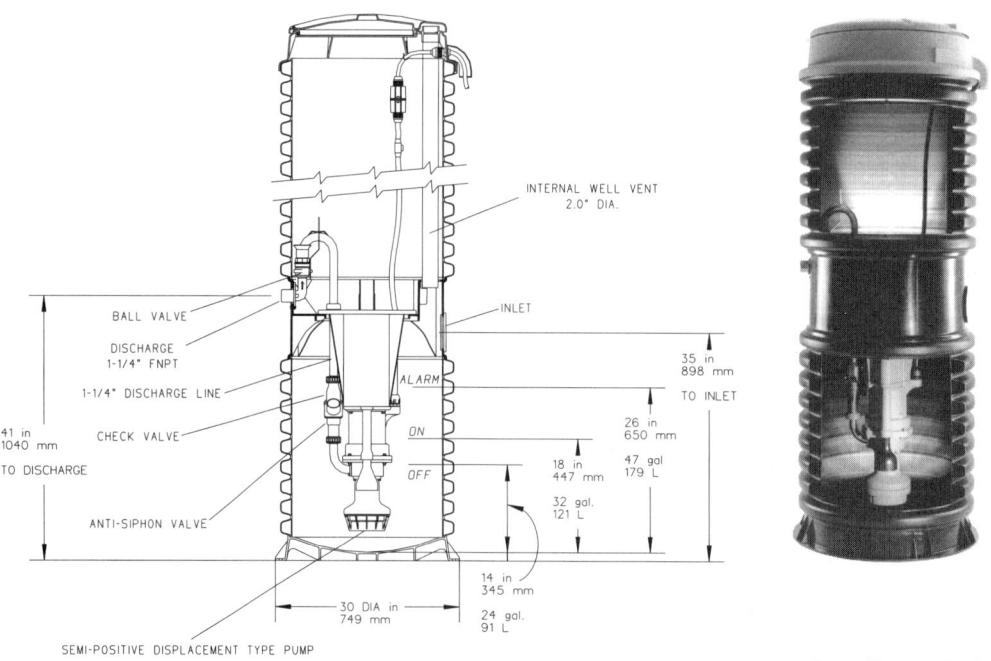

Figure 13.2 Engineering drawing and cutaway view of a pressure sewer pump system.

Service Lines

The service line connecting the pump to the main contains a check valve and a manual isolating valve. For residential customers, the service line is usually 1.25 in. (32 mm) and is made of plastic. The velocities in service lines are typically about 4 ft/s (1.2 m/s). The pressure in the system is usually about 35 psi (240 kPa) (Crites and Tchobanoglous, 1998; US Environmental Protection Agency, 1991). The discharge piping should be at least the same size as the pump outlet.

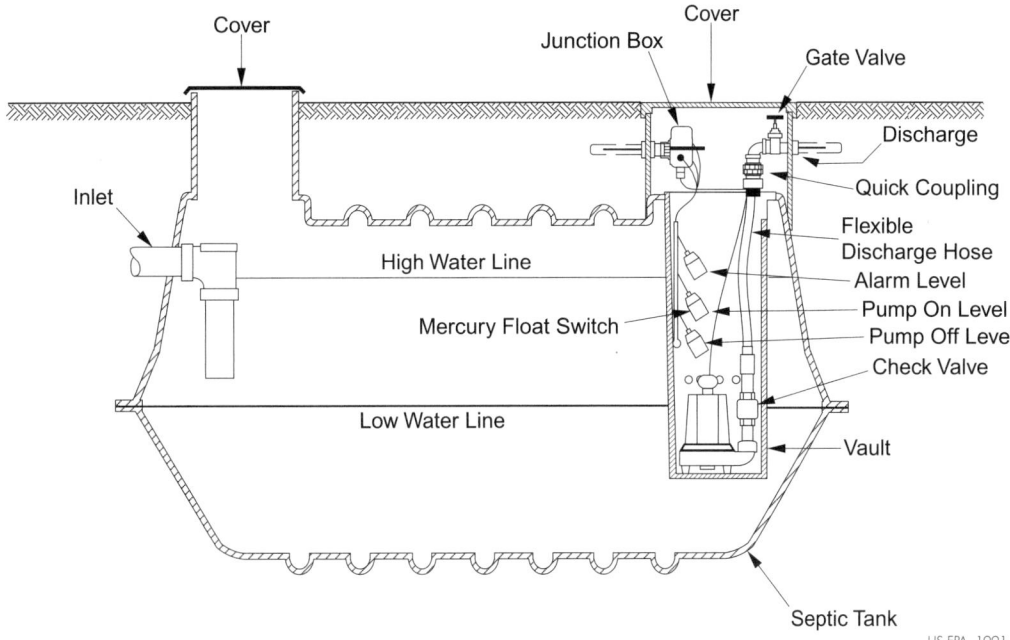

Figure 13.3 Septic tank and pump vault in a STEP system.

Pressure Mains

The pressure sewer main in the street or right-of-way is usually plastic pipe, but, unlike gravity sewers, the slope of the line is not very important. The sizing of the pipe should be based on a hydraulic analysis to ensure that the pipe is large enough to carry the design flow without excessive head loss, yet small enough to maintain self-cleansing velocities.

Air-Release/Vacuum-Breaker Valves

High points along a pressure sewer system can collect pockets of gases, so combination air-release/vacuum-breaker valves should be placed at these locations. A typical combination valve is shown in Figure 13.4. Gas pockets can collect not only at high points, but also in a downward-sloping closed pipe anywhere the slope increases significantly. The potential for collecting gas pockets can be estimated using Equation 12.12 on page 448.

The engineer should look for high points in the system and install combination valves. These valves should also be installed every 2000 ft (610 m), even on lines without high points (e/one, 2000). Because these valves can become clogged with grease, maintenance is necessary to insure proper function.

Discharge Points

A pressure sewer system usually discharges to a gravity sewer at a manhole located at a high point. Alternatively, the pressure system may discharge to a pump station wet well or at the wastewater treatment plant.

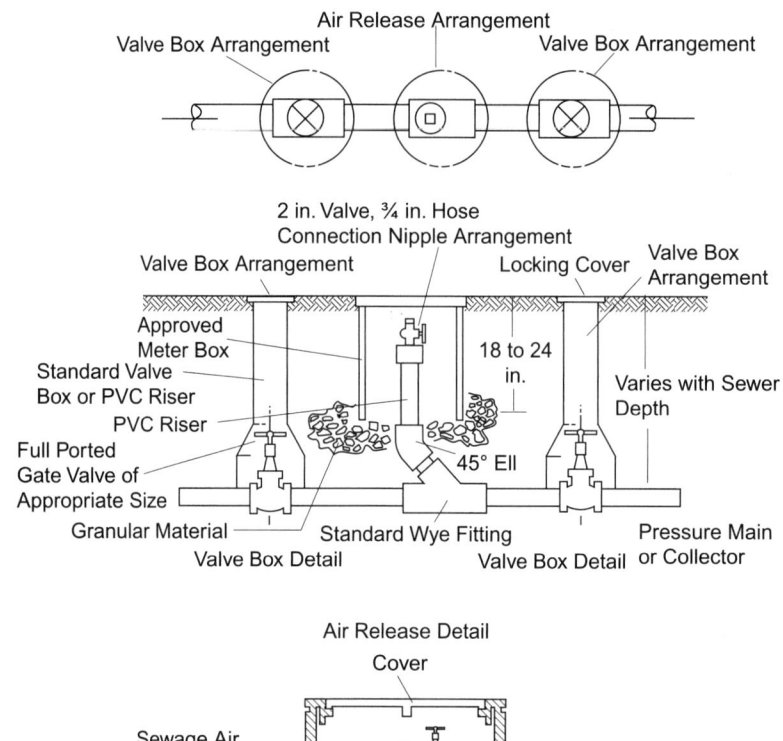
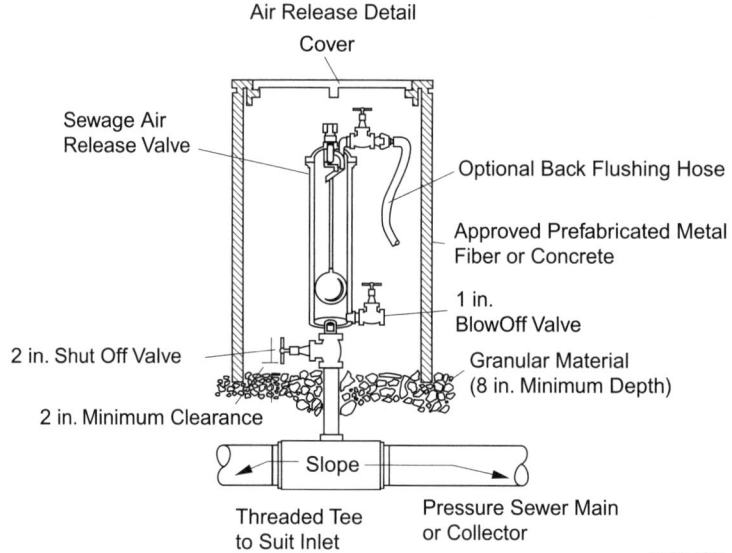

Figure 13.4 Typical air-release valve installations.

13.2 Estimating Flows

The rate of generation of wastewater in pressure sewer systems (e.g., 100 gpcd, 380 Lpcd) (GLUMRB, 1997) should be the same as in gravity-flow systems. However, because of the lower potential for I/I due to positive sewer pressures, some engineers use lower values, such as 50–70 gpcd (190–260 Lpcd), to model pressure sewer systems (Thrasher, 1988). Although these lower average inflow rates may be used, the ratio of peak inflow to average inflow will typically be higher in pressure systems since these systems tend to serve fewer customers.

Flows change gradually in gravity systems; however, the discharge from an individual customer in a pressure sewer system is zero until the water in the customer's storage tank reaches a preset level, causing the pump to turn on. The customer then discharges to the sewer at a peak (or near-peak) flow rate for a short time, the tank drains, and the discharge drops back to zero.

Much of the challenge of estimating flows in pressure sewers relates to predicting how many customers will be discharging to the system simultaneously (that is, how many pumps will be on at the same time). Research on contributions to pressure wastewater systems from individual homes has been published in numerous sources (Bennett, Lindstedt, and Felton, 1974; Jones, 1974; Watson, Farrell, and Anderson, 1967). Some more-sophisticated methods based on statistical analysis of water-use patterns from individual homes are given by Buchberger and Wu (1995) and Buchberger and Wells (1996).

Although there is very little opportunity for infiltration and inflow to enter the system along the mains and service lines, pump vaults (tanks) do provide a potential avenue for flow increases during wet weather. These need to be inspected during installation to prevent connections from downspouts and French drains. Directly metering the flow from customers is difficult and expensive. If customers are suspected of discharging wet-weather flow to the system, a simple run-time meter can be placed on the pump to determine if the pumped volume increases significantly during wet weather.

Empirical Approaches

A detailed analysis of pressure-sewer flows is based on the probability that a given number of pumps out of the population are running at any one time. Therefore, peaking-factor formulas commonly used with gravity sewers, such as those of Babbitt (1953) or Harmon (1918), do not apply to pressure sewers. A simple rule of thumb for computing design flow in a pressure sewer uses *equivalent dwelling units* (determined based on the average load from a typical residence in the area of interest) and is given by (US Environmental Protection Agency, 1991)

$$Q = 0.5\,N + 20 \qquad (13.1)$$

where Q = design flow (gpm)

N = equivalent dwelling units upstream

(For flow in L/s, replace the constants 0.5 and 20 in Equation 13.1 with 0.032 and 1.3, respectively.)

Alternatively, various sources have provided representative curves for determining design flow. Several such curves are plotted in Figure 13.5.

Using data from a study in Albany, NY, e/one (2001) developed a table relating the number of pumps running at peak times to the total number of pumps. These values are listed in Table 13.1.

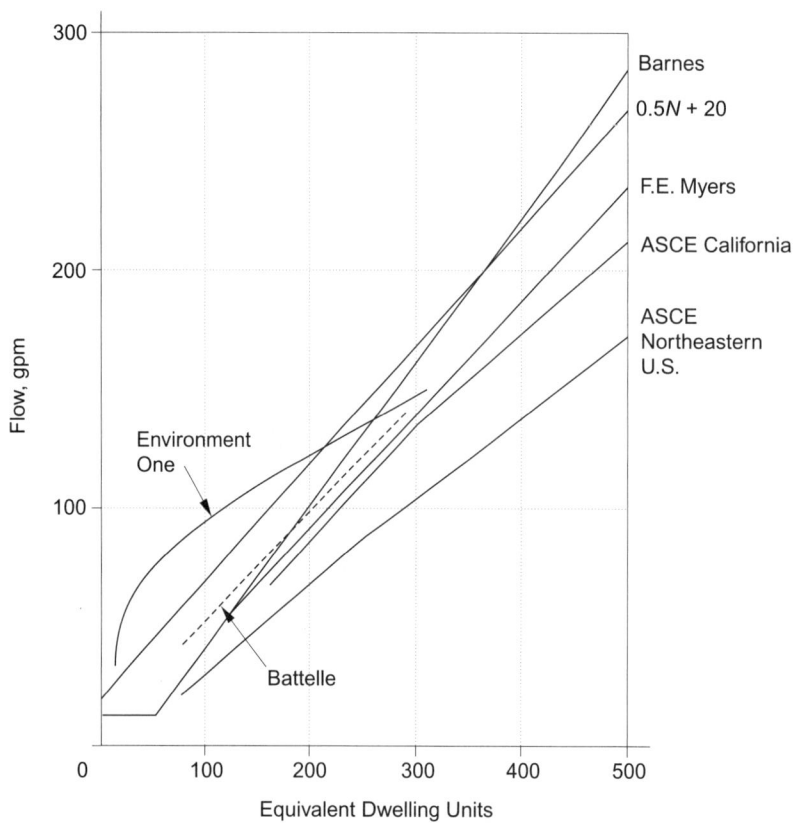

Figure 13.5 Various curves for estimating sanitary design flows.

Table 13.1 Number of pumps operating during peak conditions (e/one, 2001).

Number of Pumps in System	Max. Number of Pumps Operating Simultaneously	Number of Pumps in System	Max. Number of Pumps Operating Simultaneously
1	1	114–149	9
2–3	2	150–179	10
4–9	3	180–212	11
10–18	4	213–245	12
19–30	5	246–278	13
31–50	6	279–311	14
51–80	7	312–344	15
81–113	8		

This table can be used to estimate the peak flow at any point in a system by counting the number of pumps upstream, looking up the number that are likely to run at any one time, and multiplying that value by the flow from a pump.

Walski (2002) adapted these data to account for population and number of users per residence to derive the following expression for peaking factor:

$$PF = \frac{q + 0.71q\left(\dfrac{P}{n} - 1\right)^{0.53}}{uP} \tag{13.2}$$

where PF = peaking factor
  q = average discharge from a single pump (gpm, L/min)
  P = population
  n = number of persons per pump
  u = average demand per capita (gpcm, Lpcm)

For a relation for peaking factor that is independent of units, Equation 13.2 can be rewritten as

$$PF = \frac{a + (bP)^{0.53}}{P} \tag{13.3}$$

where $a = q/u$

and

$$b = \frac{\left(0.71\dfrac{q}{u}\right)^{1.88}}{n} \tag{13.4}$$

Values for q, u, and n vary depending on the system. Typical ranges are q = 9–15 gpm (35–60 L/min), u = 0.035–0.056 gpm (0.13–0.21 L/min), and n = 2–4 persons per pump. The value for a ranges between 200 and 500 and b ranges between 6000 and 20,000. The value of q is lower for systems with centrifugal pumps rather than positive-displacement pumps. During peak flow times, the pressure in the system increases; therefore, the flow from individual centrifugal pumps decreases accordingly. The plot in Figure 13.6, calculated using some typical values for the parameters, compares the peaking factors obtained from Equation 13.2 with those obtained by methods discussed in Chapter 6 for traditional gravity systems.

Poisson Distribution to Estimate Loads

One method commonly used in Europe to estimate the number of pumps running is based on the fact that the probability that any number of pumps are running simultaneously can be determined with the Poisson statistical distribution (Soderlund, Jonsson, and Nilsson, 1994). Given the probability that any one pump will run, the number of pumps in the system, and the an assumed number of pumps running, the probability that exactly that number of pumps is running is given by

$$PP = \frac{N!}{N_r!(N-N_r)!}(1-P_r)^{N-N_r}P_r^{N_r} \tag{13.5}$$

where PP = probability that exactly N_r pumps are running simultaneously during the wastewater generation period
  N = number of pumps in the system
  N_r = number of pumps running simultaneously
  P_r = probability that a single pump is running

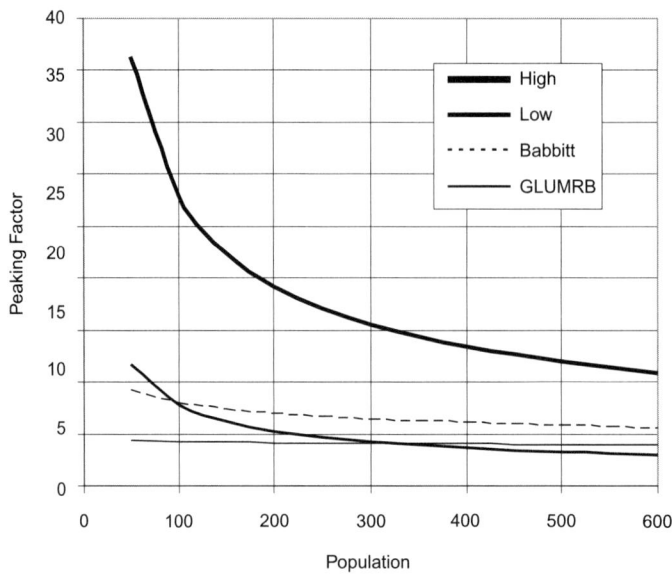

Figure 13.6 Peaking factors for pressure sewers.

The probability that any single pump is running at a given time during the wastewater generation period is a ratio of the flow into the sump divided by the rate at which the wastewater is pumped out when the pump is running, which is given by

$$P_r = \frac{Q_{in}}{Q_p} \tag{13.6}$$

where Q_{in} = effective inflow rate to the pump facility (gpm, L/s)
          Q_p = pump discharge rate (gpm, L/s)

A typical single-family pump discharge rate Q_p is approximately 10–15 gpm (0.6–1.0 L/s), depending on the type of pump and the location. The effective inflow rate Q_{in} depends on the number of users at the location, the per capita wastewater flow production, and the number of "wastewater-producing hours." It is given by

$$Q_{in} = \frac{V_w N_u}{c_f n_h} \tag{13.7}$$

where V_w = volume of wastewater per inhabitant (gpcd, Lpcd)
          N_u = number of inhabitants per pump
          c_f = unit conversion factor (60 for gpm, 3600 for L/s)
          n_h = number of wastewater-producing hours per day, usually 8–12 (hr/d)

For typical values, such as three inhabitants per pump, 80 gpcd (300 Lcpd), and 10 wastewater-producing hours per day, the inflow rate to a single-residence pump may be 0.4 gpm (0.025 L/s). For a 15 gpm (1 L/s) pump, the probability that a single pump is running is approximately 0.025 during the 10-hour wastewater generation period, which corresponds to a pump running roughly 15 minutes per day.

Figure 13.7 shows the probability of a given number of pumps running simultaneously for systems with 10 through 160 pumps for $P_r = 0.2$. Soderlund, Jonsson, and Nilsson (1994) recommend using the number of pumps running at a 10-percent probability for the design flow. A more useful value for design may be the cumulative probability of at least that number of pumps running, as shown in Figure 13.8.

Overall, this method gives somewhat lower estimates of the number of pumps running than methods based on the Albany, NY, data (e/one, 2001).

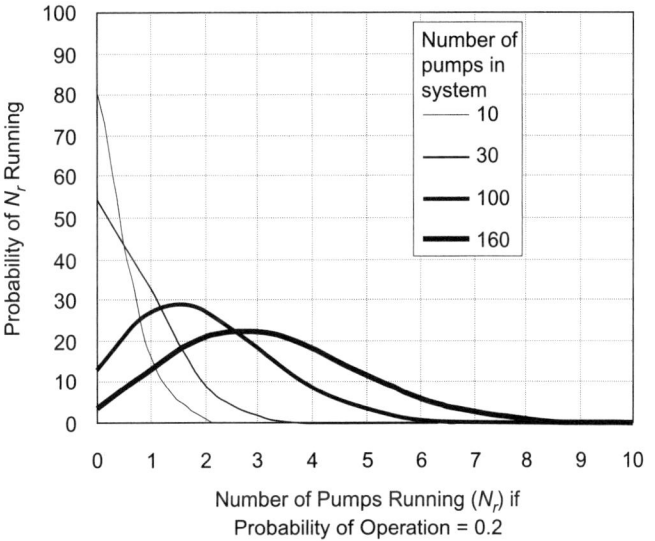

Figure 13.7 Probability of N_r pumps running at one time.

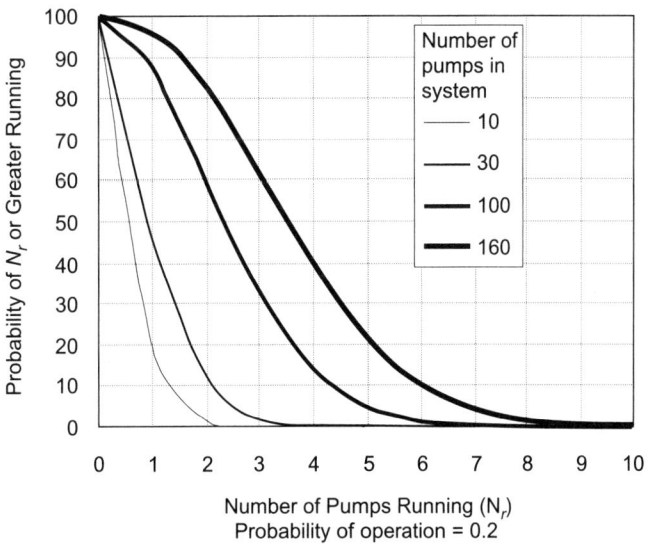

Figure 13.8 Cumulative probability or Nr or more pumps running.

13.3 Pressure Sewer Design Considerations

The design of a pressure sewer requires a layout of the piping, which should preferably be done on a CAD- or GIS-based map, much like any other sewer design. The use of an electronic base map makes it much easier to import the geometry and distances into the model for hydraulic calculations. If necessary, the design can be based on paper maps or drawings, but then the representation of the system in the model will not be exactly to scale; therefore, the modeler must input pipe lengths manually.

The key design parameter for pipe sizing is the velocity. For the system to work effectively, the velocity at peak flow should be kept below 5 ft/s (1.5 m/s) (Hydromatic Pumps, 2001), although there are some situations, such as short runs of pressure pipe, in which higher velocities can be tolerated. More important, velocity should be greater than 2 ft/s (0.6 m/s) in all pipes for at least some part of the day to prevent solids deposition.

The European Standard for pressure sewers, EN 1671, states that a minimum velocity of 0.7 m/s (2.2 ft/s) must be achieved at least once every 24 hours (CEN, 1996). Periodic flushing is recommended when this velocity cannot be maintained. The pipe bore must be the same size as the pump outlet or larger. The standard also states that detention time in the system should be less than 8 hours.

Oversizing of pressure sewers (e.g., due to assuming that all pumps are running at once) is discouraged, as it has been documented that grease and fibrous material can then block the pipe (Carcich, Hetling, and Farrell, 1972).

The sizing of individual pumps is based primarily on the peak flow from that customer or group of customers. Individual home pumps are usually sized for 10–15 gpm (0.7–1.0 L/s). The methods described in Chapter 6 and the fixture unit method described by American Water Works Association (2003) can be used to determine peak flow in commercial and industrial buildings.

With positive-displacement pumps, standard pumps can operate with line pressures as high as 60 psi (475 kPa) at low points, and standard pumps will still operate. However, the pressure in the main must be considered when selecting centrifugal pumps. High-horsepower pumps with large impellers may be required at low points. There is no minimum pressure that must be maintained in the system.

If the hydraulic model predicts negative pressures (see "Modeling Pressure Sewers" on page 479), this is an indication that a combination valve may be needed at that location to prevent air blockage or pipe collapse. Many of these situations are a result of pumping downhill and can be avoided if the pressure sewer terminates at a high point. These issues are discussed in Chapter 12 with respect to force mains, and in this regard, pressure sewers act as force mains.

It is usually desirable to draw a profile of the ground and pipe. The profile views from computer models can provide insight into pressures along the line. It may be better to use gravity sewers in areas with long stretches of downhill slope and only use pressure sewers in the portions of the system where the terrain undulates. Although the gravity section may have a higher construction cost, it should be easier to operate and does not require replacement and repair of pumps. An example of a mixed gravity and pressure system uses pressure sewers on one side of a drainage divide, but switches to a gravity sewer on the other side to flow down to the plant, as shown in

Figure 13.9. Additional information about pressure sewer design can be found in Thrasher (1985) and Flanigan and Cadmik (1979), as well as in manuals provided by pump manufacturers (e/one, 2000; Hydromatic Pumps, 2001).

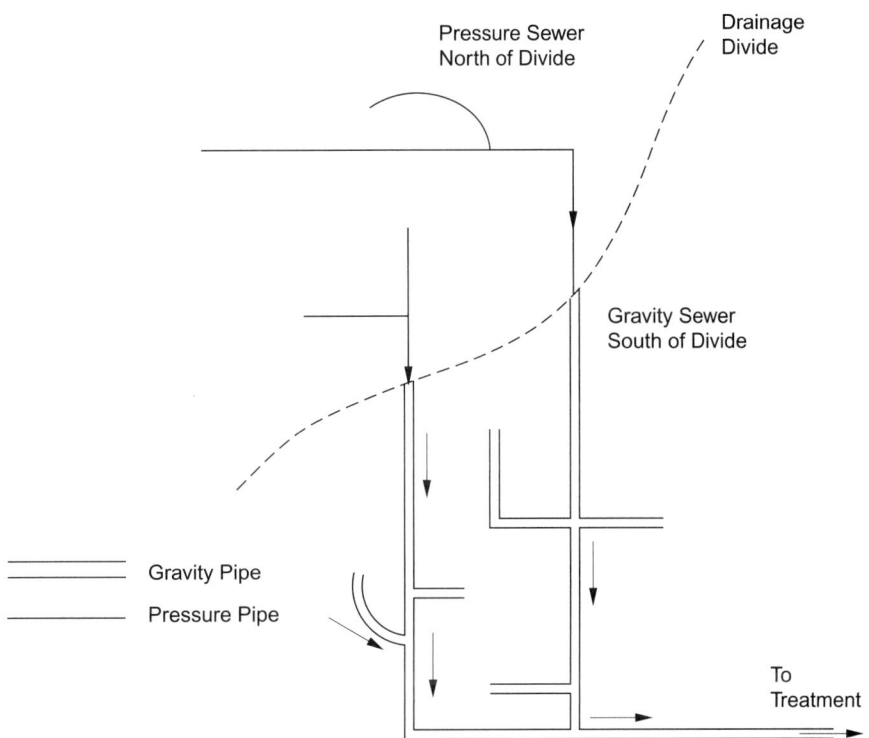

Figure 13.9 Mixed gravity and pressure sewer system.

13.4 Modeling Pressure Sewers

The fundamental hydraulic concepts involved in modeling pressure sewers are the same as those of force mains and pump stations. The primary difference between the two types of systems is that, with a pressure sewer, each customer has their own storage tank and pump; thus, the pressure system pump stations are smaller and much more numerous.

While a manual or spreadsheet hydraulic analysis may be sufficient for a system with only a few customers, a hydraulic analysis model becomes necessary as the number of customers and the complexity of the system increase. Of course, if the pressure sewers are integrated into a system with gravity sewers, then a hydraulic sewer model that can handle both types of flow is necessary if all sewers are to be analyzed simultaneously. A typical model of a pressure sewer discharging into a gravity sewer at a high point is shown in Figure 13.10.

Pressure sewers can be modeled using different levels of detail, depending on whether the modeler is interested only in the overall sizing of mains or in pump cycling and the unsteady nature of the flows. Most design work can be done with a steady-state model, whereas operational studies typically require extended-period simulations. Three basic modeling options, in order of increasing complexity, are described on the following pages.

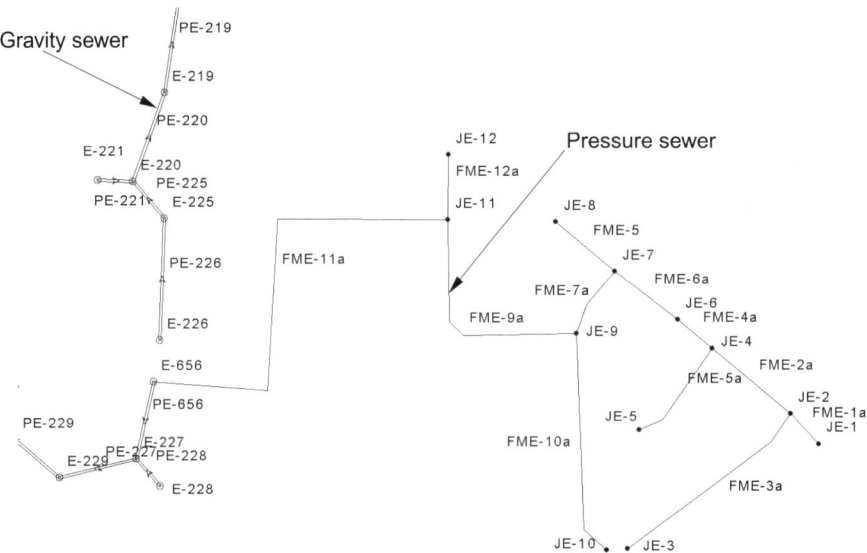

Figure 13.10 Pressure sewer discharging to a gravity sewer.

In all three of the options described, the modeler should look for situations where the pressures at low elevations are too high during peak flow conditions. Excessively high pressures may be unavoidable at very low elevations. In such cases, pipe with a higher pressure rating and/or a pump with a higher head may be required in some locations. If the high pressures are due to a steep system head curve, larger piping may be needed downstream. Model runs should also be checked to insure that velocities of at least 2 ft/s (0.7 m/s) are achieved at least once daily.

Modeling to Size Pressure Mains

If the modeler is simply trying to size the pressure mains as part of a system design, a steady-state simulation that omits individual customer pumps is often sufficient. Peak system loads are modeled by allocating multiple users to model junction nodes, much as multiple users are placed at junction nodes in water distribution models or at manholes in gravity sewer models. The corresponding peak loads are entered as known inflows.

Model nodes need only be placed at pipe intersections and changes in diameter, and at system low points and high points (which correspond to combination-valve locations) to check pressures. The modeler reviews the results to evaluate head losses and velocities, and sizes the pipes accordingly.

If local high points exist along the pressure sewer, the modeler must be aware that the pressure calculations may not be accurate. The model may report an unrealistic negative pressure (HGL dropping below the pipe) when, in actuality, a combination valve prevents the negative pressure from occurring. If a negative pressure is computed, the combination valve at this location cannot be modeled as a simple junction node. Instead, the pipe on the upstream side of the valve may be modeled as terminating in a reservoir open to atmospheric pressure and set to a hydraulic grade elevation equal

to the elevation of the valve. An inflow equal to the discharge into the reservoir is then placed on the junction node representing the downstream side of the valve. For alternative modeling techniques that can be applied in this situation, "Modeling a Pipeline with Multiple High Points" on page 444.

Representing All Service Connections as Nodes

At an intermediate level of detail, the modeler can represent each service line (e.g., house connection) as a junction node. This network configuration can be used with a steady-state run to identify the pump head required at any service connection. Determining the head at service nodes is not a major issue for positive-displacement pumps (which have steep performance curves) if the maximum pressure required is below the pump's threshold, but it can be important for centrifugal pumps.

In the steady-state model, nodes representing services with pumps running are assigned fixed inflows. By varying the number of pumps running at one time (i.e., the number of services with inflows), the modeler can determine the pressure range for any number of pumps and select the needed pump head and horsepower. Table 13.1 provides guidance on the number of pumps assumed to be running during a peak condition.

A model with all service connections represented as nodes can also be used with extended-period simulation runs to provide information on unsteady flows and how the system performs over time. With an extended period simulation, inflows and dimensionless flow patterns should be assigned to reflect the changing on/off status of the pumps.

Because the pumps themselves are not included, an extended-period simulation with this level of detail can only be used to assess system operations insofar as the pumping rates can be assumed to be relatively unaffected by fluctuations in tank level and discharge pressure. This assumption generally works well for positive-displacement pumps, but is less accurate for centrifugal pumps.

In addition to simulating normal operations, the modeler can examine extreme situations such as all pumps turning on simultaneously following an extended power outage. When the system is being initially filled, transients can damage piping, so velocities should be kept below 1 ft/s (0.3 m/s) during filling to prevent water hammer (Hydromatic Pumps, 2001).

Detailed Models

At their most complex, models can include each individual pump and tank and can be analyzed with an extended-period simulation. Runs that simulate each pump provide insight into the range of conditions that the system will experience, including the rise and fall of water in the storage tanks, changing pump status, and fluctuations in pressure and flow. This type of model is also useful for designs with centrifugal pumps because their discharges may be significantly affected by fluctuating system conditions.

A detailed model requires significantly more information, including

- Base loads and patterns for loading at storage tanks
- Volume and elevation data for individual storage tanks (may be modeled as small wet wells)
- Individual pump performance curves
- Junction node and pipe connecting the pump discharge to the pressure main for each service connection.

Figure 13.11 is a model view of a small pressure sewer system with 10 pumps. The discharge point of this network is on the far right side. The pipes are annotated with the flow rate in gpm, and the nodes are annotated with the pressure in psi. The water level and pump status for every pump are explicitly considered in a model of this detail. Figure 13.12 shows the discharge at the downstream end of this system over a

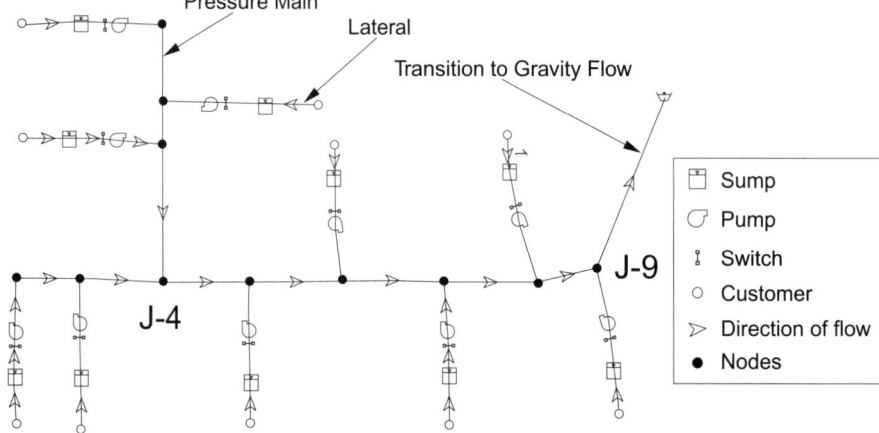

Figure 13.11 Pressure sewer model with a pump and tank at each residence.

3-hour period. Note that, with such a small system, there is no flow in the pipes for much of the time. Figure 13.13 shows the pressure at nodes J-4 and J-9. J-9 is further downstream and at a higher elevation, so it has a lower pressure and less pressure variation. J-4 is further upstream and has a lower elevation, so the pressure is consistently higher than that of J-9. In general, the most-upstream nodes experience the greatest pressure variations.

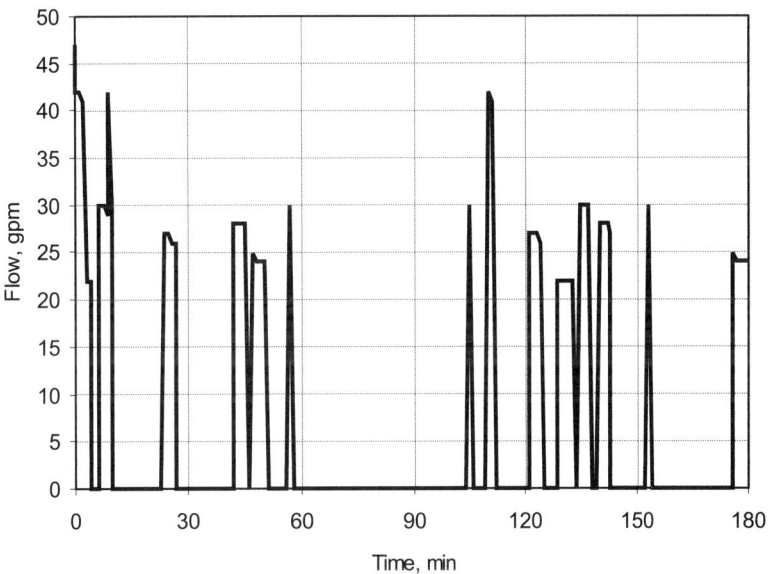

Figure 13.12 Plot of discharge versus time in a sewer model.

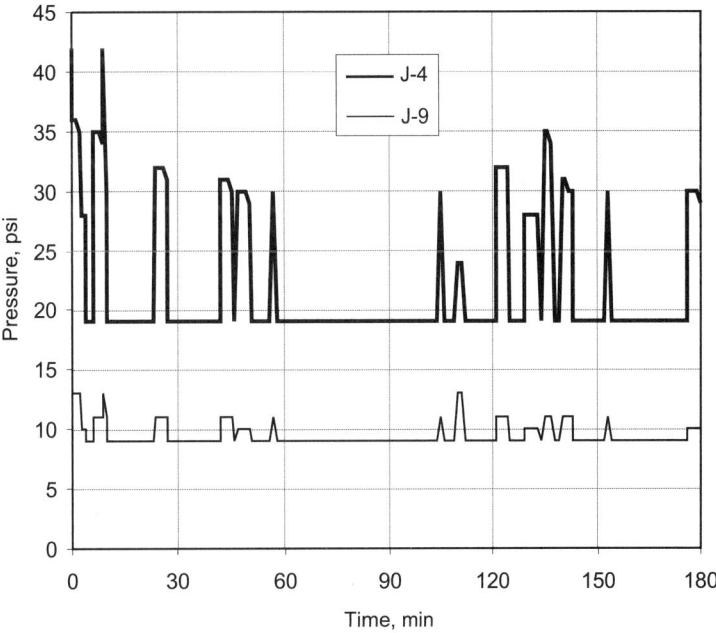

Figure 13.13 Plot of pressure versus time in a pressure sewer model.

References

American Water Works Association. 2003. *Sizing Water Service Lines and Meters*. Publication M-22. Denver, CO: American Water Works Association.

Babbitt, H. E. 1953. *Sewerage and Sewage Treatment*. 7th ed. New York: John Wiley and Sons.

Bennett, E., K. Linstedt, and J. Felton. 1974. Rural home wastewater characteristics. *Proceedings of the National Home Sewage Symposium*, American Society of Agricultural Engineers.

Buchberger, S. G. and L. Wu. 1995. A model for instantaneous residential water demands. *Journal of Hydraulic Engineering* 121, no. 3: 232.

Buchberger, S. G., and G. J. Wells. 1996. Intensity, duration and frequency of residential water demands. *Journal of Water Resources Planning and Management* 122, no. 1: 11.

Carcich, I. G., L. J. Hetling, and R. P. Farrell. 1972. *Pressure Sewer Demonstration*. US EPA, R2-72-091. Washington, DC: US Environmental Protection Agency.

Clift, M. A. 1968. Experiences with pressure sewage. *ASCE Sanitary Engineering Division* 94, no. 5: 865. Alexandria, VA: American Society of Civil Engineers.

Comité Européen de Normalisation (CEN). 1996. *Pressure Sewer Systems, Outside Buildings*. EN 1671. Brussels: Comité Européen de Normalisation.

Crites, R., and G. Tchobanoglous. 1998. *Small and Decentralized Wastewater Treatment Systems*. New York: McGraw-Hill.

e/one. 2000. *Low Pressure Sewer Systems Using Environment One Grinder Pumps*. Niskayuna, NY: e/one Corporation.

e/one. 2001. *Specifications for GP 2010*. Niskayuna, NY: e/one Corporation.

Farrell, R. P., and G. G. Darrah. 1994. Pressure sewers – A proven alternative solution for a variety of small community sewage disposal challenges. *International Symposium of Individual and Small Community Sewage Systems*. Atlanta, GA: American Society of Agricultural Engineers.

Feuss, J. V., R. P. Farrell. and P. W. Rynkiewicz. 1994. A small community success story. *The Small Flows Journal* 1, no. 1: 11.

Flanigan, L. J. and C. A. Cadmik. 1979. Pressure sewer system design. *Water and Sewage Works* April: R25.

Great Lakes-Upper Mississippi River Board of State Public Health and Environmental Managers (GLUMRB). 1997. *Recommended Standards for Wastewater Facilities*. Albany, NY: Great Lakes-Upper Mississippi River Board of State Public Health and Environmental Managers.

Harmon, W. G. 1918. Forecasting sewage at Toledo under dry weather conditions. *Engineering News Record* 80: 1233.

Hydromatic Pumps. 2001. *Pressure Sewer Manual and Engineering Guide*. Ashland, OH: Hydromatic Pumps.

Jones, E. 1974. Domestic water use in individual homes and hydraulic loading and discharge from septic tanks. *Proceedings of National Home Sewage Symposium*, American Society of Agricultural Engineers.

Langford, R. E. 1977. Effluent pressure sewer systems. *Proceedings of WPCF Annual Conference*.

Rezak, J. W. and I. A. Cooper. 1985. *Investigations of Existing Pressure Sewer Systems*. EPA/600/2-85/051.Washington, DC: Environmental Protection Agency.

Thrasher, D. 1988. *Design and Use of Pressure Sewer Systems*. Boca Raton, FL: Lewis Publishers.

US Environmental Protection Agency (US EPA). 1991. *Alternative Wastewater Collection Systems*. EPA 625/1-91/024. Washington, DC: US Environmental Protection Agency.

Walski, T. M. 2002. Estimating peaking factors for small diameter pressure sewers. Accepted for *Keystone Water Quality Manager*, Pennsylvania Water Environment Association.

Watson, K. S., R. P. Farrell, and J. S. Anderson. 1967. The contribution of individual homes to the sewer system. *Journal of the Water Pollution Control Federation* 39, no. 12: 2039.

Problems

13.1 List three advantages and three disadvantages of pressure sewers.

13.2 Of the two pump head curves in the figure, which is more likely to be a centrifugal pump and which is more likely to be a semipositive displacement pump?

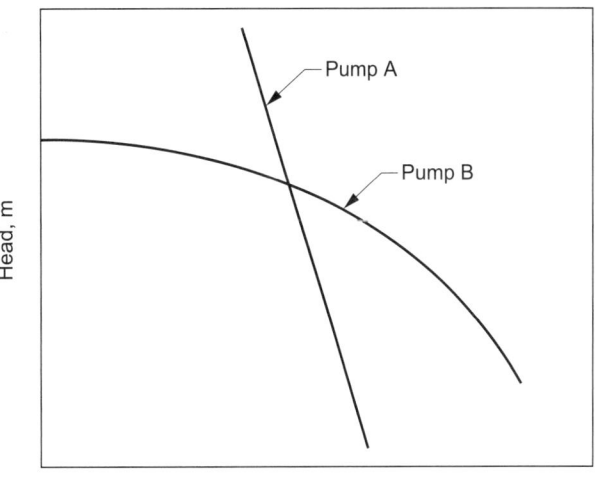

13.3 Using the Babbitt formula and the Great Lakes Upper Mississippi River Board formulas for peaking factors, determine the peaking factors they predict for the populations given in the following tables and compare with Equation 13.3 in this chapter. Use average typical values for q, n, and u.

	Peaking Factor		
Population	Babbitt	GLUMRB	Equation 13.3
20			
100			
500			

Given an average daily flow of 70 gal/capita, what is the peak flow rate in gpm?

	Peaking Flow, gpm		
Population	Babbitt	GLUMRB	Equation 13.3
20			
100			
500			

Why are the peaking factors for pressure sewers from Equation 13.3 higher than those from the other two methods?

13.4 Consider the pressure sewer being shown in the figure, which is to be installed in an industrial area with insufficient slope for a gravity sewer. When operating, each pump discharges the flow listed in the table. The discharge manhole (R-1) water level is at an elevation of 16 ft.

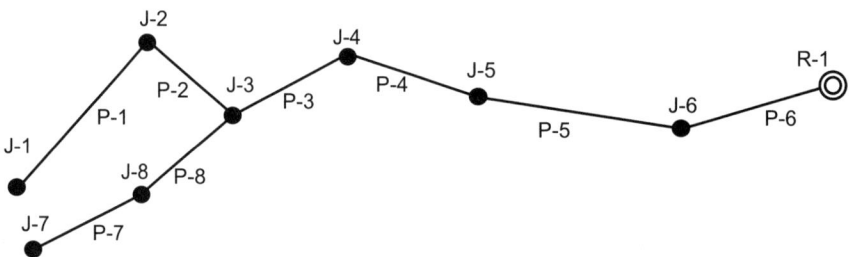

a. Select a diameter for each pipe segment; possible diameters are 2, 2.5, 3, 4, 6, and 8 in. Assume a C-factor of 130 for each pipe. Find the velocity in the pipes and the pressure and HGL at the junctions indicated when

• All pumps are running.

• Only the pumps at J-1 and J-4 are running.

The velocity should be about 4 ft/s when all pumps are running. The pressure should be less than 40 psi at all times. Complete the following tables.

| | Ground | Pipe | Inflow, | All Pumps | | Pumps J-1 and J-4 | |
| | | | | Pressure, | | Pressure, | |
Junction	Elev. ft	Elev., ft	gpm	psi	HGL, ft	psi	HGL, ft
J-1	12	7	30				
J-2	26	19	20				
J-3	20	15	15				
J-4	23	18	45				
J-5	19	14	15				
J-6	17	12	15				
J-7	10	5	35				
J-8	12	7	15				

Label	Length, ft	Diameter, in	Velocity, All Pumps, ft/s	Velocity 2 Pumps, ft/s
P-1	225			
P-2	165			
P-3	350			
P-4	425			
P-5	180			
P-6	270			
P-7	605			
P-8	420			

b. Prepare a profile drawing of the piping from J-1 to R-1 showing pipe elevation, ground elevation, and the two HGLs.

13.5 A pressure sewer serves 45 homes (one pump per home) with an average daily load of 200 L/home, 10 hours of production per day, and a typical pump discharge of 0.8 L/s when the pump is running.

a. Determine the probability that any pump is running.

b. Determine the probabilities that zero, one, two, three, or four pumps are running.

c. Determine the cumulative probability that zero, one, two, three, or four pumps are running.

Number of Pumps	Probability of Running	Cumulative Probability
0		
1		
2		
3		
4		

d. What is the maximum number of pumps running, based on Table 13.1?

CHAPTER

14

Utilizing GIS

A *geographic information system* (GIS) is a powerful configuration of computer hardware and software used for compiling, storing, managing, manipulating, analyzing, and mapping (displaying) spatially referenced information. It integrates database operations such as data storage, query, and statistical analysis with visual and geographic analysis functions enabled by spatial data. A GIS can serve as an integral part of any project that requires management of large volumes of digital data and the application of special analytical tools.

In the past, most hydraulic sewer models were developed with a batch-run philosophy in which a text file (or card deck) containing the model data was required to run the model. Gradually, hydraulic collection system models gained the ability to interact with databases. Finally, because a GIS is essentially a spatially-aware database, ongoing development has led to models that are highly integrated with GIS. Shamsi (2001) describes the evolution of model/GIS integration as a three-step process:

1. *Interchange* – Data are exchanged through an intermediate file, which may be an ASCII text file or a spreadsheet. Data are written to this intermediate file, which is reformatted for the model, if necessary, and then read into the model. The model and GIS are run independently.

2. *Interface* – Links are built to synchronize the model and the GIS. The data are duplicated on each side of the link, and the model and GIS are run independently. One common approach is the use of shapefiles (data files that contain location, shape, and attribute information for a geographic feature), which can be used to pass data between the model and the GIS and optionally update either with data contained in the other.

3. *Integration* – A single repository for the data is used. The model can be run from the GIS and vice versa.

This integration of a hydraulic model with a GIS leads to the following benefits:
- Time-savings in constructing models
- The ability to integrate disparate land-use, demographic, and monitoring data using GIS analysis tools to more accurately predict future system loads
- Visual, map-based quality control of model inputs
- Map-based display and analysis of model outputs in combination with other GIS layers
- Quality assurance
- Tracking and auditing of model changes.

From a planner's perspective, the most powerful feature of a GIS is the ability to integrate, through their spatial relationships, databases that would be difficult or impossible to integrate outside of a GIS environment. For example, a GIS can overlay soil data, repair data, and hydraulic modeling output to assign a condition rating to pipes and manholes.

Although many designers and utility managers are using GIS in their sewer models, few references describe how to automate the process. Shamsi (2002) presents two case studies on the application of GIS technology to sewer systems. Greene, Agbenowoshi, and Loganathan (1999) describe a program that was used to automatically integrate GIS data into the design of a new sewer network.

This chapter describes how GIS can be used to help create and use a collection system model. Those familiar with GIS can skip Section 14.1, which introduces the basic concepts of GIS. Section 14.2 describes how an enterprise GIS is constructed and discusses its key benefits. Section 14.3 gets to the heart of using GIS data for model building, and Section 14.4 discusses how GIS can help in visualizing model results.

14.1 GIS Fundamentals

An easy way to think of GIS is to imagine it as a set of transparencies that are layered so that any point in a layer appears at the same location in any other layer, as shown in Figure 14.1. In an actual GIS graphical user interface (GUI), these layers appear together, and the modeler can change the order in which they appear.

Within a GIS, *features* (objects on a map) are not simply points, lines, and polygons; they are linked to data tables containing associated *attributes* (information about the feature). In a wastewater collection system, facilities such as pipes, manholes, and pumps are features possessing attributes.

By selecting which layers are displayed, the order in which layers are displayed, and the *symbology* (size, shape, and color of symbols), the modeler can control the appearance of the resulting map. Figure 14.2 shows a GIS map containing streets, lots, buildings, and sewer lines in a residential community.

In addition to map-making, a GIS can be used to perform system analysis, answering questions about such things as
- Location (using proximity, buffer, or overlay analysis)
- Condition
- Temporal and spatial patterns (trends)
- What-if scenarios.

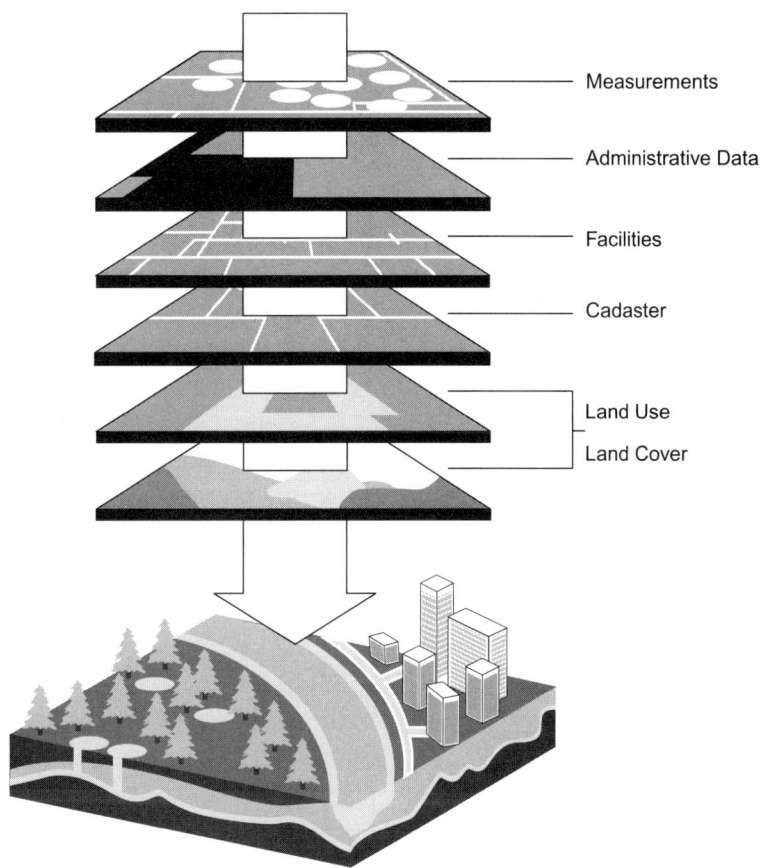

Figure 14.1 A conceptual layout of a geographic information system (GIS).

Data Management

Two primary and opposing data management paradigms are in use today: *centralized* and *decentralized data management*. Mainframe computers provide centralized data management, while PCs provide decentralized data management. In a mainframe environment, all applications and data reside on a central server. While this approach is practical, the hardware and software are often quite expensive to develop and maintain. Within the PC environment, special-purpose applications and databases are less expensive than their mainframe counterparts, and data and applications can reside on different networked PCs. The decentralized management philosophy is therefore very practical in terms of economics; however, it can lead to the creation of *data islands*. This term refers to the tendency of data sets that are maintained by individuals or small groups to remain disconnected from related data sets that would otherwise be integrated in a centralized data management environment.

The data developed within these islands are often generated and maintained redundantly, since other users needing the data do not have access and, as a result, develop and maintain their own versions (more islands). For example, the diameter (10 in., 250 mm), length (250 ft, 76 m), and material (concrete) for a pipe can be entered into the hydraulic modeling application, asset management system, and maintenance management system, and the pipe can be drawn and annotated on a map. Very few links

Figure 14.2 A GIS map showing streets, lots, buildings, and sewer lines.

to a master database or other data islands are ever developed. As a result, the utility is unable to tap the knowledge and efficiency that can be gained by analyzing and acting upon this information centrally. Additionally, the contents of these islands of data tend to diverge over time, making them difficult to consolidate into a single, current data set. Unfortunately, the data management situation of many wastewater utilities around the world is characterized by data islands and the consequent redundancy and/or inconsistency between databases. Best management practices suggest that the work flow of an organization be reviewed, with one department or group becoming responsible for maintaining and updating the various data sets. This results in data being entered once and used by many (*data interoperability*).

The computer industry has created technology such as SQL (Structured Query Language) and ODBC (Open Database Connectivity) to assist in centralizing or connecting these data islands. However, because they were designed and developed independently, data islands often do not have the key identifiers needed to form meaningful data relationships. For example, the billing system may use account number as its primary identifier, while the hydraulic modeling software uses pipe and node numbers. It is therefore difficult to relate the billing information to the hydraulic model for customer service and system planning. Identifying and addressing these issues early leads to increased efficiency and effective use of data throughout an organization.

What do the systems and databases for billing, customer service, asset management, work management, inspections and permits, water quality testing, facility mapping, hydraulic modeling, and document management have in common? The answer is geography. All of these systems have information (for example, permits, work orders, and test reports) that can be tied to a geographic location such as parcel number, address, or facility number. Geography is the essence of what is known as GIS-centric data management, a compromise between centralized and decentralized data management.

Using GIS-centric data management, features that cannot be linked explicitly through database table-to-table relationships can be associated geographically by determining their *proximity* (connectivity, distance, closeness) to one another. This aspect of GIS uniquely qualifies it as the preferred integration technology and unifying information resource within an organization.

The compromise that GIS can attain between centralized and decentralized data management is that only the GIS layers (spatial data and key identifier to link to the central database) need to be centralized. Therefore, the only limitation to the integration of specialized systems using a GIS-centric model is that they must have some reliable means of geographic referencing, such as facility ID, parcel number, or street address, and these IDs, numbers, and addresses must have a set of x-y coordinates attached to them. Virtually any type of system or database can be linked to a GIS layer if a geographical association, consistency, and high-quality data are present in both systems.

The centralized versus decentralized data management approaches are alternatively referred to as *data-centric* and *application-centric* respectively (Figure 14.3). With an *application-centric* approach, data is maintained separately for each application. For example, model data are stored and maintained in one database, and GIS data are stored in a separate, disconnected database. With a *data-centric* approach, there is a data management hub, and applications such as the GIS and the model are spokes. In this management system, the spatial data might be contained within the centralized database, if the database is spatially enabled, or it might reside in separate files that are either linked or joined to data in the central database.

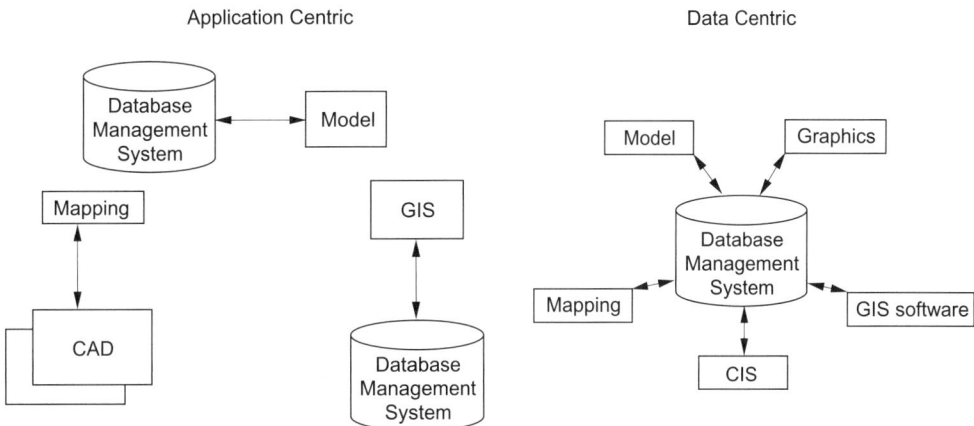

Figure 14.3 Application-centric and data-centric approaches to data management.

Geographic Data Representations

Three representations have emerged to handle most geographic data: raster, vector, and TIN. The following list describes these representations, which are shown in Figure 14.4.

- *Raster* – This representation stores data as discrete grids in which a single value for each attribute is associated with each grid cell. Each grid cell has an attribute value and location coordinates. Because the data are stored in a matrix, the coordinates for each cell need not be stored explicitly (ESRI, 2001). Rather, they can be determined "on the fly" because the origin of the raster model, the grid cell size, and the rotation are known.

- *Vector* – This representation stores discrete features as points, lines, or polygons. Each feature has attribute values and a set of *x-y* coordinates (and possibly a *z* coordinate) associated with it. In this way, vector data differ from raster data, which have coordinates intrinsically associated with the cells (ESRI, 2001).

- *Triangulated irregular network (TIN)* – TINs divide space into a set of contiguous (nonoverlapping) triangular faces. The triangular faces are derived from irregularly spaced sample points, breaklines, and polygon features, and each sample point has coordinates (*x, y*) and attributes (*z* coordinate or other feature to be modeled) associated with it. Attribute values at other locations (along breaklines and polygon features, or even on the triangular faces themselves) are calculated using interpolation within the TIN. TINs are sometimes considered a special case of a vector model, but Zeiler (1999) presents them as a separate data model.

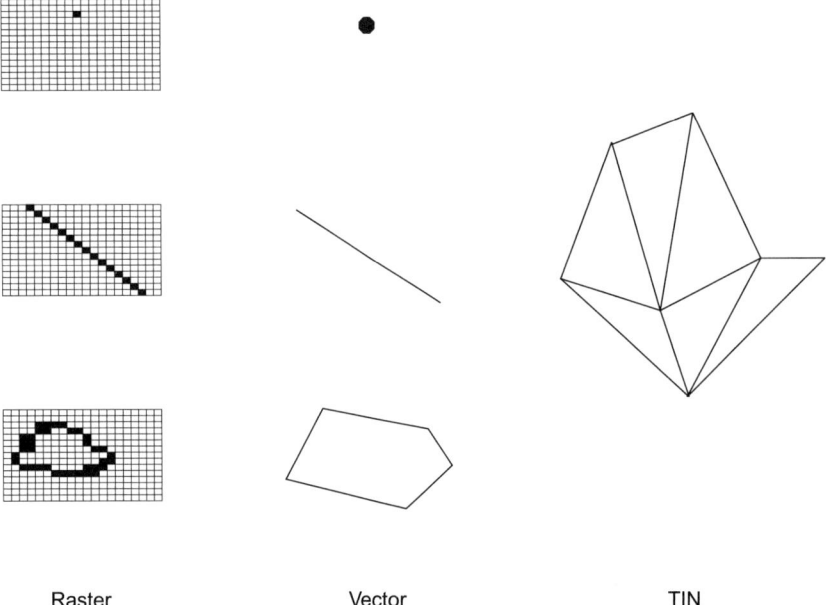

Raster   Vector   TIN

Figure 14.4 Geographic data representations.

Most data used in hydraulic modeling are vector data. For example, junction nodes are points, pipes are lines, and subbasin areas are polygons. However, modelers also use raster and TIN data for tasks such as extracting elevation data or providing background imagery.

14.2 Developing an Enterprise GIS

Many publications describe the process of developing a GIS in the water and wastewater industries, including Orne, Hammond, and Cattran (2001) and Przybyla (2002). The Water Environment Federation published a Manual of Practice titled *Implementing Geographic Information Systems* that also addresses this issue (WEF, 2004). The pace of technological advancement and the diversity of commercial implementations outstrip the ability of any general text to provide detailed guidelines on the configuration and management of a specific GIS-based modeling system. Consequently, this section provides a general discussion of the GIS development process and outlines the major steps involved in developing an enterprise GIS.

A GIS is generally implemented at one of four levels:

- *Project* – Supporting a single project objective
- *Departmental* – Supporting the needs of one department
- *Enterprise* – Interdepartmental sharing of data
- *Interagency* – Sharing of application and data with external agencies.

Building a GIS on a project basis for the sole purpose of using it with a hydraulic model is quite rare, since an organization derives a variety of benefits from a GIS, such as

- Elimination of redundant data maintenance activities
- Streamlining of workflow processes with GIS functions
- Improvements in access to quality information
- Ability to use spatial analysis to solve problems.

For these reasons, a GIS is often implemented at the departmental or enterprise level. An example of an enterprise GIS is illustrated in Figure 14.5. The subsections that follow discuss some of the key steps that should be taken to ensure a successful enterprise-level GIS implementation. For more information on planning, developing, and maintaining a GIS for modeling and other applications, see the references at the end of this chapter.

Keys to Successful Implementation

An enterprise GIS integrates geographic data across multiple departments and serves the entire organization while providing access to other information systems using a map or other application as the integrator of the organization's information (Landrum, 2001). A community or wastewater utility that commits to developing an enterprise GIS must consider several key factors:

- Development of a GIS that is capable of supporting a hydraulic model requires a high level of data quality, accuracy, and detail.

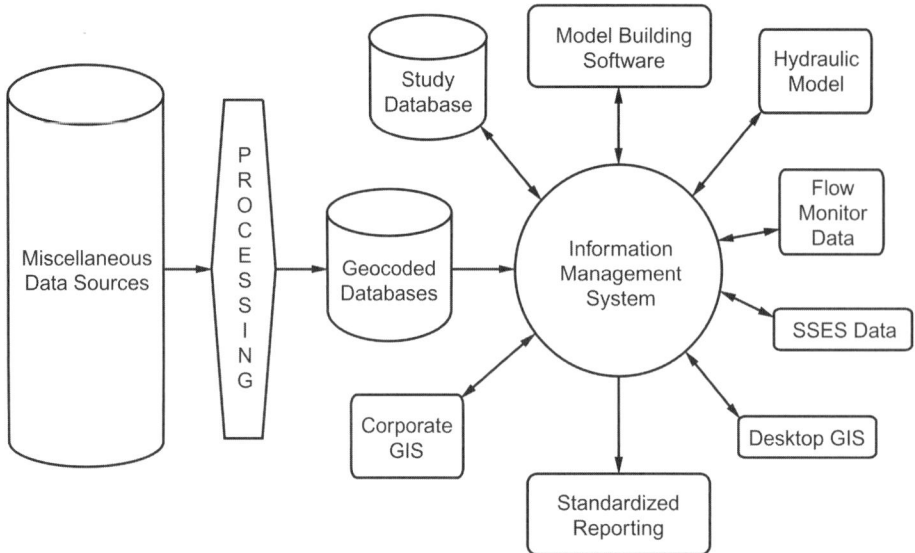

Figure 14.5 Schematic diagram of an enterprise GIS.

- Creation of a GIS requires a review of existing hardware and software and does not imply that legacy systems will go away. Systems such as a customer information systems (CIS), maintenance management systems (MMS), and supervisory control and data acquisition (SCADA) systems are usually fixtures on the landscape.

- Enterprise GIS development calls for a high level of interdepartmental cooperation. All departments involved in enterprise GIS development should share the same vision for the system. The "people" aspect of GIS development can be more challenging than the technological aspects.

- Enterprise GIS development demands a GIS leader—someone to champion the effort. The GIS leader must build communication bridges between departments so that people talk, cooperate, and share.

- The largest expense of the GIS project is usually the data development, which often requires expensive conversion from paper map sources. If an organization fails to consider all the cartographic, asset database, and hydraulic modeling needs during database development, then its GIS system will either (a) fail to meet future application demands or (b) require an expensive future data upgrade. For example, the GIS must be able to reproduce the map sources used in its creation, or all that will have been accomplished is the creation of a new, redundant data set needing maintenance.

Needs Assessment

Critical to a successful GIS implementation is a detailed understanding of the workflow of business processes and the operational and management needs of the organization. An understanding of the specific GIS functions required by individual users is also crucial. This information is gathered through a needs assessment.

A needs assessment has three components:

- *User needs assessment* – This assessment answers the following questions:

- Who is going to use the system?
- What roles do they fill?
- What tasks or functions do they need to accomplish with the GIS?
- What are their skill levels?
- Where are they?
- How often will they use the GIS applications?

- *Data source assessment* – This assessment determines what data sources are available to support the GIS data development, including their formats (e.g., electronic or paper), geographic extents, spatial (x, y, z) and attribute accuracies, coordinate system for the base map, update frequencies, and dates last updated.

- *System design assessment* – This assessment determines the types, locations, and characteristics of existing servers, individual workstations, and computer networking components. This includes operating system platforms, current applications being served, and current levels of use.

The needs assessment is an essential part of creating any IT system and is usually accomplished by conducting detailed surveys and interviews with all potential GIS users (including hydraulic engineers) and the appropriate organization decision makers. It can also be accomplished as part of an overall utility or agency business process workflow analysis.

A thorough needs assessment is crucial for developing a GIS that will provide adequate service now and in the future. It should reveal specific problems or constraints associated with present systems and identify project implementation requirements. A properly conducted needs assessment will culminate in an integrated GIS with the following benefits and advantages:

- Increased operational and management efficiency and staff productivity
- Better sharing of data
- Quicker access to timely information of high quality
- Full leveraging of the capabilities of the system
- Support for organizational operations that reflect the organization's mission and priorities
- Staff endorsement and regular use
- Immediate value to the organization
- Functionality that supports all current and future needs.

Design

The second phase of the GIS development process is the design, which may include the following tasks:

1. *Application design* – Describes the commercial software and custom programs that will be combined to create the applications required to support user needs.
2. *Database design* – Describes the format for the layers and individual features that will comprise the new GIS database, as well as their attributes.

3. *Data development plan* – Describes the techniques, methods, and procedures that will convert the data sources into the desired GIS database.
4. *System design* – Describes the hardware and software to be installed on new servers, workstations, and network components, as well as the reorganization and redeployment of existing hardware and software components. (Beyond the scope of this book.)
5. *Implementation plan and schedule* – Describes tasks and provides a schedule for developing the GIS. (Beyond the scope of this book.)

Application Design. When the responsibilities and workflow within a department have been evaluated, certain tasks that can be performed more efficiently or effectively in a GIS can be identified. Opportunities to connect the GIS with other enterprise applications may become evident. These tasks form the basis of GIS applications, and application descriptions prepared as part of the needs assessment will document these tasks.

A GIS may have interfaces to the following:
- Hydraulic and hydrologic modeling
- Customer service and maintenance management systems
- Customer information (billing) systems
- Laboratory information systems
- SCADA systems
- Document management/workflow

Popular GIS-based applications (often using or integrating the above system interfaces) include the following:
- Facility mapping (GIS data maintenance)
- Service request tracking/work management
- Asset management (GASB, 1999)
- Crew dispatch/vehicle routing
- Field data collection/inspections
- Leak detection (compare master meter to individual account data)
- Link to record/intersection drawings (computer assisted drafting [CAD] or images)
- Isolation tracing/customer notification
- Demand projections/demographic data
- CIP (Capital Improvement Programs) planning/construction monitoring
- One-call/underground service alert response
- New connection processing
- Cross-connection (backflow) test tracking
- Customer complaints

Database Design. The database design for a GIS developed for a wastewater utility should strive to accomplish three fundamental goals that will enable the GIS to become a strategic asset for the organization:

- *Cartographically represent the wastewater collection facilities (assets)* – This representation can be used to create map products.

- *Inventory the network* – The GIS is often the primary record for geographically distributed assets (that is, assets outside the plant).

- *Model the network* – The GIS should be able to support the integration of hydraulic modeling software.

Assuming that hydraulic modeling will be one of the activities supported by the GIS, the GIS analyst should identify the entire range of related hydraulic applications that may be used. The analyst can then determine the types of data required for these applications (for example, SCADA data and record drawings) and how the various types of data relate to one another. This information is essential if the database design is to meet all functional and relational requirements.

An important step in the database design process is the compilation of information about the data set, called *metadata*. Metadata provides the user with the following information:

- Source of the data
- Data reliability, quality, and quality confidence levels
- Methods used in collecting and associating the data
- QA/QC (quality assurance/quality control) and validation procedures
- Other applications and software systems with which the data might interact.

Metadata (see sidebar on page 500) is becoming more important as the ability to share data between organizations over the Internet using eXtensible Markup Language (XML), a programming language for structured information, becomes common. Portal sites use metadata so that users can search for data layers and determine whether the data sets listed meet their accuracy and spatial extents needs.

As GIS applications mature, the major GIS vendors have advanced their software from relational-relational architectures (application/database) to object-relational architectures. In the older relational-relational environment, connectivity, attribute-domain validation, and relationships between features were implemented as relationships between tables (executed by the database management system [DBMS]). In the new architecture, relationships between features, connectivity, and attribute-domain validation are implemented as object-oriented components executed by client-side software with the raw objects stored in the relational database management system (RDBMS). The principal advantage of the new object-relational structure is the compatibility of the GIS applications and data to other object-oriented software applications.

This evolution provides new opportunities and poses new challenges for integration with modeling. Objects can be more complex, with more-sophisticated connectivity, than with older GIS data types (points, lines, polygons). Because the data-modeling effort in an object world is so much more involved (Zeiler, 1999), the hydraulic modeler has to be even more involved at the GIS database design stage when using an object-relational GIS.

As an example, consider a GIS that has been developed for a wastewater collection system using the older relational-relational system. In this model, a typical pipe segment runs from one manhole to the next. But if service laterals are connected to the

Metadata

Metadata is defined as data about data—descriptive and practical information about a particular data set, database, or GIS layer. The Federal Geospatial Data Committee (FGDC) has defined a Content Standard for Digital Geospatial Metadata[1]. The Content Standard was derived as a part of the FGDC's creation of the National Spatial Data Infrastructure (NSDI) to promote the sharing of geospatial data throughout federal, state, and local governments. FGDC-compliant metadata allows for the inclusion of GIS data in the FGDC's national clearinghouse. The metadata standard outlines a formal and structured document that contains data set information and provides facts pertaining to its use in GIS, such as projection information, file format, and the sources of the data. It also includes information about how to acquire the data and whom to contact for more information about the data.

Metadata information is stored in a text (*.txt) or HTML (*.htm or *.html) file. Most USGS metadata files made before 1999 do not conform to any formal standard for physical format. The files are simple ASCII text, and the information is organized to mirror the FGDC content standard. Digital Raster Graphics (DRGs) made since 1999 use a similar but more stable format based on conformance with the "metadata parser" (mp) software tools. This format is also ASCII text but has more rigorous rules for text arrangement.

The metadata are organized into sections which include the following:

Identification information – includes the title, creator or originator of the data, abstract describing the content of the data set, keywords for search engines, and contact information for a person or organization for questions about the data itself.

Data quality information – includes information such as time period and cloud cover.

Spatial data organization – states whether the data are vector or raster and provides details about the vector objects or pixel dimensions.

Spatial reference information – contains projection or coordinate system and associated encoding details.

Entity and attribute information – describes the attributes or fields contained in a database and the corresponding domain data.

Distribution information – describes the distributor and details on availability of the data.

Metadata reference information – describes how recently the data were acquired.

Example of a section of metadata:

Metadata_Reference_Information:
  Metadata_Date: 20040318
  Metadata_Contact:
    Contact_Information:
      Contact_Organization_Primary:
      Contact_Organization: Haestad Methods, Inc.
      Contact_Person: Joe Engineer
      Contact_Address:
        Address_Type: 37 Brookside Road
        City: Waterbury
        State_or_Province: CT
        Postal_Code: 06708
      Contact_Voice_Telephone: 203 555 1666
Metadata_Standard_Name: FGDC Content Standards for Digital Geospatial Metadata
Metadata_Standard_Version: FGDC-STD-001-1998
Metadata_Time_Convention: local time
Metadata_Extensions:
  Online_Linkage: http://www.haestad.com
  Profile_Name: Haestad Metadata Profile

[1] Federal Geospatial Data Committee, Content Standard for Digital Geospatial Data (CSDGM) www.fgdc.gov/metadata/contstan.html

pipe segment, additional nodes are needed at each service lateral connection. To a hydraulic modeler, this level of detail is unnecessary and can be problematic. (See Section 14.3 for further discussion of this issue.)

Object-relational systems provide powerful new opportunities for the hydraulic modeler. In the model for the previous case, the gravity main was divided into two sections at every node, meaning that a 250-foot section of gravity main with 10 service connections is represented by 11 pipe segments. In traditional data models, these 11 pipe segments would each need their own attributes, which would, in all likelihood, be identical. It would be impractical to model an entire gravity system that is structured in this manner, owing to the large number of pipes and nodes that would be required. Representing single runs of gravity sewer with multiple segments also increases the likelihood of data-entry errors, depending on how data are created and maintained. The modeler of such a system is therefore faced with the issue of combining segments into single pipes for modeling purposes. An object-relational system can improve this situation as follows:

- The modeler can develop connectivity rules that dictate how the system is structured during model creation, so that the addition of a service lateral will not break the gravity main into two segments. The rules could also be structured so that a relationship is established between the gravity main and all of its connecting service laterals, so that a list of connections along any main could quickly be generated. In older data models, this relationship would have to be generated through proximity analysis and/or data entry. Additionally, a rule could be set so that if the location of the gravity main is modified, the endpoints of the service laterals can move with the main. The user of a legacy GIS would have to redraw each lateral manually to accomplish the same result.

- Additional rules can be established to enforce the valid relationships between different types of features in a network. For example, a rule can be developed to ensure that a 10-in. pipe can only be connected to a 16 in. pipe through a specific transition element. Another example is a rule that requires every manhole at the upstream end of a pipe run to have an associated flow.

- In addition to these types of rules, the object-relational system also allows *domains* that require attributes to be present in a validation list (for example, material can only be vitrified clay, concrete, or plastic) or in a validation range (invert elevation must be greater than 500 feet and less than 900 feet).

In older data models, the modeler would likely have to develop code to perform tasks such as merging small pipe segments and establishing connectivity rules. This code would not only rely on a programmer's expertise to properly process the myriad conditions, but also rely on a high level of data quality to avoid unintentional errors during the translation. With object-oriented data storage, the processing of data can be established at the database design stage, making the extraction of features needed to model a system a basic function of the GIS.

Although it is quite easy to define the characteristics of a buried piping system needed to support hydraulic modeling, simulating the behavior of a complex pump station within the GIS is more difficult and may not make sense. In many cases, the information needed by the modeler for pump stations will not be stored in the GIS and will have to be acquired from other sources, such as record or design documents. Ideally, all necessary input data for the model exist in the GIS, and the data format and content are capable of supporting all of the modeling goals and applications identified in the needs assessment. In practice, however, not all the data needed by modelers is in a readily available format, nor is it economical to develop it during the initial GIS implementation. Therefore, many hydraulic model interface implementations are staged to address the most urgent or time-saving modeling priorities first with the goal of having the GIS capable of generating, in a repeatable manner, a high percentage of the data required for model development.

It is important to realize that GIS is often part of a wider information-management program that may include maintenance-management systems, SCADA, facility automation, CAD, flow-monitoring databases, a wastewater asset database, as-built maps and drawings, and other elements. Developing a database design that supports the multiple needs of an organization is sometimes difficult to accomplish, but the end result should not be compromised.

Data Development Plan. This subsection describes the main components and issues of the data development plan.

Land Base (Base Map) – A sewer utility GIS must use some type of land-base layer as a spatial reference. Some design issues that must be considered with the base map are the accuracy (± *x* ft or m), the scale, the *projection* (latitude and longitude, state plane coordinates, UTM [Universal Transverse Mercator]), the vertical datum (NAD27 [North American Datum], NAD83), the methods used to create the land base, the frequency of updates, and the timeliness of the data.

The details of these decisions are beyond the scope of this book, but modelers must realize that they cannot simply make a quick decision about using a United States Geological Survey (USGS) quadrangle map, aerial photo, or commercially produced map without giving serious consideration to the long-term potential implications of the choice of land base. An appropriate land base often already exists and can be used as-is, but the accuracy of the land-base data must be validated to ensure usefulness.

Developing the land base is expensive and must be done correctly and accurately in the initial stages of the project; otherwise, costs can escalate when problems arise. Often times, development costs are shared between agencies or departments to ease the financial burden. The lack of an accurate land base is the most common problem in developing an accurate GIS, because multiple data sets developed without a common land base will almost always be inconsistent and therefore not suitable for use together.

For example, if spatially accurate sewer facilities (such as those located with a differential global positioning system [GPS]) are used in combination with inaccurate base-map layers, a good map will not be produced (for instance, pipes may not fall on the correct side of the street centerline or property line, or manholes may be shown inside buildings). The inability to produce reliable maps is more than a nuisance; it could be a legal liability.

Consider a GIS that includes a series of sewer pipes originally placed by scaling from the street centerline. If the sewer pipes are known to be exactly 10 feet off the centerline and are shown exactly 10 feet off the centerline, they would have a high degree of *relative accuracy* (the accuracy of one feature relative to another, without regard to its true position in space; Chernin and LeRoux, 1999). If the centerline location is not accurate, then both the centerline and the sewer pipes will have a low degree of *absolute accuracy* (the accuracy of the coordinate position of a mapped feature compared to its true position in space). Further, assume that a new, highly accurate data source for the street centerline is provided in the future, but the sewer pipe positions are not updated. Now the street centerline has a high degree of absolute accuracy, and the sewer pipes have a poor degree of both absolute and relative accuracy. A worker unaware of the centerline shift and using the updated map to excavate and repair a pipe collapse may well have difficulty location the sewer line, and could potentially damage other utilities.

Data Conversion — The GIS database design must be matched to the specific needs of the applications that the GIS is to serve, such as hydraulic models. Through data conversion, data are made to conform to a uniform format that supports all desired functional requirements. If necessary, the GIS database design is modified to effectively integrate it with the hydraulic modeling software, information management system, as-built drawing records, GPS, and CAD.

In some cases, the information necessary to support current and future hydraulic modeling applications is not available in digital form. It will therefore be necessary to convert paper maps to a digital format or collect data in the field with a GPS. If multiple data sources exist, the analyst should identify the sources that are best suited for the intended use, as well as the method for entering this data into the GIS.

The data conversion issues faced by developers of a new GIS or hydraulic model usually involve one of the following:

- Creation of new vector data (points, lines, and/or polygons) from paper map sources
- Migration of vector data from existing formats such as CAD files.

The creation of new vector data may require raster and/or vector conversion. Raster conversion, or *rasterization*, is the conversion of vector data (that is, points, lines, and polygons) to cell or pixel data. To the modeler, rasterization usually involves scanning paper maps (vector) to produce a digital image (raster) using a process known as *rectification* to enable the resulting image to be viewed in its approximate true coordinate space within a GIS or CAD environment. The process of vector conversion or *vectorization* is then applied to capture the visible points (manholes, lift stations) and lines (gravity mains and force mains) in the raster image as vector features compatible with the GIS and model requirements.

Some software packages can automate the vectorization process by recognizing the arrangement of pixels in a scanned image and creating the vector points and lines that represent manholes and pipes. This technology, although improving, can require a great deal of manual cleanup and generally only works well with high quality data sources.

Since many data conversion projects involve old maps that are difficult to read, most vectorization efforts are performed manually using either heads-up or heads-down digitizing. *Heads-up digitizing* refers to the process of comparing the locations of features on a paper map or scanned and rectified map and visually placing them into the GIS. This is done by using the relative position of sewer-system features to base-map features, such as a road edge or building that appears on both the source drawing and the GIS base map. *Heads-down digitizing* refers to the process of *registering* a paper map on a digitizing tablet, so that tracing map features as points and lines will result in their being added to the GIS base map in the approximate location. Heads-down digitizing by experienced conversion personnel does not require that the technician look at the computer screen, since all spatial and attribute information can usually be captured directly from the map. Heads-up digitizing is often more efficient, produces superior results, and is rapidly becoming the industry standard. The reader should note, however, that in some cases the base-map features may have changed significantly since the original production of the map.

Rasterization and vectorization should only be used when the quality of the data sources support them, which means that the information to be captured is easily distinguishable by the vectorization software. Dealing with the errors of the vectorization process can be onerous for the majority of GIS development projects. In supporting the data development process, the GIS analyst must develop and maintain data-accuracy standards and implement QA/QC procedures to ensure data integrity. The higher the required accuracy, the higher the cost of the data conversion.

Migrating map data from CAD files into the desired GIS format is quite common, yet can also pose a number of challenges. For example, a single line in a CAD file may actually represent several pipe segments in the GIS. When this element is converted to GIS format, the line must be divided into multiple lines representing individual pipe segments. As an additional hurdle, map annotations such as pipe diameter and invert elevation in a CAD drawing often do not have any data records associated with them and are not linked to the CAD features. To be turned into attribute information in the GIS, these floating graphics must be associated with the nearest pipe, and the text strings must be filtered to produce the correct attribute. For instance, "1987 – 12" may have to be converted into "1987" for the year-installed attribute and "12" for the pipe-diameter attribute.

In some cases, paper and CAD data sources are insufficient to create a model of the system that meets a jurisdiction's accuracy needs. In these instances, global positioning system (GPS) equipment can be used to create highly accurate maps of the sewer collection system. The basic process includes field work using a GPS to capture the locations of manholes, lift stations, and other features. The accuracy of the GPS system must be consistent with the accuracy requirements of the GIS.

Pilot Study

After design, the next phase of the GIS development is usually to perform a pilot study, which can include the following activities:

1. Create a pilot database following the data development plan.
2. Develop prototypes of high-priority applications following the application design.
3. Provide core software training to key staff.
4. Test the applications and data during several pilot review sessions with end users and management.
5. Finalize the database design, data development plan, and system design documents as appropriate, incorporating what was learned from the pilot review sessions.

Production

The next phase is the production phase, which can include the following tasks:

1. Finalize the QA/QC software and techniques that will be used during the entire service-area data conversion.

2. Perform the service-area-wide data conversion following the data development plan.
3. Procure the necessary hardware and software.
4. Finalize the applications.
5. Develop end-user and system-maintenance documentation.
6. Begin user training and rollout of high-priority applications (such as facility mapping).

Rollout

The final phase is rollout, which can include the following tasks:

1. Install a full complement of operational hardware and software.
2. Provide user and system-maintenance training, which will likely be a combination of core GIS software courses and application training.
3. Perform acceptance testing (formal testing to determine whether the system satisfies the acceptance criteria and thus whether the customer should accept the system).
4. Roll out the final system, which may include transition from any legacy systems being retired.

14.3 Model Construction

Constructing a sewer model and maintaining it over time can be one of the most time-consuming, costly, and error-prone steps of a hydraulic modeling project. Before widespread integration of GIS and modeling, building a sewer model was a specialized activity, separate from an organization's routine business procedures and workflows. Engineers created model input files by gathering, combining, and digitizing data from a variety of hard-copy source documents, such as sewer system plan maps, as-built maps, topographic maps, and census maps, among others. If CAD data were available, features required for modeling had to be extracted for use with the hydraulic modeling software. The process was manual and required great attention to detail and many engineering judgments along the way. Once a model was developed, calibrated, and run, the modeler generated the required outputs and what-if scenarios, and typically produced a master plan so that a utility could begin making the required capital improvements.

Despite rapid advances in hydraulic modeling software over the last decade, which have included tools for the automatic translation of CAD data into modeling data and for linking the model to external data sources, many communities and wastewater utilities have found it difficult to build, update, and maintain anything but highly skeletonized models. Although organizations may have intended to keep models current, time constraints or business-process issues have often interfered. Even if CAD layers have been updated or record drawings marked up with changes, model maintenance has usually been ignored because model input data were maintained separately from system drawings. Thus, in communities experiencing rapid growth, sewer models could quickly become outdated and have often had to be recreated from scratch when a new system model was required.

A GIS-trained engineer/modeler can use a GIS to create and maintain a model more efficiently, more accurately, and more cost-effectively than an engineer building a model inside a traditional modeling environment. Consider the following:

- Because GIS tools can automate the process, model building can be faster and more efficient, especially for large systems.

- Because GIS can manage large volumes of data, the model can incorporate more detail.

- Both hydraulic modeling software and GIS have advanced editing tools. The modeler needs to look at each task and decide if it is better done in the model or the GIS.

- In the ideal case, where GIS data entry has a consistent spatial reference and a high level of quality control, the GIS-integrated model should contain more accurate data and should therefore be easier to calibrate. This should lead to better decision-making.

- Data collected and stored in the GIS for other applications can be extracted and incorporated into the model input file, if needed.

- As long as the GIS is routinely updated, GIS data needed for reconstructing the model input file should be available.

- Digital orthophotos available in the GIS can be overlaid with the model to provide a base-map reference.

- *Georeferenced* land-use and/or zoning maps can be used to generate and allocate wastewater loads for the model.

- If modeling results are returned to the GIS, further analyses can be run, and other users, such as planners and developers, can utilize modeling data in conjunction with other GIS data.

Model Sustainability and Maintenance

By working with GIS professionals to build a sewer model from a properly constructed GIS, the engineer can spend time evaluating the sewer system and making engineering decisions rather than constructing—and, over time, reconstructing—the sewer model. If the GIS is used as the foundation for building the sewer model, and assuming the GIS is maintained over the long term, the sewer model can be rebuilt easily in the future using up-to-date GIS data, as illustrated in Figure 14.6.

For instance, a model may be constructed by using the GIS to select and extract all relevant network elements that are located in a specific basin of interest (using an overlay analysis). To ensure that these elements are readily available for rebuilding the model in the future, they can be tagged appropriately in the GIS. It may also be necessary to summarize flows from upstream basins that flow into the basin. Regardless of the methodology adopted, it should be implemented such that features and attributes can be updated in the GIS without compromising the ability to quickly reconstruct the model in the future.

The GIS professional and the modeler should determine where certain features required for the model will reside: in the GIS or in the model. For example, should pump curves be stored in the GIS? Ideally, the required data should be specified from the outset so that they can be stored and maintained in the GIS. This helps to ensure

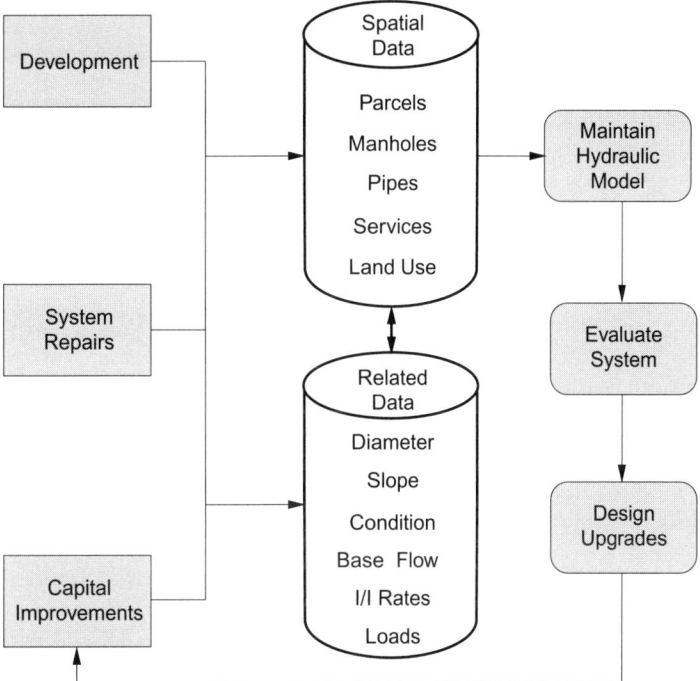

Figure 14.6 Procedure for maintaining a hydraulic model.

that the model-building process can be repeated and minimizes the adjustments that the modeler must make to the data delivered by the GIS professional.

Making good decisions about whether new pipes added to the collection system should be marked for inclusion in the model requires engineering judgment that accounts for pipe size or other criteria. The GIS professional can use GIS tools to do much of the sorting and selecting required for skeletonization, but the modeler must review the entire network carefully to ensure that the model reflects reality. This process can be made easier by placing the service laterals, gravity sewer mains, and force mains on separate layers in the GIS.

Communication Between the GIS and Modeling Staff

In some small systems, the modeler and the GIS professional are the same person; however, they are usually two individuals, or groups of individuals, in different departments or companies. Successful model development is a coordinated effort between the two parties.

During the model-building process, the GIS professional must confer regularly with the modeler to ensure that the model is developed efficiently. Both should acknowledge their differing perspectives to help ensure effective communication. The GIS professional understands GIS technology, what it can do, and how to manipulate data from various systems and databases, while the modeler understands how the model works, what data are required, and how to ensure that the model generates meaningful results.

Because the modeler is the user or consumer of the data to be developed or managed by the GIS professional, he or she should take time to explain the data needs of the model. Similarly, the GIS professional should explain GIS capabilities and limitations and what is technologically feasible. For example, a GIS containing gravity sewers may have been constructed with the pipes digitized in random directions—some upstream and some downstream. The modeler may require significant time to orient the pipes in the downstream direction, which many models require. The GIS professional, given a list of pipes that constitute model outfalls, should be able to use tracing algorithms to automatically orient all pipes in the downstream direction, thereby saving the modeler time.

Sufficient time spent with model planning and design ensures a smooth model-development process. Specifically, the GIS professional and the modeler should discuss the following issues at the outset of the project:

- *Modeling basics* – The modeler should share modeling basics with the GIS professional (for instance, that flow into the collection system occurs only at nodes; pipes should be oriented in the direction of flow; and gravity mains must be properly sloped, as determined by upstream and downstream inverts and pipe length). Before using the GIS to develop the model input file, the GIS professional must have a fairly complete understanding of input-data requirements, types of model calculations, and the basics of how the model operates. In most instances, the GIS professional can benefit from model training. With an understanding of the model and a vision of the intended outcome, the GIS professional can determine which GIS tools will best serve the modeler's needs. Merely listing required features and attributes will not suffice; the modeler must explain why these elements are crucial.

- *Modeling terminology* – For successful model development, each professional must have a basic understanding of the relevant terminology familiar to the other. The GIS professional is comfortable discussing fields, tables, and technology, while the modeler deals with pipes, roughness coefficients, and hydraulic grade lines. Both must discuss common terms, their meanings, and how they are applied. For example, they need to discuss terms such as *load* (the GIS professional may view load as the contribution of an individual dwelling unit, whereas the modeler views load as the aggregate contribution of a tributary area assigned to a particular node) and *node* (the GIS professional may think of a node as being synonymous with every service connection point along a gravity main, whereas a modeler may consider a node as only a manhole or another junction of collection system piping).

- *Standard units of measure* – The modeler must understand the units used in the GIS and the required conversions for consistency with the model. For example, pipe diameters might be expressed in inches or millimeters in the GIS but needed in feet or meters in the model. As another example, base wastewater flows might be expressed in a variety of units, depending on the underlying billing system.

Network Components

Even if hydraulic modeling is considered during the development of the GIS, unless the GIS was created solely to support modeling, it is likely to include a greater level of detail than is needed by the model. For example, it is not uncommon for the GIS to include every pipe, including service laterals to each dwelling unit. Such information is not needed for most modeling applications and should be disregarded to improve model runtime, reduce file size, and save money.

On the other hand, there are details important for modeling that may not be contained in the GIS. For example, pipe grade changes between manholes may not be reflected in the GIS, but may be significant for hydraulic modeling. Since most models allow only one slope for each pipe, in this situation it may be necessary to split the pipe and add a dummy node for modeling purposes. Additionally, the GIS is unlikely to contain details on wet wells, pump curves, and pump on/off switch levels.

Conversion of the GIS into the model therefore involves careful filtering of GIS elements to arrive at an appropriate level of detail for modeling, as illustrated in Figure 14.7.

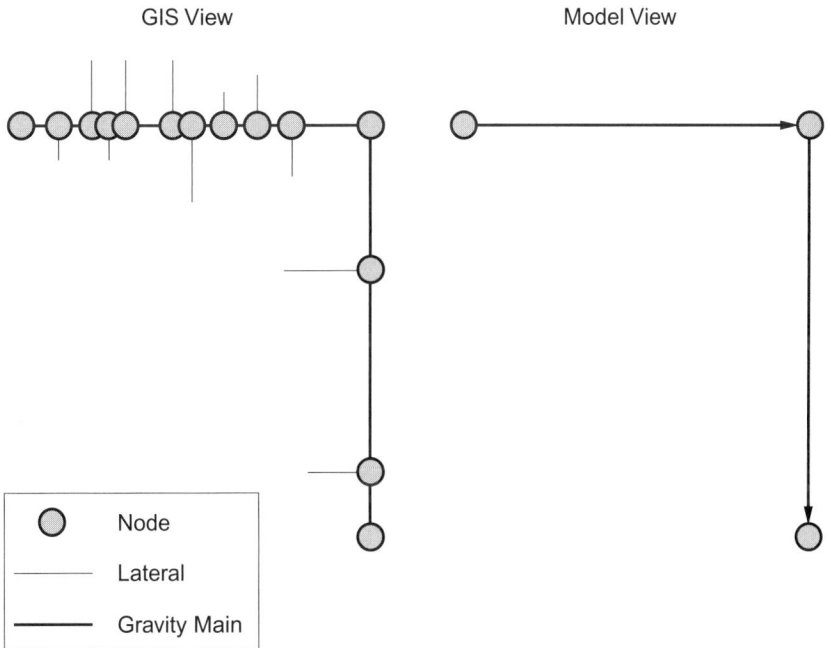

Figure 14.7 GIS view versus model view.

There are two points at which the GIS data can be cleaned up for model use—importing and *skeletonization* (simplification). When the data are imported from the GIS to the model, extraneous GIS features such as service laterals must be filtered out. This usually requires rules for mapping GIS features to model features. Typical relationships are shown in Table 14.1.

After the GIS data are imported into a model, the number of elements can sometimes be further reduced by skeletonization or simplification. In wastewater collection system models, the number of elements can be reduced considerably by representing entire subbasins as single loading points, as discussed in Chapter 5.

Some would argue that with the increasing power of models and the ease with which models can share data with GIS, skeletonization has become less important and the state of the art is evolving toward all-pipe models. Different levels of skeletonization are still appropriate, however, depending on the type of model (static versus dynamic) and how the model will be used. The GIS professional and the modeler should discuss specific skeletonization criteria in detail, including the importance of network connectivity.

Table 14.1 GIS features and their corresponding model elements.

GIS Feature	Model Elements
Gravity main	Modeled as a gravity pipe.
Force main	Often modeled as a pipe for conveyance, unless the model handles force mains explicitly.
Siphon	Often modeled as a pipe for conveyance, unless the model handles siphons explicitly.
Service lateral	Not usually modeled.
Cleanout	Not usually modeled.
Manhole	Modeled as a node or manhole.
Diversion manhole	Modeled as a node or manhole, unless the model handles diversions explicitly. Some models may support various rules for flow splitting.
Split or summit manhole (manhole that usually occurs at the crest of a road and has pipes that flow out in two directions; uncommon)	Modeled as a node or manhole; flow can be split between pipes or loaded into one as the model permits.
Drop manhole	Modeled as a node or manhole; some models may support more detail than others for this type of structure
Pump station	Wet wells and pumps are modeled as separate elements. Many models support individual pumps and various types of pump-curve definitions.
Catch basin/inlet	Loading node, inlet, or manhole depending on model.

With the automation of model building from GIS, it may be possible to construct individual models from the GIS for each type of study. For example, there may be a "Central Business District" model with a great deal of detail in that portion of town, and only a few loading points for areas upstream. There may also be an interceptor model that only considers the major interceptors. There is not necessarily a single model of the system.

Wastewater Loads

To model a sewer system it is necessary to determine both the location and quantity of the various flows (or loads) that enter the system. Loads come from three primary sources: base wastewater, infiltration, and inflow. Base wastewater flows are a byproduct of human activity, whereas infiltration and inflow stem from environmental, pipe construction, and deterioration factors.

Base Wastewater Loads. Every home or business produces wastewater that enters the sewer system. However, as wastewater loads are not usually metered at the source, quantifying them requires estimation. The three most common methods for estimating base wastewater loads (also known as dry weather flow or sanitary flow) are

- Water demand rates (the fraction of purchased water that enters the sewer) or wintertime water use (*water use x factor*)

> ## Georeferencing
>
> Before it can be used in any GIS system, an element needs to have its x-y coordinates in a known coordinate system (e.g., latitude/longitude, state plane coordinates, Universal Transverse Mercator [UTM]). The process of assigning x-y coordinates to an element based on its address or some similar characteristic (e.g., zip or postal code) is known as *georeferencing* or *geocoding*.
>
> Georeferencing is widely used in emergency response, parcel delivery, and marketing studies, and it also has applications in wastewater modeling, especially for loading models based on billing or census information.
>
> Street addresses themselves are not georeferenced. A GIS does not know where to place an element (e.g., a sewage service lateral) that is located at 250 South Adams St. For the GIS to locate that address, x-y coordinates must be assigned. Elements can be georeferenced using surveying or global positioning systems. Georeferencing can be done manually by overlaying and registering a street map on top of a GIS land base. More sophisticated, automated methods are available to greatly simplify this work.
>
> Most automated georeferencing tools in the United States use the Census Bureau's TIGER (Topologically Integrated Geographic Encoding and Reference) files (Marx, 1990). In the United Kingdom, Ordinance Survey files are used. Software is available to link any street address to x-y coordinates.
>
> While automated georeferencing is useful, there are still pitfalls in the process. One is that post office box numbers cannot be located. Another is that different naming conventions tend to cause problems. For example, it may be easy to georeference "250 South Adams Street," but "250 S. Adams St." may not be as successful. Another pitfall is that it may take some time for new land developments to be included in TIGER files. Also, some addresses may encompass large areas, so assigning a point to these areas is imprecise.
>
> Another system used for georeferencing is based on postal codes (zip codes). Knowing a zip code, it is possible to assign a customer in a wastewater system to a polygon defined by that postal code. Overlaying the postal code polygon with a loading polygon can help in loading the hydraulic model.

- Land-use flow rates using a land-use or parcel map (*area x flow/area*)
- Per capita flow rates using population and employment data (*population x volume/capita/day*).

The following is a typical procedure showing how GIS can be applied to estimate wastewater loads from land-use flow rates. The procedure suggests identifying the nodes that will be loaded first, then creating the tributary areas to those nodes. Another, and perhaps more-common method, is to delineate the tributary subbasins first based on topography and pipe network layout, and then allocate the flow from each subbasin to one or more load-point nodes. Either method is acceptable and should result in similar loadings given a similar subbasin size.

Step 1 – Identify load-point nodes. After the network has been defined, load-point nodes are designated by setting a node attribute in the GIS. Usually, nodes at the top of sewer branches, at confluences, and at the locations of major flow contributors are designated as load-point nodes (Figure 14.8). The goal is an appropriate level of granularity, such that the resulting tributary-area polygons are reasonably sized (generally between a few acres and a few hundred acres, depending on the intended level of detail).

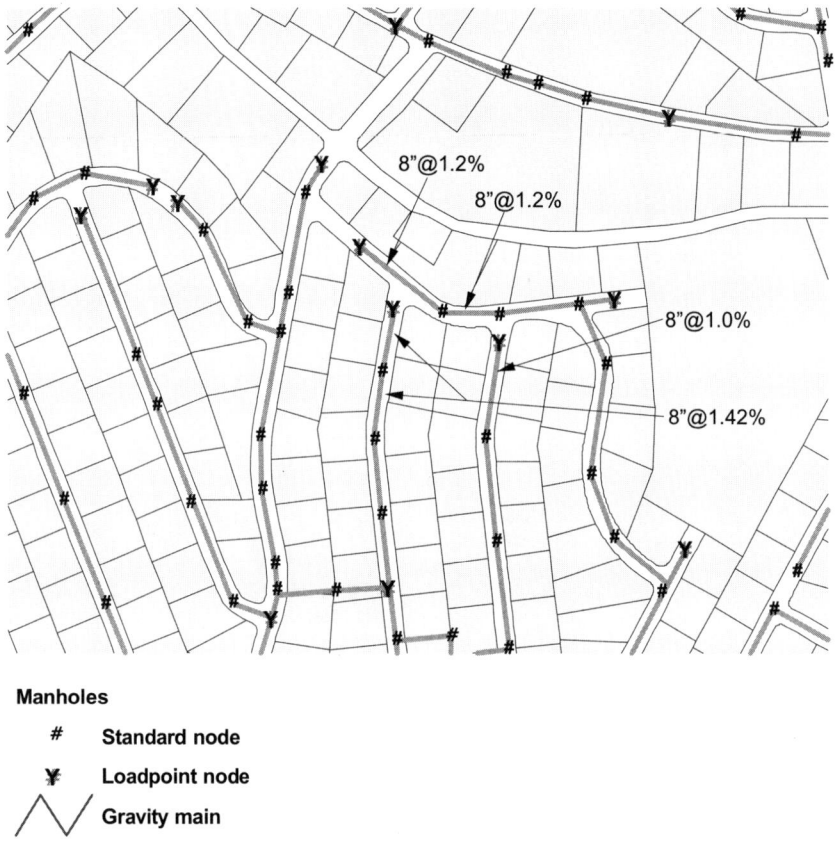

Figure 14.8 Load-point nodes and standard nodes.

Step 2 – Create tributary-area polygons. A tributary-area polygon represents the geographic region that would logically flow to a load-point node. One technique for delineating the tributary-area polygons is to overlay a topographic map with the modeled network to clearly visualize the drainage paths. Including the small pipes that are not part of the modeled network can help provide more accurate results. Advanced GIS tools can, with sufficient data, semi-automate the process of creating tributary-area polygons. For example, many GIS packages can generate Thiessen polygons (also known as a Veroni network) from a set of load-point nodes that can then be overlaid on a land-use map to generate flows to each load-point node, as illustrated in Figure 14.9.

An alternative approach is to use a parcel map on which the modeler encodes each parcel polygon with the ID of the load-point node to which it is tributary. This process can be largely automated through GIS analysis by associating each parcel with the closest node.

Step 3 – Create/obtain load polygons. Either land-use or parcel maps in GIS format should be obtained from local agencies or municipalities. There may be several versions of land-use maps, representing different development scenarios, as illustrated in Figure 14.10. Each load polygon (whether a parcel or a land-use area) must be encoded with its land-use type.

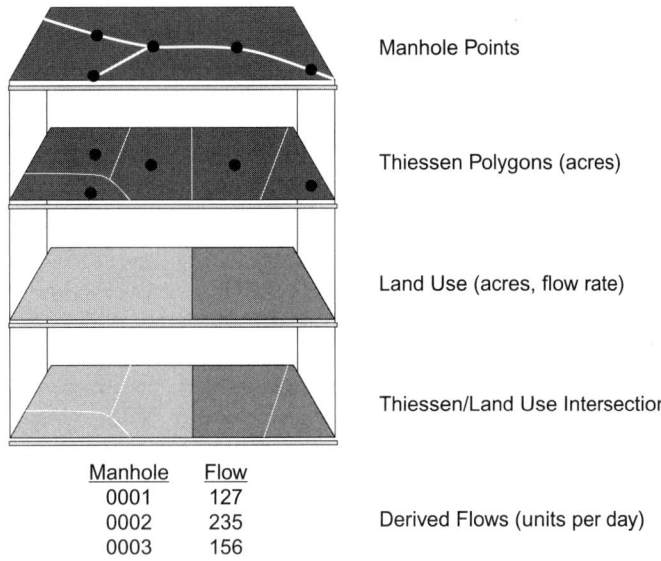

Figure 14.9 Tributary-polygon method of using GIS to generate load-point flows.

Figure 14.10 Typical land-use map.

Step 4 – Determine daily load rates. To estimate daily loads from land-use data, area-based flow rates (such as gallons/day/acre or liters/day/hectare) for each land-use category are used. Using factors to estimate wastewater flow rates from given land-use categories is described in Chapter 6.

Step 5 – Aggregate loads at load-point nodes. If the loading polygons are parcels, this step is straightforward and does not necessarily require GIS. Wastewater flow totals are calculated for parcels based on the load-point node to which they are assigned. If, however, the loading polygons are land-use polygons, GIS tools can be used to intersect the load polygons and the tributary-area polygons and to establish the aggregate daily wastewater loads for each tributary-area polygon. It should be noted that when large parcels or tributary areas are used, especially in undeveloped areas, a single parcel may load to multiple load-point nodes in the system. The modeler should take care to verify that large users' flows are appropriately loaded to the model. This can usually be verified with the municipal billing department. Similarly, the modeler should ensure that large undeveloped areas are not automatically loaded to the single closest nodes, but rather take into account predominant drainage patterns. Either the load should be allocated to multiple node or the undeveloped areas should be excluded from the loading process.

These same basic steps can be used to estimate loads for future conditions based on population or land-use projections. Custom GIS operations enable modelers to compute future wastewater loads by overlaying data, such as population projections and future land-use polygon layers, with the load-point node layer.

Infiltration and Inflow Loads. Ideally, wastewater base loads are the only loads entering a sanitary sewer system. In reality, though, there are other methods by which flow enters a sewer system—*infiltration and inflow* (also known as wet weather flow or I/I). As described in Section 7.1, hydraulic sewer models simulate I/I as two separate components—groundwater infiltration and rainfall derived infiltration and inflow. Groundwater infiltration (GWI) enters the system through defects in pipes, pipe joints, connections, and manhole walls and is usually considered to be constant over the duraion of a single precipitation event. Rainfall derived infiltration and inflow (RDII) is the wet weather flow portion of the sewer hydrograph and represents sewage flow above the normal dry weather flow pattern. GIS may be used to develop both GWI and RDII for the sewer model.

A variety of modeling techniques can simulate RDII (see Chapter 7), and many of them require the use of spatial data. The data requirements depend upon the modeling approach and can include parameters such as subbasin area, slope, and overland flow distance—all of which can come from the GIS. Other parameters such as runoff coefficients, depression storage depths, and infiltration rates can be developed from an analysis of GIS data. RDII is typically minimal for the design of new sanitary sewers.

In the case of GWI, some allowance may be required by regulatory agencies when designing new sanitary sewers. Typically these allowances are specified in terms of unit load factors such as gallons per day per mile of pipe for US customary units and liters per day per kilometer of pipe for SI units. Table 7.13 on page 262 presents ranges of GWI allowances. These values may be modified by factors such as soil type, depth of pipe, pipe diameter, or season. For existing systems, site specific unit load factors may be developed by analysis of flow data collected during dry weather using the procedures described in Chapter 9.

Building the Model

This section describes the steps involved in building a GIS-based sewer model.

Extract, Transform, Load. An enterprise GIS houses the centrally managed data shared by individuals and various departments within the organization. Modelers typically see the GIS as the primary data source or hub from which they derive their models, but they also need access to other important data sources managed outside the GIS. Often, this information does not reside in the same database or physical server that contains the GIS and may be maintained by a mix of database technologies and/or proprietary file formats. The data sources may be distributed across the enterprise and hosted on various servers and client workstations.

The key to successful modeling in the enterprise is to use automation tools to facilitate the flow of data between these pathways whenever possible, avoiding manual intervention or transcription of data between the GIS and the original data sources. The modeler can accomplish this automation in several ways:

- By using general utilities to extract the data from one source, transform it as required by the target source, and then load it into the target source. Such extract/transform/load utilities (ETLs) are readily available and are extremely valuable to modelers.

- By using programming and application programming interfaces (APIs) provided by the GIS and the database vendors to develop custom extensions of the standard GIS commands for accomplishing the ETL steps.

- By using commercially available technologies that are specialized for modeling within GIS. These technologies usually focus on some of the intensive and key data-transformation services (for example, automation of the processes for skeletonization and load estimation).

- By using data-manipulation tools within hydraulic models to transform data into the desired format.

Modeling Features. Several aspects of hydraulic modeling must be taken into account when using a GIS for this purpose. These considerations often lead to the separation of the enterprise GIS layers from the modeling GIS layers. These aspects of modeling are

- Network granularity
- Scenarios
- Time-series data
- Ownership.

Network granularity – For many hydraulic modeling applications, the model network does not need to contain every pipe in the actual system to obtain accurate results. For example, a simplified or skeletonized version of the system is often sufficient to make informed planning decisions and is often desirable for improving the efficiency of the hydraulic modeling software. In this case, providing fields in the enterprise GIS layers to manage the hydraulic results is wasteful, because many of the GIS features are eliminated during the model-building and skeletonization process. However, a single identifier can allow the extraction or skeletonization software to make the link between the GIS feature and model feature. This link then provides a trail back to the GIS feature for the analysis of hydraulic results.

Scenarios – In sewer system planning, the modeler is most often dealing with what-if conditions, not the conditions that the GIS actually contains. The what-if conditions may include future loads or proposed pipes and system facilities.

The GIS can be designed to incorporate the various what-if conditions and phases of a sewer system facility. For example, a given pipe goes through many stages:

1. Alternative pipe in the model
2. Proposed pipe in a planning study or budget
3. A pipe under design, bid, and then construction
4. An installed pipe that has not been tested or placed in service
5. A pipe placed in service.

Ideally, the enterprise GIS is designed to manage Steps 2 through 5 in this life cycle by including them on separate layers or by using subtypes to identify them. A tremendous amount of activity within a wastewater utility involves planned or proposed pipes, thus the sharing of data on planned or proposed pipes is an area where inter-agency GIS needs are high. However, papers on modeling (such as Deagle and Ancel, 2002) typically describe how models use GIS, but few describe incorporation of model information in the GIS. An exception is the Indianapolis Water Company (Schatzlein and Dieterlein, 2002), which has a separate area in its GIS for proposed projects. Many managers of enterprise systems do not want to become bogged down maintaining proposed projects and may not allow a pipe to be added until it is placed in service. In such cases, the proposed pipes need to be managed in the scenario manager of the model.

Time-series data – Most sewer models are dynamic, meaning they can be used to predict the response of the sewer system over an extended period of time. The modeler needs to visually analyze this time-series data in an efficient manner. Although an enterprise GIS can be designed to handle time-series data, it often lacks the tools to work with it efficiently, as most attributes for GIS features contain a single value (such as invert elevation). With time-series data, it is not uncommon to have several years of 5-minute-interval flow data at 100 monitoring locations. The modeling software is set up to handle these large numbers of values, but the enterprise-wide GIS is usually not the best repository.

Ownership – In an enterprise-level GIS, the most of the data are not "owned" by the hydraulic modelers, and changes to this data are often outside the modeler's direct control. Several issues arise from this lack of control. First, the enterprise GIS will often have data inaccuracies or omissions that are insignificant for maintenance or asset management but are important for hydraulic modeling. The owners of the GIS may not be able to make these corrections as quickly as the hydraulic modeler requires, so the modeler is forced to make these corrections directly in the modeling GIS layers. An opposite but equally problematic issue is that the hydraulic modeler often does not want changes to the GIS to be immediately reflected in the model. For example, when calibrating flow rates using flow-meter data, it is important that the modeler use data that reflect the actual conditions at the time of the metering. The GIS owners may be updating land-use layers for recently installed subdivisions, and this could have a significant effect on the model's results. The bottom line is that the modeler needs to be in control of the data used for modeling.

Pitfalls in Constructing Models from GIS

A common misconception is that if a utility has a sewer system GIS data set, using the GIS to generate data for the model will be easy, if not automatic. If hydraulic modeling were identified as a potential application of the GIS during the needs assessment and if these needs were considered in creating the GIS, this would be true. However, if the GIS was designed only for such purposes as hardcopy mapping, asset management, maintenance management, and capital-improvement planning, it might not be easy to use the GIS to generate a hydraulic model. This is most pronounced when the GIS is used primarily for hardcopy mapping, and its users never interact directly with the underlying GIS database. The GIS data are not necessarily bad, but they may not be suitable for hydraulic modeling purposes even though they satisfy the existing GIS needs. These differences can lead to problems if they are not anticipated and explicitly handled. The following are some of the more common pitfalls, with suggestions on how to avoid them.

Missing Attributes. It is not uncommon for a modeler to be informed that there is a "great" GIS data set available for modeling, only to find that the data set is anything but great from the standpoint of modeling. If the GIS data set was not created with modeling as an intended application, important modeling attributes will quite likely be missing (e.g., pipe slope and/or invert elevations), which can delay the modeling effort considerably or make it altogether impractical.

GIS data sets should be built from the start with modeling in mind. Ideally, a modeler should be consulted during GIS design to ensure that the necessary attributes are included and the required levels of data accuracy are established. For example, while x, y coordinates can be off by a few feet, invert elevations need to be accurate to the tenth [or hundredth] of a foot). The modeler may also make suggestions as to how to populate critical data fields when source data are missing or conflicting.

Features not Properly Connected. Connectivity is the lifeblood of a sewer model. Every element must be connected to other elements (e.g., node-pipe-node-pipe) for flow routing. Yet, in some cases, GIS features that look as if they are connected are, in actuality, not truly connected (or snapped). Sometimes artificial gaps between pipes were introduced because the data were created in a tiled system and pipes were not connected across sheet boundaries. This problem may not be visible at typical working scales (on-screen viewing or plotted maps) but becomes obvious when the view is enlarged, as illustrated in Figure 14.11. A snapped connection appears connected no matter how much the view is expanded.

The easiest way to identify connectivity problems is to run a network trace on the modeled system. A trace attempts to step through the network, moving from one feature to other connected features until it reaches the end of a line or reconnects to a previously traced feature. Generally, traced features are highlighted, making it obvious which pipes were not traced, as illustrated in Figure 14.12. Faulty connections should be repaired in the GIS data set so that subsequent downloads of GIS data for modeling purposes are correct.

Some modeling software automatically snaps end points when they are within a specified tolerance or alerts the modeler when pipe ends are within a tolerance, providing an opportunity to connect the pipes.

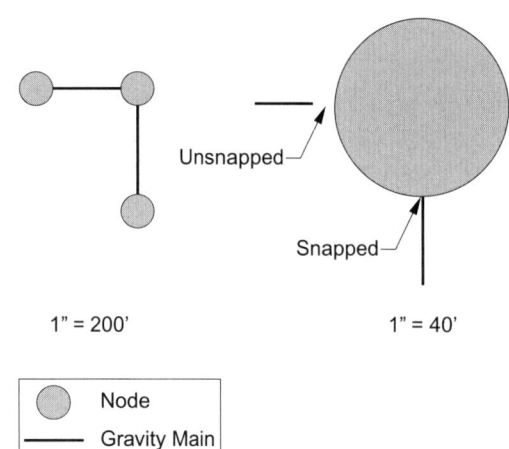

Figure 14.11 Snapped and unsnapped features in a GIS.

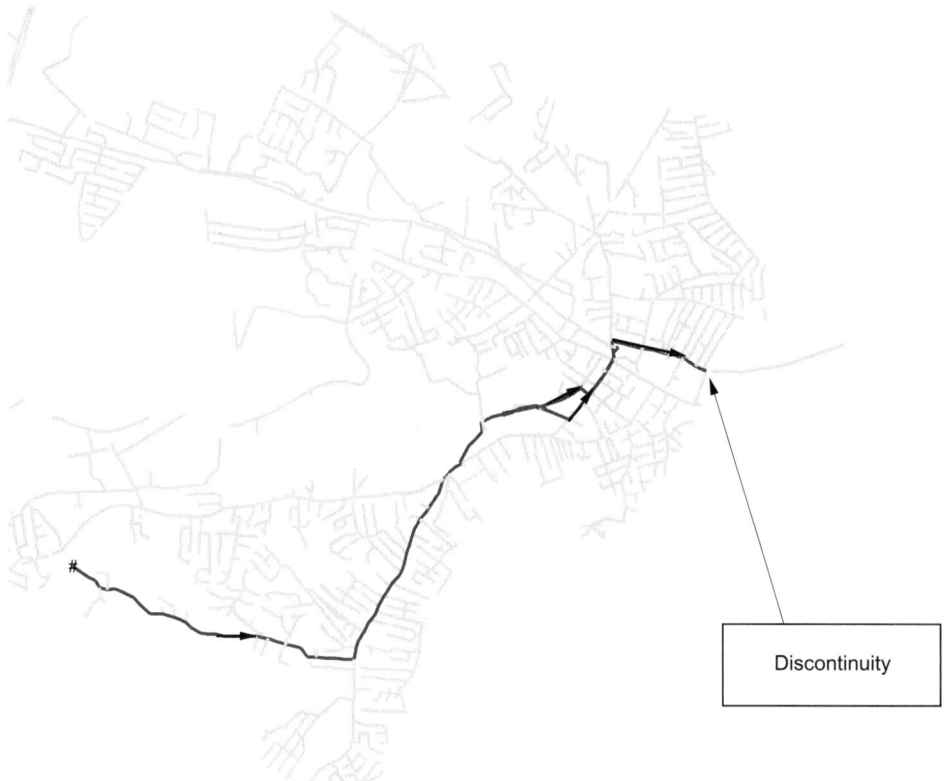

Figure 14.12 Using trace analysis to reveal a network discontinuity.

Features Digitized Backwards. Pipe direction is important for sanitary sewer systems, especially for gravity systems. Yet many GIS implementations do not consider digitizing direction, allowing pipes to be digitized in random directions—some upstream to downstream and some the reverse.

Network tracing tools can be customized to identify these conditions and, in some cases, reverse a pipe's direction of flow by swapping the node connectivity attributes (if present) and reversing the order of the graphic pipe vertices. Such tools are extremely important for the automated debugging of a sewer network. The task could easily take days or weeks to perform manually for a large system.

GIS Feature Type Has no Model Counterpart. Another common problem is that a GIS sewer data set is generally far more detailed than a modeled sewer system (although this is more prevalent with water systems). There may be a number of GIS feature types that have no counterparts in the sewer model. Simply exporting these unsupported feature types from the GIS causes problems when trying to run the model.

In these cases, it is generally best to identify an appropriate surrogate feature type that is supported by the model and convert the GIS feature on export. If a script or program is used to export data from the GIS to the model, the conversion can be done on the fly. Otherwise, the modeler may need to create a "Model Type" attribute field for export rather than the actual type.

GIS Identifiers Incompatible with the Model. Models are sometimes restrictive about the formats of feature identifiers. For example, a model may require identifiers to be numeric with no more than five digits. Such identifiers are rarely consistent with the identification standards employed by an enterprise GIS, thereby creating a potential conflict.

To avoid this problem, an attribute field called "Model ID" can be created for all GIS features to be included in the model. This field is populated with an identifier that conforms to the model requirements, as shown in Table 14.2. This identifier is used rather than the GIS identifier when data are exported from the GIS to the model.

Table 14.2 Example of storing alternative, modeled identifiers as GIS attributes.

GIS Pipe ID	Modeled ID
MH1234-MH2345	1276
MH4567-MH5678	1979

GIS Contains Short Pipe Segments. Even though a GIS can represent pipes of any length, some models, particularly dynamic models, cannot accurately model very short pipes. This problem can be alleviated while skeletonizing a system by combining short pipes.

Another method is to artificially increase the length and reduce the friction coefficient to make the pipes hydraulically equivalent. This is done by creating pipe attribute fields called "User Defined Modeled Length" and "Modeled Friction" that store the pipe length and friction coefficient to be used for modeling purposes, as illustrated in Table 14.3. These fields can be set initially to the actual pipe length and friction, then adjusted for short pipes. When data are exported from the GIS to the model, the modeled length and modeled friction are used rather than the actual values.

Table 14.3 Pipe lengths and friction may need to be adjusted for modeling.

GIS Pipe Length, ft	Friction, n	Modeled Length, ft	Modeled Friction, n
224	0.013	224	0.013
19	0.013	100	0.0057

Loading Model Results to GIS

One issue that arises in modeling with GIS is whether model results should be carried back to the source GIS. Generally, the modeling data are maintained in a separate GIS layer created specifically for modeling. For sanitary sewer systems, it may be possible to load model results directly to the source GIS data set, as it is more likely that there will be a one-to-one correspondence between raw GIS features and modeled features.

Hydraulic modeling results in an enterprise GIS can be used for a number of purposes, including the following:

- Establishing sewer main replacement priorities (when combined with other GIS layers such as soils and repair data)
- Connection permit processing (available capacity can be reviewed and future loads reserved)
- Spill/contaminant isolation/remediation (contaminant is introduced accidentally or intentionally).

14.4 GIS Analysis and Visualization

This section illustrates ways that a GIS might support a wastewater utility in the hydraulic model application cycle, from model development to capital planning, decision support, and operations support. It is important to note that a significant planning and data conversion effort may be required before a GIS can perform all of these operations.

Basic GIS Uses and Examples

In addition to providing data for sewer modeling, there are many other ways that a GIS can benefit the modeler. This section considers some examples of basic GIS capabilities and how they can be applied to the analysis and visualization of data related to sewer modeling.

Using Attributes to Create Thematic Maps. A classic, simple use of GIS is to change the appearance of features in a data set based on an underlying attribute. In Figure 14.13, this capability aids in the detection of an apparent error in GIS data that would have been imported into a model. In this figure, 8-in. (200-mm) and smaller pipes are represented by thin lines, 12-in. (300-mm) pipes by medium lines, and 16-in. (400-mm) and larger pipes by thick lines. The figure shows an 8-in. (200-mm) line in the middle of new 16-in. (400-mm) piping. Used in this manner, a GIS can serve as an excellent quality control tool before model construction for data related to the wastewater collection system piping (such as pipe length, slope, and diameter).

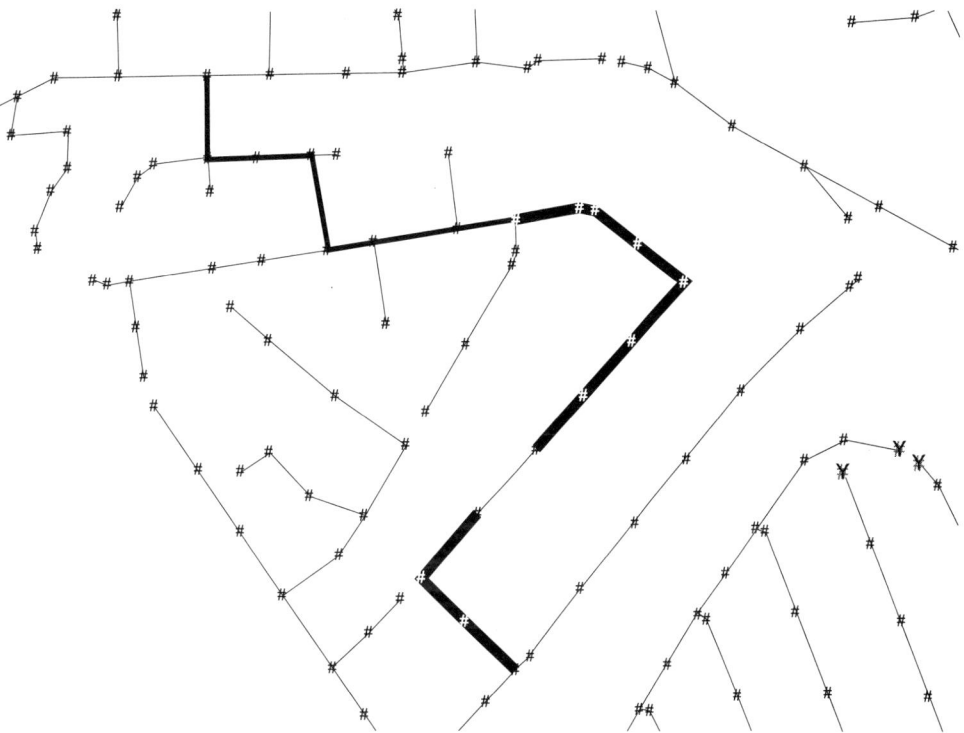

Figure 14.13 Basic thematic mapping. The thin line between thick lines suggests that there may be a diameter error in the GIS data.

Most wastewater collection modeling software can perform basic thematic mapping, but the number of available settings to distinguish between unique attribute values is usually higher in a GIS environment.

A variation of basic thematic mapping for quality control or map production may involve color-coding data according to underlying attribute ranges. Or, for example, a thematic map could be generated using different-size manhole symbols for different wastewater base-flow loads. Nodes with loads of less than 100 gpd might be shown with a small black circle, loads up to 500 gpd with a medium-size blue triangle, and loads more than 500 gpd with a large red square. These types of thematic maps can also be used effectively in quality control and debugging operations.

Communicating the results of modeling to managers, regulators, the media, and the general public is often difficult. A good map can convey the information much more clearly than long oral explanations or text. Publications such as ESRI's Map Book series contain hundreds of examples of maps drawn using GIS (ESRI).

Some examples of thematic mapping are:

- Color-coding pipes to show their age, material, or both
- Color-coding pipes to show peak flow as a percentage of available capacity under various scenarios, from existing to ultimate buildout
- Color-coding pipes to show where velocities under average flow conditions are low, possibly resulting in deposition and chronic blockage problems.

Most GIS software packages provide many options for basic thematic mapping.

Using the Spatial Coincidence of Features to Assign New Data. GIS software can analyze features on different layers to determine which coincide. In this way, data from one feature set can be transferred to other feature sets. A typical example in sewer model construction involves the overlay of load-point nodes with a layer that contains tributary-area polygons. In this way, the tributary-area polygon identifier (or other attribute) can be assigned to each point-load node, and vice versa. Other examples of this type of analysis are

- Overlaying land-use polygons on tributary-area polygons to assign aggregate land-use characteristics to the tributary-area polygons
- Overlaying soils characteristics on sewer pipes to identify areas that may be more susceptible to infiltration/inflow.

Using Spatial Relationships Among Features to Select Certain Elements and Assign New Data. In addition to using the coincidence of features to assign new data, many GIS packages can select or isolate features based on their proximity to other features. Classic cases include finding the closest feature in another data set and finding all features within a specified distance of a selected feature. The following are examples of this type of analysis are

- Finding the distance between tributary-area polygon centroids and their respective load-point nodes to help with infiltration/inflow analysis (see Figure 14.14). As discussed earlier, it is often acceptable to load tributary areas to a single node. However, in some cases, large areas should be assigned to multiple nodes to more accurately distribute the flows.
- Finding parcels within 300 ft (91 m) of a set of sewer pipes to be replaced, so that the owners of those parcels can be notified of any impending construction activities. In Figure 14.15, the dark pipes in the center of the figure were selected and buffered by 300 ft (91 m) to select the parcels to be notified.

Using Relationships to Trace Networks. When structured properly (that is, with attributes indicating which pipes are connected to which nodes), data sets such as those that make up a hydraulic model can be subjected to a process known as *network tracing*. In network tracing, GIS software uses information on which links are connected to which nodes to allow a system to be traversed. These functions are commonly applied to street networks and utility networks. The following are examples of this type of analysis:

- Generating shortest-path driving directions from point A to point B
- Tracing the network to identify segments that are disconnected, which can be a great aid in quality control of GIS and model input data
- Downstream traces to identify the exit point of a spilled contaminant into a system
- Upstream traces to identify potential sources of an identified contaminant detected in the system.

Advanced GIS Uses and Examples

Many advanced GIS analyses can be performed with the latest software and data. The examples listed in the preceding sections illustrate some of the most common uses, which can easily be accomplished using most commercial GIS packages. These basic capabilities can also be used in combination and series to perform more complex anal-

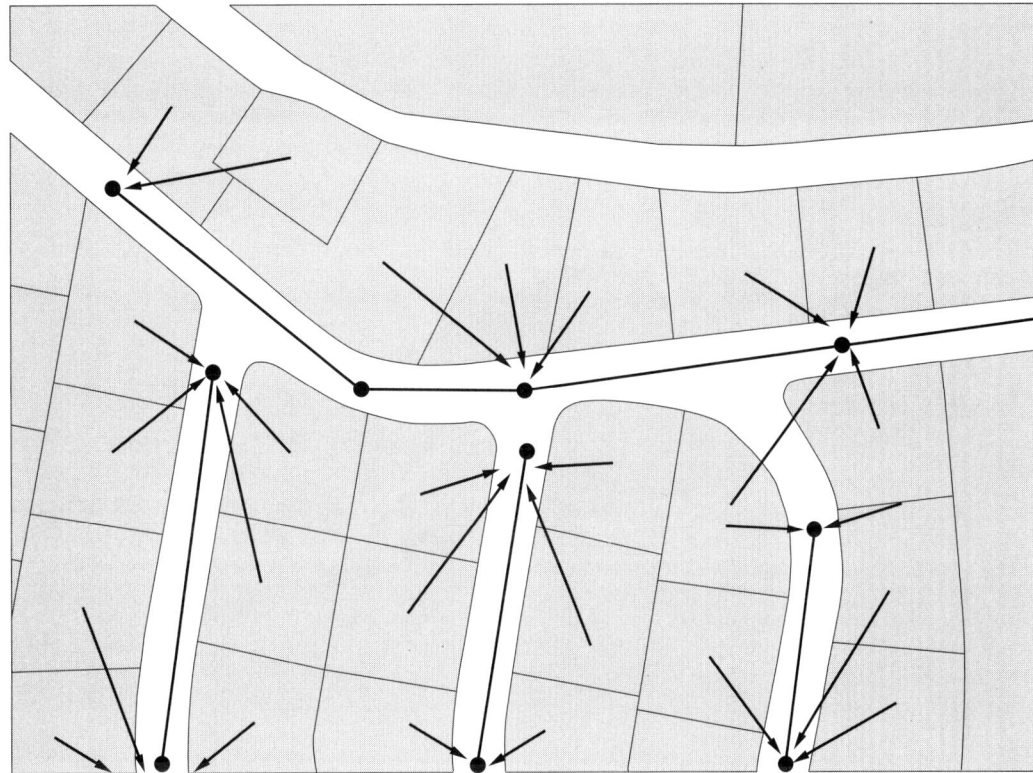

Figure 14.14 Proximity of load parcel/land use to closest loadpoint.

yses. The following examples describe some more advanced applications for wastewater collection.

- *Locating and sizing new or upgraded facilities* – Model results, especially for ultimate (or build-out) scenarios, will in most cases reveal deficiencies in the existing sewer system, suggesting the need for new or upgraded facilities. The critical questions concern the locations and sizes of the new facilities; GIS can help answer these questions.

  GIS analysis can reveal the differences between existing and ultimate land uses, thereby highlighting the areas where future development or redevelopment is expected. Correlating this information with model results highlights the nearby network facilities where deficiencies are expected. If new areas are to be served, looking at the topography reveals logical locations for new pipes. Topography also reveals where pump stations may be required.

- *Viewing the hydraulic grade line in 3D overlaying terrain and network* – Converting the modeled peak hydraulic grade line at each load-point node into a 3D GIS layer, and then overlaying that layer on a DEM or TIN showing the ground surface can help in visualizing the areas where surcharging is likely to occur. Further, converting the modeled system into a 3D GIS layer and including that in the visualization may make it possible to see ways to improve the sewer system that might not otherwise have been discerned (e.g., interconnecting an area at or near capacity to a nearby area that has excess capacity).

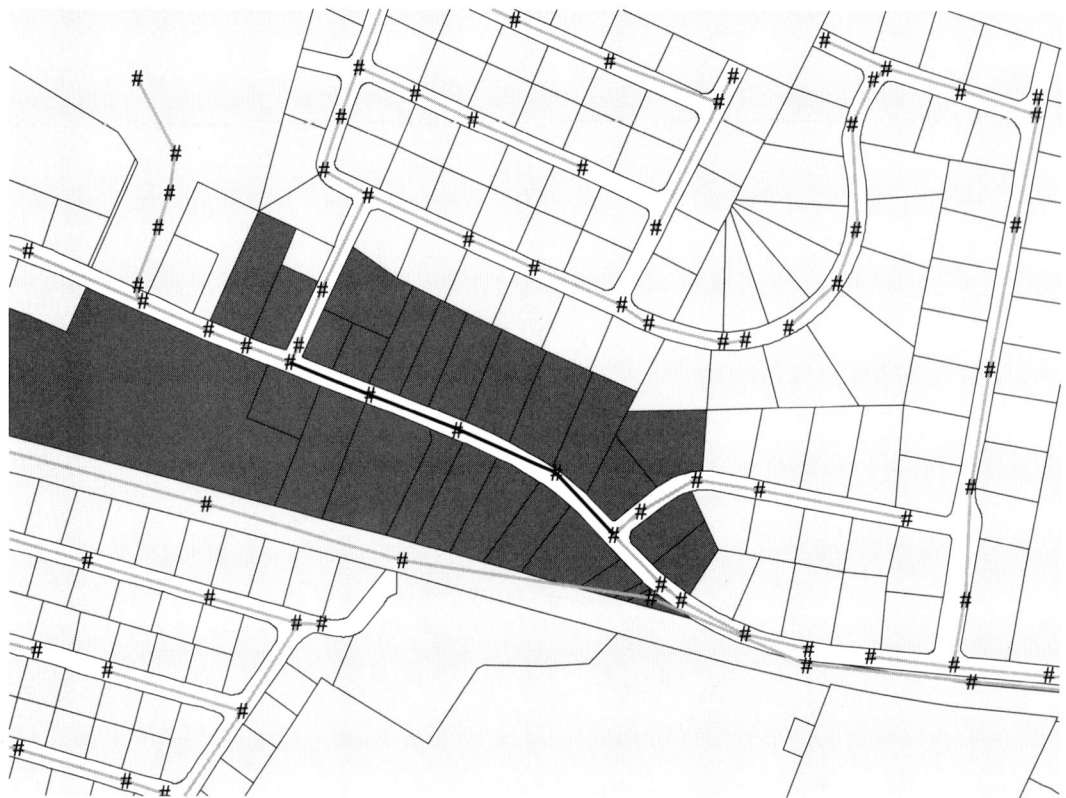

Figure 14.15 Buffer area along a pipeline project.

The potential uses of GIS in sewer modeling, analysis, and visualization keep expanding with each new advance in GIS technology and data availability. Modelers may not be aware of these GIS capabilities, and GIS professionals may not be aware that such capabilities could be applied to hydraulic modeling. Thus, modeling and GIS professionals must communicate regularly, perhaps discovering new ways to apply GIS technology to sewer modeling.

References

Chernin, P. R., and T. LeRoux. 1999. Understanding the basics of GIS: scale, accuracy and cost. *Public Works*, May.

Cowen, D. J. 1997. Discrete georeferencing. *NGCIA Core Curriculum on GIS Project*. http://www.ncgia.ucsb.edu/giscc/units/u016/u016.html (accessed 5/04).

Deagle, G., and S. Ancel. 2002. Development and maintenance of hydraulic models. Kansas City, MO: *AWWA IMTech*.

ESRI. 2001. *Dictionary of GIS Terminology*. Redlands, CA: ESRI Press.

ESRI (series). *ESRI Map Book: Applications of Geographic Information Systems*. Redlands, CA: ESRI Press.

Governmental Accounting Standards Board (GASB). 1999. *Governmental Accounting Standards Board Statement No. 34, Basic Financial Statements—and Management's Discussion for Analysis—for State and Local Government*. Norwalk, CT.

Greene, R., N. Agbenowoshi, and G. F. Loganathan. 1999. GIS based approach to sewer system design. *Journal of Surveying Engineering* 125, no. 1: 36–57.

Landrum, T. B. 2001. Enterprise GIS—building a strong foundation. Geospatial Information and Technology Association Annual Conference, San Diego, CA.

Marx. 1990. The TIGER system: yesterday, today and tomorrow. *Cartography and GIS* 17. no. 1: 89-97.

Orne, W., R. Hammond, and S. Cattran. 2001. Building better water models. *Public Works*, October.

Przybyla, J. 2002. What stops folks cold from pursuing GIS. *Public Works*, April.

Schatzlein, M. and J. Dieterlein. 2002. Finding Needles in a Haystack: IWC's Experience Optimizing Integration with Hydraulic Models. Kansas City, Missouri: *AWWA IMTech*.

Shamsi, U. M. 2001. GIS and modeling integration. *CE News* 13, no. 6.

Shamsi, U. M. 2002. *GIS Tools for Water, Wastewater and Stormwater Systems*. Alexandria, VA: American Society of Civil Engineers Press.

Water Environment Federation. 2004. *Implementing Geographical Information Systems*, Alexandria, VA Water Environment Federation.

Zeiler, M. 1999. *Modeling Our World*. Redlands, CA: ESRI Press.

Problems

14.1 Match each GIS term with the definition that most closely fits it.

1	Georeference	A	Closed two-dimensional figure
2	TIGER	B	Polygon generated around points
3	TIN	C	Unique value to even-size cells
4	Polygon	D	Feature represented by its coordinates
5	Vector	E	Assign x-y coordinates to a location
6	UTM	F	Commonly used datum in the U.S.
7	Thiessen	G	Type of projection
8	Raster	H	Data structure consisting of nonoverlapping triangles
9	NAD83	I	Georeferencing tool from the U.S. Census Bureau

14.2 Given that the average dry weather flow from a subbasin is 1.5 L/s with five loading nodes in that subbasin, assign the loads to the nodes based on the following two conditions:

 a. Based on the area associated with each nodal polygon.

 b. Based on the population in each nodal polygon.

Node	Area, hectares	Load Based on Area, L/s	Population	Load Based on Population, L/s
MH-1	11		75	
MH-2	6		92	
MH-3	15		35	
MH-4	12		81	
MH-5	9		90	

14.3 For each element in a GIS of a wastewater collection system, indicate in the following table if it is a raster, TIN, or vector element. If it is a vector, indicate if it is a point, line, or polygon.

Element	GIS Representation
Manhole	
Catchment basin	
DXF background	
Gravity sewer	
Pump	
Wet well	
Inverted siphon	

CHAPTER

15

Regulatory Issues

Modelers must be aware of the numerous laws and regulations that apply to the design, construction, rehabilitation, management, and operation of sanitary sewer networks. These regulations are used to specify design and performance standards, permitting requirements, and compliance assessment methods.

This chapter reviews the major environmental laws, policies, and regulations as they relate to sanitary sewers in the United States, Canada, and the European Union and presents examples of how hydraulic models can be used to demonstrate regulatory compliance.

15.1 United States Laws and Regulations

Until the middle of the twentieth century, water pollution was primarily considered a state and local problem. No federal goals, objectives, limits, or even guidelines existed. Initially, federal involvement was in enforcement and was strictly limited to matters involving interstate waters, but only with the consent of the state in which the pollution originated.

The first federal legislation pertaining to water pollution was the Rivers and Harbors Act of 1899, which prohibited the dumping of any material other than sewage or runoff into navigable waterways without a permit from the U.S. Army Corps of Engineers (Zwick and Bernstock, 1971). Although this law was enacted to mitigate interference with navigation, it was used to prosecute some pollution issues until later federal legislation was enacted.

Beginning in the middle of the twentieth century, a number of legislative statutes have been put in place in an effort to reduce water pollution and improve water quality.

The highlights of these policies are described in this section, with an emphasis on the relationship to sanitary sewers and wastewater discharges.

Clean Water Act

The Federal Water Pollution Control Act (FWPCA) of 1948 was the first comprehensive statement of federal interest in water pollution control, and it provided research funds and grants for state and local pollution control programs. During the 1950s and 60s, water pollution control programs were shaped by four federal laws that amended the 1948 statute. These statutes and amendments are known collectively as the Clean Water Act (CWA).

While the 1948 FWPCA provided federal assistance to municipal dischargers, the subsequent amendments extended federal involvement to enforcement programs for all dischargers. During this period, federal jurisdiction was extended to include not only navigable interstate waters, but intrastate waters as well. In 1965, water quality standards also became a feature of federal law through the Water Quality Act, which required states to set standards for interstate waters that would be used to determine actual pollution levels. Table 15.1 lists the dates of CWA legislation and subsequent major amendments, which are described in the paragraphs that follow.

Table 15.1 Clean Water Act and Amendments.

Year	Act	Public Law #
1948	Federal Water Pollution Control Act	P.L. 80-845
1956	Water Pollution Control Act of 1956	P.L. 84-660
1961	Federal Water Pollution Control Act Amendments	P.L. 87-88
1965	Water Quality Act of 1965	P.L. 89-234
1966	Clean Water Restoration Act	P.L. 89-753
1970	Water Quality Improvement Act of 1970	P.L. 91-224, Part I
1972	Federal Water Pollution Control Act Amendments	P.L. 92-500
1977	Clean Water Act of 1977	P.L. 95-217
1981	Municipal Wastewater Treatment Construction Grants Amendments	P.L. 97-117
1987	Water Quality Act of 1987	P.L. 100-4

Starting in the late 1960s, there was a growing perception that existing enforcement procedures were too time-consuming and that the water quality standards approach was flawed. Difficulties in linking a particular discharger to violations of stream quality standards, mounting frustration over the slow pace of pollution cleanup efforts, and a suspicion that control technologies were being developed but not applied to the problems increased dissatisfaction with the approach. These perceptions and frustrations, together with increased public interest in environmental protection, set the stage for the 1972 amendments.

In 1972, Congress passed the Federal Water Pollution Control Act Amendments, followed by significant amendments in 1977, 1981, and 1987 (see Table 15.1). This created a comprehensive collection of federal programs to address the serious pollution problems affecting the nation's rivers, lakes, and coastal waters.

Titles II and VI of the CWA are the primary funding-related sections and authorize federal financial assistance for the planning, design, and construction of municipal sewage facilities. Title II provides federal grants for projects based on priorities established by the states and funds as much as 55 percent of the total project cost. Congress began the transition toward full state and local government financing with the 1987 amendments. Title VI provides federal grants to capitalize state water pollution control revolving funds, which are used for sewer and treatment plant expansion and improvement projects.

U.S. Federal Regulations

The United States Code of Federal Regulations (CFR) is the codification of the general and permanent rules published in the Federal Register by the executive departments and agencies of the Federal Government. Regulations of the Environmental Protection Agency (EPA) are located in Title 40 of the CFR. Many states have adopted the federal regulations either in whole or with minor modifications.

Table 15.2 presents a list of the most important EPA regulations applicable to sanitary sewers. For example, 40 CFR 35 specifies the maximum allowable rates for inflow and infiltration. Strictly speaking, these allowable rates are only applicable to recipients of grants under the CWA. However, they have evolved into *de facto* standards for sewer systems where alternative infiltration and inflow rates are not justifiable by engineering and economic evaluations. Other related regulations found in 40 CFR 122 are associated with National Pollutant Discharge Elimination System (NPDES) permits, which are described in the next subsection.

National Pollutant Discharge Elimination System Permits. Title IV of the CWA created the National Pollutant Discharge Elimination System (NPDES) for permitting wastewater discharges (Section 402). Under NPDES, all facilities that discharge pollutants from any point source into waters of the United States are required to obtain a permit, which is a license for a facility to discharge a specified amount of a pollutant into a receiving water under specified conditions. More than 65,000 industrial and municipal dischargers must obtain NPDES permits from the Environmental Protection Agency (EPA) or qualified states. Currently, 44 states and one territory are authorized to implement the NPDES program on behalf of the EPA.

The NPDES permit program provides two levels of control: *technology-based limits* (based on the ability of dischargers in the same industrial category to treat wastewater), and *water-quality-based limits* (if technology-based limits are not sufficient to provide protection to the receiving water body). Sewage treatment plants with NPDES permits are required to submit information on their collection systems, including documentation on system operation and maintenance, and reporting on noncompliance with permit requirements.

The two basic types of NPDES permits issued are individual and general permits. An individual permit is specifically tailored to an individual facility and is usually used for more distinct and complex dischargers. Once a facility submits the appropriate application(s), the permitting authority develops a permit based on information in the application, such as type of activity, nature of discharge, and receiving water quality. The authority issues the permit to the facility for a specific time period (not to exceed five years), with a requirement that the facility reapply before the expiration date.

Table 15.2 Important Federal regulations concerning sewers.

Citation*	Title and Applicability	Regulation Text
35	Inflow and Infiltration; Definitions	35.2005(a) (16) *Excessive infiltration/inflow.* The quantities of infiltration/inflow which can be economically eliminated from a sewer system as determined in a cost-effectiveness analysis that compares the costs for correcting the infiltration/inflow conditions to the total costs for transportation and treatment of the infiltration/inflow. (20) *Infiltration.* Water other than wastewater that enters a sewer system (including sewer service connections and foundation drains) from the ground through such means as defective pipes, pipe joints, connections, or manholes. Infiltration does not include, and is distinguished from, inflow. (21) *Inflow.* Water other than wastewater that enters a sewer system (including sewer service connections) from sources such as, but not limited to, roof leaders, cellar drains, yard drains, area drains, drains from springs and swampy areas, manhole covers, cross connections between storm sewers and sanitary sewers, catch basins, cooling towers, storm waters, surface runoff, street wash waters, or drainage. Inflow does not include, and is distinguished from, infiltration.
35	State and Local Assistance; Standards applicable to recipients of federal financial assistance	35.2120(b) *Inflow.* If the rainfall-induced peak inflow rate results or will result in chronic operational problems during storm events, or the rainfall-induced total flow rate exceeds 275 gpcd during storm events, the applicant shall perform a study of the sewer system to determine the quantity of excessive inflow and to propose a rehabilitation program to eliminate the excessive inflow. All cases in which facilities are planned for the specific storage and/or treatment of inflow shall be subject to a cost-effectiveness analysis. (c) *Infiltration.* (1) If the flow rate at the existing treatment facility is 120 gpcd or less during periods of high groundwater, the applicant shall build the project including sufficient capacity to transport and treat any existing infiltration. However, if the applicant believes any specific portion of its sewer system is subject to excessive infiltration, the applicant may confirm their belief through a cost-effectiveness analysis and propose a sewer rehabilitation program to eliminate the specific excessive infiltration.
122	NPDES Permitting; Information required in an NPDES permit application for new and existing POTWs	122.21(j)(vii) *Collection system.* Identification of type(s) of collection system(s) used by the treatment works (i.e., separate sanitary sewers or combined storm and sanitary sewers) and an estimate of the percent of sewer line that each type comprises. 122.21(j)(viii) *Outfalls and other discharge or disposal methods.* Extensive list of information required for each outfall.
122	NPDES Permitting; Stormwater discharges – prohibits cross connections between storm and sanitary sewers	122.26(b)(2) *Illicit discharge* means any discharge to a separate municipal storm sewer that does not consist entirely of stormwater.
122	NPDES Permitting; Conditions applicable to all permits	122.41(d) *Duty to mitigate.* Permittee shall take all reasonable steps to minimize or prevent any discharge. 122.41(e) *Proper operation and maintenance.* The permittee shall at all times properly operate and maintain all facilities and systems of treatment and control (and related appurtenances) which are installed or used by the permittee to achieve compliance with the conditions of this permit. Proper operation and maintenance includes adequate laboratory controls and appropriate quality assurance procedures. This provision requires the operation of backup or auxiliary facilities or similar systems which are installed by a permittee only when the operation is necessary to achieve compliance with the conditions of the permit. 122.41(l)(6) *Twenty-four hour reporting.* The permittee shall report any noncompliance which may endanger health or the environment. Any information shall be provided orally within 24 hours from the time the permittee becomes aware of the circumstances. 122.41(m)(4)(i) *Prohibition of bypass.* Bypass is prohibited.

*Citation number denotes part of 40 CFR (Code of Federal Regulations).

General permits offer a cost-effective option to permitting agencies addressing a large number of facilities under a single permit. These permits typically cover categories of point sources having common elements, such as stormwater point sources, facilities that involve the same or substantially similar types of operations, facilities that require the same permit conditions, or facilities that require the same or similar monitoring.

The initial focus of the NPDES program was on treatment technology and contaminant-specific effluent limitations. Since then, two trends have developed. The first is an increase in the administrative requirements for permittees, including the development of management plans, record keeping, reporting, and public participation. Second is that the NPDES requirements have expanded from covering the discharge and treatment method to addressing the entire collection system.

Combined Sewer Overflow (CSO) Control Policy. Section 502(4) of the CWA defines a *combined sewer system (CSS)* as a wastewater collection system, owned by a state or municipality, which conveys sanitary wastewaters (domestic, commercial, and industrial) as well as stormwater through a single-pipe system to a *publicly owned treatment works (POTW)*. A *combined sewer overflow (CSO)* is the discharge from a CSS at a point before the POTW.

The US EPA issued the National Combined Sewer Overflow Control Strategy on August 10, 1989 (54 FR 37370). This strategy reaffirmed that CSOs are point-source discharges subject to NPDES permit and CWA requirements. The EPA then issued the Combined Sewer Overflow Control Policy on April 19, 1994 (US EPA, 1994) as a national framework for CSO control through the NPDES permitting program. The Policy provides guidance to municipal, state, and federal permitting authorities for meeting the CWA's pollution control goals in a flexible, cost-effective manner.

The four key principles of the CSO Control Policy are:
- Clear levels of control to meet health and environmental objectives
- Site-specific considerations to assure flexibility for developing the most appropriate solution
- Phased implementation of CSO controls to accommodate a community's financial capability
- Review and revision of water quality standards during CSO control plan development to account for wet weather impacts.

NPDES permit conditions for CSOs require an accurate characterization of the adjoining sewer systems to demonstrate adequate implementation of the following nine minimum control measures:
- Proper operation and regular maintenance programs for the sewer system
- Maximum use of the collection system for storage
- Review and modification of pretreatment requirements to mitigate CSO impacts
- Maximization of flow to the POTW for treatment
- Elimination of CSOs during dry weather
- Control of solid and floatable materials in CSOs
- Pollution prevention

- Public notification of CSO occurrences and CSO impacts
- Monitoring to effectively characterize CSO impacts and the efficacy of CSO controls.

Permittees with CSOs must submit documentation addressing each of the measures and are responsible for developing and implementing long-term CSO control plans that will ultimately result in compliance with the requirements of the CWA. The long-term plans should consider the site-specific nature of CSOs and evaluate the cost-effectiveness of a range of control options and strategies. The selected controls should be designed to allow cost-effective expansion or retrofitting.

The minimum elements of the long-term control plan are:

1. Combined sewer system characterization, monitoring, and modeling
2. Public participation
3. Sensitive area analysis
4. Evaluation of alternatives
5. Cost and performance considerations
6. Operational plan development
7. Existing POTW treatment maximization
8. Implementation schedule development
9. Postconstruction-phase compliance monitoring.

Under item 4, "Evaluation of alternatives," permittees may select from two approaches—the Presumptive Approach and the Demonstrative Approach. Under the Presumptive Approach, a program that meets any of the following three criteria is presumed to be in compliance with the water quality-based requirements of the CWA:

- No more than an average of four overflow events per year

- The elimination or capture for treatment of 85% (by volume) of the combined sewage collected in the CSS during a precipitation event in which an overflow will occur (Example 15.1) on a systemwide annual basis

- The elimination or removal of no less than 85% of the mass of pollutants.

Under the Demonstration Approach, the permittee must demonstrate that the planned control program is adequate to meet the water quality standards of the receiving body.

Sanitary Sewer Overflow Proposed Rule. A sanitary sewer overflow (SSO) is defined as an overflow, spill, release, or diversion of wastewater from a sanitary sewer system. SSOs do not include combined sewer overflows (CSOs) or other discharges from combined sewers. On January 4, 2001, the US EPA published proposed rules that address NPDES permit requirements for municipal sanitary sewer systems and SSOs. On January 24, the SSO Proposed Rule was withdrawn to give the new administration an opportunity to review it (US EPA, 2001). In the meantime, several state regulatory agencies officially adopted the SSO Proposed Rule, and portions of the rule frequently appear in regional EPA enforcement mechanisms. Even without adoption of the SSO Proposed Rule by the EPA, any discharge of wastewater from a collection system at a point not allowed under the NPDES permit is prohibited and is subject to enforcement.

The SSO Proposed Rule (US EPA, 2001) defines SSOs as:

- Overflows or releases of wastewater that reach waters of the United States

- Overflows or releases of wastewater that do not reach waters of the United States

- Wastewater backups into buildings that are caused by blockages in a sanitary sewer other than a building lateral.

Some wastewater utilities have expressed the view that the EPA has exceeded their authority under the CWA to include releases in the definition that do not reach waters of the United States. The CWA only prohibits SSOs that reach waters of the United States.

Under the SSO Proposed Rule, the standard permit conditions to be included in NPDES permits for POTWs and municipal sanitary sewer collection systems are:

- Incorporation of a *capacity assurance, management, operation, and maintenance (CMOM) program*

- Establishment of a public and health authority notification process

- Prevention of overflows.

In addition, the SSO Proposed Rule calls for expanded permit coverage to satellite systems (i.e., collection systems where no treatment is provided and the owner/operator is different from the owner/operator of the facility providing treatment).

Capacity Assurance, Management, Operation, and Maintenance (CMOM) Program. A major goal of the SSO Proposed Rule's CMOM program is to improve the ability of permitting authorities to comprehensively and proactively evaluate the management programs and performance of municipal sanitary sewer collection systems. It provides the permittee and the NPDES authority with a basis of comparison to assess how the collection system operates and performs relative to the needs and priorities of the local receiving waters and community interests. Municipalities implementing CMOM programs will have to meet the following five standards:

- Properly manage, operate, and maintain, at all times, the parts of the collection system that the permittee owns or over which it has operational control
- Provide adequate capacity to convey base and peak flows
- Take all feasible steps to stop and mitigate the effects of sanitary sewer overflows
- Provide notification to parties with a reasonable potential for exposure to pollutants associated with an overflow event
- Develop a written CMOM program summary and required program audits and make them available to the public.

Recognizing that not all requirements need the same attention, the rules allow municipalities flexibility in developing their CMOM programs. At a minimum, the permittee must implement a variety of measures, activities, and programs to meet the five performance standards above. Permittees should consider the following:

- Maintenance facilities and equipment adequacy
- Collection system map maintenance
- Information timeliness and relevance (is it up-to-date?)
- Routine preventative operation and maintenance activities
- Collection system and treatment facility capacity assessment
- Identification and prioritization of structural deficiency and rehabilitation response actions.

The SSO Proposed Rule preamble discussion states that "modeling may be a valuable tool for providing general predictions of sewer system response to various wet weather events and evaluating control strategies and alternatives." As described in Section 15.4, modeling is especially useful for identifying the capacity of the collection system and the effects of rehabilitation and maintenance.

Treatment Plant Discharges During Wet Weather. During normal operation at a sewage treatment facility, the incoming wastewater is treated by the primary units and then sent to the secondary (biological) treatment units. However, when wet weather flows exceed the capacity of the secondary treatment units, they are sometimes diverted around the flow-sensitive biological units and later recombined or blended with the wastewater that has been treated by the secondary units. These blended flows are then disinfected and discharged.

In November 2003, the US EPA issued a draft policy on the practice of blending (EPA, 2003). This proposed policy states that peak wet weather discharges from POTWs that consist of effluent routed around biological treatment units (or other advanced treatment units) blended with effluent from the biological units (or from other advanced treatment units) would not constitute a prohibited bypass and could be authorized in an NPDES permit if all of the following conditions applied. (A *bypass* is defined in 40

CFR 122.41(m) as the intentional diversion of waste streams from any portion of a treatment facility.):

1. The final discharge meets effluent limitations based on the secondary treatment regulation (40 CFR Part 133).

2. The NPDES permit application for the POTW provides notice of, and specifically recognizes, the treatment scenario that would be used for peak flow management.

3. The treatment scenario that would be used for peak flow management should provide, prior to blending, at least the equivalent of primary clarification for the portion of flow routed around biological or other advanced treatment units.

4. The peak flow treatment scenario chosen by the permittee for use when flows exceed storage/equalization, biological treatment, or advanced treatment unit capacity should be operated as designed and in accordance with the conditions set forth in the scenario-specific permit.

5. The permit must require sufficient monitoring, including type, interval, and frequency to yield data representative of the final blended discharge and ensure compliance with applicable water quality-based effluent limitations.

6. The permittee must properly operate and maintain all parts of the collection system over which the permittee has operational control in a manner consistent with 40 CFR 122.41(e).

If a POTW uses peak flow treatment scenarios consisting of effluent routed around biological or other advanced treatment units and then blended together with the effluent from the biological units prior to discharge, its permit should also address the following (EPA, 2003):

- To the extent practicable, NPDES permit requirements for discharges of peak wet weather flows at the POTW should be developed in a manner that encourages the permittee to consider the relationship between the performance of the collection system and the performance of treatment plants serving the system.

- The permit writer should ensure that the POTW adequately reflects the incidence frequency and treatment effectiveness of the peak flow treatment scenarios in developing local limits for industrial users.

The use of hydraulic sewer models to predict the magnitude and frequency of wet weather flows can be an invaluable tool for managing the flows at the treatment plant and demonstrating compliance with the regulations.

Water Quality Standards and Total Maximum Daily Loads (TMDLs)

Under section 303(d) of the 1972 CWA, states, territories, and authorized tribes are required to develop lists of impaired waters. Statewide Watershed Assessment Reports mandated by the CWA and other legislative and regulatory programs identify water quality deficiencies and prioritize watersheds for assessment. The 305(b) report, or State Water Quality Assessment, identifies and ranks waterbodies with known violations based on narrative or numeric water quality data. The 305(b) reports are prepared by the states biennially.

States are required to identify impaired water bodies through 305(b) assessments and develop total maximum daily loads (TMDLs) for each. A TMDL is a quantitative assessment of water quality problems, contributing sources, and pollution reductions needed to attain water quality standards. It further allocates pollution control or management responsibilities among sources in a watershed and provides a science-based policy for taking action to restore a water body.

Pollutant loadings from CSOs and SSOs are considered when developing the TMDL. Models may be used to estimate the frequency of overflows and the loads of pollutants to the watershed. When the TMDL is established, it may result in requirements for monitoring and/or sewer rehabilitation.

TMDLs have been required by the Clean Water Act since 1972. However, by 1996, states, territories, authorized tribes, and the US EPA had not developed many. Between 1996 and 2003, approximately 9600 were approved. The current regulations governing TMDLs were adopted in 1985 and amended 1992 (40 CFR 130.7). Many of the waters still needing TMDLs are impaired by contributions from CSOs and SSOs. Operators of wastewater collection systems should be aware of the status of the receiving waters [as per the 305(b) report] in their watersheds.

Section 404 Dredge and Fill Permits

Section 404 of the CWA requires a permit, issued by the US Army Corps of Engineers, for discharge or fill of dredge materials into the waters of the United States. This jurisdiction includes not only navigable waters, but also their tributaries and associated wetlands. The Supreme Court has held that this jurisdiction extends to lands supporting plant growth typical of wetlands. The scope of activities covered by Section 404 is much broader than the traditional dredging and filling of navigable ship channels. Regulated activities include construction in areas that affect navigable waters, such as the laying of sewers or any appurtenances. These activities may also require permits.

The Corps has streamlined the program by issuing nationwide permits for some activities (see 33 CFR 330, Nationwide Permit Program). If certain conditions are met, a specified action can proceed without an individual permit. In these instances, little paperwork is involved and permits may be obtained in a relatively short time (0-20 days).

15.2 Canadian Laws and Regulations

This section contains an overview of the Canadian laws and regulations that govern the design, expansion, and rehabilitation of wastewater collection systems, including sanitary and combined sewer systems. It is based, in part, on material in the draft Combined Sewer Overflow Treatment Technologies Manual (Environment Canada, 2004).

The management of sanitary and combined sewer systems is both a federal and provincial responsibility. At the federal level, there is no national standard. Instead, Environment Canada and Health Canada are responsible for preventing environmental and human health impacts. The provincial requirements are outlined in this section. Where applicable, guidance is also provided on the types of model analysis necessary to meet the regulatory requirements.

Sanitary Sewer Systems

Most Canadian provinces have established minimum guidelines for the sizing and construction of sanitary sewer systems and for environmental assessments. However, the detailed design, construction, and operation of sanitary sewer systems is ultimately the responsibility of individual municipalities, and their requirements may be more stringent. The following section highlights the current regulations, policies, guidelines, and practices in the Province of Ontario. Similar regulations, policies, guidelines, and practices are in place in the other provinces of Canada.

Under the Ontario Water Resources Act, the Ontario Ministry of the Environment reviews and approves applications for all new sanitary sewer works in the province. Local and regional municipalities also review and approve these applications, and in some cases, may complete the review on behalf of the Ministry. The province has prepared guidelines (Ontario Ministry of the Environment, 1985) that describe the minimum acceptable levels of sanitary servicing to assist consulting engineers and municipalities in designing sanitary sewer systems. Key elements of the provincial guidelines are:

- All new sewers are to be separate. New combined sewers or connections to existing combined sewers are not permitted, except as an interim measure where circumstances allow no alternative.

- The design of new sanitary sewers is to be based on the ultimate sewage flows expected from the tributary area. The design period is to extend a minimum of twenty years.

- Sanitary sewers should be designed using Kutter's or Manning's formula with a minimum roughness coefficient of 0.013 and sufficient slope such that a minimum velocity of 2 ft/s (0.6 m/s) will be achieved under full-flow conditions. A minimum velocity of less than 2 ft/s (0.6 m/s) will be considered appropriate where a higher slope would require extensive deepening of a sewage collection system or the addition of a pumping station, provided the municipality accepts that there may be increased maintenance requirements.

Combined Sewer Systems

All provinces in Canada have municipalities served by combined sewers, but in most cases, the construction of new combined sewers is not permitted except where there is no other alternative. Where new combined sewers are planned, they are designed to convey both sanitary and peak storm flows.

The management of CSOs in Canada is a multi-jurisdictional responsibility. The following sections present an overview of provincial regulations and guidelines and how modeling is being used to achieve compliance. Some provinces, such as Ontario and British Columbia, have established CSO procedures or regulations. In other provinces, no formal guidelines, procedures, or regulations have been developed, so individual communities have developed CSO control programs in consultation with provincial authorities.

The following provinces do not have formal CSO control policies:

- Newfoundland
- Nova Scotia

- Prince Edward Island
- Saskatchewan
- Yukon Nunavut
- Northwest Territories

New Brunswick. The Province of New Brunswick currently does not have any specific guidelines or regulations for CSO control and does not permit the construction of new combined sewers. Instead, individual municipal agencies, such as the Greater Moncton Sewerage Commission (GMSC), have identified CSOs as a wastewater management issue and developed CSO control targets and strategies to manage them. The GMSC reviewed various CSO control regulations in other North American jurisdictions, and based on their review, identified the following targets:

- A CSO abatement control target for the GMSC system of 85% wet weather flow capture. The 85% level of control corresponds to the level of control set by the US EPA and has been adopted by a number of major municipalities in Canada, such as the Cities of Winnipeg and Edmonton. Captured CSO flows are to receive equivalent-to-primary treatment, not necessarily including disinfection.

- Additional management objectives, including improving system reliability by decreasing the number of overflow structures, ensuring the proper operation of the overflows under extreme conditions, reducing the level of surcharging, and reducing the risk of flooding from the operation of the GMSC system.

GMSC has addressed these targets with the development of a short-term plan (3-10 years) and a long term plan (10-20 years). The short-term plan includes measures that address the hydraulic performance of the collector system, system reliability, and risk of basement flooding. The long-term plan includes provisions for new storage and treatment facilities.

A fully dynamic hydraulic model capable of long-term continuous simulation is used to assess the current performance of the collection system and to develop short- and long-term plans that meet control targets.

Quebec. At this time, the Province of Quebec does not have a formal CSO control policy. However, the Quebec Water Policy (Quebec, 2002) highlights issues regarding integrated management of water with a view towards sustainable development. The policy contains a commitment that the province will supplement municipal cleanup efforts. With regard to untreated urban discharges, Quebec undertakes to:

- Urge and assist municipalities to reduce, by 2007, the frequency of CSOs during wet weather by 20%. The government of Quebec will attempt to achieve this goal by encouraging the installation of control infrastructure such as retention ponds, the optimization of existing systems by utilizing retention capacities of existing sewer lines, and the implementation of more effective management systems.

- Eliminate wastewater discharges during dry weather periods by 2007. Municipalities are required to develop action plans to meet this commitment. Plans must focus on elimination of illegal connections and the intersection of sewer lines.

- Put into place a strategy governing urban discharges, such as CSOs and storm discharges. The strategy will include long-term environmental targets for discharges, a mechanism for issuing renewable depollution attestations, and environmental guidelines for grant programs.

The Quebec Urban Community (Quebec City) is now implementing a long-term CSO control plan. The plan includes the implementation of a real-time control system (RTC) to optimize the existing system with the construction of off-line and in-line storage facilities. To date, a global optimal RTC system is operational. The Quebec Urban Community has used a nonlinear hydraulic model, SWIFT, as a reference model, and MED-SOM as a dedicated application for the real-time control of its sewer networks. SWIFT models both hydrology and hydraulics. The hydrology is based on a conceptual relation between rainfall events and flows and takes into consideration pervious and impervious surface runoff, as well as pipe discharges. A Muskingum algorithm approximates hydraulic behavior, and a numerical solution of simplified Saint-Venant equations gives the attenuation of a wave traveling along a stream.

Ontario. In Ontario, the construction of new combined sewers is not permitted except where there is no alternative. Management of CSOs from existing combined sewers is governed by Procedure F-5-5, Determination of Treatment Requirements for Municipal and Private Combined and Partially Separated Sewer Systems (Ontario Ministry of the Environment, 1997). This procedure is a supporting document for Guideline F-5, Levels of Treatment for Municipal and Private Sewage Treatment Works Discharging to Surface Waters.

"You seem familiar, yet somehow strange—are you by any chance Canadian?"

Procedure F-5-5 is prescriptive and includes the following:

- Minimum CSO volumetric control and treatment criteria. The volumetric control criterion for CSOs is applied to the flow collected by the sewer system immediately upstream of each overflow location, unless it can be shown through modeling and/or ongoing monitoring that the criterion is achieved system wide. No increase in CSO volumes above existing levels at each outfall is allowed, except where the increase is due to the elimination of upstream CSO outfalls. The minimum level of treatment required for CSOs is primary treatment or the equivalent. Table 15.3 presents the specific quality and quantity guidelines specified in F-5-5.

- A requirement for the development and implementation of pollution prevention and control plans.

- Additional controls for beaches impaired by CSOs. Effluent disinfection is required where the effluent affects swimming and bathing beaches or where there are other public health concerns. Where chlorination is used, any adverse effects from chlorine residuals must be minimized.

- Provisions for new sanitary and storm connections to combined sewer systems.

Table 15.3 Procedure F-5-5 quantity and quality requirements.

Parameter	Guideline
Volumetric control	90% capture of wet weather flows[1]
Carbonaceous biochemical oxygen demand (BOD)	30% removal[1]
Total suspended solids (TSS)	50% removal[1] and not to exceed 90 mg/L for more than 50% of the time
Disinfection	Monthly geometric mean not to exceed 1,000 E. coli per 100 mL during wet weather

[1] Over a 7-month period commencing within 15 days of April 15 during an average rainfall year.

To determine specific volumetric control requirements at individual outfall locations, it is customary to utilize a continuous-simulation system model. The model can be fully dynamic to allow for the prediction of surcharge conditions or may be quasi-dynamic.

Treatment of wet weather flows from combined sewer systems may occur at a central wastewater treatment plant or at other locations, such as satellite treatment facilities. Satellite treatment facilities must provide the minimum level of primary treatment specified in Table 15.3.

Where there are combined sewage discharges to beach areas, the following additional requirements are imposed. It is customary to use a continuous system model to assess the ability of a proposed facility to meet these criteria.

- No violation of the body-contact recreational water-quality objective of 100 E. coli per 100 mL based on a geometric mean at swimming and bathing beaches (as a result of CSOs for at least 95% of the 4-month season [June 1 to September 30] for an average year).

- No more than two overflow events per season (June 1 to September 30) for an average year. The combined total duration of CSOs at any single overflow location must be less than 48 hours.

Procedure F-5-5 requires municipalities to establish and implement pollution prevention programs that focus on source pollution reduction activities. These programs are usually contained in a formal Pollution Prevention and Control Plan. To address the impact of CSOs, the plan must include the following:

- Characterization of the combined sewer system.
- An examination of the nonstructural and structural CSO control alternatives, which may include source controls, inflow/infiltration reduction, operational and maintenance improvements, control structure improvements, collection system improvements, storage, treatment, and sewer separation.
- An implementation plan with cost estimates and a schedule of all practical measures to eliminate dry weather overflows and minimize wet weather overflows.
- A sewer system monitoring program for use in assessing upgrade requirements and determining compliance with provincial requirements.

Municipalities implementing a Pollution Prevention and Control Program are expected to meet the following minimum CSO controls:

- Eliminate CSOs during dry weather periods except under emergency conditions.
- Establish and implement proper operation and regular inspection and maintenance programs for the combined sewer system to ensure continuation of proper system operation.
- Establish and implement a floatables control program for coarse solids and floatable materials.
- Maximize the use of the collection system for the storage of wet weather flows conveyed to the sewage treatment plant when capacity is available.
- Maximize the flow to the sewage treatment plant for the treatment of wet weather flow.

With respect to new sanitary and storm connections to existing combined sewers, Procedure F-5-5 gives the province the authority to:

- Stop the connection of new sanitary sewers to a combined sewer system until that system has been upgraded.
- Prevent the connection of new storm drainage to existing combined sewer systems, except where evaluations indicate there is no practical alternative.

In addition, proposed CSO control facilities such as storage tanks and treatment facilities are subject to the requirements of the Ontario Environmental Assessment Act (Municipal Engineers Association, 2000). For CSO facilities, the Municipal Engineers Association (MEA) Class EA process is followed.

Manitoba. Manitoba does not have a formal CSO control policy. However, specific municipalities, such as Winnipeg, are working to formulate a CSO management program in consultation with the Manitoba Clean Environment Commission. In setting the scope for Winnipeg's management plan, the commission considered CSO regulations across Canada, the United States, and Europe. Highlights of the proposed plan include:

- Adoption of the US EPA standard of CSO reduction (four overflows per recreational season or 85% volumetric control), and compliance with the Manitoba Surface Water Quality Objectives.

- Optimization of existing infrastructure and the development of new initiatives through a progressive, staged program.

- Enhancements to the existing collection system, including raising weirs, dewatering latent storage, modifying interception rates, and keeping a monitoring system in place.

- Establishment of an in-line storage demonstration project before the actual implementation of the in-line program.

The illustrative control program will be developed based on a 60-year period, with a projected target of three overflows per RS. Periodic reporting on the overall CSO control program, costs, improvement in control, and compliance with objectives is scheduled for review every 5-10 years. The CSO Control program is conceptual and subject to ongoing review. A brief timeline is presented in Table 15.4.

Table 15.4 Winnipeg CSO control program timeline.

Year	Planned Activities
2002–2005	Implement a SCADA system, raise interception rates, conduct an in-line storage demonstration project, and conduct additional engineering studies.
2004–2043	Integrate with basement flooding relief and sewer rehabilitation studies.
2028–2033	Access existing latent and available in-line storage.
2034–2050	Develop additional storage to meet the long-term CSO control target of four CSOs per recreational area.

A fully dynamic, continuous simulation model continues to be utilized to assist in the planning and design of the Winnipeg CSO Control Program.

Alberta. Only a few communities in Alberta have combined sewers. As a result, the Province of Alberta has not yet developed a formal CSO control policy. The City of Edmonton is the largest community served by combined sewers.

Despite the lack of a formal policy, the City of Edmonton has developed a CSO control strategy as part of its Towards a Clean River campaign for the North Saskatchewan River. The CSO control strategy is a 16-year-long program that includes an Early Action Control Plan (EACP) and a Long-Term Control Plan (LTCP). The implementation process begins with the EACP, which carries out selected CSO controls over a 10-year period. Key elements of the EACP include the following:

- In-line system storage to enable downstream sewer systems to transport and treat more wastewater with fewer overflow occurrences.

- Separation of storm and sanitary sewers as city sewers are upgraded.

- Floatables and solids control.

Key elements of the LTCP include:

- Increased system conveyance capacity.
- Construction of new storage facilities.

The City of Edmonton has developed and continues to develop a sophisticated hydrologic and hydraulic model of their sanitary and combined sewer system. The hydrologic model has been calibrated with extensive historical data and provides flow inputs into a continuous, fully-dynamic hydraulic model with the ability to simulate real-time controls, such as modulating gates and weirs.

British Columbia. Historically, CSO control in British Columbia has been accomplished on a voluntary basis through the development of municipal liquid-waste management plans. The province has moved to codify the development and implementation of these plans, making them a requirement under the new Waste Management Act, which came into force on January 1, 2004. The act applies to all municipalities, but imposes different requirements depending on the municipal population, as shown in Table 15.5.

Table 15.5 Waste Management Act requirements.

Population > 10,000	Population < 10,000
The liquid-waste management plan must address existing CSOs, including measures to eliminate overflows.	Either a liquid-waste management plan shall be developed or a study conducted to lead to implementation of measures to eliminate CSOs.

The Municipal Sewage Regulation, made under the Waste Management Act, describes municipal responsibilities concerning combined sewer systems and control of CSOs. The regulation defines a combined sewer system as ditches, drains, sewers, treatment facilities, and disposal facilities that collect, transport, treat, or dispose of a combination of municipal sewage and stormwater in a single system. The regulation stipulates that:

- No one is allowed to construct or expand a combined sewer system.
- Emergency repairs to existing combined sewer systems are permitted; however, the feasibility of sewer separation is to be assessed, and, wherever possible, the storm and sanitary sewers should be separated at the time of repair.

The regulation also states that no one shall allow a combined sewer overflow to occur during storm or snowmelt events with less than a 5-year return period. Further, an environmental impact study must be completed prior to the construction of any facility, and the study must identify any water-quality requirements as well as the treatment necessary to protect the quality and designated uses of receiving waters.

A focus of British Columbia's legislation is the eventual elimination of CSOs by replacing combined sewers with separate storm and sanitary sewers. To that end, storage or conveyance facilities may not be employed to reduce the amount of sewer separation required, unless the facilities immediately reduce and ultimately prevent the occurrence of CSOs. Furthermore, the regulation states the following:

- If storage or conveyance facilities are used, and primary and secondary treatment are available, then, at a minimum, primary treatment for flows greater than two times the average dry weather flow must be provided and the full secondary capacity of the treatment plant should be used. The primary and secondary effluent should be combined before discharge.

- A minimum receiving-environment-to-discharge dilution ratio of 40:1 should be maintained.
- Where disinfection of the effluent is required, adequate disinfection capacity should be provided to ensure disinfection of the entire discharge flow.

Within two years of the date that the Municipal Sewage Regulation comes into effect, municipalities with combined systems are required to:

- Estimate the existing flow quantity, frequency, and number of individual CSO occurrences.
- Estimate the total annual volume of all CSOs that occur during storm or snow-melt events with less than a 5-year return period.
- Develop and implement steps to reduce the quantity, frequency, and number of CSO occurrences.
- Reduce the total annual CSO volume by an average of 1% per year over each 10-year reporting period.
- Assess the potential impact on the receiving environment at all overflow locations.
- Create a database of all overflows that occur during storm or snowmelt events with less than a 5-year return period.

To address these requirements, several modeling strategies can be used. To determine annual CSO volumes, continuous modeling is required. The model can be fully or quasi-dynamic, depending on the characteristics of the system. To assess the effects of storm or snowmelt events with return periods of less than 5 years, an event model can be used.

15.3 European Union Laws and Regulations

European Union (EU) member countries have adopted several Directives for controlling urban pollution, particularly with regards to overflows. The Directives include the EU Urban Wastewater Treatment Directive (UWWTD), the proposed Water Policy Framework Directive (WPFD), the Integrated Pollution Control and Prevention Directive (IPPC), and some of the Product Directives. The following sections outline the requirements of the Directives and how they are being implemented.

Urban Wastewater Treatment Directive (UWWTD)

The UWWTD (CEC, 1991a) provides the main legislation for the control of urban pollution in the EU. The aim of the UWWTD is to avoid the pollution of fresh and marine waters from urban sewage systems, and it requires the following:

- All agglomerations greater than 2,000 Pe must discharge into collection systems for urban wastewaters. (1 Pe is defined as the organic loading with a 5-day biochemical oxygen demand [BOD_5] of 60 g/day.)
- The effluent from sewage treatment plants must meet the minimum effluent standards, which depend on the sensitivity of the receiving waters.
- Sewage discharges to "less sensitive" waters, defined as estuarine and coastal waters with a high dispersion capacity, may undergo only primary treatment.

- Sewage discharges to "normal" waters must receive biological treatment, as described in Table 15.6.

- Sewage discharges greater than 10,000 Pe to "sensitive" waters must be subjected to both biological treatment and nutrient removal (see Table 15.6).

Table 15.6 Requirements for discharges from urban wastewater treatment plants (from CEC, 1991a).

Parameter	Concentration, mg/L	Minimum Reduction[1], %
Requirements for discharges to "normal" water		
Carbonaceous biochemical oxygen demand (BOD_5 – 20° C)[2]	25 mg O_2/L or 40 mg O_2/L [3]	70–90
Chemical oxygen demand (COD)	125 mg O_2/L	75
Total suspended solids (TSS)	35[4] 35[5] 60[6]	90[4] 90[5] 70[6]
Additional requirements for discharges to "sensitive areas"		
Total phosphorus (P)	1 mg P/L (Pe of 10,000–100,000)[8] 1 mg P/L (Pe > 100,000)	80
Total nitrogen (N)	15 mg N/L (Pe of 10,000–100,000) 10 mg N/L[7] (Pe > 100,000)	70–80

1 The values for concentration or for the percentage of reduction shall apply. A look-up table shows the number of samples allowed to exceed the given values for BOD, COD, and TSS; for P and N the annual mean should not exceed the given values.

2 This parameter can be replaced by total organic carbon or total oxygen demand if a relationship can be established between BOD_5 and the substitute parameter.

3 Under Article 4 of the Directive.

4 Requirement is optional.

5 For plants >10,000 Pe.

6 For plants 2,000–10,000 Pe.

7 Alternatively, the daily average must not exceed 20 mg N/L. This requirement refers to a water temperature of 12°C or more during the operation of the biological reactor of the wastewater treatment plant. As a substitute for the condition concerning the temperature, it is possible to apply a limited time of operation, which takes into account the regional climatic conditions. This alternative applies if it can be shown that the monitoring requirements laid down in the Directive are met.

8 Pe is defined as the organic loading having a 5-day biochemical oxygen demand of 60 g/day.

- Industrial discharges into collection systems and urban treatment plants must be pretreated to ensure that:
  - The health of the staff working in collection systems and treatment plants is protected.
  - The collection systems, treatment plants, and associated equipment are not damaged.
  - The operation of treatment plants and the treatment of sludge are not impeded.
  - Discharges from the treatment plants do not adversely affect the environment or prevent receiving waters from complying with other Community Directives.
  - Sludge can be disposed of safely in an environmentally acceptable manner.

"I like Europe. They're not afraid of a few germs."

- The design, construction, and maintenance of the collection system is in accordance with the best available technical means not entailing excessive costs (BATNEEC), with particular emphasis on minimizing pollution of receiving waters due to stormwater overflows.

- All industrial, biodegradable discharges entering receiving waters from plants where the discharge contains 4,000 Pe or more are authorized and meet all national legislative requirements set for that industry.

- Sewage sludge is recycled whenever possible and is not disposed to sea by pipeline or ship (since 31 December 1998).

The UWWTD does not specify any standards for CSOs. However, the directive suggests that member states regulate them based on dilution rate, treatment capacity in terms of dry weather flow, or spill frequency.

Based on Article 5 of the UWWTD, member states are required to identify sensitive areas for waters that are, or are likely to become, eutrophic, and freshwaters intended as sources for drinking water where the nitrate content is or could become more than 50 mg N/L. Sewage treatment plants discharging to sensitive waters must also comply with the additional standards laid down for the nutrient. Five member states (Denmark, Luxembourg, the Netherlands, Finland, and Sweden) have designated all their waters as sensitive. In addition, seven member states (Belgium, Germany, Spain, France, Ireland, Portugal, and the UK) have designated parts of their waters as sensitive. Austria, Greece, and Italy have not identified any sensitive areas. The designation of the term "sensitive area" is still being considered (COM, 1999).

Member states have the option of designating certain coastal and estuarine waters as less sensitive, provided that they meet certain morphological, hydrological, or hydraulic conditions. Two member states, the UK and Portugal, have used this option.

Water Policy Framework Directive (WPFD)

In 1997, the European Commission adopted a draft proposal for a Council Directive establishing a framework for community action in the field of water policy (COM, 1997). The overall purpose of the proposed Directive is to establish a framework for the protection of freshwater, estuaries, coastal waters, and groundwaters in the EU. The main part of the directive relevant to CSOs is the requirement "to prevent deterioration of ecological quality and pollution of surface waters and to restore polluted surface waters to achieve at least 'good' surface water status in all surface waters. In order to achieve at least 'good' quality, Member States will have to establish improvement programs which may involve requirements to improve CSOs to reduce their impacts on river quality" (CEC, 1999).

Integrated Pollution Prevention Control Directive (IPPC)

The primary objective of the IPPC Directive (CEC, 1996) is to prevent or reduce emissions to air, water, and land from the most-polluting installations. The directive applies to effluents from 50 industry sectors that discharge to surface waters and to sewers. The application of Best Available Techniques (BAT) is required for the control of effluents. The application of this directive to sewage discharges will result in an improvement of effluent to sewers and of the untreated discharges from CSOs.

Product Directives

The EU Product Directives contribute to controlling pollution from non-point sources to sewers and therefore have an effect on the quality of the discharges from CSOs. Some examples include the Marketing and Use Directive (76/769/EEC) (CEC, 1976) and its amendments, which prohibit or restrict the marketing or use of certain dangerous substances and preparations containing dangerous substances, and the Detergent Directive (CEC, 1982), which requires a certain biodegradability of the surfactant before it may be marketed in detergents.

Control of CSOs in EU Member States

Whereas the effluents from sewage treatment plants are licensed in all countries, current practices for the permitting and monitoring of CSOs vary widely throughout the EU (Table 15.7). In most countries where CSOs require authorization, the permits are related to the spill frequencies. In terms of monitoring, only a low proportion of CSOs are monitored; although, depending on the country (e.g., Germany, UK), major new CSOs may require permanent monitoring facilities.

Table 15.7 CSO discharge permits in some European countries, modified from European Waste Water Group 1995 (Milne et al., 1997).

Country	Regulatory Body	Comments
Belgium (Flanders)	Environmental Agency (VLANSREM)	Discharge permit may specify overflow frequency.
Denmark	Regional Authority	Discharge permit specifies overflow frequency, but it is rarely checked. Some municipalities monitor "problem" CSOs.
France	Departments	Permit required if polluting load exceeds 500 Pe. 1–2% of CSOs are monitored, mainly near bathing waters and shellfish waters.

Table 15.7 (Continued) CSO discharge permits in some European countries, modified from European Waste Water Group 1995 (Milne et al., 1997).

Country	Regulatory Body	Comments
Germany	States (Länder)	Permits required for all wastewater discharges, including CSOs. Monitoring, regulation, and sampling procedures vary between individual states. Some states require new CSO structures to be equipped with a monitoring/telemetry facility for operational and regulatory reasons. Monitoring allows compliance with A128 guidelines.
Ireland	Environmental Protection Agency	Legislation proposed that will require discharge licenses.
Luxembourg	Ministry of Environmental Affairs	New CSOs require authorization (approval permits). Existing CSOs must be registered.
Netherlands	Water Boards	Discharge permit sets limit on overflow frequency. This is rarely checked except for problem CSOs causing public complaint (<5%). Monitoring facilities are being added to many systems.
Spain	National River Authority, Regional Authorities	All CSOs must be registered; formal permits (with conditions) are not issued at present.
UK – England and Wales	Environment Agency	Discharge consents are required for CSOs. Monitoring of "problem" CSOs only at present by Environment Agency. Spill frequencies assessed by short- or long-term monitoring, plus modeling studies by water companies. Major new CSO structures may include permanent monitoring facilities.
UK – Scotland	Scottish Environmental Protection Agency (SEPA)	Same as England and Wales, except monitoring and regulatory functions are performed by SEPA.

Design Criteria for CSOs.

Sewage treatment plants are usually designed to accept a certain maximum flow expressed as a multiple of dry weather flow (e.g., three times dry weather flow [DWF]). Any excess flow is discharged through CSOs, without further treatment, to the receiving waters. The permitting of CSOs in the different member countries usually reflects the design criteria used. Table 15.8 provides an overview of the CSO design criteria used in select EU countries.

Table 15.8 Overview of CSO design criteria in certain European countries, from European Waste Water Group 1995 (Milne et al., 1997).

Country	Design Criteria and Practice
Belgium	Minimum CSO setting has traditionally been 2–5 times mean DWF (5–10 times mean DWF for new systems). Seven overflow events allowed per year (local requirement for new CSOs in Flanders). Effects on receiving water are considered.
Denmark	Frequency of overflow, related to nature of the receiving water. Traditionally, CSO setting is 5 times daily peak DWF (equivalent to 8–10 times mean DWF). Yearly rates of BOD in spilled flow are compared to those discharged from sewage treatment works (STW). Intermittent and annual loads considered (for rivers and lakes). EQO/EQS approach has been introduced, together with modeling techniques.
France	CSO setting is 3 times peak DWF (normally equivalent to 4–6 times mean DWF). Setting for CSOs at STWs is usually 2–3 times mean DWF. Pollutant load is considered. EQO/EQS approach being introduced, together with modeling techniques.

Table 15.8 (Continued) Overview of CSO design criteria in certain European countries, from European Waste Water Group 1995 (Milne et al., 1997).

Country	Design Criteria and Practice
Germany	Minimum CSO setting is 7 times DWF where no storage is provided. 2 times mean DWF plus return to treatment. ATV Guideline A128 requirement of 90% of load to treatment, also state regulations. Storage up to 40 m^3/impervious hectare, typically 20–30 m^3/ha.
Greece	CSO setting generally 3–6 times mean DWF. Effects upon receiving waters and pollutant strength of the discharge are sometimes considered in determining the setting.
Ireland	Traditionally, 6 times mean DWF, more recently UK Formula A. EQO/EQS and modeling approach is now being introduced for some situations.
Italy	No nationally agreed upon criteria (national guidelines exist for minimum water quality standards). CSO setting generally 3–5 times mean DWF. Spill frequency criteria are being introduced on a local basis only.
Luxembourg	German ATV Guideline A128 is now the main design procedure. Traditionally, the minimum CSO setting was 3 times peak DWF (equivalent to 4–6 times mean DWF).
Netherlands	Locally negotiated frequency of overflow, usually 3–10 times per year, depending on sensitivity of receiving waters. Minimum total storage equivalent to 7 mm of runoff over impervious area. EQO/EQS approach is being introduced, together with modeling techniques.
Portugal	CSO settings are based on national guidelines. Most new CSOs have a setting of 6 times mean DWF. Receiving watercourse is considered in a few cases.
Spain	Most new CSOs have a setting of 3–5 times mean DWF. Five times mean DWF is the most frequently used setting for smaller towns.
UK – England & Wales	Historically, CSO setting is 6 times mean DWF to treatment (generally 3 times DWF to full treatment, 3 times DWF to storm tanks). 'Formula A' Setting = DWF + 1360P + 2E L/day where P = population, E = industrial effluent. (Formula A is typically 6.5–9 times mean DWF but may be higher). Storage is added where dilution is low. This is increasingly being replaced by the EQO/EQS approach and modeling techniques where appropriate.
UK – Scotland	Scottish practice is similar to England and Wales and takes into account receiving stream dilution in sizing the storage equipment.

Note: Dry Weather Flow (per capita) is broadly comparable throughout northern EU Countries.

15.4 Use of Models for Regulatory Compliance

Design engineers and utility managers use hydraulic models as tools to understand the performance of sewage collection systems. This section describes how hydraulic sewer models are used to assess and demonstrate compliance with the combined and sanitary sewer overflow regulations in the United States.

Although the CSO and SSO regulations have no specific requirement for the use of sewer models, EPA policies and guidance documents strongly recommend their use for maintaining compliance. The CSO policy (Section II.C.1.d, US EPA, 1994) states the following:

> Modeling of a sewer system is recognized as a valuable tool for predicting sewer system response to various wet weather events and assessing water quality impacts when evaluating different control strategies and alternatives. EPA supports the proper and effective use of models, where appropriate, in the evaluation of the nine minimum controls and the development of the long-term CSO control plan. It is also recognized that there are many models, which may be used to do this. These models range from simple to complex. Having decided to use a model, the permittee should base its choice of a model on the characteristics of its sewer system, the number and location of overflow points, and the sensitivity of the receiving water body to the CSO discharges.

Table 15.9 lists the type of analysis and the appropriate modeling approach for meeting the technical requirements of the US EPA's CSO policy and the SSO proposed rules.

Example 15.1 demonstrates the use of a hydraulic sewer model to determine compliance with one of the requirements in the US EPA's CSO Control Policy.

Table 15.9 Applications of software to meet CSO and SSO requirements.

Requirement	Type of Analysis Required	Model Approach
CSO – Minimum Control Measures		
Demonstrate implementation of the minimum controls: • Maximize use of collection system for storage • Maximize flow to publicly owned treatment works for treatment • Prohibit CSOs during dry weather	• RDII (rainflow-derived inflow and infiltration) quantification • Hydraulic analysis of sewer system • Operations simulation	• Calibrate model to monitored flows to determine RDII • Steady-state runs using peak dry weather flows to assess capacity • Extended-period simulation of wet weather events to determine storage and flow to treatment plant • Evaluation of real-time controls
CSO – Long-Term Control Plan – Presumptive Approach		
• Limit average number of overflow events per year or • Capture at least 85% of wet weather volume per year or • Eliminate or reduce mass of pollutants equivalent to 85% of capture volume requirement	• Simulation with design storms • Long-term simulation • Operations simulation	• Continuous simulation of design storm event • Long-term simulation of multiple events
CSO – Long-Term Plan – Demonstrative Approach		
Demonstrate that a selected control program is adequate to meet water quality requirements of the CWA	• Simulation with design storms or long-term simulation of sewer system • Use measured concentrations or transport simulations of the receiving body	• Continuous simulation of design storm event • Long-term simulation of multiple events
SSO – Capacity, Management, Operations, and Maintenance (CMOM) Programs		
Maintenance of a collection system map	Maintenance of up-to-date as-built drawings	• Use model to generate CAD-style drawings • Interface with AutoCAD and GIS
Program to assess the capacity of the collection system	• RDII analysis • Hydraulic analysis of sewer system components	• Calibrate model to measured flows to determine RDII • Model as steady-state, extended-period, or continuous simulation
System evaluation and capacity assurance plans	Simulation of control alternatives	Use model to evaluate alternatives, costs, and impacts

Section 15.4 Use of Models for Regulatory Compliance 553

Example 15.1 Capture volume analysis.

A trunk main consists of ten 300-ft long segments as shown in the following figure. A constant flow of 200 gpm enters the system at each manhole. During wet weather, RDII enters the system at manholes 2, 5, and 10.

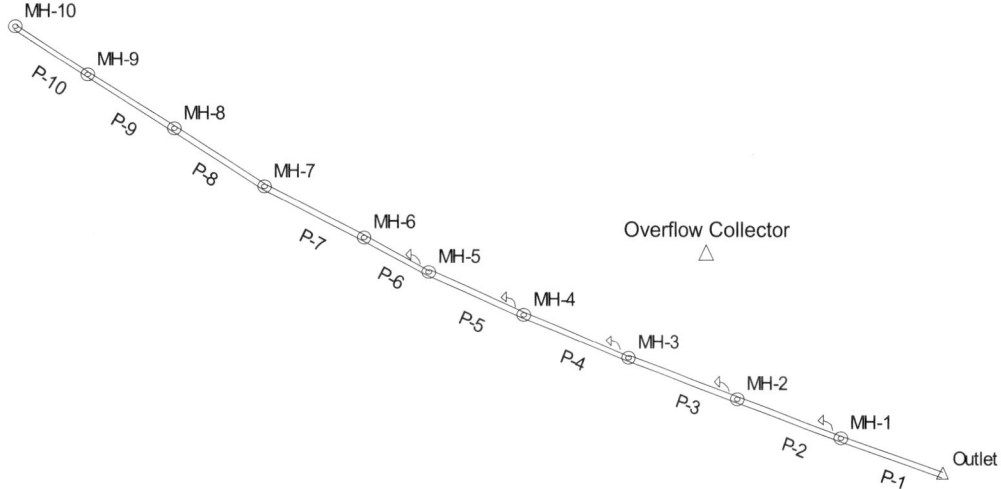

The inflow to each of the three manholes is simulated as a hydrograph having a 4.5-hour duration. This hydrograph is shown in the following figure.

A model of the system is developed and an extended-period simulation is conducted for a 5-hour event. The resulting hydrographs of the total flow entering pipe P-1, the overflow, and the flow conveyed to treatment are shown in the following figure. When

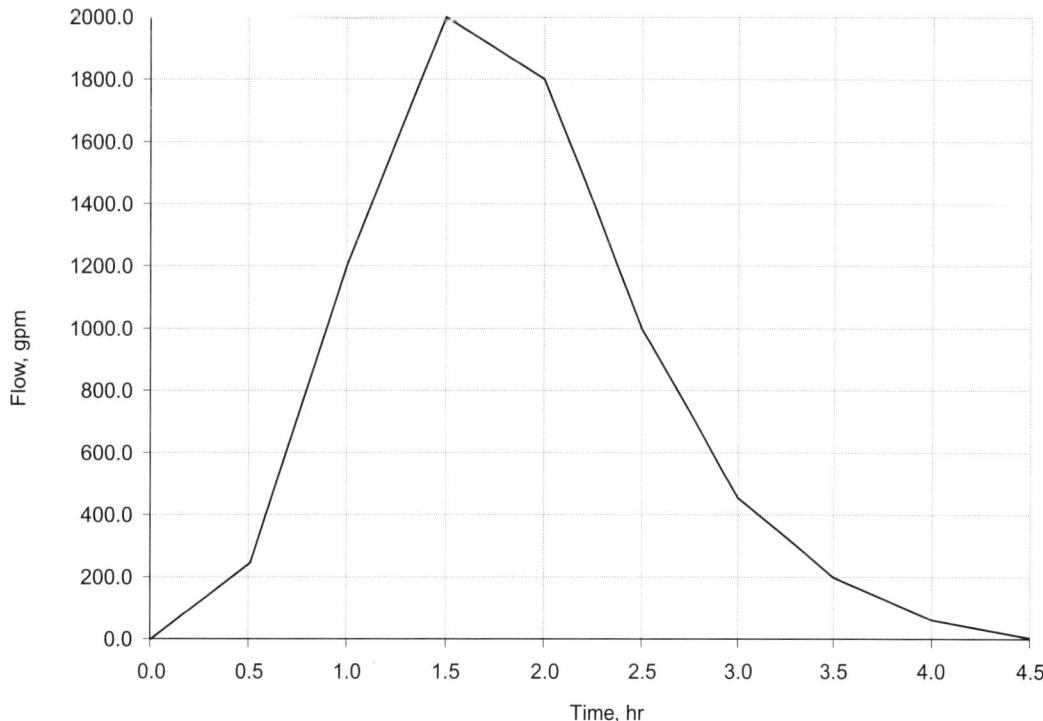

flows exceed pipe capacity, overflow occurs at the upstream end of pipe P-1. Determine if the system meets the 85% capture volume requirement in the Presumptive Approach of the Long-Term Control Plan in CSO policy.

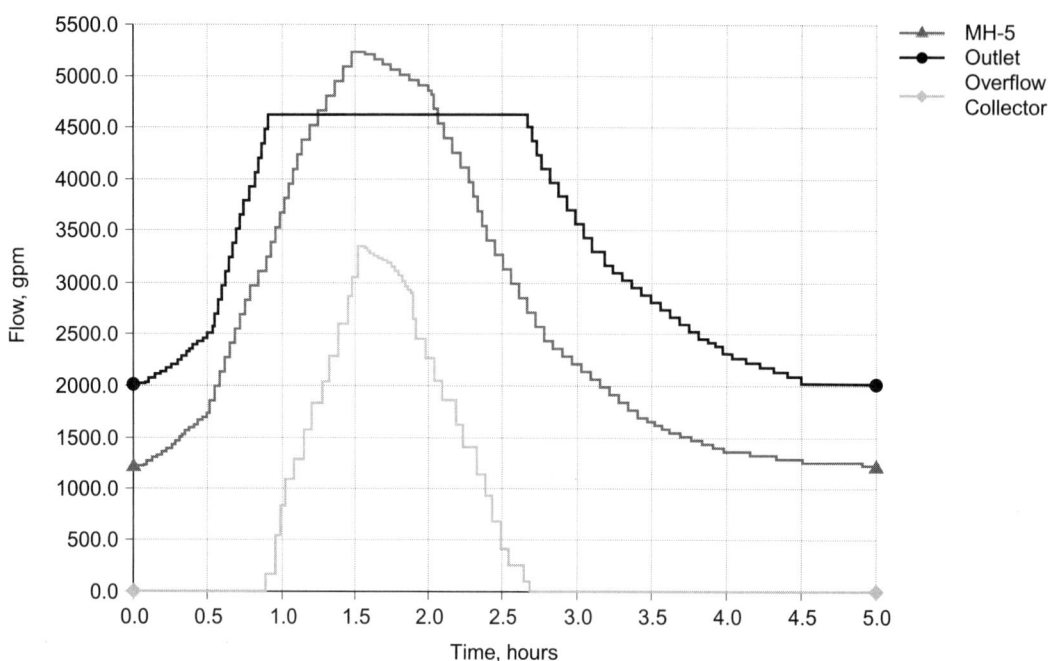

For the 5-hour simulation period, the loads are:

Sanitary flow = 811,362 gal

RDII = 417,147 gal

The discharges are:

To treatment = 1,020,147 gal

Overflow = 208,509 gal

The percent capture volume is

$$\frac{417{,}147 - 208{,}509}{417{,}147} \times 100 = 50.0\%$$

The model showed that 50% of the RDII was captured for this storm event. The regulatory requirement was to capture 85% of the wet weather flow on an annual basis. Additional simulation of storm events that occur over the course of a year will be required to assess compliance.

References

Copeland, C. 1999. "Clean Water Act: A Summary of the Law." CRS Issue Brief for Congress. RL 30030.

Commission of the European Communities (COM). 1997. Proposal for a Council Directive Establishing a Framework for Community Action in the Field of Water Policy (COM (97) 49 final). *Official Journal* C184, 17 (June).

Commission of the European Communities (COM). 1999. Water Quality in the European Union. Implementation of the Council Directive 91/271/EEC of 21 May 1991 concerning urban wastewater treatment, as amended by Commission Directive 98/15/EC of 27 February 1998. European Commission Directorate Environment. http://europe.eu.int/water/water-urbanwaste/report/chapter6.html.

Council of the European Communities (CEC). 1976. Directive on the approximation of the laws, regulations and administrative provisions of the Member States relating to restrictions on the marketing and use of certain dangerous substances and preparations (76/769/EC). *Official Journal* L262, 27 (September).

Council of the European Communities (CEC). 1982. Directive relating to the testing the biodegradability of nonionic surfactants and amending Directive (82/242/EEC). *Official Journal* L109 (22 April).

Council of the European Communities (CEC). 1991a. Directive concerning urban waste water treatment (91/271/EEC). *Official Journal* L135 (30 May).

Council of the European Communities (CEC). 1996. Directive on Integrated Pollution Prevention and Control (96/61/EC). *Official Journal* L257 (10 October).

Council of the European Communities (CEC). 1999. Common Position (EC) No 41/1999 adopted by the Council, 22 October 1999, with a view to the adoption of a Directive 1999/../EC of the European Parliament and of the Council establishing a Framework for Community Action in the field of water policy (1999/C 343/01). *Official Journal* C 343 (30 November).

Environment Canada. 2004. *Combined Sewer Overflow Treatment Technologies Manual, draft.* Ottawa, Canada.

Milne, I., B. Crabtree, S. Clarke, C. Wennberg, and J. Larson. 1997. *Best Management Practices for the Regulation of Passive Urban Wastewater.* Technology Validation Project IN10187D. Medmenham Marlow, UK: WrC.

Municipal Engineers Association. 2000. *Municipal Class EA (replaces Class EA for Municipal Road Projects and Water and Wastewater Projects).* Mississagua, ON, Canada: Municipal Engineers Association.

Ontario Ministry of the Environment. 1985. *Guidelines for the Design of Sanitary Sewage Systems.* Prepared by the Environmental Approvals and Project Engineering Branch of the Ministry of the Environment.

Ontario Ministry of the Environment. 1997. *Ontario CSO Control Procedure F-5-5.* Toronto, Canada.

Percival, R.C. and D.C. Alevizatos. 1997. *Law and the Environment: A Multidisciplinary Reader.* Philadelphia, PA: Temple University Press.

Quebec. 2002. *Water. Our Life. Our Future. Quebec Water Policy.* Envirodoq ENV/2002/0310A. Bibliotecheque national du Quebec.

US Environmental Protection Agency (US EPA). 1994. *Combined Sewer Overflow Policy.* 59 FR 18688.

US Environmental Protection Agency (US EPA). 2001. *National Pollutant Discharge Elimination System (NPDES) Permit Requirements for Municipal Sanitary Sewer Collection Systems, Municipal Satellite Systems and Sanitary Sewer Overflow.* 66 FR 7701

US Environmental Protection Agency (US EPA). 2003. *National Pollutant Discharge Elimination System (NPDES) Permit Requirements for Municipal Wastewater Treatment Discharges During Wet Weather Conditions.* 68 FR 63042.

Zabel, T., I. Milne, and G. McKay. 2001. "Approaches Adopted by the European Union and Selected Member States for the Control of Urban Pollution." *Urban Water* 3: 25-32.

Zwick, D. and M. Benstock. 1971. *Water Wasteland.* New York: Grossman Publishers.

Problems

15.1 Match each abbreviation with the appropriate description.

Abbreviation		Definition
1	CWA	a	Downstream end of a sewer
2	NPDES	b	Canadian water quality law
3	CFR	c	Pollution prevention in Europe
4	POTW	d	Problem in sanitary sewer
5	SSO	e	Law requiring permits for discharge in the US
6	CSO	f	Must have permit to overflow (in US)
7	CEAA	g	Permit to discharge in the US
8	UWWTD	h	Indicator of wastewater strength
9	IPPC	i	Repository of US regulations
10	BOD	j	European Union water quality regs

15.2 In the US, the NPDES "nine minimum controls" are applicable to what kind of system?

15.3 What are the two levels of control specified in NPDES discharge permits and how do they differ?

15.4 Name two Canadian agencies that monitor wastewater collection systems.

15.5 What type of collection system is most commonly found in urban areas of Europe?

APPENDIX

Symbols

This appendix contains a list of all the symbols and their definitions as used in this book. Typical units of measurement, in both US Customary and SI units, are provided for each symbol.

a speed of pressure wave (ft/s, m/s)
A cross-sectional area of flow (ft², m²)
     area (ac, ha)
     area of subbasin (ft², m²)
A_c cross-sectional area of the flow at critical depth (ft², m²)
A_i cross-sectional area of an inlet pipe (ft², m²)
A_o cross-sectional area of an outflow pipe (ft², m²)
     area of an orifice opening (ft², m²)
b width of a Preissmann slot (ft, m)
B structure diameter (ft, m)
c coefficient for wave translation (ft/s, m/s)
     speed of a pressure wave (ft/s, m/s)
C roughness coefficient
     runoff coefficient (dimensionless)
     melt rate factor (in/°F/day, mm/°C/day)
C_B correction factor for benching
C_{D1} correction factor for the pipe diameter
C_{D2} correction factor for the flow depth
C_d discharge coefficient (depends on the orifice edges)
C_{eq} equilibrium concentration of tracer at the downstream monitoring station (mg/L)
C_f unit conversion factor
C_P correction factor for plunging flow
C_Q correction factor for relative flow

C_s	concentration of tracer in the wastewater (mg/L)
C_t	initial concentration of tracer in the discharge (mg/L)
C_v	valve coefficient (gpm/psi$^{0.5}$, m^3/s/kPa$^{0.5}$)
C_x	coefficient estimated from regression
C_1	coefficient for the relative access-hole diameter
C_2	coefficient for the water depth in the access hole
C_3	coefficient for lateral flow, the lateral angle, and plunging flow
C_4	coefficient for the relative pipe diameters
$C(energy)$	annual pumping energy cost ($/yr)
$C(pipe)$	cost of pipe installation ($)
$C(PW)$	present worth of pipe and energy cost ($)
cv	control volume (ft^3, m^3)
d	depth of flow normal to the channel bottom (ft, m)
d_p	depression storage (ft, m)
d_s	depth of snow (in, mm)
D	diameter (ft, m)
	depression storage (in.)
D_e	diameter of an equivalent pipe (ft, m)
D_h	hydraulic depth, area/surface width (ft, m)
D_i	inlet pipe diameter (ft, m)
	diameter of the i-th pipe (ft, m)
D_o	outlet pipe diameter (ft, m)
	depth of water in a structure (ft, m)
	particle size (mm)
D_1, D_2	diameter of the (first, second) pipe out of a split (ft, m)
E	bulk modulus of elasticity (lb/in^2, kPa)
	specific energy (ft, m)
e_m	motor efficiency (%)
e_p	pump efficiency at operating point (%)
EFF_i	extreme flow factor for the i-th type of user
f	Darcy-Weisbach friction factor (dimensionless)
	infiltration rate (in./hr, cm/hr)
f_c	minimum or ultimate value of f_p (ft/sec)
f_o	maximum or initial value of f_p (ft/sec)
f_p	infiltration capacity into soil (ft/sec)
F	total accumulated infiltration (in., cm)
F	vector force acting on a fluid element (lb, N)
F_{min}	minimum flow factor
F_x	force acting on the water in a control volume in the x-direction (lb, N)
Fr	Froude number (dimensionless)
g	gravitational acceleration constant (32.2 ft/s^2, 9.81 m/s^2)
h	depth of fluid measured from the free surface (ft, m)
	difference in elevation between the highest inlet pipe invert and the centerline of the outlet pipe (ft, m)
h_f	friction head loss (ft, m)
h_l	lift head (ft, m)
	head loss between wet well and pump (ft, m)
h_L	energy loss (head loss) between cross sections (ft, m)
h_m	minor head loss (ft, m)
h_o	effective head (ft, m)
	shutoff head (ft, m)

h_p	pump head (ft, m)
h_T	energy lost to a turbine between cross sections (ft, m)
h_1	static lift (ft, m)
H	total head (ft, m)
	upstream head (ft, m)
H_c	conductive exchange of sensible heat between air and snowpack
H_e	release of latent heat of vaporization by condensation of atmospheric water vapor
H_g	conduction of heat to snowpack from underlying ground
H_p	advection of heat to snowpack by rain
H_{rl}	net longwave radiation entering snowpack
H_{rs}	net (incoming minus outgoing) shortwave radiation entering snowpack
H_s	static head (ft, m)
$H(bar)$	barometric pressure at the elevation of the pump (ft, m)
$H(vap)$	vapor pressure of water (ft, m)
HGL_o	hydraulic grade elevation at the upstream end of an outlet pipe (ft, m)
HMC_i	horizontal momentum check for pipe i
i_{ave}	average rainfall intensity (in./hr or mm/hr)
i_{10}	running 10-minute average of rainfall intensity (mm/hr)
I	inflow (ft^3/s, m^3/s)
	precipitation intensity (in./hr, mm/hr)
$I(t)$	volumetric inflow rate at time t (ft^3, m^3)
k	unit conversion factor
K	adjusted minor loss coefficient
	storage constant
	decay coefficient (s^{-1})
K_i	ratio of the time to recession to the time to peak for hydrograph i
K_L	minor loss coefficient
K_M	minor head loss coefficient (s^2/ft^5, s^2/m^5)
K_o	initial head loss coefficient based on the relative size of the structure
K_p	pipe head loss coefficient (s^z/ft^{3z-1}, s^z/m^{3z-1})
K_s	saturated hydraulic conductivity (permeability) (in./hr, cm/hr)
L	pipe length (ft, m)
	length of overland flow (ft)
M	meltwater rate, (in/day, mm/day)
$\mathbf{M}_{in}$	momentum inflow rate into a control volume (lb, N)
$\mathbf{M}_{out}$	momentum outflow rate from a control volume (lb, N)
M_x	momentum flow rate in the x-direction (lb, N)
$Mult_i$	demand multiplier at the ith time step (dimensionless)
n	Manning's roughness coefficient (dimensionless)
	pump speed (1/s)
	number of persons per pump
n_e	Manning's n for an equivalent pipe
n_f	Manning's n for a full pipe
n_i	Manning's n for the i-th pipe
n_1, n_2	Manning's n for the (first, second) pipe out of a split
N	number of weir end contractions
	perimeter of pipeline cross section (ft, m)
	number of sewer pipe deflections
	pump rotational speed (rpm)
	equivalent dwelling units upstream
N_s	specific speed

$NPSH_a$	net positive suction head available (ft, m)
p	pressure (lb/in², kPa)
	price of energy (cents/kw-hr)
	wetted perimeter (ft, m)
p_{atm}	atmospheric pressure (lb/in², kPa)
p_{abs}	absolute pressure (lb/in², kPa)
p_{gage}	gauge pressure (lb/in², kPa)
P	contributing population
	power (hp, kW)
P_{tot}	total rainfall (in., mm)
PF	peaking factor
R_h	hydraulic radius (ft, m)
Re	Reynolds number
q	average discharge from a single pump (gpm, Lpm)
q_i	unit flow for the i-th type, gal/unit
Q	pipeline flow rate (ft³/s, m³/s)
	runoff rate (ft³/s, m³/s)
	subcatchment outflow (ft³/s, m³/s)
$Q(t)$	volumetric outflow rate at time t (ft³, m³)
Q_a	average flow rate to pump station when pump is running (gpm, L/s)
Q_A, Q_B	discharges for the pair of inflow pipes that produce the largest value of C_{3D} (ft³/s, m³/s)
Q_{avg}	average flow rate (ft³/s, m³/s)
Q_{base}	average daily flow rate (gpd, Lpd)
	base demand (gpm, m³/s)
Q_{GWI}	groundwater infiltration (ft³/s or gpd, m³/s)
Q_i	discharge from an inflow pipe
	demand in the ith time step (gpm, m³/s)
Q_N	flow under normal conditions (ft³/s, m³/s)
Q_o	flow in the outflow pipe
Q_p	pump discharge (ft³/s, m³/s)
Q_{peak}	peak hourly flow rate (gpd, Lpd)
Q_{pi}	peak discharge for hydrograph i (ft³/s, m³/s)
Q_{RDII}	rainfall derived inflow and infiltration (ft³/s or gpd, m³/s)
Q_s	wastewater flow (ft³/s or gpd, m³/s)
Q_t	tracer injection rate (ft³/s, m³/s)
	total flow in sewer (ft³/s or gpd, m³/s)
Q_t	total flow into a splitter node (ft³/s, m³/s)
Q_2	flow diverted into a parallel pipe (ft³/s, m³/s)
R	ratio between precipitation and RDII
	radius of curvature (ft, m)
R_h	hydraulic radius (ft, m)
R_{hm}	average of the hydraulic radii at sections 1 and 2 (ft, m)
R_i	volumetric runoff coefficient for hydrograph i
R_1, R_2, R_3	fraction of rainfall entering the sewer system from the fast, intermediate, and slow components
$Rain_{i-j}$	cumulative rainfall for the specified range of hours
s	specific gravity
	volume of rainfall on the subcatchment (m³)
S	friction slope (ft/ft, m/m)
	slope of overland flow (ft/ft)

	storage (ft³, m³)
	catchment slope (percent)
$S(t)$	storage at the beginning of a time interval (ft³, m³)
	fluid volume (ft³, m³)
$S(t + \Delta t)$	storage at the end of a time interval (ft³, m³)
S_e	slope of an equivalent pipe
S_f	slope of the energy grade line (ft/ft, m/m)
S_i	slope of the i-th pipe
S_{min}	minimum slope to move particles
S_o	slope of a channel bottom (ft/ft, m/m)
S_x	slope of the channel bed in the longitudinal direction (ft/ft, m/m)
S_w	slope of the hydraulic grade line (ft/ft, m/m)
S_1, S_2	slope of the (first, second) pipe out of a split
$spwf$	series present worth factor (yr)
SWE	snow water equivalent (in, mm)
t	time (s)
	hours pump runs at operating point during the year (hr)
	minimum pump cycle time (min)
t_c	time of concentration (min)
t_d	total design storm duration (hr)
t_0	beginning time of storm (s)
T	top width (ft, m)
T_a	daily average air temperature (°F, °C)
T_d	period of duration around the storm's peak (hours)
T_i	time to peak for hydrograph i (hr)
T_m	threshold temperature (32°F, 0°C)
u	velocity in the longitudinal direction (ft/s, m/s)
	average demand per capita (gpcm, Lpcm)
U_{ij}	units of the i-th use type at the j-th node
V	average fluid velocity (ft/s, m/s)
$\mathbf{V}$	vector velocity (ft/s, m/s)
V_f	volume of fluid (ft³, m³)
V_m	average of the velocities at sections 1 and 2 (ft/s, m/s)
V_{min}	minimum velocity (ft/s, m/s)
V_o	velocity in an outlet pipe
V_{Rain}	volume of rainfall (ft³ or gal, m³)
V_{RDII}	volume of RDII (ft³, m³)
V_x	x-component of the velocity of the fluid in the control volume (ft/s, m/s)
$Vol(active)$	fill volume (ft³, m³)
w	subcatchment width (ft, m)
W	weight of fluid (lb, N)
	throat width (ft, m)
x	distance in the longitudinal direction (ft, m)
	number of people per household
X	relative importance of inflow and outflow in determining storage
y	depth of flow at a point (ft, m)
	indoor water use per household (gpcd, Lpcd)
y_c	critical depth (ft, m)
Z	elevation above an arbitrary datum plane (ft, m)
	channel bottom elevation (ft, m)
Z_o	elevation of an outlet pipe invert (ft, m)

α	velocity distribution coefficient
	angle of a pipe to horizontal
β	velocity distribution coefficient
γ	fluid specific weight (lb/ft^3, N/m^3)
Δ	total deflection angle of curve (degrees or radians)
ΔH	change in heat storage in snowpack
ε	equivalent sand grain roughness (ft, m)
θ	channel slope angle (radians)
$\theta_{A,B}$	angle between the outlet main and inflow pipes for the pair of inflow pipes producing the largest value of C_{3D} (degrees)
θ_i	angle between the outlet pipe and inflow pipe i (degrees)
	volumetric moisture content under initial conditions
θ_s	volumetric moisture content (water volume per unit soil volume) under saturated conditions
μ	absolute (dynamic) viscosity (lb-s/ft^2, N-s/m^2)
ν	kinematic viscosity (ft^2/s, m^2/s)
ρ	fluid density (slugs/ft^3, kg/m^3)
ρ_s	density of snow (slugs/ft^3, kg/m^3)
ρ_w	density of water (1.94 slugs/ft^3, 1000 kg/m^3)
τ	shear stress (lb/ft^2, N/m^2)
	tractive tension (lb/ft^2, Pa)
τ_0	shear stress along a pipe wall (lb/ft^2, N/m^2)
ψ	capillary suction (in., cm)

APPENDIX

B

Conversion Factors

To use the tables in this appendix, locate the "from" unit in the row and the "to" unit in the column and multiply the number you want to convert by the factor in that cell of the table. For example, to change kilometers to feet, look in the cell corresponding to the kilometer row and the feet column to find 3281 and multiply the number of kilometers by 3281 to get the number of feet.

Table B.1 Length conversion factors.

From/To	m	mm	km	in.	ft	yd	mi
meter (m)	1	1000	0.001	39.37	3.281	1.094	0.0006215
millimeter (mm)	0.001	1	1.0×10^{-6}	0.03937	0.003281	0.001094	6.214×10^{-7}
kilometer (km)	1000	1,000,000	1	39,370	3281	1094	0.6214
inch (in.)	0.0254	25.4	2.54×10^{-5}	1	0.08333	0.02778	1.578×10^{-5}
foot (ft)	0.3048	304.8	3.048×10^{-4}	12	1	0.3333	1.894×10^{-4}
yard (yd)	0.9144	914.4	9.144×10^{-4}	36	3	1	5.682×10^{-4}
mile (mi)	1609	1,609,000	1.609	63,360	5280	1760	1

Table B.2 Volume conversion factors.

From/To	m³	L	ft³	gal	Imp gal	ac-ft
cubic meter (m³)	1	1000	35.31	264.2	220.0	8.107×10^{-4}
liter (L)	0.001	1	0.03531	0.2642	0.2200	8.107×10^{-7}
cubic foot (ft³)	0.02832	28.32	1	7.481	6.229	2.296×10^{-5}
US gallon (gal)	0.003785	3.785	0.1337	1	0.8327	3.069×10^{-6}
Imperial gallon (Imp gal)	0.004546	4.546	0.1605	1.201	1	3.686×10^{-6}
acre-foot (ac-ft)	1233	1,233,487	43,560	325,900	271,329	1

Table B.3 Pressure conversion factors.

From/To	Pa	kPa	bar	atm	psf	psi	ft H₂O	mm H₂O	mm Hg	kg/cm²
pascal (Pa)	1	0.001	1.0×10^{-5}	9.869×10^{-6}	0.02089	1.451×10^{-4}	3.346×10^{-4}	0.1020	0.007501	1.020×10^{-5}
kilopascal (kPa)	1000	1	0.01	9.869×10^{-3}	20.89	0.1450	0.3346	102.0	7.501	0.01020
bar	1.00×10^{5}	100	1	0.9869	2,089	14.50	33.46	10,197	750.1	1.0204
atmosphere (atm)	1.013×10^{5}	101.3	1.013	1	2,116	14.70	33.90	10,332	760	1.0337
pounds per square foot (psf)	47.88	0.04788	0.0004788	4.725×10^{-4}	1	0.006944	0.01602	4.882	0.3591	4.886×10^{-4}
pounds per square inch (psi)	6895	6.895	0.06895	0.06805	144.0	1	2.307	703.1	51.71	0.07035
feet water (ft H₂O)	2,989	2.989	0.02986	0.02989	62.43	0.4335	1	304.8	22.42	0.03048
millimeters water (mm H₂O)	9.807	0.009807	9.807×10^{-5}	9.678×10^{-5}	0.2048	0.001422	0.003281	1	0.07356	1.000×10^{-4}
millimeters mercury (mm Hg)	133.3	0.1333	0.001333	0.001316	2.784	0.01934	0.04465	13.60	1	0.001360
kilograms per square centimeter (kg/cm²)	98,000	98	0.98	0.967423	2,046.78	14.22	32.81	10,000	735.56	1

Table B.4 Flow conversion factors.

From/To	m³/s	l/s	m³/hr	ft³/s	MGD	gpm	ac-ft/day
cubic meter/second (m³/s)	1	1000	3600	35.31	22.82	15,850	70.05
liter/second (l/s)	0.001	1	3.6	0.03532	0.02282	15.85	0.07005
cubic meter/hour (m³/hr)	2.778×10^{-4}		1	9.810×10^{-3}	6.340×10^{-3}	4.403	.01946
cubic foot/second (cfs)	0.02832	28.32	101.94	1	0.6463	448.8	1.983
million gallon/day (MGD)	0.04381	43.81	157.73	1.547	1	694.4	3.070
gallon (US)/minute (gpm)	6.309×10^{-5}	0.06309	.22713	0.002228	0.001440	1	0.004419
acre-foot per day (ac-ft/day)	0.01428	14.28	20.55	0.5042	0.3259	226.3	1

Table B.5 Viscosity conversion factors.

From/To	Pa-s	cP	lbf-s/ft²
pascal-second (Pa-s)	1	1,000	0.02089
centipoise (cP)	0.001	1	2.089×10^{-5}
pound force-second/sq. ft (lbf-s/ft²)	47.88	47,880	1

Table B.6 Kinematic viscosity conversion factors.

From/To	m²/s	cS	ft²/s
square meter/second (m²/s)	1	1,000,000	10.76
centistoke (cS)	1.0×10^{-6}	1	1.080×10^{-5}
square feet/second (ft²/s)	0.09290	9.290×10^4	1

Table B.7 Velocity conversion factors.

From/To	m/s	km/hr	fps	mph
meter/second (m/s)	1	3.600	3.281	2.237
kilometer/hour (km/hr)	0.2778	1	0.9113	0.6214
feet/second (fps)	0.3048	1.097	1	0.6818
miles/hour (mph)	0.4470	1.609	1.467	1

Table B.8 Power conversion factors.

From/To	W	kW	hp	ft-lbf/s	BTU/hr
watt (W)	1	0.001	0.001341	0.7376	3.415
kilowatt (kW)	1000	1	1.340	737.6	3415
horsepower (hp)	749.7	0.7457	1	550.0	2547
foot-pound force/sec (ft-lbf/s)	1.356	0.001356	0.001818	1	4.630
BTU/hour (BTU/hr)	0.2928	2.929×10^{-4}	3.926×10^{-5}	0.2160	1

APPENDIX

C

Physical Properties

Table C.1 Density, viscosity, and kinematic viscosity of water.

Temperature		Density		Viscosity		Kinematic Viscosity	
°F	°C	kg/m^3	slugs/ft^3	N-s/m^2	lb-s/ft^2	m^2/s	ft^2/s
32	0	999.8	1.940	0.001781	3.746×10^{-5}	1.785×10^{-6}	1.930×10^{-5}
39	4	1000.0	1.941	.001568	3.274×10^{-5}	1.586×10^{-6}	1.687×10^{-5}
50	10	999.7	1.940	.001307	2.735×10^{-5}	1.306×10^{-6}	1.407×10^{-5}
68	20	998.2	1.937	.00102	2.107×10^{-5}	1.003×10^{-6}	1.088×10^{-5}
86	30	995.7	1.932	.000798	1.670×10^{-5}	0.800×10^{-7}	0.864×10^{-5}
104	40	992.2	1.925	.000547	1.366×10^{-5}	0.553×10^{-7}	0.709×10^{-5}

Compiled from Bolz and Tuve (1973), Henry and Heinke (1996), Hughes and Brighton (1967), and Tchobanoglous and Schroeder (1985).

Table C.2 Standard vapor pressures of water (compiled from Hydraulic Institute, 1979).

Temperature		Vapor Pressure	
°F	°C	ft	m
32	0.0	0.20	0.061
40	4.4	0.28	0.085
50	10.0	0.41	0.12
60	15.6	0.59	0.18
70	21.1	0.84	0.26

Table C.2 (Continued) Standard vapor pressures of water (compiled from Hydraulic Institute, 1979).

Temperature		Vapor Pressure	
°F	°C	ft	m
80	26.7	1.17	0.36
90	32.2	1.61	0.49
100	37.8	2.19	0.67

Table C.3 Standard barometric pressures (compiled from Hydraulic Institute, 1979).

Elevation, ft	Elevation, m	Barometric Pressure, ft	Barometric Pressure, m
0	0	33.9	10.30
1000	305	32.7	9.97
2000	610	31.6	9.63
3000	914	30.5	9.30
4000	1220	29.3	8.93
5000	1524	28.2	8.59
6000	1829	27.1	8.26
7000	2134	26.1	7.95
8000	2440	25.1	7.65

Table C.4 Equivalent pipe roughnesses for various sewer pipe materials (compiled from Lamont, 1981; Moody, 1944; and Mays, 1999).

Material	Equivalent Sand Grain Roughness, ε	
	ft	mm
Wrought iron, steel	$1.5 \times 10^{-4} - 8 \times 10^{-3}$	0.046–2.4
Asphalted cast iron	$4 \times 10^{-4} - 7 \times 10^{-3}$	0.1–2.1
Galvanized iron	$3.3 \times 10^{-4} - 1.5 \times 10^{-2}$	0.102–4.6
Cast iron	$8 \times 10^{-4} - 1.8 \times 10^{-2}$	0.2–5.5
Concrete	$10^{-3} - 10^{-2}$	0.3–3.0
Uncoated cast iron	7.4×10^{-4}	0.226
Coated cast iron	3.3×10^{-4}	0.102
Coated spun iron	1.8×10^{-4}	0.056
Cement	$1.3 \times 10^{-3} - 4 \times 10^{-3}$	0.4–1.2
Wrought iron	1.7×10^{-4}	0.05
Uncoated steel	9.2×10^{-5}	0.028
Coated steel	1.8×10^{-4}	0.058
PVC	5×10^{-6}	0.0015

Table C.5 Hazen-Williams C-factors (compiled from Lamont, 1981).

Type of Pipe	Discrete Pipe Diameter, in. (cm)				
	3.0 (7.6)	6.0 (15.2)	12 (30)	24 (61)	48 (122)
Uncoated cast iron, smooth and new	121	125	130	132	134
Coated cast iron, smooth and new	129	133	138	140	141
30 years old					
Trend 1 – slight attack	100	106	112	117	120
Trend 2 – moderate attack	83	90	97	102	107
Trend 3 – appreciable attack	59	70	78	83	89
Trend 4 – severe attack	41	50	58	66	73
60 years old					
Trend 1 – slight attack	90	97	102	107	112
Trend 2 – moderate attack	69	79	85	92	96
Trend 3 – appreciable attack	49	58	66	72	78
Trend 4 – severe attack	30	39	48	56	62
100 years old					
Trend 1 – slight attack	81	89	95	100	104
Trend 2 – moderate attack	61	70	78	83	89
Trend 3 – appreciable attack	40	49	57	64	71
Trend 4 – severe attack	21	30	39	46	54
Miscellaneous					
Newly scraped mains	109	116	121	125	127
Newly brushed mains	97	104	108	112	115
Coated spun iron, smooth and new	137	142	145	148	148
Old – take as coated cast iron of same age					
Galvanized iron, smooth and new	129	133			
Wrought iron, smooth and new	137	142			
Coated steel, smooth and new	137	142	145	148	148
Uncoated steel, smooth and new	142	145	147	150	150
Coated asbestos cement, clean	147	149	150	152	
Uncoated asbestos cement, clean	142	145	147	150	
Spun cement-lined and spun bitumen-lined, clean	147	149	150	152	153
Smooth pipe (including lead, brass, copper, polyethylene, and PVC), clean	147	149	150	152	153
PVC wavy, clean	142	145	147	150	150
Concrete – Scobey					
Class 1 – Cs = 0.27; clean	69	79	84	90	95
Class 2 – Cs = 0.31; clean	95	102	106	110	113
Class 3 – Cs = 0.345; clean	109	116	121	125	127
Class 4 – Cs = 0.37; clean	121	125	130	132	134
Best – Cs = 0.40; clean	129	133	138	140	141
Tate relined pipes – clean	109	116	121	125	127
Prestressed concrete pipes – clean			147	150	150

[1] D = pipe diameter, θ = downstream bend angle

Table C.6 Minor loss coefficients[1] (compiled from Walksi, 1984).

Fitting	K	Fitting	K
Pipe Entrance		90° Smooth Bend	
Bellmouth	0.03-0.05	Bend radius/D = 4	0.16–0.18
Rounded	0.12-0.25	Bend radius/D = 2	0.19–0.25
Sharp Edged	0.50	Bend radius/D = 1	0.35–0.40
Projecting	0.78		
		Mitered Bend	
Contraction – Sudden		$\theta = 15°$	0.05
$D_2/D_1 = 0.80$	0.18	$\theta = 30°$	0.10
$D_2/D_1 = 0.50$	0.37	$\theta = 45°$	0.20
$D_2/D_1 = 0.20$	0.49	$\theta = 60°$	0.35
Contraction – Conical		$\theta = 90°$	0.80
$D_2/D_1 = 0.80$	0.05		
$D_2/D_1 = 0.50$	0.07	Tee	
$D_2/D_1 = 0.20$	0.08	Line Flow	0.30–0.40
		Branch Flow	0.75–1.80
Expansion – Sudden			
$D_2/D_1 = 0.80$	0.16	Cross	
$D_2/D_1 = 0.50$	0.57	Line Flow	0.50
$D_2/D_1 = 0.20$	0.92	Branch Flow	0.75
Expansion – Conical			
$D_2/D_1 = 0.80$	0.03	45° Wye	
$D_2/D_1 = 0.50$	0.08	Line Flow	0.30
$D_2/D_1 = 0.20$	0.13	Branch Flow	0.50

Table C.7 Manning roughness values, n, for various conduit materials.

Conduit Material	Manning's n[1]
Closed conduits	
Asbestos-cement pipe	0.011–0.015
Brick	0.013–0.017
Cast iron pipe	
Cement-lined and seal coated	0.011–0.015
Concrete (monolithic)	
Smooth forms	0.012–0.014
Rough forms	0.015–0.017
Concrete pipe	0.011–0.015
Corrugated metal pipe ½ in (13 mm) × 2⅔ in (68 mm) corrugations	
Plain	0.022–0.026
Paved invert	0.018–0.022
Spun asphalt	0.011–0.015
Plastic pipe (smooth)	0.011–0.015
Polyethylene	0.009[2]
Polyvinyl chloride	0.010[2]
Vitrified clay pipe	0.011–0.015
Vitrified clay liner plates	0.013–0.017
Open channels – lined	
Asphalt	0.013–0.017
Brick	0.012–0.018
Concrete	0.011–0.020

[1] modified from American Society of Civil Engineers (1982) unless
[2] French (2001)

Bibliography

3-Waters Technical Services. 1996-2004. *Hydraulic Modeling for Improved Collection System Management Training Documents*. Salana Beach, CA.

Abbott, M. B. 1979. *Computational Hydraulics: Elements of the theory of free surface flows*. London: Pitman.

Abwassertechnische Vereinigung (ATV [Wastewater Technical Association]). 1988. *Richlinien für die Hydraulische Dimensionierung und den Leistungnachweis von Abwasserkanalen und Leitungen* (Guidelines for Hydraulic Design of Sewers). Arbeitsblatt A110 (Worksheet A110). St. Augustin, Germany: Abwassertechnische Vereinigung.

American Iron and Steel Institute (AISI). 1999. *Modern Sewer Design*. 3d ed. Washington, DC: American Iron and Steel Institute.

American Public Works Association. 2003. *Preparing Sewer Overflow Response Plans: A Guidebook for Local Governments*. Kansas City: American Public Works Association.

American Society of Civil Engineers (ASCE). 1993. Task Committee on the Definition of Criteria for Evaluation of Watershed Models of the Watershed Management Committee. Criteria for evaluation of watershed models. *Journal of Irrigation Drainage Engineering*. ASCE 119, no. 3: 429-443.

American Society of Civil Engineers (ASCE). 1930. *Design and Construction of Sanitary and Storm Sewers*. ASCE Manual 37 and WPCF MOP 9. New York: American Society of Civil Engineers.

American Society of Civil Engineers (ASCE). 1982. *Gravity Sanitary Sewer Design and Construction*. ASCE MOP 60 and WEF MOP FD-5. New York: American Society Civil Engineers and Alexandria, Virginia: Water Environment Federation.

American Society of Civil Engineers (ASCE). 1989. *Sulfide in Wastewater Collection and Treatment Systems*. ASCE MOP 69. New York: American Society of Civil Engineers.

American Society of Civil Engineers (ASCE). 1992. *Design and Construction of Urban Stormwater Management Systems*. ASCE MOP 77 (WEF MOP-FD-20). Reston, VA: American Society of Civil Engineers.

American Society of Civil Engineers (ASCE). 1992. *Pressure Pipeline Design for Water and Wastewater*. New York: American Society of Civil Engineers.

American Society of Civil Engineers. 2004. *Sanitary sewer overflow solutions*. Washington, DC: US Environmental Protection Agency. www.epa.gov/npds/pubs/sso_solutions_final_report.pdf.

American Water Works Association (AWWA). 2003. *Sizing Water Service Lines and Meters*. 2d ed. AWWA Manual M-22. Denver, CO: American Water Works Association.

Anderson E. A. 1976. *A Point Energy and Mass Balance Model of Snow Cover*. Report NWS 19. Washington, DC: US Department of Commerce.

Arbour, R. and K. Kerri. 1998. *Collection Systems: Methods for Evaluating and Improving Performance*. US EPA Grant No. CX924908-01-0. Sacramento, CA: California State University.

Argaman, Y., U. Shamir, and E. Spivak. 1973. Design of optimal sewerage systems. *Journal of Environmental Engineering Division*, ASCE 99, EE6, 703.

Arnell, V. 1982. *Rainfall Data for the Design of Sewer Pipe Systems*. Report Series A: 8. Göteborg, Sweden: Chalmers University of Technology, Dept. of Hydraulics.

Ashley, R., B. Crabtree, A. Fraser, and T. Hvitved-Jacobsen. 2003. European Research into sewer sediments and associated pollutants and processes. *Journal of Hydraulic Engineering* 129, no. 4: 267.

Associação Brasileira de Normas Técnicas (ABNT). 1986. Projeto de redes coletoras de esgoto sanitario. *Brazilian Design Standard 9649/1986*. Rio de Janeiro, Brazil: Associação Brasileira de Normas Técnicas.

Association of Metropolitan Sewerage Agencies (AMSA). 1996. *Performance Measures for the National CSO Control Program*. Washington, DC: Association of Metropolitan Sewerage Agencies.

Babbitt, H. E. 1953. *Sewerage and Sewage Treatment*. 7th ed. New York: John Wiley and Sons.

Babbitt, H.E., and E. R. Bauman. 1958. *Sewerage and Sewage Treatment*. 8th ed. New York: John Wiley & Sons.

Bachus, L. 2004. The mechanical seal game. *World Pumps*, no. 449: 38.

Barlow, J. F. 1972. Cost optimization of pipe sewerage systems. *Proceedings of the Institution of Civil Engineers* (London), no. 2: 57.

Barnes, D., P. J. Bliss, B. W. Gould, and H. R. Valentine. 1981. *Water and Wastewater Engineering Systems*. London: Pitman.

Bechman, G. 1905. *Hydrologique agricole et urbaine* (*Agricultural and Urban Hydraulics*). Paris: Belanger.

Bennett, D., R. Rowe, M. Strum, D. Wood, N. Schultz, K. Roach, M. Spence, and V. Adderly. 1999. *Using Flow Prediction Technologies to Control Sanitary Sewer Overflows*. Alexandria, VA: Water Environment Research Foundation.

Bennett, E., K. Linstedt, and J. Felton. 1974. Rural home wastewater characteristics. *Proceedings of the National Home Sewage Symposium*. American Society of Agricultural Engineers.

Betamio de Almendia, A., and E. Koelle. 1992. *Fluid Transients in Pipe Networks*. London: Elsevier Applied Science.

Bos, M. G., ed. 1989. *Discharge Measurement Structures*. 3d ed. Wageningen, The Netherlands: International Institute for Land Reclamation (ILLR).

Bosch, D. D., and F. M. Davis. 1999. *Rainfall Variability and Spatial Patterns for the Southeast*. Tifton, GA: Southeast Watershed Research laboratory, United States Department of Agriculture - Agricultural Research Service. http://www.cpes.peachnet.edu/sewrl/Papers/Paper001.PDF. (Accessed 5/04).

Brown and Caldwell Consulting Engineers. 1984. *Residential Water Conservation Projects – Summary Report*. Washington, DC: US Department of Housing and Urban Development.

Brown, S. A., S. M. Stein, and J. C. Warner. 2001. *Urban Drainage Manual.* Hydraulic Engineering Circular 22, 2nd ed. Washington, DC: Federal Highway Administration.

Buchberger, S. G. and L. Wu. 1995. A model for instantaneous residential water demands. *Journal of Hydraulic Engineering* 121, no. 3: 232.

Buchberger, S. G., and G. J. Wells. 1996. Intensity, duration and frequency of residential water demands. *Journal of Water Resources Planning and Management* 122, no. 1: 11.

Bureau of Reclamation. 2001. *Water Measurement Manual, A Water Resources Technical Publication.* Washington, DC: United States Department of the Interior, Bureau of Reclamation.

Burton, G. A. and R. E. Pitt. 2002. *Stormwater Effects Handbook A Toolbox for Watershed Managers, Scientists, and Engineers.* Boca Raton, FL: Lewis Publishers.

Butler D., R. W. P. May, and J. C. Ackers. 1996. Sediment transport in sewers Part 2: Design. *Proceedings of the Institution of Civil Engineers: Water, Maritime & Energy* 118: 113–120.

Butler D., R. W. P. May, and J. C. Ackers. 2003. Self-cleansing sewer design based on sediment transport principles. *Journal of Hydraulic Engineering* 129, 4: 276–282.

Camp, T. R. 1940. Discussion – Determination of Kutter's *n* for sewers partially filled. *Transactions of the American Society of Civil Engineers.* 109: 240–247.

Camp, T. R. 1946. Design of sewers to facilitate flow. *Sewerage Works Journal* 18, no. 3.

Carcich, I. G., L. J. Hetling, and R. P. Farrell. 1972. *Pressure Sewer Demonstration.* US EPA, R2-72-091. Washington, DC: US Environmental Protection Agency.

Cave, K., E. Harold, and T. Quasebarth. 1996. *Preliminary Pollution Loading Projections for Rouge River Watershed and Interim Nonpoint Source Pollution Control Plan,* RPO-NPS-TR07.00. Detroit, MI: Rouge River National Wet Weather Demonstration Program

Cembrowicz, P. G., and G. E. Krauter. 1987. Design of cost optimal sewer networks. *Proceedings of the Fourth International Conference on Urban Storm Drainage.* Lausanne, Switzerland, 367–72.

Chaudhry, M. H. 1987. *Applied Hydraulic Transients.* New York: Van Nostrand Reinhold.

Chaudhry, M. H. 1993. *Open-Channel Flow.* New York: Prentice-Hall.

Chernin, P. R., and T. LeRoux. 1999. Understanding the basics of GIS: scale, accuracy and cost. *Public Works,* May.

Chow, V. T. 1964. *Handbook of Applied Hydrology.* New York: McGraw-Hill.

Chow, V. T. 1973. *Open Channel Hydraulics.* New York: McGraw Hill.

Chow, V. T., D. R. Maidment, and L. W. Mays. 1988. *Applied Hydrology.* New York: McGraw-Hill.

Clift, M. A. 1968. Experiences with pressure sewage. *ASCE Sanitary Engineering Division* 94, no. 5: 865. Alexandria, VA: American Society of Civil Engineers.

Coleman, S. E., J. J. Fedele, and M. H. Garcia. 2003. Closed conduit bed-form initiation and development. *Journal of Hydraulic Engineering* 129, 856.

Comité Européen de Normalisation (CEN). 1996. *Pressure Sewer Systems, Outside Buildings.* EN 1671. Brussels: Comité Européen de Normalisation.

Commission of the European Communities (COM). 1997. Proposal for a Council Directive Establishing a Framework for Community Action in the Field of Water Policy (COM (97) 49 final). *Official Journal* C184, (17 June).

Commission of the European Communities (COM). 1999. Water Quality in the European Union. Implementation of the Council Directive 91/271/EEC of 21 May 1991 concerning urban wastewater treatment, as amended by Commission Directive 98/15/EC of 27 February 1998. European Commission Directorate Environment. http://europe.eu.int/water/water-urbanwaste/report/chapter6.html.

Copeland, C. 1999. "Clean Water Act: A Summary of the Law." CRS Issue Brief for Congress. RL 30030.

Council of the European Communities (CEC). 1976. Directive on the approximation of the laws, regulations and administrative provisions of the Member States relating to restrictions on the marketing and use of certain dangerous substances and preparations (76/769/EC). *Official Journal* L262, 27 (September).

Council of the European Communities (CEC). 1982. Directive relating to the testing the biodegradability of nonionic surfactants and amending Directive (82/242/EEC). *Official Journal* L109 (22 April).

Council of the European Communities (CEC). 1991. Directive concerning urban waste water treatment (91/271/EEC). *Official Journal* L135 (30 May).

Council of the European Communities (CEC). 1996. Directive on Integrated Pollution Prevention and Control (96/61/EC). *Official Journal* L257 (10 October).

Council of the European Communities (CEC). 1999. Common Position (EC) No 41/1999 adopted by the Council, 22 October 1999, with a view to the adoption of a Directive 1999/../EC of the European Parliament and of the Council establishing a Framework for Community Action in the field of water policy (1999/C 343/01). *Official Journal* C 343 (30 November).

Cowen, D. J. 1997. Discrete georeferencing. *NGCIA Core Curriculum on GIS Project*. http://www.ncgia.ucsb.edu/giscc/units/u016/u016.html (accessed 5/04).

Crites, R., and G. Tchobanoglous. 1998. *Small and Decentralized Wastewater Treatment Systems*. New York: McGraw-Hill.

Cunge, J. A. 1969. On the subject of a flood propagation computation method (Muskingum method). *Journal of Hydraulic Research* 7, no. 2: 205–230.

Cunge, J. A., F. M. Holley, and A. Verwey. 1980. *Practical Aspects of Computational River Hydraulics*. London: Pitman.

Dajani, J. S., and Y. Hasit. 1974. Capital cost minimum drainage networks. *Journal of Environmental Engineering Division,* ASCE 100, EE2, 325.

Dawdy, D. R., J. C. Schaake, and W. M. Alley. 1978. *Distributed Routing Runoff Models*. US Geological Survey Water Resources Investigation Report. 78-90. Reston, VA: US Geological Survey.

Day, T. J. 2000. *Sewer Management Systems*. New York: John Wiley & Sons.

Deagle, G., and S. Ancel. 2002. Development and maintenance of hydraulic models. *Proceedings of the AWWA Information Technology Conference*. Kansas City, MO: American Water Works Association.

Deb, A. K. 1974. Least cost design of branched pipe network system. *Journal of Environmental Engineering Division,* ASCE 100, EE4, 821.

Delleur, J. W. 2001. Sediment movement in drainage systems. In *Stormwater Collection Systems Handbook*, edited by L. W. Mays. New York: McGraw-Hill.

Delluer, J. W. 2003. The evolution of urban hydrology: Past, present and future. *Journal of Hydraulic Engineering* 129, no. 8: 563–573.

Dent, S., L. Wright, C. Mosley, and V. Housen. 2000. Continuous simulations vs. design storms comparison with wet weather flow prediction methods. From conference *Collection Systems Wet Weather Pollution Control*. Rochester, NY. Alexandria, VA: Water Environment Research Foundation.

DeSutter, R., P. Rushford, S. J. Tait, M. Huygens, R. Verhovern, and A. J. Saul. 2003. Validation of existing bed load transport formulas using in-sewer sediment. *Journal of Hydraulic Engineering* 129, 325.

Diogo, A. F., G. A. Walter, E. R. de Sousa, and V. M. Graveto. 2000. Three-dimensional optimization of urban drainage systems. *Computer-Aided Civil and Infrastructure Engineering* 15, 409–426.

e/one. 2000. *Low Pressure Sewer Systems Using Environment One Grinder Pumps*. Niskayuna, NY: e/one Corporation.

e/one. 2001. *Specifications for GP 2010*. Niskayuna, NY: e/one Corporation.

Ecenbarger, W. 1993. Flushed with success. *Chicago Tribune*, 4 April.

Elimam, A. A., C. Charalambous, and F. H. Ghobrial. 1989. Optimum design of large sewer networks. *Journal of Environmental Engineering* 115, no. 6: 1171.

Environment Canada. 2004. *Combined Sewer Overflow Treatment Technologies Manual, draft*. Ottawa, Canada.

ESRI (series). 1984-2004. *ESRI Map Book: Applications of Geographic Information Systems*. Redlands, CA: ESRI Press.

ESRI. 2001. *Dictionary of GIS Terminology*. Redlands, CA: ESRI Press.

Fair, G. M., and J. C. Geyer. 1954. *Water Supply and Wastewater Disposal*. New York: John Wiley & Sons.

Farrell, R. P., and G. G. Darrah. 1994. Pressure sewers – A proven alternative solution for a variety of small community sewage disposal challenges. *International Symposium of Individual and Small Community Sewage Systems*. Atlanta, GA: American Society of Agricultural Engineers.

Federal Water Pollution Control Act [commonly referred to as Clean Water Act], Public Law 92-500, October 18, 1972, 86 Stat. 816; 33 *US Code* 1251 et seq. Amended by PL 100-4, February 4, 1987.

Feuss, J. V., R. P. Farrell. and P. W. Rynkiewicz. 1994. A small community success story. *The Small Flows Journal* 1, no. 1: 11.

Field, R., and T. P. O'Connor. 1997. Control strategy for storm-generating sanitary sewer overflows. *Journal of Environmental Engineering*. 12391: 41.

Field, R., D. Sullivan, and A. N. Tafuri. 2004. *Management of Combined Sewer Overflows*. Boca Raton, FL: Lewis Publishers.

Flanigan, L. J., and C. A. Cadmik. 1979. Pressure sewer system design. *Water and Sewage Works* April: R25.

Foil, J., J. Cerwick, and J. White. 1999 Where we've been—wastewater collection. *Missouri Water Environment Association Newsletter* (Fall).

French, R. H. 1985. *Open Channel Hydraulics*. New York: McGraw-Hill.

Frühling, A. 1910. Die entwasserung der stadte (Drainage of Cities). In *Handbuch der Ingenieurwissenschauften* (*Handbook of Engineering Studies*). Leipzig: Englemann.

Gayman, M. 1996. A glimpse into London's early sewers. *Cleaner*, March.

Geyer, J. C., and J. L. Lentz. 1964. *An Evaluation of the Problems of Sanitary Sewer System Design*. Baltimore, MD: The Johns Hopkins University Press.

Gifft, H. M. 1945. Estimating variations in domestic sewage. *Waterworks and Sewage* 92: 175.

Gill, E., M. A. Parker, D. A. Savic, and G. A. Walters. 2001. Cougar: A genetic algorithm and rapid integrated catchment modeling application for optimizing capital investment in combined sewer systems. *World Water & Environmental Resources Congress* (Orlando, Florida).

Gill, M. A. 1987. Hydraulics of partially filled egg shaped sewers. *Journal of Environmental Engineering* 113, no. 2: 407–425.

Governmental Accounting Standards Board (GASB). 1999. *Governmental Accounting Standards Board Statement No. 34, Basic Financial Statements—and Management's Discussion for Analysis—for State and Local Government*. Norwalk, CT.

Grant, D. M. 1989. *ISCO Open Channel Flow Measurement Handbook*. Lincoln, NB: ISCO Environmental Division.

Great Lakes and Upper Mississippi River Board of State Public Health and Environmental Managers (GLUMRB). 1997. *Recommended Standards for Wastewater Facilities*. Albany, NY: Health Research, Inc.

Greene, R., N. Agbenowosi, and G. V. Loganathan. 1999. GIS-based approach to sewer system design. *Journal of Surveying Engineering* 125, no. 1: 36–57.

Haestad Methods, and S. R. Durrans. 2003. *Stormwater Conveyance Modeling and Design*. Waterbury, CT: Haestad Press.

Haestad Methods, G. Dyhouse, J. Hatchett, and J. Benn. 2003. *Floodplain Modeling Using HEC-RAS*. Waterbury, CT: Haestad Press.

Haestad Methods, T. M. Walski, D. V. Chase, D. A. Savic, W. Grayman, S. Beckwith, and E. Koelle. 2003. *Advanced Water Distribution Modeling and Management*. Waterbury, CT: Haestad Press.

Haestad Methods. 2001. *SewerCAD Sanitary Sewer Modeling Software*. Waterbury, CT: Haestad Methods.

Haestad Methods. 2000. *StormCAD User's Guide*. Waterbury, CT: Haestad Methods.

Haestad Methods, Walski, T. M., D. V. Chase, and D. A. Savic. 2001. *Water Distribution Modeling*. Waterbury, CT: Haestad Press.

Haestad Methods. 2003. *HAMMER Transient Analysis Model*. Waterbury, CT: Haestad Methods.

Haestad Methods. 2003. *WaterGEMS Geospatial Water Distribution Modeling*. Waterbury, CT: Haestad Methods.

Hager, W. H. 1994 (English edition 1999). *Wastewater Hydraulics*. Berlin: Springer.

Hager, W. H. 1998. Minimalgeschwindigkeit und sedimenttransport in kanalisationen (Minimum velocity and sediment transport in sewers). *Korrespondenz Abwasser* (*Wastewater Correspondence*) 36, no.1: 29.

Hager, W. H. 1999. *Wastewater Hydraulics: Theory and Practice*. Berlin: Springer.

Hammer, M. J., and M. J. Hammer, Jr. 2001. *Water and Wastewater Technology*, 4th ed. Upper Saddle River, NJ: Prentice-Hall.

Harmon, W. G. 1918. Forecasting sewage treatment at Toledo under dry weather conditions. *Engineering News Record* 80: 1233.

Harold, E. M. 2001. "System evaluation and capacity assurance." *Ecoletter* (Water and Waste Operators Association of Maryland, Delaware and the District of Columbia; and the Chesapeake Water Environment Association), Summer 2001.

Hathaway, G. A. 1945. Design of drainage facilities. *Transactions, American Society of Civil Engineers* 110: 697–730.

Heaney, J. P., W. C. Huber, and S. J. Nix. 1976. *Stormwater Management Model, Level I, Preliminary Screening Procedures*. EPA 600/2-76-275. Cincinnati, OH: US Environmental Protection Agency.

Horton, R. 1933. Separate roughness coefficients for channel bottom and sides. *Engineering News-Record* 111, no. 22: 652–653.

Horton, R. 1939. Analysis of runoff plot experiments with varying infiltration capacity." *Transactions, American Geophysical Union* 20: 693–711.

HR Wallingford. 1998. *The Wallingford Procedure: Volume 2 – Practical Application of the Wallingford Procedure*. Wallingford, England: HR Wallingford.

HR Wallingford. 2001. *HydroWorks, v7.0* (Build 42). Wallingford, England: HR Wallingford.

Huber, W. C., and R. E. Dickinson, 1988. *Storm Water Management Model* Version 4: *User's Manual*. Athens, GA: US Environmental Protection Agency

Huff, F. A. 1967. Time distribution of rainfall in heavy storms. *Water Resources Research* 3, no. 4: 1007–1019.

Huff, F. A. and J. R. Angel. 1992. *Rainfall Frequency Atlas of the Midwest*. Bulletin 71. Champaign, IL: Illinois State Water Survey.

Hunter, R. B. 1940. *Methods of Estimating Loads in Plumbing Systems*. Report BMS 65. Washington, DC: National Bureau of Standards.

Hydraulic Institute. 2000. *Hydraulic Institute Standards*. Parsippany, NJ: Hydraulic Institute.

Hydraulic Institute. 2000. *Pump Standards*. Parsippany, NJ: Hydraulic Institute.

Hydraulic Institute. 2001. *Pump Life Cycle Costs: A Guide to LCC Analysis for Pumping Systems*. Parsippany, NJ: Hydraulic Institute.

Hydrologic Engineering Center (HEC). 1990. *HEC-1 Flood Hydrograph Package*. Davis, CA: US Army Corps of Engineers, Hydrologic Engineering Center.

Hydromatic Pumps. 2001. *Pressure Sewer Manual and Engineering Guide*. Ashland, OH: Hydromatic Pumps.

Imhoff, K. 1907. *Tashenbuch der Stadtentwasserung* (*Pocket Guide for City Drainage*). Berlin: Oldenburg.

International Association of Plumbing and Mechanical Officials. 1997. *Uniform Plumbing Code*. Los Angeles: CA. International Association of Plumbing and Mechanical Officials.

Jacquet, C., E. Piatyszek, and S. Lyard. 2002. "Radar-based rainfall input requirements synthesis of US and French 10 years experience." In *Proceedings of the Ninth International Conference on Urban Drainage*. Reston, VA: American Society of Civil Engineers.

Jakovlev, S. V., J. A. A. Karlem, A. I. Zukov, and K. Siki. 1975. *Kanalizacja*. Moscow: Stroizdat.

James, W., ed. 2002. *Best Modeling Practices for Urban Water Systems*. Monograph 10. Guelph, ON: CHI Publications.

Jewell, T. K., T. J. Nunno, and D. D. Adrian. 1978. Methodology for calibrating sewer models. *J. Environmental Engineering* 104: 485.

Johnstone, D., and W. P. Cross. 1949. *Elements of Applied Hydrology*. New York: Ronald Press.

Jones, E. 1974. Domestic water use in individual homes and hydraulic loading and discharge from septic tanks. *Proceedings of National Home Sewage Symposium*, American Society of Agricultural Engineers.

Karassik, I. J., J. P. Messina, P. Cooper, and C. C Heald, eds. 2000. *Pump Handbook*, 3d ed. New York: McGraw-Hill.

Kibler, D. F., ed. 1982. *Urban Stormwater Hydrology (Water Resources Monograph)*. Washington, DC: American Geophysical Union.

Kilpatrick, F. A and E. D. Cobb. 1985. "Measurement of discharge using tracers." In *Techniques of Water-Resources Investigations of the United States Geological Survey*, Book 3, Chapter A16. Washington, DC: US Government Printing Office.

Knight, D. W. and M. Sterling. 2000. Boundary shear in circular pipes running partly full. *Journal of Hydraulic Engineering* 126, no. 4: 263.

Kuichling, E. 1889. The relation between rainfall and the discharge in sewers in populous districts. *Transactions of the American Society of Civil Engineering* 20, no. 1.

Lamont, P. 1981. Common pipe flow formulas compared with the theory of roughness. *Journal of the American Water Works Association* 73, No. 5: 274.

Landrum, T. B. 2001. Enterprise GIS—building a strong foundation. Geospatial Information and Technology Association Annual Conference, San Diego, CA.

Langford, R. E. 1977. Effluent pressure sewer systems. *Proceedings of WPCF Annual Conference*.

Liebman, J. C. 1967. A heuristic aid for the design of sewer networks. *Journal of Sanitary Engineering Division,* ASCE 93, SA 4, 81.

Linsley, R. K. Jr., M. A. Kohler, and J. L. Paulhus. 1982. *Hydrology for Engineers.* 3d ed. New York: McGraw-Hill.

Lui, G., and R. G. S. Matthew. 1990. New approach for optimization of urban drainage systems. *Journal of Environmental Engineering* 116, no. 5: 927.

Lukas, A., M. S. Merrill, R. Palmer, and N. Van Rheenan. 2001. Search of Valid I/I Removal Data: The Holy Grail of Sewer Rehab? *Conference Proceedings, Water Environment Federation 74th Annual Conference and Exposition*. Alexandria, VA. Water Environment Foundation.

Mackay, R. C. 2004. ANSI vs. API? *Pumps and Systems* 12, no. 3: 36.

Macke, E. 1983. Bemenssung ablagerungsfier stromungszustande in kanalisaationsleitungen (Design flows with no deposits in sewers). *Korrespondenz Abwasser (Wastewater Correspondence)* 30, no. 7: 462.

Maidment, D. R. 1993. *Handbook of Hydrology*. New York. McGraw-Hill.

Mara, D., A. Sleigh, and K. Talyor. 2000. *PC-Based Simplified Sewer Design*. http://www.efm.leeds.ac.uk/CIVE/Sewerage/sewerage_index.html (accessed May 13, 2004).

Marx. 1990. The TIGER system: yesterday, today and tomorrow. *Cartography and GIS* 17. no. 1: 89-97.

Matheussen, B. R., and S. T. Thorolfsson. 2001. Urban snow surveys in Risvollan-Norway. In *Urban Drainage Modeling*, Proceedings of the Specialty Symposium of the World and Water Environmental Resources Conference. Alexandria, VA: American Society of Civil Engineers.

May, D. K. 1986. *A Study of Manning's coefficient for commercial concrete and plastic pipes.* Edmonton, Alberta, Canada: T. Bench Hydraulics Laboratory, University of Alberta.

May, R. W. P. 2003. Preventing sediment deposition in inverted sewer siphon. *Journal of Hydraulic Engineering* 129, no. 4: 283

May, R. W. P. 1994. Transport of sediment in sewers: Application to design of self-cleansing sewers. *European Water Pollution Control* 4, no. 5: 57–64.

Mayer, P. W., W. B. DeOreo, E. M. Opitz, J. C. Kiefer, W. Y. Davis, B. Dziegielewski, and J. O. Nelson. 1999. *Residential End Uses of Water.* Denver, CO: American Water Works Association Research Foundation.

Mays, L. W. 1975. Optimal layout and design of storm sewer systems. Ph.D. Diss., University of Illinois, Urbana.

Mays, L. W. ed., 1996. *Water Resources Handbook.* New York: McGraw-Hill.

Mays, L. W. , ed. 2000. *Water Distribution Systems Handbook.* New York: McGraw-Hill.

Mays, L. W. 2001. *Stormwater Collection Systems Design Handbook.* New York: McGraw-Hill.

Mays, L. W. 2001. *Water Resources Engineering.* New York: John Wiley & Sons.

Mays, L. W. ed. 1999. *Hydraulic Design Handbook.* New York: McGraw-Hill.

Mays, L. W., and B. C. Yen. 1975. Optimal cost design of branched sewer systems. *Water Resources Research* 11, no. 1: 37-47.

Meeneghan, T. J., M. D. Loehlein, R. E., Dickinson, R. D. Myers, and T. Prevost. 2002. "Impacts of rainfall data on model refinements in the greater Pittsburgh area." In *Proceedings of the Ninth International Conference on Urban Drainage.* Reston, VA: American Society of Civil Engineers.

Meredith, D. D., 1971. Dynamic programming with case study on planning and design of urban water facilities. In *Treatise on Urban Water Systems.* Colorado State University.

Merritt, L. B. 1998. Sewage generation rates and peaking factors in central Utah. Brigham Young University. Provo, Utah: Unpublished paper presented at the 1998 Water Environment Association of Utah annual conference.

Merritt, L. B. 1999. Obstacles to lower cost sewer systems. Sewer Design Paper #99-1. Provo, UT: Civil and Environmental Engineering Department, Brigham Young University.

Merritt, L. B. 2000. Example cost sensitivity curves from case studies. In *Proceedings of WEAU Annual Conference.* Salt Lake City, UT: Water Environment Association of Utah.

Merritt, L. B., and R. H. Bogan. 1973. Computer-based optimal design of sewer systems." *Journal of Environmental Division,* ASCE 99, EE1, Proc. Paper 9578.

Metcalf & Eddy, Inc. 1972. *Wastewater Engineering.* New York: McGraw-Hill.

Metcalf & Eddy, Inc. 1981. *Wastewater Engineering: Collection and Pumping of Wastewater.* ed. by G. Tchobanoglous. New York: McGraw Hill.

Metcalf, L., and H. Eddy. 1914. *American Sewerage Practice.*

Milne, I., B. Crabtree, S. Clarke, C. Wennberg, and J. Larson. 1997. *Best Management Practices for the Regulation of Passive Urban Wastewater.* Technology Validation Project IN10187D. Medmenham Marlow, UK: WrC.

Miralles, F., S. W. Miles, and A. I. Perez. 2001. A methodology for the evaluation and design of improvements in wet weather sanitary sewer system in the municipality of Luquillo, Puerto Rico: A pilot case study. *WEFTEC Latin America 2001.* Alexandria, VA: Water Environment Federation.

Mockus, V. 1969. Hydrologic soil-cover complexes. *National Engineering Handbook*, Section 4: Hydrology: Chapter 9. Washington, DC: US Soil Conservation Service.

Moffa, P. E. 1997. *The Control and Treatment of Combined Sewer Overflows.* 2d ed. New York: Van Nostrand Reinhold.

Montgomery Watson. 1998. *City of Baton Rouge/Parish of East Baton Rouge Sanitary Sewer Overflow (SSO) Corrective Action Plan.* Baton Rouge, LA: Montgomery Watson.

Moody, L. F. 1944. Friction factors for pipe flow. *Transactions of the American Society of Mechanical Engineers* 66.

Moody, N. R. 2001. Water Environment Federation Collection Systems Technical Discussion. Group posting, October 2.

Mulvaney, T. J. 1851. On the use of self-registering rain and flood gauges in making observations of the relation of rainfall and of flood discharges in a given catchment. *Transactions of the Institute for Civil Engineers, Ireland* 4, Part 2: 18.

Municipal Engineers Association. 2000. *Municipal Class EA (replaces Class EA for Municipal Road Projects and Water and Wastewater Projects).* Mississagua, ON, Canada: Municipal Engineers Association.

National Oceanic and Atmospheric Agency, National Weather Service. 2000. FLDWAV Computer Program, Version 2-0-0.

Natural Resources Conservation Service (NRCS). 1997. *National Engineering Handbook.* Washington, DC: US Department of Agriculture. http://www.info.usda.gov/CED/ (accessed 6/16/04).

Nelson, R. E., A. Habibian and H. O. Andrews. 2000. *Protocols for Identifying Sanitary Sewer Overflows.* ASCE/EPA Cooperative Agreement CX 826097-01-0. Reston, VA: American Society of Civil Engineers.

Nelson, R.E. 1987. Sanitary sewer modeling. Paper presented at the *37th Kansas University Environmental Engineering Conference.* Lawrence, KS: Kansas University.

Nix, S. J. 1994. *Urban Stormwater Modeling and Simulation.* Boca Raton, FL: CRC Press.

Norman, J. M., R. J. Houghtalen, and W. J. Johnston. 2001. *Hydraulic Design of Highway Culverts.* McLean, VA: Federal Highway Administration.

Novotny, V., K. R. Imhoff, M. Olthof, and P. A. Krenkel. 1989. *Karl Imhoff's Handbook of Urban Drainage and Wastewater Disposal.* New York: John Wiley & Sons.

Ohlemutz, R. and M. Walkowiak. 2002. A case study at Vallejo Sanitation and Flood Control District: A methodology for assessing the effectiveness of sanitary sewer rehabilitation on reducing infiltration and inflow. In *Pipelines 2002: Proceedings of the Pipeline Division Specialty Conference*. Reston, VA: American Society of Civil Engineers.

Ontario Ministry of the Environment. 1985. *Guidelines for the Design of Sanitary Sewage Systems*. Prepared by the Environmental Approvals and Project Engineering Branch of the Ministry of the Environment.

Ontario Ministry of the Environment. 1997. *Ontario CSO Control Procedure F-5-5*. Toronto, Canada.

Ormsbee, L. E. and S. Lingireddy. 1997. Calibrating hydraulic network models. *Journal of the American Water Works Association* 89, no. 2: 44.

Orne, W., R. Hammond, and S. Cattran. 2001. Building better water models. *Public Works*, October.

Ota, J. J., and C. Nalluri. 2003. Urban storm sewer design: Approach in consideration of sediments. *Journal of Hydraulic Engineering* 129, 291.

Parker, M. A., D. A. Savic, G. A. Walter, and Z. Kappelan. 2000. SewerNet: A genetic algorithm application for optimizing urban drainage systems. *International Conference on Urban Drainage*.

Percival, R.C. and D.C. Alevizatos. 1997. *Law and the Environment: A Multidisciplinary Reader*. Philadelphia, PA: Temple University Press.

Pilgrim, D. H., and I. Cordery. 1975. Rainfall temporal patterns for design floods. *Journal of the Hydraulic Division, American Society of Civil Engineers* 101, no. HY1: 81–95.

Pisano, W. C., O. C. O'Riordan, F. J. Ayotte, J. R. Barsanti, and D. L. Carr. 2003. Automated sewer and drainage flushing in Cambridge, Massachusetts. *Journal of Hydraulic Engineering* 129, no. 4: 260

Pomeroy, R. D. 1974. *Process Design Manual for Sulfide Control in Sanitary Sewerage Systems*. EPA 625/1-7-005, US Environmental Protection Agency.

Ponce, V. M. 1986. Diffusion wave modeling of catchment dynamics. *Journal of the Hydraulics Division*, ASCE 112, no. 8: 716–727.

Ponce, V. M., R. M. Li, and D. B. Simons. 1978. Applicability of kinematic and diffusion models." *Journal of the Hydraulic Division*, ASCE 104, no. HY12: 1663.

Preissmann, A. 1960. *Propogation des intumescenes dans les canaue et rivieres*. Grenoble: First Congress de L'Association Francaise de Calcul.

Price, R. K. 1973. A comparison of four numerical methods for flood routing. *Journal of the Hydraulics Division*, ASCE 100, no. 7: 879–899.

Przybyla, J. 2002. What stops folks cold from pursuing GIS. *Public Works*, April.

Quebec. 2002. *Water. Our Life. Our Future. Quebec Water Policy*. Envirodoq ENV/2002/0310A. Bibliotecheque national du Quebec.

Random House. 1970. American College Dictionary, edited by C. P. Barnhart. New York: Random House.

Rantz, R. E. 1982. *Measurement and Computation of Stream Flow*. Vol. 1: *Measurement of Stage and Discharge*; Vol. 2: *Computation of Discharge*. US Geological Survey Water Supply Paper 2175. Reston, VA: US Geological Survey.

Raths, C. H., and R. R. McCauley. 1962. Deposition in a sanitary sewer. *Water & Sewage Works* (May): 192–197.

Rawls, W. J., L. R. Ahuja, D. L. Brackensiek, and A. Shirmohammadi. 1993. Infiltration and soil water movement. Chapter 5 *Handbook of Hydrology*. D. R. Maidment, ed. New York: McGraw-Hill.

Read, G. F., and I. G. Vickridge. 1997. *Sewers – Rehabilitation and New Construction*. London: Arnold.

Reid, D. 1991. *Paris Sewers and Sewermen: Realities and Representations*. Cambridge, MA: Harvard University Press

Reyburn, W. 1971. *Flushed with Pride: The Story of Thomas Crapper*. Englewood Cliffs, NJ: Prentice-Hall.

Rezak, J. W. and I. A. Cooper. 1985. *Investigations of Existing Pressure Sewer Systems*. EPA/600/2-85/051.Washington, DC: Environmental Protection Agency.

Roesner, L. A., and E. H. Burgess. 1992. The role of computer modeling in combined sewer overflow abatement planning. In *Proceedings of the Symposium on Water Resources and River Basin Management of the International Association on Water Pollution Research and Control* (16th Biennial Conference and Exposition). Washington, DC: International Association on Water Pollution Research and Control.

Roesner, L. A., J. A. Aldrich, and R. E. Dickinson. 1989. *Storm Water Management Model User's Manual Version 4: Extra Addendum*. EPA 600/3-88/001b. US Environmental Protection Agency.

Rogers, J. R., A. J. Fredrich, and Environmental and Water Resources Institute, eds. 2002. *Environmental and Water Resources History*. Reston, VA: American Society of Civil Engineers.

Rouse, H., and S. Ince. 1957. *History of Hydraulics*. Iowa Institute of Hydraulic Research.

Rushforth, P. J., S. J. Tait, and A. J. Saul. 2003. Modeling the erosion of mixtures of organic and granular in-sewer sediments. *Journal of Hydraulic Engineering* 129, 308.

Salvato, J. A. 1992. *Environmental Engineering and Sanitation*. 4th ed. New York: Wiley Interscience Publishers.

Samani, H. M. V. and S. Jebelifard. 2003. Design of circular urban storm sewer systems using multilinear Muskingum flow routing methods. *Journal of Hydraulic Engineering* 129, vol. 11: 832.

Sander, T. 1994. Zur dimensionierung von ablagerungsfreien abwasserkanalen unter besonderer berücksichtigung von neuen erkenntnissen zum sedimentations – varhalten (The design of sewers with no deposits with particular attention to new results relative to sedimentation). *Korrespondenz Abwasser (Wastewater Correspondence)* 37, no. 6: 689.

Sanks, R. L., ed. 1998. *Pumping Station Design*. 2d ed. London: Butterworth.

Saul, A. J., P. J. Skipworth, S. J. Tait, and P. J. Rushforth. 2003. Modeling total suspended solids in combined sewers. *Journal of Hydraulic Engineering* 129, 298.

Savic, D. A., and G. A. Walters. 2001. Evolutionary computing in water distribution and wastewater systems. *World Water and Environmental Resources Congress* (Orlando, Florida).

Schaake, J. C. Jr., J. C. Geyer, and J. W. Knapp. 1967. Experimental examination of the rational method. *Journal of the Hydraulics Division, American Society of Civil Engineers* 93, No. HY6.

Schatzlein, M. and J. Dieterlein. 2002. Finding Needles in a Haystack: IWC's Experience Optimizing Integration with Hydraulic Models. Kansas City, Missouri: *AWWA IMTech*.

Schmidt, O. J. 1959. Measurements of Manning's coefficient. *Sewage and Industrial Wastes* 31, no. 9: 995.

Schultz, N. U., D. M. Wood, V. Adderly, and D. Bennett. 2001. RDI/I quantification research results. Helsingør, Denmark: 4th DHI Software Conference. http://www.dhisoftware.com/uc2001/Abstracts_Proceedigs/Proceedings/Conference_Proceedings.htm (accessed 6/16/04).

Semadeni-Davies, A. 2000. Representation of snow in urban drainage models. *Journal of Hydrologic Engineering* 5, No. 4: 363–370.

Shamsi, U. M. 2001. GIS and modeling integration. *CE News* 13, no. 6.

Shamsi, U. M. 2002. *GIS Tools for Water, Wastewater and Stormwater Systems*. Alexandria, VA: American Society of Civil Engineers Press.

Sherman, L. K. 1932. Stream flow from rainfall by the unit graph method. *Engineering News Record*. No. 108: 501.

Shields, A. 1936. Anwndung der aehnlichkeitsmechanik und der turbulenz forschung auf die geschiebebeweung (Application of Similarity Mechanics and Turbulence Research upon Bedload Movement). *Mitteilungen der Preussischen Versunchsanstalt fur Wasserbau und Schiffbau* (Prussian Research Institute for Hydraulic Engineering and Shipbuilding) 26.

Sinak, D. 2002. "O&M capacity assurance: Case studies in flow data." In *Pipelines 2002: Proceedings of the Pipeline Division Specialty Conference*. Reston, VA: American Society of Civil Engineers.

Sirapyan, N. 2001. A history of personal computing. *PC Magazine* 20, No. 15.

Smith, J. A. 1993. "Precipitation." In *Handbook of Hydrology*, ed. by D. R. Maidment. New York: McGraw-Hill.

Snider, D. 1972. Hydrographs. *Hydrology*, National Engineering Handbook, Section 4. Washington, DC: US Soil Conservation Service.

Snyder, W. M. 1955. Hydrograph analysis by method of least squares. *Proceedings of American Society of Civil Engineers*. No. 81: 73

Speer, E., R. Swarner, Z. Vitasovic, M. S. Gelormino, and N. L. Ricker. 1992. Real-time control for CSO reduction. Paper presented at Water Environment Federation Conference, New Orleans, LA.

Steel, E. W. 1938 & 1947. *Water Supply and Sewerage*. New York: McGraw-Hill.

Stevens, P. and H. M. Sands. 1995. Sanitary sewer overflows leave telltale signs in depth-velocity scatttergraphs. *National Conference on Sanitary Sewer Overflows (SSOs)*. EPA 625-R-96-007. Washington, DC: U.S. Environmental Protection Agency.

Stevens, P., M. Lopez, and G. Jacquet. 2002. "Evaluation of gauge adjusted radar for rainfall measurements in RDII programs." In *Proceedings of the Ninth International Conference on Urban Drainage*. Reston, VA: American Society of Civil Engineers.

Stirrup, M., Z. Vitasovic, and E. Strand. 1997. Real-Time Control of Combined Sewer Overflows in Hamilton-Wentworth Region. *Water Quality Research Journal of Canada* 32, No. 1: 155–168.

Straub, L. G., C. E. Bowers, and M. Puch. 1960. Resistance to flow in two types of concrete pipe. Technical Paper No. 22, Series B. Minneapolis: St. Anthony Falls Hydraulic Laboratory, University of Minnesota.

Submersible Wastewater Pump Association. 1997. *Submersible Pumping Systems Handbook*. Highland Park, IL: Submersible Wastewater Pump Association.

Swamee, P. K. and A. K. Jain. 1976. Explicit equations for pipe flow problems. *Journal of Hydraulic Engineering*, ASCE 102, No. 5: 657.

Tait, S. J., G. Chebbo, P. J. Skipworth, M. Ahyerre, and A. J. Saul. 2003. Modeling in-sewer deposit erosion to predict sewer flow quality. *Journal of Hydraulic Engineering* 129, 316.

Tang, W. H., L. W. Mays, and B. C. Yen. 1975. Optimal risk-based design of storm sewer networks. *Journal of Environmental Engineering Division*, ASCE 101, EE3, 381.

Tarr, J. A. 1996. *The Search for the Ultimate Sink: Urban Pollution in Historical Perspective*. Akron, OH: University of Akron Press.

Tchobanoglous, G. 1981. *Wastewater Engineering: Collection and Pumping of Wastewater*. New York: McGraw-Hill.

Tchobanoglous, G., F. L. Burton, and H. D. Stensel. 2003. *Wastewater Engineering, Treatment, and Reuse*. 4th ed. New York: McGraw-Hill.

Tekeli, S., and H. Belkaya. 1986. Computerized layout generation for sanitary sewers. *Journal of Water Resource Planning and Management* 112, no. 4: 500.

Thrasher, D. 1988. *Design and Use of Pressure Sewer Systems*. Boca Raton, FL: Lewis Publishers.

Toebes, G. H., ed., 1970. *Natural Resource Systems Models in Decision Making*. Purdue University: Water Resources Center.

Tullis, J. P. 1986. Friction factor tests on concrete pipe. Hydraulic Report No. 157. Logan, Utah: Utah Water Research Laboratory, Utah State University.

US Army Corps of Engineers. 1998. *Engineering Design Runoff and Snowmelt*. Manual No. 1110-2-1406. Washington, DC: US Army Corps of Engineers.

US Environmental Protection Agency (US EPA). 1991. *Alternative Wastewater Collection Systems*. EPA 625/1-91/024. Washington, DC: US Environmental Protection Agency.

US Environmental Protection Agency (US EPA). 1994. *Combined Sewer Overflow Policy*. 59 FR 18688.

US Environmental Protection Agency (US EPA). 1995. *Combined Sewer Overflows: Guidance for Long-Term Control Plan*. EPA 832-B-95-002. Washington, DC: US Environmental Protection Agency.

US Environmental Protection Agency (US EPA). 1999. *Combined Sewer Overflows: Guidance for Monitoring and Modeling*. EPA 832-B-99-002. Washington, DC: US Environmental Protection Agency.

US Environmental Protection Agency (US EPA). 2000. *Compliance and Enforcement Strategy Addressing Combined Sewer Overflows and Sanitary Sewer Overflows*. Washington, DC: US Environmental Protection Agency.

US Environmental Protection Agency (US EPA). 2001. *National Pollutant Discharge Elimination System (NPDES) Permit Requirements for Municipal Sanitary Sewer Collection Systems, Municipal Satellite Systems and Sanitary Sewer Overflow*. 66 FR 7701. Washington, DC: US Environmental Protection Agency.

US Environmental Protection Agency (US EPA). 2002. *Guidance on Environmental Data Verification and Validation*. EPA QA/G-8, EPA/240/R-02/004. Washington DC: US Environmental Protection Agancy.

US Environmental Protection Agency (US EPA). 2003. *National Pollutant Discharge Elimination System (NPDES) Permit Requirements for Municipal Wastewater Treatment Discharges During Wet Weather Conditions.* 68 FR 63042. Washington, DC: US Environmental Protection Agency.

US Environmental Protection Agency. (US EPA) 1999. *Private Inflow/Infiltration source control program helps reduce SSOs*. Washington, DC: US Environmental Protection Agency Fact Sheet.

US Environmental Protection Agency. (US EPA) 2001. *Affordable Large Scale Sewer Line Replacement*. Washington, DC: US Environmental Protection Agency Fact Sheet.

US Environmental Protection Agency. (US EPA) 2002. *Implementing Integrated CMOM*. Washington, DC: US Environmental Protection Agency Fact Sheet.

US Environmental Protection Agency. (US EPA) 2004. *CMOM Program Self Assessment Checklist*. Washington, DC: US Environmental Protection Agency.

US Federal Register. 2003. *National Pollutant Discharge Elimination System Permit Requirements for Municipal Treatment Discharges During Wet Weather Conditions*. 68 no. 216: 63042.

US Soil Conservation Service. 1986. *Urban Hydrology for Small Watersheds*. Technical Release 55. Washington, DC: US Department of Agriculture.

Veissman, W. Jr., G. L. Lewis, and J. W. Knapp. 1989. *Introduction to Hydrology*. New York: Harper-Collins.

Walski, T. M. 1984. *Analysis of Water Distribution Systems*. New York: Van Nostrand Reinhold.

Walski, T. M. 1984. Estimating O&M costs when costs vary with flow. *Journal of Water Resources Planning and Management* 110, no. 3: 355.

Walski, T. M. 2003. Estimating peaking factors for small diameter pressure sewers. *Keystone Water Quality Manager*, 36, no. 3: 14. Pennsylvania Water Environment Association.

Walski, T. M., T. S. Barnhart, J. M. Driscoll, and R. M. Yencha. 1994. Hydraulics of corrosive gas pockets in force mains. *Water Environment Research* 66, no. 6: 772.

Walters, G. A. 1985. The design of the optimal layout for a sewer network. *Engineering Optimization*, no. 9: 37.

Wastewater Planning Users Group (WaPUG). 1998. *Code of Practice for the Hydraulic Modeling of Sewer Systems*. 2d ed. Wallingford, England: Wastewater Planning Users Group.

Water Environment Federation (WEF). 1993. *Design of Wastewater and Stormwater Pumping Stations*. WEF MOP FD-4. Alexandria, VA: Water Environment Federation.

Water Environment Federation (WEF). 1994. *Existing Sewer Evaluation and Rehabilitation*. WEF MOP FD-6. Alexandria, VA: Water Environment Federation.

Water Environment Federation (WEF). 1997. *Energy Conservation in Wastewater Treatment Facilities*. WEF MOP MFD-2. Alexandria, VA: Water Environment Federation.

Water Environment Federation (WEF). 1999. *Prevention and Control of Sewer System Overflows,* 2d ed. WEF MOP FD-17. Alexandria, VA: Water Environment Federation.

Water Environment Federation. 2004. *Implementing Geographical Information Systems.* Alexandria, VA: Water Environment Federation.

Water Research Centre (WRc). 1987. *A Guide to Short Term Flow Surveys of Sewer Systems.* Swindon, UK: WRc Engineering.

Water Research Centre (WRc). 2000. *Sewerage Rehabilitation Manual.* 4th ed. Wiltshire, England: Water Research Centre.

Watson, K. S., R. P. Farrell, and J. S. Anderson. 1967. The contribution of individual homes to the sewer system. *Journal of the Water Pollution Control Federation* 39, no. 12: 2039.

Watt, W. E. 1989. *Hydrology of Floods in Canada: A Guide to Planning and Design.* Ottawa: National Research Council of Canada.

Watters, G. Z. 1984. *Analysis and Control of Unsteady Flow in Pipelines.* Stoneham, MA: Butterworth.

Weinmann, D. E., and E. M. Laurenson. 1979. Approximate flood routing methods: A review. *Journal of the Hydraulics Division,* ASCE 105, no. HY12: 1521.

Williams, G. S., and Hazen, A. (1920) *Hydraulic Tables.* New York: John Wiley and Sons.

Wright, L., S. Dent, C. Mosley, P. Kadota, and Y. Djebbar. 2001. "Comparing rainfall dependent inflow and infiltration simulation methods." In *Models and Applications to Urban Water Systems Monograph 9,* ed. by W. James, Guelph, Ontario: CHI.

www.epa.gov/npdes/pubs/cmomselfreview.pdf (accessed 8/12/04).

Wylie, E. B., and V. L. Streeter. 1993. *Fluid Transients in Systems.* Englewood Cliffs, NJ: Prentice-Hall.

Yang, D., B. E. Goodison, and J. R. Metcalfe. 1998. Accuracy of NWS 8" standard nonrecording precipitation gauge: Results and application of WMO intercomparison. *Journal Atmospheric and Oceanic Technology* 15 (Feb): 54–68.

Yao, K. M. 1974. Sewer line design based on critical shear stress. *Journal of Environmental Engineering* 100, no. EE2: 507–520.

Yen B. C., and V. T. Chow. 1980. Design hyetographs for small drainage structures. *Journal of the Hydraulic Division, American Society of Civil Engineers* 106, No. HY6: 1055–1076.

Yen, B. C., ed. 1982. *Urban Stormwater Hydraulics and Hydrology.* Highlands Ranch, CO: Water Resources Publications.

Yen, B. C., and A. S. Sevuk. 1975. Design of storm sewer networks. *Journal of Environmental Engineering Division,* ASCE 101, EE4, 535.

Zabel, T., I. Milne, and G. McKay. 2001. "Approaches Adopted by the European Union and Selected Member States for the Control of Urban Pollution." *Urban Water* 3: 25-32.

Zeiler, M. 1999. *Modeling Our World.* Redlands, CA: ESRI Press.

Zwick, D. and M. Benstock. 1971. *Water Wasteland.* New York: Grossman Publishers.

Index

A

absolute pressure 29, 30
    equation for 30
absolute viscosity 26
Abwassertechnische Vereinigung (ATV) method 71
access structure. *See* manholes
advancement coefficient for storms
    equation 221
    values 221, 222
affinity laws, for variable-speed pumps 129–130
air-release valves 459, 471, 472
alignment of pipes. *See* pipe alignment
alternatives. *See* scenarios
atmospheric pressure 29–30
average flow rate, in models 167–168

B

Babbitt calculation method for peaking factors 188
backwater curves 77–78
base flow hydrographs 216
base wastewater flows 205, 272
    in model calibration 305
benches in manholes 160, 161
    to reduce head loss 161, 166
benching
    of manholes 355–356
    of structure invert 57
best efficiency points
    for variable-speed pumps 130
    in equation for specific speed of pumps 431
    use in selecting pumps 431–432
boundary shear stress. *See* tractive tension
broad-crested weirs 79, 82, 83, 276
    coefficient of discharge 84
    discharge equation 84
    See also weirs
bubbler systems to measure depth 285–286
bubbler systems, in wet wells 433
buffer strip, along pipelines 524

bulk modulus of elasticity 27
    equation 27

C

calculation for peaking factors calibration. *See* model calibration
Camp formula 69
    calculation example 69
Canada
    combined sewer system control policies 539
        Alberta 544
        British Columbia 545
        Manitoba 543
        New Brunswick 540
        Ontario 541
        Quebec 540
    sanitary sewer system requirements 539
    wastewater collection systems, laws and regulations 538
Capacity Assurance, Management, Operation, and Maintenance programs 536
    See also CMOM program
capacity overflows 324
capital improvement planning. *See* long-range master planning
capture volume analysis (example) 553–554
catchments 203
cavitation 28, 128
    in pumps 433
    solutions to 435
    See also closed-conduit flow
central vacuum stations 338
    See also vacuum sewer systems
centrifugal pumps 126, 164, 429, 468, 469
    axial-flow 164, 429, 430
    mixed-flow 164, 429
    pump characteristic curves 429
    radial-flow 164, 429
    See also pumps
C-factor. *See* Hazen-Williams equation
channel slope
    as sewer design variable 38
    steep 75
check valves 435, 458
Chézy equation 44

Chézy's C 44
Chicago method for synthesizing hyetographs 220, 221–222
　　calculation example 222
　　design storm constants 221
　　equations for 221, 222
Chicago, Sanitary and Ship Canal 8, 10
circular cross section 45, 46
　　hydraulic element chart for 47
Clean Water Act 530, 538
　　legislative history 530
closed-circuit television (CCTV), for sewer inspections 380
closed-conduit flow 23, 113
　　Darcy-Weisbach equation for calculating head loss 116
　　Hazen-Williams equation for calculating head loss 118
　　head loss, calculation example 118
　　Manning equation for calculating head loss 120–121
　　minor loss, calculation example 124
　　See also cavitation, hydraulic transients
CMOM program 536
Colebrook-White equation 117
　　relative roughness in 117
　　Swamee-Jain equation compared 120
　　using the Moody diagram with 117
collection system models. See wastewater collection system models
collectors 2
column separation in pipes 458
　　prevention of 458–459
combined sewer overflow (CSO) 209
　　design criteria 550
　　estimating 325
　　sewer separation and 400–401
combined sewer systems 203, 338, 371
　　historical aspects 9
　　hydrology 208–209
　　manhole inspections 380
　　modeling 210–211
　　potential advantages 338
　　rehabilitation options 398
　　separate sewers vs. 10–11, 12
　　sewer separation 400–401
　　wet weather capacity 209
　　wet weather hydrographs 211
　　wet weather wastewater flow in 205–206
　　See also Canada, combined sewer system control policies, National Combined Sewer Overflow Control Policy (US)
compliance. See regulatory compliance
composite energy-loss method, for estimating minor losses 60–63
comprehensive planning studies. See long-range master planning
compressibility of fluids 27
computer models 5, 11, 137
conditions 385
conditions simulated by sewer network models 149–150
conjugate depths 72, 75
conservation of energy 33–36
　　general equation for 33
conservation of mass 32–33
　　general equation for 33
conservation of momentum 36–37
　　applied to pipe bends 37
　　general equation for 36
　　steady flow equation for 37
constant-speed pumps 129, 429, 432, 456
　　brake power equation 449
　　curve fitting to pump performance data, example 450–451
　　cycle time of 432
　　efficiency equations 449–450
　　head characteristic curve equation 448–449
　　in multiple pump station systems 456
　　See also pumps
construction 1
continuous flow measurements 272
continuous hydrologic simulations 216
contracted weirs 80
　　discharge equation 82
　　See also weirs
control points 77
control structures. See flow-control structures
convex routing 100, 102
　　discharge equation 100
convex routing coefficient 100
corrosion of pipe wall, effect on pipe roughness 121
critical depth of flow 72–74
　　equation for 73
　　example 73–74
cross sections
　　area 45
　　circular 45
　　closed-top 46–49
　　hydraulic element chart for circular 47
　　hydraulic radius 45
　　noncircular 49
　　open-top 45, 46
　　rectangular 45, 46
　　top width 45
　　trapezoidal 45, 46
　　triangular 45, 46
　　wetted perimeter 45
　　See also open-channel cross sections
CSO. See combined sewer overflow (CSO)
curved sewer alignment 349, 350

D

Darcy's law 233
Darcy-Weisbach equation 43
　　calculation with Moody diagram, example 118
　　for calculating Manning's n 50
　　for head loss in closed-conduit flow 116
　　friction factor in 116
Darcy-Weisbach friction factor 43, 116
　　relative roughness in 116
　　Reynolds number in 116
data accuracy, for GIS 502
data assessment criteria 147
data collection 146–147, 271
　　calibration data 147
　　for models 146
　　operations data 147
　　sanitary loading data 147
　　wet weather flow 147
data conversion, for GIS 503–504
data gap analysis 148
data islands 491–492
data management 491–493
　　application-centric 493

centralized 491, 493
data interoperability 491–492
data-centric 493
decentralized 491, 493
geographic data representations 494–495
GIS and 493
data models 5
data requirements
for design of wastewater collection systems 340–341
for modeling wastewater collection systems 143–144
data schema 5
data sources for models 144–146, 174
dry weather wastewater flow data 173, 174
field inspections 145
field surveys 145
operational records 145
precipitation data 293
record drawings 145
system data 216–217
system maps 145
data validation 147
decentralized wastewater treatment systems. *See* wastewater treatment systems
deep sewers 352
defect flows, indicated by high R-values 313
degree-day method of snowmelt estimation 263, 264
demand multipliers
use in defining flow patterns in models 196
use in models 196
demands
on wastewater collection system 173
See also flows, loads
density 24
of snow 263
depressed sewers. *See* inverted siphons
depression storage 206, 230–232
data 231
equation relating storage to slope 231, 232
depth of flow
as sewer design variable 38
critical 72–74
for various pipe slopes 48
in closed-top cross sections 46
in open-top cross sections 45
in partially full circular pipe, example 47–48
depth of pipe cover 349–352
depth sensors 284–286
bubbler systems 285–286
floats 284
pressure transducers 285
staff gauges 284
ultrasonic devices 286
design codes
for wastewater collection systems 339–340
Ten State Standards 339
design criteria, for wastewater collection systems 339–340
design storms 219
Chicago method 221–222
constants, Chicago method 221
Huff and Angel method 224
methods 220
NRCS storm distributions 225–228
procedure for constructing 220
selection criteria 219

synthetic and historical design-storm hyetographs compared 226–228, 229
to calibrate sewer models 219
uniform rainfall procedure 220–221
design. *See* wastewater collection system design
design. *See* wastewater collection system design
diffusion wave routing 97, 102
dilution method for flow measurement 276, 282
discharge
Parshall flume equation for 279
sewer design variable 38
See also flows
discharge measurements. *See* flow measurements
discharges 33
diurnal demand patterns 193–195
diurnal flow curves 193–195, 306
developing customer curves 195
establishing time increments for 195
system wide 195
diversions, routing model complications 104
documentation of model 151–152
domestic water use. *See* residential water use
double-linear reservoir approach to hydrographs 248
downstream flooding, of gravity sewers 444, 445
drop manholes 107, 162–163
dry pipes, complications in routing models 107
dry weather wastewater flows 173–174
data sources for 173
design loads 346
hydraulic design 352–358
methods for determining 174, 175–186, 386
minimum flows 190
model calibration 305–307
model calibration example 307–309
peak flows 187, 188
peaking factors for 187–192
selection of peaking factors 191
time-varying flows 193–198
waste sources 173
wastewater generation rates 176–186
See also diurnal flow curves, flow patterns, wastewater loads
dry wells 426
cavitation in pumps 433
dynamic modeling. *See* extended-period simulation
dynamic viscosity. *See* absolute viscosity

E

EGL. *See* energy grade line
electromagnetic velocity meters 287–288
elevated crossings 359, 360
elevation head, in energy equation 34
empirical methods, to runoff calculations for sanitary sewer systems 204
energy equation 33
across hydraulic jumps 75
for flow profiles 76–77
for open-channel flow 35–36
for turbulent gravity flow 41
energy grade line (EGL) 35
for a backwater profile 78

through a Venturi section 34
energy losses 40
energy-loss method
    for estimating minor losses 55–57
    head losses through a manhole structure, calculation example 58–59
engineered overflows 324
enterprise geographic information systems 495, 496
    application design 497, 498
    as part of information management program 501
    base map considerations 502–503
    data accuracy 502
    data development plan for 502–504
    data ownership 516
    database design 497, 498–502
    design process 497–498
    implementation success factors 495–496
    interfaces 498
    loading models results to 520
    modeling pitfalls 517–519, 520
    modeling procedure in 515–516
    needs assessment for developing 496–497
    network granularity 515
    pilot study 504
    potential applications 498
    production phase tasks 504–505
    rollout tasks 505
    scenarios in 516
    sewer model applications in 520
    time-series data in 516
    See also geographic information systems (GIS)
EPA. *See* US Environmental Protection Agency
EPS. *See* extended-period simulation
equivalent sand grain roughness 43, 116
    for sewer pipes 116
    See also pipe roughness
European Union
    combined sewer overflow design criteria 550
    combined sewer overflows 548, 549
    Integrated Pollution Prevention Control Directive 549
    Product Directives 549
    urban pollution directives 546
    Urban Waste Water Treatment Directive 546–548
    Water Policy Framework Directive 549
event-based hydrologic calculations 216
extended-period simulation (EPS)
    applications 176, 357–358
    development of hydrograph loads for 239–248
    model calibration 305
    of force mains 441–442
    using time-varying flows in 193
    See also steady-state simulation
extreme flow factors 187, 191–192
    based on flow 191
    based on population 191
    See also peaking factors

F

Federal Water Pollution Control Act (FWPCA). *See* Clean Water Act
finite-difference equations 95–96

First Law of Thermodynamics 33
fixed-speed pumps. *See* constant-speed pumps
fixture unit method
    for estimating waste flows 181–183
    using Hunter curves 182–183
fixture value method. *See* fixture unit method
flap gates 163, 166
floats
    for measuring depth 284
    in wet wells 433
flow components, in sanitary sewers 272–273
flow conditions, types of 3
flow depth. *See* depth of flow
flow measurements 271
    considerations in making 271–275
    dilution method 276, 282
    in-pipe methods 280–281
    instrumentation for 283–291
    location of 273–274
    locations of, influencing factors 274
    manual methods 281–283
    review of existing data 273
    safety in making 274–275
    techniques 275–283
    timed flow method 276, 281
    velocity-area method 276, 282
flow metering. *See* flow measurements
flow monitoring programs 272–273
flow patterns 193–198
    continuous 196, 197
    diurnal curves 193–195
    repetition of 196–197
    residential community example 197–198
    start time 196
    stepwise 196, 197
flow profiles 76–77
    backwater curves 77–78
flow rates
    definitions 175
    See also discharges
flow regimes, velocity profiles in 32
flow reversal, complications in routing models 106–107
flow-control structures 78–84
    baffled side weir 80
    broad-crested weirs 82–84
    gates 84
    orifices 79
    parallel relief sewers 78
    sharp-crested weir 80–82
    side weirs 80, 84
flows
    dry weather wastewater 173–174
    estimates for pressure sewer systems 472–477
    using estimates in designing new systems 175
    using estimates to model existing systems 176
    wet weather wastewater 173, 203–204
    See also discharges
fluid properties 24–28
    bulk modulus of elasticity 27
    compressibility 27
    density 24
    Newtonian fluids 25
    plastic fluids 25
    specific weight 24

vapor pressure 27–28
viscosity 24–26
flumes 276, 278–280
    Parshall flumes 278–280
    See also hydraulic control sections
flushing to clean sewers 346
foot valves 435
force main system design
    determining pipe sizes 436
    equation for estimating pipe diameter 436
    flow velocity range 436
    issues 419–420
    key design parameter 436
    model use in developing head curves 455–456, 457
    model use in developing system head curves 438
    multiple pump station layout 456
    peak flows 436
    pipe size optimization 438–441
        example 440
    pipeline construction options with multiple high points 444–446
    pipeline full-flow capacity equation 446
    procedure 420
    pump selection 448, 457
    pumping energy cost equation 439
    system head curves for 437–438
force main system models
    advantages of extended period simulation 441
    identifying downstream flooding of gravity sewers 443, 444, 445
    identifying wet well flooding effects on pump performance 443–444, 445
    model components 442
    multiple pump stations 457
    pipelines with multiple high points 444–448
    pumps 442
force mains 2, 113, 338, 419–420
    alternatives for connecting gravity systems 420–421, 422
    corrosive gases in 448
    head losses 128
    hydraulic design 420
    hydraulic grade line for 128
    hydraulic transients 457–459
    pressure flow in 3
    sizing with multiple pump stations 455–457
    sizing with single pump station 435–441
    system head curve equation 128, 437
    system head curves 126–128, 437–438, 446–447
free outfall 57
friction coefficients, GIS pipe lengths and 519
friction factor
    Colebrook-White equation for 117
    equations compared 121
    in Darcy-Weisbach equation 43
    Moody diagram for 117
    Swamee-Jain equation 50
friction losses 113–122
    Darcy-Weisbach equation to calculate head loss in pipes 116
    in force mains 437
    using the Hazen-Williams equation for 118
    using the Manning equation for 120
    See also head losses
friction slope 121
Froude number 74
    critical flow depth 74
    equation for 74
    subcritical flow 74
    supercritical flow 74–75
full pipe flow. *See* closed-conduit flow
FWPCA. *See* Clean Water Act

G

gas pockets 448
gases, corrosive, in force mains 448
gates 84
    discharge coefficient 84
    discharge equation 84
gauge 30
gauge pressure, equation for 30
geographic data representations 494–495
    raster data 494
    triangulated irregular networks (TINs) 494
    vector data 494
geographic information systems (GIS)
    applications, in wastewater utilities 520–524
    architecture types 499
    architecture, hydraulic models and 499–502
    attributes 490
    data accuracy 502
    data conversion 503–504
    described 489, 490, 491, 492
    features 490
    for system analysis 490
    georeferencing 511
    hydraulic model integration with 489–490, 508–510
    hydraulic modeling software vs. 505–506
    implementation levels 495
    metadata 499
    model construction with 505–506
    model integration benefits 490
    model integration process 489
    model maintenance and 506–507
    spatial coincidence of features 522
    symbology 490
    thematic mapping 520–521
    to analyze spatial relationships among features 522, 523
    tracing networks via 522
    tributary-polygon method for generating load-point flows 511–514
    See also enterprise geographic information systems
georeferencing 511
Germany, sewer system history 8
GIS. *See* geographic information systems (GIS)
GLUMRB standards. *See* Great Lakes Upper Mississippi River Basin (GLUMRB) standard
gradually varied flow 23, 76
gravity flow 23, 338
    partially full 3
    surcharged 3
gravity sewer systems. *See* wastewater collection systems
gravity sewers, downstream flooding of 444
grease deposits 158
Great Lakes Upper Mississippi River Basin (GLUMRB) standard
    calculation for peaking factors 188–189

Green-Ampt infiltration equation 233–234
groundwater infiltration 205, 207
    control 402
        estimated using unit rates 304, 306–307
        in model calibration 305

H

Hazen-Williams equation 115, 118
    C-factors for pipes 118, 119
    head loss calculation, example 120
head characteristic curve for pumps 125, 126
head loss coefficient 55
    benching correction factors 55–57, 58
    flow depth correction factor 56
    pipe diameter correction factor 56
    plunging flow correction factor 57
    relative flow correction factor 57
head losses 40, 127
    Darcy-Weisbach equation for 43, 116
    Darcy-Weisbach equation, with Moody diagram, example 118
    due to friction in closed-conduit flow 114–115
    for inflow pipes, equation 60
    general equation for 41, 55, 60
    Hazen-Williams equation for 115, 118, 119
    in force mains 437
    in manholes, reduction by benching 57, 58
    Kutter-Chézy equation 44
    Manning equation for 41–42, 120
    See also friction losses, minor losses
HGL. *See* hydraulic grade line
high water marks 283
    chalk lines method 283
    tea cup method 283
history
    of hydraulics 8, 11–16
    of wastewater collection systems 7–11, 12
Horton infiltration equation 233
Huff and Angel method for synthesizing hyetographs 224
    example 226–228
    historical design-storm hyetographs compared 228, 229
    storm coefficients for 224
Hunter curves 182–183
hydraulic control sections
    flow measurements using 275–280
    in open channels 275–280
    See also flumes, weirs
hydraulic depth 39
    equation for 39
    open-channel cross section 45
hydraulic design 352–358
    variables for sewers 38–40
hydraulic design process
    manholes 355–356
    pipe sizing 354–355
    procedures 353–354
hydraulic grade line (HGL) 35
    for force mains 128
    through a Venturi section 34
    See also piezometric head

hydraulic grade line, visualizing in GIS 523
hydraulic jumps 75–76
    cause of odor problems 76
    energy equation for 75
    turbulence in 75–76
hydraulic models
    in sewer system design 6
    See also sewer models
hydraulic problems in sewers 158–159
    grease 158
    roots 158
    sags 159
    sediment 158, 159
hydraulic properties of sewers 28–32
    flow 30
    flow regimes 31
    static pressure 28–29
    velocity 30
    velocity profiles 31
hydraulic radius
    of open channel 45
    partially full pipe, example 47–48
hydraulic transients 27
    control mechanisms 458–459
    in force mains 457–459
    surge allowance 458
    use of air-release valves 459
    use of check valves 458
    use of transient analysis model 459, 460
    use of vacuum breaker valves 459
    See also closed-conduit flow
hydraulics
    history of 8, 11–16
    steady gravity flow 23–84
    unsteady gravity flow 91
hydrodynamic equations. *See* St. Venant equations
hydrogen sulphide gas pockets in force mains 448
hydrographs 205
    actual, from events 251
    base flow 216
    combined sewer, wet-weather 211
    empirical methods for generating 248–262
    methods for developing 239
    nonlinear reservoir approach to 246–248
    normalized 251
    NRCS dimensionless unit hydrograph 243–244, 245
    percentage of rainfall volume entering collection system 249
    time to peak-flow calculation 240
    triangular 240
    unit hydrograph approach 242–243, 249–250
    See also RTK hydrograph method, Snider triangular hydrograph method, wastewater flow hydrographs, wastewater hydrographs
hydrologic models 203
    continuous approach to wet weather flows 216
    continuous simulation 217
    event-based approach to wet weather flows 216
    event-based methods 217
    See also runoff models
hydrologic routing. *See* routing models
hydrostatic pressure 13, 14
hydrostatic pressure. *See* static pressure
hyetograph synthesis
    Chicago method 221–222

equations 221, 222
    example 222
    Huff and Angel method 224
    NRCS storm distributions 225–228
    uniform rainfall 220–221
hyetographs 217, 218
    using continuous historical records 228–229
    wastewater flow hydrographs with 386
    See also rainfall data

I

I/I. *See* infiltration/inflow
IDF. *See* intensity-duration-frequency (IDF) data
impulse-momentum principle 75
    applied to hydraulic jumps 75–76
    equation for hydraulic jumps 75
incompressible fluid 27, 32
    assumption of 33
industrial discharges, European Union requirements 547
infiltration 173, 203, 205, 206, 232–234
    defined 2
    estimated using unit rates 306–307
    Green-Ampt equation 233–234
    groundwater 272
    Horton equation 233
    in sanitary sewers, sources 212
    into manholes 213
    RDII allowances in new sewer design 261–262, 348
infiltration and inflow allowances 346–348
infiltration/inflow (I/I), defined 3
inflow 3, 173, 205
    nonwastewater 3
inflow coefficient method 250–252
initial abstraction of rainfall 237
inlet structures, equivalent structure diameter 56
intensity-duration-frequency (IDF) data for rainfall 217, 218
    used to develop synthetic design storms 219
interbasin transfers 405
interception 206, 230
interceptors 2
internal energy 33
invert elevation of pipes 157
inverted siphons 159–160, 360–361
isolation valves 435

J

junction structures. *See* manholes

K

kinematic viscosity 26
    equation 26
kinematic wave routing 97–98, 102
    equation 97–98, 247
kinematic wave solution 97–98
kinematic wave speed 97
kinetic energy 33
Kutter's n 44
Kutter-Chézy equation 44

L

laminar velocity profile 32
land-use
    estimating wastewater flows from 511–514
level pool routing 100, 102
life-cycle costs 353
lift stations. *See* pump stations
linear regression. *See* multiple linear regression analysis
loading points 173
    determining flows at 173
loads 173
    assignment to model nodes 187
    bottom-up approach to estimates 174
    See also demands, flows
location tape 349
London, sewer system history 7, 8, 10
long-range master planning 5
    use of models for 140
loops, in sewer pipes, routing model complications 106
low-pressure sewer systems. *See* pressure sewer systems

M

maintenance 374
maintenance overflows 324
manholes 2, 160, 161
    benching 160, 161, 355–356
    condition of 380, 381
    construction materials 336
    covers 336
    crown elevations of pipes 356
    design 335
    drop 162–163
    energy dissipation in 355–356
    head losses, reduction by benching 57–58
    hydraulics 54–57
    infiltration into 213
    invert elevations 160–161
    minor losses in 54–63
    outlet 163
    pipe junctions at 337
    rim elevation 161–162
    routing model complications 103
    sizes 162, 336
    weirs to regulate flows 163, 164, 165, 166
    with 90-degree bends 162
Manning equation 15, 41, 120–121
    for closed-conduit flow 42–43, 120
    for head loss in force main, example 121
    for open-channel flow 41

to estimate average energy grade line slope 77
Manning's n 44
    assumption for pipes 120
    Darcy-Weisbach equation for 50
    Darcy-Weisbach equation for, example 50–51
    factors affecting value 49–50
    for open-channel materials 42
    for overland flow 247, 248
    for pipe materials 42
    pipe wall roughness effect on 49
    recommended values for sewer design 53–54
    variation with depth 52–53
    variation with depth equation 52–53
    variation with pipe roughness 51–52
    variation with velocity 51–52
    See also pipe roughness
Manning's roughness coefficient. *See* Manning's n
mathematical models 5
maximum flow rates with pumping 358
maximum flows. *See* peak flows
maximum velocity, in sewers 39
melt rate factor of snow 263
meltwater rate 263
metadata 499, 500
metallic location tape 349
microtunneling
    with laser-guided boring 352
    with pipe jacking 352
mild channel-slope 74
minimum flow factors 190
    equations for 190
minimum flows 190, 347
minimum velocity for sediment transport (in sewers) 39–40, 347
    Abwassertechnische Vereinigung (ATV) method 71
    Camp formula 69
    examples 69, 71
    Yao's method 70
minor loss coefficients
    adjusted 60
    for fittings 122
    for force mains, calculation example 124
    for lateral flow/lateral angle/plunging flow 60–62
    for relative pipe diameter 62
    for relative-access hole diameter 60
    for valves 123
    for water depth in manholes 60–61
    in junction structures 55
minor losses 122–124
    composite energy-loss method 60–63
    energy-loss method of calculation 55–57
    in inlet structures 54–63
    in manholes, calculation example using energy-loss method 58–59
    in pipes, equation for 122
model archiving 152
model calibration 148, 301–305
    adjustment of parameters 303, 304
    components of flow 305
    concepts 302
    data collection for 147, 322
    dry weather flow example 307–309
    dry weather flows 305–307
    extended-period simulations 305
    overflow problems in 324–328
    procedure 302–303
    special considerations 320
    steady-state simulations 305
    timing shifts of diurnal curve 323, 324
    volume differences 321–322
    wet weather wastewater flow example 318–319
    wet weather wastewater flows 309–320
    See also modeling process, overflows
model calibration events 219
    shape adjustments of diurnal curve 322–323
model construction
    CAD data in 505
    feature connectivity 517
    friction coefficients 519, 520
    GIS pitfalls 517–519
    hydraulic modeling software vs GIS 505–506
    issues in 508
    measurement units 508
    missing attributes 517
    network components not in GIS 508–510
    pipe direction 518–519
    pipe lengths 519, 520
    procedure for 515–516
    staff communication importance during 507–508
    terminology and 508
    See also sewer models
model data requirements 143–144
model elements 152
    inverted siphons 159–160
    manholes 160–164
    outlet manholes 163
    outlet nodes 163
    pipes 154–160
    pump stations 167–168
    pumps 164–168
    wet wells 168–169
model maintenance, GIS and 506–507
model objectives 138, 140
    macroscale 142
model processing
    defining flow patterns in models using demand multipliers 196
model validation. *See* model verification
model verification 302
model, software-use training 143
modeling 5, 356
    combined sewer systems 210–211
    computer models, defined 5, 137
    defined 5
    macroscale models 142, 153–154, 155
    mathematical models, defined 5, 137
    microscale models 142–143, 153
    overflows 324
    pumped systems 441–448
    purposes 138–141, 153, 175–176, 203–204
    sanitary sewer systems 213–216
    scale of 141
    system models, defined 5, 137
modeling process 16–18, 137, 138, 139
    assessment of model utility 149
    assignment of loads to model nodes 187
    bookkeeping for 151–152
    caveats 150
    data collection for 146–147

data requirements 143–144, 161
data sources 144–146, 174
data validation for 147
documentation of 151–152
elevation accuracy importance 161
interpretation of results 150
model building 148, 152
model simulation runs 149–150
model verification 148
plan contents 137–138
planning 137
scale of 141, 153
sensitivity analysis 148
software selection 143
solution development 150, 151
See also model calibration, model elements, software
modeling terminology, staff communications and 508
models
    hydrologic 203
    parameters 303, 304
    pressure sewers 479–483
    purpose of 138–141
    rainfall-runoff 203
    runoff 229–239
    scenarios in 141
    sewer network 137
    simulation runs 149–150
    snowmelt 262–264
    types of 5, 7
    updating 152
    wet weather wastewater flows 206–208
    See also modeling process, runoff models, sewer models
Modified Puls routing. *See* level pool routing
momentum flow rate 37
Moody diagram 16
    for calculating friction factor, example 118
    for solving Colebrook-White equation 117
multiple linear regression analysis
    example 253–254
    for estimating wet weather wastewater flows 252–256
    See also rainfall-derived infiltration and inflow (RDII)
Muskingum routing method 98, 102
    discharge equation 98, 99
    storage equation 98
Muskingum-Cunge routing method 98–100, 102
    discharge equation 99
    See also Saint Venant equations

N

National Combined Sewer Overflow Control Policy (US) 533–535
National Pollutant Discharge Elimination System (NPDES) 531
    permit program 531, 532
Natural Resources Conservation Service storm distributions. *See* NRCS (SCS) storm distributions
Navier-Stokes equations 14
needs assessment, for developing an enterprise 496–497
net positive suction head (NPSH) 128, 131, 433–435
    available in the system equation 434
network granularity 515
networks, tracing with GIS 522

Newton's law of viscosity 26
Newtonian fluids 25, 26
NEXRAD (Next Generation Weather Radar) 295
nodes 512
nonlinear reservoir approach to hydrographs 246–248
non-Newtonian fluids 26
nonuniform flow 23
normal depth 23
NRCS (SCS) method of estimating runoff 236–239
    curve numbers 237–239
    equation 237
NRCS (SCS) storm distributions 225–228
    storm coefficients 225–228
    synthesizing hyetographs, example 226–228
NRCS dimensionless unit hydrograph 243–244, 245
    calculation example 246

O

object models 5
objectives, of models. *See* model objectives
odor problems, caused by turbulence 76
of gravity sewers 443
on-site wastewater treatment systems 337
open-channel characteristics 44–46
open-channel cross sections
    area 45
    hydraulic depth 45
    hydraulic radius 45
    top width 45
    wetted perimeter 45
    See also cross sections
open-channel flow 23
    backwater curves 77–78
    classification 23
    control points 77
    critical depth 72–74
    energy equation for 35–36
    flow control structures 78–84
    Froude number 74
    gradually varied 23
    hydraulic jumps 75–76
    nonuniform 23
    specific energy 72–74
    steady 23
    subcritical flow 74
    supercritical flow 75
    uniform 23
    unsteady 23, 91
operations and maintenance, using models for 141
optimization techniques
    in sewer design 361, 363
    in sewer design, trial and error adjustments 362
orifices 79
    discharge coefficients 79
    equation for discharge 79
    horizontal orientation 79
    vertical orientation 79
outfalls, for stormwater runoff 204
outlet manholes 163
outlet node. *See* outlet manholes

overflows 272, 324–326
    capacity overflows 324
    detecting 326–328
    engineered 324
    interbasin transfers of 405
    maintenance overflows 324
    modeling 324
    routing model complications 104–105
    See also model calibration, sanitary sewer overflows
overland flows, routing of 246–248

P

parallel pipes, routing models and 105–106
parallel relief sewers 78, 105–106
Paris, sewer system history 8, 9
Parshall flumes 278–280
partial depth 38, 39
peak discharge equation
    unit hydrograph 244
peak flow attenuation 93
peak flow measurements 272
peak flows (dry weather)
    calculation example 192
    equations 187, 189, 191
    See also peaking factors
peak flows (wet weather)
    computed from runoff depth 240
    equations for 235–236, 240–241, 244, 250, 259
    modified rational method of estimating 236, 250–252
    NRCS dimensionless unit hydrograph 245
    NRCS dimensionless unit hydrograph method 243–246
    RTK hydrograph method of estimating 254–260
    Snider triangular hydrograph method for 240–241
    time of concentration 235, 240
    time to peak, equation 240
    time to peak, runoff depth and 240–241
    See also rational method for estimating peak runoff
peak sanitary flows. *See* peak flows (dry weather)
peaking factors
    Babbitt equation 188
    charts, limitations of 188
    compared 190
    downstream adjustments for 191
    example 192
    for dry weather flows 187–192
    for pressure sewer flows 474, 474–475
    Great Lakes Upper Mississippi River Basin (GLUMRB) standard equation 188–189
    Harmon equation 188, 189, 190
    Tchobanoglous curve 189–190
percent full depth 38, 39
permit program 531
permits
    CMOM program 536
    dredge and fill 538
    National Pollutant Discharge Elimination System (NPDES) 531, 532
    Sanitary Sewer Overflow (proposed) 535
    wet weather treatment facility discharges, blending policy 536–537

phased construction of sewers 348
piezometric head 35
pipe age
    effect on Manning's n 49
    effect on pipe diameter 155
pipe alignment 348
    criteria for depth 349–350
    curved 349, 350
    depth and 350–351
    horizontal 348
    limitations on depths 352
    maximum depths 352
    minimum depths 349–351, 352
    minimum slopes 348–349
    slopes 348–349
    vertical 348
    vertical misalignment 355
pipe cover depth 349–352
    criteria for 349–350
    in nontrafficked areas 350–351
    in trafficked areas 350–351
    limiting factors for 352
    maximum 352
    minimum 349–352
pipe deflection limits 349
pipe diameter 155
    age effects on 155
    effect on Manning's n 49
    rehabilitation effects on 156–157
    specifications of 24-inch concrete pipe 156
pipe flow. *See* closed-conduit flow
pipe friction
    accounted for by roughness coefficient 157
    depth of flow effect on 48, 157
    friction loss, equations compared 121
pipe invert elevations 157
pipe joints 334
pipe length 155
pipe linings 156–157
pipe materials 3, 155–157, 334
pipe roughness 116, 157
    changes in 121
    wall roughness, effect on Manning's n 49
    See also equivalent sand grain roughness, Manning's n
pipe shapes 157, 158
pipe sizes 157
    pressure mains 471
    pressure sewer service lines 470
    reductions downstream 354
    selecting 354–355
    small-diameter sewers 354
pipe slope
    as sewer design variable 38
    assumed constant between manholes 157
    factor in type of flow 75
    minimum for sewer sediment self-cleansing 39–40, 63–69
    sediment self-cleansing, calculation examples 64–65, 67–68
pipelines, buffer areas along 524
pipes 334, 335
    corrosion and 3
    crown elevations in manholes 356
    flexible 156
    force mains 2
    grease deposits in 158

Hazen-Williams C-factors for 118, 119
head loss in 114–115
in models 154–160
installation 335
invert elevation of 157
Manning's n and 120
minor losses in, equation for 122
rigid 156
rising mains 2
roots in 158–159, 380, 382
sags in 159
scale deposition effects on roughness 121
sediment in 158–159
shear stress in 113, 115
standards for 334, 335
turbulent flow in 115
velocity in partially full, example 47–48
See also model complications
pipe-wall corrosion, effects on pipe roughness 121
piping laterals 2
plastic fluids 25
point flow measurements 272
Poisson distribution, for estimating pressure sewer system loads 475–477
potential energy 33
precipitation 205
data sources 293
measurement 292–297
See also rainfall data, rainfall measurement
Preissmann slot 103–104
width, equation for 103
pressure
absolute 30
atmospheric 30
gauge 30
pressure flow 113
in force mains 3
pressure head 29
equation for 29
example 29
in energy equation 34
pressure hydraulics 113
pressure sewer flows 472–477
design flow estimates 473, 474
equivalent dwelling unit estimates of design flows 473
peak flow estimates 474, 474–475
peaking factor equation 474
pressure sewer mains 471
pressure sewer models 479–483
detailed extended-period simulation of each service connection 482–483
discharge into gravity sewer 479, 480
representing service connections as nodes 481–482
steady-state simulation to size pressure mains 480–481
pressure sewer system components 468–471
air-release valves 471–472
discharge points 471
pressure mains 471
pumps 468–469, 470
service lines 470
storage tanks 470, 471
vacuum-breaker valves 471
pressure sewer systems 2, 3, 113, 338
See also wastewater collection systems

pressure sewer, components of 468–471
pressure sewers 467
advantages of 467
description of 468–471
design considerations 478–479
disadvantages of 467
estimating flows in 472–477
mixed gravity-pressure systems, profile views 478, 479, 480
pressure transducers 285
in wet wells 433
pump characteristic curves 127, 131
equations for 448–449
for axial-flow pumps 429, 430
for constant-speed pumps 448–451
for radial-flow pumps 429
for variable-flow pumps 451–452, 453
model representations 442
See also pumps
pump curves. *See* pump characteristic curves
pump efficiency 448
constant-speed pumps 448–451
variable-speed pumps 451–454
WaterCAD for calculating 455
pump head characteristic curves. *See* pump characteristic curves
pump performance, wet well flooding effects on 443–444, 445
pump station flows, in gravity sewers 358
pump stations 2, 419–420
alternatives for connecting gravity systems 420–421, 422
applications of 420–421, 422
characteristics of 425
components 423, 424
configuration 426–427
design considerations 419–420, 425
dry well 426
estimates of loads on 436
flow attenuation downstream of 442–443
information sources for design details 425
metering flow from 435
pre-engineered packaged stations 425
pump capacities 425
system head curves 437–438, 439
wet-well 427
See also force mains
pumping flow rate, use in model 167–168
pumping hydraulics 113
pumps 125–132, 164–168, 423
affinity laws for variable-speed pumps 129–130
as pressure sewer components 468–469, 470
axial-flow 429, 430
best efficiency points 130, 131, 429, 430, 432
brake power of 128, 131
capacities 425
cavitation in 128, 433–435
characteristics of 425
control by flow matching 442
control levels in wet wells 168
controls 167
coverage charts 431
cycle time of 432
design flow rate 431–432
efficiency 128, 131
efficiency curves 127, 131, 166–167
energy costs 448–455
field testing, need for 132

for dry wells 426
for wet wells 426–427
grinder 468
head characteristic curve 127
head characteristic curves for 126, 127, 165–167, 453, 468, 469
horsepower curves for 131
impeller 125, 131, 132
information sources for 166
input power of 130, 131
mixed-flow 429
motor efficiency of 131
multistage 430
operating points of 127, 431–432, 453–454
overall efficiency 131
positive-displacement 429
progressive-cavity 468–469
radial-flow 429
screening of solids by 427
screw 429
selection of 431–432, 448
self-priming 426
semipositive-displacement 468–469
septic tank effluent 468, 470, 471
simultaneously running, estimating the number of 475–477
specific speed of 430–431
specific speed of, equation 430
submersible 426, 427, 428
system head curves 438, 439
types of 164, 427–432
verification of selection with model runs 431–432
vertically mounted 429
water power 131
wet-pit 426, 428
wire-to-water efficiency 131
See also centrifugal pumps, constant-speed pumps, pump characteristic curves, self-priming pumps, variable-speed pumps

Q

quality assurance/quality control (QA/QC)
for wastewater collection system characterization 379

R

R value method 240, 249
evaluation of method 313
use of 249
See also rainfall-derived infiltration and inflow (RDII), RTK hydrograph method
R values, as large defect flow indicators 313
radar imagery 295–297
See also rainfall measurement
radar velocity meters 291, 292
rain gauges
nonrecording 293
operation of 294–295
recording 293–294
See also rainfall measurement
rainfall
depression storage 206, 230–232
infiltration 206, 232–234
rainfall abstractions 206, 207, 230–233
initial abstraction 237
rainfall data 217–229
continuous records 219, 228–229
intensity-duration-frequency (IDF) data 217, 218
preparation for modeling wet weather wastewater flows 217–229
sources 293
See also hyetographs, precipitation
rainfall interception 206, 230
rainfall measurement 293–294
See also precipitation, radar imagery, rain gauges
rainfall retention 237
rainfall volume
percentage entering sewer system 249
R-values 249, 255, 256
rainfall-derived infiltration and inflow (RDII) 3, 205, 214–216, 272
allowances for new sewer design 261–262
components 205
control practices 402–404
estimating peak RDII flows, probabilistic method 316
hydrograph calculation example 318–319
hydrograph generation methods 386, 387
hydrographs 309–310
in model calibration 305
methods for generating hydrographs of 248–262
mitigation strategies 396, 397, 398
prediction, from percentage of streamflow 313–314, 315
rainfall-flow regression to predict 316–317
reduction, methods for predicting 403–404
RTK hydrographs for 315–316
RTK method evaluation 315
simulation 514
through manholes 380
unit loading rates 310–311
variables affecting volume and rate of 389–390
See also multiple linear regression analysis, R value method
rainfall-runoff models 203
response hydrographs 215, 215–216
rapid flow. *See* supercritical flow
rapidly varied flow 77
raster data 494
rational method for estimating peak runoff 234–236
inflow coefficient method 250–252
peak runoff equation 235
runoff coefficients 236
time of concentration equation 235
RDII. *See* rainfall-derived infiltration and inflow (RDII)
real-time controls 405
limitations 405–406
modeling and 406
recession time, equation for 221
regional wastewater treatment systems. *See* wastewater treatment systems
regression analysis. *See* multiple linear regression analysis
regulators of flow 163, 164, 165
regulatory compliance
modeling applications in 6
using models for 141, 551, 552
using models for (example) 553–554

regulatory prescribed loads, to determine dry weather flows 174
rehabilitation studies, modeling applications in 6
rehabilitation, of sewer systems. *See* wastewater collection system rehabilitation
relative roughness 116
    in the Colebrook-White equation 117
    in the Darcy-Weisbach friction factor 116
    in the Moody diagram 117
    in the Swamee-Jain equation 120
relief sewers 2
residential water use 176–177
    diurnal wastewater flows from 194
    household size effect on 177
    low-flush toilets 183, 184
    relation to household size 177
    water conservation effects 177
    See also unit load factors, water use
restrained pipe joint 38
retention of rainfall 237
return period
    of rainfall intensity 218, 220, 221
return period, of rainfall intensity 217
Reynolds number 31
    calculation example 31
    equation for 31
    for classifying flow regimes 31
    in the Colebrook-White equation 117
    in the Darcy-Weisbach friction factor 116
    in the Moody diagram 117
    in the Swamee-Jain equation 120
rising mains. *See* force mains
Rivers and Harbors Act of 1899 529
roots
    in manholes 380, 381
    in pipes 158–159, 380, 382
roughness coefficients
    Kutter's n 44
    Manning's n 41–42
routing model complications 101–107
    drop structures 107
    dry pipes 107
    flow reversal 106–107
    loops in sewer pipes 106
    manholes and junctions 103
    overflows and diversions 104–105
    parallel pipes 105–106
    surcharging 103–104
    surcharging sewer pipes 103–104
    See also pipes
routing models 94, 102
    convex method 100, 102
    limitations of 94
    Muskingum method 98, 99, 102
    Muskingum-Cunge method 98–100, 102
    storage equation for 94
RTK hydrograph method 254–260
    applications 254
    calculation of flows 259
    definition of parameters 255–259
    evaluation 315–316
    example 260
    for RDII prediction 315–316
    limitations 255
    parameter calculation example 258–259

    parameter calculation from field data 258
    Snider triangular hydrograph compared 242
    See also hydrographs, R value method, Snider triangular hydrograph method
runoff coefficients
    for development types 236
    for surface area types 236
runoff collection 207
runoff curve numbers 237–239
runoff depth, computing runoff volume from 240
runoff generation 206–207
runoff models 229–239
    choosing a method 229–230
    using double-linear reservoirs 248
    using nonlinear reservoirs 248
    See also hydrologic models
runoff volume
    determination of hydrographs from 239–248
    equation for 240
    relation to runoff depth 240
R-value method 312
    identification of basin for I/I reduction 388
    mapping values from calibrated sewer model 390, 391
R-values
    for comparing monitored basins 388
    for initial percent-impervious values of subbasin 388
    incremental R 388
    mapping observed values by subbasin 389
    peak R 388
    total R 388

S

safety, during flow measurement 274–275
sags, in pipes 159
Sanitary and Ship Canal (Chicago) 8, 10
sanitary flows.
sanitary sewer load data. *See* wastewater loads
sanitary sewer models. *See* wastewater collection system models
Sanitary Sewer Overflow Proposed Rule (US) 533–535, 536, 552
sanitary sewer overflows (SSOs) 212
    detecting 326–328
    estimating 326
    See also overflows
sanitary sewer system requirements
    Canadian requirements 539
sanitary sewer systems 203, 204, 338
    design 204
    hydrology 212–213
    infiltration sources 212
    modeling 213–216
    rehabilitation options 396, 397, 398
    wet weather overflows 403
    See also separate sewer systems
sanitary sewers, flow components 272–273
scale deposition, effect on pipe roughness 121
scattergraphs, detecting overflows from 326–328
scenarios 516, 523
    in models 141
scouring sediment in sewers 71–72
SCS curve numbers. *See* runoff curve numbers

SCS method of estimating runoff. *See* NRCS (SCS) method of estimating runoff
SCS storm distributions. *See* NRCS (SCS) storm distributions
sediment
    in pipes 158–159
    suspended in wastewater 63
sediment carrying capacity of sewers 65–72
sediment deposition in sewers
    effect on Manning's n 50
    effect on models 159
    mitigation of 39–40, 63
    research sources 72
sediment transport
    Camp formula 69
    Camp formula calculation, example 69
    in sewers 63–72
    minimum velocity for 69
self-cleansing sewers
    design 63–72
    velocity in inverted siphons 160
    velocity needed for 158
self-priming pumps 426
    cavitation in 433
    need for check valve 435
    need for foot valve 435
    See also pumps
sensitivity analysis
    applied to sewer design 363
    of models 148
separate sewer systems
    potential advantages 338
    See also sanitary sewer systems
septic tank effluent pump systems (STEP) 468, 470, 471
sequent depths. *See* conjugate depths
series present worth factor 439
service area 348
sewer 1
sewer cleaning equipment, need for 71
sewer design. *See* wastewater collection system design
sewer inspection 379–380
    closed-circuit television (CCTV) for 380
    dye studies 382
    internal conditions 380
    manholes 380, 381
    plug-and-weir techniques 382, 384
    smoke investigations 381–382, 383
sewer layout 342
sewer models
    applications 138–143, 153, 175, 175–176, 203–204
    applications in enterprise GIS 520
    hydraulic modeling software vs GIS 505–506
    See also model construction, modeling process, models
sewer scanning and evolution technology (SSET) 380
sewer service, factors to consider in providing 337–338
sewer surcharging 151
sewer system operations, modeling applications in 6
sewer systems, design
sewer systems. *See* combined sewer systems, sanitary sewer systems, separate sewer systems, wastewater collection systems
sewers
    collectors 2
    conveyance types 3
    interceptors 2
    laterals 2

    main 2
    relief 2
    trunk 2
    vacuum 2
shaping. *See* benching
sharp-crested rectangular weirs 80–82
    discharge coefficient equation 81–82
    discharge equation 81
    See also weirs
shear stress 25
    general equation for 25
    in pipes 113, 115
    See also tractive tension
simulation runs, of models 149–150
simulation. *See* extended-period simulation, models, steady-state simulation
siphons, inverted 159–160, 360–361
small-diameter sewers 354
Snider triangular hydrograph method 240–242
    equation for peak flows 240–242
    RTK method compared 242
    See also hydrographs, RTK hydrograph method
snow
    albedo 264
    density 263
    melt rate factor 263
    metamorphism 263
    water equivalent 262–263
snowmelt 262
    degree-day method of estimating 263, 264
    energy-balance model 263–264
    models 262–264
    runoff potential 262–263
    temperature-index method of estimating 263
software
    design engineers' use in modeling 356
    factors considered by 356
    selection criteria 143
    WaterCAD, for calculating pump efficiency 455
Soil Conservation Service (SCS) storm distribution. *See* NRCS (SCS) storm distributions
source controls 399–400
specific energy
    critical depth 72–74
    equation for 72
    example 73–74
specific weight 24
    equation for 24
SSOs. *See* sanitary sewer overflows
St. Venant equations 14, 95–96
    approximations 96–97
    continuity equation 95
    diffusion analog solution 97
    finite difference method solution 95
    kinematic wave solution 97–98
    method of characteristics solution 95
    momentum equation 95
    time-step size 96
    See also Muskingum-Cunge routing method
staff gauges 284
staged construction of sewers. *See* phased construction of sewers
Standard 374
static head 126, 127
static lift. *See* static head

static pressure 28–29
    equation for 28
steady flow 23
    assumption of 33
steady-state simulation 7, 356–357
    model calibration 305
    See also extended-period simulation
steep channel slope 75
steep terrain, sewers in 358–359
stems 1
storage equation 94
storage facilities 2, 406
    in-line 405, 406
    modeling of 407
    offline 407, 408
    tunnels 407
    See also wet weather flows
storage tanks, in pressure sewer systems 470
storm advancement coefficients
    equation for 221
    values for 221–222
storm depths 219, 224
storm hydrographs 216
storm sewers, in Paris 8, 9
stormwater runoff 204
streamflow, as RDII predictor 313–314
subbasin delineation 154, 155, 213
    guidelines for 154
subbasins, characteristics by runoff parameters 214
subcritical flows 74–75
supercritical flows 74–75
surcharged gravity sewers 113
surcharging sewer pipes, routing model complications 103–104
suspended sediment, in wastewater 63
Swamee-Jain equation 50, 120
    Colebrook-White equation compared 120
synthetic unit hydrographs, peak discharge equation 244
system characterization. *See* wastewater collection system characterization
system data for models 216–217
system head curves for force mains 126–128, 437–438
    discontinuous curve example 446–447
    equation for 128, 437
system models 5, 137
    See also sewer models

T

tea cup method, for determining high water marks 283
temperature-index method of snowmelt estimation 263
Ten State Standards 339
thematic mapping 520–521
time-flow method for flow measurement 276, 281
time-series data 516
time-varying flows 193–198
    diurnal wastewater curves 193–195
TIN. *See* triangulated irregular networks
toilets
    impact on wastewater quality 8
    low flush 183, 184
total dynamic head. *See* pump head

total head 35
total maximum daily loads (TMDLs), water quality standards and 537–538
tractive force. *See* tractive tension
tractive tension
    equation for 63–64
    on pipe wall 63
    sediment carrying capacity and 65
tractive tension method
    minimum slope calculation for gravity sewers, examples 64–65, 67–68
    to calculate minimum pipe slope 64
training in model use 143
tranquil flow. *See* subcritical flow
transit-time velocity meters 289–291
treatment plants
    location of 420, 421, 422
    regional 420
triangular hydrograph method. *See* Snider triangular hydrograph method
triangulated irregular networks (TINs) 494, 495, 523
tributary-polygon method, for generating load-point flows 511–514
turbulence 15
    in hydraulic jumps 75–76
turbulent flow
    Hazen-Williams equation for calculating head loss 115, 118–120
    head loss in pipes 115
turbulent flow, use of Manning equation to calculate head loss 120–121
turbulent velocity profile 32

U

ultrasonic devices to measure depth 286
ultrasonic devices, in wet wells 433
ultrasonic velocity meters 288–291
    coherent Doppler meters 289, 290
    full-pipe meters 291
    random Doppler meters 288
    transit-time meters 289–291
uniform flow 23
Uniform Plumbing Code 183
uniform rainfall
    equation for 220
    in design storms 220
uniform rainfall procedure 220–221
uniform steady flow. *See* uniform flow
uniform velocity profiles 32
unit flow factors
    See also residential water use, water use
unit hydrograph method 242–243
    based on flow records 249
    convolution process to develop 242
    deconvolution process for developing 249
    simplifications to 250, 251
unit hydrographs, peak discharge equation 244
unit load factors 176
    average daily flow rates, calculation example 186–187
    based on fixtures 181–183
    based on land use 183, 185

based on water-use measurements 185–186
    for commercial sources 177, 178
    for industrial sources 179
    for residential sources 176
unit loads
    estimates from literature 174
    to determine dry weather flows 174
unsteady flow 23, 91–92
    conditions leading to 91–92
    modeling complications 101–107
    routing (modeling) 93
    See also extended-period simulation
US Army Corps of Engineers 529
    dredge and fill permits 538
US Environmental Protection Agency (EPA)
    Capacity Assurance, Management, Operation, and Maintenance (CMOM) program 536
    National Combined Sewer Overflow Control Policy 533–535, 552
    NPDES permits 531
    regulations 531, 532
    Sanitary Sewer Overflow Proposed Rule (US) 533–535, 536, 552

V

vacuum sewer systems 113, 338
    See also wastewater collection systems
vacuum sewers 2, 3
vacuum-breaker valves 459, 471
validation. *See* model verification
valves
    air-release 459, 471, 472
    check 435, 458
    foot 435
    isolation 435
    vacuum-breaker 459, 471
vapor pressure 27–28
variable-speed pumps 129, 429, 432, 451, 456, 457
    affinity laws for 129–130, 451–452
    best efficiency points for 130
    efficiency equation 452
    efficiency of operation 454
    head equation
    in multiple pump station systems 456, 457
    operating points of 453–454
    power equation 452
    pump characteristic curves 452, 453
    relative speed factors for 130
    wet-well size effect on 432
    See also pumps
vector data 494, 495
velocity 30
    as sewer design variable 39–40
    effect on Manning's n 49
    equation for 30
    in partially full pipes, example 47–48
velocity distribution coefficient 37
velocity head 35
    in energy equation 34
velocity meters 287–291
    coherent Doppler 289, 290
    electromagnetic 287–288
    radar 291, 292
    random Doppler 288
    ultrasonic 288–291
velocity profiles 31, 32
    laminar 32
    turbulent 32
    uniform 32
velocity-area method for flow measurement 276, 282
Venturi meters 34
verification. *See* model verification
viscosity
    absolute 26
    effect on Manning's n 49
    kinematic 26
    kinematic, equation 26
volume of rainfall. *See* rainfall volume
volume of wet wells 169

W

wall roughness, of pipe 49
waste loads. *See* loads
wastewater collection system analysis, history 7–16
wastewater collection system characterization 372, 376
    benchmarking 373
    capacity analysis 395, 396, 397
    construction methods used 378
    core components 374–375
    data analysis 386–390
    data cleanup 377
    data collection 377, 379, 385–386
    data sources 379
    data types required 378–379
    design criteria used 378
    environmental data 375
    European Standard EN 752-2 1997 373–374
    field investigations of system condition 379–380, 385–386
    hydraulic control facilities 382, 384
    hydraulic performance data 375
    hydraulic performance investigation procedure 384–385, 394–395
    investigation level determination 375–376
    model simulations and 372
    operations and maintenance data 375, 378
    performance categories 375
    performance requirements 373–374
    planning procedure 372
    problem prioritization 376
    quality assurance/quality control 379
    records review 376–378
    smoke investigations 381–382, 383
    structural data 375
wastewater collection system components 334–337
    flow diversion structures 337
    inverted siphons 360–361
    manholes 335–336
    permanent flow meters 336
    pipe junctions 337
    pipes 334–335

wastewater collection system design 333–334
    along streams 359
    alternate system configurations 341
    cleaning by flushing 346
    codes, standards, and criteria 339–340
    combined versus separate sewers 338
    components 334–337
    computer modeling for 333, 356–357
    conveyance types 338
    costs 340
    data requirements 340–341
    dry weather flow estimation 173–174
    easements 343–344
    elevated crossings 359, 360
    environmental considerations 340
    extended-period simulation (EPS) 357–358
    factors affecting system layout 341–342
    for steep terrain 358–359, 442–443
    hydraulics 352–358
    infiltration and inflow, allowances for 346–348
    initial planning 337–338
    inverted siphons 360–361
    life-cycle costs 353
    manhole location and spacing 342, 343
    maximum flow rates with pumping 358
    minimum flows 347
    operation and maintenance considerations 340
    optimization techniques in 361, 363
    phased construction 348
    pipe alignment 348
    procedures 333
    project schedule 340
    pumping facility location 343
    regulatory compliance 340
    rules-of-thumb 204
    sanitary flows 346–348
    sewer network layout 342, 344–346
    special installation types 358–361
    steady flow modeling for 356–357
    using models for 140
wastewater collection system models
    applications 5–7
    types of 7
wastewater collection system models. *See* modeling process, models
wastewater collection system overflows. *See* overflows
wastewater collection system rehabilitation 371–372
    best management practices (BMPs) 399–400
    combined sewer system options 398, 400–401
    evaluating strategies for 395–399
    model simulations and 372
    pipe rehabilitation 401–402
    pipe replacement 401–402
    preventive maintenance 399
    RDII control practices 402–404
    RDII mitigation 396, 397, 398
    real-time controls 405–406
    sanitary sewer system options 396, 397, 398
    sewer separation 400–401
    source controls 399–400
    using models for 141
wastewater collection systems 1, 2
    defined 2
    elevated crossings 359, 360
    facility upgrading 523

    flow components 272–273
    flow rates 173
    GIS use in 490
    hydrology 208–209
    installation in steep terrain 358–359
    modeling procedure 16–18
    preventive maintenance 399
    sediment carrying capacity 65–72
    technological advances in 11, 16
    terminology 2
    US federal regulations for 532
    See also combined sewer systems
wastewater flow hydrographs 386
    components of flow 386
    data analysis for system evaluation 386–390
    rainfall hyetographs with 386
wastewater flows
    base flow estimation methods 510
    daily load rate estimation 514
    estimation from land-use, GIS procedure for 511–514
    I/I simulation and 514
    sources 510
wastewater hydrographs 205
    components of flow 204–206, 309–310
    quantification of RDII 309–310
    See also hydrographs
wastewater loads
    for models 147
    per capita 176
    using fixture unit method 181–183
    using land-use methods 183, 185
    using measured-flow methods 185–186
    using unit load factors 176–179
    See also dry weather wastewater flows, wet weather wastewater flows
wastewater management, technology and 1
wastewater monitoring data, used to determine dry weather flows 174
wastewater treatment facilities, history 9
wastewater treatment systems
    choice of 337–338
    on-site 337
wastewater utilities, GIS applications in 520–524
wastewater, sources 3
water bulk modulus of elasticity 27
water conservation
    impacts on residential use 177
    low-flush toilets 183, 184
water consumption, per capita rates 176
water demand, estimating peak flows in dry weather 182–183
water density 24
water pollution, US federal government and 529
water quality
    TMDLs and 537–538
    wet weather collection system overflows and 11
water quality investigations, modeling applications in 6
water specific weight 24
water surface profiles 76
water use
    billing date, to determine dry weather flows 174
    consumption, per capita rates 176
    industrial 179
    See also residential water use, unit load factors
water vapor pressure 27

606 Index

water viscosity 26
WaterCAD, for calculating pump efficiency 455
water-quality studies, use of models for 141
wave celerity. *See* kinematic wave speed
weighted translation routing 100, 102
    discharge equation 100
weirs 79–80, 81, 82, 83, 163
    baffled side 80
    contracted rectangular 82
    curved 163, 165
    discharge coefficients for 80, 81, 82, 84
    for flow measurement 277–278
    leaping 163, 164
    portable 277–278
    rectangular 277
    rectangular suppressed 277
    sharp-crested 79, 276
    side 80, 84, 163, 164
    suppressed 80
    to regulate flow in manholes 163, 164, 165, 166
    transverse 163, 165, 166
    trapezoidal 277
    types of 80
    uncontracted weirs 80
    V-notch 277
    See also broad-crested weirs, contracted weirs, hydraulic control sections, sharp-crested rectangular weirs
wells. *See* dry wells, wet wells
wet weather capacity, of combined sewer system 209
wet weather discharges, EPA blending policy (proposed) 536–537
wet weather flows
    excess I/I and 11
    system storage modeling 407
    treatment facilities 407–409
    See also storage facilities
wet weather overflows, in sanitary sewer systems 403
wet weather wastewater flow generation 206–207
    in combined sewers 205–206
    methods for quantifying 207, 207–208
wet weather wastewater flows
    allowance for RDII in sewer design 261–262
    data collection for models 147
    defined 204
    development of hydrographs for 239–262
    hydrographs 216
    model calibration 309–320
    model calibration example 318–319
    modeling 206–208, 229–239
    modeling approaches to 203–204, 215, 216–217
    multiple linear regression analysis for estimating 252–253
    rainfall data preparation for modeling 217–229
    See also wastewater loads
wet wells 2, 168–169, 423, 426–427, 428
    alarms 433, 434
    bubbler systems in 433
    constant-speed pumps and 432
    floats in 433
    flooding effects on pump performance 443–444, 445
    inactive volume 169
    irregular-shaped 169
    minimum volume equation 432
    odor control 433
    pump control levels in 168
    sizing of 432–433
    ultrasonic devices in 433
    variable-speed pumps and 432
    volume 169, 432–433
wetted perimeter of open channel 45
what-if-conditions. *See* scenarios

Y

Yao's method 69–70

CD-ROM Contents

Included with this book is a CD-ROM containing software and documentation. The specific items that can be found on the CD are as follows:

- A 25-pipe version of SewerCAD (Stand-Alone interface) that can be used to work many of the exercises in this book. Note that the SewerCAD software is licensed for ACADEMIC PURPOSES ONLY. Professional or commercial application is strictly prohibited under the license agreement.
- Installation instructions containing CD-ROM contents and advanced installation details.
- *SewerCADUsersGuide.PDF*, an Adobe Acrobat file of the complete SewerCAD User Manual. The information in the manual and the latest documentation on the newest features are also available in SewerCAD's online Help.
- *Exam_book.pdf*, an Adobe Acrobat file of the examination booklet, which can be filled out and submitted to Haestad Methods for grading and award of CEUs (refer to "Continuing Education Units" in the front matter for more information).
- Adobe Acrobat software required to view the SewerCAD User Manual and exam booklet. Installing Acrobat is an option included in the installation routine.

Installation Instructions

Insert the CD into your CD-ROM drive. If you have Autorun enabled on your computer, the installation menu will appear automatically after the CD-ROM is inserted. If Autorun is not enabled, click the Start menu, select Run, enter D:\Autorun, and click OK (if D: is not your CD drive, enter the appropriate letter instead).

A menu will open with installation options. Follow the on-screen instructions.

Haestad Methods On-Line KnowledgeBase

KnowledgeBase is an on-line FAQ database on the Haestad Methods website.

Free access to the Haestad Methods SewerCAD KnowledgeBase is provided with the SewerCAD Academic Version for one year from the date of purchase of this book. To enter the KnowledgeBase, open SewerCAD and click the Globe button in the upper right portion of the SewerCAD window.

System Requirements

To run SewerCAD Stand-Alone, your computer should have at a minimum:

- Pentium III 750 MHz processor
- 64 MB RAM
- 25 MB hard disk space, plus room for data files
- 800 x 600 display resolution with 256 colors

The following are the recommended specifications:

- Fastest available processor
- 128 MB RAM

Technical Support

If the CD-ROM or software provided is not functioning as expected, e-mail Haestad Methods technical support at support@haestad.com, or call +1-203-755-1666 for assistance.

SewerCAD End-User License Agreement: Academic License

IMPORTANT, PLEASE READ THIS LICENSE CAREFULLY BEFORE USING THE SOFTWARE. YOU ARE AGREEING TO BE BOUND BY THE TERMS OF THIS LICENSE AS SET FORTH HEREIN. This Haestad Methods, Inc. (HAESTAD METHODS) End-User License Agreement (Agreement) is a legal agreement between HAESTAD METHODS and YOU (either an individual or a single entity, such as a partnership, corporation, LLC, or other entity) for the HAESTAD METHODS software product contained in this package (SOFTWARE). The SOFTWARE includes computer software on associated media and printed materials, and may include on-line or electronic documentation. BY INSTALLING, COPYING, OR OTHERWISE USING THE SOFTWARE, YOU AGREE TO BE BOUND BY THE TERMS OF THIS AGREEMENT. IF YOU DO NOT AGREE WITH THE TERMS OF THIS AGREEMENT, DO NOT INSTALL, COPY, OR USE THE SOFTWARE, AND PROMPTLY RETURN THE PACKAGE AND UNUSED SOFTWARE TO HAESTAD METHODS.

GRANT OF LICENSE: HAESTAD METHODS hereby grants to YOU a non-exclusive license to use the SOFTWARE in accordance with the terms of this Agreement. HAESTAD METHODS reserves all rights not expressly granted herein. The SOFTWARE is licensed, not sold, from HAESTAD METHODS to YOU. HAESTAD METHODS retains ownership of the SOFTWARE and any and all authorized and unauthorized copies that YOU make of it. The different types of SOFTWARE licenses YOU may obtain are: an Individual User, Local Area Network (LAN), Wide Area Network (WAN), or an Academic Edition of said licenses. The type and number of users for each purchased license shall be designated in a ClientCare certificate or other written document sent to YOU from HAESTAD METHODS. Install shall mean loading the SOFTWARE into temporary memory, on a hard disk, or other permanent storage device of the computer. Install shall not mean loading the SOFTWARE on a network server for the sole purpose of distributing the SOFTWARE to other computers.

INDIVIDUAL USER LICENSE: The SOFTWARE is licensed for use by one user at the original location, on a single computer.

LAN LICENSE: The SOFTWARE is licensed for multiple users at one geographic location. SOFTWARE may be loaded on a single network server for the sole purpose of distributing SOFTWARE to other computers at the same geographic location. YOU must ensure that the number of concurrent users of the SOFTWARE does not exceed the number of users designated in your license.

WAN LICENSE: The SOFTWARE is licensed for multiple users at multiple Branch Office location(s) as designated in your license. The Branch Office(s) may be in different geographic locations. SOFTWARE may be loaded onto a single network server for the sole purpose of distributing SOFTWARE to other computers. YOU must ensure that the number of concurrent users of the SOFTWARE does not exceed the number of users designated in your license. YOU may obtain licenses for additional Branch Offices not designated in the original WAN License by contacting HAESTAD METHODS.

ACADEMIC EDITION LICENSE: In addition to the license restrictions of the Individual User, LAN, and WAN licenses, the Academic Edition license is granted for educational purposes only. Professional, commercial, or any other use not specifically granted herein is strictly prohibited under the terms of this Agreement.

SOFTWARE ASSIGNMENT OR TRANSFER: This SOFTWARE license is not for resale, assignment, or transfer. This SOFTWARE is licensed for the sole use of the original licensee at the original location(s), as designated in accordance with this Agreement.

RENTAL: YOU may not rent, lend, or lease the SOFTWARE.

TERMINATION: Without prejudice to any other rights, HAESTAD METHODS may terminate this Agreement if YOU fail to comply with its terms and conditions. If HAESTAD METHODS notifies YOU in writing that it has terminated this Agreement, YOU agree to immediately destroy or return all copies of the SOFTWARE and all of its component parts.

Any violation of usage restrictions, including but not limited to usage beyond the approved number of pipes, nodes, and/or number of users, constitutes a breach of this Agreement. It is a violation of this Agreement to employ, use, and/or enter any serial numbers, registration numbers, and/or product ID strings that HAESTAD METHODS has not supplied to YOU. Any breach or violation of this Agreement will result in the termination of this Agreement in addition to any other penalties or recourse available under applicable law.

UPGRADES: If the SOFTWARE is an upgrade of an older HAESTAD METHODS software product, YOU agree to destroy or return to HAESTAD METHODS all copies of the older HAESTAD METHODS software product within thirty (30) days of installing the upgrade.

CUSTOMIZATIONS, ADD-ONS, AND EXTENSIONS: If HAESTAD METHODS creates or provides herewith or in future products, a modification of the software, in whole or in part, such as a customization, add-on, and/or extension of the software for a particular application, then this SOFTWARE agreement equally applies to such a modification, and by installing, copying or otherwise using the modification, YOU agree to be bound by the terms of this SOFTWARE agreement without further written notice. If YOU do not agree, then do not install, copy or use the modifications, and return the package and all unused software products to HAESTAD METHODS.

CUSTOM APPLICATIONS: Custom Applications developed by YOU using the WaterObjects API set and redistributed for any commercial purpose shall incorporate the "Built using WaterObjects® Technology" logo in the application's "About Box" and documentation, and shall be subject to HAESTAD METHODS' custom application guidelines, which shall be available upon request.

INTELLECTUAL PROPERTY: The SOFTWARE is protected by copyright, trademark, and other intellectual property law in the United States of America and in other countries by international treaties. Therefore, YOU may not make or sell copies of the SOFTWARE, except that YOU may either (a) make one copy of the SOFTWARE solely for backup or archival purposes, and in so doing YOU must reproduce on such copy any HAESTAD METHODS copyright notice and any other proprietary legends that were on the original copy of the SOFTWARE, or (b) install the SOFTWARE on a single computer and keep the original copy solely for backup or archival purposes. YOU may not make or sell copies of the printed, electronic, or on-line materials accompanying the SOFTWARE. YOU may not reverse engineer, decompile, disassemble or create derivative works for, or competing products with, the SOFTWARE.

WARRANTY: For a period of one (1) year after YOU receive this SOFTWARE (regardless of whether YOU use the SOFTWARE during the one year period), HAESTAD METHODS warrants that the media on which it is contained will not be defective. In the event that during this warranty period the media containing the SOFTWARE is defective, your sole remedy is to contact HAESTAD METHODS and HAESTAD METHODS in its sole discretion will (a) replace or repair the defective media or (b) refund your money upon your returning to HAESTAD METHODS the original and all copies of the SOFTWARE.

DISCLAIMER OF WARRANTIES: EXCEPT FOR THE EXPRESS WARRANTY STATED ABOVE, THE SOFTWARE IS PROVIDED "AS IS" AND WITHOUT WARRANTIES AND CONDITIONS OF ANY KIND, EXPRESSED OR IMPLIED, INCLUDING BUT NOT LIMITED TO ANY IMPLIED WARRANTIES OF MERCHANTABILITY OR FITNESS FOR A PARTICULAR PURPOSE AND NON-INFRINGEMENT. THE ENTIRE RISK AS TO THE QUALITY AND PERFORMANCE OF THE SOFTWARE LIES WITH YOU.

LIMITATIONS OF LIABILITY: TO THE MAXIMUM EXTENT PERMITTED BY APPLICABLE LAW, HAESTAD METHODS SHALL NOT BE LIABLE FOR ANY DAMAGES TO YOU OR ANY OTHER PERSON OR ENTITY IN CONNECTION WITH THE USE OF THIS SOFTWARE. UNDER NO CIRCUMSTANCES WILL HAESTAD METHODS BE LIABLE FOR ANY SPECIAL, DIRECT, INDIRECT, INCIDENTAL, CONSEQUENTIAL, OR OTHER DAMAGES WHATSOEVER (INCLUDING WITHOUT LIMITATION, DAMAGES FOR LOSS OF BUSINESS PROFITS, BUSINESS INTERRUPTION, LOSS OF BUSINESS INFORMATION, OR ANY OTHER PECUNIARY LOSS) ARISING OUT OF THE USE OR INABILITY TO USE THE SOFTWARE EVEN IF HAESTAD METHODS HAS BEEN ADVISED OF THE POSSIBILITY OF SUCH DAMAGES. IN NO EVENT SHALL HAESTAD METHODS LIABILITY FOR ANY DAMAGES OR LOSS TO YOU OR ANY OTHER PARTY EXCEED THE PURCHASE PRICE PAID FOR THE ORIGINAL SOFTWARE. PAYMENTS MADE UNDER THIS AGREEMENT DO NOT INCLUDE ANY CONSIDERATION FOR ASSUMPTION OF RISK. DO NOT USE THIS SOFTWARE IN ANY WAY OR FOR ANY PURPOSE IF YOU DESIRE HAESTAD METHODS TO TAKE ANY LIABILITY FOR ITS USE.

CONTROLLING LAW: This license shall be governed by and construed in accordance with the laws of the United States, and the laws of the State of Connecticut. If this SOFTWARE was acquired outside the United States, then local law may apply. If a court of competent jurisdiction finds any provision of this license or portion thereof to be unenforceable, that provision of the license shall be enforced to the maximum extent permissible so as to affect the intent of the parties, and the remainder of this license shall continue in full force and effect.

CONTACT US: If YOU have any questions or comments, please contact HAESTAD METHODS at the address listed in or on this or the accompanying material.